CRIMINOLOGY

CRIMINOLOGY

A CROSS-CULTURAL PERSPECTIVE

VOLUME II

Edited by

Dae H. Chang

Chairman
Department of Administration of Justice
Wichita State University, Wichita, Kansas

CAROLINA ACADEMIC PRESS
DURHAM, NORTH CAROLINA

Published in the United States and Canada by
CAROLINA ACADEMIC PRESS
2206 Chapel Hill Road, Box 8791 Forest Hills Station
Durham, N.C. 27707

Published in India by Vikas Publishing House Pvt Ltd

ISBN: 0-89089-053-6

Library of Congress Catalog Card No. 75-5478

PRINTED IN INDIA

CONTRIBUTORS

Dr THOMAS WURTENBERGER, Director, Institut fur Kriminologie und Strafuollzugs Kunde, University of F reiburg, Gunterstalstrasse 70, Freiburg, West Germany.

Dr PAUL KOCH, Assistant to Dr Wurtenberger, Freiburg, West Germany.

Dr MARIA CRISTINA GIANNINI, Assistant Professor, Instituto di Diritto Peale Criminologica University Degli Studi di Roma, 00185 Roma, Italy.

Dr TARO OGAWA, Professor, Department of Law University of Asia, 5-24, Sakai, Masashino, Tokyo, Japan. He is also Deputy Director, United Nations Asia and the Far East Institute on Prevention of Crime and Treatment of Offenders.

Mr LESLIE C. S. LEE, Ministry of Welfare Service, Jalan Semantan, Kuala Lumpur 23-04, Peninsular, Malaysia.

Mr ALEJANDRO F. DE SANTOS, Professorial Lecturer and Bar Reviewer, Ateneo de Manila University and San Beda College; Chief Legal Counsel, Metropal (Association of Police Chiefs in Manila and Metropolitan Areas).

Dr JUAN MANUEL MAYORCA, H., Director, La Prevencion del Delito es tarea de todos, Venezuela.

CONTENTS

CHAPTER 6

FEDERAL REPUBLIC OF GERMANY

THOMAS WURTENBERGER
PAUL KOCH

Dr Thomas Wurtenberger was educated in Germany and Switzerland. He attended elementary and secondary schools in Zurich, Switzerland, and Karlsruhe, Germany (1914-1927). Then he studied jurisprudence at the University of Zurich, Frankfurt, Freiburg i. Br., Munich, and Berlin (1927-1932). During the years 1933-1954, he served as Scholarly Assistant at the Legal Faculty of the universities of Heidelberg and Freiburg; Lecturer in criminal law at the University of Erlangen; and Professor of criminal law at the University of Mainz. Since 1955, he is Professor of criminal law and criminology and Director of Freiburg. He is also a member of the International Society of Criminology in Paris, and of the Penology Commission of the Federal Ministry of Justice in Bonn. His works have been translated into different languages and he is well known in criminological circles all over the world. Some of his published works include The System of Classification of the Laws of Property in German Penal Legislation Since 1532 *(1933),* Art Forgery *(1940),* German Criminal Reports *(1941),* The Struggle Against Art Forgery in German and Swiss Penal Law Practice *(1951) (this book is translated into Italian, Japanese, and Chinese), and* Personal and Juridical Law: Contribution to the Future Study of Man and His Law *(1967). He is also the Editor of* Criminology and Execution of Imprisonment X, International Course of Instruction in Breiburg i. Br. *(1961),* International Colloquium on Criminology and Penal Law

Reform (*1967 with Jescheck*), Criminology, Papers on the Suppression of Social Deviation (*1964*), Contributions to Studies on the Execution of Punishment (*with Muller-Dietz, since 1967 and* Excerpta Criminologica (*with Nagek and others since 1961*).

Dr Paul Koch is presently serving as Assistant to the Director Surtenberger at the Institute of Criminology and Penology, University of Freiburg. He attended elementary and secondary schools in Eschwege and Neustadt from 1944 to 1958. From 1958 to 1963, he attended universities of Heidelberg, Berlin, and Breiburg. He received his doctorate in jurisprudence in 1968 after completing a series of examinations. He is author of the book entitled Prison Work and Rehabilitation (*1969*). *He has also published the article entitled "Papers on Penal Scholarship," edited by Thomas Wurtenberger and H. Muller-Dietz.*

THE GENERAL PICTURE OF German criminology in its historical development since the Franco-German war of 1870-71 is characterized by the upheavals of the cultural and social data that are evident in this era of changing political and economic conditions. The strong environmental conditioning of crime is visible in the criminality curve of the last 100 years, which in a continuing rising and sinking showed a constant change in its nature and expression.

The beginning of official crime statistics in the German Reich (1882), which supplies the numerical basis of the picture of criminality, fell into the epoch of an all too rapid cultural and economic growth and a radical political reorganization. However, the economic crises of the waning 19th and the early 20th century (1882, 1890, 1900, 1908) with their subsequent depressions had little effect on the movement of criminality. It was not until the World War of 1914 that a more significant change in the picture of criminality took place. The war at the same time formed the transition to a period of political and, above all, economic decline.

The nature and direction of crime in the period around 1900 was characterized by a predominance of simple offenses of assault and offenses against property. Conspicuous was the increase in alcohol delicts in the form of aggravated bodily injury and other offenses of violence. Until 1918, the regularly occurring sequence of economic booms and depressions found their strongest reaction in theft and receiving of stolen goods. It is during and after the years of crisis that the criminality curve reached its respective high point. In general, the wavy curve of criminality—until World War I—showed a tendency to decline, probably due to the rising standard of living. In contrast to this, among the offenses against property, fraud and embezzlement increased threefold and two fold, respectively.

The First World War showed two phases with respect to crime. Until about 1916 it had a favorable effect in almost every respect on the movement of crime. The feeling of solidarity under the pressure of war conditions and a strict control of the State resulted at first in a strong reduction in the number of crimes. In the area of violent and moral offenses especially, i.e. of the typically "male" crimes, there was only a seeming reduction, since almost all younger men were removed from civilian criminal justice by military service. Due to the war, the intensity of criminal prosecution by the State was relaxed. Since 1916 a recessive movement took place in the development of criminality, the causes of which can be seen only indirectly in the war condition, but directly in the worsened general economic condition. The lack of necessary goods, the realization of extreme sacrifices, and the spreading disappointment and discontent caused the curve of criminality to rise threateningly. The main characteristic of the last war period was the increase of offenses of physical need, above all, theft, fraud, and infidelity. Furthermore, an increasing number of youths, women and members of more educated classes were identified as perpetrators.

The years between the end of World War I until the beginning of World War II can be called a period of German reconstruction attempts. The economic collapse (1922-1923) which followed the collapse of the military and political structure, the subsequent stablilization of the currency with an apparent prosperity (1923-1928), the then beginning unemployment, and the rule of the National Socialists were the landmarks of this period—landmarks that were also relevant criminologically. The rate of criminality in general rose at the

outcome of World War I, when there was an advance in
the offenses of physical need and, at the same time, a decrease
in the offenses of assault, especially of violence. Consequent to
the collapse, the decrease of the authority of the State, the
feeling of devaluation of human life and of real property, and
the onset of inflation caused a further rise in the curve of
criminality in the directions indicated. The demoralization of
youth, which had begun during World War I, was aggravated
by the increased number of orphaned and illegitimate children.

Among the offenses of physical need, crime was rising
especially due to the then prevailing "flight to the real values."
In the cases of plain theft and receiving of stolen goods,
criminality reached record heights in 1923. The offenses of
theft in this period accounted for about half of all sentences,
while receiving of stolen goods moved suddenly from eleventh
(1899) to second place on the frequency scale. The change in
moral attitude caused by the general economic plight manifested itself further in a rise of moral delicts.

The period of deflation and the apparent economic prosperity (1924-1929) caused by the influx of foreign capital resulted
in a change from the prevailing "real value delicts" to
"monetary value delicts." Theft and receiving of stolen goods
decreased; fraud, embezzlement, and forgery increased. Serious
offenses showed a general rising tendency. Aggravated bodily
injury increased only slightly until 1927. During the period
of mass unemployment, which began in 1938, crime showed
the familiar structure of depressed social conditions. In contrast to earlier economic depressions, now the aggravated
offenses of physical need—such as grand theft, robbery, and
blackmail—were considerably on the increase until 1932.

Any representation of the increase in crime during the
time of the National Socialist regime until the beginning of
World War II has to take into account the amnesty laws of
that period (especially in 1936 and 1938) which dismissed approximately 500,000 criminal cases, thereby significantly
changing the picture. With this reservation, one can speak of a
remarkable reduction in the total amount of criminality of this
time. However, the development of a few important offenses
showed a marked upward trend. Increases are noted parti-

cularly in the delicts of infidelity, false accusation and slander, and also in delicts with a high secret criminality—especially moral offenses—which reached a rare high point in 1937. The number of murders also rose steadily since 1933. In other areas, the improvement in economic conditions and the authoritative execution of governmental power led to a constant reduction in crime. By the 1933 law against habitual criminals, and the 1937 law of preventive detention by the police, many professional criminals were prevented from committing further offenses.

The sparse criminality data that are available on the Second World War confirm basically the observations that were made in the First World War period. During World War II period, also, there are two different phases. At the beginning of the war the increase of national strength led to a reduction of offenses of violence and property. Later, under the influence of growing conditions of distress and war-weariness, offenses of physical need and violence increased. At the same time a lowering of morals and an advance of criminality into a social strata that had not previously been in conflict with the law were noticable. This manifested itself in an increase in crime among the youth and the women.

Radical changes in environment after the war influenced the crime scene in general. The return of soldiers and later of prisoners of war, the departure of foreigners, and the influx of refugees led to a change of the population structure and of the social strata. Added to this was the insecurity of Germany's legal situation, the blockade of the capital, Berlin, a frightening lack of all necessary goods and also of jobs, and finally a general shortage of money. Under these circumstances it is not surprising that criminality in the post-war era was particularly rampant. As a typical phenomenon of the post-war era, the "black market" exchange of goods formed a considerable source of criminality, which for some time even survived the monetary reform of 1948. Thus, while the countryside and provincial towns fared better and overcame more easily the damages of war, the big cities showed a steep rise in crime-rate. However, due to the shortage of goods and shelter, the food stamp system, and the black market, offenses of physical need increased significantly. As after the First World War, the strong rise in theft and moral offenses formed the main characteristic of crime. The numerical reduction of fraud and receiving of stolen goods is to be explained by a corresponding higher secret criminality, especially due to the attraction of the black market. Conspicuous also, in contrast to the World War I, was the increase in corruption among public servants.

In 1949, Germany was particularly penalized by the creation of the Federal Republic of Germany in the west and the German Democratic Republic in the east. In the Federal Republic the picture of crime was determined by the total economic development, which in the early sixties was already being described as the "German economic miracle." Two decades of economic and political stability made the achievement of affluence possible, resulting in the near disappearance of the crime of physical need. However, in its place completely new forms of criminality appeared, and the term "criminality of affluence" attained a special meaning. Crime statistics, which are being published annually since 1953 for the entire federal area by the Federal Crime Bureau in Wiesbaden, show that the development of crime in the Federal Republic of Germany (exclusive of traffic violations) is dominated by the continual increase in theft. In 1968, theft represented more than 60 per cent of the total criminality. The growing affluence manifested itself in an increase of the so-called "criminality of greed." At the same time crime changed its forms of appearance and adapted itself to the new economic conditions. The various types of fraud and the appearance of "white-collar criminality" in all its varieties were proof of that. In view of the considerable damage caused by this typically economic crime, it is all the more regrettable that in this area obscurity is a particular problem. Included in the white-collar crimes are, among others, tax evasion, bribery, price-fixing in the allocation of government contracts, subsidy frauds, and the defrauding of savings and loan institutions.

Due to high demand for labor, Germany has had a strong influx of foreign workers in highly industrialized areas since 1960. This population group has nearly doubled between 1962 and 1966 (in 1968 there were almost 1.5 million foreign workers). The crime rate of the foreign-worker during this period is about 50 per cent higher than that of the German population. While the situation is about the same as that of German criminality in the case of theft, the share of offenses of violence and morals committed by foreigners is conspicuously high. Thus crime figures in cases of robbery, aggravated body injury, rape, prostitution, and man-slaughter are approximately four times as high as those of the Germans.

In the course of the last two decades, juvenile crime has been continually on the increase. In this area there is overlapping from criminal to non-acceptable, non-criminal modes of behavior, as for example, "degeneracy." In a modern industrial society, the institutionalization and collectivization of certain psycho-social tendencies results in the development of new social habits and a dismissal of personal responsibilities among young people. Thus the rise in juvenile criminality could be an indication of an incongruity between traditional legal norms and modern morality.

With regard to the scope of juvenile crime, the official statistics show that the overall frequency of the number of offenses committed by the younger generation (up to 21 years of age) is higher than ever before and that it is continuously increasing. Apparently, most of these delinquents are juveniles who are sensitive to differences in status between themselves and the affluent sections of society—a fact which is leading to group self-consciousness. It is a fact worth noting that at least half of the juveniles offenses are committed in some kind of group. Depending upon the situation their primarily non-directed aggressiveness also turns occasionally against standards of law.

Consequently, in the area of aggressive offenses (robbery, extortion, rape, prostitution, body injury, and coercion), there has been a tremendous increase on the side of the younger population while the overall frequency remains essentially the same. Even in the area of car thefts (from 1953 to 1962 the number of such offenses per inhabitant rose by about 400 per cent) and vending machine thefts, the sharp increase was due mostly to juvenile delinquency. In offenses connected with motor vehicle traffic, the 18-25 age group increased disproportionately in the time after World War II. During the years 1954-1958 it constituted on the average about 50 per cent of all offenses in connection with traffic regulation.

CRIMINAL LAW

In its legal definition, the term "crime" has a twofold
meaning. In the first place it is used by the legal scholars,
including criminologists, to denote a delinquent act. Every
human act which calls for punishment by the legal order is
considered a crime. In the German criminal law, on the other
hand, the term "crime" also denotes the most severe offenses. It
is so defined in the German Code of Criminal Law of 1871, as
also in its September, 1969 version. According to the Code
of Criminal Law, "Verbrechen" (crimes) are acts which call for
imprisonment of one year or more; "Ubertretungen" (violation) are acts which call for imprisonment up to six weeks or for
fines up to 500 DM; and "Vergehen" (misdemeanors, petty
crime) are all other acts threatened with imprisonment or fines.
Thus, the type of punishment laid down in the Code of Criminal Law is decisive for various categories of offenses.

Besides those acts which are punished by criminal law,
there are the minor offenses called "Ordungswidrigkeiten" (cf.
the law for minor offenses—OWiG—from 5/24/68). Such a
minor offense, as opposed to a major one (felony), does not
call for imprisonment or monetary penalty but only for a small
fine, the amount of which can range between 5.00 DM and
1,000 DM (cf.§§1; and 13 OWiG).

In the body of law, there is no other definition of the
features of a punishable act. However, jurisdiction and research have developed three essential features: (*i*) "Tatbe-
standmabigkeit" (evidence), (*ii*) "Rechtswidrigkeit" (offense of
law); and (*iii*) "Schuld" (guilt).

A punishable act (offense) is *evident*, if it can be subsumed
under the legal features of a certain type of offense. An act is
against the law if it represents a fact punishable under the law
and if there does not exist any special reason for justification.

Guilt is the personal-psychological relation of the offender to
his transgression. Guilt means that the offender can be
accused of an evident and unlawful act.

Most offenses can be committed by *anyone*. Only in special
cases are the offenders treated differently according to
their sex. Thus, the evidence of grave homosexual offenses
can only be established for men, not for women (§175, STGB).

On the other hand, only the mother of an illegitimate child can become guilty of infanticide (§217, STGB). Also only a woman can fulfil the condition of abortion by the pregnant woman (§218, Sec. 1, STGB). With regard to *age* the same, regulations of the general penal code apply to offenders of all age groups. Neither for the juvenile delinquent nor for the elder do there exist special categories of offenses.

With regard to *nationality*, residents and foreigners are equally responsible to the standards of German law as specified in the regulations of the international penal code. According to the *principle of personality* (§3, STGB), the German Penal Code applies to the offense of a German national, irrespective of where it was committed. The *territorial principle*, which forms the basis of §4 of the STGB, stipulates that offenses of foreigners within Germany are treated according to the German Penal Code.

As for as the *social status* of the offender is concerned, there are offenses that can be committed by anybody; and special offenses which are restricted to a special group, as those committed by government officials (i.e. passive bribery according to §331 and 332, STGB).

In essence, the present German criminal law is a factual criminal law (Tatstrafrecht). In special cases, however, the personality of the offender is considered as an important criterion for the punishment, i.e. when dealing with offenders of lessened accountability or the dangerous habitual offenders. Besides, there are also laws which are geared towards certain criminological types of offenders, such as the regulations governing the punishability of the panderer or the tramp.

At the same time, the German criminal law is a law of guilt, which takes into account the freedom of decision vested in man for all his acts. According to this philosophy an offense can only be punished if it is possible to construe an accusation of personal guilt against the offender. Thus, every punishment presupposes guilt on the part of the offender. The establishment of guilt means an ethical judgment of unworthiness for the offender, because he has decided against the law, although he could have stayed within its borders.

Legal Definitions of Juvenile Delinquency

The German law differentiates between children (up to 14 years), juveniles (14-18 years), and adolescents (18-21 years). Children are not responsible at all in a legal sense. The offense of a juvenile is treated as an offense under the general criminal law. The term "juvenile delinquency" of the American law, according to which offenses of children and juveniles are not considered as "crime" (Honig, Das amerikanische Strafrecht; in: Das auslandische Strafrecht, der Gegenwart, Bd. 4 1962, S. 78), has on equivalent in the German criminal law. Since the enactment of the first German Juvenile Penal Code (JGG, 2/16/23), however, the criminal law for juveniles is independent, in many respects, of the criminal law for adults. Thus according to the present Juvenile Criminal Law of 8/4/53, special regulations are in force governing the responsibility of juvenile offenders and court sanctions. A juvenile offender is responsible in a legal sense (according to §3, JGG) only if he is mature enough to understand the injustice of his offense, and if he is able to act according to this moral and intellectual understanding. In case this maturity is lacking the judge cannot punish the offender, however, he can order educational measures like the judge of of a court of Chancery. If the juvenile is responsible for his offense before the law, special sanctions which are not available under the criminal law for adults are imposed. There can be handed down educational measures (§9, JGG), disciplinary measures, i.e. juvenile detention (§13, JGG) and juvenile punishment (§17, JGG). In any case, preference is given to educational measures over punitive ones.

The adolescent is fully responsible to the law for every offense he commits. For the legal consequences of such an offense, however, the juvenile penal code is to be used, whenever the adolescent at the time of the offense is on the level of a juvenile in his moral and intellectual development, or if his offense is a typical juvenile offense.

CRIME STATISTICS

Since 1953, the Federal Office of Investigation of Criminal Offenses in Wiesbaden has issued annually a statistical report of crimes in the Federal Republic of Germany, including West Berlin. All offenses are categorized in the first place according to the single types of major or minor according to the German criminal law, including all offenses against the criminal side— and State laws. For every group of offenses, the total offenses and the solved cases are shown. In addition to that many sub-divisions can be found, such as distributions according to male and female, or adult and adolescent offenders. Specially listed are foreign and ubiquitous offenders. Finally, a distribution according to the locality of the offenses is given: metropolitan area, medium and small town, and rural areas. A special listing shows also whether a car was used for the offense. The criminal statistics of the police intend to inform about the offense and about the offender.

In addition to the statistics of the Federal Office, the State Offices of Criminal Offenses issue their own official statistics on the number of crimes which have become known. They are subdivided similarly as those of the Federal Office.

Further important statistical material can be gathered from the statistics of prosecution (Strafverfolgungsstatistik), which are the yearly compilations of the Federal Office for Statistics in Wiesbaden. The statistics for the administration of justice have been compiled since 1959 in the series entitled "Population and Culture." Here all offenses and all offenders are registered. This is a survey of all statistics in the area of crime prosecution. All prosecuted offenders are divided according to the type of their offenses, their age, and sex. Furthermore, statistical material on the execution of the sentence and help while on probation is shown. The results of the statistics on crime prosecution are published by the corresponding State offices of statistics.

The following statistical data on crime were compiled according to crime statistics of the Federal Office of Criminal Offenses, and the yearly statistics for the administration of justice by the Federal Office of Statistics.

Table I provides data about the crimes which have become known, crimes which have been solved, and about the arraigned offenders. However, since 1963, these statistics have not included the offenses against the security of the State, nor traffic offenses. This explains the marked decline of known crimes in

TABLE I

CRIME STATISTICS OF THE POLICE

	1958	1960	1961	1962	1963	1964	1965	1966	1967
	2,158,510	2,034,239	2,120,419	2,106,469	1,678,840	1,747,580	1,789,319	1,917,445	2,074,322
	+4.1%	+4.3%	+4.2%	−0.7%	(−20.3%)	+4.1%	+2.4%	+7.2%	+8.2%
	3,588	3,660	3,771	3,699	2,914	2,998	3,031	3,213	3,465
	+3.6%	+3.2%	+2.4%	−1.9%	(−21.4%)	+2.8%	+1.1%	+6.0%	+7.8%
	1,118,493	1,333,697	1,374,306	1,359,448	932,307	961,827	951,115	1,015,467	1,082,009
	51.8%	65.6%	64.8%	64.6%	(55.5%)	55.0%	53.2%	53.0%	52.2%
	824,947	1,102,398	1,127,171	1,111,739	686,964	693,536	685,700	734,289	769,485
	155,186	158,757	159,878	159,355	127,763	129,517	125,529	131,411	143,455
	980,133	1,261,155	1,287,049	1,271,094	814,727	823,053	811,229	865,700	912,940

NOTE: *Row A*—Offenses which have become known. This comprises all crimes and offenses against the German criminal law which have been reported to the police or have come to their attention in some other way, and which have been processed by the police up to the point where the prosecution or the courts have assumed responsibility. Offenses are judged here as completed acts even if only attempt was made. In cases of murder or man-slaughter the attempt is considered separately. The offense is being treated according to the section of the law which the police consider as having been broken regardless of whether the prosecution or the courts judge it differently at a later point.

Row B—Number of total frequency. This means the number of offenses prorated per 100,000 inhabitants of the total population.

Row C—Solved crimes. An offense is considered solved if at least one of the following conditions is fulfilled: (*i*) the offender must be considered as convicted either by confession or other proof; (*ii*) the identified or unidentified offender must be apprehended in the criminal act, even if he denies the offense; and (*iii*) the offender must be known or be identified as a person, regardless of whether he has been apprehended, whether he is left free or whether he is fleeing.

An offense is not solved, e.g. if a stolen object has been found, but not the thief.

Row D—Rate of solution. This is the relation between the solved offenses and those which come within the period of the yearly report.

Row E—Offender. Offenders are persons over 14 years of age who can be convicted of a punishable act by the police. Every offender is counted only once in one preliminary proceeding, and only for that act which calls for the most severe punishment. However, because the person who has become known as an offender is being listed not only once a year, but again and again in preliminary proceedings at different times, the 980,133 offenders of the year 1968, for example, can *not* be considered as 980,133 different persons.

TABLE II

Categories of offenses without traffic offenses	1963	1964	1965	1966	1967	1968
Murder and man-slaughter (includes attempted infanticides)	1,391	1,548	1,634	1,864	1,991	1,910
Accidental homicide (without traffic accidents)	1,019	982	922	888	865	851
Bodily injury resulting in death	295	312	274	236	229	194
Dangerous and heavy bodily injury	30,239	29,858	30,403	30,663	31,860	32,668
Robbery, extortion, car theft, assaulted robbery	6,721	7,218	7,655	9,010	9,784	9,737
Grand theft	268,135	299,586	336,988	398,878	448,409	460,346
Simple theft	675,288	695,128	697,969	741,886	794,101	847,721
Embezzlement, aiding and abetting, receiving stolen property	58,232	58,571	54,980	55,286	56,590	53,871
Fraud and malfeasance	184,298	184,043	180,757	180,075	195,574	193,570
Falsification of documents, offenses against transportation fees	14,725	16,899	18,586	16,819	17,102	18,085
Rape	6,572	6,159	5,923	6,060	6,255	6,319
Indecent assaults	56,149	57,641	53,079	52,555	52,819	52,173
Abortion	2,784	2,388	2,165	1,773	2,369	1,687
Arson (intended or accidental)	14,185	15,334	11,029	11,437	12,761	14,462
Offenses against personal freedom	8,313	9,943	11,694	13,210	14,941	16,036

Property damage: willful destruction,						
vandalism	154,264	136,539	117,860	107,236	93,267	85,497
Narcotic offenses	1,891	1,349	1,080	1,003	992	820
Other offenses	293,225	290,784	227,865	267,022	267,711	264,213
TOTAL	2,158,510	2,074,322	1,917,445	1,789,319	1,747,580	1,678,840

NOTE: The table deals with criminal statistics of the police, and informs about the frequency of individual and groups' offenses. The number relate to the cases which have become known to the police in the respective year. The division of the groups of offenses follows the standards of German criminal law. As these are different from the American standard, the numbers can be compared with the data of the "F.B.I. Uniform Crime Reports" only with certain reservations. Here, also, the fact should be considered that offenses against the security of the State, and against traffic regulations, are not included.

1963 for traffic offenses which constitute according to the statistics of sentenced offenders, about one-half of all offenses (cf.
Table II). Due to this fact, the number of known offenses and
the rate of their solutions in the year 1963 cannot be properly
compared with the results of the year 1962. Therefore, the
corresponding percentages for the two years are put into
brackets.

THEORIES OF CRIME CAUSATION

From the beginning, German criminology was caught in the
contradiction between the Italian crimino-anthropological
school and the French crimino-sociological school. Franz von
Liszt, who can be legitimately associated with the start of the
development of a scientific criminology in Germany, attempted
to bridge the one-sidedness of both schools by the following
compromise formula: "The crime is the product of the indivi-
duality of the offender in the moment of the offense, and of
the circumstances which surround him in this moment."

In his criminal-political Marburg program, he demanded
that criminal anthropology, criminal psychology, and criminal
sociology be included in the total criminology. In addition to lawmen, the development of criminology in Germany owes most to
the medical field, especially psychiatrists, such as Kraft-Ebbing,
Kraepelin, Wilmans, Birnbaum, Hoche, Sommer, and especially
Aschaffenburg. During the time after World War I, criminology
as a whole was largely a domain of psychiatrists in Germany.

The teachings of constitutional biology by Kretschmer, and
the psychiatric research of K. Schneider on psychopathy, were
used for the purposes of study in criminology. A branch of
hereditary biology gained dominant influence during the thirties,
with the twin and geneology research of Lange, Stumpfl, Kranz,
Riedel and others. Attempts to utilize Freud's psychoanalysis
and the individual psychology of Adler and Jung were also
made.

With the exception of the statistical men, teachers of criminology like Exner, Mezger, Sauer, and v. Weber were dealing
predominantly with problems of criminal sociology. They
focused attention on the question of what influence the surroundings and the milieu have on the commitment of a crime.

TABLE III
CONVICTED OFFENDERS

	1967	1966	1965	1964	1963	1962	1961	1960
Men	553,557	541,446	506,546	518,682	501,458	528,697	514,514	487,866
Women	70,897	66,306	63,846	67,584	65,225	68,501	63,781	61,088
TOTAL	624,454	607,752	570,392	586,266	566,683	597,198	578,355	548,954

THE NUMBER OF CONVICTIONS ON OFFENSES AGAINST TRAFFIC REGULATIONS

	1967	1966	1965	1964	1963	1962	1961	1960
Men	301,011	293,908	262,355	255,588	241,603	258,291	254,254	216,052
Women	19,379	18,007	16,883	17,315	15,812	17,421	17,208	15,023
TOTAL	320,390	311,915	279,238	272,903	257,415	275,712	271,462	231,075

NOTE: The table gives us information about the number of convicted offenders. Convicted persons are all those who have been sentenced legally by the verdict of a German court, either according to the criminal law to imprisonment or to a fine, or whose offense has been punished according to the Juvenile Penal Code. These figures include adult, adolescent and juvenile persons. In order to emphasize the great number of traffic offenses, they were listed separately.

Table IV

CONVICTED ADULT OFFENDERS

	1966	1965	1964	1963	1962	1961
Male	441,168	412,200	416,208	397,365	410,279	393,104
Female	56,698	55,185	58,122	55,630	58,164	53,622
TOTAL	497,866	467,385	474,330	452,995	468,443	446,726

OF THESE PREVIOUSLY CONVICTED

	1966	1965	1964	1963	1962	1961
Male	198,496	184,167	189,073	179,975	187,436	176,684
Female	12,546	12,873	13,661	13,815	13,302	13,829
TOTAL	211,042	197,040	202,734	193,790	200,738	190,513

TABLE V
ADULT OFFENDERS WHO HAD RECEIVED PRISON SENTENCES OF LESS THAN 10 MONTHS ELIGIBLE FOR PROBATION

	1966	1965	1964	1963	1962	1961
Male	162,555	137,436	126,974	118,833	117,292	111,639
Female	11,974	12,576	13,682	13,874	14,594	13,908
TOTAL	174,529	150,012	140,656	132,707	131,886	125,547

THOSE ACTUALLY PLACED ON PROBATION FROM THE ABOVE GROUP

	1966	1965	1964	1963	1962	1961
Male	54,068	46,559	44,740	42,948	43,529	42,926
Female	7,474	7,967	8,073	8,596	8,829	8,348
TOTAL	61,542	54,526	52,813	51,544	52,358	51,274

NOTE: A deferment of the sentence, probation, means that the verdict of imprisonment for not more than nine months (12 months since the law of September, 1969) is not executed, in order to give the offender the chance to be free of punishment because of good conduct during a specified period of time. This institution can be compared with the American "probation." The table shows first all sentences which could have been eligible for the granting of probation according to the law. The second part shows the number of sentences which actually have been placed on probation.

These studies were initially suggested by the problems of war and post-war crime. Exner and Liepmann investigated the influence of World War I on the development of criminality. The findings of this investigation, that the mass-statistical method has to be supplemented by individual observation of great scope, led to a multitude of special crimino-sociological studies which were published mostly in the series, "Kriminalistische Abhandlungen" (edited by Exner); "Untersuchungen zur Kriminalitat in Thuringen" (Investigations to the Criminality of Thuringia), and "Untersuchungen zur Kriminalitat in Deutschland" (both edited by v. Weber); and currently in "Kriminologischen Untersuchungen" (Criminological Studies). In these studies factors like personality, sex, age, profession, family status, social origin, economic conditions, education and residence of the offender were investigated, as was the special situation at the moment of the offense—as far as it could be read from the acts. It was attempted to consider psychological, psychiatric, and genetic factors.

An excellent survey of the development of German criminology up to World War II can be found in the books of Exner (*Kriminalbiologie;* 1. Aufl., 1939; 3. Aufl. edition, 1949); Mezger (*Kriminalpolitik auf kriminologischer Grundlage* [Special Criminosociological Studies, Results and Tasks], 1939).

After World War II, the attempt was made to catch up with the international developments in the area of crime causation research; here the American criminology gained considerable influence. But criminology's position in the wider frame of social sciences has not been fully clarified. The confrontation between criminologists of the psychiatric and the sociological schools continues to be there. However, in recent years there have been signs of a beginning of an interdisciplinary co-operation.

Within the criminological research of the group getting its orientation from sociology, the dialectic relationship which has been placed into the foreground by such sociologists as Wurzbacher, Scharmann, and Claessens is gaining increasing importance as a scientific model. Within the dynamic playing together of these correlative factors, the processes determining the build up of the socio-cultural personality of man—socialization, enculturation and personalization—gain increasing importance as a starting point for research. In this structure a possibility is being seen to reach beyond the narrowness of the prevalent multifactor model, and to arrange the found factors in an all comprising theory. Such a theoretical criminology also tries to utilize anthropological categories. In doing so it starts from the knowledge that the criminologist—if he views the criminal as a being who is determined by hereditary factors, hormones, milieu, and cultural forces—is not allowed to forget that all these factors constitute only a partial aspect of the human being, and that man in the last analysis is not a completely determined creature. An anthropological point of view is supposed to prevent the researcher from overestimating the results he has found in his narrow area of specialization, in their rank value for the total understanding of human existence and of human acting.

Therefore, one-sidedness of perspective has to be avoided in investigating the personality of the offender and his behavior. Those sides of human existence, which up to now have been largely neglected, will also have to be taken into consideration, with special emphasis on the social and cultural dimensions of man.

At present, sociologists are looking from different angles at the attempts of criminological scientists to grasp theoretically the many empirical research studies of the factors which determine criminal behavior. Starting with the formation of the socio-cultural personality, the attempt is being made to isolate those factors which are decisive in the process of socialization. The realization that deviant behavior can be interpreted as pathological behavior only in exceptional cases, and that it normally follows the same principles as normal behavior, led to the fact that the terms and concepts of a general theory of social acting were transferred to criminological problems. Socio-legal considerations caused investigations about the functionality of the standard for the social system and about the meaning of social control.

From here starts the attempt to abandon the confinement of the classic aetiological questioning and to place criminal behavior into the more comprehensive concept of the process of interaction with social control. However, these methodological problems of the aetiological research are just beginning to be clarified. Already, a new theoretical orientation of "pure" criminologists, dependent on their criminological research, can be discerned.

PENAL PHILOSOPHY

The problem of justification of penalty has been the subject of the science of criminal law since earliest times. On the one hand are the absolute theories of penalty and, on the other, the relative or purpose theories. In the view of the absolute theories, the penalty is only compensation or retaliation for the respective committed offense, and not a means of crime prophylaxis. As compared to this, the relative theories claim that the penalty should not exhaust itself simply by inflicting something harsh on the offender. On the contrary every penalty would have to be seen from the aspect of crime prevention. General prevention has to be discerned from special or individual prevention. According to general prevention, the mere threat of a penalty is supposed to exercise a deterrent effect on every potential offender. The goal of special prevention can be reached by such deterring factors, by education, or by safeguarding the population from the criminal.

Philosophical Foundation and Historical Development

Any survey of the historical development of the penal philosophy in Germany has to start with the often cruel and hard penalties of the Middle Ages. During the period of the Enlightment, the traditional system of punishment was mitigated almost everywhere in Europe due to the expanding thoughts of humanism. The goal was first to find a fair relation between the gravity of the committed offense and the appropriate penalty. In the beginning of the 19th century, the thinking about criminal law was influenced mainly by the demands of the German idealistic philosophy from Kant to Hegel.

The teachings of Kant and Hegel furthered the notion that the highest meaning of penalty was to retaliate for an act the offender had committed in wilful fault. The German codes of criminal law of the 19th century were determined in their spirit and in their crimino-political powers by liberalism and conservatism. The Code of Criminal Law of 1870, which became effective on the first of January 1872 and which is in effect up to the present, tried to arrive at a synthesis of these political discrepancies. It connected the ideas of retaliation by Kant and Hegel with the theory of general prevention by Feuerbach. The guiding principle of criminal law in those days was "general prevention by just retaliation." But already at the end of the century, new intellectual powers like the social welfare movement were beginning to exercise influence on the general thinking regarding crime. At that time, it was the great German teacher of criminal law, Franz von Liszt (1851-1919), who placed the idea of special prevention into the foreground.

The penalty as retaliation changes to a purposeful social penalty. Its purposes, however, are not rigidly predetermined; on the contrary, they have to be combined and chosen according to the personality of the respective offender. The endeavors of von Liszt started a far-reaching new orientation in the system of sanctions of the German criminal law. He was the first to recognize crime as a phenomenon of social reality and on this basis he looked for a connection between criminal law and criminology—an idea which had remained largely isolated up to that time. He was a co-founder of the modern "sociological school of criminal law" that met the bitter resistance of the conservative "classic school." In spite of this opposition, the ideas for which von Liszt fought, such as the concept of education, have gained more and more ground, particularly in the Juvenile Penal Code. Correspondingly, numerous amendments to the Penal Code have been enacted.

During the "Third Reich," between 1933 and 1945, the ideas of retaliation and of the protection of existing law (Rechtsgut) were emphasized more strongly. In addition, the criminal law was increasingly deemphasized by administrative measures (cf. confinement in concentration camps or preventative confinement). Also, especially during the war, the concept of deterring and safeguarding was strongly pushed into the foreground. At the same time the "protection of the people" served more and more as a pretext for disproportionately hard and brutal penalties. The most important result with regard to criminal politics was the introduction of measures for the security and improvement of the Penal Code in 1933, which had been conceived long before the NS period. These measures were placed beside the actual penalties and were meant to supplement them (e.g. confinement in mental institutions or protective custody for dangerous and habitual criminals).

After 1945 the attempt was made to continue the criminal policies of the twenties which had been interrupted so suddenly by the NS period. The first aim had to be the elimination of the traces of National Socialism in the German Penal Code, and to return to the principle of a strictly constitutional state. Furthermore, the great need for reformation of the Penal Code was recognized fully by the public, the science of law, and the legislature. The reform of the Penal Code started in 1953 with the formation of the grand commission for criminal law. On the basis of their suggestions up to 1962, several drafts of a new Penal Code were worked out. The 1962 draft of the Federal Office of Justice followed a conservative line in the reform of the criminal law. The alternative 1966 draft, submitted by several teachers and scholars of criminal law, agreed much more with the demands of a rational modern policy in criminology. In recent years, the special committee of the German "Bundestag" for the reform of the criminal law drafted a new general part of the STGB (Penal Code), with a comprehensive system of penalties and corrective measures, and reformed individual parts of the special section of the STGB. These endeavors resulted in the first reform law of 6/25/69, of the Penal Code and in the second reform law of 7/4/69.

Present Trends in Penal Philosophy

The guiding principles of the present day criminal law in the Federal Republic of Germany are laid down in the constitution of the Federal Republic, the "Grundgesetz" of 1949. According to Article 103 of this constitution, an act can be punished only if a penalty for it has been prescribed by law before the offense was committed (the same wording can be found in § 2, Section I of the Penal Code; compare also Article 7 of the Convention of Human Rights). Article 103 of the constitution states that nobody can be punished for the same crime more than once. Furthermore, capital punishment is abolished according to Article 102 of the constitution.

There is no clear-cut definition of the meaning and purpose of punishment in the Penal Code or in the constitution at the moment. However, it is generally agreed upon that such a definition will have to get its orientation from the idea of esteem for human dignity and the rights of man.

According to this body of thought, it has to be the final purpose of every penalty to enable an orderly and unendangered social life for all citizens. The starting point for these considerations has to be the polarity between the individual and society. Society has to be protected from breaches of law by an individual. At the same time, however, the individual as a free and responsible personality must not be disregarded. Decisive criteria in the search for the goal and the essence of punishment by the State are the protection of the rights, the personality and the guilt of the offender, as well as the thoughts concerning special and general prevention. As a synthesis of these different points of view, the goal of maintaining law and order by the State has to be seen in the protection of the personality, and this has to be accomplished in such a frame as defined by the degree of personal guilt.

Looking ahead toward a future penal code of the Federal Republic, it has to be stated that the two above-mentioned reforms of criminal law (of 1969) do not contain any clear definition about the meaning and purpose of punishment. This question, therefore, continually falls to the interpretation of legal science and jurisdiction. However, in the alternative draft of the criminal law (1966), prepared by the German teachers, it was stated clearly that penalties and measures for protecting the rights serve to re-incorporate the offender into the community of right. This re-incorporation was declared to be the superior goal of inflicting punishment. Only such a definition of the meaning and the purpose of criminal law agrees with the idea of a social and constitutional state in the present time.

FUNCTION OF THE COURT

In Article 20 II, p. 2, of the "Grundegesetz" (GG=constitution), it is formulated that the power of legislation and the executive power are separate.

Organization of Courts in Relation to Government Agencies

As far as the principle of independence of the courts is concerned, a dependency of jurisdiction on other powers exists
only in so far as the courts have to use the laws which have
been enacted by the legislature. In addition, the courts are
free from any outside influence, regardless of whether it is
being attempted by the government or Parliament. According
to Article 97, I, GG, the judges are independent and subject
only to the law. The principle of autonomy of the courts
serves to strengthen the personal and objective independence
of the judge. Neither the government nor the Federal Office
of Justice as a governmental agency are allowed to determine
the order of business of the courts. It is considered to be the
duty of the courts themselves, as they are not bound by directions from outside. The principle that the body of jurisdiction
(court) is not formed from case to case, but always for one
business year in advance, is also a measure to safeguard this
independence. Thus, the government has no influence whatsoever on the composition of a court in individual cases.

Let us now consider the possibility of the above principles
being thrown overboard.

Federal Administration of the Law. The freedom from
direction of the judge does not encompass administrative
matters of law. To this area belongs the administrative activity which creates those outer conditions which enable jurisdiction, such as matters of personnel and the entire administration. Even the supervision of personnel is a matter of the
administration of law. The head of the administrative body
is formed by the Federal Departments of Law; for the Supreme
Court it is the Federal Office of Law and the Federal Office
of Prosecution; whereas for the courts and offices of prosecution
of the individual states, the state offices of law are responsible.
The presidents of the highest state courts report to them,
while the presidents of the Assize Courts (Landgericht) report
to the president of the highest State court. The senior judges
of the county courts are finally responsible to the president of
the Assize (district) Court.

Other Possibilities of Influence. The Government can influence an individual case by giving directions to the prosecution—which are bound to be followed—to propose certain
motions or to suggest specific measures of correction. Also,
the highest representative of the State power (Federal President, Prime Minister or government of the states) has the
final power of decision in matters of amnesty and pardon.

Classification of Courts and their Objectives

The personnel make-up and the area of competence of the
courts is essentially regulated by the law of the constitution
of courts.

"Amtsgericht" (*County Courts*). These are courts for
smaller districts. They are occupied by the number of professional judges which is required in every case. Depending
upon the size, the professional supervision is in the hands of
the president, the director or senior judge of the County Court.

"Landgericht" (*District Courts*). They comprise several areas
of County Courts. They consist of a president and the necessary number of directors and members or judges.

"Oberlandesgericht" (*Supreme Courts of the States*). These
are for larger districts which do not always coincide with the
boundaries of the states. They consist of a president and the
necessary number of senate presidents and judges.

Qualifications, Duties, Ranks, and Obligations of Judges, Prosecutors, and Other Court Members

Only somebody equipped with the qualification for the position
of a judge can be a professional judge.

Professional Judges. They qualify by passing two examinations. The first examination must be preceded by a course
of studies at the law school of a university. Between the first
and the second examination a practical internship of two and
a half years at several courts, or at the office of posecution, or
with an attorney and in the area of administration has to be
completed.

Whoever has served at least three years as a judge, after
having acquired the qualifications for such a position, can be

TABLE VI

"AMTSGERICHT"

Division	Distribution of personnel	Area of competence	Source of law
County judge	1 professional judge	Minor offenses (up to one year of prison), crimes which are crimes only because of repetition	§§24,25 GVG
Court of jurors	1 or 2 professional judges and 2 jurors	Minor offenses of little importance; crimes for which no other court is responsible	§§24, 25, 28, 29 GVG
County judge as judge of a juvenile court	1 professional judge	Offenses of juveniles which are not punished by imprisonment	§§33, 39 JGG
Court of jurors for juveniles	1 professional judge and 2 jurors for juvenile courts (1 male 1 female)	All offenses which do not belong to the area of competence of another juvenile court	§§33, 40, 41 JGG

NOTE: GVG—Gerichtsverfassungsgesetz=law for the constitution of courts, from 1/27/1877 in its form of 12/19/1964.
JGG—Jugendgerichtsgesetz=law for juvenile courts of 8/4/1953.

TABLE VII
"LANDGERICHT"

Division	Distribution of personnel	Area of competence	Legal source
Small criminal court	1 professional judge and 2 jurors	Appeals to sentences of the county judge	§§74,65 GVG
Large criminal court	3 professional judges and 2 jurors	First trials of offenses and crimes of special importance; appeals to sentences of the court of jurors	§§74,76 GVG
Assize court	3 professional judges and 6 jurors	Crimes which involve human lives	§§80,81 GVG
Juvenile court	3 professional judges and 2 jurors for juvenile courts	First trials of especially grave and comprehensive crimes; appeals to sentences of the judge for juveniles and of the court of jurors for juveniles	§§33,41 GVG

TABLE VIII
"OBERLANDESGERICHT"

Division	Distribution of personnel	Area of competence	Legal Source
Senate for revisions and complaints	3 professional judges	Revision of those sentences of the county judge which cannot be reversed by appeal; revisions of appealed sentences of the small and large criminal court; revisions of sentences of the assize court	§§121,122 GVG
Senate for first trials	5 professional judges	Political crimes directed against a state of the federation	§§120,122,134 GVG

appointed with a lifelong tenure. Usually the courts only
employ judges who do not have tenure. The regular procedural system allows for the appointment of the judges by the
government or by the Prime Minister of the State. Judges of
the Federal Supreme Courts are elected.

The independence of the judge is guaranteed by Article 97,
I GG. The judge is bound only to the law. He is not even
bound by decisions of the higher courts. He has the freedom
from directions, and the freedom of responsibility for the
contents of his decisions in view of possible disciplinary measures. The objective independence of the judge is guaranteed
by his personal independence. This implies that a professional
judge can be dismissed or placed on retirement against his
will only by authority of the decision of a court. The principles of irremovability and of a fixed renumeration safeguard
his personal independence.

The social status of the German judges is not as eminent
as that of their Anglo-American counterparts. Their number
is also considerably higher than in countries in the sphere of
Anglo-American law.

According to Article 92, GG, regarding the total jurisdiction
in matters of crimes, every pronouncement of a genuine penalty is reserved to the judges. They represent the final power of
decision. As stipulated in Article 104, II GG, the decision
over the personal freedom of the individual is in the hands
of the judge.

Lay Judges. The election of lay judges includes several
steps. The local community council prepares a list of candidates. From this list a special committee chooses the required
number of jurors. This committee consists of the county
judge as chairman, one administrative officer of the State
government, and 10 people from the court district who are
trusted by its inhabitants. The sequence in which the jurors
participate in the court sessions is determined by a lottery
system during a public session of the County Court.

The lay judges exercise their duties during a main session
to the full extent and with the same right to vote as the
professional judges. In contrast to the juror courts existing
before 1924, where the task of establishing the guilt and of
measuring the penalty was distributed between lay and pro-

fessional judges, today the jurors and the professional judges arrive at their decision together. Courts consisting entirely of lay judges do not exist. The judging of laymen does not play such an important role in Germany as it does in the Anglo-American law. Jurisdiction is largely the duty of professional judges.

The lay judges are technically as independent as professional judges. They are obligated to exercise this honorary duty. They are reimbursed for loss of earnings and for the cost of transportation. They can be excluded and rejected like professional judges.

Prosecutors. At every court an office of prosecution is supposed to exist. Thus the Federal Prosecutor General is assigned to the Supreme Court, the Prosecutors General to the Supreme Courts of the states, the district prosecutors to the County Courts. The Court and the office of the prosecution are two administrative bodies on the same level, without having the right of direction for each other. The superior prosecutors themselves have to follow the directions of their respective secretaries of justice. The senior prosecutors at the Supreme Courts of the states and at the district courts have the right to give directions to all prosecutors in their district. Within the system of prosecution, the police officers are helpers to the office of prosecution.

The emphasis of the activity of the prosecution is on the preliminary proceedings. The prosecution must decide whether to drop the case or to formulate an official accusation. In the usual course the prosecution has to represent the accusation, it has no part in the criminal trial. It is not supposed

TABLE IX
"BUNDESGERICHTHOF"

Divison	Distribution of personnel	Area of competence	Legal source
Senate	5 professional judges	For first trials of political crimes; revisions of sentences of the large criminal courts when the competence of the "Oberlandesgericht" is not justified.	§§134, 134a, 135, 139, GVG

to accuse the offender one-sidedly, but has also to take into consideration evidence that might exonerate the accused.

"*Bundesgerichtshof.*" Supreme Court in Karlsruhe is the highest court for criminal offenses. This consists of a president and the necessary number of senate presidents and federal judges.

Legal Counsel, Attorney, and Lawyer System

Admission, Legal position, and organization of the attorneys of law are regulated by Federal Regulations.

Admission. Attorneys of Law can associate with every legal court in the Federal Republic of Germany. An attorney of law is allowed to plead only at courts for which he is admitted.

Legal Position and Duties of the Attorney of Law. The lawyer is not a government official, on the contrary, he is the representative of a free but legally bound profession. As an independent voice of the law he has a position which is similar to an official government position. In the proceedings of the trial his duty is mainly to defend the accused. The British differentiation between "Barrister" and "Solicitor" is not known in the German Law.

Organization. The attorneys of a district, which encompass that of a supreme court of a state, form a chamber of attorneys. Its duty to further the interests of all lawyers and to supervise its individual members. If violations of professional duties have to be judged, an honorary court of lawyers is competent for that purpose.

Method of Trial

Following are the principles for the starting of a trial:

"*Offizialprinzip*' (§ *152, I, StPO*). The prosecution is opened by the prosecutor because of his office, and without any consideration of the will of the offended. Popular accusations are permitted only in rare and less grave cases (§374, StPO).

"*Akkusationsprincip*" (*Principle of Accusation*). The opening of a court investigation depends on an accusation (§ 151, StPO). Usually the prosecution makes all accusations.

"*Legalitatsprinzip*" (*Principle of Legality*). The prosecution is normally obligated to follow up all acts which are punishable and can be prosecuted, as long as there exists sufficient evidence (§ 152, II, StPO).

Contrary to Anglo-American ways of proceedings where the method of trial is predominant, the principle of preliminary proceedings is valid in Germany. The court investigates the facts itself and is not bound to declarations of trial participants (§ 244, II, StPO). Unlike the Anglo-American ways of proceedings, there exist only a few legal rules for providing evidence. The principle of free evaluation of the evidence is in force here (§ 261, StPO).

In *dubio pro reo* the accused does not have to prove his innocence, on the contrary he has to be proved guilty. The burden of material evidence consequently is always carried by the prosection.

The basis for the sentence is only what has been said during the main trial. In other words, the oral principle is generally applied. The main trial is open to the public.

Course of the Proceedings (Regulated by the StPO)

The regular trial proceedings, which are separated from the execution proceedings by the legal sentence, are divided into preliminary, intermediate, and main proceedings.

Preliminary Proceedings. The simple preliminary proceedings are supposed to be undertaken by the prosecution, which is mostly done by the police. The preliminary proceedings end with the decision of the prosecution—either to accuse or to close the investigation. In cases where the preliminary proceedings by the prosecution are followed by an investigation of a professional judge, the case of accusation is followed by another step.

Intermediate Proceedings (§ *198—212 b, StPO*). The intermediate proceedings are done by the court which decides to have them carried out. They begin with the arrival of the document of indictment, and end with the decision of the court whether the main trial shall be opened or whether the accused shall be freed of prosecution. A case of opening would be followed by the next step.

Main Proceedings or Trial (§ *226-275, StPO*). The prepara-

tion of the trial (§ 213—225 StPO) consists mainly of setting
dates, inviting witnesses, and possibly scheduling hearings of
witnesses. The conduct of the trial is up to the presiding
judge. He has to examine the accused and the witnesses
(§ 238, I, StPO). In the Germain main trial, the judge is
considerably more prominent than in the Anglo-American
law. Cross examinations are rare and are to be permitted
by the chairman only if the prosecution and defense both
ask for it (§ 239, StPO). After the hearing of witnesses is
finished, the prosecutor and the defense have the opportunity for their final speeches. The accused always has the
last word. The main trial ends with the pronouncement of
the sentence which has been reached in secret consultation.

Right to Appeal

Sentences of the county judge and of the court of jurors can
be challenged (§312, StPO) if the decision is felt to be unjust.
The appeal has to be placed with the court of the first trial
(judex a quo: §314, StPO). The court of appeals is the small
or the large Criminal Court.

The court of appeals re-examines the case with regard to the
facts and the legal procedure of the trial. If the appeal is justified, the sentence is nullified. Normally the court of appeals
takes the decision itself in such cases. The sentence is not
allowed to be changed to the disadvantage of the accused as
long as the accused, or in his favor the prosecution, has appealed the sentence (inhibition of the reformation in peius: §331,
StPO).

Revision. This is possible for all sentences from the court of
jurors, all first sentences of the Criminal Courts, the appeal
sentences of the Criminal Court, and the sentences of the
County Court (§§333—335, StPO). The request for revision
has to be placed with thec ourt whose sentence is felt to be unjust. The court of revision for sentences from the court of
jurors, and for first sentences, is the Supreme Court; for all other
cases, it is the Supreme Court of the State. The revision leads
to a re-examination of the law which can be justified only
if the sentence is in violation of law (§337, StPO). The wrong
statement or appraisal of facts, however, cannot be rectified

by revision. If revision is possible, and if it proves to be justified, the revision court declares the sentence null and void. In contrast to the procedures of appeal the court of revision normally refers the sentence back to another division of the court whose sentence has been overruled (§354, II, StPO). Also in the realm of revision, the inhibition of the reformation in peius is valid (§358, II, StPO).

Complaint. This has been made possible in order to re-examine decisions of courts of first sentences and courts of appeal, and to re-examine ordinances with regard to the facts and the legality. Complaints are directed to the *judex a quo*, in urgent cases they can also be brought to the court of complaints directly. In contrast to the appeal and to the revision, it does not hinder the execution of the decision which caused the complaint. The decision about the complaint is made without hearing on the basis of acts (legal documents) alone.

Reopening of a Case. Legal decisions can be reversed only on very few conditions by reopening a case (§359, StPO). The decision on such a request is not made by a higher court, but by the same court that has made this decision (§367, StPO). The execution is not hindered by the request for reopening a case (§361, StPO).

FUNCTIONS OF THE POLICE

The principal duty of the police is to counteract, in the interest of the population, all disturbances of public order and security. The police, therefore, are part of executive power of the State. Police power does not participate in jurisdiction. There are no police courts.

Police Organization

There are two types of police: the administrative police and the security police. Here, we are concerned only with the security police. One of their main duties is the prevention and the repressive prosecution of criminal offenses. With regard to organization, the police force is part of the administration of inner affairs and not of the administration of justice. This holds true even if, as is the case with the criminal police, its

occupation consists exclusively in prosecuting criminal offenses. However, under certain circumstances, which have been
described earlier, the police are technically subordinated to
organs of the law like the prosecution or the investigation
judge. On the basis of the general administrative competency
of the federal states (Article 30, GG), the function of the police
is up to the individual states of the federation. The police
force is subordinated to the respective secretary or senator of
the interior. The organizational structure is different in the
individual states. There are common features, however, in
matters of the basic structure. In the states, which are larger
in terms of area and population, four horizontal levels can be
discerned: the government, district, county, and local level.
Vertically, the security police are divided essentially into the
criminal police (not wearing uniform), the protection police,
the water protection police (coast guard), and the stand-by
police, all of which wear uniforms.

The criminal police have become most independent because
of the special duties they have to perform. With their specially
trained personnel, they have to prosecute all of the more important criminal offenses, while the prophylactic prevention of
criminal offenses and the prosecution of less important offenses
is done by all other types of police officers. The center for all
criminal police officers is the criminal office of each state. These
transmit all information and documents that are necessary to
the federal office of crime. It has not only the obligation to
collect all material for the respective state, but also to prepare
the criminal statistics, to inform the police offices, to inform
the population, to maintain all equipment necessary for communication and identification, and to follow up on certain
crimes (like narcotics, counterfeiting).

The protective police in uniform is the agent of execution,
the general branch of the total police executive power. That
holds true also for the coast guard and the stand-by police,
which live in camps, and whose duties it is to do the job of
the protective police in state or nation-wide emergencies.

In spite of the federal structure of the Federal Republic,
the federation itself has police groups. First of all, we shall
take up the Federal Office of Crime Investigation in Wiesbaden. Its duty is to fight criminals who are operating beyond

the borders of an individual state. The office has to collect all information and data pertaining to the fight against crime led by the police and to the prosecution of crime; it has to inform the government agencies of the states and to maintain equipment for communication, identification, and of criminological technology. The prosecution of criminal offenses is normally a duty of the police of the states. However, the Federal Office of Investigation can follow up on a criminal offense itself, if a state agency so requests, or if the secretary of the interior orders it because of "serious reasons."

In such cases the federal office of investigation is allowed to give directions to the state agencies. It maintains its own officials, who are allowed insofar as they are capable to operate in the area of the entire Federal Republic. If possible, however, they shall co-operate with the local police. An important duty of the Federal Office of Investigation is the international co-operation in the frame of "Interpol."

Objectives, Policies, and Duties of the Police

The prosecution of criminal offenses is the duty of the office of prosecution, which is an independent agency of the law. The office of prosecution investigates suspects and, if necessary, accuses them. The office does not have its own organs of execution which could hear witnesses, execute warrants for arrest, preliminary arrests, confiscations, and raids. The office of prosecution therefore co-operates closely with the police. The method of co-operation and the duties and the rights of the police are defined by the regulations for the proceedings of criminal trials (StPO), and the Law for the Constitution of Courts (GVG).

According to §163, StPO, the agencies and officers of the police have to investigate criminal offenses, and arrange all undelayable measures to prevent the danger of prejudicing the course of justice. In doing so the police have to follow up, except for unimportant exceptions on the grounds of the principle of legality, *every* suspicion which is based on sufficient actual clues. This means that the police are not allowed to neglect a prosecution on the basis of their own judgment. According to law, the police are supposed to act principally upon request or on behalf of the office of prosecution, because it is the highest authority in all preliminary proceedings. However, according to §163, StPO, the police have the right and the duty of the first seizure, which means that they are allowed in urgent cases to proceed on their own and independently.

In such cases the police have to submit the findings of their investigations to the office of prosecution immediately, so that it has the opportunity to take over the proceedings.

In practice, however, things have evolved differently. Thus, normally, the police lead the investigations without the participation of the office of prosecution except in cases of extremely serious crimes. After termination of its investigation, it submits the results to the office of prosecution, which decides on the bas s of the evidence whether to accuse or not. This practical course is based on the criminalistic superiority of the police over the prosecutors who are usually lacking in a crimino-technological and tactical training.

Within the organization, besides co-operation with the office of prosecution, two groups of police have to be discerned who have different rights. In principle all agencies and officers of the police are obligated—according to §161, StPO—to help the office of prosecution or request without being subjected to an immediate power of order. Certain officers of the police have been declared by law, according to §152, GVG, as "helping officers" of the office of prosecution. This means that the office of prosecution can give directions to these officers directly, regardless of the fact that these officers continue to remain within the organizational frame of the police. As far as the execution of their orders and disciplinary law is concerned, they are responsible to the office of prosecution. Besides being bound by such directions, the position of the helping officers differs from that of the others in view of the fact that the helping officer can employ a number of means for investigation and compulsion which normally only the judge or the office of prosecution can use.

An important activity of the police, in addition to investigation, is the preventive fight against crime. This encompasses the collection and evaluation of criminalistic materials with regard to certain types of crimes and offenders, in order to gain a criminalistically founded basis for a successful prevention of crime. To the realm of this activity belongs also the information of the population as to the danger or the methods of certain offenders, i.e. swindlers' and sexual criminals.

Powers of the Police

The police enjoy the following powers in terms of arrest, search, etc.

Temporary Arrest. Normally only a judge can order the arrest of a suspect. Prerequisite for the issue of a warrant for arrest by a judge is the urgent suspicion of having committed an offense, and either danger of flight or danger of prejudicing the course of justice, or (in the case of certain sexual offenses), the danger of repetition. The police also operate under these conditions of imminent danger (not only the helping officers of §127, Section 2, StPO). Imminent danger means that the suspect would probably flee or or prejudice the course of justice without the immediate action of the police. The person temporarily arrested has to be presented to a judge immediately, at the latest on the day after the arrest. The judge in turn has to issue a warrant for arrest or to release the person (Article 104, Section 2-3, GG, §128, StPO). If it is impossible to get a decision of a judge by the end of the day after the arrest, the person has to be released.

In the area of the preventive fight against crime, the police also have the right on certain conditions—which differ in the individual states—to arrest a person temporarily (custody of police). Here the same limit has to be met. The arrest must be necessary in order to prevent an immediately serious danger of public security—i.e. an imminent commitment of a crime— if the prevention of this crime is not possible in any other way.

Search. A suspect and his living quarters (including clothes and other personal possessions) can be searched only if this leads to his arrest, and also if it can be assumed that the search will lead to material evidence (§102, StPO). The search of an apartment or house at night is allowed provided the offender is being followed in the very act of committing a crime, or if danger is imminent. A judge alone can issue a warrant for search. However, if the search promises success if done immediately, the police can also issue the warrant, but this can be done only by the helping officers of the office of prosecution.

Confiscation. Objects which can be of importance as evidence for the investigation are allowed to be confiscated upon the order of a judge. Such orders can also be issued by the helping officers of the office of prosecution, if danger is imminent. Orders of this type are supposed to be confirmed by a judge within three days. The concerned individual can demand at any time a confiscation warrant by a judge.

Search of the Body. A suspect's body can be searched only with the purpose of establishing facts which are of importance for the criminal proceedings (§81 a, StPO). Thus it is allowed to have a sample of blood taken by a physician without the consent of the accused, provided that it does not endanger the health of the person. The order for search of the body is to be issused by a judge. If the success of the investigation is endangered by delay, it can also be issued by the office of prosecution or its helping officers. Other persons than the accused have to submit to a search of their bodies only if they are possible witnesses, and it has to be established whether their bodies show a certain trace of a crime (§81 c, StPO.)

Measures Serving Identification. For the purpose of a criminal trial or identification, the police (not only the helping officers) are allowed to take pictures and fingerprints against the will of the accused. (§81 b, StPO).

Rights of Punishment. The pronouncement of criminal punishment, regardless of the type, is the exclusive right of the judge. The police are only allowed to issue fines for less serious violations of traffic regulations. They are issued in a process which is similar to that of a court, and they cannot be higher than 1,000 DM. However, the person who has been fined can appeal against such decisions at a court. A single officer can issue on the spot fines for unimportant violations up to 20 DM.

Internal Structure of the Police

The Federal Office of Investigation issues a search book which contains all wanted persons. The "BundesKriminalblatt" (Bulletin of the Federal Office of Investigation) appears five times a week and lists all unsolved crimes, and crimes of known criminals, especially of travelling offenders.

Patrol Activities, Search. The general security police in uniform carry out motor patrols regularly under the supervision and control of traffic as well as the general fight against crime. The criminal police entertain special divisions which are occupied exclusively with the search for wanted criminals. There are existing special search patrols whose activities focus on special areas and places. Larger local offices, the state offices of investigation, and also the federal office of investigation, keep special search files for search of objects, especially stolen cars, and persons. The files are being supplemented daily.

Special Divisions of Criminal Technology. The local criminal offices, especially the state offices and the federal office of investigation, maintain special places for criminal-technological investigations which deal with the study and evaluation of traces of medical, chemical, physical, or biological types. They have at their disposal modern technological equipment and laboratories.

Operation of Prisons. Prisons (jails) operated by the police—as found in the USA—do not exist in the Federal Republic of Germany. The police, therefore, are not involved immediately with the execution of imprisonment.

Police Ratio per 1,00,000 Population

In 1967, there were, in the Federal Republic of Germany (without West Berlin), approximately 107,000 police officers in uniform (protective police, coast guard, and stand-by police), and about 12,000 officers of the criminal police. For every 1,00,000 inhabitants, 208 police officers were available, based on the population of about 57 million. This calculation does not consider the special police of the Federal Railroad system, 24,000 officers, the police troops of the federation, the border guards—comprising 20,000 men—whose duty consists exclusively of guarding the federal borders.

Generally, the total number of police officers is considered to be too low to master the rising wave of crime. An increase in personnel is being demanded from many sides.

FUNCTION OF THE PRISON

Since 1945, the execution of the court sentence is the duty
of the individual states of the federation. The present organization, as well as the ways of executing the sentence, is patterned on the regulations for duty and execution issued by the
state administrations of justice (12/1/61).

Prison Organization

According to the above-mentioned regulations, the independent institutions of detention which have a full-time director
have to be distinguished from the court-prisons, which are
led on a part-time basis by a judge or a prosecutor. The independent institutions serve the fulfilment of imprisonment
and measures of protection or improvement. In the court-
prisons, detention pending investigation and shorter periods
of imprisonment are being executed. The period of imprisonment is not to exceed three months. In the Federal Republic
of Germany there existed (on 1/1/67) a total of 302 justice-
owned prisons including all court-prisons, labor camps, and
institutions of detention pending investigation. These institutions had a total of 54,883 inmates, among whom 2,288 (or
about 4 per cent) were women. The supervision of these
institutions is exercised by the respective state secretaries of
justice, partly also by the attorney generals. Furthermore, so-
called "Gefangnisbeirate" (prison councils) exist in several federal states. They consist of a group of free citizens who visit
the prisons occasionally in order to get an independent picture
of the process of execution and of possible grievances.

Internal Arrangement of Prisons

There are different types of independent institutions of detention. Most common are the general prisons, in which sentences
for the penitentiary and for the prison are fulfilled. There are
also institutions or divisions specially meant for the execution
of measures of protection and improvement.

Besides special institutions for those offenders who are serving for the first time, there are juvenile detention institutions,

institutions for detention pending investigation, and prisons for women. There also exist so-called open or half-open institutions and houses for sick prisoners. The space situation in the Federal Republic of Germany is responsible for the fact that prisoners in detention pending investigation, young prisoners, persons in protective custody, women and sick prisoners can not always be accommodated in special institutions. In such cases an orderly separation within the institution has to be provided.

Of the already mentioned 302 institutions for imprisonment owned by the department of justice in 1967, 191 were smaller court-prisons of County or District Courts which can seldom hold more than 40-50 prisoners. These are for short period imprisonments and detentions pending investigation. However on grounds of simplifying the administrative process and saving costs, the number of court-prisons is gradually being reduced.

The following is a distribution of prisoners serving in institutions owned by the department of justice (that means exclusive of prisoners being detained pending investigation) for a specific day, i.e. 3/31/67 (the portion of women has been indicated in brackets): Of a total of 48,031 (2,025) prisoners, 8,296 (319) served in a penitentiary, 32,635 (1,302) in a prison, 5,292 (92) in a prison for juveniles, and 1,808 (312) in other types of detention institutions. Among these, 1,028 (124) persons had to serve lifelong imprisonment.

Methods of Rehabilitation

According to point 57 of the already mentioned regulations for duty and execution (of 1/1/61), the meaning of the prison sentence is to protect the population, to help the prisoner recognize that he has to pay for a committed crime, and to resocialize him. Within the science of justice it is generally accepted today that the chief purpose of a sentence has to be to integrate the offender into society again. For every resocialization is a step towards the realization of the principle of protecting the goods of law which is being aimed at by material execution of a sentence. In the course of practice, however, the execution of a sentence is often still being done as a security measure.

In the process of resocialization, measures during the stay

in aprison and measures after the release of a prisoner are to be distinguished. Within the institution of detention, the foremost goal of resocializing is to accustom the prisoner to regular work. In doing so the attempt is made to utilize the socializing effects of work and job for the prisoner.

In German prisons there exist two types of work places. On the one hand, there are the so called "Unternehmerbetriebe," which are operated by companies of the free business world within the prisons and provide the prisoners with jobs. These are mostly industrial or similar work halls, in which assembly jobs for the companies are done, or half or ready-made products for sale on the free market are being produced. On the other hand, there are the state-owned operations, which do mainly jobs of a manual or agricultural type.

The work operations in prisons, although an improvement on the past, are nowhere near the standards of free enterprise with regard to its technological and economic organization. Most often, orders and trained personnel are lacking. That is the reason why the prisoners in many institutions are still being employed with "Verlegenheitsarbeiten" (jobs to fill the time) like making nets or paper bags. In some selected institutions, a few specially chosen prisoners are given the opportunity to work outside the prison in industrial operations during the day and to return in the evening. The institution of "Freigangertum" (free-walker) provides encouraging experiences, for the prisoner is working in an environment he will find after having been released. At the same time the negative effects of the prison sub-culture are eliminated.

The prisoner does not receive any wages, but only a nominal recompense for his work which lies somewhere between 0.50 DM and 1.20 DM per day. Added to that, he can get a certain "Leistingspramie" (efficiency premium) up to 20.00 DM per month. The average earnings of a prisoner in the year 1966-67 amounted to not quite 30.00 DM per month. Half of this money the prisoner can use for himself, the other half is kept for the time of his release. However, there does not exist any legal right for this recompense.

The job training and development facilities available to the prisoners leave much to be desired. Only in a few institutions can one learn an apprenticeship for a trade and a corresponding final examination. Increasing attempt is being made to train the prisoners for jobs in industry in order to facilitate their transition into the world of free enterprise.

Thus, not only the work but also the correct ways of filling the prisoners' free time are important in the area of execution of sentences. The prisoner can choose from among a growing choice of leisure-time occupations. Sports, games, hobbies, and discussion groups are being formed. The prisoner has also the opportunity to participate in home study courses, to use the library of the institution, or to contribute to the prison newspaper. Besides that the prisoners can also listen to the radio and watch TV and films occasionally.

Special methods of treatment for the process of resocialization are still seldom to be found in the practice of German imprisonment. The use of individual or group therapy as well as other psychotherapeutic methods is still in its infancy, mainly because the necessary personnel and the money for equipment is lacking. Very few institutions have a psychologist or a psychiatrist. In the year 1966-67, only 10 psychiatrists and 13 psychologists were available for 53 independent institutions with 39,000 inmates. Therefore, the task of personality study and the treatment of prisoners is mostly left to the social workers and teachers. By and by, in some institutions group-counselling is being done.

Juvenile Detention Homes or Prisons

The punishment of juveniles (14-18 years) was completely reorganized by the first German "Jugendgerichtsgestz," the law for juvenile courts (2/16/23). Since that time the criminal law for juveniles has been an independent entity beside the criminal law for adults. According to this law, measures of education have to be given preference to penalties.

The criminal law for juveniles (8/4/53) describes the types of arrest of juveniles: the arrest during leisure time (up to four days), the short arrest (up to six days), and the continuous arrest (up to four weeks). This is executed in special institutions for juvenile arrest (juvenile detention homes), and in special rooms for the leisure-time arrest.

Similarly, the juvenile punishment is executed in special

institutions meant for this purpose. A special form of juvenile penalty is the punishment for an undetermined period of time. The time is indicated only as a frame from at least six months to, at the most, four years. After the lapse of the minimal period, the appropriate judge will determine whether the sentenced person can be released and considered for resocialization, or whether he will have to serve time in the institution. The foremost goal of such sentences is to educate the youth to a legal and responsible way of conduct. This also means accustoming the juvenile to regular work and a meaningful way of spending his leisure time. Furthermore, in every juvenile detention home there are special teachers, who instruct the youth as in school. Even if the methods of execution in the realm of juvenile jurisdiction are more progressive and less strict than in the area of adult jurisdiction, the fact remains that the execution of juvenile sentences needs to be reformed still further.

Methods of Capital Punishments

In the Federal Republic of Germany the capital punishment was abolished by Article 102 of the Constitution. The Penal Code of 1871 (§13) had provided for capital punishment, first, in the case of a completed murder; and secondly, in the case of an assassination attempt on the emperor or another head of a country. During the "Third Reich," the application of capital punishment was extended to a number of other political offenses. For the first time, however, it provided for lifelong imprisonment in case of murder in exceptional cases. After the war, from 1945-1949, capital punishment was pronounced only in case of murder, but not executed any longer.

In spite of the abolition of capital punishment, the discussion about its re-establishment has never ceased in Germany. Nationwide polls show that even today more than half of the population would like to see capital punishment reintroduced for especially detestable crimes. However, within the realm of jurisdiction and within parliaments, there is a growing conviction that capital punishment does not have greater deterrent power than lifelong imprisonment. Practically speaking, a re-establishment of capital punishment would only be possible today by means of a change in the Constitution, for which two-thirds of the representatives of Parliament would be needed.

PROBATION AND PAROLE SYSTEM

In the Federal Republic of Germany the "Strafaussetzumg zur Bewährung" (probation), which can be compared to the Anglo-American institution of "probation" without being identical with it, is regulated in the §23 through 25 of the Penal Code (StGB).

Probation for Adults

The basic philosophy behind probation is to give an offender—who has been sentenced to a short-term in prison—the opportunity to remain free of punishment after the offense, if he behaves well. This furthers the process of resocialization and avoids the dangers which lie outside the purpose of the penalty but which could not be avoided if the short-term sentence would have to be served in prison. According to §23 StGB, the court places on offender on probation if the penalty does not surpass 12 months, and if the prognosis of the court with regard to the offender justifies the expectation that, under the impact of probation, he is likely to lead a legal and orderly life in future. This means that the pronouncement of the sentence was enough to warn him and its execution can be waived. Therefore, a sentence of over six months is not eligible for probation if the defense of the legal order demands its execution.

The time of probation lasts not less than two years and not longer than five years. The following table provides data regarding the number of sentences with probation (adults):

TABLE X

1966	1965	1964	1963	1962	1961
61,542	54,526	52,813	51,544	52,358	51,274

According to §42a and 24b StGb, the probation can be coupled with certain injunctions and directives. These injunctions serve the purpose of giving satisfaction for the committed offense.

The following injunctions are provided for in §24a: (*i*) Reparation of damages connected with the offense; (*ii*) Payment of fines in favor of an institution of public benefit (nonprofit organizations); and (*iii*) to do other work beneficial to the public.

The directives have the purpose of helping the sentenced person find the way to a legal and orderly life. They aim at a merely individual prevention, as for example sojourn, education, training, work, leisure time, order in economic state of the sentenced person; agreement to special doctors' care or treatment for drug and other addicts; agreement to pay alimony; and submission to the supervision of a probation helper.

If the sentenced person is successful in the probation period, his penalty is waived. If he does not fulfil the expectations of probation, the latter is repealed. According to §25 if the sentenced person violates the injunctions placed upon him, or if he is sentenced to imprisonment during the period of probation for another crime, or if he indicates in another fashion that the trust placed in him was not justified the probation is repealed.

Probation of Juveniles and Adolescents

The probation of juvenile penalties is regulated in the §§20-26 of the Juvenile Penal Code (JGG). According to them the judge can place a sentenced juvenile or adolescent on probation if the penalty is not more than one year, so that the person can attain waiver of penalty during the period of probation. The sentenced juvenile can be considered for this only if his personality and previous life, in conjunction with his behavior after the offense, warrants the expectation of such a favorable change in the ways of life that he will show a legal and orderly conduct under the educational impact of the period of probation. The latter consists of at least two or, at the most, three years. Under certain circumstances it can be shortened afterwards to one year or lengthened to four years.

During the period of probation the conduct of the juvenile is to be influenced by injunctions and directives that guarantee a comprehensive educational impact. These injunctions encompass directives concerning the place of sojourn, the place of work, the company of certain persons, or the use of tobacco and alcoholic beverages. The judge can also place certain duties on the juvenile, as reparation of damages, or the payment of a certain sum to an institution of public benefit. While adults are placed under the supervision of a probation helper only in the rarest instances, this is always the case with juveniles (§24, JGG).

If the juvenile has passed probation, his penalty is waived after the period of probation is over. The repeal of the probation by the judge occurs if circumstances become known which would have led, considering the essence of probation, to its being denied. Probation is also repealed if the juvenile, who is older than 16 years, refuses to promise the fulfilment of his injunctions; if he is guilty of not complying willfully with the probation directives, or if he indicates in another way that he was not worth the trust placed in him.

It also needs to be pointed out that for adults as well as for juvenile offenders probation can be pronounced by way of an act of grace.

Conditional Release (Parole) of Adults

The conditional release can be compared, to a certain degree, with the American institution of "parole." In contrast to probation, the sentenced person has the possibility of proving his legal conduct under the conditional release system only after having served a part of his penalty.

The law restricts itself to only two positive conditions which can make a conditional release possible: first, the serving of at least two-thirds of the total penalty, or a minimum of two months (in special cases only after half of the penalty has been served, or at least one year); and, secondly, a favorable prognosis for a future legal and orderly conduct outside the prison.

The period of probation is variable. Its minimum is not allowed to be shorter than that part of the penalty which has not yet been served. Its upper limit is equal to a normal probation of five years. The decision over the conditional release has to be made—exactly like the decision on probation according to 23 StGB—by the court which has sentenced the offender for the first time. For the shaping of the period of probation the same regulations apply as for the probation itself. The court can give injunctions and directives to the released, it can put him under the supervision of a probation helper, and can also repeal the probation if the released person has a relapse. In case he passes the probation period, the remaining penalty is waived.

The crimino-political importance of the conditional release lies in the following points. First, it is supposed to be a stimulant for the sentenced person to earn waiver of the rest of his penalty by good conduct. Secondly, the conditional release forms the last step of an orderly, progressive procedure, which starts with a strict beginning phase and is being eased progressively. In this sense the period of conditional freedom is logically and practically the last step before the transition into total freedom. Thirdly, the conditional release shall help the sentenced person in completing the transition to total freedom. He needs help especially in the early period after his release from prison, during which, as experience has taught us, the danger of a relapse is greatest. This opportunity is offered only by the system of conditional release because of the combination of injunctions, conditions with probational help and supervision, and the threat of repeal in case of failure. Few of these conditions can be applied once the person has served out his full sentence.

Parole for Juveniles

The judge for juveniles, as the execution director, can release the juvenile who has been sentenced to a certain penalty, if he has served part of his sentence and if the circumstances warrant the expectation that he will lead a responsible life in future (§88, JGG). Before a period of six months has elapsed, release on probation can be ordered only on very special grounds. This release is permitted for sentences of more than one year, if the sentenced juvenile has served at least one-third of his penalty. The juvenile released on probation is placed by the execution director under supervision. For that period of probation the regulations for the conditional release apply. correspondingly. In the case of a sentence for an undetermined period of time, where only a minimum and a maximum time limit is specified, the release on probation is possible only if the juvenile has served the minimum period of his penalty, and if the circumstances warrant the expectation that in future he will show an orderly conduct (§89, JGG). Besides that, the regulations of §88, JGG also apply in this case.

Like the regular probation, the conditional release for probation can be pronounced via an act of grace.

For the regular probation, as well as for the conditional release, one of the injunctions for the sentenced person consists in the promise to accept the supervision and the directives of a probation helper (§24c, StGB). While this is done rarely for adults—due to lack of able supervisors—juvenile offenders on probation are always placed under the supervision of a helper who supervises their conduct in a general way and sees to it that they fulfill the injunctions. In doing so he acts as a caretaker and tries to help the probationer overcome difficulties during the early period. In the case of juvenile probationers, the helper is also supposed to co-operate on a basis of trust with the parents or guardians, the school, and the director of job training.

The following statistics show that during recent years the number of helpers and probationers has remained approximately constant; and on an average, one helper takes care of 50 probationers.

TABLE XI

	1967	1966	1965	1964
Number of helpers	519	516	518	511
Number of probationers	26,203	25,095	26,149	26,739

Of the yearly additions of paroled, those on probation are in the majority, as is clear from the following table:

TABLE XII

Additions per year	1967	1966	1965	1964
On probation	8,063	6,662	6,440	7,101
On conditional release	5,078	4,511	5,144	4,929
TOTAL	13,141	11,173	11,584	12,030

The number of successful probations is always in excess of the number of repeals because of failure. As we shall see, on the whole, approximately 55 per cent of the probationers were successful. The majority of repeals were caused by a new offense on the part of the probationer.

TABLE XIII

Reductions	1967	1966	1965	1964
End of the help because of successful probation	6,290	6,540	6,702	7,004
Repeals	5,427	5,456	5,196	5,386
TOTAL	11,717	11,996	11,898	12,390

STUDY OF CRIMINOLOGY: A GENERAL SURVEY

Almost all universities of the Federal Republic of Germany offer courses, lectures, seminars, and colloquia in the areas of criminology, juvenile criminology, and science of execution of sentences. These are normally one or two weekly credit-hour courses.

Universities Offering Courses in Criminology

The universities of Berlin, Bochum, Giessen, Frankfurt/M., Freiburg/Br., Hamburg, Heidelberg, Koln, Mainz, Mannheim, Munchen, Saarbrucken, and Tubingen offer courses in all areas. Special lectures on juvenile criminology are available at the universities of Frankfurt/M., Hiedelberg, and Mannheim; and lectures on the science of sentence execution at the universities of Berlin, Freiburg/Br., and Saarbrucken.

Outside the universities, criminological questions and problems are being investigated and taught by the Federal Office of Investigation in Wiesbaden and the different offices of investigation of the states, as well as by police schools and institutes. These institutions are meant especially for the training and education of police officers. They regularly exchange ideas with the university law schools and assist them by providing research, statistics and other important data. Finally, criminological research is furthered by the German Criminological Society (headquartered at Frankfurt/M.), the Society for Criminology, the Society of Crime Prevention, the German Association for Juvenile Court and Helpers of Juvenile Courts, the German Association for Sexual Research, the German Association for Court and Social Medicine, the German Juvenile Institute in Munich, and the Academy for Basic Criminological Research in Kassel.

Most criminological lectures, colloquia, and seminars are offered by the faculty of the law school, but occasionally also by the institutes of sociology, medicine or criminal medicine. There are indications of an interdisciplinary co-operation at some universities of the Federal Republic. Thus the University at Hamburg formed a special research group to discuss criminological problems on an interdisciplinary level. The criminological institute of the University of Tubingen is carrying out studies which involve lawmen, psychiatrists, psychologists, criminologists, and sociologists. A similar group consisting of lawmen and psychiatrists has been formed at the University of Ulm. At the University of Munster, criminological questions are discussed on an interdisciplinary level between professors of law, psychology, sociology and others. Also at the University of Freiburg/Br., regular seminars between scientists of the criminological institutes and the psychiatric clinic are taking place.

Current Problems

The fight over the scientific subject matter of criminology continues to be undecided in the Federal Republic of Germany. A conservative and narrow view considers the ways of behavior, as typified by the Penal Code, to be the subject of criminological research. This conception, however, is limited to a few only. More and more, the study of "socially abnormal behavior," which is situated in the so-called "perimeter of crime," is considered as the prime subject matter of the science of criminology. This is so because criminological science has not only to deal with crime *per se*, but also with questions of alcoholism, prostitution, neglect of juveniles, and suicide. It has also been seen that analyses of the problems of creating and using penal standards, the effects of the penalty in and outside the process of execution, and questions concerning the treatment of law offenders belong to the field of criminology. The basic understanding of this wider conception is that the development and the behavior of offenders can only be seen properly in the context of a continuous contact with the standards and institutions of law and with the representatives of law enforcement. On the other hand, the "Kriminalistik," the technical teachings about the actual detection of crime are not included in the area of criminology.

With regard to the correct ways of study, the leading question is whether only the methods of natural sciences—or also those of the humanities—are to be legitimately used in the field of criminology. This problem also dominated its neighboring sciences like sociology or psychology for a long time. In the beginning of criminological research in Germany, scientific methods were being mostly used. However, this concept turned out to be too narrow and gradually the methods of humanities and social sciences found their way into criminological research.

The problems facing criminological science of the Federal Republic of Germany today are of a very common nature. The focus is on the relationship between empirical criminology and criminal politics, especially on the effects of criminological research on the jurisdiction and the penal legislation. These questions have tremendous importance at the moment as a new penal code and a new code for the execution of sentences is being prepared in the country. Unfortunately, the courts and the organs of penal legislation do not always fully evaluate and use the contributions of scientific criminology and penology. In the area of empirical criminology, the problems of increasing juvenile delinquency and white-collar crimes are in the foreground. In the realm of empirical investigations, interview, questionnaire, description of life, and the testing procedure are of special importance. For the study of criminality as a social mass-phenomenon, statistics are being used, and general, critical analyses of a culture or time are being done.

Research Projects

At the various universities and other institutes of higher edu cation, investigations in different areas of criminology and sentence execution are being carried out. Some of the most important studies from the recent past are enumerated below.

The institute of sociology at the Free University of Berlin did one major study in each area, viz. the situation of criminal sociology in the Federal Republic; the process of resocialization in families of alcoholics; and the theory of differential association in the framework of abnormal sociology. At the psychological institute of the University of Erlangen-Nurnberg, a study of family and evironmental data for juvenile criminals and depraved juveniles is in progress. This is an individual investigation in the framework of a more comprehensive project with the preliminary title: "The Effects of the Family Constellation on the Person, his Social Relations and the Following Generation." At the institute of sociology and social-anthropology of the same University, a preliminary study of the number of roles (Rollenfeld) of the probation helper is being done. At the institute for criminology of the University of Frankfurt/M., the various offenses—and the factors that can alter them—are being investigated. Questions pertaining to criminality among children and juvenile arsonists, and the education and psychotherapy of criminals are also under study. Besides this, sociological and criminological studies in a slum area of Heidelberg are underway. Since 1965 this institute has been responsible for the so-called "Heidelberg Documentation" of the entire literature of criminology in German language.

In the criminological seminar of the University of Kiel, the interrelationship between the length of imprisonment and the process of resocialization of juveniles is being analyzed. At the University of Mainz, criminological research projects are currently in progress on the examination of the prognosis tables of Glueck with regard to German persons, and an investigation of fraudulent behavior in gambling. Also, being studied are the murders of cab-drivers, the white-collar crimes of real estate agents, crime among waiters, criminality in connection with orders of the Federal Army, and the stand of criminology during the "Third Reich." The institute for criminal and social psychiatry at the University of Marburg is exploring the after-effects on serious criminals who have been sentenced to lifelong penitentiary or mental institutions. At the institute for criminal sciences of the University of Munster, among other topics, the possibilities of fighting white-collar crimes are being studied. At the institute of social research of the same University, the delinquency of juveniles, and also the problems of abnormal behavior and the social hierarchy (levels), are being examined. The structure of roles and the conflict of roles in a prison are under exploration. An investigation of the social situation of released prisoners is being planned.

At the institute for criminal psychology and psychiatry of the University of Saarbrucken, a research program is in progress with the title: "Psychological, Biological and Catamnestical Investigations in the Framework of Sexual Delinquency." At the criminological institute of the same university, studies on the criminology of juvenile sexual delinquents, as well as on the criminological prognosis and the effectiveness of child welfare work are being done. The institute for criminology at the University of Tubingen is investigating the factors leading to criminality and the possibilities of resocializing juvenile offenders. The problems of prisoners sentenced to lifelong terms are being considered on an inter-disciplinary level. Also the criminology of casuals (paupers), of children, and of juvenile thieves is under study. At the neurological clinic of the same University, the possibilities of prognosis for children and juvenile offenders are being analyzed. Juvenile murderers and children who became the victims of sexual crimes are examined for the purposes of research.

The institutes of criminal medicine at the universities of Koln, Gottingen, Frankfurt, Kiel, Berlin, Mainz, Heidelberg, and Marburg are also occupied with criminological studies, which is reflected in the publication of their dissertations. Often a special scientific series is available for the publication, as the "Kriminologischen Untersuchungen" (Criminological Studies), the "Kriminalwissenschaftlichen Abhandlungen" (Studies in the Science of Criminology), The "Kriminologischen Forschungen" (Criminological Research), or the series "Kriminologie."

Government agencies are also doing research in criminology. Notable are the numerous criminological studies of the Federal Office of Investigation in Wiesbaden, which are published in the "Schrifteneihe des Bundeskriminalamtes" (Publications of the Federal Office of Investigation). The agencies of the individual federal states are also involved in criminological research, as in the case of studies on arsonists, and on suicides within the institutions of execution (Senator for Justice in Berlin), or on robbery, and rape delinquencies (Department for the Interior of Hamburg).

Almost all persons doing criminological research agree that much too little is being done in this area in the Federal Republic of Germany. The urgently needed financial means necessary for the development of criminological positions and department are provided with some hesitation. Also the co-operation between the individual groups doing research, the institutions, the governmental agencies and organizations needs to be improved considerably.

A certain discord and rivalry among the scientific criminological organizations in Germany adds to the difficulties. In order to overcome these shortcomings, the erection of a central research institute is being generally advocated where basic criminological research can be done on an interdisciplinary level. Parallel to such a development, a certain professional image and goal would have to be created for the criminologists.

General Social Policies

The great importance of socio-political measures for the criminal policies were recognized in Germany relatively late, as until recent years it was dominated by the idea of retaliation in the criminal law. A systematic crime prevention, which started with the personality of the offender and his social environment, was thought of still less.

It was the merit of Franz von Liszt, and the "Sociological School of Criminal Law" founded by him, to have helped modern prevention-oriented criminal policies emerge in Germany. With this change, for the first time in history, criminopolitical considerations were focused on the individual, and on the personal and social factors that surrounded him at the time of crime. In order to achieve the protection of the population by preventive measures, the general social politics of the State were considered more and more relevant to the area of criminal policies.

The crimino-political importance of socio-political measures can be seen in the area of special prevention, as also more prominently in that of general prevention. Effective crime prevention cannot exclusively focus on people who have already committed crimes; nor can it be satisfied with stopping further offenses among such people, even though the measures of special prevention—especially in the different forms of probation helps—are very important. Measures that do not allow a crime to be committed in the first place appear to be more effective.

In terms of crimino-political goals, the legislators seemed to have greater trust in the deterrent effects of the legal penalties and, for special cases, in harsh prison penalties. This type of thinking, however, has proved to be thoroughly unrealistic. It is true that the majority of population consists of law-abiding citizens, but this is hardly because of any particular criminal policies of the State. Criminality as a predominantly social phenomenon is being influenced decisively only by social policies (Sieverts). Social policies are understood today more and more as the comprehensive "policies of society" (Achinger), and as such comprise also financial and economical, cultural and educational policies. It does not aim any longer, as it did at the time of Franz von Liszt, solely at the socially deprived and underprivileged lower classes; on the contrary, it is aimed at all citizens.

The wide field of these socio-political measures is not any more the sole responsibility of the agencies of criminal law. They can exercise, therefore, only an "exemplary supporting function" (Sieverts). There can be no doubt about the crimino-political relevancy of the socio-political activity of the State. For the Federal Republic of Germany—which accord- ing to its constitution is a social and constitutional state—the famous statement of Franz von Liszt is applicable today: "Good social policies are at the same time the best criminal policies."

Development of Socio-political Measures for Crime Prevention. The narrow understanding of social policies of the end of the 19th century focused primarily on "Arbeiterfrage" (the problem of the industrial workers). Franz von Liszt, with a crimino-political perspective, demanded from the State socio-political measures which would abolish the prevalent poverty among the proletarian masses. This poverty was for him one of the most important, if not even the most decisive, factors causing the frightening increase of criminality which accompanied the development of the modern industrial state. Crime showed more and more the signs of being a social mass phenomenon. Typical was the rapid increase in recidivism and juvenile criminality.

The first crimino-political measures of the State with a socio-political flavor were aimed at these two phenomena of crime. Due to the untiring demands of the "Sociological School of Criminal Law," a juvenile penal code and a juvenile welfare code were created in the twenties. The fine sytem, and later on a system of measures for protection and betterment, were also introduced. Parallel to this, the different types of help for criminals were developed—social help in court, help for probation, and welfare for prisoners and released prisoners. Finally, there was the attempt to introduce principles of education and resocialization in the realm of execution of sentences. In toto, this can be called the period of the fight for a "social criminal law" (Redbruch).

These innovations, mainly of the special preventive type, were supplemented by numerous socio-political measures of the general preventive kind. Related to this was the development of a model system of social security which started with the introduction of the laws of social insurance in 1883. Further milestones in the crimino-political development were the "law for procuring jobs and insuring the unemployed"—which became effective in 1927, and the transition of the poverty laws of the State into a welfare law—which must be considered modern for that time. This was accomplished by the "Verordnung uber die Fursogepflicht" (Law on Welfare Obligation), and the accompanying "Principles of the Prerequisites, Types and Extent of Public Welfare" (1924). The public measures in the area of working law, housing and health-welfare, and education, were also important.

This broad spectrum of socio-political activities characterizes the decades-long endeavors of the State in creating a basis of existence compatible with the dignity of man, and in accomplishing the social integration of those underprivileged classes that produced the maximum number of criminals. The two world wars and the economically troubled times that followed them—as also the interlude of national socialist regime—interrupted the development of such criminal policies that would reach far into the area of general social upliftment. The type of criminality caused by genuine want, of which Franz von Liszt was thinking and which was justifying his crimino-political demands, is a thing of the past. Today, crimino-political considerations have to cope with the problem of how to stop the opposite phenomenon—the criminality caused by the high standard of living.

Present State of Crime Prevention and Corresponding Demands for the Future. The starting point for the present situation is Article 20 of the Constitution of 1949. According to this the Federal Republic of Germany is a social and constitutional state. The idea of a social state however, was not taken into account sufficiently in the area of crime prevention. However, the standard of living of the working part of the population has constantly improved after the last World War, and has reached a peak it had never attained before.

Total employment has been achieved. The housing shortage caused by the war is almost over; the system of social security has been generously expanded during the last twelve years, especially in the areas of retirement payments and social help (formerly welfare). In the sector of health and education policies, at least the most serious shortcomings have been eradicated, although not all legitimate wishes could be fulfilled.

All this has probably abolished the old criminality caused by physical need. However, it was not able to stop a further increase in crime rate. The picture and the causes of criminality have changed basically as compared with the past. The "civilization conflict," the "psychologically decisive criminogenic life conflict," moves more clearly into the foreground today. The consequences are an increasing "social helplessness," and "difficulties in socializing" under the life conditions of the largely depersonalized, anonymous, industrial, mass state (Hellmuth Mayer).

The 19th century was still completely dominated by the

social question which has been overcome in the meantime. Its place has been taken today by the socio-educational question that demand new answers. To find these answers is the task of the social policies of the State. They go beyond the mere material security of the citizen and deal especially with cultural and educational problems. In this new dimension their crimino-political, i.e. crime preventing, mission has to be seen. The idea of personal help and counselling gains greater importance within the area of social legislation. The federal law of 6/30/61 for social help expressly gives preference to this kind of personal help before material support. Within the area of community (public) and free welfare, more and more advisory services are being made available. Their working areas comprise marriage, family, and educational counselling.

Other institutions try to help all types of addicts and mentally ill persons, or maintain telephone counselling services. In some rare instances, such services for sentenced or released fellow citizens are also available.

Youth work is important for the prevention of crimes. It is being done either by public agencies, by the community, or in "free," unstructured social areas. The greatest increase in crime can be observed among juveniles and children. One reason for this phenomenon is the frequent failure of filling leisure time meaningfully. Thus the local leisure-time institutions and enterprises—such as open houses, educational enterprises for juveniles, youth clubs, youth work of unions, organized travelling and vacationing, and vacations outside the cities—are especially important for the young people. There are several measures for the protection and welfare of already endangered juveniles and children. The public welfare agencies, who are responsible for such juveniles, try to influence the youth without coerced education. They have shifted their operations more and more into the open spaces of the country. In doing so they focus on areas of social concentration as the highly populated areas in cities, camps, and other places endangering juveniles.

In this connection the socio-political measures for the support of families with many children (so-called family reparation) can also be mentioned. They range from tax exemptions to providing appropriate living quarters.

Among the criminals, juveniles as well as adult, are many with defective education and job training. The reasons for these deficiencies are to be found mostly in the environment, but often also in physical or intellectual shortcomings. Socio-political measures—such as expansion to health supervision, rehabilitation work with inhibited persons, special education and other therapeutic and educational institutions—have a great role to play in the prevention of crime. The possibilities in these areas, however, are far from exhausted. That can also be said for the political education of juveniles and adults.

The task of a comprehensive law education is not yet generally recognized and much less successfully accomplished. The road to the application of a criminal law, which is guided by the principles of a social and constitutional state, will become open only if in the area of criminal and social policies, the reform of the criminal law and the execution of its sentences is understood as an integral part of the great social reform of our times.

BIBLIOGRAPHY

ACHINGER, HANS. *Sozialpolitik als Gesellschaftspolitik.* Rowohlts deutsche Enzyklopädie. Band 47, Hamburg: Rowohlt, 1958.

AKTUELLE KRIMINOLOGIE. Mit 25 Beiträgen in-und ausländischer Autoren. Hamburg: Kriminalistik Verlag, 1969.

ANTILLA, INKERI. "Uber Ursachen der Kriminalität im Wohlfahrtsstaat." *Monatsschrift für Kriminologie und Strafrechtsreform.* Band 47, 1964, pp. 252-258.

BAUER, FRITZ. *Das Verbrechen und die Gesellschaft.* München: Ernst Reinhardt Verlag, 1957.

BAUMANN, JÜRGEN. (Hg.). *Programm fur ein neues Stafgesetzbuch.* Der Alternativ-Entwurf der Strafrechtslehrer. Frankfurt u. Hamburg: Fischer, 1968, (Fischer Bücherei Nr. 952).

BAUMANN, JÜRGEN UND ANDERE. *Alternativ Entwurf eines Strafgesetzbuches.* 2. Auflage, Tübingen: Mohr, 1969.

BLAU, GÜNTER. "Sozialpädagogische Tendenzen im Strafrecht der Gegenwart." *Monatsschrift für Kriminologie und Strafrechtsreform.* Band 45, 1962, pp. 141-157.

BRÜCKNER, GÜNTHER. "Die Ursachen des Widerrufs der Bewährungsaufsicht." *Bewährungshilfe.* Jahrgang 7, 1960, Heft 3, pp. 173-184.

BRUNS, HANS JÜRGEN. "Die Strafaussetzung zur Bewährung." *Goltdammer's Archiv für Strafrecht,* 1956, pp. 193-240.

BUNDESKRIMINALAMT (Hg.). *Polizeiliche Kriminalstatistik für die Bundesrepublik Deutschland einchliesslich West-Berlin.* Wiesbaden: Bundeskriminalamt, 1953-1968.

BUNDESKRIMINALAMT (Hg.). *Grundfragen der Wirtschaftskriminalität.* Wiesbaden: Bundeskriminalamt, 1963.

BUNDESKRIMINALAMT WIESBADEN (Hg.). *Vorbeugende Verbrechensbekämpfung.* Wiesbaden: Bundeskriminalamt, 1964.

BUSCH, MAX UND EDEL, GOTTFRIED (Hg.). *Erziehung zur Freiheit durch Freiheitsentzug.* Internationale Probleme des Strafvollzugs an jungen Menschen. Neuwied und Berlin: Luchterhand, 1969.

CHRISTIANSEN, KARL O. "Kriminologie (Grundlagen)." *Handwörterbuch der Kriminologie* (hg. von A. Elster und H. Lingemann; 2. neubearbeitete Auflage von R. Sieverts). Band 2, Berlin: Walter de Gruyter u. Co., 1968, pp. 187-220.

DAHM, GEORG. *Deutsches Recht.* Die Geschichtlichen und dogmatischen Grundlagen des geltenden Rechts. 2. Auflage, Stuttgart: W. Kohlhammer, 1963.

DALLINGER, WILHELM UND LACKNER, KARL. *Das Jugendgerichtsgesetz.* 2. Auflage, München und Berlin: C. N. Beck, 1965.

DIECKHOFF, ALBRECHT. "Englisches und Deutsches Strafverfahren-ein kurzer Rechtsvergleich." *Strafrechtspflege und Strafrechtsreform.* Hg.

von Bundeskriminalamt. Wiesbaden: Bundeskriminalamt, 1961, pp. 159-166.

DREWS, BILL UND WACKE, GERHARD. *Allgemeines Polizeirecht der Lander und des Bundes*. 7. Auflage, Berlin: Heymanns, 1961.

ELSTER, ALEXANDER UND LINGEMANN, HEINRICH. *Handwörterbuch der Kriminologie*. 2. vollig neu bearbeitete Auflage herausgegeben von R. Sieverts. Band 1, Berlin: Walter de Gruyter u. Co., 1967.

EXNER, FRANZ. *Kriminologie*. 3. Auflage, Berlin/Göttingen/Heidelberg: Springer, 1949.

FRIEDRICH, KARL. "Stellung, Aufgabe und Arbeitsweise des Bewährungshelfers." *Bewährungshilfe*. Jahrgang 9, 1962, Heft 1, pp. 3-21.

GEERDS, FRIEDRICH. *Die Kriminalitat als soziale und als wissenschaftliche Problematik* (Recht und Staat in Geschichte und Gegenwart, Heft 315/316). Tubingen: Mohr, 1965.

————. *Kriminalphenomenologie.*—Ihre Aufgaben und Möglichkeiten. Festschrift fur Hellmuth Mayer, hg. von F. Geerds und W. Naucke. Berlin: Duncker und Humblot, 1966, pp. 605-627.

GÖPPINGER, HANS E. *Die gegenwärtige Situation der Kriminologie* (Recht und Staat in Geschichte und Gegenwart, Heft 288/289). Tubingen: Mohr, 1964.

————. *Problem interdisziplinärer Forschung in der Kriminologie*. (Tübinger rechtswissenschaftliche Abhandlungen, Band 24). Tubingen: Mohr, 1968.

GROSSRAU, EBERHARD. "Ordnungswidrigkeiten." *Handwörterbuch der Kriminologie*. (hg. von A. Elster und H. Lingemann; 2. neubearbeitete Auflage von R. Sieverts). Band 2, Berlin: Walter de Gruyter u. Co., 1968, pp. 254-258.

HAGEMANN, MAX, "Verbrechensverhütung." *Handwörterbuch der Kriminologie* und der anderen strafrechtlichen Hilfswissenschaften; hg. von A. Elster und H. Lingemann. Band 2, 1. Auflage, Berlin u. Leipzig: Walter de Gruyter u. Co., 1936, pp. 886-893.

HARBORDT, STEFFEN. *Die Subkultur des Gefängnisses* Beiträge zur Strafvollzugswissenschaft, hg. von Th. Würtenberger und H. Müller-Dietz, Heft 1. Stuttgart: F. Enke, 1967.

HEISING, MICHAEL. *Die Entlohnung der Gefangenenarbeit*. Basler Studien zur Rechtswissenschaft, Heft 83. Basel und Stuttgart: Helbing ung Lichtenhahn, 1968.

HELLMER, JOACHIM. "Sozialisation, Personalisation und Kriminalität." *Der Mensch als soziales und personales Wesen*, hg. von G. Wurzbacher. Stuttgart: F. Enke, 1963, pp. 202-224.

HENKEL, HEINRICH. *Strafverfahrensrecht*. 2. Auflage. Suttgart: Kohlhammer, 1968.

HERING, KARL HEINZ. *Der Weg der Kriminologie zur selbständigen Wissenschaft*. (Kriminologische Schriftenreihe, hg. von A. Mergen, Band 23). Hamburg: Kriminalistik-Verlag, 1966.

HEYDE, LUDWIG. *Abriss der Sozialpolitik*. 12. Auflage, uberarbeitet und ergänzt, von St. Münke und P. Heyde. Heidelberg: Quelle u. Meyer, 1966.

HOLLE, ROLF. "Die Kriminalität in der BRD Deutschland (1955-1964)." *Schriftenreihe des Bundeskriminalamtes.* 1968/2. Wiesbaden: Bundeskriminalamt, 1968.

JESCHECK, HANS-HEINRICH. *Lehrbuch des Strafrechts.* Allgemeiner Teil. Berlin: Duncker und Humblot, 1969.

KAISER, GÜNTHER. "Zur kriminalpolitischen Konzeption der Strafrechtsreform." *Zeitschrift für die gesamte Strafrechtswissenschaft.* Band 78, 1966, pp, 100-152.

————. "Probleme interdisziplinärer empirischer Forschung in der Kriminologie." *Monatsschrift für Kriminologie und Strafrechtsreform.* Vol. 50, 1967, pp. 352-366.

————. "Die Beziehungen zwischen Kriminologie und Strafrecht." *Goltdammer's Archiv.* 1967, pp. 289-315.

KERN, EDUARD. *Gerichtsverfassungsrecht.* München: C. H. Beck, 4. Auflage, 1965.

KERN, EDUARD UND ROXIN, CLAUS. *Strafverfahrensrecht.* Ein Studienbuch. 9. Auflage, München und Berlin: C. H. Beck, 1969.

KLEINKNECHT, THEODOR; MÜLLER, HERMANN UND REITBERGER, LEONHARD. *Kommentar* zur Strafprozessordnung und zum Gerichtsverfassungs und Ordnungswidrigkeitengesetz. 6. Auflage, Nürnberg/Dusseldorf/Berlin: Stoytscheff, 1966.

KOCH, PAUL. *Gefangenenarbeit und Resozialisierung.* Beitrage zur Strafvollzugswissenschaft; hg. von Th. Würtenberger und H. Müller-Dietz, Heft 4. Stuttgart: F. Enke, 1969.

KOENIGER, HANS. *Die Hauptverhandlung in Strafsachen.* Koln-Berlin-Bonn-München: C. Heymanns Verlag, 1966.

Kriminologische Wegzeichen. Festschrift für Hans von Hentig zum 80. Geburtstag. (Kriminologische Schriftenreihe, hg. von A. Mergen, Band 29). Hamburg: Kriminalistik-Verlag, 1967.

LEFERENZ, HEINZ. *Die Aufgaben einer modernen Kriminologie* (Schriftenreihe der juristischen Studiengesellschaft Karlsruhe, Heft 76). Karlsruhe: C. F. Müller, 1967.

MAUCH, GERHARD. "Psychotherapie im Strafvollzug." *Monatschrift für Kriminologie und Strafrechtsreform.* Vol. 47, 1964, pp. 108-121.

MAURACH, REINHART. *Deutsches Strafrecht.* Allgemeiner Teil. Ein Lehrbuch. 3. Auflage, Karlsruhe: C. F. Müller, 1965.

MAYER, HELLMUTH. *Strafrechtsreform für heute und morgen.* Kriminologische Forschungen. Band 1. Berlin: Duncker u. Humblot, 1962.

MEINERT, FRANZ. "Die Entwicklung der kriminalpolizeilichen Verbrechensbekämpfung seit den Reichsjustizgesetzen." *Strafrechtspflege und Strafrechtsreform.* Hg. von Bundeskriminalamt. Wiesbaden: Bundeskriminalamt, 1961, pp. 177-195.

MERGEN, ARMAND. *Die Kriminologie.* Eine systematische Darstellung. Berlin und Frankfurt/M.: Franz Vahlen, 1967.

MITTERMAIER, WOLFGANG. *Gefängnis unde.* Ein Lehrbuch fur Studium und Praxis. Berlin und Frankurt/M.: Vahlen, 1954.

Mörs, Klaus-Jürgen. *Das Freizeitproblem im deutschen Erwachsenstraf-vollzug*. Beiträge zur Strafvollzugswissenschaft; hg. von Th. Würtenberger und H. Muller-Dietz, Stuttgart: F. Enke, 1969.

Müller-Dietz, Heinz. "Strafvollzug und Strafvollzugsdienst heute." *Monatsschrift für Kriminologie und Strafrechtsreform*, Vol. 50, 1967, pp. 281-297.

————. *Strafbegriff und Strafrechtspflege*. Berlin: Duncker u. Humblot, 1968.

Müller-Dietz, Heinz und Würtenberger, Thomas (Hg.). *Fragebogenenquete zur Lage und Reform des deutschen Strafvollzugs*. Bad-Godesberg: Eigenverlag Bundeszusammenschluss für Straffälligenhilfe, 1969.

Nass, Gustav. *Bewährungshilfe*. Untersuchungen zur Resozialisierung junger Straftäter. Forschungsberichte zur forensischen Psychologie, Heft 4. Berlir: Walter de Gruyter u. Co., 1968.

————. *Der Staat und seine Verbrecher*. Eine Gesamtkonzeption der Kriminalpolitik. Wiesbaden: Limes-Verlag, 1968.

Niggemeyer, Bernhard. "Kriminalpolizei." *Handworterbuch der Kriminologie* (hg. von A. Elster und H. Lingemann; 2. neubearbeitete Auflage von R. Sieverts). Band 2, Berlin: Walter de Gruyter u. Co., 1967, pp. 19-47.

Noll, Peter. *Die ethische Begrundung der Strafe*. Recht und Staat in Geschichte und Gegenwart, Heft 244. Tübingen: Mohr, 1962.

Peters, Karl. *Grundprobleme der Kriminalpädagogik*. Berlin: Walter de Gruyter u. Co., 1960.

————. *Strofprozess*. Ein Lehrbuch. 2. Auflage, Karlsruhe: C. F. Müller, 1966.

Quensel, Stefan. *Sozialpsychologische Aspekte der Kriminologie*. (Kriminologie, Abhandlungen über abwegiges Sozialverhalten, hg. von Th. Würtenberger, Heft 1). Stuttgart: F. Enke, 1964.

Radzinowicz, Leon. "Strafrecht und Kriminologie (unter besonderer Berücksichtigung heutiger Strömungen in der Bundesrepublik Deutschland)." *Strafrechtspflege und Strafrechtsreform*. Hg. vom Bundeskriminalamt. Wiesbaden: Bundeskriminalampt, 1961, pp. 17-34.

Rangol, Alfred-Johannes. "Die Straffälligkeit nach Hauptdeliktsgruppen und Altersklassen 1884 bis 1958." *Monatsschrift für Kriminologie und Strafrechtsreform*. Vol. 45, 1962, pp. 157-175.

————. "Der internationale Kriminalitätsvergleich." *Monatsschrift für Kriminologie und Strafrechtsreform*. Vol. 48, 1965, pp. 114-134.

Ritter, Kurt-Lennart. *Der practische Gang der Strafrechtspflege*. (Kriminologische Untersuchungen, hg. von Th. Würtenberger und H. von Weber, Heft 9). Bonn: L. Röhrscheid, 1960.

Rollmann, Dietrich. (Hg.). *Strafvollzug in Deutschland*. Situation und Reform. Frankfurt/M. und Hamburg: Fischer, 1967 (Fischer Bücherei Nr. 841).

ROXIN, CLAUS. "Sinn und Grenzen staatlichen Strafens." *Juristische Schulung*. 1966, pp. 377 ff.

SACK, FRITZ UND KONIG, RENÉ (Hg.). *Kriminalsoziologie*. Frankfurt a. M.: Akademische Verlagsgesellschaft, 1968.

SACK, FRITZ. *Die West-Ost Wanderung der Kriminalität*. Grundlagen der Kriminalistik, Band 4. hg. von H. Schafer. Hamburg: Steintor-Verlag, 1968; pp. 245-293.

————. "Probleme der Kriminalsoziologie." *Handbuch der Empirischen Sozialforschung*, hg. von R. König, II. Band, Stuttgart: F. Enke, 1969, pp. 961-1049.

SANGMEISTER, WOLFRAM. "Die heutige Situation der deutschen Kriminalpolizei." *Kriminalpolitische Gegenwartsfragen*, hg. vom Bundeskriminalamt. Wiesbaden: Bundeskriminalamt, 1959, pp. 115-120.

————. "Polizei." *Handwörterbuch der Kriminologie* (hg. von A. Elster und H. Lingemann; neubearbeitete Auflage von R. Sieverts). Band 2, Berlin: Walter de Gruyter und Co., 1968, pp. 295-306.

SCHÄFER, H. "Wesen und Entwicklung des Vorbeugungsgedankens—Ein Beitrag zur Geschichte der Kriminalprophylaxe—". *Vorbeugende Verbrechensbekämpfung* (hg. vom Bundeskriminalamt Wiesbaden). Wiesbaden: Bundeskriminalamt, 1964, pp. 27-46.

SCHÄFFER, NORBERT. "Bewährungshilfe, ein Erfolg oder Misserfolg." *Bewährungshilfe*. Juergang 8, 1961, Heft 4, pp. 323-329.

SCHAFSSTEIN, FRIEDRICH. "Die Jugendkriminalität in der industriellen Wohlstandsgesellschaft." *Monatsschrift für Kriminologie und Strafrechtsreform*, Vol. 48, 1965, pp. 53-67.

————. *Jugendsstrafrecht*. Eine systematische Darstellung. 2. Auflage, Stuttgart-Berlin-Köln-Mainz: Kohlhammer, 1966.

SCHAFSSTEIN, FRIEDRICH (Hg.). *Weg und Aufgabe des Jugendstrafrechts*. Darmstadt: Wissenschaftliche Buchgesellschaft, 1968.

SCHMIDT, EBERHARD. *Lehrkommentar zur Strafprozessordnung* und zum Gerichtsverfassungsgesetz. Teil I, 2. Auflage 1967; Teil II, 1957 mit Nachträgen und Ergänzungen 1966; Teil III, 1960, Göttingen: Vandenhoeck und Ruprecht.

————. "Geschichte der Strafröchtspflege." *Handwörterbuch der Kriminologie* (hg. von A. Elster u. H. Lingemann; 2. neubearbeitete Auflage von R. Sieverts). Band 1, Berlin: Walter de Gruyter u. Co., 1966, pp. 317-333.

SCHONKE, ADOLF UND SCHRODER, HORST. *Strafgesetzbuch*. Kommentar. 14. Auflage, München u. Berlin: C. H. Beck, 1969 mit Nachtrag 1969.

SCHÜLER-SPRINGORUM, HORST UND SIEVERTS, RUDOLF. *Sozial auffallige Jugendliche*. Munchen: Juventa Verlag, 1964.

SCHÜLER-SPRINGORUM, HORST. *Strafvollzug im Übergang*. Studien zum Stand der Vollzugsrechtslehre. Göttingen: O. Schwarz und Co., 1969.

SCHWARZ, OTTO UND DREHER, EDUARD. *Kommentar zum Strafgesetzbuch*. 29. Auflage, Munchen und Berlin: C. H. Beck, 1967.

SCHWARZ, OTTO UND KLEINKNECHT, THEODOR. *Strafprozessordnung*,

Gerichtsverfassungsgesetz und ergänzende Bestimmunge. 28. Auflage, München und Berlin: C. H. Beck, 1969.

SEELIG, ERNST. *Lehrbuch der Kriminologie.* 3. Auflage neubearbeitet und ergänzt von H. Bellavic. Darmstadt: Stoytscheff, 1963.

SELGE, EDGAR. "Die Jugendstrafe von unbestimmter Dauer in der Praxis der Rechtsprechung der Jugendgerichte und des Jugendstrafvollzuges." *Monatsschrift für Kriminologie und Strafrechtsreform.* Vol. 45, 1962, pp. 129-140.

SIEVERTS, RUDOLF. "Kriminalpolitik." *Handwörterbuch der Kriminologie* (hg. von A. Elster und H. Lingemann; 2. neubearbeitete Auflage von R. Sieverts). Band 2. Berlin: Walter de Gruyter u. Co., 1967, pp. 1-19.

STATISTISCHES BUNDESAMT WIESBADEN (Hg.). Bevolkerung und Kultur. Reihe 9: *Rechtspflege.* Stuttgart und Mainz: W. Kohlhammer, 1960 bis 1967.

STEINER, J. M., SCHUMACHER, H. UND QUENSEL, STEPHAN. "Group-Counseling im Erwachsenenstrafvollzug—Erfahrungen aud einem Experiment—." *Monatsschrift fur Kriminologie und Strafrechtsreform.* Vol. 49, 1966, pp. 160-172.

SUTTINGER, GUNTER. "Jugendkriminalitat." *Handwörterbuch der Kriminologie* (hg. von A. Elster u. H. Lingemann; 2. neubearbeitete Auflage von R. Sieverts). Band 1, Berlin: Walter de Gruyter u. Co., 1966, pp. 401-436.

SYDOW, KARL-HEINZ. *Erfolg und Misserfolg der Strafaussetzung zur Bewahrung* (Kriminologische Untersuchungen, hg. von H. v. Weber und Th. Würtenberger, Vol. 13). Bonn: L. Röhrscheid Verlag, 1963.

TERSTEGEN. "Die sog. 'Weisse-Kragen-Kriminalitat' unter besonderer Berücksichtgung des Entwurfs." *Strafrechtspflege und Strafrechtsreform,* hg. vom Bundeskriminalamt. Wiesbaden: Bundeskriminalamt, 1961, pp. 81-118.

WAHL, ALFONS. "Statistik und Bewahrungshilfe." *Bewährungshilfe,* Jahrgang 8, 1961, Heft, 3, pp. 276-290.

————. "Zehn Jahre Bewahrungsaufsicht und Bewährungshilfe in der Bundesrepublik Deutschland." *Bewährungshilfe,* Jahrgang 11, 1964, Heft 1, pp. 5-31.

————. "Bewährubgshife fur Erwachsene in der Bundesrepublik Deutschland." *Bewährungshilfe,* Jahrgang 14, 1967, Heft 2, pp. 67-80.

WEISS, WALTER. "Bewahrungshilfe heute und morgen." *Bewährungshilfe,* Jahrgang 15, 1968, Heft 1, pp. 4-25.

WENZKY, OSKAR. "Krinaltechnik." *"Handworterbuch der Kriminologie* (hg. von A. Elster und H. Lingemann; 2. neubearbeitete Auflage von R. Sieverts). Band 2, Berlin: Walter de Gruyter u. Co., 1967, pp. 92-138.

WURTENBERGER, THOMAS. *Die geistige Situation der deutschen Strafrechtswissenschaft* (Freiburger Rechts—und Staatswissenschaftliche Abhandlungen Band 7). 2. Auflage, Karlsruhe: C. F. Müller, 1959.

WURTENBERGER, THOMAS (Hg.). *Kriminologie und Vollzug der Freiheitsstrafe.* Stuttgart: F. Enke, 1961.

WURTENBERGER, THOMAS UND HALL, JEROME. "Strafrecht." *Staatslexikon*, hg. von der Görres-Gesellschaft. Band 7, 6. Auflage, Freiburg i. Br. : Herder, 1962, pp. 743-778.

WURTENBERGER, THOMAS. "Das Menschenbild unserer Zeit und die Kriminalität als sozialkulturelles Phänomen." *Bewahrungshilfe*, Jahrgang 13, 1966, Heft 1, pp. 3-16.

WURTENBERGER, THOMAS (Hg.). "Reform des Strafvollzugs im sozialen Rechtsstaat." *Juristenzeitung*. 1967, pp. 233 ff.

WURTENBERGER, THOMAS. "Notwendigkeit und Möglichkeit einer koordinierten kriminologischen Forschung." *Grundlagenforschung und Kriminologie*, hg. vom Bundeskriminalamt. Wiesbaden: Bundeskriminalamt, 1969, pp. 225-241.

CHAPTER 7

ITALY

MARIA CRISTINA GIANNINI

For more than one hundred years, Italy has continued to make many valuable contributions not only in general sociology, but also in the field of criminology. Cesare Lombroso (1836-1909), Enrico Ferri (1856-1928), Roffaele Gerofalo (1852-1934), and others, to name a few, made an early start on scientific approach to the study of crime, delinquency, and laws. Although much of the early "positive school" theories have been shifted to "environmental" or "learning" theories, Italian school of criminology is still felt in Europe and to a certain degree in the United States, Canada, and South America.

The present article on Italian criminology is authored by Dr Maria Cristina Giannini. She received her Gymnasium and Liceum in Rome in 1959. Then she entered the University of Rome and completed her Doctorate in Law in 1965. From 1967 to 1969 she continued her training as a post-doctoral trainee and became an Assistant in Criminology, Faculty of Law, University of Rome. For the next year, 1968, she served as Research Assistant, United Nations Social Defense Research Institute, Rome. In September, 1969, Dr Giannini was promoted to Assistant Professor in Criminology, Faculty of Law, University of Rome. Some of her published articles include "Incest: Note on Comparative Legislation" in Sessuologia (*Sexology*) *in 1967; "Criminological Aspects of Recidivism and Principal Criminolgenetic Theories of Such Recidivism" in* Recidivism and Young Adult, *Nationai Center for Prevention and Social Defense, Roma, 1969; and "Economy and Criminality" in* Workbook on Clinical Criminology, *1969.*

ITALY IS A PARLIAMENTARY republic whose President (Chief of State) is elected for seven years with a two-thirds majority (at the third voting however an absolute majority only is required) by an Assembly consisting of the two branches of Parliament, and also Delegates elected by the Regional Councils. The President of the Council and the ministers— who are nominated by the President of the Republic, and who must also obtain a vote of confidence from Parliament—exercise the executive power. Legislative power is given to Parliament. It is formed by the Chamber of Deputies, elected for five years through direct general election by proportional representation; and the Senate of the Republic whose members are elected for five years by direct election on the basis of regions; while ex-Presidents and other personalities, who are particularly distinguished for their scientific or artistic merits, are nominated for life.

The country extends to 301,245 square kilometers. For administrative purposes it is divided into 93 provinces, which are grouped into 20 regions, of which five have a special statute. The national language is Italian. The prevailing religion is Roman Catholicism, with small Protestant and Hebrew minorities.

The population in 1966 was calculated to be 53,129,000 (according to the latest census of October 15, 1961 the population was 50,623,569), with an annual increase of 0.6 per cent.

Table I shows the composition of the resident population, both active and non-active, according to age, sex, and civil status, taken from the last census.[1]

Concerning economic structure and development in Italy, it can be seen from a recent publication of the Central Institute of Statistics,[2] that in 1966 in a resident population of 53,129,000 those in the pool of potential labor were 20,322,000, i.e. 38 per cent. By pool of potential labor we mean all those who are disposed in one way or another to produce material benefits or to give service, and as this disposition may be manifested by the possession as well as by the request for work, the pool of potential labor who are em-

---

[1] Istituto Centrale di Statistica, *10° Censimento Generale della popolazione 15 ottobre 1961*, Vol. VI, Professioni, Roma, 1967.

[2] Istituto Centrale di Statistica, *I conti degli italiani—compendio della vita economica nazionale*, Roma, 1967.

TABLE I

RESIDENT POPULATION ACTIVE AND NON-ACTIVE BY SEX, AGE, AND CIVIL STATUS

Age	Active population		Non-active population		Total	
	Male	Male and female	Male	Male and female	Male	Male and female
Up to 10 years	—	—	4,183,432	8,176,099	4,183,432	8,176,099
10—15	267,411	425,889	1,891,116	3,802,912	2,158,527	4,228,801
15—20	1,320,197	2,050,478	596,934	1,727,085	1,917,131	3,777,563
20—25	1,830,626	2,647,206	229,751	1,426,320	2,060,377	4,073,526
25—30	1,819,066	2,389,525	80,541	1,404,476	1,899,607	3,794,001
30—35	1,864,887	2,400,009	54,450	1,462,931	1,919,337	3,862,940
35—40	1,793,799	2,325,337	65,442	1,482,551	1,859,241	3,807,888
40—45	1,250,895	1,620,158	63,060	1,108,914	1,313,955	2,729,072
45—50	1,500,193	1,915,672	96,405	1,370,901	1,596,598	3,286,573
50—55	1,414,498	1,784,835	142,975	1,405,209	1,557,473	3,190,044
55—60	1,061,617	1,293,753	206,277	1,356,872	1,267,894	2,650,625
60—65	341,280	696,434	468,706	1,522,587	1,009,986	2,219,021
Over 65 years	480.845	623,606	1,559,456	4,203,810	2,040,301	4,827,416
TOTAL	15,145,314	20,172,902	9,638,545	30,450,667	24,783,859	50,623,569

BY CIVIL STATUS

	Active population		Non-active population		Total	
	Male	Male and female	Male	Male and female	Male	Male and female
Bachelors and spinsters	5,407,341	8,050,000	7,275,133	16,450,234	12,682,474	24,500,234
Married and separated	9,530,480	11,617,509	1,915,404	11,304,158	11,445,884	22,921,667
Widowed and divorced	207,493	505,393	448,008	2,696,275	655,501	3,201,668
TOTAL	15,145,314	20,172,902	9,638,345	80,450,667	24,783,859	50,623,569

ployed may be distinguished from those unemployed. In 1966, the number of employed was 19,553,000 and the unemployed 769,000. The following table shows the relative data for 1966:

TABLE II

	Thousand	Per cent
Resident pool of potential labor	20,322	38.3
(a) Present in Italy	19,926	37.6
(i) Employed	19,157	36.1
(ii) Unemployed	769	1.5
(b) Temporarily employed abroad	396	0.7
Remainder of the population	32,807	61.7
Resident population	53,129	100.0

From 1951 to 1966 the number of Italians increased (resident population) by more than five and a half million, the pool of potential labor on the other hand decreased by almost one and a half million. As a consequence, the population not forming the pool of potential labor (children, students, housewives, pensioners) increased by more than seven million. The principal causes of this change in situation are: the fact that many women who were formerly partially employed in agriculture have left the pool of potential labor in increasing numbers and returned to housekeeping, the greater tendency of young people to study and the longer duration of these studies, the extension of pension funds to new categories of workers, and the lowering of the pensionable age limit. Thus, a number of causes are responsible more or less directly for the transformation of the Italian economic structure, and the slight improvement in the conditions of life of the population.

Passing on to examine the employment figures especially the distribution of the employed—permanent and temporary— and also the relationship between independent and dependent workers in the various sectors of economic activity, it can be noted from Table III that in 1966 the employed were in all about 19,157,000. From the point of view of sectoral division, it can be said that for every 100 employed Italians there are nine in the armed forces and civil service, 40 in industry, 24 in agriculture and 27 in other activities. As for the temporarily employed (which only exist in the private sector) 18 per cent of these are employed in agriculture, seven per cent in industry and four per cent in other activities.

TABLE III
THE EMPLOYED IN ITALY IN 1966
(IN UNITS OF A THOUSAND)

Sector	Permanent			Marginal workers	Total
	Independent	Dependent	Total		
(a) Private sector	5,994	9,921	15,915	1,575	17,490
(i) Agriculture	2,733	1,107	3,840	820	4,660
(ii) Industry	1,164	5,934	7,098	523	7,621
(iii) Other activity	2,097	2,880	4,977	232	5,209
(b) Armed Forces and Civil Service	—	1,667	1,667	—	1,667
TOTAL	5,994	11,588	17,582	1,575	19,157

The percentage of independent workers in the total number of permanent workers is therefore 71 per cent in agriculture, 16 per cent in industry and 42 per cent in other activities. Concerning the occupational structure it can be noted that from 1951 onwards this has been greatly modified. The two most important changes concern those employed in agriculture who have decreased by almost four million, and the percentage of dependent workers in the total employed which has greatly increased. These two phenomena are interrelated, for many independent agricultural workers have shifted to other sectors to become dependents of industrial enterprises and to carry out other work. This transferring has had a definite beneficial effect on all sectors, giving rise to an increase in general productivity and income.

Concerning the latter, it has been calculated that in 1966 the national net income was 35,029 billion lire and given a population of 53,129,000, the pro capital net annual income was about 659,000 lire. The contribution of the various sectors of economic activity to the formation of the internal gross

TABLE IV

Sectors	Billions of lire	Per cent
(a) Private sector	29,431	87.2
(i) Agriculture, forests, and fisheries	4,225	12.5
(ii) Industry	13,536	40.1
(iii) Other activity	11,670	34.6
(b) Armed Forces and Civil Service	4,333	12.8
Internal gross income	33,764	100.0

income is, in total and percentage figures, shown in Table IV.

Regarding criminality in Italy the following graph gives the trend and amount from 1900 to 1965.[3]

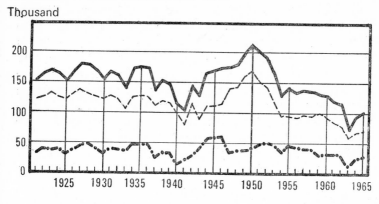

Thousand

━━━━━━ Total

‒ ‒ ‒ ‒ ‒ ‒ Detentive punishments

━•━•━•━ Pecuniary (fine) punishments

It would be too long and complex to speak of it in detail, and it is preferable to give only the actual picture of penal justice by referring to the address made by the Attorney General of the Supreme Court of Cassation on the occasion of the inauguration of the judicial year 1969[4]. It is affirmed therein that the penal picture on June 30, 1968 compared with that of June 30, 1967 shows a decrease of 28 per cent in the "preture," 19 per cent in the "uffici di istruzione" and of 11 per cent in Cassation. In the other "uffici giudiziari" a small increase is shown—57 per cent in the Tribunals— but this must be returning to normal after the Amnesty of 1966 which eliminated many processes, being the great number of appeals proposed in the hope of the Amnesty. With respect to the preceding period there was also a relevant decrease in the Tribunal proceedings for minors. The crimes reported to the "preture" and to the "procure della Repubblica" have decreased in all by 7.5 per cent. The following in parti-

[3]Istituto Centrale di Statistica, *Sommario di statistiche storiche dell' Italia, 1861-1965*, Roma, 1968.

[4]M. Duni, *Discorso per l' inaugurazione dell'anno giudiziario 1969*, Tip. Morara, Roma, 1969.

cular are the ones indicated as having decreased: 25 per cent in
commerical smuggling; 33 per cent in the selling of foodstuffs
no according to Health Regulations; 7 per cent in crimes of
apte; 11 per cent for acts of lust and obscenity; and 18 per
crent for man-slaughter. Reports of homicide with intent have
increased by 4 per cent; burglary by 3 per cent, and reports
on the writing of cheques with insufficient funds by 8 per cent.

However, the phenomenon of criminality, i.e. reports to the
general attorneys, remains stationary in many districts, in
others they are on the increase. For some this increase concerns offenses which do not provoke excessive social alarm;
for others, however, this increase concerns violent crimes
against the person and against property.

CRIMINAL LAW

The word "crimine" which is the equivalent of the English
expression "crime" is no longer used in modern Italian law. In
fact, the old tripartition of offenses into crimes, felonies, and
misdemeanors has been abandoned and the general category of
crime[5] according to Italian law is divided into two specific
types: "delitti" and "contravvenzioni" (to some extent corresponding to felonies and misdemeanors, Art. 39, Penal Code).

Legal Definition of Crime

The expression "crimine" comes from Roman law (which is
the source of various expressions to indicate illicit actions) often
with the same meaning (scelus, fraus, maleficium, flagitium faci-
nus, peccatum, probrum, delictus, crimen); the most used were
"maleficium," "crimen" and "delictum." Crime in that law was
used to indicate the infraction of a juridical norm in general.[6]

"Crimen" according to its etymology ($\kappa\rho\acute{\iota}\nu\omega$) means

---

[5] "Reato" is derived from the Greek $\rho\iota\tau\iota\alpha$ = Guilt, which corresponds to the Sanskrit atyaya = transgression from ati+i, transire, In
Pictet, Les origines indo-europeennes, p. II, Paris, 1863, p. 434.

Quintiliano, Inst. orat., VIII, 3, states that the word "reatus," in
today's sense was first used by M. Messala, who acquired it from
"reus." "Quaedam in usu perquam recentia, ut Messala primus reatum
dixit." "Reatus," previously, signified reactive action for defense subjected to the judge, and only recently the act of the offender.

[6] C. Ferrini, Diritto Penale Romano, Hoepli, Roma, 1898 pp. 35-37.

"object of research and decision," i.e. something which relies on the decision of the judge. In the Latin language of the Imperial Age the term assumed the meaning "imputation, penal trial" and thereafter also included the illicit fact which constitutes the object of the trial. The expression, however, was used exclusively for the illicit fact, the object of public prosecution, as opposed to the word "delictum" which indicated the "privata crimina."

The different usage of "delictum" and "crimen" is linked to the evolution of the concept of penal violation and punishment, while there was an antithesis between private punishment and public punishment. Thus, during the classical period, "delictum" signified the illicit act, the source of "obligatio," punished by "jus civile" with private punishment; and "crimen" the illicit act punished by "just pubblicum" with public punishment. The antithesis ceased and the two words became equivalent when public penal law covered private penal law (the post-classical and "Giustinianeo" period).[7]

In Italian intermediate law the terms "crimen" and "delictum" are conserved, as sub-categories under the general term "maleficium." However, as can be seen[8] the distinctions are

---

[7]E. Albertario, *Delictum e crimen nel diritto romano classico e nella legislazione giustinianea*, Milano, 1924.

[8]"Differentia est inter crimen et delictum et maleficium. Crimen itaque dicitur esse quotiescumque adest animus ad delictum committendum. . . Delictum tunc demum dicitur esse, et quando est animus ad delinquendum, et quando etiam non est animus. . . . Delictum est genus generalissimum, et crimen subalternum. . . . Delictum ordinarie non punitur, ubi non est dolus. . . . Quamvis fiat aliquid illicitum, si tamen poenam non meretur, non appellatur delictum. Intelligendo tamen istud esse verum interpretatione iuris, sed quoad bonos mores dicitur esse delictum. . . . Maleficium autem ex lata significatione comprehendit omne malegestum, sive fiat re, sive verbis; si vero sumitur stricte, tunc accipitur pro eo quod committitur facto. . . et ideo non comprehendit male dictum vel male scriptum." (A.N. Blancus, *Practica Criminalis*, Venetiis, 1955, p. 47.)

"Dicitur maleficium esse reale factum. . . . Crimen vero dicitur peccatum accusatione et correctione dignissimum. . . . Excessus autem potest dici legis transgressio. . . . Delictum vero est genus generalissimum, comprehendens omne genus deliquendi." (Bonifacius De Vitalinis, *Tractatus super maleficiis*, Venetiis, 1555, p. 104.)

"Delictum generale nomen est. . . . Crimen autem tunc proprie dicitur, quando quis dolo malo et prava intentione delinquit. . . . Maleficium

anything but precise and concording, and they do not respond to the sense afterwards assumed by the terminology under examination.

The distinction between "crimini" and "delitti" accepted in the Napoleonic legislation seems to come from the "Grand Coutumier" of Charles VI (1380-1422), in which it was used to separate the more serious offenses from the less serious ones. It became less clear when it was adopted by the French Penal Code in 1810 which added another category called "contravvenzioni" misdemeanors—a tripartition which was already known in Italy by another terminology as proved by the extract from Bonifacio de Vitalinis (excessus, transgressio),[9] and also existed in Germany.

The tripartition can be found in the Sardo-Italian Penal Code of 1859 according to which "crimini" crimes were offenses punished with criminal punishment, "delitti" felonies those punished with correctional punishment, and "contravvenzioni" misdemeanors offenses punished by the police (Art. 2.) The Tuscan Penal Code of 1853, however, divided offenses into "delitti" and "transgressioni" (transgressions) and the latter were foreseen in punitive police regulations and in other laws.

The bipartition of "delitti" and "contravvenzioni" was maintained in the Italian Penal Code of 1889 and is also there in the present one (in force since 1930).

Concerning the meaning of "reato" offense it can be noticed how, during the course of the 18th century, the Italian criminalistic science—inspired by the ideology of the "Illuminism" —followed a utilitarian concept of penal law, and by merit of the work of Cesare Beccaria obtained the first dogmatic systematisation. Towards the middle of the 19th century an important train of thought was outlined which has a certain influence even today, called the Classical School; this found in Francesco Carrara the first theoretical basis. According to this school, the offense is not a factual reality but a juridical one

---

accipitur pro damno iniuria et pro facinore. . . et pariter non nisi cum dolo et malo animo contrahitur. . . . Crimen requirit non solum dolum et malum animum, sed etiam contenionem (criminationem); maleficium vero sine contentione dicitur." (Farinacius, *Praxis et theoricae criminalis*, Francoforte, 1622, p. 251.)

[9]*Ibid.*

resulting from the contradiction between the human fact and the law. The offense may be represented as a "harmonic discord." It is a juridical reality which, in order to exist, has need of certain material and moral elements, but that which completes its real being is the contradiction between these elements and the law. The definition of offense according to this conception is that of a human action contrary to the law and punished by the latter.

This definition is opposed by that of the "Scuola Criminale Positiva" (Criminal Positive School) which found its major exponents in Cesare Lambroso and Enrico Ferri. According to their conception, the offense is a human and social fact, a permanent substratum from which the juridical aspect cannot be separated. It is therefore a variable reality in time and space. In addition, while according to the traditional and Classical School the offense has a value in itself, the Criminal Positive School considers the offense in relation to, and almost in function of, its author pointing out the symptomatic value of his dangerousness. Consequently, according to the Positive School the offense is not sufficient in itself to apply the penal sanction, but the dangerousness of its author is also to be considered.[10]

These two conceptions of the offense are included in equal measure in the Italian Penal Code, which sometimes considers the offense as a juridical fact formed by precise elements both essential and occasional (circumstances), and otherwise considers it exclusively as a pathological expression or even as a social dangerousness.

In the law, however, an explicit definition of crime cannot be found, but can be extracted from the context of the whole Code. It can be said that according to Italian Penal Code the following elements make up the definition: (*i*) a material fact committed by man (either action or omission); (*ii*) a psychological element which has determined this fact (intention, imprudence, negligence etc.); (*iii*) a contrast between this fact and the law (the existence of a norm which prohibits it); and (*iv*) the provision of a sanction for the committing of the material fact accompanied by the psychological element.

---

[10]E. Florian, *Trattato di Diritto Penale*, Vol. I, Vallardi, Milano, 1934.

In a synthesis it can be defined as "a fact committed by man and supported by a certain psychological element, contrary to the law and subject to penal sanctions."

In the Italian penal law the principle of legality predominates, according to which it is impossible for the judge to define new crimes even with an analogy to those foreseen by the law. This principle comes from the Roman statement "nullun crimen nulla poena sine lege," and is currently expressed both by the Constitution ("nobody may be punished if not according to a law which was in force before the fact was committed") (Art. 25) and the Penal Code ("nobody may be punished for an action which is not expressly provided for as offense by the law, nor given a punishment for an action which according to the law of the moment in which it was committed, did not constitute an offense") (Art. 1).

Therefore an offense is only that behavior which is specifically described by the law and subjected to sanctions of a penal nature. These sanctions are divided into punishments and security measures. The following are the punishments: life imprisonment, detention, fine ("multa" for "delitti"), "arresto," and fine ("ammenda" for "contravvenzioni"). The security measures are: judicial mental hospital, house for care and custody, agricultural open institution and work house, judicial reformatory, supervised liberty, expulsion from one or more municipalities or provinces, exile from the State for foreigners, caution of good conduct, and confiscation. Punishment or security measures presuppose the commitment of a crime. Complete or diminished mental sanity is required for the application of punishment, whereas security measures are applied either in the case of insanity or when the social dangerousness of the author has been ascertained. In some cases the punishment and the security measures are applied one after the other (diminished mental sanity, habitual or professional offenders).

In the law there is provision of a punishment following all forbidden behavior. The offense must be considered a "delitto" if the sanctions provided for are life imprisonment, detention, or fine ("multa"); whereas it must be considered a "contravvenzioni" if the provided sanctions are "arresto" or fine ("ammenda"). While punishments have a determined duration, security measures have no stated maximum duration.

The psychological element which completes the offense, also called the subjective element, may be one of the following three types: intentional, preter-intentional, or without intention of the consequences ("colposo").

The offense is intentional if done with intent, when the damaging or dangerous result—which is the consequence of the action or the omission and on which the law states the offense depends—is foreseen by the author and willed as the consequence of his own action or omission. It is preter-intentional, or exceeds the intent, when a damaging or dangerous result succeeds the action or omission which is more serious than that willed by the author. It is "colposo," or contrary to intent, when the result, even if foreseen, is not willed by the author and is the consequence of negligence, recklessness, or lack of the needed skill, or of not abiding by the law, rules, orders, or disciplines.

When the law does not expressly provide that the offense is punishable as preter-intentional or "colposo," it may be punished only if it was done with intent.

The author may be punished if, when committing a crime, he was capable of understanding and willing, being conscious of the action or omission (Art. 85 and 42, Penal Code). In this case it can be said that the author, besides being "imputabile," is also socially dangerous because the law or the judge, according to his discretion, presumes that he might commit other offenses in the future (Art. 203 and 204, Penal Code).

In cases of insanity or minors under the age of 14, only security measures may be applied. In some cases the law contains a compulsory provision for the application of a security measure. This is called dangerous presumed by the law.

Between capability (Art. 85, Penal Code) and insanity (Art. 88, Penal Code) there is an intermediate state known as diminished sanity (Art. 89, Penal Code). It is recognized that the individual, when committing the crime, "was because of insanity in such a mental state as to largely diminish, without completely excluding, his capacity for understanding and willing, he has to answer for the offense committed, but the punishment will be diminished." In the most serious cases security measures like detention in a house of care and custody are added to the diminished punishment.

Legal Definition of Juvenile Delinquency

According to the present Italian legislation, a juvenile delinquent is one who when committing the offense is under 18 years of age (Art. 98, Penal Code). In the field of juvenile delinquency there are two categories of offenders, the first is of those who are below 14 years (Art. 97, Penal Code) and the second consists of those who when committing the offense were over 14 but under 18 years.

The two categories are differently regulated by the law. Those under 14 years may not in any circumstances be subjected to punishment. If the offense committed is serious, they may be considered socially dangerous and subjected to security measures, or may be committed to a judicial reformatory, or given supervised liberty. Minors between 14 and 18 years receive sanctions adapted to the stage of maturation of their personality which is ascertained by a rigorous scientific examination. If they are immature their treatment is the same as that of the first category; if mature. i.e. capable of understanding and willing, then they are subjected to diminished punishment; and if dangerous, also to security measures.[11]

Since 1934 juvenile delinquents are judged by special courts for minors.

Besides the above given definition of juvenile delinquency, "strictu sensu," a "latu sensu" may be also given which includes another category of young people who are judged by the juvenile courts, not for having committed offenses, but for behaving in other deviant ways which suggest inclination towards crime. These cases concern purely preventive intervention which will determine the application on non-penal re-education measures such as the commitment to re-education centers, or the passing over to the judicial social service for re-educative treatment on probation.[12]

Often minors who have committed offenses, when they are not subjected to punishment because they benefit from judicial pardon or the conditional suspension of the punishment, may be subjected to non-penal re-education measures. Such measures

[11] I. Baviera, *Diritto minorile*, Milano, Giuffre, 1965.
[12] *Law*, No. 1404 (July 20, 1934); and *Law*, No. 888 (July 25, 1956).

may also be applied to young people who are not yet 18 years old, and may be extended until they are 21 years of age.

CRIME STATISTICS

The crime statistics in various categories for the years 1960-1966 are given in Tables V and VI.

THEORIES OF CRIME CAUSATION

For a long time there was no interest to go deeper into a criminal etiology because the problem of penal law received its definition from religious philosophical and moral theories, which were connected with Christianity and in particular with the concept of free will. According to this concept, the sole cause of criminality (except the clear cases of insanity) was to be found in the responsible will of the subject, i.e. his voluntary choice to do wrong. From this a rigid and reactive punishment system was conceived in terms of moral retribution.

This concept was severely attacked by Lombroso resulting in a deep shift in the traditional view. Attention was then focused on pathology, and following from that the punishment is no longer seen as retribution but as punishment-defense, to be applied according to the dangerousness of the criminal.

Lombroso had forerunners among the physiognomists and the phrenologists, but these were only marginally occupied with the study of criminal behavior.

According to the theories of the ancient philosophers, the basis of criminality was identified as moral degeneration correlated to physical degeneration. In fact the studies on the relationships between the physical and moral aspects were numerous. It was believed that by observing the physiognomic traits, the relevant psychic elements—and therefore the way of thinking and feeling of any individual—could be discovered. It can be affirmed that physiognomy began with Aristotle, Socrates, Galeno, and Seneca, and then continued more intensively in the Middle Ages. On the same line of thought is the thinking of more recent scholars, such as the

TABLE V
INDEX OF CRIME

Categories	1966	1965	1964	1963	1962	1961	1960
Homicide with intent	494	470	536	484	471	542	—
Infanticide	21	19	19	17	20	21	—
Preter-intentional homicide	51	35	32	44	51	73	—
Homicide without intent	4,805	4,710	4,394	4,289	3,519	3,279	—
Libel and slander	1,279	1,712	1,621	926	2,234	2,318	—
Grievous bodily harm with intent	3,235	4,633	4,214	3,175	10,731	11,148	—
Grievous bodily harm	5,116	11,136	9,563	2,316	10,984	9,905	—
Rape, etc.	2,370	2,450	2,288	2,044	2,724	2,758	—
Offenses concerning prostitution (enticing of women to prostitution, etc.)	1,243	1,049	1,070	949	871	860	—
Offenses against the family and children	3,178	3,395	3,505	3,270	3,694	3,935	—
Theft	17,244	18,996	18,032	15,909	17,092	20,550	—
Robbery, extortion, and kidnapping	1,366	1,195	1,207	1,120	1,082	1,096	—
Embezzlement and other frauds	8,081	8,427	7,756	7,357	10,319	10,395	—
Trade fraud	235	294	269	180	438	365	—
Selling foodstuffs not according to health regulations	176	261	373	774	456	483	—
Bankruptcy	2,388	3,023	2,421	1,448	4,472	4,265	—
Bad cheques	9,310	10,484	10,468	6,527	8,670	10,525	—

Abuse of public money by officials	278	289	264	311	266	330	—
Violence. against persons charged with public functions	3,933	4,052	4,069	3,753	4,916	4,745	—
Other felonies	22,939	25,566	23,774	20,474	31,251	32,666	—
TOTAL	87,742	102,196	95,875	75,367	114,261	120,259	130,928

NOTE: The published statistics in Italy are up to 1966 and are incomplete for 1960. Istituto Centrale di Statistica, *Annuario di Statistiche Giudiziarie*, Vol. X, 1960; Roma 1962; Vol. XI, 1961, Roma 1964; Vol. XII, 1962, Roma 1965; Vol. XIII, 1963, Roma, 1966; Vol. XIV, 1964, Roma 1967; Vol. XV, 1965, Roma 1968; Vol. XVI, 1966, Roma 1968.

TABLE VI

		1966	1965	1964	1963	1962	1961	1960
Number of crimes reported to the judicial authority*	Male	—	—	—	—	—	—	—
	Female	—	—	—	—	—	—	—
	Total	2,768,751	2,618,883	2,281,659	2,088,247	1,988,768	1,924,197	1,668,024
Number of persons committed to prison for detention awaiting trial, or for serving sentences, or as a security measure	Male	—	—	—	—	—	—	—
	Female	—	—	—	—	—	—	—
	Total	53,443	62,280	61,286	53,108	66,239	63,446	66,182
Number of convictions†	Male	74,823	86,547	81,450	61,061	94,486	98,966	—
	Female	12,919	15,649	14,425	11,306	19,775	21,293	—
	Total	87,742	102,196	95,875	75,367	114,261	120,259	130,928
Number of crimes (prisoners) known as recidivists	Male	37,616	40,027	39,690	35,803	45,706	51,131	—
	Female	3,897	4,422	4,124	3,653	5,789	6,612	—
	Total	41,513	44,449	43,814	39,456	51,495	57,743	—
Number of suspended sentences	Male	—	—	—	—	—	—	—
	Female	—	—	—	—	—	—	—
	Total	28,349	34,088	30,888	23,098	38,294	41,436	51,924
Number of persons on parole	Male	—	—	—	—	—	—	—
	Female	—	—	—	—	—	—	—
	Total	94	223	414	167	223	270	199

*Offenses (felonies and misdemeanours reported to the judicial authority (Preture and Procure della Repubblica) by public authorities and private persons.

phrenologists of the beginning of the 19th century, who—influenced by the research of Gall on the correlation between cerebral functions and psychological activity—believed that from the protuberances and depressions of the skull could assessed the level of intelligence and the various individual tendencies including morality, madness and criminality. According to them (Dalla Porta, Spurzheim *et al.*) the latter should be considered as the consequences of irregularities in the development of various regions of the brain and the skull.[13]

Lombroso, although principally influenced by German materialism which studied the objective data, and Compte's positivism which required a broad basis of positive facts and perceived the importance of the biological factors at the root of the social phenomena, was also influenced by the evolutionistic biological theory of Darwin, extended to the concept of social evolution by Spencer. Under this influence Lombroso studied, worked, conducted research, and taught, and found himself to be the heir to a growing complex of medical, clinical, and psychiatric ideas which directly or marginally were concerned with the criminal.[14]

According to the general Lombrosian theory the delinquents are distinguished from the non-delinquents on the basis of the existence of various physical anomalies which are by origin atavistic and degenerative. The concept of atavism, which postulates a reversion to a primitive or subhuman type of man is characterized by physical features reminiscent of a variety of inferior morphological aspects belonging to apes and lower primates. It is implied that the mentality of an atavistic type is that of a primitive man who has biologically "reversed," and is inevitably against the norms of civil modern society. Successively, Lombroso enriched this concept with the *theory of degeneration*, which concerns the existence of pathological conditions in the delinquent.

Lombroso reached these conclusions on the basis of an extended observation of delinquents detained in prison. On the occasion of the autopsy of the famous bandit, Vilella, he

[13]*G. Antinori, I precursori di Lombroso,* Torino, 1900.
[14]M. E. Wolfgang, "Cesare Lombroso," *Quaderni de Criminologla Clinica,* 1961.

found a depression in the interior of the lower back part of the skull which he called "Median occipital fossa" (a characteristic of inferior animals) as well as another depression correlated with an over-development of the "ipertrofia del vermis" which is usually found in birds in the "cerebellum." Looking at that skull he believed to have understood the problem of the nature of the delinquent; an atavistic being in whom the ferocious instincts of primitive humanity and of inferior animals are reproduced.

While the case of Vilella was a clear example of physical reversion, the studies carried out on Verzeni (a delinquent sentenced for sadism and rape), who showed cannibalistic instincts, confirmed the existence of a cultural reversion. However, Lombroso found the final key to his systemization after the case of Misdea, a young soldier, unintelligent, but not vicious, subject to epileptic fits, who suddenly for some trivial cause killed eight comrades.

Continuing his research, Lombroso submitted his theory on atavism to deep criticism, and all those anomalies found in the delinquent which could not be explained by atavism were put down to epilepsy. Thus Lombroso no longer considered the born delinquent only in terms of an atavistic reversion to primitive man, but also spoke of the break in development of the nervous centers, illness, mingled atavism, degeneration, and epilepsy in his etiological analysis of the born delinquent.[15]

Pushed by critics and friends, particularly Ferri, Lombroso began, towards the end of the century, to give attention to economic and social factors in criminal etiology, but continued to underline a changing interaction between heredity and environment.[16] It is in this post-Lombrosian phase that the work carried out by Ferri is specially important. To make clear the presumed biological absolutism of the Lombrosian theory, Ferri divulged his bio-sociological concept of crime, according to which the offense is always the result of personal conditions which react to given environmental factors.[17]

[15]C. Lombroso, *L'Uomo delinquente*, Ved. 1897.

[16]C. Lombroso, *Crime, its Causes and Remedies* (Boston: Little, Brown and Co., 1912).

[17]E. Ferri, *Sociologia Criminale*, 2nd ed. (Torino, 1900).

In Italy, the strong biological tradition of Lombroso—after the ideological conflicts between defenders of positivism and the conservatives of the Classical School—was continued by studies and researches in the endocrinological, constitutionalistic, psychological, and forensic-psychiatric fields and by the works of scholars such as Ottolenghi, De Sanctis, Lugaro, Vidoni, P-ende and Di Tullio.[18]

An interesting development was the convergence of concern in the study of delinquent behavior on the part of the legal medicine schools, and of criminologists with a general medical orientation. All this, however, has not diminished the relevance given to sociological factors as shown by the writings of Di Tullio.[19]

The prestige of the medical profession and the large amount of empirical material put at the disposal of professionals in both fields, together with their expert work, favored the continuous development of the medical aspect of criminology. On the other hand, the slow development of social science, due to the prominence of idealistic philosophers, prevented the rising of a sociology-oriented criminology, with the exception of the writings of Niceforo.[20] In psychology, the biological tradition and the professional and academic links with medicine lined up the psychologists with the criminologists of a medical orientation, and the forensic psychiatrists.[21]

However, the great development of the theory of social factors must not be forgotten, especially in the field of juvenile delinquency in the post-war period. The collision between the

---

[18]B. Di Tullio, *La constituzione delinquenciale nella etiologia terapia del delitto*, A.R.E., Roma, 1928; B. Di Tullio, *Manuale de Antropologia e Psicologia Criminale*, A.R.E., Roma, 1931; and E. Monachesi, "Trends in Criminological Research in Italy," *American Sociological Review*, 1, 1936.

[19]B. Di Tullio, *Medicine et Sociologie en Etiologie Criminelle* (Paris: Societe Internationale de Criminologie, 1951).

C. Gerin, F. Ferracuti, and A. Semerari, "Evaluation medicolegale de l'imputabilite et de la dangerosite sociale dans les anomalies et dans les maladies psychiques: ses repercussions criminologiques," *Zacchia*, 26, 1963.

[20]A. Niceforo, *Criminologia*, Bocca, Roma, 1949.

[21]L. Meshcieri, "Osservazioni critiche sull 'applicazions dei metodi psicologici nello studio della personalita del delinquente," *Archivio Penale*, 1951.

two concepts (both constitutionalistic and environmental) has recently resulted in an attempt at agreement in the clinical direction, which, accepting the multifactoral approach, has been widely and validly used in the criminal etiological sector. In fact facing the evident impossibility of finding a sole cause —sociological, psychological, or biological, or criminal—the casual research should be directed towards a group of factors, which altogether affect criminal behavior. This view, indicating the individual approach in order to resolve a concrete criminal problem in a particular subject, is widely supported by Di Tullio and his School of Criminology.[22] More recently, this multifactural trend has tried to conduct an integrated interdisciplinary approach.[23]

PENAL PHILOSOPHY

The Italian legal tradition has its origin in ancient Greece and Rome.

Philosophical Foundation and its Historical Development

It was during the period of most intensive development of Greek philosophy that the problem of justification of punishment arose. In the writings of Plato there is the assumption that justification of punishment is based on the principle of atonement, i.e. punishment is considered a necessary retribution which follows crime, applied in the name and in the interests of the community.[24] There is also the concept of social defense in the sense that the State threatens and applies the punishment for its own survival and protection.[25] Plato in

[22]B. Di Tullio, *Principi di Criminologia Clinica e Psichiatria forense*, 3rd ed. (Roma: Istituto Italiano di Medicina Sociale, 1963).

[23]F. Ferracuti and M.E. Wolfgang, *Il comportamento violente— Modern iaspetti criminologici*, Milano, Giuffre, 1966. This approach is widely accepted in the clinical field, also see Di Tullio, "High imports for American Criminology," *Criminologica*, Vol. VI, 3, 1968.

[24]This affirmation is to be found in "Goegia." (E. Sacchi, "Sulla teoria platonica del delitto e della pena," *Rivista filosofica*, Anno II⁰, Vol. III, 1900), pp. 30-40.

[25]Concepts that are to be found in "Repubblica," "Le Leggi," and

fact bases the justification of penal law on social utility; one punishes not for the offense already committed, but more for probable future offenses, so that on the one side the guilty person does not return to crime, and on the other, learning from the punishment inflicted, others refrain from it. The Platonic doctrine therefore moves away from prevention towards atonement, and the concept of defense is confined to the ethical criterion of individual improvement.[26] The practical effect of punishment, more or less obscured in Plato's system, is accentuated and becomes prevalent in Aristotle, to find itself functioning as moral education and directing towards virtuous activity which is the duty of the State.[27]

The Roman "giureconsulti," conforming with their practical views, did not express a precise theory on the justification of punishment. They affirmed that punishment had various goals like deterrence by means of example—a doctrine also adopted by Cicero, the aim of amendment, and the concept of atonement.[28] In the last period of Roman law these various goals overlapped and were summarized in the supreme principle of public utility and public order.[29]

The Church gave a new orientation to the conception of punishment according to which the human power to punish is nothing but a divine delegation. The religious authorities, in inflicting punishment, acted in the name of and on behalf of the Divinity. Sin is crime, and penitence the punishment. This penal theory, born in the "Patristica" and perfectioned by the "Scolastica" culminates in the thinking of St Agostino and in the system of St Thomas d'Aquino.[30]

During the Middle Ages and up until the rising of rationalistic philosophy, no scientific theory can be found outside that

---

"Protagora." (Bortolucci, "Il delitto e la pena nei dialoghi di Platone," *Archivio Giuridico*, Serie III, Vol. III, 1905), pp. 117-258.

[26]E. Florian, *Trattato di Diritto Penale*, Vol. I, Vallardi, Milano, 1934.

[27]Especially in the works "Politica" and the "Etica Nicomachea."

[28]Marciano, *Digesto*, 48, 3, 6, 1, "ut Vindicet in exemplum; ne quid et aliud postea tale facere miliatur"; Marciano, *Digesto*, 48, 19, 6, par. 1, "ut exemplo deterriti minus delinquant"; and Paulus, *Digesto*, 48, 19, 20, "quod poena constituitur in emendationem hominum."

[29]C. Ferrini, *Diritto Penale Romano*, Roma, Hoepli, 1898, pp. 36-37.

[30]Saint 'Agostino (354-430), *Civitas Dei, Confessioni*; Tomaso (1226-1274), *Summa theologica*.

of the "Scolastica" on the justification of punishment. Two principles dominated in practice, first, the reason of State, public vendetta, which led to violent intimidations and the use of the most cruel punishments; and secondly, the moral principle of atonement in the religious sense conforming to the teaching of the Church.[31]

In the period of "Umanesimo" and "Rinascimento" the concept of punishment assumed characteristics nearer to reality and, thanks to the works of Grozio, scientific research on the principle of criminal law was begun. According to this scholar, who explains the genesis of human society by referring to the hypothesis of a social contract—either tacit or expressed, the principle of primitive law is also contractual: he who commits an offense implicitly agrees to subject himself to punishment because for the good results of human association a crime cannot remain unpunished.[32]

This doctrine of the contractual origin of criminal law, taken up and perfected by the "Enciclopedisti" in particular, was dominant during the second half of the 18th century and was accepted in Italy—where during the period of "Illuminismo" Italian penalistic science was developing rapidly.

In our country, before Beccaria, no autonomous penal theory had been developed which was really organic and which could become the basis for a complete criminal justice system. All penal theories came from works of philosophy and were therefore applications of more general principles. The merit of elevating criminal law to the level of science and giving penal theories a practical foundation must be given to Beccaria. However, to identify him as the founder of the Classical School is an arbitrary opinion. Beccaria indicated the prevention of delinquency by means of education and concerned himself with the delinquent by pointing out his insensibility, affirmations which would be taken up and widely developed afterwards by scholars of the Positive School.

As has already been mentioned, until Beccaria's time all types of abuse dominated in practice: torture, absolute power

[31]Calisse, *Svolgimento storico del diritto penale in Italia dalle invasioni barbariche alle riforme del secolo XVIII°*, Milano, 1934.
[32]Grozio, *De jure belli ac pacis*, 1625.

of the judges, and most atrocious inequalities; while in theory
it was intended to lift human justice towards divine justice
or to derive justice from the law of war and vendetta which
degenerated into the most terrible deterrents. Beccaria was the
first to go against theoretical aberrations and abuses in the
practice of criminal justice and gave it a human and social aim.

Beccaria, following Grozio, affirmed that human justice has
nothing to do with divine justice. Criminal justice finds its
basis in common utility, in the general interest for the good of
the majority. This foundation, essentially utilitarian, must be
corrected, limited, and fortified by the moral law; thus the
fundamental principle of Beccaria is in fact the lining up of the
criminal law with the moral law.[33]

Filangeri,[34] Pagano, and Romagnosi may be considered to
have given fillip to the movement that had its origin in the
works of Beccaria, while Rossi and Carmignani provided
another noteworthy impulse to penal doctrine.

Towards the mid-point of the 19th century a new orientation arose in Italian criminalistic science by means of the
abandonment of the utilitarian concept of criminal law. This
new orientation was derived from the ideology of the "Illuminismo" dscisively affirming the ethic-retributive character of
punishment. Carrara was the best representative of this trend
known as the Classical School of Criminal law.[35]

This school studied crime and punishment as abstractions
and considered them immutable in time and space. Crime is a
legal conception, a simple relationship of contradiction between
the human fact and the violated law. The investigation must
be aimed at the fact, while the person of the offender was
considered according to the average standard of ordinary
man, and not that of criminals. The criminal was therefore
considered morally free, endowed with a free will as any
other man. As a consequence punishment is an entity correlated to the offense, adopted to restore the legal order in

[33]C. Beccaria, *Dei delitti e delle pene* (a facsimile of the original edition
published anonymously in Livorno in 1764) (Torino; U.T.E.T., 1964).

[34]G. Filangeri, *La scienza della legislazione,* Capolago, Tiporgrafia e
Libreia Elvetica, 1834.

[35]F. Carrara, *Programmi di diritto criminale,* 1859.

proportion to the offense as far as it is possible. There is non-imputability, only if the freedom of will does not exist.

Contrary to the classical approach, there arose an important new movement that took the name of the Positive School. While the Classical School considered crime as a legal fact disregarding the offender, the new school affirmed that, before or together with the fact, a study of the man who committed it must be made. The creator of this idea was Cesare Lombroso.

Starting from the Lombrosian concept of the criminal being abnormal, and externally recognizable by special somatic and psychic characteristics.[36] Garofalo,[37] and Ferri[38] elaborated on and developed the principles and the doctrine of this new school, rejecting individual responsibility, proposed a radical change in the legislation. Maintaining that the criminal was inevitably brought to crime because of the effect of the forces that work inside and outside him, the school affirmed that punishment is useless and that the author of a crime should not be punished but segregated from society, thereby being just in a position where it is impossible for him to do harm, and within possible limits, readapted to social life. They suggested that the sanctions to be adopted concerning the criminal should not be measured according to the seriousness of the committed crime, but according to the dangerousness of the subject (indeterminate sanction).

The sanction, which for the Classical School by being linked to the presupposition of free will is punishment and an afflictive measure, ceased to be so for the Positive School and became a legal means of defense against crime, an institution of social security. It therefore became a criminal sanction to be applied to the offenders on the basis of their characters, and the various contingencies of the crime.

In this way, the Positive School, although in many essential ways diverging from the classical line of thought, in substance complemented it, integrated it, and overtook it, thus widening

[36]C. Lombroso, *L'uomo delinquente studiato in rapporto all'antropologia alla medicina legale e alle discipline carcerarie*, 1876.

[37]R. Garofale, *Criminologia*, Torino, 1885.

[38]E. Ferri, *Sociologia Criminale*, 2nd ed., Torino, 1900.

the context and the limits of penal discipline.

Present Trends in Penal Philosophy

The fundamental lines of thought of the Positive and the Classical Schools provoked wide comments and discussions. While these two schools developed, supporters of an intermediate school arose,[39] who incorporated many practical ideas of the Positive School, but maintained strongly the fundamental statutes of the Classical School. As a consequence of the Third School," the advocation for the maintenance of punishment in its traditional form was made, but the proposal was to institute, alongside other provisions, security measures designed to combat dangerousness of the offender.

Mention should also be made of the Technical Legal School with prevailing methodological orientation[40] headed by Rocco.

By this time, the prevailing opinion was moving in the direction of the distinction within the area of criminal law between the imputable and the non-imputable offender and between punishments and security measures; a tendency widely realized by the criminal Code in force at present.

During the last few years, there has been a great flowering of writings in Italy in which the numerous problems connected to the coming into force of the new criminal Code have been studied in detail. In addition, freeing itself from traditional thoughts, the Italian doctrine has made serious efforts to adjust itself to the development of the conception of punishment and to systems of fighting criminality which are common to all civilized people, and with notable success.[41]

This tendency is strongly supported by "Social Defense" movement which as a criminological school of thought, that has developed in Europe as a result of the conflict between the

[39]E. Carnevale, *La terza sc ola e la concezione unitaria del diritto criminale*, Progr. del dir. crimin., 1915; *Diritto criminale*, Vol. I° Roma 1932; B. Alimena, *Note filosofiche d'un criminalista*, Modena, 1911; and V. Manzini, *Trattato di diritto penale* (Torino : U.T.E.T., 1963).

[40]A. Rocco, *Il problema e il metodo della scienza del diritto penale*, 1910.

[41]F. Antolisei, *Manuale di diritto penale*, parte generale, Giuffre Milano, 1960.

Classical and the Positive School, is considered by many authors as a synthesis of the two.

FUNCTION OF THE COURT

The Italian legal system provides for different types of courts for different purposes.

Organization and Classification of Courts

Criminal justice is administered by the following bodies: the "Pretura"; Tribunal, and Assize Court; Court of Appeal, and Assize Court of Appeal; Cassation Court; and the Public Prosecutor.

"*Pretura*." This is located in the chief town of every "mandamento"[42] usually comprising a group of municipalities. The "pretore" (one single judge) takes direct charge of the investigation and of the trial. In some of the more important towns (Rome, Naples, Milan etc.) the "pretura" is divided into sections.

The "pretore" has power in both civil and criminal matters. Regarding criminal matters he is a judge of first instance for offenses for which the law established detentive punishment (reclusion or arrest) for not more than a maximum of three years, or a pecuniary punishment[43] whatever the amount, this being apart from, or together with the above mentioned detentive punishment.

The trial before the "pretore" is preceded by an investigation which is always 'sommaria" (i.e. investigation directly carried out by the p'ublic prosecutor).[44]

Tribural. This body has its seat in every chief town of each "circondario."[45] It is a collegiate body made up of a chairman

---

[42]The "mandamento" is the smallest territorial judicial set.

[43]There are two types of pecuniary punishments, the first being "multo" which is applied for "delitti" (felonies), and the second "ammenda" for "contravvenzioni" (misdemeanors).

[44]The "pretore" acts himself as public prosecutor during the investigation phase.

[45]A "circondario" is a territorial set consisting of several "mandamenti."

and two "puisne" judges who have power in both civil and criminal matters—with more than one section existing in the same Tribunal. Concerning criminal matters it has power in the first instance, for cases which pertain neither to the "pretore" nor to Assize Court, and, in the second instance, for the examination of proceedings against decisions from the "pretore" which are subject to appeal.

Assize Court. This is a special section of the Tribunal, which has specific powers for more serious crimes, i.e. for those considered in Article 29 of the Penal Procedure Code. It is made up of a chairman, a "puisne" judge and six popular judges. Attached to each Tribunal there is an investigation of penal proceedings either to be dealt with by the Tribunal, or by the Assize Court. Within the investigation office there are one or more investigating judges. The investigation of each case is accomplished by a single judge at the request of the public prosecutor, either for cases within the competence of the Tribunal or the Assize Court. In some cases the investigation may be carried out directly by the public prosecutor. The investigating judge has the power to discharge the defendant or to submit him to the successive trial.

In the chief town of each "distretto"[46] there is also a Tribunal for Minors. This functions as a collegiate body composed of a chairman, a "puisne" judge, and two popular members (a man and a woman) chosen from among the experts in psychology and psychiatry. The Tribunal has powers over all crimes committed by minors of 18 years or less. The procedure before the Tribunal for Minors does not provide for an investigating judge. The investigation so far has always been committed by the public prosecutor.

Court of Appeal. The Court of Appeal has its seat in every chief town of each "distretto." It is a collegiate body composed of a chairman and four "puisne" judges. It is divided into criminal and civil sections. It has power in both criminal and civil matters of appeal against Tribunal decisions and in addition has competence in some specific matters such as enforcement of foreign sentences and rehabilitation.

In each appeal court a special section for minors is put

---

[46]"Distretto" is a territorial set consisting of several "circondario."

aside which judges in the second instance crimes committed by minors under 18 years. Another special section is the Assize Court of Appeal which judges appeals against decisions of the Assize Court; it is composed of a chairman, a "puisne" judge, and six popular judges.

There is an investigation section attached to the court of appeals which consists of a chairman and two judges and has power concerning the appeals brought against acquittals of the investigating judges.

Court of Cassation. This is a unique collegiate body and is located in Rome. It functions by separate sections, each with a chairman and six judges. It has power in criminal matters and its competence is limited. On request from the prosecutor or private parties, it assesses the conformity of decisions of the judiciary with the provisions of the law, without discussing matters of fact. It examines decisions taken by the Court of Appeal or pronounced in the first instance, against which no other appeal is possible.

The Court of Cassation, as the supreme judicial body, ensures the exact observance and a uniform interpretation of the law, states the limits of the various judicial authorities and directs the distribution of functions of judiciary and other powers of the State. Decisions from the Court of Cassation are not subject to appeal.

Office of the Public Prosecutor.[47] This is attached to the Court of Cassation, the Court of Appeal, and the Tribunal. For the former it is represented by the Attorney General. There is no such office attached to the "preture" because in criminal matters the "pretore"—in the investigation phase and during the execution of the provisions—has the role of public prosecutor, while during the trial he is exclusively concerned with jurisdictional functions and the public prosecutor is represented by another person (usually a lawyer appointed for each case).

The Public Prosecutor at the Tribunal is chief of the criminal police of the "circondario" and therefore directs and

[47]In the Italian system the public prosecutor is defined as a "magistrato requirente" and belongs to the judicial order together with the judges ("magistrati giudicanti") constituting the above listed bodies.

controls the activities of the criminal police. In any case, having received information on a crime he has a duty either to introduce penal action or to request from the investigating judges attached to the Tribunal a decree of "impromovibilita" for the penal action. The investigating judge, if he accepts the request, declares that the prosecution is closed, otherwise he continues with the investigation.

The Attorney General of the Appeal Court is chief of the criminal police of the "distretto" and normally has the same duties in the appeal instance as the public prosecutor at the Tribunal in the first instance.

Qualifications of Court Members

The Judicial System Act (R.D. 30-1-1941, No. 12) gives the rules for the legal status of judges and prosecutors, i.e. access to the career, promotions, special prerogatives which are part of the judicial function, discipline, salaries, and rights and duties of judges and prosecutors.

Article 104 of the Constitution establishes that the "judiciary constitutes an autonomous body independent from any other authority." The norms which establish the autonomy of the judiciary, and those which state the judge's special prerogatives, derive from the above mentioned article of the Constitution which settles the two characteristics (autonomy and independence) of the judicial system.

The judicial body is composed of all magistrates (judges and public prosecutors) appointed by a competitive examination and assigned to the judicial rank by the High Council of the Magistracy. In fact, Article 106 of the Constitution states that "appointments of magistrates should take place by competitive examination." The above mentioned examinations are established by the High Council of the Magistracy following a request from the Ministry of Justice or "ex-officio" and graduates in jurisprudence are admitted. According to the existing rules, it is necessary to undergo training for at least two years as a judicial "observer."

According to Article 107 of the Constitution, "magistrates can be distinguished only because of their different functions." With law Number 392 of 1951, three categories of magistrates

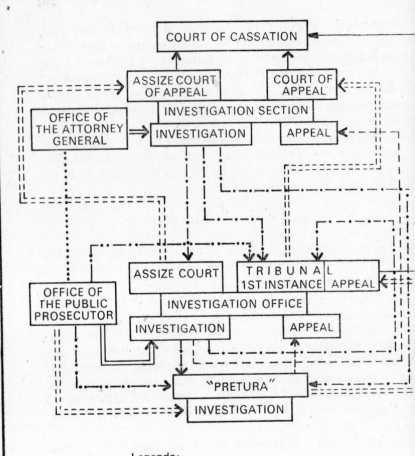

Legenda:

– – – – – – –	Appeal against decisions pronounced during the investigation in the first instance.
–·–·–·–·–	Forwarding of the case by the investigating judge and the investigation section for further trial.
··············	Claiming of proceedings by the Attorney General.
–··–··–··–	Summons from the public prosecutor to appear before the tribunal or the assizes Court and request to the "Pretore" to start proceedings.
═══════	Request for investigation "formale" (carried out by the investigating or by the investigation section) or "sommaria" ('pretore')
=========	Appeal against decisions pronounced in the first instance.
────────	Appeal against decisions pronounced in the second instance

were established: judges of the Tribunal, judges of the Appeal Court and judges of the Cassation Court. This tripartition indicates the position that judges reach after acquiring a certain seniority of having passed examinations.

The present organization of key posts of the administrative functions of the Ministry of Justice are carried out by judges; such an assignment gives them a position outside the organic role of magistracy.

The judges, besides being obliged to fulfill their functions in accordance with the law, are subject to specific duties, such as the obligation to reside permanently in the same municipality as the judicial office where they work; the obligation of reporting the existence of possible reasons for incompatibility in deciding specific cases; the prohibition of the assumption of any public or private professional commitment; the prohibition of working in industry, commerce or other professions; and the prohibition of accepting assignments without authorization (Arts. 12, 18, 19, 16, 17 of the judicial system).

The judge may be freed from his duties to undertake the function of deputy, senator, municipal, and provincial counsellor. The most important right however is that of "inamovibilita" in which his special prerogatives are summarized. It has two objects: one, that the function itself of judging involves the fact that the judge may not, against or without his will, be excluded from the judicial order, even temporarily, when exercising his functions; and secondly, regarding his place of assignment it concerns the prohibition of his being removed from his position or being assigned to another function without his own consent.

In fact, Article 107 of the Constitution establishes that "judges are cinamovibili. They may not be dispensed or suspended from their duties nor sent to other places or given other functions, but following the decision of the High Court of the Magistracy, adopted with the defense guarantees established by the judicial system and with their consent. The public prosecutor is given the guarantees forseen for him by the norms of the judicial system."

According to this provision, it is easy to understand the following principles as stated in the Constitution: first, it establishes the content of guarantee for the "inamovibilita" of the judges only; secondly, it establishes that public prosecutors have also the right to be given guarantees of which the regulation depends however on the ordinary law; and thirdly, it conforms that "inamovibilita" has two objects—the functions and the seat.

The Italian Constitution ratifies the fundamental principles that assure autonomy and independence to the judiciary as per Article 1 which states that judges are not subject to supremacy but that of the law. Article 104 affirms that the judiciary constitutes an autonomous body independent from any other power, and, for the concrete realization of such principle it places at the top of the judicial power a relevant organ, the High Council of the Magistracy, which deals with all matters related to magistrates' status, thus excluding any possible dependence on organs of another power.

The Council's Chairman is the President of the Republic; and the First President of the Court of Cassation and the Attorney General (at the Court of Cassation) are its permanent members. The other members (21) are elected by magistrates, two-thirds from among the members of various categories, and one-third by parliament in a common meeting among university professors in juridical subjects and lawyers with 15 years career.

Referring to competence, Article 105 of the Constitution involves the High Council in the employments, assignments, transfers, promotions, and disciplinary provisions concerning magistrates. The Ministry of Justice merely takes care of the organization and functioning of services related to justice (Art. 110 of the Constitution).

The High Council lasts for four years but the President of the Republic has the power of dissolving it with anticipation if its functioning is impossible.[48]

Lawyer System

The defense intervenes during the penal proceedings with a twofold function as an assistant and a representative.

The function of assistance has a wider or smaller field of

[48]*Nuovissimo Digesto Italiano*, Vol. XII, Torino: U.T.E.T., 1965.

action depending on the phase the procedure has reached: in the investigation phase the lawyer has, even if only in part, the right to participate in several important investigation acts. The function of representation is outlined with relation to the accomplishment of certain actions.

During the investigation, the defendant has the right to only one defender, while for the actual trial (both at the moment of preliminary acts and during the discussion) he has the right to two defenders. The lack of a defender for the defendant during the trial—the presence of a defender being compulsory in every trial for the total duration of it—involves the nullity of the trial itself.

Lawyers have to observe the rules for professional morality and corrections and they may be subject to disciplinary sanctions as per the law dispositions regarding the forensic professional exercise.

According to the source of the investiture the defender is appointed by the defendant or provided by the judge. The nomination can be made in any of the acts of the proceedings, received by the judicial authority, or with personal declaration to the clerk of the judicial office charged with the proceedings. The nomination of the defender is made by the investigating judge when the investigation is "formale," by the public prosecutor when the procedure is "sommaria" or when it is the case of a "procedimento direttissimo," by the "pretore" when the trial is of his own competence, and by the chairman of the collegiate organ at the stage of preliminary acts and in the discussion. The work of the defense is free of charge only for defendants who have no money.

The unlawful abandonment of the defense brings two consequences: the suspension of the exercises of the profession for a certain period, and the charging of trial expenses arisen because of the abandonment of the defense.[49]

Besides the lawyers, the "procuratori" (solicitors) may participate in the defense of private parties (the defendant or civil parties) in the penal trial. The difference between lawyers and 'procuratori" is practically non-existent (the "procuratore"

[49]G. Leone, *Diritto Processuale Penale*, 7th ed., Jovene, Naples, 1968.

cannot defend outside his place of residence nor before the Appeal Court and the Cassation Court).

Method of Trial

The principal types of penal processual activity are: the "giudizio direttissimo," the "giudizio per decreto," and the "giudizio ordinario."

"*Giudizio Direttissimo.*" When a person is caught while committing a crime which falls under the competence of the "pretura" or tribunal, the "pretore" or the prosecutor—if he decides to proceed and if special investigations are not necessary—may put him or her under arrest (in cases when the law makes provision for arrest) after a general interrogation before the "pretura" or the tribunal within the fifth day from the arrest. If it is not possible to proceed in this way, the "pretore" or the public prosecutor proceeds as usual. If the crime falls under the competence of the Assize Court, a "processo direttissimo" may be initiated only in case the court is at that time in session or if it has to meet within five days from that of the arrest.

"*Guidizio per Decreto.*" The "pretore" whose duty is to inflict a fine, may sentence the person with "decreto" without proceeding to the discussion. Opposition to this penal sentence can be proposed. If the person opposing is not present at the discussion, without a legitimate justification the "pretore" orders the execution of the "decreto," but if the opposition is present, the "decreto" is repelled and the "pretore" follows the formal procedure.

"*Guidizio Ordinario*". The penal action, apart from the above mentioned instances, must be taken by the investigating judge at the Tribunal (procedure "formale") or by the public prosecutor (procedure "sommaria") according to the complexity of the investigation. At the end of the procedure "sommaria" if the public prosecutor believes that the defendant should be released, he asks the investigating magistrate to acquit him; otherwise he asks the Chairman of the Tribunal to proceed with the trial.

Proceedings against juveniles are taken up at the juvenile tribunal by the public prosecutor who promotes the pena action and takes care of the investigation by means of procedure "sommaria."

The investigating judge, at the end of the investigation, acquits the accused or tables the trial and refers it to the "pretore" if it falls under his competence, and to the Tribunal or the Assize Court when the "pretore" examines the proceedings from a "sommario" point of view.

The Attorney General may refer the investigation of crimes which come under the Assize Court or the Tribunal to the "investigating section" and in this case he takes care of the relevant indictment. Judgment takes place at the judicial offices which have competence in the matter.

In Italy the procedure for appeal or cassation is the same and when the appeal is presented by the defendant there is a principle of prohibition of the reformation "in peius" of the appealed sentence.

FUNCTION OF THE POLICE

The present structure of the police force in Italy is composed of the "Arma dei Carabinieri"; the "Corpo delle Guardie di Pubblica Sicurezza"; and the "Corpo delle Guardie de Finanza."

The "Arma dei Carabinieri" and the "Corpo delle Guardie di Pubblica Sicurezza" have general assignments. The former comes organically under the Ministry of Defense, and the latter under the Ministry of Internal Affairs. They have similar tasks and assignments consisting of: maintenance of public order, safeguarding of citizens' security, preservation of property, prevention and control of crime, seeing to the observance of the laws and regulations of the State, and helping in case of public or private accidents. The "Corpo delle Guardie di Finanza" has specific duties; it has the assignment of preventing, discovering, and reporting the evasion of fiscal payments and financial violations. It participates in the political and military defense of the frontiers and in the maintenance of public order and security. It is part of the Armed Forces of the State and comes under the Ministry of Finance.

Powers and duties attributed to members of the above mentioned bodies can be divided on the basis of their qualifications as officers or policemen, commitments for public security, and criminal matters. The public security police are encharged with the protection of public order, general security, public morality, social peace and tranquility; the activity of the criminal police, on the other hand, does not have a preventive character, it is only related to violations of the penal law which have already taken place.

While the public security police can take initiatives of action, and function using dynamic methods and procedures with wide discretionary powers, the criminal police carry out the activities which have previously been assigned to them and are obliged to follow rigid norms established by the Penal Procedure Code. Article 109 of the Constitution establishes that "the judicial authority directs criminal police"; and Article 220 of the Penal Procedure Code states that officers and policemen of the criminal police must exercise their functions under the supervision of the Attorney General (at the Court of Appeal) and the public prosecutor (at the Tribunal). They must also carry out the orders of the investigating judge and of the "pretura." The powers conferred on the criminal police are limited to the activities necessary for the urgent gathering of information or evidence of a crime; however, the activity of this police body is generally subject to the Penal Procedure Code which confers less powers on policemen and submits the operations they carry out to major restrictions compared to those carried out by officers.

The criminal police duties may be defined as those of investigating and gathering information regarding crimes and coercion; the action by means of which these duties are carried out can be considered an activity of the above mentioned police body itself, or as an activity delegated or ordered by the judicial authority, or as mere police assistance to the latter. The distinction is important, because when an activity is carried out by the judicial authority in the presence of the criminal police, then they are considered as accessories; when the activity is carried out by delegation of the judicial authority, it is considered as being accomplished by the latter; but when this activity is carried out by the criminal police in the course of their ordinary functions because of their specific power, then this activity is subject to the control of the judicial authority.

The activity assigned to the criminal police—being limited to cases of urgent intervention for serious crimes—are as follows:

First, according to Article 222 of the Penal Procedure Code, an officer may proceed on his initiative with arrest if the offender is caught in the act, and may also so proceed outside these circumstances if there is a well-founded suspicion of escape and it concerns persons seriously suspected of a crime for which a warrant of arrest is compulsory. They may detain the persons arrested for the time strictly necessary for the interrogation, and then must immediately take the suspect to the judicial authority. As soon as they have arrested a person they must immediately inform the public prosecutor and communicate within 48 hours the reasons for the arrest as well as the result of any "somaria" investigation already carried out.

Secondly, the officers should take care that the material evidence and traces of crime are preserved and that the scene is not altered before the judicial authority arrives on the spot. In cases there is a well-founded reason that objects and traces may be altered or dispersed in the meanwhile, they may proceed with the necessary control and confiscation of material evidence (Art. 222, PPC). Also they may directly proceed with markings, making descriptive and photographic notes and any other technical operations in relation to their functions.

Thirdly, in the case of the offender being caught while committing a crime or in case of escape, officers may proceed, even at night, with personal or domicile searching if they have reason to think that the individual has taken refuge there, or that objects which should be confiscated are to be found there. The officer in charge must give reasons why he carried out the search and communicate the report within 48 hours to the judicial authority which will approve it if the necessary conditions for such a search existed.

Fourthly, in the case of the offender being caught while committing a crime and when it is urgent to gather evidence of the crime or preserve its traces, officers may proceed with a "somaria" interrogation of the arrested person, take information from witnesses and carry out the necessary recognition, inspection, and confrontation procedure (Art. 225, PPC).

Fifthly, according to Article 226, the officers in the course of their duty may not open sealed papers, but must transmit them to the competent judicial authority. Concerning the interception or the prevention of telephone communications officers must have authorization from the judicial authority.

Sixthly, Article 227 provides that at the end of these operations, officers must immediately transmit to the judicial authority a note on the action carried out and any object collected, i.e. it is their duty to present a report (as stated in Art. 2, PPC) for all crimes with which officers are acquainted, provided that they are not crimes for which a charge may only be made by the victim.

Seventhly, Article 228 provides that officers, who have knowledge that somebody has been unlawfully deprived of his personal liberty, must go to the spot and if there is no legal motive for the detention they must free the detained person and make an immediate report to the judicial authority.

To a certain extent, criminal policemen have similar powers and duties as those conferred on officers, but because of the difference in rank and qualifications the law has enforced certain limits to their activities.

Criminal police according to Article 219, may, on orders from the judicial authority, carry out direct or indirect investigations into the dangerousness of the author of a certain crime.

Besides the above mentioned activities that the criminal police perform in the course of their ordinary duties, they may also carry out activities delegated or ordered by the judicial authority, or activities assisting the latter.[50]

FUNCTION OF THE PRISON

The prison system in Italy is organized in the following manner.

Prison Organization

It is composed of jails, special and ordinary prisons for execution of punishment, institutions for security measures and institutions for juveniles.

"*Stabilimenti di Custodia Preventiva*" (*Jails*). These may be divided into (*i*) central or branch judicial prisons, the former

---

[50]*Novissino Digesto Italiano*, Vol. XIII (Torino: U.T.E.T., 1966).

being established in each chief town where there is a tribunal
and the latter in the same town of the same "circondario";
and (*ii*) "Mandamentali" prisons are established in the municipality where the "pretura" is located. In these jails, persons
awaiting trial or prisoners in transit are normally detained.

Persons guilty of "delitti," sentenced to detention for a
period of not more than two years may also be sent to a
central judicial prison as well as those guilty of "delitti" or
"contravvenzioni," sentenced to detention less than six months
may be sent to a "mandamentali" prison.

Arrested persons awaiting trial must be kept apart from
those already sentenced. Persons accused of the same crime
must be kept separated if the judicial authority has so ordered,
and even if such an order is not given, the separation must be
provided by the Governor of the prison if the prison
permits it.

Sentenced prisoners who have been declared habitual or
professional offenders, or those with an inclination to crime,
either "delitti" or "contravvenzioni," may not be assigned to
judicial prisons.

Prisons for the Execution of Punishments. This category of
prisons can be divided into (*i*) ordinary prisons, i.e. corresponding to the three types of detentive punishment provided
for in the Penal Code: prisons for those serving life sentences;
prisons for those sentenced for "delitti" (reclusione); and
prisons for those sentenced for "contravvenzioni" (arresto);
and (*ii*) special prisons which are used in relation to the prisoner's record age, sex, physical and mental condition, e.g.
there are prisons for habitual and professional offenders, or
those with a tendency to crime; prisons for physically and
mentally ill offenders (i.e. persons sentenced to a decreased
punishment because of insanity or deafness and dumbness,
chronic alcoholism or drug addiction, habitual drunkenness,
and addiction to narcotics); prisons established for disciplinary measures, i.e. special security; for medical purposes; for
work purposes; as well as institutions for the progressive
treatment of the offender where prisoners sentenced to more
than five years and under the conditions provided in Article
227 of the Correctional System Act are transferred.

In addition to the external division of the prisons, there is also a division of the prisoners within the prison itself, or within one section of it. Prisoners are divided into similar groups with a view to ensure the moral and physical homogeneity of each group, with the purpose of re-educating the prisoners as individuals. Women serving detentive sentences are placed in institutions different from those of men.

Institutions for Security Measures. These serve to execute security measures and function according to the provisions of the Penal Code. They are divided according to the different categories of socially dangerous persons.

(*i*) *Agricultural colonies and workhouses.* These are two correctional methods aimed at re-educating by work offenders who are sane and over 18 years of age. The offenders are committed to one of these institutions by the "giudice di sorveglianza" (Juge de l'Application des peines) according to their character and position, their previous occupation and the milieu in which they will have to return afterwards to live. Those who have been declared habitual or professional offenders, or those with a tendency to crime—who are no longer under security measures and commit other intentional crime which is considered as a new demonstration of their dangerousness—are sent to the above mentioned institutions, as also persons sentenced to detention or security measure when specifically indicated by the law (Art. 223 and 226, Penal Code).

(*ii*) *Judicial mental hospitals.* In the case of intentional crimes which are to be punished with imprisonment for a period of more than two years, the offender who is not imputable because of insanity, chronic alcoholism or narcotic addiction, or deafness and dumbness, is always sent to these institutions to serve a security measure.

(*iii*) *"Casa di cura" and "casa di custodia".* Those sentenced for an intentional crime whose punishment has been decreased because of mental illness or chronic alcoholism or narcotic addiction, or because they are deaf or dumb, are sent to these institutions.

With regard to the above mentioned institutions it must be underlined that, in accordance with the general principles as laid out in Article 211 of the Penal Code, persons are taken thereafter they have served their sentence to detention except when the conditions of their illness are such that they do not permit the immediate expiation of the punishment, and in such a case the judge may order that they be taken to hospital before the punishment is initiated or completed.

(*iv*) *Judicial sanatorium*. Prisoners suffering from tuberculosis or with a tendency to it are sent to these institutions.

Methods of Rehabilitation

Having eliminated any kind of physical punishment which leads to the mortification, either physical or mental, of the person, the Italian penal system is now based on measures of restriction of personal liberty and on measures which limit such liberty. In the first case, however, this privation of liberty is limited to the minimum necessary for social defense and is directed towards the social rehabilitation of the individual.

The principle of punishment as re-education, already substantially adopted in the regulations of the Prison System in force since 1931 and modified in accordance with the dispositions and the aims of the present Penal Code, has been definitely confirmed in the Constitution. Article 27 states that "punishment may not consist of inhuman treatment and must be aimed at the re-education of the sentenced person." It is therefore in conformity with the Constitution and the ordinary law that the orientation of correction administration gives particular attention to the re-education of the prisoners who are committed to it for the serving of detentive sentences.[51]

Whether the restriction on personal liberty is punishment or a security measure, and even having different aspects, it is always based on treatment aimed at the re-education of the person and must be considered according to the most modern concept, as a measure of social readaptation.

The assignment of treatment most relevant for the offender may only be achieved after observation and classification. The latter, following the modern trend, is made in accordance with the concept of not dividing the groups only on the basis

[51]Regio Decreto, June 18, 1931, *Regolamento per gli Istituti di Prevenzione e di Pena.*

of their negative aspects (i.e. potential danger, narcotic addiction, and psychopathic trend), but also in view of their positive qualities of rehabilitation (professional attitude, morality, cultural level, and collaborating capacity). This division must be made after the indispensable objective grouping of age, sex, etc. and works on two levels; one, choice of the suitable correctional institution; and secondly, choice, once inside the latter, of an efficient and concrete program of treatment. However, an essential premise to the treatment is the observation of the offender's personality which must be carried out before his assignment to an institution. Because of the difficulties of general observation of all offenders, the correctional administration tries to organize it in a centralized way, following unitarian methodological lines.

The first centralized institution with this aim was established in Rome (Rebibbia), and now two more have come up in Milan and Naples. The method of observation adopted by the different experts (social workers, educators, electroencefalographists, endocrinologists, doctors, neurologists, psychiatrists, psychologists, and radiologists) consists of as wide a conception as possible of the personality—such as the integration of the known, affected, physiological and morphological aspects of the individual transferred to the social reality—and linked to the role that the subject has in this same social reality.[52]

The observation begins with an anamnestic-biographic investigation which is composed of a social inquiry, the specific anamnesi of each specialist, as well as the examination of the juridical and correctional records of the sentence. The evaluation continues in the sectors of morphological and endocrinological examination, functional examination, psychical examination, and behavioral examination. Each report is presented and discussed in a group meeting in which a general evaluation of the subject is given and a hypothesis for treatment is formulated.[53]

[52]Agostino Gemelli, "Delitto e Personalita," *La concezione dinamica della personalita nello studio dei delinquenti*, Giuffra, Milano, 1955.

[53]Giuseppe Di Gennaro, Franco Ferracuti, and Mario Fontanesi, "L' esame della personalità del condannato nell'Istituto di osservazione di Rebibbia," *Rassengna di Studi Peniteziari*, No. 3, Roma, 1958.

The "group counciling" in each institution is quite gene-
ralized; in some institutions more precise methodologies are
applied, as for instance the psychotherapy of a group or of an
individual.

In addition, there are several norms in the prison rules
which aim at improving prisoners both morally and intellectually. There is constant religious assistance; the establishment
of school courses is prescribed (which are compulsory for
illiterate prisoners) and other kinds of study and education
are forseen and carried out. Professional education is particularly emphasized. Prisoners usually lack a qualification or
specialization in an occupation. This fact is often the cause of
criminal action, because it is difficult for unqualified men to
find employment in modern society and they must endure
troublesome and long periods of unemployment and poverty.

Professional training is, however, only one aspect of the
work-obligation of the prisoner as stated by Italian law. This
obligation is not an afflictive measure aimed at making the
punishment harder to bear; it represents a duty of the prisoner related to his subsistence and a means by which he is led
to rehabilitation. In fact regular work creates a habit which
the prisoner will maintain until he leaves the prisons; and this
is the most important consequence because it reflects itself
outside prison life—it is the final result of the expiation of the
punishment.

Besides work there is recreation which does not consist in
an occasion for disordered explosion of energy, but is, in itself,
an element of socialization. There are regulations concerning
sports, radio and television which, in practice, have considerable application; libraries and films are also provided.

In addition to the educator, there is also the social worker
—who constitutes the "trait d'union" between the loneliness
of the prisoner and liberty—and through whom prisoners
maintain contacts with their own families, being assured that
their relatives are helped and that they are not abandoned to
misery. In fact, the assistance to the families of prisoners, and
of those subjected to security measures as also the released
prisoners and their families, is another important way of helping in the rehabilitation of offenders and is carried out by
the "Consigli di Patronato."

Assistance to prisoners' families does not only stem from a sense of charity or justice to reduce the needs of those who, without guilt, bear deprivations caused by the loss of means of subsistence due to the imprisonment of the head of the family; it is also part of the rehabilitating treatment. To assist these families means in fact working to remove the unfavorable surrounding conditions which are such an important aspect in the etiology of delinquency; it means smoothing out situations which embitter the social in-adaptation of the individual; and, finally, to create a milieu ready to receive the released person and support him in the difficulties to be faced in liberty.[54]

Juvenile Detention Homes or Borstals

Institutions for juveniles are divided into: re-education institutions; prison schools; judicial reformatories; and special reformatories.

Institutions for Re-education. The following institutions and re-education services have been created: institutions for personality observation; re-education homes and psycho-pedagogical medical institutions; social-service offices, half-way houses and juvenile hostels; schools, laboratories and special recreation centres (Act. 25/7/56, No. 888). These execute the provisions which the judicial authority has been encharged to adopt in its role as administrator of the juvenile court regarding juveniles of irregular conduct who have not committed an action considered by the law as a crime.

Prison Schools. The judicial authority establishes within its penal role a relevant section in the observation institutions destined to receive minors in "preventive custody"; and the prison schools, where juveniles who are to be punished for a crime are sent. These institutions have been established in place of the old juvenile prisons, which used to receive juveniles serving a sentence.

Judicial Reformatories. In case a juvenile is to be submitted to a detentive security measure according to the provisions of the Penal Code, he is committed to this type of institution.

[54]Reale Nicola, "Rieducazione del condannato," *Rassegna di Studi Penitenziari*, No. 4, 1957.

Special Reformatories. Minors who constitute a social danger according to the law, because of the seriousness of the crimes committed—as well as those who having been taken to an ordinary reformatory have shown themselves to be particularly dangerous—are assigned to these special reformatories.

With a view to obtaining more precise individual treatment within each institution, special sections of agricultural open schools or work houses may be established for habitual and professional delinquents; or special sections of judicial mental hospitals and homes may be set up for the care and custody of the deaf, the dumb, the customary drunkards or the addicts. Separate sections are also provided in ordinary and special reformatories for minors under 14.

In all these institutions there are separate sections for women.

Capital Punishment. Article 21 of the Penal Code stated that "capital punishment is executed by shooting inside the prison, or in another place indicated by the Ministry of Justice. The execution is not public."

However, this Article has been repealed and capital punishment has been eliminated by the Act of August 10, 1944. According to Article 27 of the Constitution, "Capital punishment is not admitted except in the cases provided by military war laws."

PROBATION AND PAROLE

Probation generally consists of two elements: on the one hand, the suspension of the punishment, and on the other the treatment in liberty but under supervision.

The suspension of the sentence is carried out in three different ways by European legislations: *suspension of prosecution* (Norwegian law); *suspension of the sentence* (Anglo-American law which is also applied in Sweden for adults and juveniles and in Austria for juveniles); and *suspension of the execution of the punishment*, i.e. conditional suspension of the punishment (peculiar to the "sursis," of the Franco-Belgian system which is adopted by the Italian penal law both for adults and minors).

The second element of probation is the treatment in liberty

under supervision. It is obviously preceded by a preliminary psychiatric, psychological, medical, and social examination. The fundamental legal problem in this connection is the inclusion of such an examination in trial, before or after the sentence. Agreement from the defendant solves this difficulty because in this case the examination may be carried out at any stage of the trial. With regard to such agreement, it is generally requested as a requirement in those countries which follow the English system and less often when probation is connected with the "sursis" system. In Italy this is compulsory for juveniles, while for adults the traditional system of "sursis" without supervision is still in force.

The conditions required by the Italian penal law for the concession of conditional suspension of the punishment are the following: (*i*) absence of recidivism (i.e. the offender has not previously been sentenced for a "delitto"); (*ii*) the punishment must not be followed by security measures; (*iii*) the law states that the prison sentence must not be of more than one year for "delitti" (three years for juveniles, and two years for persons of more than 70 years of age) and two years for "contravvanzioni," also the fines must not exceed the corresponding limit taking into account the criteria of convertibility into detentive punishment; and (*iv*) sometimes this concession is dependent upon the fulfilment of restitutions deriving from the crime.

The suspension of the execution of punishment is ordered for a period of five years if the sentence is for a felony (delitto, intentional or otherwise); and for two years if the sentence is for a "contravvenzioni." The revocation of the suspension is mandatory when the offender commits another "delitto" or "contravvenzioni" of the same kind during the above mentioned period of time, if he does not carry out his civil obligations, or if he is sentenced for the "delitto" previously committed.

Generally probation is referred either to the situation of suspension of the sentence and its execution or to the situation following an anticipated release of the prisoner before the complete fulfilment of the detention period.

Articles 176 and 177 of the Penal Code regulate the concession of "liberazione condizionale" (parole): (*i*) the offender must give proof of good behavior; (*ii*) he, or she must have served 30 months or at least half of his sentence when the remainder does not exceed five years (the recidivist, however, must have served at least four years and not less than three-fourth of the sentence, the offender sentenced to life imprisonment can benefit from "liberzione condizionale" only after having served at least 28 years of his sentence); and (*iii*) the concession of this benefit depends on the fulfilment of restitution deriving from the crime, except in cases in which the offender demonstrates his inability to do so.

The offender being granted "liberazione condizionale," the execution of detentive security measures, forseen by the sentence, must also be considered as suspended. The "liberazione condizionale" is revoked if the person concerned commits another "delitto" or a "contravvenzione" of the same kind, or does not fulfil the obligations related to parole.

The trial judge has the power to grant the conditional suspension of the sentence while "liberazione condizionale" is granted by the Minister of Justice after consultation with the "giudice di sorbeglianza."

For "liberzione condizionale" i.e. parole under supervision, Article 177 states that "the person in parole under supervision is subjected to obligations aimed at avoiding the possibility of committing new crimes and the supervision must be exercised in such a way as to facilitate, through an occupation, the re-adaptation of the person to social life."

Concerning "supervision," it is completely absent in cases of conditional suspension of the sentence, while for the person on parole it is exercised by the police (Art. 228, Penal Code). Nevertheless, the institution of a national service of social workers makes it possible to give persons on parole real assistance. In the field of adults social assistance is in an experimental phase but it is already in force for juveniles who are always supervised by a social worker.[55]

STUDY OF CRIMINOLOGY IN ITALY

Academic teaching of criminology—there are no specific courses for penology, juvenile delinquency, probation or parole,

---

[55]P. Nuvolone, La "*probation*" nella prospettiva del diritto comparato e nel diritto italiano, II Giornate Italo-Francesi di Difesa Sociale.

but very often these subjects come into the criminology program—is primarily carried out in the Medical Faculties and Law Faculties. The official title is generally "criminal anthropology." This title has recently been changed to "criminology" in two places; in some other "criminal sociology" is taught (in Italy there are many Faculties of Political Science, but only one for the Social Sciences, which has only recently been established).

Criminal anthropology is taught at the Medical Faculties of the more important Italian universities (Turin, Genova, Milan, Padau, Pisa, Modena, Parma, Naples, Pavia Cagliari, Sassari, Palermo, Messina, Bologna, and Bari) to fifth year or sixth year students and is considered an autonomous course, as it is complementary and not compulsory.

In the Law Faculty, besides courses of a juridical, historical, and sociological character, there are generally three complementary courses of a criminological character: criminal anthropology, psychology, and legal medicine—all usually taught to third year students.[56]

The establishment of departments within the university structure is at present awaiting parliamentary approval and the various faculties are made up of sections in which subjects of more or less the same kind are found. Therefore, within the Medical Faculty criminal anthropology comes under the legal medicine section, while the same subject in the Law Faculty comes under the section of penal law (i.e. in the University of Rome the criminological course is held at the Faculty of Law).

There is no criminological degree—only degrees in law or medicine—but the subject matter of the thesis may be criminological.

Criminology is also taught in two specialized schools in Rome. The first has a juridical criminological character, and its aim is specialization in penal law and criminology, the second has a more specific clinical character, and aims at specialization in clinical criminology.

[56]G. Canepa, "L'insegnamento della criminologia e della antropologia criminale," *Quaderni di Criminologia Clinica*, No. 1, 1965, pp. 31-35. "L'enseignement universitaire de la criminologie et de la medecine criminologique," *La revue canadienne de criminologie*, Vol. 9, No. 1, 1967.

The development, prospects, and the current situation of criminological research have recently been the subject of a study.[57] This study reveals how difficult it is to carry out such a task satisfactorily, specially in view of the complexity of the situation concerning the criminological sciences in the academic field, as also in the areas of application and research. Part of the work is dedicated to the examination of all criminological writing published in Italy from 1965 to the beginning of 1969. By classifying the 560 works, the areas in which research is lacking have been brought to light. It also helps in underlining the influence of the close ties existing between criminology and the psychological, psychiatric, and medico-legal disciplines on the one hand, as well as the concentration of scientific activity on the more practical aspects—with particular emphasis on diagnosis and treatment—on the other. Equally evident is the limited interest in sociological and cross-cultural research.

Criminological research has naturally felt the influence of the academic identification and denomination of the disciplines, but the major problem is posed by the lack of financial resources, which is one of the principal obstacles in its development. This research relies on the financial support of university institutes and some non-academic centers. Among these the "Centro Nazionale di Prevenzione e Difesa Sociale" and its Criminological Section (the Center has studied, among other topics, female criminality and recidivism);[58] the Section on "Documentation, Study and Research for the Prevention of Adult Criminality" of the Italian Penitentiary Administration (which collaborated in the above mentioned research on female criminality and, with the Italian Social Defense Group, in investigations into crime and the automobile,[59] and has also undertaken research activities on correctional topics); and

[57]F. Ferracuti and M.C. Giannini, "Le teneenze della ricerca criminologica in Italia negli ultimi cinque anni," *Quaderni di Criminologia Clinica*, No. 4, 1969.
[58]Centro Nazionale di Prevenzione d Difesa Sociale, *Gli aspetti generoli della criminalita femminile*, Milano, 1968; *Recidivismo e giovani adulti*, Roma, 1969.
[59]"Criminalita e automobile" (Atti delle Prime Giorante Italiane di Difesa Sociale, promoted by the Italian Group of the International

the Judicial Commission of the "Consiglio Nazionale delle Richerche," which has funded various studies, need to be mentioned specifically.

As far as research carried out by university centers is concerned, several studies—on subjects like Sardinian criminality, recidivism, mental illness in juvenile delinquents, socio-cultural causes of criminality in areas undergoing social change, psycho-farmaceological treatment of criminal subjects, genetic anomalies, correctional-clinical research, aggression and the effects of violence in the mass media—are underway.

In conclusion it can be affirmed that the methodology utilized in all the above mentioned studies is based on a clinical and sociological approach for operative solutions, and very often an integrated inter-disciplinary methodology is directly used.

Social Defense Society, Roma, March, 29-31 1968), *Quaderni di Criminologia Clinica*, No. 4, 1968.

BIBLIOGRAPHY

A. A. "Criminalita e automobile," Proceedings of the first Italian Days of Social Defense, promoted by Italian Group of International Association of Social Defense, March 29-31, 1968, *Quaderni di Criminologia Clinica,* Roma, 1968, No. 4.

ALBERTARIO, EMILIO. *Delictum e crimen nel diritto romano classico e nella legislazione giustinianea,* Milano, 1924.

ALIMENA, BERNARDINO. *Note filosofiche d'un criminalista,* Modena, 1911.

ANCONA, LEONARDO. "Agostino Gemelli e la concezione psicologica della Criminologia," *Quaderni di Criminologia Clinica,* Roma, 1959, No. 4.

ANTINORI, G. *I precursori di Lombroso,* Torino, 1900.

ANTOLISEI, FRANCESCO. *Manuale di diritto penale,* parte generale, Giuffre, Milano, 1960.

AUGUSTINUS (Sanctus). Aurelius, La citta di Dio, Stamperia A. De Rossi, Roma, 1743.

——.*Le confessioni,* Milano, Hoepli, 1923.

BARTOLUCCI. "Il delitto e la pena nei dialoghi de Platone," *Archivio Giuridico,* Roma, Serie III, Vol. 3⁰, 1905, pp. 177-258.

BAVERIA, IGNZAIO. *Diritto minorile,* Milano, Giuffre, 1965.

BECCARIA, CESARE. *Dei delitti e della pene.* Fascimile of the original edition published anonymous in Livorno, 1764, Torino, U.T.E.T., 1964.

BLANCUS, A.N. *Practica criminalis,* Venetiis, 1955, p. 47.

CALISSE, CARLO. *Svolgimento storico del diritto penale in Italia dalle invasioni barbariche alle rigorme del sec. XVIII⁰,* Milano, 1934.

CANEPA, GIACOMO. "L'insegnamento della Criminologia e della Anthropologia criminale," *Quaderni di Criminologia Clinica,* Roma, 1965, No. 1, pp. 31-53.

——."L'enseignement universitaire de la Criminologie et de la Medecine criminologique," *Le revue canadienne de Criminologie,* 1967, Vol. 9, No. 1.

CARMIGNANI, GIOVANNI A. *Juris criminalis elementa.* Milano, 1863.

CARNEVALE, EMANUELE. *La Terza Scuola e la concezione unitaria del diretto criminale,* Progr. del dir. crimin., 1915.

——.*Diretto criminale,* Vol. I⁰, Roma, 1932.

CARRARA, FRANCESCO. *Programmi di diritto criminale,* 1859.

Centro Nazionale di Prebenzione e difesa sociale, *Gli aspetti generali della criminalita femminile,* Milano, 1968.

——.*Recidivismo e giovani adulti,* Roma, 1969.

DE VITALINIA, BONIFACIUS. *Tractatus super maleficiis,* Venetiis, 1555, p. 104.

DI GENNARO, GIUSEPPE, FERRACUTI, FRANCO and FONTANESI, MARIO. "L'esame della personalita del condannato nell'Istituto di osservazione di Rebibbia," *Rassegna di Studi Peniteziari,* Roma, No. 3, 1958.

Dɪ ᴛᴜʟʟɪᴏ, Bᴇɴɪɢɴᴏ. *La costituzione delinqueziale nella etiologia e terapia del delitto*, A.R.E., Roma, 1928.
——. *Manuale di Antropologia e Psiolgia Criminale*, A.R.E., Roma, 1931.
——. *Medecine et Sociologie en Etiologis Criminnelle*, Parigi, Societe Internationale de Criminologie, 1951.
——. *Principi di Criminologia Clinica e Psichiatria forense*, 3 edi. Istituto Ital. di Medicina Sociale, Roma, 1963.
——. "High imports for American Criminology," *Criminologica*, Vol. VI⁰, No. 3, 1968.
Dᴜɴɪ, Mᴀʀɪᴏ. *Discorso per l'inaugurazione dell'anno giudiziario 1969*, Tip. Morara, Roma, 1969.
Fᴀʀɪɴᴀᴄɪᴜs. *Praxis et theoricae criminalis*, Francoforte, 1622, p. 251.
Fᴇʀʀᴀᴄᴜᴛɪ, Fʀᴀɴᴄᴏ and Wᴏʟғɢᴀɴɢ, Mᴀʀᴠɪɴ E. "L'integrazione della Criminologia," parte I e II, *Quaderni di Criminologia Clinica*, 1965, No. 2 e 3.
——. *Il comportamento violento. Moderni aspetti criminologici*, Milano, Giuffre, 1966.
Fᴇʀʀᴀᴄᴜᴛɪ, Fʀᴀɴᴄᴏ, Fᴏɴᴛᴀɴᴇsɪ, Mᴀʀɪᴏ and Wᴏʟғɢᴀɴɢ, Mᴀʀᴠɪɴ E. "The diagnostic and classification Center at Rabibbia-Rome," *Federal Probation*, 1963.
Fᴇʀʀᴀᴄᴜᴛɪ, Fʀᴀɴᴄᴏ, Gɪᴀɴɴɪɴɪ, M. Cʀɪsᴛɪɴᴀ. "Le tendenze della ricerca criminologica in Italia negli ultimi cinque anni," *Quaderni di Criminologia Clinica*, 1969, No. 4.
Fᴇʀʀɪ, Eɴʀɪᴄᴏ. *Sociologia criminale*, II ediz., Torino, 1900.
Fᴇʀʀɪɴɪ, Cᴏɴᴛᴀʀᴅᴏ. *Diritto Penale Romano*, Roma, Hoepli, 1898, pp. 35-37.
Fɪʟᴀɴɢɪᴇʀɪ, Gᴀᴇᴛᴀɴᴏ. *La scienza della legislazione*, Capolago, Tipografia e Libreria Elvetica, 1834.
Fʟᴏʀɪᴀɴ, Eᴜɢᴇɴɪᴏ. *Trattato di Diritto Penale*, Vol. I⁰, Vallardi, Milano, 1934.
Gᴀʀᴏғᴀʟᴇ, Rᴀғғᴀᴇʟᴇ. *Criminologia*, Torino, 1885.
Gᴇᴍᴇʟʟɪ, Aɢᴏsᴛɪɴᴏ. *La concezione dinamica della personalita nello studio dei delinquenti*, in "Delitto e Personalita," Giuffre, Milano, 1955.
Gᴇʀɪɴ, Cᴇsᴀʀᴇ. Fᴇʀʀᴀᴄᴜᴛɪ, Fʀᴀɴᴄᴏ and Sᴇᴍᴇʀᴀʀɪ, Aʟᴅᴇ. "Evaluation medico-legale de l'imputabilite et de la dangerosite sociale dans les anomalies et dans les maladies psychiques: Ses repercussions criminologiques," *Zacchia*, 26, 1963.
Gʀᴏᴢɪᴏ, Uɢᴏ. *De jure belli ac pacis*, 1625.
Istituto Centrale di Statistica. *Annuario di Statistiche Giudiziarie*, Vol. X⁰, 1960, Roma, 1962.
——. *Annuario di Statistiche Giudiziarie*, Vol. XI⁰, 1961, Roma, 1964.
——. *Annuario di Statistiche Giudiziarie*, Vol. XII⁰, 1963, Roma, 1965.
——. *Annuario di Statistiche Giudiziarie*, Vol. XIII⁰, 1963, Roma, 1966.
——. *Annuario di Statistiche Giudiziarie*, Vol. XIV⁰, 1964, Roma, 1967.
——. *Annuario di Statistiche Giudiziarie*, Vol. XV⁰, 1965, Roma, 1968.
——. *Annuario di Statistiche Giudiziarie*, Vol. XVI⁰, 1966, Roma, 1968.
——. *10⁰ Censimento Generale della popolazione 15 ottobre 1961*, Vol. VI⁰, Professioni, Roma, 1967.

Istituto Centrale di Statistica. *I conti degli italiani-Compendio della vita economica nazionale*, Roma, 1967.

———. *Sommario di statistiche storiche dell' Italia, 1861-1965*, Roma, 1968.

LEONE, GIOVANNI. *Diritto Processuale Penale*, VII edi., Jovene, Napoli, 1968.

LOMBROSO, CESARE. *L'uomo delinquente studiato in rapporto all'antropologia, alla medicine legale, e alle discipline carcerarie*, 1876.

———. *L'uomo delinquente*, Ved., 1897.

———. *Crime, its Causes and Remedies*, Boston, Little, Brown & Co., 1912.

MANZINI, VINCENZO. *Trattato di diritto penale*, U.T.E.T., Torino, 1963.

MARCIANO. *Digesto*, 48, 3, 6, L.

———. *Digesto*, 48, 19, 6, par 1.

MESCHIERI, LUIGI. "Osservazioni critiche sull'applicazione dei metodi psicologici nello studio della personolita del delinquente," *Archivio Penale*, Roma, 1951.

MONACHESI, ELIE. "Trends in criminological Research in Italy," *American Sociological Review*, 1, 1936.

NICERFORO, ALFREDO. *Criminologia*, Bocca, Roma, 1949.

Novissimo Digesto Italiano, U.T.E.T., Torino, Vol. IV⁰, 1959.

———. U.T.E.T., Torino, Vol. XII⁰, 1965.

———. U.T.E.T., Torino, Vol. XIII⁰, 1966.

NUVOLONE, PIETRO. *La "probation" nella prospettiva del diritto comparato e nel diritto italiano*, II Giornate Itale-Francesi di Difesa Sociale, in corso di stampa.

PAGANO, MARIO. *Sul processo criminale*, Napoli, Marotta, 1824.

PAULUS. *Digesto* 48, 19, 20.

PICETE, ADOLFO. *Les origines indo-europeennes*, p. II, Paris, 1863, p. 434.

QUINTILLANO. *Inst. orat.* VIII, 3.

REALE, NICOLA. "Rieducazione del condannato," *Rassengna di Studi Penitenziari*, Roma, 1957, No. 4.

Regio Decreto 18 Giugno 1931. *Regolamento per gli Istituti di Prevenzione. e di Pena.*

ROCCO, ARTURO. *Il problema e il metodo della scienza del diritto penale*, 1910.

ROMAGNOSI, GIAN DOMENICO. *Genesi del diritto penale*, ed. Prato, 1837.

ROSSI, PELLEGRINO. *Traite de droit penal*, Paris, 1828.

SACCHI, E. *Sulla teoria platonica del delitto e della pena*, filosofica, Anno II⁰, Vol. 3⁰, 1900, pp. 30-40.

TOMMASO (SANTO) D'AQUINO. *Summa theologica*, Mediolani, T. Pagnoni, 1881.

WOLFGANG, MARVIN E. "Cesare Lombroso," *Quaderni di Criminologia Clinica*, 1961.

CHAPTER 8

JAPAN

TARO OGAWA

Dr Taro Ogawa, a graduate of the Tokyo Imperial University, and a recipient of LL. D. from Tokyo University, is a distinguished scholar, administrator, researcher, and writer in the field of criminology in Japan. He has held many important positions, some of which are: Deputy Director, United Nations Asia, and Far East Institute for Prevention of Crime and Treatment of Offenders; Director, the Second Division, the Research and Training Institute, Ministry of Justice; Superintendent, the Kanto Medical Facilities for Boys and Girls; Executive Director, the Japan Prison Association: Chairman, the Kanto Adult Rehabilitation Commission; Director, Bureau of Adult Correction, Ministry of Justice; and lecturer on the subject of criminal policy in several universities (Hosei, Chuo, and Waseda universities and Tokyo Women's College). At present he is Professor in the Department of Law, the Asia University, Tokyo. Dr Ogawa has published many articles and monographs relative to criminology and penology largely in Japanese and some in English. His published works include Hoan Shobun [*Security Measures*], Tokyo: *Nihon Hyoronsha* (1952); Hanzai to Jiyukei [*Crime and Imprisonment*], Tokyo: *Ichiryu-sha* (1954); Keiji-seisaku Ron [*Notes on Criminal Policy*], Tokyo: *Hosei University Press* (1952); Jiyukei no Tenkai [*The Development of Imprisonment*], Tokyo: *Ichiryu-sha* (1964); *and* Keiji-seisaku Ron Kogi [*Textbook on Criminal Policy*], Vol. 1 & 2, Tokyo: *Hosei University Press* (1958).

JAPAN IS A COUNTRY of islands, lying, like a festoon, from north-east to south-west along the eastern edge of the continent of Asia. It runs from lat. 45°31′ N to lat. 26°59′ N which is the same as the latitudes covered by the whole of the USA or, to give another example, the latitudes covered from Switzerland to the middle of the Sahara desert. It has, therefore, a climate enriched by the variety which comes from four seasons.

The population is over 100 million. The area of the country is 369,662,04 square kilometers, but the population is not evenly distributed because of rapid urbanization in recent years.

The people of Japan are of one race, all speaking Japanese except for a very small number of Ainu, and foreigners coming from Korea, the USA and elsewhere. There is, therefore, no serious racial problem such as we see in other countries.

The Japanese settled in these islands at a very early stage in history. An archaeologist tells us that the early Japanese settled in these islands in the neolithic era. They appear in history towards the end of the first century B.C. when they began to have contact with China. Many of the tribes among the original Japanese began to form a community during the 3rd and 4th centuries; and between the 6th and 7th centuries all tribes combined to form a national community.

A patriarchal state, with *Tenno* (Emperor) as a patriarch, existed for the next 1,300 years, sometimes powerful, sometimes weak. Early in the 7th century Tenno issued some revolutionary statutes called "Taiho Ritsu-Rei" which derived from Chinese laws. This sort of legal state continued until the middle of the 10th century, when the political power of Tenno began gradually to decline. The middle ages in Japanese history were dominated by the warrior class, who continued to rule the country until one hundred years ago, though naturally the clan in power changed from time to time owing to continuing political feuds. The last one was the Tokugawa which lasted for about 300 years.

What are the personality traits of the people, if any? In the "Period of Enlightenment," French philosophers such as Robespierre and Montesquieu reproached the Japanese, claiming that they had a hidden streak of cruelty in their make-up.

During a debate in the National Assembly on May 23, 1791, when the abolition of the death penalty was discussed, Robespierre (a man who became famous in French history as a terrorist), speaking on behalf of a group of abolitionists against the retention of the death penalty, severely criticized the Japanese as a nation, saying "Look at Japan! There is no country where the death penalty has been so abused and such cruel punishments adopted as in Japan." Robespierre's opinion seems to have been derived from a statement in Montesquieu's *Spirit of Law* in which there is a reference to the cruel character of the Japanese especially in connection with the treatment of Christians.[1]

The Japanese do not accept these criticizms. They consider themselves tolerant by nature, giving as an example their long experience of the abolition of the death penalty. In the early days of their history and under the influence of Buddhist principles no one suffered the death penalty for 347 years from 818 to 1155.[2] Sorai Ogiu (1666-1723), a famous thinker in the middle period of the Shogunnate, declared that cruelty was foreign to the Japanese way of thinking. He said: "There have not been any thoughts of putting people to death by burning as a punishment in either China or Japan. This type of punishment seems to originate from Christian methods."[3] This view is also supported by a contemporary scholar, Dr S. Ono, Special Consultant to the Ministry of Justice and a main drafter of the Draft Penal Code, 1960.[4] He comments that the cruelty, characteristic of penal practice in Japan during the Middle Ages, seems to owe its origin to the European practices during the Middle Ages.

Another piece of evidence to show the tolerant attitude of the Japanese is their method of incorporating into the Penal

[1]Kameji Kimura, *Shikei-Ron* (On Capital Punishment) (in Japanese) (Tokyo: Kobundo, 1949), pp. 11 and 14.

[2]Akira Masaki, *Shikei* (Capital Punishment) (in Japanese) (Tokyo: Nippon Kyoron-sha, 1964), p. 7.

[3]Taro Ogawa, *Hanzai to Jiyukei* (Crime and Imprisonment) (in Japanese) (Tokyo: Ichiryu-sha, 1952), p. 50.

[4]Seiichiro Ono, *Keibatsu no Honshitsu Sonota* (The Fundamental Nature of Punishment and Others) (in Japanese) (Tokyo: Yuhikaku, 1955), p. 364.

Code only the milder measures used by other countries, as for example China.[5]

The Japanese may not be extraordinarily tolerant people, but certainly they are not extraordinarily cruel, as the French thinkers would have us believe. It seems that these thinkers were too much prejudiced in their views about the Japanese traits by seeing the measures which the Japanese adopted as a matter of policy during the period of Isolation. The policy of Isolation was the only way of escape from the aggressive mercantilism of European countries. The policy was especially severe in its attitude towards aliens. The treatment of foreigners shipwrecked on Japanese soil and the persecution of Christians were an inevitable result of this policy and gave the French thinkers the impression that the Japanese were a cruel race. However, it was not a true indication of the Japanese native character.

The period of Isolation is a key to the understanding of Japanese modern society. In one sense it was the preparation period for modern industrial Japan. Just as in Europe mercantilism opened the way to modern capitalism, so in Japan the resistance to mercantilism paved the way for later development For criminologists it is interesting to note that during this period of resistance to invasion by European mercantilism new ideas about punishment appeared in Japan, whilst in Europe mercantilism itself was the motive power in promoting new thoughts about punishment.

The national Isolation Policy of the Tokugawa Shogunate (i.e. (a) forbidding the propagation of Christianity (b) prohabiting private communication with foreigners and preventing travel abroad (c) strictly controlling foreign trade (d) excluding foreigners, except Dutch and Chineses merchants) lasted for nearly 220 years between 1633-1853. Then came the American Admiral Perry to the shores of Japan to awaken her from sleep under this policy. This lengthy experience of isolation made possible not only a primitive accumulation of wealth which prepared the way for the later industrial development, but also helped to form certain aspects of the Japanese character. Among

[5] Ryosuke Ishii, *Keibatsu no Rekishi* (History of Punishment) (in Japanese) (Tokyo: Nippon Kyoron-sha, 1952).

the Japanese characteristics depicted by cultural anthropologists, some may have been acquired, so to speak, during this period of more than two hundred years.[6]

Over a 100 years have passed since this Isolation was legally abolished. The Meiji restoration created a modern form of government following the collapse of the Tokugawa Shogunate. It tried to change the feudalistic system into the modern set-up of an industrial society. W.W. Rostow, in his book, *The Stages of Economic Growth*, makes a comparative survey of many countries from the viewpoint of special theories of economic growth (i.e. a traditional society, the preconditions necessary for "take off," the period of "take off," the period of maturity and the period of high mass consumption.) As to Japan, it rushed according to Rostow, into the period of "take off" in the year 1878.[7]

Some of the leading characteristics of the social system of Japan may be enumerated as follows: (*a*) the patriarchal family system; (*b*) the bureaucratic concentration of power; (*c*) a capitalistic class system; (*d*) a democratic system; and (*e*) a society subject to mass media and other mass phenomena.

The patriarchal conditions in the family, the community, and the State were characteristic of Japanese "traditional society," to use Rostow's expression.

An emotional relationship similar to that found between parents and children existed in every aspect of society. Some authors call this a "Vertical Society" to distinguish it from the "Horizontal Society" which is a Western pattern, and in which the individual in society has equal rights. Some remnants of the "Traditional Society" are still at work in the emotional life of the Japanese people.[8]

Preparations for industrial development, the "take off" in Rostow's expression, were made between 1878 to 1900. During this period the Meiji government had set up a strong bureaucratic system. The government, with the aid of this bureau-

[6]Ruth Benedict, *Chrysanthemum and Sword: Patterns of Japanese Culture* (Tokyo: Charles E. Tuttle Co., 1954).

[7]W.W. Rostow, *The Stage of Economic Growth, a Non-communist Manifesto* (New York: the Cambridge University Press, 1960), p. 9.

[8]Cf. Chie Nakane, *Kinship and Economic Organization in Rural Japan* (London: Athlone Press, 1967).

cracy, succeeded in abolishing the "Unequal Treaty" in 1899.[9]

The treaty had been a great hindrance not only to the independence of the State but also to industrial development. There followed the period of "maturity" which lasted until 1940 and during which Japan built up her capitalistic system through national endeavor. The capitalistic class distinction between capitalists and laborers became a new feature necessary for the understanding of Japanese society at this period.

Revolutionary changes were made after the war by the introduction of a new Constitution. Compared with the old Constitution, the new Constitution had three very distinctive features: it renounced war, it established the sovereignty of the people, and the security of human rights. The spirit of democracy, as also the democratic organizations, have gradually begun to flourish under the new Constitution.

Economic growth since the war, however, has been extremely fast, keeping pace with the democratic trends. Rostow maintains that Japan entered the high mass consumption period in 1955.[10] Characteristic of this period are the large-scale heavy chemical industries and the service industries (the so-called third industries). This, however, does not mean that the small industries, which were once the stabilizing factor in Japanese society, have disappeared. Thus in Japanese society two different motivations prevail, resulting from large and small-scale industries; this has been described as the dual construction of Japanese society.

It may be useful to draw attention to the relationship between this economic growth and the general trend of crime. The Western type of Penal Code came into force in 1882 after the "take off" period had already begun. To use Engels' expression, the rapid increase in crime at the beginning of the period may be the result of the "proletarianization of the people,"[11] a social phenomenon which appears in the "take off" period. In the graph of criminal statistics, which shows the number of persons convicted of offenses under the penal law

[9]See section entitled "Criminal Law."

[10]Rostow, *op. cit.*, p. 88.

[11]W.A. Bonger, *Criminality and Economic Conditions* (Boston: Little, Brown and Co., 1916).

in the first instance, we find two peaks: one in 1885, and the other in 1894. From about 1900 to 1930 or 1940 there another upward curve.

Theft and gambling were the main offenses, and any upward or downward trends in the graph have been due to increases or decreases in these two forms of crime.

After World War II, crime rose from 1948 and then fell from 1951 onwards. When the currency was stabilized crime began to decrease. The phenomena of crime, which we find after our economy was said to have entered the high mass consumption period, seem to be somewhat different from those of an earlier stage. As compared with crime in the Meiji era, when crime was "a crime of poverty," today's crime may be described as "the crime of prosperity."

CRIMINAL LAW

The present Penal Code in Japan came into force in 1908. It was already subject to a few amendments before the last war, but most of the important amendments were made after World War II. The penal philosophy prevailing in Europe towards the end of the 19th century took on a new form which separated it from the classic thinking which had formed the basis of thought in the Japanese first Western style Penal Code of 1880.

It is said that the main provisions of the Japanese Code of 1908 were adopted from the progressive measures in the penal codes of the Netherlands, Finland, Italy, Portugal, and Austria. In fact the foundations upon which it rested were derived from the German philosophy which permeated Japanese legal fields since the Meiji Constitution in 1889.

Legal Definition of Crime

The term "Restoration" which means the revival of the old peaceful state that had existed in the days of the direct government of the Emperor Tenno, was used by the proponents of the Meiji revolution. The fundamental aim of the new government was to establish an organization derived from the Chinese proto-type similar to that of the old regime. As for the Penal Code, the Meiji Government promulgated it under the title

"Shinritsu-Koryo" in 1870. It followed the Chinese system where a statutory penal code had been in existence for a long time, a code which the Japanese had adopted in earlier days. The Chinese Code had provisions for different types of crime and punishment in much the same style as the modern European penal codes but it differed from them in that it was essentially a bureaucratic product and much influenced by Eastern culture.

The Government soon found that this Penal Code was not suitable for the new regime and promulgated another Code entitled "Kaitei-Ritsu-Rei" in 1873. In this the French philosophy of penal thought was introduced and combined with the Chinese provisions. However it still proved to be unsuitable. Besides, the reasons which were compelling Japan at this time to modernize her penal code on Western lines were of a special nature. Although the advance of the imperialistic powers during the last period of the Tokugawa did not succeed in completely colonizing Japan, unfavourable treaties had been concluded between the Shogunate and several countries, treaties to which the Meiji Government was later forced to accede.

Of importance to Japan under these unfavorable treaties were the deprivation of her customs autonomy, and the jurisdiction of extraterritoriality. By the latter is meant that Westerners were tried for misconduct in Japan not by Japanese courts and according to Japanese laws, but by the consular courts and in accordance with the laws of the countries from which they came. Naturally it was degrading for a nation to be obliged to give such extra-territorial exemption to foreigners, and it was a mark of inferiority which the Japanese wished to remove. For that purpose it was very necessary to revise her legal system, especially her penal code, in conformity with the Western pattern.

Two penal codes, a Chinese-style Code and a mixed-style Code were in use for some time. Then, a French scholar, Gustave Boissonade (1826-1910), was invited to draw up a new Penal Code on the Western pattern. He used the "Napoleonic Code" of 1810 as his model for the draft. This was the first Western-style Code. It was promulgated in 1880 and brought into force from 1882. In 1907, however, a wholly revised

Penal Code was issued. This time it followed not the French but the German style.

The important alterations made after the last war were of two types: one was concerned with types of crime, and the other with the treatment of offenders. Those crimes which were peculiar to the status of Tenno and incompatible with the new Constitution, and the concept that such an offense as adultery was illegal only if committed by the wife, were abolished. Probation according to the Anglo-American pattern was introduced along with the Continental practice of *sursis* (suspension of the execution of a sentence).

In Japan crime is analyzed following German theory of criminal law which has three constituent elements. In France crime is considered as consisting of two elements, i.e. *élément matériel* and *élément moral*. There are two elements, *actus reus* and *mens rea*, in Anglo-American law.

The three elements in Japanese law are (*i*) an act penalized by law, (*ii*) the illegality of this act, and (*iii*) culpability. In Japan, there is no common law crime; all crimes are defined in the statutes. A person may have committed an act that is defined by law as an offense, for example intentional homicide, but he may have done this in self-defense, in which case the court may judge that his act was not "illegal." Culpability may be deemed somewhat similar to *mens rea* in the Anglo-American system. It includes intent, negligence, and criminal responsibility. Three kinds of persons shall not be held criminally responsible under the Japanese Penal Code: insane persons, deaf-mutes, and infants under 14 years of age. Acts by these persons are not punishable. There is no discrimination in defining crime according to sex, nationality, or social status except for the age limit mentioned above. Under the penal law all persons are treated equally.

Besides the penal law which covers offenses that we call "penal law offenses," there are many special laws dealing with crimes which we call "special law offenses." There are nearly fifty groups of important special penal laws at present; among them those dealing with road traffic offenses show the greatest number of violations.

Legal Definition of Juvenile Delinquency

The Juvenile Law of 1948 provides that any person under 20 years of age shall be legally considered as a juvenile. As to the term "delinquency," no clear-cut definition is provided in any law, but juveniles falling under the jurisdiction of Article 3 of the Law are generally referred to as juvenile delinquents, and are primarily dealt with by the Family Court. Article 3 of the Law defines who shall be subjected to the jurisdiction of the Family Court distinguishing the following three categories:

(*i*) "Juvenile offenders," or those aged 14 to 19 who have committed an offense.

(*ii*) "Law-breaking children," or those who are under the age of criminal responsibility, that is under 14 who have committed a breach of law, and who have been referred to the Family Court from the authorities under the Child Welfare Law.

(*iii*) "Pre-delinquent," this refers to a person under 20 years of age who is prone to commit an offense in view of his or her character or surrounding circumstances, because of the existence of the following reasons:

(*a*) that he or she habitually disobeys the reasonable control of his or her guardian; (*b*) that he or she repeatedly deserts his or her home without good reason; (*c*) that he or she associates with a known criminal or an immoral person, or frequents any place of dubious reputation; and (*d*) that he or she habitually acts so as to injure or endanger his or her own morals or those of others.

CRIME STATISTICS

In Japan the collection of data concerning crime is carried out by various agencies such as the National Police Agency, the Ministry of Justice, or the Supreme Court. They issue an annual report of crime statistics. The following statistics (pp. 596-602) are mainly based on these reports.

THEORIES OF CRIME CAUSATION

In accordance with the generally accepted views on criminology

TABLE I
PENAL CODE OFFENDERS INVESTIGATED AND CLEARED BY THE POLICE, 1960-1967

	1960	1961	1962	1963	1964	1965	1966	1967
I. PROPERTY OFFENSES								
(1) Larceny	180,899	187,372	183,921	187,065	193,931	188,821	184,432	169,669
(2) Fraud	28,743	26,881	23,337	21,441	22,811	22,428	22,075	18,785
(3) Embezzlement	12,345	11,682	9,458	8,006	8,619	8,044	8,012	6,287
(4) Stolen property	8,352	8,016	6,288	5,447	5,610	5,096	4,793	3,820
(5) Breach of trust	241	295	270	223	280	288	296	196
TOTAL	230,580	234,246	223,274	222,182	231,251	224,677	219,608	198,757
II. OFFENSES OF VIOLENCE								
A. NON-HEINOUS CRIMES								
(6) Physical violence	38,445	39,648	38,488	41,702	45,238	45,029	45,532	44,415
(7) Bodily injury and man-slaughter	83,449	85,056	79,202	73,612	76,791	73,802	74,222	73,633
(8) Intimidation	4,388	4,548	4,227	4,470	5,035	4,603	4,320	3,762
(9) Extortion	25,268	26,099	25,333	24,289	24,824	21,784	18,968	15,310
(10) Unlawful assembly with weapon	568	558	701	939	888	471	787	724
TOTAL	152,218	155,909	147,951	145,012	152,776	145,689	143,649	137,844
B. HEINOUS CRIMES								
(11) Murder (including patricide, infanticide and attempt)	2,844	2,921	2,503	2,452	2,501	2,379	2,278	2,122
(12) Robbery	2,983	2,460	2,268	2,269	1,968	2,036	1,824	1,377
(13) Homicide or injury in the execution of robbery, and rape in the course of robbery	2,577	2,514	2,273	1,931	2,051	2,070	1,975	1,766
TOTAL	8,404	7,895	7,044	6,652	6,520	6,485	6,077	5,265

III. SEX OFFENSES

(14) Rape (including those resulting in injury and death)	8,080	8,123	7,750	7,579	8,284	8,444	8,210	8,039
(15) Indecent assault, obscene matters: distributing, selling, etc.	4,039	4,299	4,434	5,205	5,844	7,240	7,669	7,387
TOTAL	12,119	12,422	12,004	12,784	14,228	15,684	15,879	15,426

IV. OFFENSES OF NEGLIGENCE

(16) Negligent homicide and injury in business conduct	118,937	129,728	139,713	181,176	228,680	266,264	308,731	402,368
(17) Simple negligent homicide and injury	2,087	1,959	1,743	1,627	1,520	1,330	1,166	1,070
(18) Fire caused by negligence	8,476	8,998	8,957	7,986	7,950	8,466	6,940	7,176
TOTAL	129,500	140,685	150,413	190,789	238,150	276,060	316,837	410,514

V. OTHERS

(19) Arson	969	925	758	936	772	729	700	638
(20) Betting	6,050	7,031	7,343	7,530	12,669	15,900	15,541	13,121
(21) Kidnapping	133	169	230	295	263	240	258	295
(22) Documentary forgery and counterfeiting securities	1,949	2,044	1,919	1,836	2,034	2,041	2,114	1,733
TOTAL	8,101	10,169	10,250	10,597	15,738	18,910	18,613	15,787

SOURCE: The National Police Agency, *Hanzai Tokei-Sho.*

NOTE: In tables I, II, III, and IV, the expression "investigated and cleared by the police" means that the police could identify the individual who was the criminal suspect in a particular case, and eventually could investigate and interrogate him, but it does not necessarily mean that all suspects involved in a case were arrested by the police. In the case where the suspects were investigated and interrogated by the police as mentioned above around 80 per cent of them were not "arrested"; they voluntarily appeared before the police so that the police officers could interrogate them. This percentage has been stable during last ten years.

TABLE II

MAJOR SPECIAL LAW OFFENDERS INVESTIGATED AND CLEARED BY THE POLICE, 1960-1967

	1960	1961	1962	1963	1964	1965	1966	1967
Narcotic Control Law	2,081	1,954	2,349	2,288	847	859	692	476
Sword and Firearm Possession Control Law	16,827	16,462	18,346	21,392	22,190	22,211	21,383	17,576
Anti-Prostitution Law	16,203	13,955	12,430	11,153	11,031	10,671	9,670	8,230
Customs Law	2,226	2,622	2,083	2,102	2,505	2,545	1,868	1,868
Road and Traffic Control Law	3,093,695	3,703,179	5,014,544	4,650,118	5,061,328	5,243,166	4,614,438	4,569,570

SOURCE: The National Police Agency, *Hanzai Tokei-Sho.*

TABLE III
PENAL CODE OFFENDERS

	1960	1961	1962	1963	1964	1965	1966	1967
Number of penal code offenses known to the police	1,495,888	1,530,464	1,522,480	1,557,803	1,609,741	1,602 430	1,590,681	1,603,471
Number of penal code offenses investigated and cleared by the police	958,629	1,019,963	1,022,512	1,045,417	1,069,617	1,051,708	1,051,608	1,077,103
Number of penal code offenders investigated and cleared by the police								
(i) Male	526,765	543,597	526,308	556,157	613,629	651,480	696,513	748,175
(ii) Female	34,699	37,717	43,558	50,492	54,993	55,307	53,542	54,403
TOTAL	561,464	581,314	569,866	606,649	678,522	706,827	740,055	802,578
Number of penal code offenders prosecuted by public prosecutor								
(i) Male	257,613	280,783	284,635	282,666	336,933	370,044	400,918	438,917
(ii) Female	6,046	6,910	7,170	7,558	9,068	10,930	12,345	13,718
TOTAL	263,659	287,693	293,805	290,224	346,001	380,972	413,264	452,635
Number of convictions of penal code offenders								
(i) Male	238,280	244,994	258,447	265,945	305,389	349,930	379,643	NA
(ii) Female	5,027	5,161	5,509	5,803	6,588	8,546	9,454	NA
TOTAL	243,307	250,155	263,956	270,748	311,977	358,476	389,097	NA

SOURCE: The National Police Agency, *Hanzai Tokei-Sho*; The Ministry of Justice, *Kensatsu Tokei Nenpo*; and The Supreme Court, *Shiho Tokei Nenpo*.

TABLE IV
SPECIAL LAW OFFENDERS

	1960	1961	1962	1963	1964	1965	1966	1967
Number of special law offenses investigated and cleared by the police	3,270,577	3,871,729	5,200,007	4,893,948	5,268,387	5,483,113	4,827,133	4,965,047
Number of special law offenders investigated and cleared by the police								
(i) Male	3,188,885	3,767,603	5,079,156	4,786,998	5,113,066	5,297,786	4,655,756	4,774,939
(ii) Female	63,949	66,460	85,386	105,737	96,576	117,369	114,991	134,299
TOTAL	3,252,834	3,834,063	5,164,542	4,892,735	5,209,642	5,415,155	4,770,747	4,909,238
Number of special law offenders prosecuted by public prosecutor								
(i) Male	68,753	74,025	70,174	94,271	75,294	81,351	82,279	112,241
(ii) Female	15,810	15,141	15,865	18,508	16,306	18,136	17,775	20,866
TOTAL	84,563	89,166	86,039	102,779	91,600	99,487	100,054	133,107
Number of traffic offenders prosecuted by public prosecutor	1,893,710	2,266,001	3,259,483	3,398,497	3,738,908	4,136,895	3,793,433	3,916,609
Number of convictions of special law offenders	83,135	94,070	85,834	105,687	85,638	88,507	80,480	NA
Number of convictions of traffic offenders	1,854,662	2,200,958	3,211,328	3,408,938	3,473,150	4,172,661	3,811,895	NA

SOURCE: The National Police Agency, *Hanzai Tokei-Sho*; The Ministry of Justice, *Kensatsu Tokei Nenpo*; and The Supreme Court, *Shiho Tokei Nenpo*.

TABLE V
RECIDIVISTS

	1960	1961	1962	1963	1964	1965	1966	1967
Total number of newly committed prisoners								
(i) Male	39,929	36,179	34,749	33,484	31,810	31,397	31,557	27,486
(ii) Female	1,079	1,106	1,247	1,119	947	968	982	871
TOTAL	41,008	37,285	35,996	34,603	32,757	32,365	32,539	28,357
Number of Recidivists among newly committed prisoners								
(i) Male	22,621	20,697	19,619	18,251	17,085	17,488	16,553	14,180
(ii) Female	474	507	619	578	485	503	495	436
TOTAL	23,095	21,204	20,238	18,829	17,570	17,991	17,048	14,616

SOURCE: The Ministry of Justice, *Kyosei Tokei Nenpo*.

NOTE: The term "recidivist" follows the definition described in the Penal Code, that is, a recidivist is a person who has been sentenced to imprisonment at forced labor and who is sentenced again to imprisonment at forced labor for a limited term within five years from the day on which the execution of the former sentence was completed or remitted.

TABLE VI
NUMBER OF POPULATION WHOSE AGE ARE OVER 14 (IN THOUSANDS)

	1960	1961	1962	1963	1964	1965	1966	1967
Number	66,860	68,560	70,356	72,209	73,825	75,163	76,461	77,638

SOURCE: The Ministry of Justice, *Hanzai Kaku-sho*, 1968.

TABLE VII
JUVENILE PENAL CODE OFFENDERS INVESTIGATED AND CLEARED BY THE POLICE

	1960	1961	1962	1963	1964	1965	1966	1967
Number of offenders	147,899	158,884	162,941	174,351	190,442	190,864	193,121	186,000
Number of offenders 1000 per inhabitants over 14 and under 20 years of age	13.7	14.1	13.9	14.2	15.1	14.8	14.3	14.4

SOURCE: *Hanzai Hakusho* (White Paper on Crime) (in Japanese), 1968, p. 129.

it would not be too much of an exaggeration to say that, while penology made its first appearance in England and America, criminology originated in Italy, France, and Belgium. That is to say, criminology was very much the concern of Latin countries, and, in contrast, penology the result of the Anglo-American way of thinking. The concept of German criminology and the so-called "Criminal Policy" of Germany developed later than that of other countries. It is the German idea of criminology that has played a great part in the development of Japanese criminology.

Before the effects of Western culture came to be felt, the basic theory of crime and punishment in Japan was that crime was the result of poor governing techniques, and punishment part of the art of government. As the interchange of cultures between East and West increased, Japan began to adopt her ideas in order to bring them into line with those of the West. The Japanese penology and criminology were influenced to a great extent by the Penal Law of 1881 which was modeled on the French pattern. Thus the ideas of Latin criminology began to gain ground. However, in the field of penology the English system was preferred because of the English colonial prison system, and this had some influence in the setting up of Japan's new prison system.

There were good reasons why the French system was adopted at that time. When the introduction of foreign elements was deemed necessary at the beginning of the Meiji government, the selection of the types of elements from each country was carefully considered. For example, those to be introduced from England were machines, trade, geology, the manufactures of iron, building and construction, ship-building, cattlebreeding and social work; those to be introduced from France were law, jurisprudence, international law, economics, biology, statistics, astronomy, mathematics, ethics, chemistry, and building.[12] With such an approach, it is easy to understand why France was chosen as the country from which penal law and criminology were to be introduced, and England was

---

[12]Yoshio Mizuta, *Seio-ho Kotohajime* (The Beginning of the Western Laws) (in Japanese) (Tokyo: Seibundo, 1967), p. 172.

chosen for penology which was thought of as a kind of social work.

Under the influence of the Latin countries, the criminal statistical research first began soon after the Penal Law was brought into force. Attempts were made to translate the works of Lambroso and Garofalo, and these translations formed the basis of Japanese criminology, although English books such as *Golden Liran* and Macdonald were also used as textbooks. Then, from 1897 to 1907 the German idea of criminology was further developed by those Japanese scholars who studied in Germany and adopted to conform to their needs. At that time European criminology was changing from classical thinking of punishment to a new positive way of thought. The three leaders of this new movement were Ferri, v. Liszt, and Van Hammel whose major works on the subject were *Criminal Sociology* (1881), *The Concept of Objective in the Penal Law* (1882), and *Crime and Repression* (1886). Among Japanese scholars who studied in Europe and brought back these new ideas on punishment was Dr Eiichi Makino who studied under Ferri and Liszt. He was a firm believer in the new ideas, and despite his youth, was representing the New School of penal law jurisprudence in Japan.

To understand the trend of criminology in Japan it will be useful to refer to the so-called "school-fight" (Schul-Streit) in the jurisprudence of penal law. Almost everywhere there had been a fight between the progressive theories and the conservative theories. In Germany, a fight of this sort had been fought very powerfully by the dispute between v. Liszt and v. Birkmeyer.[13] The former had alleged that the object of punishment was to maintain law and order in society, the latter regarded punishment as revenge itself. When the 1907 Penal Code was drafted in Japan, progressive ideas were included, especially the theory of social defense. The Code was said to be the most progressive penal code of that time.

After its promulgation, the "school-fight" intensified following the pattern found among the jurists in Germany. A powerful rival of Makino appeared. He was Shigema Oba who had

---

[13]v. Liszt, *op. cit.*; v. Birkmeyer, *Schutzstrafe and Vergeltungsstrafe*, 1906.

studied under v. Birkmeyer, himself a rival of v. Liszt. Oba made studies of criminals in order to show that there was nothing of such a criminal trait as suggested by the theory of the classical school. An intensive study of 1,000 prison-inmates was made in 1909.[14] This might be described as the first positive work in Japanese criminology, though there had been some studies on a smaller scale before. It is odd and of interest that these "positive" studies, which belonged to the new school of thought or at any rate were connected with it, were undertaken by a lawyer of the classical school in Japan.

No worthwhile criminological research works appeared before the end of 1925 except for articles, monographs or textbooks which followed the way of the Latin, and later the Latin-German type of criminology. During this period, not only statisticians and lawyers but also psychiatrists, psychologists, and sociologists began to take part in criminological studies. They made, however, no contribution of note except in a few cases. For example Takano, a statistician showed that there was a close correlation between the statistical curve of the trend of price of corn and that of crime.[15] Toward the end of 1925, Gillin or Aschaffenburg's books were popular with those interested in criminology.

The preparation of a law for the treatment of juvenile offenders which was begun in 1922 gave a stimulus to the study of criminology. During the 20th century research was done in the field of criminal-biology in Germany and this trend influenced Japan. Around this period the prison authorities adopted a new line for the classification of inmates by scientific methods and they also began to employ psychiatrists, psychologists, and educators in an advisory capacity. The Japanese criminology which had thus begun to take on a new look was unfortunately set back by the outbreak of war.

In USA where, it is said, criminology was not studied until 1910, research was being conducted in the sociological as well as in the psycho-analytical field. However neither of these attracted the interests of Japanese criminologists. The ground

[14]Shigema Oba, *Saikin Keijiseisaku Konpon Mondai* (Recent Important Problem in Criminal Policy) (in Japanese) (Tokyo: Sansho-do, 1911).

[15]Iwasaburo Takano, *Tokeigaku Kenkyu* (The Statistical Studies) (in Japanese) (Tokyo: Okura-Shoten, 1915), p. 564.

was not ready. Both sociology and psychiatry were too much under influence of the German approach. But after World War II, American criminology quickly entered the Japanese society, and its practical and clinical sides attracted the minds of local experts in this field.

Though there are many prominent researchers at the present time, the names of two of them need to be mentioned here. Dr Shufu Yoshimasu, now President of the Association of Japanese Criminology, has been one of the propelling powers of criminological research, and he himself is an efficient research professor. His achievement covers a large variety of studies, but three of them are quite remarkable: a study of twin offenders, a study of the life curves of criminals, and a study on crime prediction.[16]

He examined 28 pairs of one-egg twins and 18 pairs of two-egg twins, and found that 50 per cent of the one-egg cases are concordant with respect to committing crime, while no cases are concordant in two-egg twins. This figure, if compared with the figures found in the study made by Lange[17] and in other Western studies, shows less concordance of one-egg twins. Yoshimasu is still continuing the study. According to his recent findings, the concordance rate comes somewhat closer to the Western findings, because the twins which he had studied before were young, but are older now, and some of them have become criminals.

An important conclusion of Yoshimasu appears to be that the concordance rate for one-egg twins is larger in the case of early offenders (under 25 of age) than in the case of late offenders; that is to say, in the case of early offenders, hereditary factors are more influential than environmental factors.

His second study is about the prediction of recidivism, in which he was already interested in the early stage of the development of such studies. In 1936, he published "A Psychiatric Study about the Social Prognosis of Criminals," and in 1951, "A Prognosis of Criminals Careers" was written. In the latter

---

[16]Shufu Yoshimasu, *Hanzaigaku Gairon* (Outline of Criminology) (in Japanese) (Tokyo : Yuhikaku, 1958), pp. 81, 227 and 247.

[17]Johannes Lange, *Verbrechen also Schicksal* (Studien an Krimminellen Zwillingen, Leipzig, 1929) (English translation by Charlotte Haldane, *Crime and Destiny*, New York, 1930).

article, he used seven factors for prediction at the time of the sentence, viz. psychopathic traits, early crimes, frequent repetition of crimes, broken home, incomplete school, frequent change of jobs, and hereditary factors. A person who has six or seven of these factors may be predicted to become a repeater with a certainty of 91.7 per cent. If three factors are present the certainty is 79.2 per cent. But for a complete prediction, it is necessary to add some predictive devices at the time of the offender's release to the prediction made for at the time of his sentence. This is the main result of his study in this field.

His third study of the life curve of criminals is interesting for probing into the type of recidivism. He invented the following indices in examining the criminal process: (*i*) age of first crime; (*ii*) repetition of crime and interval between crimes; and (*iii*) type of crimes repeated (property crime, violent crime, and so on), and he applied this idea by writing a life curve of a criminal. It allows case-researchers to understand the case more clearly. Scholars who belong to his school are always using this method.

The other scholar is a young sociologist, Dr Hiroyuki Iwai. Criminological studies in the field of sociology are not yet developed in Japan, as pointed out before, when compared with other fields of criminology. In this situation, his work on anti-social groups is very important; it is a sociological approach to organized crime in the country. Japan has her special organized criminal groups which had their origin in the feudal society. The Bakuto (Gamblers), Tekiya (Racketeers), and similar groups are the violent groups who get their revenues from gambling, prostitution, narcotics, boot-legging, and protection rackets. Iwai, while examining these groups in detail, concludes that clinically organized criminals are psychopathic persons.[18] They have been drifting into those anti-social groups the structure of which gave them an opportunity to compensate for their low self-respect due to their "Yakuza" (worthless) personality.

[18]Hiroyuki Iwai, *Byori Shudan no Kozo* (The Structure of Deviate Groups) (in Japanese) (Tokyo: Seishin Shobo, 1961).

PENAL PHILOSOPHY

When Japan tried to centralize her political power in the 8th century, she adopted, with little change, the Chinese law which was very advanced in its provisions on penal matters. There is a general saying that if Roman law was of a particularly civil nature, Chinese law was of a particularly penal nature.[19] China has had a long history of statutory penal law which originated in a statutory code entitled "Ho-Kyo" in 407 B.C.

It is perhaps necessary to compare, very briefly, the characteristics of the Chinese law with the modern Western penal code. These are as follows: (i) the punishment inflicted would depend upon class and status; (ii) for the construction of a crime, analogical inference was applied; (iii) a certain act might be punished if it was regarded as contrary to the moral sense of the people, although such an act was not defined as a crime in the code; (iv) there were five types of punishment, whipping, striking with a stick, hard labor, transportation, and death; and (v) torture was allowed.

For a short period only the Japanese Penal Code as derived from Chinese law was applied, but soon it fell into disuse for about 1000 years under the impact of feudalism.

During the regime of Tokugawa Shogunnate emerged the concept of a penal policy which would contribute to the maintenance of social law and order in a peaceful period, a penal policy which was the result of the Isolation policy. Some of the ideas were comparable to the modern penal thoughts in Europe. That is to say that while modern European thoughts on punishment developed under the influence of mercantilism, Japanese ideas were stimulated by the influence of Isolation which was set up in strong opposition to European mercantilism. Among the most prominent thinkers of those days was Sorai Ogiu (1666-1723). He attempted to draw up a new policy suitable to the times following the Chinese pattern of punishment, but it eventually turned out to be fairly modern.[20]

We find several modern notions present in his propositions,

---

[19] Seiichiro Ono, *op. cit.*, p. 323.
[20] Taro Ogawa, *op. cit.*

for example the distinction between law and morals, the theory of social accountability which made the function of punishment not retributive but preventive, the use of imprisonment as a method of punishment, the enactment of penal law (there was no statutory law at his time), the distinction of detention pending trial from punishment by imprisonment, the separation of courts from the police and so forth. As can be imagined, the ideas found amongst these propositions made it easy later on to adopt a modern penal code.

As already pointed out, the Meiji government finally adopted a French style Penal Code in 1880; the theories behind the Code were obviously influenced by French penal lawyers. The most important characteristic of this Code was its principle of legality. Article 2 of the Japanese Code stated that no act was to be punished which was not prescribed in the laws, a provision derived from Article 4 of the French Code. The old Constitution which was promulgated in 1890 had a provision containing the legality principle (Article 23). It came from the Prussian Constitution (Article 8) which was drawn up along the lines of the French Declaration of Human Rights (Article 8). As a result of the adoption of the principle of legality, most of the traditional provisions of the Chinese penal code, for example, analogical inference, punishment of minor offenses without penal provisions etc., were entirely abolished.

The penal philosophy prevailing at this time was that of the neo-classical school (*école néo-classique*). One of the prevailing philosophies in France at that time was that of Réné Garraud (1849-1930).[21] It differed from the classical theory of Beccaria and was eclectic in concept. It claimed that while the intrinsic element of punishment should be retribution, its function should have two aims—one being the restoration of the wrong done to society by atonement, and the other social defense. A famous Japanese penal lawyer of that time, Dr Seisho Tomii, studied under Garraud and mostly followed his eclectic theory.

After the Constitution came into force in 1890, the German penal theories were gradually felt in Japan. Shortly before

---

[21] *Traité théorique et pratique du droit pénal* (1889-94).

1890, as already shown, the new theories of Enrico Ferri, Franz v. Liszt and others appeared.[22] Following were the main points suggested by this new school: (*i*) crime shall be studied not as a product of free-will but as a necessary causal phenomenon; (*ii*) dangerous characteristics of the criminal can be recognized from the nature of the crime committed; (*iii*) punishment is not retributive but reformative and preventive; and (*iv*) punishment shall be awarded according to the character of an offender; "not the act, but the actor is to be punished."

After 1890 scholars and lawyers tended to move closer to this new school, and the Japanese penal law revisions were carried out under the overwhelming influence of this trend. The new law was drawn up in 1907. After that came the "school-fight" already mentioned. Various problems arising from the fight were discussed during the course of making a temporary draft penal code which was published in 1931 and 1940.

The new democratic Constitution after World War II introduced a great change, but there were fewer changes made in the field of penal philosophy as compared with other fields. The penal philosophy of Japan is still greatly influenced by the German way of thinking. The principle of legality in Article 31 of the new Constitution is substantially the same as that declared in the old constitution. As far as penal affairs are concerned, the Constitution has no special new ideas except an abundant provision of human rights in criminal procedures. Thus no revolutionary change has been brought about in the fundamentals of penal philosophy.

The typical antagonism of the "school-fight," is now gradually beginning to disappear especially after the war. The two schools are drawing closer together in their ideas.

New theory along the line of the classic school is now trying to reconcile the antagonism of both schools. It asserts that a man is conditioned by his constitution and environment, but on the other hand, he has freedom of conduct and can control some of these aspects by his personality. Therefore, a crime is not only an act but may be deemed as an expres-

[22]Enrico Ferri, *La sociologia criminale*, 1884; Franze v. Liszt, *Der Zweckgedanke in Strafrecht*, 1882.

sion of personality.[23] This so-called theory of "culpable personality" is very different from the old theory of "Tatschuld" (act-culpability) and is coming closer to the theory of dangerousness of offenders as laid down by the new school.

On the other hand, scholars belonging to the new school are establishing a new theory of "normative responsibility" (normative Schuldlehre), which is based on the idea that it is reasonable to expect for an actor to follow legal acts. Why is an offender culpable? He is culpable (responsible) because he is expected to follow a norm in a certain situation, but dares to offend it.[24] The structure of this theory is far beyond the social accountability theory of the school and comes nearer to the ideas of the opposite school.

Formerly the main points of difference of both schools were that one emphasized the punishment of an "act" and the other, the punishment of "an actor." However due to recent developments in the schools one cannot find as much difference as was obvious formerly.

The Japanese dogma of penal law, as said before, lists three elements in the concept of crime: an act penalized by law (Tatbestand)—actus reus, the illegality of this act, and culpability—mens rea. In this connection, the problem of whether a criminal intention comes under "Tatbestand" or culpability is being discussed. Dr Kimura, an eminent professor of penal law, asserts that criminal intention should be included in "Tatbestand"; he is for the German theory of "finalistische Handlungslehre" (the final act theory).[25] Around this theory there are many controversies—this is also a new trend in Japanese criminal law circle.

One of the most important things being discussed among criminal lawyers in Japan is the Penal Draft Code of 1961.[26] Subjects of discussion in this connection are as follows:

[23]Shigemitsu Dando, *Keiho-Koyo* (Textbook of Penal Law) (in Japanese) (Tokyo: Sobunsha, 1957).

[24]Kameji Kimura, *Shinkeiho Tokuhon* (New Textbook of Penal Law) (in Japanese) (Tokyo: Yuhikaku, 1956).

[25]Kameji Kimura, *Keiho Soron* (General Principles of Penal Law) (in Japanese) (Tokyo: Yuhikaku, 1959), pp. 139 and 203.

[26]A Preparatory Draft for the Revised Penal Code of Japan, the American Series of Foreign Penal Code, 8, Sweet & Maxwell Limited London, 1964.

(a) provision of crime committed by omission; (b) provision of self-induced mental disorder; (c) provision of crime aggravated by results; (d) provision of impossible offense; (e) provision of indirect principles; (f) provision of conspiratorial co-principles; (g) the death penalty; (h) to retain or not the distinction between imprisonment with forced labor and imprisonment without forced labor; (i) the indeterminate sentence for habitual offenders; (j) the fine; and (k) security measures for mentally disordered defendants of a dangerous nature, and for alcoholic or narcotic addicts.

FUNCTIONS OF THE COURT

The termination of World War II led to radical changes in Japanese society as well as in the Japanese judicial system. Even before the War, Japan had adopted the doctrine of separation of the three powers of administration, legislature, and judicature. However, the power of the judicature was not as strong and independent as it is today. For instance, the courts at that time had no power to determine the constitutionality of law, order, regulation, or official act. Furthermore, the power of the general administrative supervision over the judiciary remained in the hands of the Minister of Justice, although he had no authority over the judges in the exercise of their judicial functions. The new Constitution of Japan, enacted in 1946, came into effect on May 3, 1947. Under this Constitution the separation of powers is completely realized without any restrictions. The whole judicial power is vested in a Supreme Court and in such inferior courts as may be established by law. The courts are the exclusive adjudicators of all legal disputes including administrative actions as well as both civil and criminal ones. Administrative agencies are not allowed to make more than preliminary determinations.

As a result of this reform, the power of courts has been remarkably expanded in content. The courts are empowered to determine the constitutionality of any law, order, regulation, or official act. In view of the important functions assigned to the court, the independence of the judiciary has acquired a deeper meaning than before. All judges are independent in the exercise of their conscience and are bound only by the Constitution and the laws. No disciplinary action against judges is to be administered by any executive organ or agency. Furthermore, for the purpose of strengthening the autonomy of the court, the new Constitution has vested the Supreme Court with the authority of judicial administration, such as assignment and transfer of judges to the specific courts, appointment and removal of court personnel other than judges, and financial affairs of the courts—which under the old Constitution was in the hands of a member of the Cabinet, the Minister of Justice. Under the present system, the Chief Justice of the Supreme Court ranks on the same level as the Chairman of both Houses of the Diet and the Prime Minister. This reflects the fact that the judicature in Japan stands on equal footing with the administration and the legislature.

Court Organization

Following the promulgation of the new Constitution, the new Court Organization Law was enacted in 1947. According to the Law, there are five kinds of courts: the Supreme Court is the highest; the High Courts rank next to the Supreme Court. Then follows the District Courts and Family Courts and the Summary Courts are on the lowest level. There are no special courts in Japan such as commercial courts, administrative courts, or military courts.

Supreme Court. The Supreme Court is the court of last resort. The number of justices of the Supreme Court is fixed at 15 including a Chief Justice.

The Supreme Court has appellate jurisdiction only. The grounds of appeal are not unlimited. With regard to criminal cases the grounds of appeal are as follows:

(*i*) An appeal may be lodged against a judgment rendered by a High Court on the ground that there is a violation of the Constitution or an error in construction, interpretation, or application of the Constitution, or on the ground of an error of law which is material to the judgment, or an improper imposition of punishment, or a gross error in fact-finding, or on the ground that a judgment has been pronounced that is incompatible with the judicial precedents formerly established by the Supreme Court.

(*ii*) As to a judgment rendered in the first instance by a District Court, Family Court, or Summary Court, appeal may be taken to the Supreme Court on the ground that a conclusion in the judgment is to the effect that laws, ordinances, regulations, or official act are in violation of the Constitution.

High Courts. These are located in eight large cities of Japan, and each has territorial jurisdiction over one of the eight parts of the country.

In criminal cases High Courts have jurisdiction for appeals against judgments rendered by the District Court, Family Court, or Summary Court. Exceptionally the High Court has the original jurisdiction as a court of first instance in criminal or insurrection cases. In the High Court cases are handled by a three-judge panel, except insurrection cases which must be handled by a five-judge panel.

District Courts. There are 49 District Courts having territorial jurisdiction over judicial districts each of which corresponds to the area of a prefecture except four districts in Hokkaido.

A District Court has original jurisdiction over all offenses except those involving crimes punishable by a fine or less. It has concurrent jurisdiction with summary courts over cases in which a fine is an optional penalty, or in cases of theft, and certain other specific crimes. Cases in the District Court are dealt with by a single judge or by a three-judge panel depending on the nature and importance of the case.

Family Courts. The Family Courts and their branches are located in the same places as the District Courts and the branches of the District Courts.

The Family Court was established on January 1, 1949, for the purpose of placing both family and juvenile problems under the jurisdiction of one tribunal because the adjustment of a family's situation was considered an absolute prerequisite for the protection of children and the prevention of delinquency. The Family Court consists of the juvenile division, and the family affairs division. In the juvenile division it handles the cases involving delinquent juveniles under 20 years of age and adults who have injured in certain ways the welfare of juveniles. All cases in the Family Court are handled by a single judge.

Summary Courts. There are 570 Summary Courts in cities towns, and villages throughout the country.

A Summary Court has the power to try criminal cases punishable by a fine or less, cases in which a fine may be fixed at the discretion of the court, and certain specific crimes like habitual gambling, operating a gambling establishment, theft, embezzlement, or receiving stolen property. The punishment that a Summary Court may impose is limited to relatively short imprisonment or fine. All cases in the Summary Court are handled by a single judge.

Structure of the Legal Profession

The Japanese legal profession consists of three categories of lawyers—judges, public prosecutors, and practising attorneys. As of 1967, there were 2,500 judges, including 15 Supreme Court justices, 8 High Court chief justices, 520 assistant judges, and 740 Summary Court judges. In the same year, there were 1,082 public prosecutors and 762 assistant public prosecutors. The total number of practising attorneys who belong to 51 local Bar Associations is 7,998 as of June, 1967.

Qualification and Selection in the Legal Profession. In order to become a lawyer of whatever category, it is necessary to pass the bar examination and complete legal training as a legal apprentice at the Judicial Training and Research Institute for two years. Graduates of the Institute may become assistant judges, public prosecutors, or practising attorneys according to their own choice.

Selection of Judges and Related Matters. Qualifications for the appointment of judges are described in the Court Organization Law.

The Chief Justice of the Supreme Court, designated by the Cabinet, is appointed by Tenno (Emperor). Other justices of the Supreme Court are appointed by the Cabinet and attested by the Emperor. Justices of the Supreme Court are appointed from among persons of broad vision and extensive knowledge of law, who are not less than forty years of age. At least ten of them must be persons who have made a career in the legal profession or as a professor of law. There is no provision for a term of office, but the justices have to retire from office at the age of seventy.

Judges of the High Courts, District Courts, and Family

Courts are appointed by the Cabinet from a list of persons nominated by the Supreme Court. Nominees must have legal experience as assistant judges, public prosecutors, and practising attorneys, or as professors of law. Judges may hold office for a term of ten years and may be reappointed. They must retire from office on attaining 65 years of age. The Emperor attests the appointment of the presidents of the High Courts. As to assistant judges, they are appointed by the Cabinet from a list of persons nominated by the Supreme Court. As already mentioned, the nominees must have completed a two-year term of legal training. Those who have held the position of an assistant judge for not less than ten years are eligible to become full judges. Assistant judges, as a rule, cannot take decisions independently.

As for a judge of a Summary Court, although he is usually required to have practical experience of not less than 10 years as an assistant judge, public prosecutor, or practising attorney, the way is open for a man of ability other than a jurist. More than half of them formerly held positions as court clerks, court probation officers, or other officials and were especially appointed through selection by the Selection Committee for Summary Court Judges. Summary Court Judges hold office for a term of 10 years and retire from office upon the attainment of 70 years of age.

A judge cannot, against his will, be dismissed or removed to any other official position, or be transferred from one court to another, or suspended from exercising his judicial function, or have his salary reduced, except by public impeachment, or under the provisions of the statute relating to national review, or unless judicially declared mentally or physically incompetent to perform official duties.

All judges receive, at regular stated intervals, adequate compensation which is regulated by a specific law separate from that regulating the general civil service. The compensation of judges is considerably higher than that of general government officials.

Selection of Public Prosecutors and their Duties. Public prosecutors are government officials who are competent to perform prosecutorial duties. The officials titles of public prosecutors are the Prosecutor-General, the Assistant Prosecutor-

General, Superintending Public Prosecutors, Public Prosecutors, and Assistant Public Prosecutors. Public Prosecutors are appointed from among those qualified to be judges or assistant judges. However, the selection and appointment as assistant public prosecutors are different from those of public prosecutors. The selection is made through a decision by the Assistant Public Prosecutors Selection Committee which is attached to the Ministry of Justice.

There are four levels of public prosecutor's offices: the Supreme Public Prosecutor's Office, high public prosecutor's offices, district public prosecutor's offices and local public prosecutor's offices, corresponding to the Supreme Court, High Courts, District Courts and Summary Courts. Public prosecutor's offices are under the jurisdiction of the Minister of Justice.

Public prosecutors carry out their duties within the jurisdictional territory of their court. Assistant public prosecutors can be assigned only to prosecute duties in local public prosecutor's offices. Public prosecutors conduct the prosecution of criminal cases, request the court to make proper application of the law, and supervise the application of the judgment. The guarantees of status and remuneration of public prosecutors are similar to those of judges. Political neutrality and impartiality of the prosecution serves as a powerful support for the independence and impartiality of the judiciary. Furthermore, public prosecutors in Japan have the discretionary power to prosecute or not. Even if they are convinced of the guilt of their suspects, they may drop the prosecution by refraining from filing the information—if they find that the prosecution is not essential in view of such criminological factors as the personality, age, environmental background of the suspect, the nature and circumstances of the crime, the circumstances after the offenses, and the possibility of rehabilitation of the suspect.

Qualification of "practising attorneys" and their system. Matters relating to practising attorneys are provided in the Lawyers Law. According to the Law, a practising lawyer has the duty to protect the fundamental human rights and to realize social justice. He shall also perform his functions sincerely and use his endeavors for the maintenance of social order and improvement of the legal system.

The qualifications to become a practising lawyer are almost the same as those for an assistant judge or a public prosecutor. A person who wishes to practice as a "practising attorney" must apply for registration with the Bar Association. If there is apprehension that the person may injure good order or the reputation of the Association, or if he behaves in such a manner so as to render himself unfit to practice, the Bar Association may refuse to forward his request for registration which depends upon the decision of its Qualification Examination Committee.

There exists no distinction among practising attorneys, such as that between barristers and solicitors. However, practising attorneys are prohibited from taking part in specified acts which may raise a doubt about the fairness of their business, or from holding concurrently full-time public offices for payment.

Court Officials other than Judges. Besides judges, the courts have such officials as judicial researchers, court clerks, family court probation officers, court stenotypists, bailiffs, marshals, and court secretaries.

Judicial research officials conduct the necessary research in connection with the hearing and the deciding of cases as assistants to the justices of the Supreme Court. Court clerks are responsible for attending hearing and recording proceedings as well as for preparing and keeping in custody records and other documents concerning the cases of the court. Family Court probation officers conduct investigation concercing domestic cases and juvenile cases.

Method of Trial

The trials in Japan are classified into three categories, that is trials of first instance, trials of second instance, and trials of third instance. One of the basic principles that govern the trial is that of a public trial. This principle has been established in order to protect the fairness of judicial administration.

More than 90 per cent of the cases are processed by a single judge. The collegiate court—which consists of three judges— tries serious offenses, such as murder, rape, and arson, but also other cases if the court deems them proper to be tried in that way. Incidentally, there are no jury trials in Japan now, although jury trial had been introduced in 1923 by the Jury Law. This law, however, was suspended altogether in 1943.

Among the participants in the court proceedings are the Judge the court clerk, and the public prosecutor. As to the defendant, the general rule is that the trial cannot be opened unless the defendant is present. Concerning the defense counsel, the trial will be opened in some minor cases without him. In practice, however, there are many instances in which defendants are assisted by defense counsel. If the defendant is unable to select a defense counsel of his own because of poverty or some other reasons, he is entitled to ask the court to designate his defense counsel at the expense of the State. The Public Prosecutor and the defendant have the rights to request the examination of evidence, to question witnesses, to contest the credibility of evidence, and to state objections to measures taken by the presiding judge. Moreover, the defendant has the privilege to remain silent and to refuse to make a statement.

Ordinary trial proceedings are divided into four stages as follows: (*i*) opening proceedings, (*ii*) examination of evidence, (*iii*) closing statements, and (*iv*) judgment.

In the opening proceedings the court has first to inform the defendant of his rights to remain silent and to refuse to answer individual questions. After the information has been read aloud by a public prosecutor, the defendant and his defense counsel are given the opportunity to make a statement about the case at issue. Unlike the Anglo-American Law, there is no arraignment system in Japan. Even if the defendant pleads guilty the Public Prosecutor has to prove the conviction of the defendant by evidence other than the defendant's confession, which however is admissible as evidence.

The examination of evidence is initiated by an opening statement of the Public Prosecutor. It is the first duty of the latter to apply for the examination of evidence. According to the rule of evidence provided by the Code of Criminal Procedure, a written statement either of a witness or of the accused to police or the Public Prosecutor is admissible as evidence if the defendant and the defense counsel give consent for its submission to the court.

When the examination of evidence has been completed, the Public Prosecutor must state his opinion on the facts and the application of law to them. As a rule he also makes a recommendation for the sentence to the court. Generally, the defendant or his counsel have the right to make the last statement.

Then the case is closed, and the judgment is pronounced to the accused. It must be announced orally in open court. In Japanese criminal procedure, the process of sentencing is not clearly separated from that of finding guilty or not. Accordingly, in the judgment the court will pronounce the decision regarding both the facts charged and the sentence. The system of presentence investigation has not yet been introduced in criminal courts except for juvenile delinquents who come before the Family Courts.

Generally, there are two types of appeals in Japanese criminal procedure. One is the appeal from the judgment of a court of first instance to a High Court, and the second is the appeal from the judgment of a High Court to the Supreme Court.

The Public Prosecutor and the defendant have the right of appeal. The defense counsel can exercise the defendant's right of appeal so long as it is not contrary to the former's express wishes. When the only party who made an appeal is the defendant, the appellate court cannot pronounce a sentence more severe than the original one.

FUNCTIONS OF THE POLICE

The Police Law, enacted in 1954, provided for the supremacy of law, and a democratic administration for the organization and activities of the police in Japan. This law also intended to provide a more efficient police organization, paying considerable attention to the principle of local autonomy.

Police Organization

There are 3 principal divisions of the fundamental structure of the police system.

(i) *Central organ of the police.* The National Public Safety Commission and the National Police Agency were established as the central organ of the police. The National Public Safety Commission is subject to the control of the Prime Minister, and is composed of a cabinet minister as the chairman and of five commissioners. The Commission takes charge of police operations relating to the public safety of the nation, administers matters concerning police education, police communication, criminal identification, criminal statistics, and police equipment. It also coordinates matters concerning police administration and supervises the National Police Agency.

The National Police Agency is headed by a Director-General who is appointed by the National Public Safety Commission with the approval of the Prime Minister. It co-ordinates the police administration of all the prefectural police agencies throughout the country, and performs prescribed duties which cover the same scope as those of the National Public Safety Commission. There are seven Regional Police Bureaus which serve as the local agencies of the National Police Agency.

(*ii*) *Local organs of the police.* In each prefecture there is a Prefectural Public Safety Commission and a Prefectural Police Headquarter. Under the jurisdiction of the Prefectural Governor, the Prefectural Public Safety Commission is established and is usually composed of those members who are appointed by the Governor with the consent of the Prefectural Assembly. The Prefectural Police is supervised by this Commission which has the duty to keep close contact at all times with the National Public Safety Commission and with other Prefectural Public Safety Commissions.

Throughout Japan there are 46 Prefectural Police Headquarters which take charge of the affairs of Prefectural Police. Under their jurisdiction police stations are established in the major cities or towns. The jurisdictive area of each police station is subdivided into numerous police "boxes" and residential police boxes. Police boxes are small box-like police substations, mainly placed in urban districts; several police officers are assigned to each police box. Residential police boxes are established in rural communities such as farm-villages or fishing villages.

(*iii*) *Relationship between police and other government agencies.* In Japan the police is not placed under a specific central government agency, such as the Ministry of Interior, Ministry of Justice or the courts. As has been pointed out earlier, the police is controlled by the Prime Minister through the National Public Safety Commission.

As to the activities of criminal investigation, the police is checked by the courts through the issuance of warrant of arrest or search. The Code of Criminal Procedure describes the relationship between the police and Public Prosecutor.

Internal Structure. In order to understand the internal structure of the Japanese police it will be useful to illustrate the organization and activities of Prefectural Police Headquarters and police stations.

We can take up the organization of the Tokyo Metropolitan Police Department—which is one of the largest Prefectural Police Headquarters in Japan as an example. It is divided into several divisions such as Police Administration, General Affairs, Criminal Investigation, Crime Prevention, Traffic, Security, Public Safety and Police School.

The Criminal Investigation Division supervises or controls criminal investigation conducted by the police stations concerned, and furthermore itself conducts the investigation of serious or peculiar or difficult cases. This division is divided into several sections, including laboratory and flying squad section. In the laboratory section forensic medicine, physics, and chemistry for the identification of offenders, or evidence are conducted with the co-operation of the Scientific Police Research Institute which is attached to the National Police Agency. The flying squad section is composed of a considerable number of trained officers and equipped with radio cars, movable telephone cars, walky-talkies, etc. in order to suppress crimes which either occur frequently in cities or in succession over wide areas.

A police station consists of several sections. Crime prevention and investigation of juvenile offenders is the responsibility of the Crime Prevention Section. It is well known that intensive patrolling is very effective for the prevention and suppression of crime. A reasonable number of patrol cars are assigned to each police station according to the size of its jurisdiction and population. Patrol men are usually dispatched to police boxes to carry out patrol in their areas.

The Scientific Police Research Institute was established in 1948 and its chief services are composed of study-tests and examinations in the field of scientific detection and other identification work, prevention of juvenile delinquency and other crimes, prevention of traffic accidents, as well as traffic police activities. The Institute is divided into several divisions.

One of them is the Scientific Detection Division which is engaged in research of identification theories and the practices that serve the on-the-spot activities of local police authorities —especially identification and examination of evidence by means of every scientific technique derived from legal medicine, physics, chemistry, electrical and mechanical engineering, psychology, radio-isotope, and photography.

Police Manpower. Japan having a population of 100,250,000 as of December, 1967, the authorized strength of the police force is 161,590. The rate of police officers computed per 100,000 inhabitants was 162 for 1967. As has been pointed out already, each Prefectural Police Headquarter and police station has a Criminal Investigation Section which is a basic unit for investigation activities. Throughout the country, the total number of criminal investigators who belong to either Prefectural Police Headquarters or to police stations is about 30,000 as of 1967. Of this number, 5,044 police officers are assigned to the Tokyo Metropolitan Police Department.

Responsibilities, Duties, and Powers of the Police

The Police Law describes the principal duties of police as (*i*) protection of life, body, and property of the people; (*ii*) prevention, suppression, and investigation of offenses; (*iii*) arrest of suspects; (*iv*) traffic control; and (*v*) other affairs concerning the maintenance of public safety and order. Police activities for the maintenance of public peace and order are known as the preventive action of the police; the scope and limits of the preventive action are defined by law. The police has the responsibility to check a person when he is committing or about to commit an offense. It also has the authority to investigate crimes and to arrest offenders. This is one of the most important functions of the police in all countries.

In Japan too, criminal investigation is one of the primary

duties of the police. As a matter of course criminal investigation must conform to the provisions of the laws and regulations such as the Code of Criminal Procedure and the Rule of
Criminal Procedure issued by the Supreme Court. According
to these provisions police officers are required to investigate
offenders and the evidence when they deem an offense has
been committed. There are two methods of police investigation, one based on voluntary co-operation, the other on compulsory measures. In the former case the police officer will
carry out the investigation without arresting the offender. If
he needs to interrogate the suspect he may ask him to appear
at the police station for an interview; the suspect has the freedom to refuse to do so. This is the principal method for investigation in Japan. In the latter case the investigation is
conducted by arresting the offender or searching and seizing
the property.

However, when police officers believe that they should
arrest offenders they have to get a warrant of arrest which has
to be issued beforehand by a judge, except for the so-called
flagrant offense during which a police officer is authorized to
arrest the offender without warrant. After arresting the offender the police officer is authorized to detain him for 48 hours
in the detention room of the police station. During this time
he can interrogate the suspect after cautioning him that he has
the privilege of refusing self-incrimination and the right to
select his defense counsel.

Unless the police officer believes the suspected person should
not be detained any more, he must hand over the suspect to
the Public Prosecutor within 48 hours with the evidential
documents or real evidence. After receiving the suspect the
Public Prosecutor decides within 24 hours whether the suspect
should be detained or not. Even in detaining the suspect the
Public Prosecutor must apply for the issue of a warrant of
detention by a judge; the detention period is basically 10 days
during which the police officer can proceed with the investigation. Neither the police nor the Public Prosecutor are required
to get the approval of a judge for the release of a suspect.

Concerning the preventive activities of the police, the Police
Duties Execution Law of 1948 plays an important role. The
object of this law is to provide the necessary measures for the

faithful execution of the authority and duties of a police officer in protecting the life, physical integrity and property of individuals, in preventing crimes, maintaining public safety in accordance with the Police Law, and in enforcing other laws and regulations. According to the Police Duties Execution Law, a police officer may stop and question a person whom he has reasonable ground to suspect of having committed, or being about to commit, a crime. However, the persons mentioned above may not be detained or taken to a police station, or compelled to answer questions against their will. In the case where a police officer finds a person, who judging reasonably on the basis of his unusual behaviour must be feared to inflict an injury on his own life, on the life of others, or on property because of mental derangement or drunkenness, and who must also be reasonably believed to need emergency aid and protection, the police must give him immediate protection at any place, such as a police station or a hospital.

It must be noted, here, that in Japan the Public Prosecutor is also authorized to engage in investigative activities. So, the relationship between the police and the Public Prosecutor is an important one. Though basically their relationship is of a cooperative type, the Public Prosecutor is thought of as a semi-judicial officer because of his qualifications. His main job in the course of an investigation is to reinforce the evidence from the legal standpoint and give the necessary advice to the police officer so that he may submit the best evidence to prove the guilt of the accused at the trial.

FUNCTIONS OF THE PRISON

In Japan, all prisons are administrated at the national level by the Correction Bureau of the Ministry of Justice. The Correction Bureau is one of the 7 major bureaus of the Ministry, and is responsible for the administration of all penal and correctional institutions including juvenile training schools, juvenile remand homes, and women's guidance homes for prostitutes. Probation and parole services fall under the jurisdiction of the Rehabilitation Bureau of the Ministry of Justice.

Prison Organization

For the purpose of administration and supervision of the penal and correctional institutions, the whole territory of Japan is divided into 8 correction districts, and each district has its own headquarters. The Superintendent of Correction Headquarters is vested with the authority to administratively supervise all the institutions in the district, and is responsible to the Minister of Justice.

Prisons are administrated under such basic laws and regulations as the Prison Law of 1908; the Prison Law Enforcement Regulation (Ministry of Justice Ordinance of 1908); the Ordinance for Progressive Grade Treatment (Ministry of Justice Ordinance of 1933); and Compendium of Rules for the Classification of Prisoners (Correction Bureau Directive of 1948); and by numerous other directives issued by the Minister of Justice and the Director of Correction Bureau. The Prison Law provides for 4 kinds of penal institutions: prisons for persons sentenced to imprisonment at forced labor; prisons for persons sentenced to imprisonment without forced labor; houses of penal detention for persons convicted to penal detention under 30 days; and detention houses to detain, accused persons and suspects. Thus in Japan, "prison" is the general term for all these institutions; the majority of the prisons combine the functions of all 4 types in one institution, except in the larger cities where separate and independent detention houses are provided.

Throughout Japan, there are 7 major detention houses; 57 major prisons with 98 branch detention houses in smaller cities; 16 branch prisons; and 9 juvenile prisons. As of May 30, 1968, the total inmate population of these institutions was 56,691, including 1,371 females. A detailed breakdown of this number reveals that 48,393 were convicted prisoners including 1,077 females, 1,403 juveniles (i.e. under 20 years of age), and about 1,500 prisoners sentenced to imprisonment without forced labor; 7,917 were unconvicted prisoners including 238 females; there were 72 persons condemned to death, including 3 females; 281 workhouse detainees (who are in default of payment of a fine) including 8 females; and 24 others.

The number of officers working in prisons and detention

houses as of January 1, 1967 was 16,762, consisting of 269 wardens and executives, 810 captain guards, 1,186 assistant captain guards, 2,580 senior guards, 9,515 guards, 616 industrial specialists, 424 medical and classification specialists, 106 teachers, and 1,253 clerical workers, maintenance workers, drivers, and other employees.

Classification of Prisoners and Prisons

Convicted prisoners who constitute the great majority of the penal population are classified into the following 11 major categories:

Category	Standards	Number of prisoners falling in the category (as of December 20, 1967)
Class A	Those of generally normal or near-normal personality who are expected to respond well to correctional treatment	8,345
Class B	Those of quasi-normal personality who offer a rather poor prospect for good response	24,236
Class C	Those who have a long term sentence (generally more than 8 years)	3,769
Class D	Prisoners under the application of those under the age of 20 to whom the penal measures of the Juvenile Law are applied	1,230
Class E	Those under 23 years of age who are considered treatable as juvenile prisoners	1,008
Class G	Those under 25 years of age who fall under Class A	5,059
Class H	Those who have a mental defect (psychosis, psychopathy or feeble-mindedness) and need specific treatment and care	1,435
Class K	Those who have a physical disease, deformity, injury or senility and need specific treament	915
Class J	Females	1,106
Class M	Foreigners who need specific foods and manner of living	61
Class N	Those sentenced to imprisonment without forced labor	1,142

Each prison is designated to receive one or a few of these classes, and some of the 57 prisons are specified as being a medical prison, a women's prison, or a long-term prison. Prisons are also generally referred to A, B, or C class prisons.

The nine juvenile prisons receive all criminally convicted persons under the age of 20, and are characteristically more treatment-oriented than adult prisons. They comply with both the Juvenile Law and the Prison Law. An inmate of a juvenile prison may remain in the same institution until he reaches the age of 26. Incidentally, other types of institutions (non-penal) are also provided for juvenile delinquents by the Juvenile Law and the Chief Welfare Law.

The 16 branch prisons include several open farm camps, a camp for a ship-building yard, medical institutions for specific types of illness, and special training centers for traffic offenders.

The Treatment Scheme of the Prison

Reference has already been made to the classification which guides the distribution of the inmates to the various prisons.

Classification. Within each institution, a more detailed classification is carried out, and the best treatment plan is worked out for each inmate with respect to workshop assignment, grouping, custody, family and environmental pressures, and individual needs, so that his welfare as well as his rehabilitation should be promoted.

Progressive Grade System. The first Article of the Ordinance of "Progressive Grade Treatment" 1933 says: "The aim of this Ordinance is to reform convicted persons and rehabilitate them to social life, alleviating their treatment according to their efforts and exertions." In this system, inmates are assigned upon admission to the fourth grade, in principle, and are promoted toward the first grade as they prove to be deserving more freedom through good conduct, industry, and sense of responsibility. The privileges increase as one is promoted, and those who are assigned to the first grade are assumed to be prepared to accept responsibility for their own behavior. The system is related to parole selection, though the parole is not limited to the first graders.

Education. Prisoners receive upon admission general orientation to institutional life for the first few weeks. Conversely, pre-release orientation is provided at the end of their stay in the prison to alleviate the barrier which they will face in readjusting themselves to normal social life. Chances for academic training are provided outside work hours especially for those who were school drop-outs, and more intensive programs are organized in juvenile prisons. Social education in prisons embodies lectures by visiting experts from various walks of life. Inmates are encouraged to take correspondence courses, and, in 1965, 4,091 inmates persued such courses either at their own expense or with financial support from the government. Programs of religious guidance, radio and TV service, library service and reading guidance, are actively conducted, and are intended to promote the chance of rehabilitation of prisoners.

Counselling and Psychotherapeutic Services. Counselling and psychotherapeutic programs have recently been introduced in penal and correctional institutions in Japan. As yet there has not been established a standardized system of such service. Prisons, however, have organized programs of counselling and psychotherapy in order to meet the individual needs of prisoners, help them to improve their personality, and rehabilitate them for a lawful life in community.

One of the most influential methods in Japanese prisons— a method which may be considered as belonging to the category of psychotherapeutic treatment—is called the *naikan* method. It appears to be indigenous to Japanese culture to some extent, and was initiated and advocated by Rev. Yoshimoto. *Naikan* when literally translated means "introspection." Naikan leaders encourage prisoners to introspect themselves recalling their past life from their early childhood, first in relation to the mother, and then to the father, brother, friend, and so on. A client is not to think back about what his mother did to him or how she was to him (this is called extra-spection), but he is taught to reflect upon himself how he was or what he did to his mother. In other words, he is to look at himself from the viewpoint of his mother, father and so on.

The client is required to live in a solitary room throughout the period of treatment, generally for a week. During that period, he does nothing but introspective meditation except for three meals, sleep, toilet, and an occasional interview with the leader. The method has proved to be effective in generating certain changes in the client's self-image and worldview so that he can overcome egocentricity, and eventually adjust to social life. Under the system of voluntary prison visitors, prisoners can have chance to be assisted by them through counselling and individual interviews when troubles occur.

Vocational Training and Prison Industry. Vocational training programs in prisons are intended to provide prisoners with a better opportunity for employment and eventual rehabilitation through improved work attitudes and skills. In 1965, 712 inmates were qualified and attained certificates by passing National or Prefectural examinations in such fields as automechanics, boiler operation welding, laundry operation, and barbering.

The total value of production by the prison industries in 1965 was 5,103 million yen, which was equivalent to approximately 27 per cent of the total budget for the administration of prisons including payment to prison officials, and was 247 per cent of the cost of operating the industries. The net profit equalied 89.9 per cent of the amount directly required for the maintenance of prisoners. Breaking down the value of production by type of work done, 56 per cent was obtained from manufacturing, 28 per cent from provision of labor, and 16 per cent from repair work. In 1965, 13.7 per cent of the prisoners were engaged in metal work, 14.4 per cent in paper work, 9 per cent in tailoring, 7.4 per cent in woodcraft, 5 per cent in printing, and 3.7 per cent in leather and hide work.

Nearly a quarter of the prisoners were engaged in maintenance and 1.6 per cent of prisoners stayed in camps and went every day outside the walls with minimum custody to work in water and forest conservation, ship-building, and many other types of production. Prisoners employed in prison industries are paid a remuneration according to the results of their work and good behavior. The amount, however, is not satisfactory, a monthly average being 642 yen in 1967.

Institutions (Non-penal) for Juvenile Delinquents

The Juvenile Law of 1948 stipulates that all persons under 20 years of age are juveniles, and are subject, within the scheme of treatment of offenders, to special procedures and re-educative measures that favor protection and treatment rather than punishment. Juvenile offenders aged 14 to 19 are first tried by the Family Court, and may be sent to a juvenile training school if they are found to be in need of such a measure. These schools—which are 60 in number—are operated under the Reform and Training School Law of 1948, involving about 2,700 officials and a daily average of approximately 9,000 inmates. The Family Court may detain juveniles in a juvenile remand home during a few weeks for the purpose of a pre-investigation. There are 50 juvenile remand homes in the country involving about 1,200 officials including about 200 classification and diagnosis specialists. The annual total admissions amount to approximately 35,000 juveniles.

The Family Court may refer the case to a Public Prosecutor for criminal trial, if the offender is over 16 years of age. A juvenile thus tried and sentenced to imprisonment by the Criminal Court is sent to a juvenile prison.

Children who have not reached the age of criminal responsibility, i.e. below 14, and have violated the law are dealt with by agencies and institutions under the Child Welfare Law. Child Education and Training Homes are institutions under that Law, and receive children and juveniles under the age of 18. Admission to and release from the Homes are not judicially regulated but are authorized administratively by the Governor of the Prefecture, who is responsible for the operation of such institutions and agencies under the supervision of the Ministry of Health and Welfare. There are 53 Homes of this kind built by the prefecture, two Homes built by the State, and two Homes built privately.

There are also three Women's Guidance Homes which are operated in compliance with the Anti-Prostitution Law of 1956, and are under the jurisdiction of the Correction Bureau.

Capital Punishment

The authorized method of capital punishment at present is that of hanging. The execution is carried out in a section of prison specifically designated for that purpose, in a closed

situation so that nobody except those who are directly responsible for the execution are admitted to the scene. This was the
sole procedure adopted for capital punishment in the old Penal
Code promulgated in 1880 shortly after the Meiji Restoration.
Before that, other methods were also used, and during the
Tokugawa Shogunate there were six kinds of capital punishments: *Geshinin* (simple beheading), *Shizai* (beheading for the
purpose of testing a new sword), *Gokumon* (beheading and
public exhibition prior to execution and public exposure of the
head after execution for three days), *Haritsuke* (crucification),
Kazai (burning, a special punishment for arson), and *Nokogiri-
biki* (a kind of crucification after touching the neck with a
bamboo saw in public). For a person belonging to the Warrior,
Seppuku known in Western countries under the name of
Harakiri (suicide by cutting abdomen) was employed as a
kind of capital punishment.

PROBATION AND PAROLE SYSTEM

The oldest correctional institution in Japan which was
primarily aimed at the rehabilitation of offenders was established as early as 1790 in Edo, the present Tokyo. Known by the
name "Ishikawajima Ninsoku-yoseba" (Work-house), it
accommodated vagrants and certain other types of misdemeanants for about three-quarters of a century. The work-
house is renowned for its progressive approach to inmates such
as vocational training, education, and religious counselling.
What is more significant, however, in relation to the history of
non-institutional treatment is the fact that this establishment
provided discharged inmates with well-organized aftercare
services with the assistance of village heads and volunteers.
Not infrequently the aftercare included control and assistance
similar to parole in modern society.[27]

Development of Probation and Parole in Japan

Other precursors of non-institutional methods also began to

---

[27]Akira Masaki, *Shin Kangoku-gaku* (New Penology) (in Japanese)
(Tokyo: Yuhikaku, 1941), p. 113.

take place during the latter part of the last century. First, the old Penal Code of 1881 provided in a modest way for a system of conditional release whereby a prisoner who had served three-quarters of his sentence was to be legally eligible for conditional release to be followed by police surveillance. Although the above eligibility had been in the new Penal Code of 1907 by reducing the requirement of having served part of the sentence to one-third, the practice showed that until promulgation of ordinance relating to conditional release in 1931, conditional release was regarded as an exceptional mercy and was awarded only on a very limited scale.

Secondly, Japan has long been accustomed to the use of *sursis* (suspension of the execution of a sentence). The first statute for *sursis* was enacted in 1905 and later the system was incorporated into the new Penal Code of 1907. Through a few amendments of the Code, the eligibility for such dispositions was remarkably expanded. For a fairly long time, Japan had been prepared for the introduction of adult probation that took place in 1953-1954, by means of the *sursis*. The *sursis* had been stipulated a few decades earlier. It was not yet probation in the full sense of the word because it lacked an essential aspect, the supervision and assistance of a probation officer.

Thirdly, the old Juvenile Law 1922, which authorized a quasi-judicial authority called "Shonen Shinpan Sho" (the juvenile investigation and determination office) to investigate and dispose of juvenile delinquents, provided for a system of protective supervision as one of several alternative dispositions available to the office. The office was empowered to place the juvenile delinquent under the supervision and guidance of a protective supervisor attached to the office or any other appropriate individual or agency. This is generally regarded as the advent of the probation scheme in the country.

Following these developments, the drastic social reform after World War II finally led to the establishment of a comprehensive structure for non-institutional treatment of offenders as an essential counterpart of institutional correction. The Offenders Rehabilitation Law which was promulgated in 1949 opened up a new way to probation and parole. It gave effect to the establishment of parole commissions and probation-parole supervision offices. At the same time, the law set forth juvenile probation as well as parole supervision of juvenile and adult offenders. Adult probation, however, was not instituted until the amendment of the Penal Code in 1953-55. Later the full enforcement of the Anti-prostitution Law in 1958 resulted in the addition of a new category to the caseload of parole supervision.

At present the subjects of probation and parole supervision consist of the following five categories: (i) juvenile probation—the juvenile delinquent for whom probation has been ordered by the Family Court; (ii) adult probation—the offender who has been put on probation "together" with a suspended sentence by the criminal court (This category may be called adult probation because substantially all persons in this category are adult offenders); (iii) prison parol—the offender who has been released on parole from prison; (iv) training school parole—the juvenile delinquent who has been released on parole from a training school; and (v) guidance home parole—the woman who has been released on parol from a woman's guidance home.

Organization

Under the Rehabilitation Bureau of the Ministry of Justice which is responsible at the central level for the administration of nation-wide probation and parole services, there are eight parole commissions located in each of the eight districts of the country. The number of commissioners varies from three to nine primarily in accord with the population of the institutions in each district. Acting for the commission, a panel of three commissioners is authorized to grant and revoke parole, suspend supervision, terminate indeterminate sentences, and decide on other pertinent issues. The commissioners are fulltime officials who generally have professional knowledge and experience in the administration of correctional institutions, the probation service, prosecution, or other related fields. As of January, 1968, there were 44 commissioners. Eighty-eight parole (cum probation) officers assisted the commissioners in the examinations that take place prior to granting parole.

As to the administrative structure, the probation-parole

supervision offices are under the parole commission. Being situated in each of the 49 districts of the country, these offices are responsible for the operation of pre-release investigation and preparation, probation and parole supervision, aftercare aid for discharged offenders and released suspects, application for pardon, crime prevention activities and the like. In discharging these duties, full-time probation officers are assisted to a large extent by volunteer probation officers in each community. These volunteer probation officers are suitable persons appointed by the Minister of Justice. Recent figures of the number of probation officers and volunteers are 700 and 50,000, respectively for the entire country.[28]

All probation officers are civil servants. Generally they are recruited from those who have been educated in the social sciences at a college or university and passed the national examination for the civil service. Initial training courses and refresher courses of various length and levels are conducted for them regularly at the Research and Training Institute of the Ministry of Justice.

In relation to the organization of probation and parole services, further reference should be made briefly to two other organizations providing voluntary rehabilitation service in cooperation with public probation-parole agencies. In the first place, the Big Brothers and Sisters Association has about 10,000 members in the country consisting of university students and working youths. Closely keeping in touch with the probation-parole supervision office in the locality, they assist volunteer probation officers in guiding and helping juvenile delinquents under probation or parole.

Another important type of voluntary organizations are the rehabilitation aid societies approved by the Ministry of Justice.

[28]Aside from the 700 probation officers employed by the Ministry of Justice and engaged primarily in the supervision of probationers and parolees, there is another group of about 1,300 probation officers who are appointed by the Supreme Court and work at the Family Court. In contrast to the former group, the major function of the latter consists in pre-hearing investigations of family and juvenile delinquency cases, whereby it is estimated that about two-thirds of the pre-hearing manpower is being devoted to juvenile delinqueney cases. Incidentally, it should be noted that there exists as yet no system of pre-sentence investigation for the criminal court in Japan.

As of May, 1966, 135 societies of this nature in the country were equipped with rehabilitation hostels to accommodate certain probationers and parolees as well as discharged offenders in need of residential care. Being specialized in terms of sex and age of offenders in most cases, they had a total of 3,888 beds. These societies are subsidized by the national government on a day-capita basis.

As for as probation and parole eligibility, and the duration of supervision are concerned, following are the rules and regulations as provided by the law.

Juvenile Probation. The Juvenile Law prescribes no restriction upon the Family Court judge in placing the juvenile delinquent on probation. In other words, any juvenile who is adjudicated to be delinquent may be put on probation no matter how serious the offense he has committed if he is recognized as being in need of such treatment. The duration of probation is up to the twentieth birthday, or for two years whichever is longer, subject to early discharge or extension in certain cases.

Adult Probation. In contrast, the criteria for the application of probation in the criminal courts are much more complex, partly because the probation system in criminal cases is based on the traditional system of *sursis.* In brief, the restrictions are twofold, that is they relate to the length of the sentence to be suspended and to the offender's previous criminal record. The Penal Code describes the criteria for the use of probation as follows: When the court sentences an offender to imprisonment with or without forced labor for not more than three years or to a fine not exceeding 50,000 yen, it may, with due consideration for extenuating circumstances, suspend the execution of the sentence and, in its discretion, place him under probationary supervision for a period between one and five years. In this case, however, the offender must be a first offender. A person who has been previously convicted may be awarded a suspended sentence and be placed on probation only, if five years have passed since his previous sentence was completed or remitted.

If a person commits another crime during the period of suspended sentence, the court may again suspend the sentence for the new offense, but only if he is sentenced to imprisonment for not more than one year and there are extenuating circumstances especially favorable to him. If the court does suspend the sentence in such a case, it is legally bound to decree probation.

The duration of adult probation is equivalent to that of the suspended sentence, but the former may actually be shortened by means of a tentative discharge by the authority of the parole commission.

Prison Parole. According to the Penal Code, a person sentenced to imprisonment may be released on parole after one-third of his fixed term sentence, or ten years of a life sentence have been served, provided that the offender appears to have reformed himself. The period of parole supervision is equivalent to the unserved part of his sentence, and there is no way to reduce it except by pardon.

Training School Parole. Any inmate of a training school becomes eligible for parole when six months have elapsed since his admission. However, statistics show that, in practice, inmates are generally held in the school for more than a year before parole is granted. In principle, supervision following release on parole from the training school lasts until the age of twenty though it may be extended either by the superintendent of the school or by the Family Court, depending on the degree of extension, or it may be curtailed by a decision of the parole commission.

Guidanced Home Parole. Those women who come into conflict with the Anti-prostitution Law may be committed to the women's guidance home by the judgment of the criminal court for a period of six months. Inmates of the home, however, may be released on parole at any time during the above statutory period of confinement and subjected to the supervision of the probation officer for the remaining part of the six months.

Probation Statistics

During 1966, 39,160 persons were placed on probation, of whom 30,647 (78.3 per cent) were those adjudicated by the Family Court as delinquent juveniles while the other 8,513 (21.7 per cent) were sentenced by the Criminal Court. During the decade preceding 1966, the incidence of probation orders had increased tremendously particularly in juvenile cases. The above two figures of juveniles and adults in 1966 represent 180 and 123 per cent of the corresponding figures for 1956. This trend is apparently the consequence of a general rise in crime and delinquency rather than due to a change in sentencing policy in favor of probation.

Of all the juveniles who appeared before the Family Court in 1966 for any delinquency except traffic violations, 9.3 per cent were placed on probation while the other major dispositions were as follows: referred to the public prosecutor (for criminal trial), 8.6 per cent; commitment to a training school, 3.2 per cent; and absolute discharge before or after hearing, 62.8 per cent. The percentage of probation orders has remained approximately the same for the last several years.

As to criminal cases, of a total of 79,542 offenders who were sentenced to imprisonment in 1966, 54.8 per cent, or 43,573 persons had their sentences suspended. Of this number, 8,795 persons were placed on probation. Thus the rate of probation orders to the number of suspended sentences amounted to 20.2 per cent, standing at 11.1 per cent of the total number of sentences of imprisonment. These percentages had been more or less stable for preceding years.

As of December 31, 1966, there were 65,628 juvenile and 23,968 adult probationers under supervision throughout the country. These figures represent as much as 173 per cent of the probation caseload of ten years before.

Parole Statistics

The number of parolees released from prison has been showing a gradual decline. In 1966, a total of 18,953 prisoners were released on parole, representing 71 per cent of the number in 1961. A similar trend is noted also in the number of parolees from training schools. The total of 6,423 boys and girls so released in 1966 was only 89 per cent of the corresponding figure in 1961. Number of release on parole from women's guidance home has decreased sharply since 1961, and in 1966 it recorded only six.

The total of 18,953 persons released on parole from prison in 1966 represented 55.8 per cent of all releases from prison in the year. Similarly, the 6,423 parolees from training schools accounted for 83.2 per cent of a total of 7,723 inmates released in the same year.

As of December 31, 1966 the total of 18,218 parolees under supervision were broken down as follows: 7,834 from prision, 10,383 from training school and one from a women's guidance home.

Results of Probation and Parole—Their Problems

The results of parole appear to be promising at first sight. Of 19,396 prison parolees discharged from supervision in 1966, 94.2 per cent were discharged successfully at the end of the specified term while only 4.7 per cent were revoked. However, the low rate of revocation is not necessarily related to the positive effect of treatment during parole at present. It should be noted that, of those who completed a parole term in 1966 83 per cent of the prison parolees and 24 per cent of the training school parolees were only six months or less under supervision. A recent research which compared the community conduct of parolees to that of those released after serving a full sentence showed that within 18 months after release, one-third of the former group had committed further offenses while more than one-half had done so in the latter group.[29]

As regards adult probation, 2,209 persons, or 27.3 per cent of the total of 8,098 persons who ended their probation in 1966 had their probation revoked. In the same year, the rate of revocation of juvenile probation computed in a similar manner was 15.7 per cent. However, a recent follow-up study covering a span of five years in average revealed that 46.5 per cent of the 903 sample cases had committed further offenses, and another 9.2 per cent had done so after probation.[30]

[29]*Hanzai Hakusho* (White Paper on Crime) (in Japanese) (Tokyo: Homusogo Kenkyusho, 1967), p. 276.

[30]*Homu-sogo-Kenkyu-sho Kiyo* (Annual Report of Studies made by the Institute of Research and Training, Ministry of Justice) (in Japanese), 1968, p. 200.

STUDY OF CRIMINOLOGY IN JAPAN

In universities it has been a long tradition that criminology and penology are seen as a part of the subject matter to be dealt with by the Department of Law under the name of criminal policy. Such a tradition undoubtedly hindered the development of scientific approaches to crime problems, leaving other disciplines relatively ignorant about the contributions they might make toward this area of study.

Institutions for Teaching Criminology

In recent years, nearly half of the fifty-odd universities in the country which have law departments offer a course in criminology and penology. The situation is more or less the same with respect to graduate study. While criminology is taught in law schools at selected universities, there is not a single graduate school concentrating on criminology and penology per se.

However, the preceding paragraphs are not intended to imply that there is no other department or school concerned with the subject of crime and delinquency. A few universities have special sections within a faculty or institutes in the departments of medicine, psychiatry, psychology, or sociology which show a special interest toward problems of the causation of crime, and clinical aspects of criminals and juvenile delinquents. Some of these sections and institutes are carrying on extensive research activities as well as teaching the criminological aspects of human behavior from viewpoints of their particular disciplines. A few universities have also been teaching correctional theory and practice as one of their optional courses for the past few years.

Researchers of Criminology

Researchers of criminology are found mainly among government and university staff. Under the new arrangement of the juvenile, correctional, and probation system after the war, their number has increased a great deal. They may be divided into the categories of lawyers who are more inclined to penology, or toward the so-called criminal policy; criminal biologists who have medical training; criminal psychologists who have played an important part in criminological research since the beginning of criminology in this country—this field having recently attracted a large number of researchers; psychoanalysts of whom there are still very few; sociologists; and statisticians.

Criminological Associations and Research Institutes

The precursor of the Japan Criminology Association was organized early in the 1910s. Its tremendous development and contribution thereafter in the field of criminal biology is mainly due to the personal dedication of Dr T. Furuhata, and Dr S. Yoshimasu.

The Japanese Association of Correctional Medicine which forms a part of the Japan Medical Association is now presided over by Dr M. Ohtsu. It has maintained close liaison with its American counterpart, American Correctional Medical Association, eversince they held joint convention in 1960.

While the Association of Criminal psychology, presided over by T. Endo, was founded in 1963, criminal sociologists have not yet reached the stage of forming their own association. There are many other professional associations in which a section of members are involved in one way or another in criminological studies. The Japan Penal Law Association has a comparatively long history, being presided by Professor S. Dando. It has held frequent discussions on criminology.

At present there are only a few public institutes for criminological research. Since its establishment in 1959, the Research and Training Institute of the Ministry of Justice has conducted numerous research projects. The subjects of study vary widely, ranging from sentencing to parole follow-up. Important subjects which it took up at its inception were delinquency prediction, and effects of short-term imprisonment. It has also been engaged in extensive research programs regarding the causation and prevention of crime and delinquency. Research projects in recent years include a variety of areas such as criminal typology, organized crime, sex offenses, impact of various environmental factors upon juveniles, and the formulation of delinquency prediction tables.

Studies of clinical approaches to delinquents were also pursued vigorously by a number of practitioners. Psychotherapy and counselling either for individuals or groups are one of the major areas of this category. Another remarkable development has been in the field of criminal sociology. Particularly important are those researches on crime which are related to urbanization, mobility, gangs, and the like.

Recently developments have also taken place in the sphere of victimology. An international research project on "the relationship between boys' expectation of their future as adults and their behavior problems in industrialized societies" has been in operation in collaboration with universities in the United States (Rutgers) and Sweden.

The National Institute of Educational Research and the National Institute of Mental Health also devote a part of their efforts to the prevention and treatment of juvenile delinquency. Their recent projects include a comparative analysis of delinquent and normal pupils in the secondary school; stepmother-child relationships in relation to behavior disorders of children; and delinquency in a coal mine town including a follow-up for ten years.

According to Hoshino and Matsumoto in their report to the Annual Conference of the Association of Sociology in Japan in October, 1968, the following researches have been made in Japan since 1945 in connection with crime and delinquency, causation, and other problem of criminology.

Table I indicates the following characteristics as seen during the years 1945-1968. First, during the period from 1945 to 1954 a comparatively large number of studies on juvenile delinquency as well as on the relations between crime and war appeared. Secondly, the really positive studies began to appear in the period from 1955 to 1959. Thirdly, the studies made during the following period showed variety and, among them, the studies of delinquency in particular family situations (parental situations), of types of crime and delinquency, of recidivism, and of anti-social groups, are noteworthy. The Glueck's prediction studies were discussed, and gave stimuius to similar studies.

TABLE I

Subject of researches	Number of researches				Total
	1945-1954	1955-1959	1960-1964	1965-1968	
(a) Family	4	1	10	4	19
(b) Anti-social groups	—	1	6	6	13
(c) Areas	2	3	16	10	31
(d) Classes	—	—	2	2	4
(e) Social organization and its changes	2	—	4	3	9
(f) Education	1	2	5	1	9
(g) Process of delinquency	—	2	3	11	16
(h) Delinquents and criminals	2	—	3	1	6
(i) Type of crime	1	1	6	5	13
(j) Criminal damages	—	—	3	2	5
(k) Recidivism	—	2	7	3	12
(l) Treatment and prevention	2	6	11	8	27
(m) Prediction	2	—	7	1	10
(n) Sex, ages	1	—	1	3	5
Others	—	1	1	1	3
TOTAL	17	19	85	61	182

NOTE: Unpublished materials distributed by Hoshino and Matisumoto at the Annual conference of the Japanese Association of Sociology, held at Waseda University on October 20, 1968.

GENERAL POLICIES WITH RESPECT TO CRIME PREVENTION

The humanistic efforts to prevent crime in some societies may be listed under the following five headings.

Reforming Criminals

In a patriarchal society, such as Japan was, the education and training of the people played a very important part in the social policy. Confucianism which taught feudal people how to live in society was the main resource in this connection. When the Tokugawa Shogunate drew up the statutory penal regulations for the first time, called the "Osadamegaki Hyak-kajo" (the Hundred Regulations), it did not overlook the need to distribute a citizens' manual called "Rikuyugengi" which showed how to live and which was drawn up with Confucianism as its basis.

The importance of education, particularly for the convict, was especially emphasized. When the Shogunate established a workhouse for vagabonds and ex-convicts under the name of Ninsoku-yoseba in 1790 (which later became a prison in the Meiji era), emphasis was placed on the moral education of the inmates. Sekimon-shingaku, one of the moral philosophies at that time and derived from Confucianism, Shintoism and Zennism, was used for this purpose. It is said that as a result of this moral education many inmates were reformed and became good farmers, merchants, and sometimes officers of the institution itself.

The Meiji Government was one of the governments which attached a great deal of importance to education. It had the simplified opinion that cause of crime should be sought in the lack of education, and that if education was widely spread among the population, the number of crimes which at that time were on the increase, would be lessened.

However, in the prison system as modernized by the Meiji government, the significance of education was under-estimated when compared with more recent experience. The custodial function was the most important. Nevertheless, there were a few provisions made for education and religion, and there were many discussions about the function of a prison. Some emphasized the reformative function, others claimed that retribution was the main function, but no provision was made for either of these functions in the laws and regulations which expressed the policy of the State. In the prison regulations there was a simple statement that the aim of the administration was to maintain peace and order within the prison. It was not until 1934 that expression was given to the reformative function of prison by the introduction of the Progressive Grade System. And soon after the war, in 1946, the Ministry of Justice declared again that the function of the prison was to reform and rehabilitate. In addition it was made clear, by the introduction of the Offenders Prevention and Rehabilitation

Law, that the purpose of any extramural and intramural treatment of offenders was reformative and rehabilitative.

Reforming Delinquents

Reforming juvenile delinquents is obviously a very important way of preventing crime. In this field of treatment for children also the French system was once adopted. In the French Penal Law of 1810, provision was made for a House of Correction to be set up in a separate corner of a prison to which children who were delinquent, had committed a crime, or were beyond the control of their parents, might be sent. The same provision was adopted in Japan in the Penal Code of 1880. With our present knowledge it is obvious that such a system would not be successful in treating young people. Judge Demetz, dissatisfied with the system, built in France in 1839, his own private institution called the Mettray Institution.[31] The Mettray experiment was copied by Shinkyo Takase who had a keen desire to rehabilitate young delinquents and considered the system adopted by the penal law to be inadequate. He opened a private reformatory school in Tokyo in 1885. This was the first institution for delinquent children in Japan.

In 1900 the Government passed the Reformatory School Law for delinquent children following the pattern of the Industrial School System in England, but it received no support from society. The prefectural government which had responsibility for building institutions was not enthusiastic because of lack of funds. During this period the House of Correction and the Reformatory School were engaged in treating young delinquents. Then in 1907 the new Penal Code abolished the House of Correction which used to be attached to a prison.

The Penal Code of 1907 made no reference to the treatment of delinquent children. It was not until 1922 that a general system for treating juvenile delinquents was put forward in the form of the Juvenile Law. The law was based on a mixture of American and German legislation. It provided that (i) the establishment of Shonen-Shinpan-Sho (the Juvenile

---

[31]Barnes and Teers, *New Horizons in Criminology* (New York: Prentice Hall, Inc., 1947), p. 911.

Investigation and Determination Office) in which an officer who had been a prosecutor or a judge would deal with the cases sent there; (*ii*) those delinquents under 18 years of age who had committed an offense but who had been released by suspension of prosecution or who were prone to commit an offense, should be sent to the center; (*iii*) the center administered one of the measures of protection to the youth who was sent there; (*iv*) the indeterminate sentence was adopted as a special punishment of young people; and (*v*) a child under 16 could not be sentenced to death.

On the basis of this law, various preventive measures against juvenile delinquency were started. For example various types of homes for homeless delinquent children were established, and there were vigorous campaigns once a year for the prevention of juvenile crime.

After the war, the need for a complete revision of the system became imperative with the setting up of the new Constitution. It was important that the treatment of juveniles should have a constitutional basis. The principle of Article 32 of the Constitution which states that no person should be denied the right of access to the courts, ought naturally to apply to juvenile delinquents also. In 1948 the new Juvenile Law was promulgated and came into force in 1949.

It provides in the first place that juvenile delinquents and offenders under the age of 20 are subject to the jurisdiction of the Family Courts which were newly set up for this purpose. By juvenile delinquents are meant children under 14 who commit offenses and pre-delinquents who are prone to commit offenses.

Secondly, there are two measures of treatment; a penal measure and a protective measure.

Thirdly, every case shall be sent to the Family Court in the first instance. This procedure is entirely different from that of ordinary criminal cases. A Family Court considers the case and if it finds that the case should be dealt with by a penal measure, it sends it to a prosecutor for public prosecution.

Fourthly, there are three kinds of methods used by a family court as protective measures: (*i*) probation or juvenile probation, a literal translation is "protective supervision"; (*ii*) commitment to a child education training home under the jurisdiction of Health and Welfare Ministry; and (*iii*) commitment to a reform and training school under the jurisdiction of the Ministry of justice.

Fifthly, prior to a final decision, a Family Court may place juveniles under the supervision of a family court probation officer for further investigation, a disposition called temporary probation.

Helping Ex-Prisoners

The care and protection of the ex-convict is also very important for the prevention of crime.

There are various aspects to the field of prison aftercare, such as giving money or food, securing a shelter, finding a job, providing medical service, or, in a word, giving relief support to prisoners. From the early days of the Meiji period the need to help ex-convicts in order to prevent crime was keenly appreciated by a certain section of society, but public opinion and the lack of funds for government activities prevented this need being realized. Therefore the government of the day devised a strange system of allowing ex-convicts to stay in prison.

The prison regulations of 1882 provided that those who had nowhere to go on discharge might be permitted to remain in a separate part of the prison and to earn their livelihood (Article 30). This was an entirely bureaucratic arrangement and in the course of time the government got into serious financial difficulties due to the gradual increase of ex-prisoners remaining in prison. The system was repealed in 1889 and the government hoped that a voluntary service of this nature organized by private citizens would replace it.

It was in 1888 that the first prisoners' aid society was established in Shizuoka city under the sponsorship of Meizen Kinpara, a businessman noted as a moralist for his part in reformation. In the same year the Japan Prison Association was organized, copying the French Precedent of "Societe des Prisons," to promote the aftercare of prisoners.

People, however, were not very enthusiastic about its activities until amnesty granted at the death of the Emperor's mother in 1897 led to the release by pardon of more than 12,000 prisoners at one time. In order to take care of these people, more than 60 aid societies were started which have gradually increased in number. The government issued a decree to subsidize these societies in 1907. The number of societies amounted to 745 in 1927 and to 1,220 in 1937.

An epoch-making step was taken by the enactment of the Law for Services of Judiciary Protection (Shiho-Hogo Jigyo Ho) in 1939. This law not only clarified the legal framework of aid and assistance to the discharged and standardized the methods, it also provided for the supervision and guidance of the voluntary aid societies. In addition, the most important step was the provision of the employment of volunteers for the aftercare of individual cases. The volunteer was then called Shiho-Hogoiin (a judiciary patron), and now is called Shiho-Hogoshi (a volunteer probation officer). The system originated from a local practice in the Fukui Prefecture where the Discharged Prisoner's Aid Society, Fukudenkai, asked an influential section of the community in towns and villages to become patrons for discharged prisoners. This occurred at the time of the pardon given in the memory of the death of Meiji Emperor in 1913.

After the war, great strides were made in the development of aftercare, and extramural treatment of offenders. In this connection three laws promulgated after the war, need to be mentioned: (i) the Offenders Rehabilitation Law, 1949; (ii) the Law for the Aftercare of Discharged Offenders, 1950; and (iii) the Law for Probationary Supervision of Persons under Suspension of the Execution of Sentences, 1954.

The first deals with parole, the second with aftercare, and the third with probation. Among these three, the law dealing with aftercare supersedes the Law for Services of Judiciary Protection mentioned above. It makes available and and assistance to those discharged prisoners who ask for it, while the other two laws provide supervision and aid during the terms of probation or parole. The former law makes provision for optional assistance, while the character of the latter is mandatory.

The law makes several important stipulations on aftercare:

First, the government is made responsible by this law for providing rehabilitation aid to the persons mentioned in it.

Secondly, the persons entitled to aid and assistance in emergency situations by this law are the persons who have been discharged from imprisonment.

Thirdly, the approval for the establishment of an aid society, as well as the matter of a subsidy to, and the supervision of such a society are regulated by this law.

Fourthly, the aid provided by this law is of a temporary character and cannot be extended beyond six months.

Fifthly, there are two types of aids: (*i*) temporary aid such as helping a prisoner to return home and giving or lending money or articles to him; and (*ii*) continuous aid such as helping offenders to obtain the necessary education, training, medical treatment, recreation or employment, to better themselves and to adjust to their environment, e.g. by means of taking them into a hostel established by an aid society.

General Social Policies

General social welfare services are, of course, one of the most important factors in the prevention of crime. The Meiji government in its early period was too occupied with other important matters to consider any welfare services to the people. In 1874 the government issued regulations for helping the poor called "Jikkyu Kisoku," but the cases falling within the regulation were strictly limited to the extremely poor who were living alone and could not work on account of old age (over 70 years of age), illness, deformity, or tender age (under 13 years). People qualifying under these regulations could be given just the necessary food.

From 1900 onwards people became conscious of the government's responsibility for the welfare of the poor and the underprivileged. This was due to the influence of "social policy" of European countries. "Social policy" and "criminal policy" entered around the same time into the conscience of the Japanese people. "Criminal policy," in one sense, led to the enactment of the new Penal Code of 1907, while the "social policy" had merely led to an awakening of ideas in a section of society. The first strike of the laboring classes took place in a textile factory in Osaka in 1894. The government did nothing much in the social welfare services until 1933.

The government enacted the relief law in 1933 which extended the relief activities to other needs than just food supply (livelihood aid, birth aid, occupational aid, and death aid), and provided a voluntary worker's service for the first time. As for the latter, there was an experimental attempt at this sort of service in Osaka. Dr S. Ogawa, who was once an important promoter of prison reform, was invited after his retirement from the prison service by the Osaka prefectural government as a consultant to the governor, and there he initiated a voluntary workers system—a system with which he had become familiar by studying the European experience of social welfare services. This was adopted in Osaka at the time of the economic depression in 1917.

It is not unnatural that Dr Ogawa, being deeply impressed with the need for social welfare services while he was working as a prison reformer, eventually came to be a powerful influence in the field of social welfare.

In addition to the relief law of 1933, which was limited to the relief of the extremely poor, the government recognized the necessity of relief for widows and other distressed people, and enacted the law for the protection of mothers and children, and other laws. And in 1938, in order to supervise, and subsidize private institutions, the Law of Social Services (Shakai-Jigyo-Ho) was enacted.

Remarkable changes were made in this field after the war. The new Constitution put emphasis on the importance of social welfare services by means of Article 25, saying that (i) all people shall have the right to maintain the minimum standards of wholesome and cultured living; and (ii) in all spheres of life, the State shall use its endeavors for the promotion and extension of social welfare and security, and of public health. Based upon this provision, laws were enacted in various fields.

First came the Law of Livelihood Assistance in 1946 in which the following fundamentals of social welfare were laid down: (i) the State shall be responsible for assistance of livelihood for distressed people; (ii) people shall be given equal opportunity for access to social welfare services; and (*iii*) The degree of livelihood to be provided and obtained by this law shall be on the level of wholesome and cultured living.

When implementing this law, the government felt the need to amend it with the result that a large-scale amendment was promulgated in 1950, and was supplemented by the Law dealing with Social Welfare Services (Shakai-Fukushi Jigyo-Ho) which was enacted in the following year. The latter was fitted into the context of the Law of Social Services of 1938. It defined the items which were common to the various services, and it also set up local social welfare agencies and other organizations.

With these two laws as fundamental to the system, other social service laws were passed to supplement them: the Child Welfare Law (1947), the Welfare Law dealing with Cripples (1950), the Law on the Feeble Minded (1960), and the Laws dealing with Mothers and Children (1964).

These social welfare laws are obviously contributing in varying degrees to crime prevention. In addition, the Mental Hygiene Law (1950) which laid down the treatment of mental patients, the Employment Security Law (1947), and other laws are also helping to prevent crime.

As a result of these laws, certain social agencies and officers have been supplied to communities, e.g. the social welfare agency mentioned before, voluntary social officers, child welfare centers, child welfare officers, voluntary child welfare officers, consultants to mothers, welfare officers for the crippled, and so forth.

Mention should also be made of a law which was enacted for the purpose of delinquency prevention, through the co-ordination of government agencies in a community at the levels of central, prefectural, and town or village government. This law was called the Law of the Councils for Discussing Youth Problems. Such councils were established at the central and local levels. The central council was established in the cabinet, and the local councils exist in both the prefectural office and the town or village office. Every council must consist of representatives of government departments and youth experts.

Police Prevention

The police are an agency directly involved in the prevention of crime. On the one hand, the quick arrest of an offender acts as a warning to potential criminals, and, on the other, the information and advice which the police gives to the general public also acts as a preventive measure.

The Japanese police force was established in 1871. At the beginning of the Meiji government, military forces which belonged to the feudal lords had been brought to Tokyo in order to maintain order. But soon the government learned of the police forces in Europe.

In 1857 the Regulations of the Executive Police were issued. These regulations played a very important part in the government of the country; they based on the principle that the executive police had the task of protecting the people from danger and also maintaining public order.

As regards the police force before the war, there were two characteristic features: the wide range of its activities, and the strong powers given to the police. After the war, it was the first concern of the democratic government to avoid the danger of a police state, so that the Police Law which limited police activities to the necessary minimum was enacted in 1947. Due to the limitation of police activities, the rate of apprehensions of criminals decreased from 90.3 per cent to 63.8 per cent after the war.[32] However, this may be taken as an unavoidable price a democratic society has to pay.

To make up for their loss of the right to arrest offenders brought about by changes of the system after the war, the police have tried to increase their efficiency by using scientific methods in all their activities. For instance, they are using computers in the finger-print system or the card system of *modus operandi* of offenders. The Scientific Police Research Institute mentioned before is now contributing in a big way towards finding the criminals.

[32]Shoko Takeyayu, "Nishi Doitsu ni okeru Hanzai Sösa, Kensatsu oyobi Saiban ni tsuite" (On Criminal Investigation, Prosecution and Judgment in West Germany), (in Japanese). *Jurist*, No. 189 (Tokyo: Yuhikaku, 1959).

As regards general preventive services, telephone, radio, and TV are used to the full extent. The police are sometimes broadcasting the forecast of a crime in a certain area. Community organization services are also carried on by voluntary persons at the request of the police.

In 1950, a special program of juvenile police activities was drawn up.[33] The prevention of delinquency as well as the rehabilitation of juvenile delinquents is the special object of the program. Juvenile police units have been established in the police organization, and juvenile centers have been built in the main cities under the auspices of police in accordance with this project.

CONCLUSION

The foregoing analysis shows that the Japanese systems and practices in the field of crime and punishment, as well as the philosophy underlying them, have been largely derived from the West. This westernization has been achieved mainly during the course of last 100 years. In fact, the whole system can be understood now in the light of Western criminology and penology. Many common grounds of discussion can be found, if only the linguistic barrier is overcome. Law systems can be classified into several families, such as the Anglo-American, the European Continental, the Chinese, the Hindu, the Islamic, and the African. The present system of law in Japan is modelled on the pattern of the Anglo-American and the European Continental laws.

However, a further examination reveals some unique features reflecting the historical remnants of the feudalistic age and the bureaucratic structure of the modern age. These can be summed up in the following manner.

It can be said that the public in Japan is rather indifferent to the government's actions in relation to the treatment of offenders—an attitude which grew mainly during the feudalistic period. The principle of "keep the public uninformed and dependent" was widely adopted in the Tokugawa Shogunate

---

[33]*Shonen Keisatsu Katsudo Yoko* (The Programme for Activities of Juvenile Police) issued by the National Police Agency in 1960.

regime and embraced by the administrators in those days as the essence of their tenet. Exporting the public to the treatment muted out to the offenders was most intolerable for the authorities. Though appreciable improvements have been made in this field since the beginning of the Meiji era, the credit should be given largely to modern bureaucracy—the general public made little contribution in this direction. It seems that the people have been accustomed to merely expecting the government authorities to do something for penal reform. The Japanese society is often referred to as a "vertical society." No organization for penal reform has ever been formed by virtue of suggestions by citizens themselves. Take as an example the Japan Correctional Association. It was initially organized as the Prison Association and was brought about as a result of the initiation and leadership shown by the authorities of that time. This shows a remarkable contrast to the Western countries where individuals contributed much to penal reform. There were citizens who organized homes for delinquent juveniles or ex-prisoner aid societies in Japan too, but it is evident that even in those private organizations, encouragament and advice from persons in the government had a vital role to play.

It can be said that in Japan modern knowledge and techniques in criminology have not been used fully as far as the practices of crime prevention and treatment of offenders are concerned. Even to this day, persons working in this area of governmental function seem to be frequently preoccupied by traditional legal ideology, and sometimes resort to inflexible and stereotyped ways of thinking. This is reflected, in the first place, by the fact that the system of pre-sentence investigation has not been introduced yet in the Criminal Courts. Parenthetically the system of probation could only be established upon the principle that pre-sentence investigation and probation are inseparable. Secondly, few experiments have been conducted so far in the treatment of offenders. This is significant in view of the fact that it was such experiments that led to improvements of the penal system in many other countries. Thirdly, mass-congregational prisons are still maintained in spite of the strong objections against them.

However, there are two hopeful signs in the form of the

"Preparatory Draft for the Revision of the Penal Code," and an unpublished draft for the revision of the Prison Administration Law. In the former there are advanced devices for the prevention of crime representing progressive thinking. But it is feared that even now it lags far behind the level of advancement of European countries, e.g. there is no provision for the new sanction of semi-detention in the draft. As far as the draft for the Prison Administration Law is concerned, certain new measures and semi-institutional type of treatments like leave for working in the community, prison hostel, and weekend detention are being considered.

DANDO SHIGEMITSU. *Japanese Criminal Procedure*, South Hackensack, N.J., Fred B. Rothman & Co., 1965. Trans. by B.J. George, Jr.

————. *Keiho Kyo* [An Outline of the Penal Code] in Japanese, Tokyo, Sobunsha, 1957.

Homusho [Ministry of Justice, Japanese Government]. *Hanzai Hakusho* [White Paper on Crime] in Japanese, 1967; Ministry of Justice, *Summary of White Paper on Crime*, 1967.

Japanese Ministry of Justice. *Criminal Justice in Japan*, 1965.

Hogo Tokei Nenpo [Rehabilitation Statistics] in Japanese, Tokyo, n.d.

Homu Sogo Kenkyu Sho Kiyo [Annual Report, The Rerearch and Training Institute] in Japanese.

Kensatsu Tokei Nenpo [Annual Crime Statistics on Public Prosecution] in Japanese, 1966.

Kyosei Tokei Nenpo [Annual Statistics on Correction] in Japanese, 1967.

NAKAMURA, HAJIME. *Ways of Thinking of Eastern People*, Honolulu, Hawaii, Tibet-Japan, East-West Center Press, 1964.

National Police Agency. *Hanzai Tokei-sho* [Annual Crime Statistics] in Japanese, 1966.

Office of Prime Minister. *Statistical Handbook of Japan*, Tokyo, Japan Statistical Association, 1967.

OGAWA, TARO. *Hanzaigaku Hyaku-nen* [Hundred Years of Criminology] in Japanese, Horitsu no Kiroba, Vol. 21, No. 10, Tokyo, Teikoku Chiho Gyosei Gakkai, 1968.

ONE, SEIICHIRO. *Keibatsu no Honshitsu Sonota* [The Fundamental Nature of Punishment and Others] in Japanese, Tokyo, Yuhikaku, 1955.

REISCHAUER, EDWIN O., *The United States and Japan*, Cambridge, Mass, Harvard University Press, 1965.

SOJI, KUNIO, *Keiho-Gakusetsu Hyakunenshi* [Penal Law—Theories During One Hundred Years] in Japanese, *Jurist* Tokyo, Yuhikaku, No. 400, September 15, 1968.

Supreme Court of Japan. *Courts in Japan*, 1965.

————. *Guide to the Family Court of Japan*, 1966.

CHAPTER 9

MALAYSIA*

LESLIE CHIN SENG LEE

Leslie Chin Seng Lee is at present serving as a govern-ment Social Welfare Officer in the District of Kinta, Perak, West Malaysia. He began governmental service in 1950, first serving as a Probation Officer and later as Principal of Approved Schools (Juvenile Offenders' Rehabilitation Centers). He obtained his Diploma in Social Studies, Part I and II, from the University of Malaya in Singapore, and became a Book Prize Winner. In 1964, Mr Lee was a guest of the British government and studied Great Britain's social welfare works. In the same year he attended the International Training Course at the United Nations Asia Far East Institute in Tokyo, to study Prevention of Crime and Treatment of Offenders. He has published a number of articles including "A Study of the Problems of Disabled Persons," (1961); "A Study of Therapeutic Group Work for Emotionally Disturbed Children," (1961); and contribu-ted an article on "The Young Adult Offender in Malaya" to National of Crime and Delinquency, in New York, in 1963.

*Several persons have been of great helf to me in the preparation of this article. My particular thanks go to M. Mahalingam, Deputy Public Prosecutor, Perak; Chong Sik Kwong, a practising lawyer; S. Krishnan of the Criminal Investigation Department, Ipoh; and Miss Tan Kim Cho, Librarian Assistant, Public Library, Ipoh. I would also like to thank the numerous people representing various professions, from the

THIS STUDY IS ABOUT West Malaysia (the former Federation of Malaya) and does not include the states of Sabah and Sarawak because information from these two states is not easily available.

Malaysia was established on September 16, 1963. It comprises the Federation of Malaya consisting of eleven states, Sabah and Sarawak. Malaysia has a diversity of races and cultures in the population of just over 10 million. Besides the indigenous people of the component states like the Malays, Sea Dayaks or Land Dayaks of Sarawak, Dunsuns, Kadazans, and other minor groups of Borneo, there are the Chinese, Indians, Pakistanis, Arabs, Europeans, and Americans. Each of these ethnic groups has a distinct way of life. In Malaya the indigenous people are all Malays who lead a predominantly rural life. Against the indigenous background are the Chinese descendants of immigrants who, together with Indians, Pakistanis, and Europeans, dominate the urban scene. The Chinese are largely occupied in the tin and rubber industries and in business and commerce. The Indians, largely Tamils from South India, work on the rubber plantations. Of late, however, increasing numbers of people of all races have entered the professional and civil services. The Europeans, mainly British, continue to play an important role in the rubber and tin industry, commerce, and other professions. The Eurasians, a large number of whom are of part of Portuguese extraction from Malacca, lend color to Malaysia's racial complexity and harmony.

According to the census, the population figure on December 31, 1965, is 9,557,804.[1] The racial composition for West Malaysia is Malays just over four million, Chinese nearly three million, Indians and Pakistanis nearly one million, and others nearly two hundred thousand. There is a culture diversity for the most part created by religious influences. The

---

legal field, the courts, police force, the Social Welfare Department, the Prisons Department, and the University of Singapore, who put up with me cheerfully during my researches and whose kindness made my task easier.

[1] *Official Year Book*, Malaysia, 1966, p. 28.

Western world has also contributed its share to the cultural and religious heritage of Malaysia.

Yet despite diversity there is a distinctive pattern of Malaysian society. Links of friendship and common loyalty crossing racial and religious barriers are forged by Malaysian institutions like the sporting, cultural, social, and educational organizations.

Of the distribution of population in the Federation of Malaya (West Malaysia), 70 per cent live in rural areas. Over 60 per cent of the population is under the age of 21 years. There is free primary education, but due to lack of teachers and other facilities it has not been possible yet to make full provision for it. In 1966 there were 1,706,860 pupils in 5,725 schools with a total number of 62,183 teachers.[2]

In Malaysia approximately two-thirds of all working persons derive their livelihood from developing and exploiting resources of the country. Half of these are employed in the planting industries or industries associated with the processing of agricultural products. This illustrates the predominantly agricultural economy of the nation.

Despite the political changes in Malaysia and South East Asia in recent years, the nation has made considerable progress in economic and social development. Malaysia's productivity in the economic field has brought about one of the highest per capita incomes in Asia. The ability to expand her economy despite the high rate of population growth (3 per cent annually) is considered a great achievement by international standards.[3] But there are other problems, one of which is associated with the growing unemployment rate. This is particularly acute among the youth between 15-19 years of age, being in the region of 16.5 per cent. However, in comparison with many other countries in this region, Malaysia's social problems are not serious.

The various services provided at governmental and voluntary levels appear to be quite well equipped to deal with its social problems, particularly in the field of youth work. Through its Ministry of Youth, Sports and Culture, a number of pro-

[2]Source: Ministry of Education.
[3]*Official Year Book*, p. 127.

grams have been launched to encourage and guide the development of youth clubs and organizations through grants-in-aid and other provision for training. From 1954 to 1963 a total number of 4,421 youth club leaders have attended courses at the National Youth Training Center. The courses are specifically designed to train youth leaders in recreational facilities, cultural programs, arts and crafts, and community services with emphasis on rural development projects. A more comprehensive training program for unemployed youth was started in 1966 in the form of pioneer corps with the specific aim of placing them in employment eventually. In this connection a total number of 800 young members have been recruited from those registered as unemployed with the Ministry of Labor. An Advisory Board consisting of representatives from different Ministries, like the Ministry of Commerce and Industry and the private sector, has been formed to advise on job opportunities and types of training needed.

In so far as crime is concerned, the annual report of the Royal Malaysian Police Force for the year 1965 indicates a general decrease in the incidence of crime compared to the previous year.[4] The total number of serious crimes—such as murder, attempted murder, kidnapping for ransom, robbery, gang-robbery, extortion, house-breaking and theft—reported was 8,179 as compared to 8,581 the previous year. The number of bicycle thefts reported also decreased by 359, but other reported thefts increased by 180 as compared to the previous year.

The total value of property reported lost in 1965 was $9,920,000, of which property to the value of $2,541,000 was subsequently recovered; as compared to $9,700,000 and $1,800,000 respectively for the previous year.

Statistics on crime in general, offenses against the person and offenses against property are shown in Table I.[5]

The annual report of Department of Social Welfare, Malaya, has suggested that juvenile delinquency in general is a result of urbanization, industrialization and the gathering together with large numbers of the less favored economic strata of the community who have no satisfactory outlet for

[4] *Annual Report of Royal Malaysia Police, 1965.*
[5] *Ibid.,* p. 51.

TABLE I

Year	Under Penal Code	Under other laws	Total
1964	32,804	3,338	36,142
1965	31,934	3,806	35,740
1966	34,864	7,159	42,023

	1964	1965	1966
Offenses against the person			
Murder	162	166	127
Attempted murder	35	37	31
Voluntarily causing grevious hurt	278	291	200
Kidnapping for ransom	3	2	4
Rape	170	184	174
Offenses against property			
Gang robbery	204	195	265
Robbery	1,059	1,032	1,307
Extortion	1,018	817	824
House breaking and theft	5,982	6,199	7,708
Bicycle theft and other thefts	18,900	21,218	22,074

their natural energies. It is not a very important sociological factor in rural areas.[6] It continues to be a not so serious problem and in fact there was a slight decrease in the total number of offenses committed by juveniles in 1965 as compared with the previous year. But there is a strong view held by some social welfare and probation offices that although juvenile delinquency is not yet considered a very serious problem, it is merely a question of time. It is argued that as Malaysia develops economically and technologically it will experience an increase in juvenile crime. This projection poses difficult problems for the country with regard to planning and changes in law. The main offenses committed by juveniles were theft and house breaking which comprise more than 53 per cent of total offenses committed during the year 1965. Some of the contributing factors suggested by officials are personality defects, poverty, a lack of parental control, and broken homes but these could be only partial reasons.

Juvenile delinquency could be regarded as a relatively

---

[6] *Annual Report of Department of Social Welfare*, West Malaysia, 1965.

TABLE II
CLASSIFICATION OF OFFENSES, 1965

Against property	1,368
Against person	154
Sexual offense	15
Gambling	82
Traffic	350
Customs and excise	34
Breaches of municipal by-laws	118
Breaches of detention ordinance	36
Miscellaneous	373
TOTAL	2,530

new problem in the Malaysian community and did not occupy the attention of the Government till 1946, i.e. after the liberation.[7] It is believed that the secret societies also exert quite a strong influence on juvenile delinquency. Secret societies are traditionally Chinese institutions conceived originally on the Chinese mainland as quasi-benevolent societies. These institutions came with the early Chinese immigrants to the land of adoption in Malaysia. They gradually degenerated into parasitic bands of criminal hoodlums indulging in all types of criminal activities and specializing in the protection rackets. They terrorize prostitutes and lure young girls into prostitution. Gang clashes because of conflicting interest are a source of crime and each secret society looks to the young for its recruitment and expansion of activities.

In the main cities of Malaysia today, police claim to have had reports of secret society thugs forcing school-going juveniles under threat of assault to part with their pocket money. The more criminally inclined student may respond by joining the gang. Police methods of combating secret societies influence on juveniles include the provision of mobile patrols and beat-men in areas where students are normally way-laid by secret society thugs during hours of student movements between schools and homes.

However, this form of action has not been successful because of the impossibility of providing one hundred per

[7]Hanif Omar, "Juvenile Delinquency in Malaya" (Unpublished Report), 1964.

cent coverage. An additional police effort takes the form of giving talks[8] to children on the menace of secret societies with a view to getting students to keep away and to report on the presence of thugs. The government is urged to increase the number of trained Probation Officers to supervise youthful offenders effectively. Some parents, the police claim, are indirectly assisting the growth of the secret society menace by keeping their children—who are victims of secret societies —from coming forward to identify the oppressors and testify against them. The police constantly urge parents and teachers to co-operate in their efforts to combat the growth of the secret society menace.

TABLE III
CRIMES INVOLVING SECRET SOCIETIES

	1964	1965
Murder	22	13
Attempted murder	8	4
V.C.G.H.	16	14
Seizable forms of simple hurt	52	44
Rioting	56	30
Gang robbery	19	21
Robbery	34	55
Extortion	93	38
Offenses under the Societies Ordinance No. 28/49	3	4
Offenses under the PCO No. 13/59	34	36
Offenses under the R.R. Enact. Cap. 39	52	62
Other offenses	78	75
TOTAL	467	396

SOURCE: *Annual Report of Malaysia Royal Police Force, 1965.*

The system of law used in the country was introduced by the British. It consists of the Indian Evidence Act, the Penal and Criminal Procedure Codes (of British India) with slight alterations, and a Civil Procedure Code based on the English Judicature Acts. The common law of England and the doctrines of Equity shall apply as far as local circumstances permit.

[8]Sponsored under Police School Liaison Program, see section entitled "Probation and Parole System."

CRIMINAL LAW

Any attempt to define crime encounters a serious difficulty.
A crime may be defined as an offense against the State, capable of being followed by penal sanction. A crime differs from
an offense against an individual or individuals arising from,
e.g. breaches of contract or of trust, and from torts. The
basis of criminal law is the Penal Code largely borrowed from
India.

Legal Definition of Crime

The word "crime" is not defined anywhere in the Penal Code.
The equivalent word is "act" or "omission." The Criminal
Law as reflected in the Penal Code declares which acts of
individuals constitute crimes and prescribes the penalty to
which persons are liable if they are proved to have committed
them. The act itself, such as murder or robbery, may affect
primarily one member of the community, but it is of such a
nature that the public must be protected against the consequences of its commission and so it is treated as a public
wrong and punished accordingly. Since crimes are offenses
against the State therefore the latter takes the initiative in
prosecuting criminals. The State is in theory (though sometimes not in actual practice) always responsible for conducting prosecution, and such criminal proceedings are conducted
in the name of the Public Prosecutor.

Thus the aim of a criminal proceeding is not so much to
give relief to an injured party (though many crimes such as
causing hurt may give rise to an independent suit at the later
stage) but to determine whether the offense has been committed, and to award punishment accordingly. It is true that
crimes differ from civil wrongs but it is not correct to say
that the same set of facts can never constitute both a crime
and a civil wrong, for criminal law overlaps at many points.
For example, if X takes Y's motorcar without Y's consent, X's
act may, under certain circumstances, constitute both a crime
of theft and a tort of conversion.

Apart from the Penal Code offenses there are others known
as Statutory Offenses codified in the form of statutes called

Acts, Ordinances or Enactments, and of Rules and Regulations and by-laws made under the authority of the statutes. Unlike Penal Code offenses these statutes have dispensed with requirement of "mens rea." The penalty under Statutory Offense may be small but the damage to the public occasioned by the commission is sometimes great and therefore the legislature is aware that the state of mind of the accused would be exceptionally difficult to establish with any degree of certainty such as in offenses like operating a radio or TV without a licence, or not closing shop on a particular public holiday.

Legal Definition of Juvenile Delinquency

The Juvenile Courts Ordinance defines a juvenile offender as one who is above the age of 7 and under 17 years of age.[9] The Malayan Penal Code enacts a presumption of innocence in children under seven years of age. Again from 7—12 years, the child is presumed to be incapable of crime intellectually if it can be shown to the court that he has not attained sufficient maturity to judge the nature and consequences of his act.

A significant distinction exists between a child and a young person. A child is a person between the age of 7 and 14 years, while a young person is between 14-17 years. Approved School Order is generally made for children while Henry Gurney School Order is only used for young persons. Two types of juvenile offenders can be classified (*i*) those who commit offenses under the Penal Code, and Statutory Laws like Ordinances or Enactments; and (*ii*) those who are termed as being in need of care and protection, and beyond parental control.

The latter are not so much offenses as actions requiring preventive measures. They give opportunities to the Court to help the offenders become law-abiding. The definition of "in need of care and protection" is broad and loose, and covers children or young persons "who have no parents or guardians, or parents or guardians unfit to exercise proper care and guardianship."

[9]*Juvenile Courts Ordinance*, 38/47.

Such statutory offenses are permissive rather than mandatory. It is not incumbent on the court and the officials to treat all such children as delinquents. The enforcement agencies, judicial and correctional, are expected, however, to act when in their judgment the interest of the child and of the community compel legal intervention. In a sociological sense the delinquent act can perhaps be defined as a behavior that violates the basic norms of the community and when officially known it calls for legal sanction.

The term "young adult offender"[10] is generally used to refer to a person who has attained the age of 17 years but not reached 21 years of age. The judicial policy is, while treating him as an adult for all purposes of trial and conviction, to discourage passing a sentence of imprisonment if he is a first offender. Imprisonment is generally ordered if no other suitable method of punishing him is available, including probation. Under the Juvenile Court Ordinance, the Supreme Court has power to commit him to Henry Gurney School (Borstal Institution) until he has attained 21 years of age.

CRIME STATISTICS

The statistics under study apply to West Malaysia only (as those for East Malaysia covering the two states of Sabah and Sarawak are not available; in any case, the figures for East Malaysia are a negligible factor).

Crimes Reported to the Police

It has not been possible to obtain the figures for other agencies engaged in law enforcement like the Customs and Excise, Municipality, and Income tax, nor do the statistics obtained include traffic offenses. The figures presented in Table IV represent only true seizable offenses reported to the police—by which it is meant that the police has power to arrest ordinarily the person who is so reported under the Penal Code or under any other law.

Number of reports made to the police does not accurately

---

[10]Definition derived from a Circular of the Federal Registry of the Judicial Department, 1954.

TABLE IV
WEST MALAYSIA

	1967	1966	1965	1964	1963	1962	1961	1960
Seizable offenses reported to the police*	46,861	42,023	35,740	36,142	32,183	30,449	27,261	31,399
Number of persons involved in criminal proceedings		108,324	106,483	105,603	110,286	115,959	110,629	111,287
Number of convictions (in criminal cases only)	81,498	81,802	83,024	83,622	86,444	92,408	88,396	93,030
Number of cases (criminal) heard in courts		98,350	97,160	95,970	102,095	109,238	103,024	103,193
Yearly increase or decrease in RATE in relation to number of criminal cases		−4,843 (−4.7%)	−6,033 (−5.8%)	−7,223 (−7%)	−1,098 (−1.1%)	+6,045 (+5.9%)	−169 (−0.16%)	

SOURCE: Federal Registry, Supreme Court, Malaya; *Official Year Books*; *Annual Reports of Royal Malaysia Police*; and *Annual Reports of Department of Social Welfare*, West Malaysia.

*No statistics available of crimes/offenses reported to other agencies. It refers only to seizable offenses under Penal Code or other law.

reveal the criminality of the police districts. It is necessary to turn to other methods, like the number of investigation papers put up by the police, to get a more accurate picture of the size of the problem. For the year 1962, the number of initial reports made to police was 454,113, but out of this only 31,255 investigation papers were put up.

Number of Arrests

As mentioned earlier, Table IV shows the number of seizable offenses reported to the police. For the year 1967 there was an increase of 4,838 over the previous year, but compared with 1960, the increase was 5,462. It was not possible to give the number of arrests by police, since the figures are not available except for the year 1967. The number of persons reported to have been arrested for seizable offenses was 23,834. Court statistics, however, may be helpful in revealing the number of persons involved in criminal proceedings. It is assumed that this figure also includes non-penal code offenses, i.e. offenses under other Statutory Acts, municipal offenses and a host of others. The number of persons involved in criminal proceedings has remained somewhat constant from 1960 to 1966, beginning with 111,287 and ending with 108,324 in 1966. It is useful to compare the figures with the number of criminal cases, and there does not appear to be any significant increase from 1964 to 1966. Between these two years the drop is 2,380.

Number of Convictions

From 1960 to 1966, there is an apparent decrease in the number of convictions except for 1962, as illustrated in Table IV. The decrease began in 1963 with 86,444 to 81,802 in 1966, but it represents a negligible decrease.

Prosecution in criminal cases in the subordinate courts, like Magistrate's Courts and Sessions Courts in the country are normally carried out by police prosecutors. The number of convictions secured for 1964 and 1965 is as follows:

TABLE V

	1964	1965
Serious cases	7,712	6,500
Summary arrest and summons cases	134,668	119,039

The number of prosecuted cases for 1967 is 65,177.

Recidivists. Information regarding recidivists is not obtainable from either the police or the courts or from any published reports. In regard to juvenile offenders, however, the percentage of recidivists for 1964 and 1965 was 157 (6.4 per cent) and 179 (7.4 per cent), respectively.

Following are the various crimes according to types of crime index.

Crime against the Person

This is a seizable type of offense and generally speaking, it means the police can arrest without a warrant. The main offenses have been summarized in Table VI.

An increase of 40 murders was reported in 1967 as compared with the previous year, but compared with 1965 there was only an increase of 2 cases. According to the Annual Report of the Royal Malaysia Police for 1965, of the 166 murders committed for that year, 13 of them were the work of secret societies and criminal gangs. Rape has shown steady increase from 1960 to 1967. Between this period, there was an increase of 100 cases. In several cases involving minor girls the offenses are only reported to the police after pregnancy has been discovered. An explanation offered for the proneness in this sort of sexual crime is attributed to (*i*) the isolated working places of young girls who work on rubber estates where, when attacked especially at "unearthly" hours, it is not possible for them to summon assistance; and (*ii*) the living conditions of the village and *kampong* inhabitants is such that men who are not close relatives can gain access, especially on false pretenses.

Crime against persons can generally be attributed to activity of the secret society and other criminal gangs. It will be recalled that gang fights are usually over the control of rackets, such as illegal lotteries and gaming illegal sale of cinema tickets, prostitution, and narcotics. Such gang clashes lead to killing and maiming.

TABLE VI

CRIME INDEX: SEIZABLE OFFENSES REPORTED TO POLICE—WEST MALAYSIA

Offenses against the person	1960	1961	1962	1963	1964	1965
Murder	130	116	126	116	162	166
Attempted murder	42	42	47	41	35	37
Voluntarily causing grevious hurt with or without dangerous weapon	209	246	299	201	278	291
Seizable forms of simple hurt	1,097	1,059	1,097	1,185	1,419	1,115
Rape	118	107	126	156	170	188
TOTAL	1,596	1,560	1,695	1,699	2,064	1,797

SOURCE: *Official Year Books; Annual Bulletin of Statistics;* and *Annual Reports of Royal Malaysia Police.*

Crime against Property

This is the most prevalent type of all seizable crimes which accounts for nearly 50 per cent of those committed under the Penal Code. Table VII shows that in respect of juvenile offenders, for the year 1962, 48.2 per cent were offenses against property, while for 1964 out of a total of 2,530 offenses, the number "against property" was 1,368 which accounts for 54 per cent.

Gang robbery has been on a steady increase in West Malaysia since 1960 to 1967, as shown in Table VIII.

From 87 cases in 1960 the number has shot up to 301 in 1967. Extortion has also increased from 824 cases in 1966 to 870 in 1967, though the peak was reached in 1962 when the number recorded was 1,198. This type of offense has close connection with secret society influence and element, because together with robbery, extortion is one way by which gangs force their victims to pay up in cash or in kind. Gang robbery in Penal Code means five persons or more jointly engaged in robbing. It is common to find gang robbery consisting of four to seven in number, and armed with firearms. They frequently use motor vehicles and display considerable organization and planning in their attacks.

Extortion is reported to be particularly pernicious and a prevalent form of crime and has been practised over a very long period by Chinese secret societies observing a triad ritual.

Another offense which is on the increase is house-breaking and theft. From 5,071 cases in 1960, it has steadily increased up to 8,464 in 1964. This can be partly attributed to secret societies activity but it is not typical. The significant factor is the growth of residential suburbs in recent years, and migration of people from the countryside to the towns, with an increasing floating population in urban areas. The value of lost property reported in 1962 was $5,784,186.59, $7,870,599.54 in 1964, and for the year 1967 it rose to $11,985,822.42.

Other Crimes

Crimes that fall under this category include narcotics, pro-

TABLE VII

STATISTICS ON JUVENILE OFFENDERS (INCLUSIVE OF ALL OFFENSES) FOR WEST MALAYSIA

	1966	1965	1964	1963	1962	1961
Total juveniles brought before courts	2,402	2,411	2,530	2,234	1,922	2,342
Total convicted	1,897	2,010	2,177	1,775	1,576	1,823

CLASSIFICATION OF OFFENSES

	1962		1964		1965	
	Number	Percentage	Number	Percentage	Number	Percentage
Against property	927	48.2	1,368	54.1	1,280	53.0
Against person	118	6.1	154	6.0	116	4.8
Sexual offense	14	0.8	15	0.7	11	0.5
Customs and excise	30	1.5	34	1.3	27	1.1
Gaming	135	7.0	82	3.2	96	4.0
Municipal by-laws	226	11.8	118	4.6	165	6.8
Breach of detention order	21	1.1	36	1.4	36	1.0
Traffic offenses	282	14.7	350	13.5	368	15.0
Miscellaneous	169	8.8	373	15.0	312	13.0

SOURCE: *Annual Report of Department of Social Welfare, 1962, 1964, 1965, West Malaysia.*

Table VIII

CRIME INDEX: SEIZABLE OFFENSES REPORTED TO POLICE—WEST MALAYSIA

Offenses against property	1960	1961	1962	1963	1964	1965	1966
Gang robbery	87	142	174	203	204	195	265
Robbery	450	575	876	910	1,059	1,032	1,307
Extortion	524	702	1,198	973	1,018	817	824
Housebreaking and theft	5,071	5,044	5,378	6,190	5,982	6,199	7,708
Theft of vehicles	NA	NA	NA	NA	940	1,273	1,780
Theft of bicycles	4,107	4,384	4,379	5,334	5,922	6,093	5,739
Other thefts	10,345	10,001	14,663	11,042	12,038	13,852	16,335
Cheating	405	452	532	551	341	493	574
Criminal breach of trust	332	320	723	334	439	362	407
TOTAL	21,321	21,620	27,923	25,537	26,943	30,319	34,639

Offenses against public tranquility and justice	1960	1961	1962	1963	1964	1965
Rioting	103	46	118	110	154	106
Escaping from lawful custody	3	1	10	2	47	31
Resistance/obstruction to lawful apprehension	82	72	69	83	24	31

Counterfeiting	1950	1961	1962	1963	1964	1965
Number of reports	590	110	54	16	15	8
Number of persons arrested	17	1	—	1	1	2

SOURCE: *Official Year Books, Annual Bulletin of Statistics,* and *Annual Reports of Royal Malaysia Police.*

TABLE IX

CRIME INDEX: SEIZABLE OFFENSES REPORTED TO POLICE—WEST MALAYSIA

Gambling and betting	1960	1961	1962	1963	1964	1965	1966
Number of reports	2,146	2,084	2,651	2,897	2,379	3,118	4,552
Number of persons arrested	5,189	4,978	5,216	5,079	4,646	6,953	9,619
Narcotics	1960	1961	1962	1963	1964	1965	1966
Number of reports	1,125	973	1,070	727	566	523	485
Number of persons arrested	1,339	1,016	1,204	812	527	782	573

SOURCE: *Official Year Books, Annual Bulletin of Statistics,* and *Annual Reports of Royal Malaysia Police.*

stitution, gaining and betting, and other commercial crimes.

Narcotics. The number of such crimes remains small as can be seen from Table IX.

The number of persons arrested are 527, 782, and 573 for the years 1964, 1965, and 1966. The main drug used is opium which is consumed by smoking. Before the use of opium was prohibited by law in 1948 there were addicts who were largely the immigrant Chinese and confined to the higher age group— say 55 years onwards. Smoking opium is on the decline and does not attract young people.

Nevertheless, trafficking in narcotics is a problem from the police point of view; and it is necessary for the police to work in close liaison with the Customs Department. Annual total seizures of raw and prepared opium in Malaya for the last 5 years, as given in the Bulletin of the Central Narcotics Bureau are as follows:

TABLE X

Year	Malaya (*lbs.*)
1958	1,584
1959	2,579
1960	3,890
1961	4,408
1962	5,717

Prostitution. It is a known fact that prostitution is wide-spread in Malaya and not only is it carried out in hotels and massage parlours, but also in private houses. Unlike in some developed countries, open soliciting is relatively little. The authorities like the police and Social Welfare are not able to do more than just keep the situation within reasonable bounds.

The police, aided by the Social Welfare Department, are doing all they can to prevent young girls under 17 years from being forced to follow a career of prostitution. While the police has adequate powers to prosecute people who live on the immoral earnings of women and girls, the Social Welfare officers have power to detain all young girls under the age of 18 years in places of safety under the Women and Girls Protection Ordinance. Nearly 60 per cent of the girl delinquents brought to courts either under the Juvenile Courts Ordinance or under Women and Girls Protection Enactment can be said to be in need of some kind of care and protection.

Several factors explain why it is difficult to stamp out this form of vice. Non-cooperation of hotel keepers to keep away known prostitutes from their premises; the reluctance of witnesses, especially prostitutes and their clients, to come forward to testify; and the frequent change of addresses of prostitutes are problems faced by the police and the social welfare authorities.

Gaming and Betting. Statistics in Table IX for the year 1964-1965 and 1966 show a significant increase in the number of cases reported and the number of persons arrested for charges of gaming and betting.

Without question, the unofficial figure must be much larger than what is revealed by statistics. Occasionally, drastic action has to be taken by police against pin-table and fruit-machine operators. Another form of crime is promoting and selling "character lottery," and it is most common in both urban and rural areas. Illegal bookmaking on race days is a prevalent offense which seriously engages police attention. The table below shows the number of persons convicted for the year 1965.

TABLE XI

Character lottery	620
Illegal bookies	41
Other gaming	3,614
TOTAL	4,275

Commercial Crime. For the year 1965, 742 cases connected with commercial crime were dealt with by the police. This was an increase of 308 compared with 434 reported in the previous year. Generally, such offenses are perpetrated by agents and employees of firms and government departments, bogus companies and bogus traders, and tricksters. The increase has been attributed to the rapid growth of industry and commerce in the country.

THEORIES OF CRIME CAUSATION

The causal problem is the most difficult one in the entire realm of criminology. In Malaysia no literature which can be used as a text reference has been written or published except for small booklets and pamphlets with each author trying to cover an aspect of the problem. Working papers at seminars and annual government reports of departments concerned in services with criminal and delinquents suffer from inadequacy of materials collected, lack of depth in study, and from inconsistency in follow-up. Although they are useful materials for both professional and lay readers a good deal of further study has to be done before they can provide an objective basis for the more serious students of criminology. The theses submitted by students at the University of Singapore as a graduation exercise to qualify for the diploma in social studies are also useful, but there again, they tend to deal with the problem in an unintegrated fashion. Valuable information could be derived if it is possible for their findings to be co-ordinated and integrated by experts.

A search for causes of delinquent and criminal behavior is beset by many difficulties. Let us consider first the major handicaps to etiological research. It is common knowledge that a science of normal behavior is prerequisite to the scientific analysis of human behavior but there is no denial of the fact that such a well-systematized science is still lacking. Modern developments in psychology, social psychology, psychiatry, and psycho-analysis tend to interpret human behavior subjectively and make guesses about human dynamics.

Apart from the basic difficulty inherent in the lack of an organized behavior science, there is another serious and persisting problem presented by over-simplification of causation. There is the ready tendency to attribute complex behavior to a single cause or to a few simple factors.

Let us consider some of the theories of general causes. Shaw and Mckay[11] pointed out in their ecological studies that there is relationship between delinquency and disorganized neighborhood. This explanation, however, is too narrow and

[11]Clifford Shaw and H.D Mckay, *Juvenile Delinquency and Urban Areas* (Chicago: University of Chicago Press, 1942).

excludes consideration of the significant psychological and constitutional factors in the individual who has become socially deviant. The American criminologists,[12] Lindesmith and Dunham, attempt to divide offenders into social criminals and individual criminals. They regard the former as a group product of the sociological influences of the community and the culture upon the person. This group is considered to be the result of non-social individual forces. Walter Reckless[13] distinguishes between the constitutional and the situational factors and says that the majority of sociological criminologists support his theory of the situational delinquent. In contrast Healy and Bronner[14] have stressed mainly the relationship between the internal and external forces with regard to the emotional stresses suffered by the child, principally as a result of his subjective responses to circumstances in his immediate primary groups. For purposes of simplification the causative theories may be grouped under the following four headings: (*i*) psychological theory—the home and family in relation to crime; (*ii*) biological theory; (*iii*) psychopathy and crime; and (*iv*) sociological theory—social institutions and crime.

Psychological Etiology

Home and Family. It is an established truth that the family plays an exceptionally important role in determining the behavior of the child considering the degree and amount of exclusive contact between the child and his parents during the period of his greatest dependency—and the continuation of this intimate and exclusive contact for several years later. The theory of a born criminal is now outdated. In a world of rapid social changes the task of child training is no longer simple as it existed in the early primitive societies.

Types of Homes and of Family Relationships. The homes of delinquent children are frequently characterized by one or more of the following conditions[15]: poverty; large number of

---

[12]A.R. Lindesmith and H. Warren Dunham, "Some Principles of Criminal Typology," *Social Forces*, Vol. 19, 1941.

[13]Walter Reckless, *Criminal Behavior*, 1940.

[14]Healy and Bronner, *New Light on Delinquency and its Treatment*.

[15]These factors of a broken home were the findings of a sample survey on children in an approved school in West Malaysia, 1962.

children; absence of one or both parents by reason of death, divorce or desertion; unemployment; ineffective, immoral, alcoholic, or incompatible parents; crowded housing conditions; and parents themselves who suffer from various psychological or emotional ailments, including stresses.

Cyril Burt concluded in his study in England that vice and crime were present five times as frequently in the homes of delinquents as in homes of non-delinquents. This shows that criminologistic behavior of parents or other members in the child's family has a bearing on the child's behavior.

The broken home which has become unfavorable by reason of death, divorce, or desertion is an important contributory factor. In an approved school in Malaysia, statistics based on a survey show that 80 per cent of such children are the products of broken homes. Cyril Burt[16] also found about twice as many broken homes in the delinquent group than he did in the control group in England.

The type of home from which children come is important for another reason. In such homes training and discipline is usually characterized by indifference, neglect, or extremism of parents, who do not train or control children correctly at their early age. It is common to hear complaints in Juvenile Courts by parents, usually from the lower socio-economic class, charging their own children to be uncontrollable. This, one often finds, is due in part to the lack of affection and concern for the child.

The foregoing general processes would seem to reveal a situation in which (i) the child would assimilate within the home by observing his parents or other members' attitudes and behavior patterns; and (ii) the home would fail to train the child to deal with community situation in the law-abiding manner.

It has also been suggested that psychological tension and emotional disturbances in the home may arise from favoritism, rejection, insecurity, harshness, and irritation which will produce adverse effect upon children.

The delinquent is often considered to suffer from emotional

---

[16]Cyril Burt, *The Young Delinquent.*

disturbance which is a continuation of those occurring in his home. David Abrahamson[17] observes that such tensions and disturbances at home can drive a child away from home into contact with delinquents. Slawson[18] found that 54 per cent of the delinquents he studied had run away from home as compared with 4 per cent of the school children of the non-delinquent group. Dickson[19] in his study of 100 young offenders in Sarawak came to the conclusion that 64 of them were the products of incomplete families which in varying degrees have produced a sense of insecurity for these children. If the atmosphere is one of neglect, and extreme discipline such as beating and little or no affection is shown to the child, the youngster will possibly become withdrawn and anti-social. In the research made by Sheldon and Eleanor Glueck[20] of 1,000 boys divided equally into delinquents and non-delinquents, the writers made this observation: "The delinquent boys were largely deprived of affection by their fathers, mothers, brothers, and sisters and not so many of them as of the non-delinquents responded warmly to their fathers and mothers or develop an emotional tie leading to wholesome identification of boy with father."

Biological Causes

Although crime has often been defined as a social phenomenon, some scholars have held the view that crime and criminality are the products of non-social causes. The view has been expressed in the form of relationship between criminality and certain aspects of the biological make-up of the criminal.[21]

Heredity. In the early part of the century the discussion of causes was centered around the controversy between heredity

[17]David Abrahamson, "Family Tension, Basic Causes of Criminal Behavior," *Journal of Criminal Law and Criminology*, September-October, 1949.

[18]John Slawson, "The Delinquent Boy."

[19]M.G. Dickson, *Young Offenders in Sarawak and Sabah*, Borneo Literature Bureau.

[20]Sheldon and Eleanor Glueck, *Delinquents in the Making* (New York: Harper and Brothers, 1952), p. 64.

[21]Paul W. Tapan, *Juvenile Delinquency*, McGraw-Hill.

and environment. This controversy has continued into the present but with decreasing interest. The world renowned criminologist Lombroso and his followers used comparisons of criminals and savages as their method of studying inheritance of criminality. In their view the typical criminal was a born criminal and they attributed this to atavism or "throw back" to lower animal and savage life. Lombroso, despite his significant contribution to understanding of criminals, produced no acceptable proof or explanation of the inheritance of criminality. No one accepts today the theory that a criminal is born and not made.

Subsequently, Goring[22] attempted to prove by elaborate correlations that the criminal tendency is inherited and that environmental conditions are of slight importance to criminality. Goring made careful measurements of several thousand prisoners in comparison with the general population and reached the conclusion that prisoners differed anatomically from the general population. Prisoners, he discovered, were slightly shorter in height and slightly lighter in weight. Goring's work is generally considered as having discarded the early Lombrosian view that criminals are labelled by certain stigmata and form an inferior biological group.

The claim that criminals are produced by their physical and physiological conditions cannot be accepted. On the contrary, these conditions are important for the study of crime causations only to the extent that they affect social interaction.

Psychopathy and Crime

How far can criminal behavior be explained in terms of characteristics or traits of the personality when such personality is of a general pathological condition? For this we look to Neo-Lombrosian theory. Unlike Lombrosian theory which speaks of criminals being of a distinct physical type, the Neo-Lombrosian theory using the same logic of argument and substituting for physical type, declares criminals to be psychopathic. The mental pathologies among several classi-

[22]Charles Goring, *The English Convicted* (London: HMSO, 1913), p. 369.

fication methods can perhaps be simply classified as follows :
(*i*) mental defect or feeble mindedness, (*ii*) psychosis or insanity, and (*iii*) Neuropathic conditions including epilepsy
and psychopathic personality.

Mental Defect. This has been used as a specific explanation of crime based on the proposition that all criminals are
feeble-minded persons, and they commit crimes by reason of
their lack of sufficient intelligence to appreciate the implications of their actions. H.H. Goddard,[23] one of the most extreme adherents of this theory, states that "it is no longer to
be denied that the greatest single cause of delinquency and
crime is low grade mentality, much of which is within the
limits of feeble mindedness."

The proposition that feeble mindedness is inherited has
now been generally abandoned. It is argued that inferior
mentality is neither the specific cause nor the outstanding
factor in crime and delinquency, although it can be accepted
that a higher percentage of delinquent children come from
the ranks of those who are of border-line intelligence. It is
not the mental deficiency, but the inability of the child to
adjust himself adequately in the school or other social situations, which usually causes him to be delinquent.[24]

Psychosis. Although mental disease has been known for
many generations, much disagreement still prevails regarding
definitions, classifications, causes, methods of diagnosis,
therapy, extent in the general population, and frequency
in the criminal population. We are told that the major
characteristic which psychotics have in common is the
patient's complete breakdown or severe impairment of emotional communication. The end result of this being that they
loose contact with reality. Psychotics have been found to
produce social harm in various ways, but this does not
necessarily conclude that all psychotic patients will commit
crimes or legal crimes of any kind.

Psychopathic Personality. The terms psychopathy and
psychopathic personality appear to be used with little or no

---

[23]H.H. Goddard, *Human Efficiency and Levels of Intelligence*, Princ-
ton, University Traits, 1920.

[24]James Coleman, *Abnormal Psychology and Modern Life*, pp. 476-477.

differentiation to describe persons who are regarded as emotionally abnormal but who do not show complete break with reality that characterizes psychotics. Some psychiatrists have classified psychopathic personalities in three groups, the egocentric, the inadequate, and the vagabond. Others classify them into schizoid types, paranoid types, sexual deviants, alcoholics, and drug addicts. If such loose explanations for psychopathy are used, then the term psychopathic personality seems easy to describe anyone for which no other definition could be found. Most writers have designated this concept as a "waste basket" category when inexplicable behavior is confronted. Peru[25] touching on this concept says that the term is commonly "useless in psychiatric research. It does not refer to any specific behaviorable entity. It only serves as a scrap basket to which is relegated a group of otherwise unclassified personality, disorders and problems."

Other Personality Deviations. It is relevant to mention the other effective responses of the individual to a situation when there is a failure to meet his basic needs. These include emotional insecurity, feelings of inadequacy and inferiority, and various accounts of affectional under-nourishment. The child needs an adequate and wholesome outlet for the expression of his psychic drives and wishes as pointed out by W.I. Thomas.[26] He went on to say that the child needs some satisfying implementation of his social drives to prevent frustration.

Healy and Bronner[27] directed their findings to the relationship between personal traits and delinquency. They analyzed a group of 105 delinquents who were treated over a three-year period in three different clinics. This group was compared with an equal number of non-delinquents who lived in the same homes and neighborhood. Findings of this study show that 91 per cent of the delinquents and only 13 per cent of the non-delinquent suffered from deep emotional disturbances. This interpretation however has been questioned.

[25]P.W. Peru, *The Concept of Psychopathic Personality*, Vol. 2 (New York: Ronald Press, 1944).
[26]W.I. Thomas, *The Unadjusted Girl*, 1923.
[27]Healy and Bronner, *op. cit.*

The principal argument against it is that emotional disturbance does not in itself explain delinquent behavior, as is shown by the 13 per cent non-delinquents who were also emotionally disturbed.

Psycho-analytic Theory. Today there is a large proportion of professional persons working with delinquents and criminals who accept psycho-analytic theory to explain criminality. Many such theories emphasize unconscious emotional difficulties of some kind in the causation of crime. This theory is based on the conventional Freudian teaching[28] that the mind as a whole entity is divided into three parts, namely id, ego, and super-ego.

The id consist of instincts or impulses or original tendencies acquired at birth. The id impulses are not adaptable to social life and therefore they have to be repressed or expressed in socially acceptable manners if one is to avoid conflicts with society. Basically this is a frustration of drives common to all human beings. On the other hand the super-ego is the guardian of the moral codes of society and together with the ego it directs or checks the id. By this explanation the theory holds the criminals as a person who has failed to tame the id sufficiently or who has failed to transform the id into socially acceptable ways of behavior.

One can see the major difficulty with such theory because the variables cannot be studied scientifically, and also the elements cannot be measured.

In conclusion the Neo-Lombrosian theory claiming that crime is the result of psychopathy is no more justified than was the Lombrosian theory. No consistent statistically significant differences between the personality traits of delinquents and the personality traits of non-delinquents have been found. The explanation of criminal behavior apparently must be referred to social interaction in which both the behavior of a person and the overt behavior of other persons play their parts.[29]

---

[28]Cressy Stherland, *Principles of Criminology.*
[29]*Ibid.*

Sociological Theory : Social Institutions and Crime

Under this view, the sociological contribution from the impact of social institutions would be discussed. An increasing number of studies have been made to determine what are the effects of the general social institutions on criminal behavior. The basic general institutions such as family, economics, government, education, religion, and mass media as organized systems for meeting social needs of the community will be examined.

Economic Institution. Within this context the social scientist is interested in the relationship between crime and poverty. Two principal questions are often asked: "Do people of lower economic status commit more crimes than people of the higher economic status?" "Do crime rates increase when there is a trade depression?" Studies of the economic status of criminals do seem to confirm that the lower economic class has a much higher official crime-rate than the upper economic class. The principal sources of information giving rise to this belief are, first, that arrests, convictions and commitments to prisons appear to be concentrated on the lower income group. Nearly 70 per cent of a sample survey of the children in an Approved School in Malaysia were classed as poor or very poor.[30] The second type of data is the comparative delinquency and crime rates of various areas of differing economic status.

Shaw and Mckay[31] compared residential areas within each of 20 cities and found a large and consistent relationship between crime and poverty. In regard to the relation between crime rates and the business cycle there is a suggestion that serious crimes show a slight but inconsistent rise in periods of depression and fall in periods of prosperity. In England and Wales, according to Winifred Alkin,[32] throughout the twenties of this century the figures remained remarkably low. When the slum came the level of crime went up steadily.

How far can we accept the above explanations for criminal

[30]Survey on Population of the Sungai Besi Approved School, Selangor (Unpublished), 1962.

[31]Shaw and Mckay, *op. cit.*, p. 141.

[32]Winifred Alkin, *The English Penal System* (London: Penguin Books), p. 13.

behavior? A general positive conclusion about the relationship between poverty and crime is difficult to be established because it is generally believed that official criminal statistics is biased in favor of white-collar crimes, due to differences in arresting practices. This tends to give rise to an exaggerated view of excessive criminality among the lower class. However, poverty as a factor undoubtedly plays a significant role. Poverty in the modern city often means segregation in low-rent areas and forces dwellers to be isolated, resulting in closer contact with criminality.

In Malaysia, with 200,000 young people below the age of 21 years unemployed, there is a serious problem of creating jobs for this large group. Various programs initiated by the government and quasi-government bodies are directed towards increasing employment opportunities for the hungry job-hunting youth. Many projects stress vocational training in addition to academic courses. This seems to be a practical way of enabling young people to find employment so that they can play a useful role in the community.

Government Institutions and Crime. It is a prominent theory in some quarters that crime can be caused by lack of enforcement of laws. It is often argued that a solution of this problem lies in bringing pressure upon the police and the courts to enforce laws strictly which would lead to reduction in crime. But this process poses extreme difficulties, since there are other factors at work which are outside the control of the enforcement agencies.

It is common knowledge that the law makers and enforcers do not always command the respect of the citizens.[33] There seems to be a general contempt, suspicion, and distrust for legislative bodies because they are considered as impersonal and corporate bodies rather than as individuals. At the same time the police are always misunderstood and bear a negative public image. They are considered brutal, corrupt, and inefficient. This is also aggravated partly by the fact that policemen are not selected because of their integrity and code of conduct, rather by their physical strength. In this regard, the Royal Police Force in Malaya has initiated measures to improve

[33]Cressy Sutherland, *op. cit.*

their image and also public understanding of the law. The Police School Liaison Program,[34] among other reasons, is carried out to instil into the minds of the young school children that laws are made for good social and public order and that policemen are not only concerned with arresting "bad hats" but with helping people in general to obey the laws of the country. Other media used by governmental agencies include Police Week when campaign is conducted to educate the general public on the role of the police, and civic courses organized by the Department of Information to explain the general policy of the government in relation to new legislation which may be controversial, or not properly understood.

Crime and the Educational System. Crime and delinquency is often attributed to poor education or failure of the schools, just as they have been attributed to bad homes and poor family training. While schools in general do not have the specific function of preventing delinquency, they, like the family, are now expected to inculcate children with certain values of the law-abiding society and are expected to provide interesting activities for the child.

Dickson,[35] in a study of children committed to Approved School in Sarawak, found that 14.6 per cent of the Sarawak Chinese boys admitted to the home for the period 1953-1962 had reached an educational level above primary three. The overall result shows that the educational level of children in the Boys' home is far below the normal level for students of their ages in the community. The main reasons why the school careers were mostly brief and inglorious can be seen from the following observations gathered from their records. "Expel owing to laziness, disobedience and failure in examinations, left owing to low mental ability and laziness, left due to lack of interest, left due to laziness and truancy, very irregular attendance, truanted in school and never learning his lessons, dismissed for being a bad influence, etc."

A recent feature in the Malaysian School System is the Parent-Teacher Association which is formed, besides other

---

[34]The implications of this program are discussed in detail in Section entitled "General Social Policies."

[55]M.G. Dickson, *op. cit.*

reasons, to bring a closer contact between parents and teachers so that children who are having difficulties in school, and probably on the threshold of becoming delinquents, could be helped by the teacher and parents concerned.

It appears that crime decreases with the amount of formal education. In 1931 MacCormick[36] estimated that about 17 per cent of all prisoners could not read the newspaper or write a letter, and in 1951 it was estimated that from 10 per cent to 30 per cent of the admissions to correctional institutions throughout the State are illiterate. In the Malaysian Approved Schools nearly 50 per cent of the children committed are either illiterate or semi-illiterate although in comparison with the non-delinquent population it would mean that the child should have had at least 4-6 years of primary education on admission to Approved Schools.

Lack of formal education does not necessarily prove delinquency or criminality. Formal educational level may merely reflect the economic status, home conditions, and several other conditions which affect the probability for contact with delinquent and behavior patterns. The fact that some children play truant is undoubtedly related to poor family conditions and to other conditions outside the school as well as to the school program itself.

Newspaper and Crime. Sometimes newspapers have been severely criticized for the part they play in relation to crime. Charges made against them suggest that they promote crime by its constant advertising and by presenting crime news in such a way that it takes away the dignity of the police and court proceedings. Distortion of news causes the public to panic in regard to crime, which makes consistent and sober-judicial procedure difficult. Because little is said about the thousands of people who lead a consistent law-abiding life, the impression is sometimes created that crime is the customary mode of life. The *modus-operandi* of criminals who seemingly and successfully defeat law and justice is so played up in the newspaper that one wonders if this does not en-

[36]Austin H. MacCormick, "Education in the Prisons of Tomorrow," *Analysis of the American Academy of Political and Social Science,* September, 1931.

courage others who might be tempted with the same motive, "to get rich quick," or "to get away for nothing".[37]

Occasionally a criminal states that he got the idea from a newspaper account of the activities of another criminal. Criminals read the crime news and may be quick to attribute their own criminality to some case currently in the headlines. Newspapers do on occasion glorify specific criminals and consequently increase their prestige among their ilk and also among delinquents, who may try to seek self-esteem in an unconscious manner.

Newspapers are concerned with profits; public welfare is secondary. There is also the suggestion that comics produce adverse effect on children. A noted psychiatrist, Marjorie Bell, who is an ardent opponent of the comic has listed the following objections: "they often suggest criminal or sexually abnormal ideas, create a mental preparedness for temptation . . . and create for young readers a mental atmosphere of deceit, trickery and cruelty."

A recent report on Juvenile Delinquency[38] by the Japanese Ministry of Justice listed mass communication media as one of the structural factors producing delinquency. Inadequate control of mass media in exposing sexual or criminal behavior is also quoted in a study[39] of delinquency in Thailand as a contributory factor.

This view, some writers have asserted, has not conclusively demonstrated that comic books are detrimental in any way. Thomas Halt[40] made a study of 235 delinquents and a comparable group of non-delinquents and concluded that harmful books do not produce delinquency.

A general observation that can be made is that any individual tendencies towards delinquency which have been derived from other sources may be reinforced by the crime stories in

[37]*The Straits Times*, February 26, 1969.

[38]"The Present State of Juvenile Delinquency and Counter-Measures in Japan," Ministry of Justice, 1965.

[39]Sanga Linasmita, "Report on the Results of the Research on Causes of Certain Types of Offenses Committed by the Children and Juveniles," Bangkok, 1965.

[40]Thomas Halt, "Comic Books and Juvenile Delinquency," *Sociology and Social Research*, March, 1949.

comic books, but whether a behavior pattern is followed will depend upon the child's prior associations with delinquent and anti-delinquent behavior patterns in his primary groups.[41]

Movies and Television. Since the arrival of television, criticism of comic books and newspapers appear to have waned. Today television and movies as a mass media are subjected to the same charges which were once directed at comic books. Movies and television probably are most effective in glamourising life and stimulating desires for a life of luxury. There is no evidence that children form basic attitudes to authority or morality from exposure to motion pictures. It is true that in some poorly administered delinquency researches, children have been blamed for their deviant behavior on account of motion pictures. Such data, of course, do not provide any conclusive index of causation. Such studies have pointed out a very small proportion of offenders who are excessive in their watching of movies and television. More often motion pictures may prevent misconduct through providing a harmless outlet.

Thus, it is clear that the causes of crime lie primarily in the area of personal interaction rather than the effect of general social institutions, economics, government, education or by the media of mass communication. The proposition that the general social institutions and mass media have some significance for crime is however not to be ruled out. Crime does increase when the general institutions are suddenly disrupted as happened soon after World War II, when in Malaysia during the British Military administration it was found necessary to devise a more effective method of dealing with rising crime and delinquency. This was quickly followed by the introduction of Juvenile Courts Ordinance and legislation giving to the police wider powers to curb certain crimes like extortion, kidnapping, and activities of secret societies.

PENAL PHILOSOPHY

In primitive society the injured party inflicts punishment on the wrong-doer if the latter belongs to another tribe. This was followed by another system commonly referred to as the

[41]Cressy Sutherland, *op. cit.*

private system of punishment, expressed in the form of "an eye for an eye," "a tooth for a tooth." History has also seen the composition system of punishment whereby compensation in money or kind was paid to the injured party. This characterized the penal laws of the early Middle Ages.

Philosophical Foundation and its Historical Development

In the course of history punishment has not always been inflicted exclusively as a reaction to crime.[42] They are influenced not only because of penological, social, and humanitarian considerations, but also because of the dominant trend of political and economic history. When we examine the philosophical aspects of punishment we find that discussion has hinged upon problems of moral justification, the aims and the effect of punishment in general, and of the various methods in particular. The moral justification of punishment at one time used to be regarded as the fundamental problem of penal philosophy. This, however, has now been relegated to the background in favor of the theory that punishment derives its moral justification from the simple fact that it is necessary for the preservation of society against the criminal.

Whatever the controversy over moral justification of punishment may be, it is generally agreed that society has to make its members, with the exception of children and certain categories of mentally abnormal individuals, personally responsible for the actions—provided the methods of treatment take into account the manifold causal factors leading to crime. This theory is now evidently reflected in our criminal law. In Malaya the age of criminal responsibility is seven years and children between 7-12 years are exempted from penal prosecution if it can be proved that they have not understood the nature and meaning of their act.

What are the aims of punishment? An examination of the functions of punishment shows that it has a variety of aims: (*i*) to secure retribution; (*ii*) to secure restitution; (*iii*) to give deterrence; and to reform. The earlier theory was markedly based on retribution, and deterrence.

[42]"The Meaning of Punishment," *Chambers Encyclopedia*, Vol. 11, p. 371.

In pre-British Malaya, criminal law in the patriarchal states was a tissue of barbarities, inconsistencies and class favoritism—three of the most damning flaws in the administration of justice.[43] In medieval Malacca, a man might be impaled or burnt alive or beaten on the chest to death for murder or homicide. The Pahang digest prescribes for a traitor 360 tortures, to be followed by quartering. For treason against the ruler, a Pahang youth in 1880 was killed in the most cruel manner with his scalp down over his eyes and his body tied to a stake to be drowned by the rising tide. Alternative to the death penalty in Malacca of the 15th century were such punishments as scalping or cutting the tongue of a betrayer of royal commands.

In regard to punishment carried out on the basis of restitution, there were instances except for heinous and incorrigible offenders. Tribal penalties always took the form of restitution, a fowl or goat for assault, and a man from the slayer's tribe in the event of homicide. A man who stole a buffalo would live if he had money. The penalty was first to return the buffalo or its value to the owner, and in addition there was a fine of some object with economic value[44]

Deterrence was perhaps the main aim behind the punishment meted out. The usual penalty for theft was the loss of a hand on the first and second occasion and the loss of a foot for the third or fourth offenses.[45] Fine for stealing jack-fruit was the loss of a finger, or instead the thief could have the fruit hung from his neck, and be taken round the town or village in procession with cries and clamour for seven days.[46] Erring women were the victims of obscene tortures.

---

[43] Richard Winstedt, *Malaya and Its History* (London: Hutchinson University Library), p. 99.

[44] Richard Winstedt and P.E. Josselin de Jong, "A Diggest of Customary Law from Sungai Ujong, Negeri Sembilan," in the *Journal of the Malayan Branch of the Royal Asiatic Society*, Vol. XXVII, 1954.

[45] Richard Winstedt, *op. cit.*, p. 100. Perak's 99 laws are less severe and allowed a thief to compound for a first offense, to lose a finger for a second, and to be banished for a third.

[46] Richard Winstedt and P.E. Josselin de Jong, *op. cit.*

Life in a tribe was communal. The death penalty, imprisonment, and mutilation involved in the loss of a pair of hands to the tribe. If a tribesman was killed, the chief of his tribe chose a substitute of the same sex from the tribe of the slayer.

Richard Winstedt's account describes that not only was suppression of crime the main object of law in a port kingdom but also that fines were a profitable source of income to rulers and chiefs. When some man injured another, half the fine would go to the king and half to the complainant. They could not demand justice without the complainant taking something to the judge.

The history of penal methods is closely connected with political, religious, and economic history. As we have seen, the earliest penalties were not of a rational but of a highly emotional character. Capital and corporal punishment, and not imprisonment, were used. The principal methods of execution known to have been used in medieval Malaya were the various kinds of tortures like burning, impaling, quartering, and drowning.

The use of imprisonment as a penalty for crime became common practice just over a century ago. It was introduced by the British presumably after it had started to administer the Malay States. The outmoded cruelty of Muslim criminal law was soon replaced by the Indian Penal Code and the Indian Criminal Procedure Code. The Malay rulers, appreciating the cruel methods of punishing their wrong doers, and the impracticability of the Muslim law of evidence, were glad to adopt the new changes.

Imprisonment, we know now, has undergone profound changes in the course of penal history. Originally its object was not punishment but only safe custody before trial. As a method of punishment, prison in Great Britain became popular perhaps for the first time when criminals could not be got rid off either by mass execution or by mutiliating penalties, when banishment proved ineffective, and offenders were too poor to pay fines. In England not until the 19th century was there a movement for the improvement of prison conditions and the development of experimental methods with prisoners.

In Malaya, sweeping changes in prison reform have taken

place with the adoption of the minimum standard for treatment of prisioners as laid down by the United Nations. In 1953 the Criminal Justice Bill was passed empowering the abolition of corporal punishment with the cat of nine tails, and the abolition of rigorous imprisonment. Under the new legislation the prison authorities and not the courts will determine the conditions under which a sentence is to be carried out. With punishment conceived as also embodying reformative function, conditions have become generally more humane and social work in prisons is now considered an integral part of the prison administration.

Trends in Present Penal Philosophy

The penal philosophy still appears to contain the element of retaliation as reflected in the tendency in many instances on the part of the court to send the offender to an institution.

Retaliction. It may be argued that there is still a strong belief that putting a criminal behind bars would protect the society and prevent him from committing further offense. By and large, however, there is a growing number of enlightened judges and magistrates who appreciate that imprisonment has harmful influence and effects upon persons so treated, especially if it is a young and first offender. The Penal Code, the Criminal Procedure Code and other statutes may appear harsh and basically remain unchanged, but the court with its discretionary power could impose alternative punishment if it considers it necessary.

Misconception of Prisons. There has been a lot of criticism of public preference for degrading conditions in prisons. One such criticism[47] runs like this: "We are well aware of the not inconsiderable and frequently extremely vocal public opinion that would wish to have conditions of detention made as oppressive, degrading and humiliating as possible. These extremes are economically and morally injustifiable and they would not achieve the rehabilitative ends."

As regard the penal administration today, inconsistency and

---

[47] *Report of the Prisons Inquiry Commission* (State of Singapore: Government Printer, 1960), p. 5.

incompatibility is still apparent between theory and practice. On the one hand prisons are supposed to be run with rehabilitation of the prisoner as an objective but on the other hand prison rules, at least some of them, are designed for an opposite purpose altogether. Thus it cannot be concluded that prisons are run entirely as treatment institutions. It cannot be denied that there is ample evidence of the punitive and destructive reactions which appear more frequent than constructive efforts to rehabilitate the prisoner. The continuous high recidivism among prisoners here and elsewhere is, therefore, perhaps not a surprising element.

The New Trend. Considering the development in our criminal law and court, and penal practices, there is room for optimism, and those concerned with this matter—particularly social workers—should have reason to be pleased. There is recognition that punishment can be used to reform criminals. Within the past 10 years or so social workers aided by psychologists, sociologists, psychiatrists and psycho-analysits have made an increasing impact in the field of treatment of crime. The professional social workers, followed by lawyers and those with judicial sentencing powers, have come to realize that criminals are not born and they can be prevented from pursuing their criminal career if the right methods are used.

This gradual shift of emphasis from total punishment to reformation is to some extent reflected in legislation and in the sentencing policies of the courts. Whipping, for instance, though allowable under the law, is seldom used; and in dealing with juvenile offenders, this appears to have been discarded almost altogether. Malaysia has also seen the gradual growth of other more constructive methods. Just before World War II juveniles were for the first time sent to reformatory schools rather than prisons. After the passing of the Juvenile Courts Ordinance in 1949 and with the establishment of Approved Schools and probation service—a service administered by the Ministry of Social Welfare—the court has virtually ceased sending young persons below 17 years to prisons. The development of a more humane and up-to-date method has even gone farther. A policy was adopted in 1954 by the Supreme Court Registry to encourage the use of probation and compulsory attendance centers as an alternative form of punishment for young adult offenders between 17 and 21 years rather than imprisonment, wherever possible.

Rehabilitative Agencies. Legislators and the government have expressed their concern for the reformation of offenders in another form. Today there are agencies which the law has provided for their formation to help the government rehabilitate those subjected to due process of law or confinement. Organizations like Discharged Prisoners Aid Societies, Juvenile Welfare Committees, and Advisory members of Juvenile Court are a few examples.

The Habitual and Persistent Criminals. How do you deal with the hardcore criminals who do not seem to respond to any punishment? This is one of the crucial problems facing the government. It is argued that in such a case it is apparently necessary to give deterrence in punishment. With this in view, legislators and crime enforcement officers consider punitive but preventive laws like police supervision, Prevention of Crime Ordinance,[48] Restricted Residence Enactment, and Kidnapping Act useful. Police supervision as a form of deterrence can be imposed by a court in addition to sentence of imprisonment. This in generally meant for habitual criminals. While such drastic measures are apparently inevitable, it must not be forgotten that many criminals never consider the penalty, perhaps because they are psychopathic or feeble-minded or acting under the stress of a great emotion. Cases are known of prisoners who described their psychological reactions while committing crime and it would appear that little consideration is given to the penalty.

The trend in the statute and in current practice does not seem clear-cut, mainly because in criminal justice there are the constant conflicting demands of the general public between reforming and punishing. The whole system embodies traces of conflicting motives, as for example the imposition of fines may be interpreted as a relic of the days when retribution was upper most.

Various Forms of Punishment. Some of the more important

[48]Persons detained under this Act may be sent to a penal colony, which the government has planned to open in an island off the East Coast of Malaya.

forms of sentences which courts may pass on convicted persons can be considered here. First the death penalty is prescribed for offenses like treason, murder, and kidnapping for ransom under the Kidnapping Act. Execution is effected by hanging. Secondly, the offender may be sentenced to a term of imprisonment. The old distinction between penal servitude, rigorous imprisonment and simple imprisonment has now been abolished. It should be noted that the maximum penalties prescribed for offenses under the law need not be, and usually are not, imposed. These prescribed penalties in the Penal Code or Statutory Acts only provide the courts with the maximum period which it must not exceed. Persons under 17 years of age may not be imprisoned unless there is no other appropriate method of dealing with them. The Juvenile Courts Ordinance provides for persons under 17 years of age to be committed for a period of training[49] in the Henry Gurney School (Borstal Institution) or Approved Schools when they have been convicted of offenses for which imprisonment could be awarded. The High Court has power to commit a young offender between 17-21 years of age to Henry Gurney School.

All courts have a general power to inflict fines except in cases where they are required by law to sentence the offender to death or life imprisonment or to detention during his Majesty's pleasure. Fine is about the most popular type of sentence (70 per cent) and is substantially used in traffic offenses, gaming offenses and miscellaneous offenses under Municipal Enactments, Customs and Excise Ordinance, Income Tax Ordinance, etc. The maximum amount of the fine imposable is in many cases fixed by statute. Upon a conviction for most, though not all, crimes, the court may pass a conditional sentence discharging the offender conditionally on his own bond of good behavior, or make a probation order placing him under the supervision of a probation officer for not exceeding three years.

The probation order may be made subjected to conditions designed to ensure that the offenses will not be repeated. If any of these conditions are violated during the course of the

---

[49]The duration is three years, but it is indeterminate in that the School has power to release the inmate on licence.

probation order, or should the probationer commit a further offense while the probation order is in force, he may be recalled for sentence on his original charge. The same rule applies to persons who are conditionally discharged. The probation order is of an indeterminate nature, for the law provides for the order to be discharged before the duration expires, if the court is satisfied that further supervision is no longer necessary.

On the other hand, the deterrent theory of punishment still remains. In regard to an offender with previous convictions, the court may order him to undergo police supervision after he has completed his imprisonment.

The sentencing policy, just as in other countries, tends to be influenced by certain factors. Where the community is stable and not disturbed by any alarming crime wave, punishment tends to be less severe; but on the other hand when there is an increase in law-breaking incidents, the reaction on the legislators and courts tends to become more punitive.

FUNCTIONS OF THE COURT

Elsewhere in this chapter reference has been made to the independence of the Judiciary, as in other countries like Great Britain. Herein lies the key factor in the relationship between the courts and the government agencies.

Organizations of Courts in relation to Governmental Agencies

By virtue of the Constitution, Parliament exercises some control over the executive functions and in the same way courts also have certain rights of control to prevent and check abuses by the executive authority. The Constitution, being the supreme law of the country, provides a frame-work within which Parliament and the executive may or must perform their functions. To fill in the necessary details in order to regulate the daily life of the nation, this is left to Parliament although it does not ordinarily attempt to regulate smaller details. Therefore, of necessity, it must delegate its authority within prescribed limits to the executive.[50] The method by which this

[50]See *Official Year Book*, 1966, p. 96.

is done is known as Subsidiary Legislation. This means a Minister or a State Government or a Statutory Body such as a Municipal Corporation can, within the limits prescribed by the legislature, make rules or laws as though they had been made by the Parliament—but if they exceed these limits they will become "ultra vires" and void.

There are a number of checks to prevent or minimize an order exceeding its authorized limits. One of these is known as the machinery of judicial control. If the court is not satisfied that a ministerial order has been correctly made within the bounds approved by the legislature, the court is empowered to declare to that effect whereupon the ministerial order ceases to be lawful. The court is a body to which a person, who claims to be aggrieved by some act or omission of a member of the government agencies or an agent of some other authority, may bring an action for damages in appropriate cases or he may apply to the court for the issue of one of perogative orders or injunction.

Judicial control by means of the perogative orders and by means of injunctions depends primarily upon the application of two principles, the principle of "natural justice" and the "ultra vires" principle.

In regard to the first principle the courts have always insisted that where any person has to make a judicial or a quasi-judicial decision, he must comply with the dictates of natural justice. For example, a tribunal charged with deciding a dispute must give a fair hearing to both sides. A rule of natural justice requires that every tribunal should make known to the parties the reasons for its decision, but where administrative tribunal such as the Minister has to make a decision involving questions of policy it is not always convenient that reasons should be published. Many modern acts of Parliament have not conferred quasi-judicial powers upon Ministers and others in such a way as to preclude the necessity for the publication of reasons. This is seen in the provisions of a number of acts like Prevention of Crime Ordinance, Rent Control Act, Banishment Act, and Restricted Residence Enactment.

The "ultra vires" doctrine has many applications. The principle which underlies it lays down that no power must ever be exercised beyond the limits which the law places upon it to exercise.

Another form of control by the courts over the executive is known as the limit of judicial control. These are determined by the sovereign power of Parliament. Where an act of Parliament expressly excludes the jurisdiction of the courts, or where it confers a restricted power or an absolute discretion, the courts are powerless to intervene. The Minister, however, must act in good faith. This discretionary power is absolute and can never be challenged in the courts.

The courts have, on the whole, as far as statutory curtailment of judicial review is concerned, rallied in favor of the interest of the individual as is seen in the slight though significant relaxation in the interpretation of highly subjective terms.[51]

Classification of Courts and their Objectives

Following are the various types of courts in which is vested the judicial power of the country.

Federal and High Courts. The two High Courts which coordinate jurisdiction and status are the High Court in Malaya and the High Court in Borneo.[52] Above these two High Courts is the Federal Court with its principal registry in Kuala Lumpur [capital of Malaysia] having exclusive jurisdiction to hear appeals from decisions of any High Court. The Federal Court also has the same original jurisdiction and may exercise the same powers as exercisable by a High Court.[53]

The High Courts exercise control over subordinate courts through appellate revisionary and general supervisory jurisdiction. Each High Court in the states of Malaya and in East Malaysia is headed by a Chief Justice who under him has a number of other judges. Therefore each Chief Justice is the

[51]Huang Su Mien, "Judicial Review of Administrative Action by the Perogative Orders," *University of Malaya Law Review,* Vol. 2, July, 1960.

[52]Borneo refers to Sarawak and Sabah which became part of Malaysia in 1963.

[53]See *Courts of Judicature Act, 1963,* Section 45; and also see Constitution of Malaysia, which is the supreme law of the country.

head of the judiciary of his state. All other courts come under his administrative control.

The Lord President is the Supreme Head of the Judiciary System in Malaysia. The Federal Court consists of the Lord President together with the two Chief Justices of the two High Courts and all the other judges appointed as Federal Judges.

As mentioned earlier the High Court in the exercise of its original jurisdiction can try all offenses carrying death sentence. Every such trial is held by a jury.[54]

Subordinate Courts. The Subordinate Courts consist of *Sessions Court* and *Magistrate Court.* Both courts have criminal and civil jurisdiction but each has its own power as described by the Courts Ordinace.

The Sessions Court is presided over by a president. Sitting alone without Jury or Assessors he has only jurisdiction to try any offense which carries a maximum penalty of seven years imprisonment. In regard to civil cases the amount involved must not exceed $2,000. The President of a Sessions Court also has jurisdiction in a Juvenile Court.[55]

In the Magistrate Court[56] a first class magistrate can hear cases involving offenses which carry a maximum penalty of

[54]Except for offenses under the Kidnapping Act, 1961, for which death penalty may be imposed. Such trials are conducted with the aid of two assessors. The Jury System has been a feature of the administration of justice in the states of Malacca and Penang for a number of years even before the country attained independence in 1957. But since independence the Jury System has replaced the Assessors System in all the High Courts in the states of Malaya. But the Jury System has not been extended to the High Courts in the Borneo states where trial by the Assessors System is still maintained.

[55]Here he is assisted by two Advisers one of whom is a woman. The duty of advisers is purely advisory which concerns the punishment of any child or young person below the age of 17 years found guilty of an offense. All juvenile cases are heard in close court. The court can try all offenses except those punishable by death.

[56]The Courts Ordinance makes a distinction in magistrates who are divided into first class and second class. The first class is further subdivided into two categories. One composed of government officials appointed as ex-officio such as District Officers and the second persons appointed under the Courts Ordinance who will normally be responsible for a number of courts with him a certain area. They are known as Circuit Magistrates.

up to three years imprisonment, but he has only power of sentence up to one year imprisonment, or a fine up to $2,000, or both. The second class magistrate can try offenses which carry imprisonment of one year.

The second class magistrates, the majority of whom are District Officers or Assistant District Officers, do not as a policy hear cases but they confine their activities to dealing with persons arrested or on remand until a first class magistrate is available.

Magistrates also hold inquest into cases where people appear to have died from violent or unnatural death.

Other Courts. In this country there are Religious Courts which only try persons who embrace Islamic faith and whose offenses are punishable under Religious Enactments. Penghulu Courts have jurisdiction to hear petty offenses involving a fine not exceeding $25.

Qualifications, Duties, Ranks, and Obligations of Judges, Prosecutors and other Court Members

The qualifications for the above appointments are explained in the Malayan Constitution Documents.[57]

Judges. A judge of the Federal Court or of any High Court must be a Federal citizen; he should have been an Advocate of any High Court or Federal Court for a period not less than 10 years or a member of the Judicial or Legal Service of the Federation or of a state for a period of not less than 10 years.

The appointment shall be made by the *Yang di-Pertuan Agong*[58] acting on the advice of the Prime Minister after consulting the Conference of Rulers. The appointment of the Lord President, the Chief Justice of the two High Courts in West and East Malaysia and other judges of the Federal court is made likewise. The Constitution stipulates that any judge appointed will hold office until he attains the age of 65 years unless he resigns or is removed from his office. The Prime Minister has vigorously repudiated fears expressed in Parliament of political interference with the judiciary. "I do not

[57]See Article 122 B of *Malaysian Constitution Documents.*
[58]The Supreme Head of the States of Malaysia.

think any Prime Minister in his right sense would interfere. Once that happens there will be no more law and order and there will be no respect for the law."[59]

An apparent example of the absence of effective political interference occurred in 1964 when a government minister lost a libel case.[60]

Like the British system the judges in the country enjoy total independence, freed from the control of the executive and the legislature.

Prosecutors. The qualifications for appointment of the Attorney General are similar to that of a judge of the High Court. The Attorney General is the Principal Law Officer of the Federation under the Constitution. He is responsible for advising the Yang di-Pertuan Agong and the Cabinet upon legal matters. He has power exercisable at his discretion to institute, conduct, or discontinue criminal proceedings other than before a Muslim Court, a Native Court or a Court Martial. The Attorney General has right of audience and takes precedence over any other person appearing before any court or tribunal in the country. As the Head of the Legal Department, he is therefore concurrently the Public Prosecutor.[61] He is a member of the Malaysian Legal Service and the post is not a political appointment.

Solicitor General. He is next in command to the Attorney General and acts in his absence in public prosecution.

Deputy Public Prosecutors or Crown Counsels. They are similarly appointed by the Yang di-Pertuan Agong. They exercise all or singular the rights and powers exercisable by the Public Prosecutor in criminal prosecutions. They are qualified in law, and upon appointment become members of the Malaysian Legal Service.

Chief Registrar. He is the Chief Executive[62] of the Judicial Department of Malaysia and is under the direct supervision and control of the Lord President of the Federal Court. The Chief Registrar and Deputy Registrar are appointed by the Yang di-

[59]*Dewan Ra'ayat Debates* (House of Representatives), No. 12, August 19, 1963.
[60]*Sunday Times*, December 6, 1964.
[61]See *Criminal Procedure Code*, Section 376.
[62]See *Courts of Judicature Act, 1963.*

Pertuan Agong with concurrence of the Lord President of the Federal Court. The Chief Registrar and Deputy Registrar of the Federal Court have the same jurisdiction, powers, and duties as the Masters of the Supreme Court in England. After appointment to posts in the Judicial and Legal Service, members are eligible for promotion.

Registrars of the High Court. He is appointed by the Yang di-Pertuan Agong with the concurrence of the Chief Justice of the High Court concerned. He is the executive of the High Court and is responsible to his own Chief Justice. He has the same jurisdiction, powers and duties as the clerks of criminal courts in England. Overall control of the Registrars of High Courts is exercised by the Chief Registrar of the Federal Court. It must be remembered that they have to be citizens of the country and have to be an Advocate and Solicitor before they can qualify for appointment.

President of Sessions Court.[63] They are appointed by the Yang di-Pertuan Agong, and must be qualified in law.

Magistrates are appointed by the Rulers or Governors of the states in which they officiate and in both cases on the recommendation of the Chief Justice.

Legal Counsel, Attorney, and Lawyers' System

Lawyers in West Malaysia and lawyers in East Malaysia are called Advocates and Solicitors of the High Court and Advocates of the High Court respectively. Their functions are identical. They have exclusive right of audience in the court of their respective states. This does not, however, prevent a party involed in a suit from conducting his own case personally, if he wishes. Lawyers have the sole right to draw up legal instruments on behalf of members of the public. Entry into the profession is strictly controlled in terms of qualification and only those who have the requisite qualifications may be admitted. A qualified person[64] is defined as "an advocate and solicitor qualified in law as a Barrister at Law of England or Northern Ireland or a member of the Faculty of Advocates in Scotland

---

[63]See *Courts Ordinance*, 1948.
[64]See *Advocate and Solicitors Ordinance*, 4/47.

or a person upon whom the University of Malaya has conferred the degree of Bachelor of Laws of the University (Amendment Ordinance 35/61)."

Before any candidate can be admitted to practise, evidence of good conduct has to be furnished. He is required to serve a period of pupilage or reading in chambers under an Advocate and Solicitor of approved standing and he must also satisfy the Bar Council as to his ability to undertake his responsibility towards his future clients. The Ordinance[65] in regard to admission and enrolment of qualified person stipulates that "every qualified person who applies to be admitted as an Advocate and Solicitor shall do so by petition to the Court verified by both Statutory declaration with two recent testimonials to his character annexed."

It continues to explain that "every petitioner shall have continuously attended and received instruction in Law in the office of a practitioner of not less than 7 years standing at the Bar to read not less than 12 months except those from the University of Singapore who has attended a rapid course upon graduation with LLB."

The public and legal practitioners are both protected by the Advocates and Solicitors Ordinance because the Ordinance is designed to ensure a high standard of professional ability on the part of lawyers and to prohibit persons not sufficiently trained from practising the law.

The legal profession in Malaysia is what is termed a fused profession in that there is no distinction between the functions of a barrister at Law and a Solicitor. Both undertake the same functions of general practice although one may specialize in different branches of law.

The Bar Council can be termed as the professional association of the legal profession but it also enjoys certain rights by law, the principal of which is the examination of candidates for admission to the Bar after they have qualified as lawyers. The statutory requirement in the Ordinance stipulates that "persons applying for admission as an Advocate and Solicitor shall appear before a board appointed by the Bar Council to be tested for his adequate knowledge of the laws of the Federation of

---

[65] *Ibid.*

Malaysia, the practice and etiquette of the profession and of the English language and is a suitable person for admission."

While it is the duty of the Bar Council to establish that character and submit confidential report to the Chief Justice it is only the Chief Justice who has the final say and power to overrule. Advocates and Solicitors are controlled by the legal provision which enables the Supreme Court to disqualify a lawyer from practising after considering the report of the appropriate Bar Committee which is part of the Bar Council.

Methods of Trial

These can be summed up under four broad categories:[66] (i) summary trials by Magistrates; (ii) preliminary inquiries into cases triable by the court of a judge; (iii) trial before the High Court with Jury; and (iv) Juvenile Court proceedings.

Summary Trials by Magistrates.[67] The procedure requires the charge to be read and explained to the accused, followed by the accused being asked whether or not he pleads guilty to the charge or claims to be tried. If there is a plea of guilty, the Magistrate may proceed to convict the accused provided that before recording the plea of guilt the Magistrate has already ascertained that the accused understands the nature and consequences of his plea. If the accused claims to be tried the court will proceed to hear evidence for the prosecution. The right of the accused to cross-examine all the witnesses for the prosecution is guaranteed. Where the court is satisfied that no case has been made out, it shall acquit the accused. On the other hand, if there are grounds for presuming that the accused has committed the offense, the court will proceed to try the accused on the original charge or on an amended charge.

In summary trials the prosecuting officer need not open the case but may forthwith produce his evidence. When the accused is called upon to enter on his defense, he or his advocate may, before producing his evidence upon his case stating the facts or law on which he intends to rely and may after giving evidence or examining witnesses, sum up his case. The prose-

[66]See *Malayan Criminal Procedure Code.*
[67]Also refers to Presidents of Sessions Courts.

cution officer shall have the right of reply on the whole case when the accused has given evidence.

Preliminary Inquiries into Cases Triable by a Court of Judge. All criminal proceedings before a High Court Judge proceed from a preliminary inquiry by a Magistrate. The same procedure applies in preliminary enquiry whereby the Magistrate hears the case for the prosecution and the accused person is brought before him. Evidence produced in support of the prosecution is heard. If the Magistrate finds that there are not sufficient grounds for committing the accused person for trial, he shall discharge the accused. The Magistrate may however amend the charge and try the accused accordingly or order him to be tried before some other Magistrate. If the Magistrate is of the opinion that there are sufficient grounds for committing the accused to stand trial by court of a judge, the Magistrate shall frame the correct charge and commit the accused for trial before a High Court. The Magistrate who hears the preliminary inquiry shall forward the full record of the proceeding to the public prosecutor.

Upon the commencement of trial before the court of a single judge without jury the charge is read and explained. The accused is then asked whether or not he pleads guilty or claims to be tried. If the accused pleads guilty he may be convicted thereon, but if he claims trial then the court shall proceed to hear the case. The prosecution opens his case by stating shortly the nature of the offense charged and the evidence by which he proposes to prove the guilt of the accused. On conclusion of the case by the prosecution, if the judge finds no case against the accused has been made out, he shall order the accused to be acquitted. On the other hand if he finds that a case has been made out, the judge shall call upon the accused to enter on his defense. The accused or his advocate may then open his case stating the facts or law upon which he intends to rely, and making such comments as he thinks necessary on the evidence of the prosecution. He may then examine his witnesses, and after their cross-examination and re-examination, may sum up his case. In all cases the prosecution officer has the right to reply on the whole case. The judge will then pass sentence accordingly.

Trials by Jury before the Court of a Judge. In all cases where
the punishment of death is authorized by law the accused shall
be tried by jury.[68] Here the procedure is the same as in a trial
by a court without jury. The verdict returned shall be unani-
mous or by a majority of not less than five to two. The accused has the right to object to any juror chosen under certain
conditions such as presumed or actual partiality in the juror,
his association with the court or with police by virtue of the
jurors' duty.

After the jurors have been chosen, the prosecuting officer,
normally a Deputy Public Prosecutor from the Legal Department, shall open his case by stating shortly the nature of the
offense charged and the evidence by which he proposes to prove
the guilt of the accused. Again the difference in the Jury System lies in the fact that at the conclusion of the case for the
prosecution it is the duty of the Judge to address the Jury.
After the address, the verdict shall be returned by the Jury
and the Judge will pass sentence according to the verdict.

The essence of the judicial process lies in the application of
rules of law to the facts of particular cases. Every judicial
decision involves both questions of law and questions of fact,
e.g. to prove a charge of murder, the prosecution has to show
that the accused acted voluntarily, and although the law presumes that every man intends the natural consequences of
his acts, it may be that an examination of the facts will show
that there is some doubt whether the act causing death was
voluntary.

In "jury" trials it is, broadly speaking, the duty of the judge
to determine all questions of law, including questions as to the
admissibility of evidence, and for the jury to decide all questions of fact.

Juvenile Court Proceedings. The method of trial in the Juvenile Court in respect of Juvenile Offenders incorporates all the
features of a trial in adult court, except for the more humane
and understanding approach shown by the court towards the
juvenile accused. In trying petty offenses the court sits and
deals with the accused in a summary way. The procedure is

[68]The jury consists of seven persons. The jurors are chosen by law
from persons summoned to act.

similar to that of an adult court, except for certain differences
peculiar to the Juvenile Court. These characteristics are: first,
it is a closed court and is not accessible to public, except
persons sanctioned by the President of the Court. Secondly, the
jurisdiction of the court does not extend to juveniles charged
with an offense carrying death sentence. Thirdly, the court is
composed of a President and two Advisors whose duty is
purely advisory and affects only the consideration of the treatment or punishment of the delinquent found guilty of the
offense. Fourthly, it shall be obligatory for the Court to ask
for a pre-sentence report from a probation officer. Fifthly,
where an order is made such as fine or payments of compensa-
tions or damage to the complainant, the order can be directed
towards the parents or guardians of the juvenile offender.

In respect of proceedings involving juveniles being brought
up as being in need of care and protection or being beyond
control of parents or guardians, the atmosphere is more
friendly and the police prosecutor shall not be present. In all
Juvenile Court proceedings it shall be necessary for the
parents or guardians of the juvenile to be present unless there
is good reason for their presence to be dispensed with by the
Court.

Right to Appeal

There is a right to appeal from all Subordinate Courts to the
High Court and there is a virtually unlimited right of appeal
from the High Court to the Federal Court. Where an appeal
from the decision of a Subordinate Court in a criminal matter
has been heard and determined by the High Court, a further
appeal to the Federal Court lies only by way of reference on
a certificate from the judge who heard the appeal, or from the
Public Prosecutor that the determination of such an appeal involves a point which it is desirable in the public interest to be
determined by the Federal Court.[69]

Appeals from the Federal Court lie to the Yang di-Pertuan
Agong. Such appeals are then referred by arrangement with
the British Government to the Judicial Committee of the Privy

[69]"Justice Law and Order," *Official Year Book*, 1966, p. 99.

Council sitting in London in accordance with the usual procedure regulating appeals to the highest judicial tribunal in the Commonwealth. On receiving from Her Britannic Majesties Government the report on recommendation of the Judicial Committee, His Majesty will make such order as is necessary to give effect to the report on recommendation.

FUNCTIONS OF THE POLICE

The Royal Malaysia Police operates under the Police Act, 1967. The organization, discipline, powers and duties of the Royal Malaysia Police[70] have been consolidated as a result of this Act.

Police Organization

The Royal Malaysia Police now comprises the Police Forces of the States of Malaya, Sabah, and Sarawak, under the command of an Inspector General with his headquarters in Kuala Lumpur. He is responsible to the Minister of Home Affairs for the control and direction of the service and formulates a policy on how the service should be organized and administered.

The National Police Force is divided broadly into five departments:[71] *"A" Department*—administration, personal and training; *"B" Department*—Police filed force (para-military), public order, operations, marines, logistics, signals auxillary; *"C" Department*—finance supply source, works and capital development and transport; *"D" Department*—criminal investigation department;[72] and *"E" Department*—special branch.

This broad division is necessary because of the complexities of the responsibilities and duties of the Royal Malaysia Police and the manifold problems in the administration of a large National Force.

[70]With the separation of Singapore from the Federation in August, 1965. the Singapore Police Force ceased to be a component of the Royal Malaysia Force.

[71]See *Organization of the Government of Malaysia* (Kuala Lumpur: Development Administration Unit, Prime Minister Department, 1967).

[72]The work of this department is the main concern of this article.

Police Objectives, Policy and Duties

The police statutory functions may be summed up as follows: (*i*) maintenance of law and order; (*ii*) preservation of the peace; (*iii*) prevention and detection of crime; (*iv*) apprehension and prosecution of offenders; and (*v*) collection of security intelligence.

These functions[73] represent a very wide character, being the sole instrument of the nation for the rule of law. The Royal Malaysia Police has had to include duties which are of a specialized nature. Following are its main units and their respective functions: (1) *The Special Branch*—responsible for all aspects of security intelligence in the interest of Internal Security and Defense; (2) *The Police Field Force*—to conduct military operations against militant arm uprising in the country; (3) *The Federal Reserve Unit*—to prevent and suppress public disorders; (4) *Police Marine Branch*—to prevent breaches of the law, including illegal immigration, smuggling and traffic in firearms, to enforce certain provisions in the Merchant Shipping Ordinance, to protect Malaysian Fishing Craft; (5) *The Signals Branch*—to provide police communications network throughout Malaysia; and (6) *The Transport Branch*—to provide the force with the mobility that is vital in policing and hence the objectives, policies, and duties are clearly laid down to ensure the peace and tranquility of the country.

Police Power

Generally, the power vested with police in crime prevention, detention, and control is wide and this is defined in various statutes like the Police Act of 1967, the Criminal Procedure Code, and other Ordinances and Enactments. The preventive action of the police, as provided under the Criminal Procedure Code, grants power to the police officer to interpose for the purpose of preventing the commission of any seizable offense.[74] He

---

[73]See *Police Act, 1967.*

[74]"Seizable Offense" means an offense in which a police officer may ordinarily arrest without warrant.

may also of his own authority interpose to prevent any injury
attempted to be committed to any public property movable
or immovable. The police officer has power under the Police
Act to inspect licenses, vehicles, to retain and search aircraft,
to erect road barriers, to regulate assemblies, meetings and
processions, and to make orders to require persons to remain
indoors.

With regard to law enforcement, the further power granted
to the police is explained in the Criminal Procedure Code. The
police officer in the case of seizable offense may proceed to
make an inquiry on the spot, and to order persons involved
in the case, whether it be the accused or witnesses, to attend
before himself.

A police officer has power to search for documents believed
to be in the possession of any person in the course of investigation. He has authority to arrest and demand for right of
access to any place, vessel or building in which the person to
be arrested has sought shelter. In this connection it is lawful
for the police officer to break open any door or use reasonable
amount of force. In dealing with persons who are incapacitated by intoxication, illness, or mental disorder, the police
officer has power to search such a person for the purpose of
ascertaining his name and place of abode.[75] Any police
officer[76] may arrest without a warrant a person who has been
concerned in any seizable offense; who has in his possession
without lawful excuse any implement of house breaking; who
is the subject of a warrant of arrest issued earlier by a court;
who is found in possession of any suspected stolen property;
who obstructs a police officer on duty or who has escaped
from lawful custody; who has no reasonable means of substance; who is a habitual robber, house breaker or thief or a
habitual receiver of stolen property.

Despite wide powers being given under the law to the police
the public is protected, since no court can take cognisance
of any offense unless a complaint has been made to the police
in the more serious type of cases, and the sanction of the
public prosecutor is required for prosecution.

---

[75] *Criminal Procedure Code*, Section 23.
[76] *Criminal Procedure Code, op. cit.*, p. 29.

Internal Structute of Police

This can be best explained in a diagram as shown below:

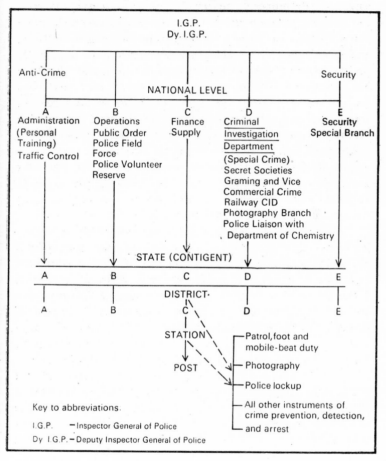

Key to abbreviations.

I.G.P. — Inspector General of Police

Dy I.G.P. — Deputy Inspector General of Police

Beat System. As can be seen from the diagram, the point of contract between the police and the public is at district and station level. The salient features of the Beat System may be summarized as follows.[77] First, each urban area is divided into a number of beats (Bicycle or Foot). Secondly, in urban areas,

[77]Source: Police circular.

traffic patrols are provided to deal with busy traffic centers, shopping and cinema areas. Thirdly, although police officers are not to act as private watchmen, nor are they supposed to patrol private property, nevertheless it is their duty to visit and examine private premises when they have reason to suppose that an offense has been or is likely to be committed. Fourthly, under the Patrol System the police are directed to pay particular attention to premises temporarily unoccupied if notice has been given to the police and consent of the owner has been obtained. Fifthly, vigilance of the police on beat duty in early morning is stressed when they are required to observe carefully persons carrying bags, parcels, and other objects under suspicion. They will pay special attention in rural areas to persons removing cattle or market produce during the night and in the early morning. Sixthly, they also will pay attention to persons who are seen to visit or leave houses in early morning under suspicious circumstances.

To implement the Beat System, power under Criminal Procedure Code has been given to the police whereby police officers are empowered to stop, search, and detain persons suspected of having or conveying anything stolen or unlawfully obtained, if there is no time to apply for a search warrant. These powers are of the greatest value in the prevention and detection of crime, and although it may cause annoyance to innocent persons, the police are required to use care and discretion in exercising their authority in spite of the risk of mistakes.

Police Lockup and Prisoners. The police lockups operate on the Lockup Rule of 1953 as provided under the Prisons Ordinance. This section of the Ordinance makes it clear that the lockups are to be used as places for the confinement of persons remanded or sentenced to such terms of imprisonment not exceeding one month, as may be specified in each case.

Such lockups are administered by the Chief Police Officer of the State who delegates his responsibilities to the man who actually has the physical control of the lockups. These lockups are not designed and should not be used for the prolonged confinement of persons. No matter whether they are on remand under the ordinary law or are subjected to orders of detention. The police lockups can also be used for legitimate custody of an arrested person who cannot furnish bail, or for a person suspected to be mentally disordered while waiting to be moved for mental treatment.

The rules also regulate the manner in which prisoners in lockups are to be treated. Facilities for prisoners are required to be printed in all languages understandable to the various races. The prisoner is allowed a visit by a close relative within 24 hours, or by a friend if he hasn't a relative, within a period of 48 hours.

Prisoners in lockup are segregated according to the various categories into which they fall. These categories include convicted and remand prisoners, drunkards, habitual criminals, political suspects, women, and juvenile prisoners. Juvenile prisoners are at all times kept separately from adults. Female prisoners are also to be kept separately from male prisoners, and cells used for the imprisonment of females are to be suitably screened. Medical examination of prisoners is also provided. All prisoners are to be afforded reasonable opportunities for exercise at least once each day. Remand prisoners and political suspects cannot be made to perform laborers' duties. The prisoner has the right to see his lawyer. The police, during visit of the lawyer to the accused, are required to exercise a reasonable discretion and to be fair to the accused. No child under three years of age may be admitted to prison with its mother. Police are required to ensure that women prisoners and any children that accompany them are examined by a Medical Officer before or immediately after they are placed in the lockup.

Laboratory. In the field of forensic science the Police Department though not having its own laboratory, receives full and unstinted support from the Department of Chemistry in West Malayasia. The Department of Chemistry further assists the police by conducting training courses for senior CID officers. These courses are greatly appreciated by the officers concerned and have proved to be of immense value to them. In the year 1965, a total of 14,872 exhibits were sent by the police to the Forensic Division and the hand-writing division of the Department of Chemistry for examination. This is an increase of 3,299 compared with 11,573 in 1964.

There is no Department of Chemistry in Sabah, and exhibits are sent to the departments of Chemistry in Kuala Lumpur and

Singapore for analysis. In Sarawak, although there is a Department of Chemistry, the majority of exhibits have still to be sent to the Chemistry Department in Kuala Lumpur because this department is still in its infancy.

Police Photographic Branch. The headquarter's Photographic Branch of the Royal Malaysia Police Force is situated in Kuala Lumpur. It is adequately equipped to deal with all types of police photography. In West Malaysia there are 18 photographic sub-branches situated in the bigger towns. During the year 1965, the headquarter's Photographic Branch and its sub-branches took a total of 152,579 photographs and produced 544,564 copies, as compared with 149,663 and 543,892 respectively in 1964.

Police Ratio per 100,000 Population

The police ratio per 100,000 population is as follows:

For the country, it is given as 338 persons per 100,000.

The polic ratio in the 3 component States is as follows : (a) States of Malaya—1 to 363; (b) Sabah—1 to 256; and (c) Sarawak—1 to 268. The ratio for the Force as a whole is 1 to 296.

The establishment of the Royal Malaysian Police as in December, 1967, was:[78] Gazetted Officers—687; Inspectors—1,453; Rank and File—26,573; and the total was 28,513.

FUNCTIONS OF THE PRISON

1946 saw significant changes when seven different sets of prison legislation, governing the administration of prisons in the Federated and Unfederated Malay States and the Settlement,[79] were unified. This marked the transformation of an entirely punitive penal system into one in keeping with the modern trend of dealing with the imprisoned. As a result of re-

---

[78] *Malaysia Year Book*, 1967, p. 135.

[79] Before the formation of Federation of Malaya in 1949—and subsequently Malaysia in 1953—the Federated Malay States and Unfederated Malay States were component states of what was then known as British Malaya. The Straits Settlement was composed of Singapore, Penang, and Malacca.

organization, a Federal Commissioner of Prisons was appointed
and entrusted with the task of administering all the prisons in
the country.[80]

Prison Organization

A complete re-organization of the Prisons Department could
be said to have been accomplished in 1949 when, for the first
time, a Prison Officers' Training Depot was established in 1952
to re-educate the Prison's Staff.[81] Prisons are a federal matter
and are within the portfolio of the Ministry of Justice.

Penal Establishments. There are 17 penal establishments in
West Malaysia—classified as follows: (1) Central Training
Prison—1; (2) Regional Training Prisons—4; (3) Prison Camp
Open Conditions—1; (4) Central Prison for Special Prisoners—1;
(5) Local Prisons (Men)—2; (6) Local Prisons (Women)—5;
(7) Henry Gurney School for Boys—2; and (8) Henry Gurney
School for Girls—1. The total number of prisoners in West
Malaysia at the end of 1966 was 2,991.

Internal Arrangement of Prisons

Classification of prisons is based upon degree of security,
length of imprisonment of prisoners, age, sex, and background
of prisoners. The majority of the prisons are of the maximum
security type, the main reason being they were built many
years ago to suit the old deterrent theory. In West Malaysia
there is only one open prison for adults.[82] The Borstal type
of Institution[83] for training of young male offenders has features of medium security. Prisoners in Malaysia are divided
into 3 categories: (a) *Unconvicted*—which includes those on
remand or awaiting trial; (b) *Civil*— persons committed for debt,

[80]With the formation of Malaysia, the administrative control over the
prisons in Sabah and Sarawak have now been delegated to the Commissioner of Prisons, Malaysia.

[81] "Treatment of Adult and Youthful Offenders," *Official Year Book,
op. cit.*, p. 101.

[82]Prisoner Camp, open type, at Kelantan.

[83]This refers to Henry Gurney School for boys between 14-21 situated
at Telok Mas, Malacca, West Malaysia.

failure to obey maintenance orders, contempt of court, etc; and
(c) *Convicted*—those serving a sentence of imprisonment.

Strict segregation is enforced in respect to the sexes, young offenders from adults, unconvicted from convicted, and civil from criminal prisoners. Within the convicted adult group there exists a further sub-classification: (*i*) *Young Prisoners Class*—those not exceeding 20 years of age; (*ii*) *Star Class*—first offenders and other prisoners who have no vicious habits or tendencies; and (*iii*) *Ordinary Class*—persons considered unsuitable for the Star Class, and are persistent offenders.

Methods of Rehabilitation and Training

These are regulated by a Prisons Ordinance and Rules based on the modern concept of treatment and training of prisoners. The new legislation is based on the Standard Minimum Rules for the treatment of prisoners prepared by the United Nations.[84]

The prison program embodies educational and industrial training, the extension of trust and responsibility, special training schemes for certain categories of prisoners, including pre-release training and parole leave. Compared with conditions existing 80 years ago, prisoners today are employed in productive and instructive occupations with the idea of assisting the discharged prisoners to earn a living. A system of payment to prisoners according to their grades is in use. Remission is awarded to all prisoners serving imprisonment exceeding one month but this remission is forfeitable for misconduct. The eligibility is equal to one-third of the sentence.

Industrial Training and Cottage Crafts. Prisoners in the central training and regional prisons in West Malaysia are employed in various trades. They are awarded Proficiency Certificates on passing a test but such certificates though useful in practice, do not seem to lead to employment. Evening classes in handicrafts and hobbies in all large prisons are held. To give incentive to prisoners, one-half of the profits from articles sold goes to the credit of the prisoners concerned and is handed to him on release.

[84]*Official Year Book, op. cit.,* p. 102.

With regard to education and recreation, the prisoners in West Malaysia spend an average of 15 hours a day outside cells. Every effort is made to keep them fully occupied in instructive activities through educational classes, group discussions, debates, dramatic societies, concerts, cinema shows, and games. The success of this type of program depends upon several factors but nevertheless it is the social climate within the prison that matters most.

The problem of rehabilitating the ex-prisoner remains crucial, particularly in job-finding for prisoners. The Discharged Prisoners' Aid Society is entrusted with the responsibility of helping the discharged prisoner live as an accepted member of the community. This attempt has not been very successful. What has to be overcome is the general public prejudice that the ex-convict is by implication a dangerous outcast to be ostracized.

Juvenile Detention Centres

In each of the three component states of Malaysia, viz. Sarawak, Sabah, and Federation of Malaya, there is a separate prison for young prisoners. In Sarawak, young convicted prisoners under 17 years of age are detained separately, and in Sabah young prisoners between 16-21 years are segregated from the other adult prisoners. In West Malaysia there is also a separate penal establishment for young prisoners between 17-21 years of age.

The pattern of training for young prisoners, though operated within maximum security conditions, embodies certain English Borstal principles. Particular attention is paid to segregation of this group from the hardened core. The rigid prison rules pertaining to communication with the outside world have been modified and rendered flexible. Vocational education training is given special emphasis in the daily work program. The position regarding the imprisonment of young adult offenders is a matter of considerable concern to the bench and to the prison authorities.

Juvenile Detention Homes may be divided into 3 categories: (a) Remand Homes and Hostels; (b) Approved Schools; and (c) Henry Gurney Schools or Borstal Institutions.

The administrative authorities for running and managing Remand Homes and Hostels, and Approved Schools, are the Ministry of Welfare Services; while Henry Gurney Schools come under the control of the Prisons Department.

Remand Homes and Hostels. They serve the same function as a Probation Hostel in Great Britain, except that the Hostel here has an added function of serving as a remand center for juvenile accused while awaiting trial. The Hostel also provides facilities for children on transit and those on licence or on after care since discharge from Approved Schools or the Borstals.

The reason why the center is also a remand center is because the court wishes to avoid detaining juveniles accused in police lockup or prison while they are on trial, if they are for some reason or other not on bail. As a Probation Hostel, it serves a useful purpose in enabling the Juvenile Court to commit the juvenile offenders for an initial period of one year while he is on probation. Such an order is made after the court is satisfied that the probationers' attitude and conduct can change for the better within the period of his residence in the Hostel. In West Malaysia, there are eight Hostels, one of which is for girls; and they are situated in the bigger towns and in different parts of the country. At the end of 1966, 152 juveniles were in residence.

Approved Schools. It must be stressed that they are open institutions, different from the Henry Gurney Schools managed by the Prison Department.

These institutions are established under the Juvenile Courts Ordinance, and in West Malaysia the Ministry of Welfare Services has set up four such Approved Schools; three for boys and one for girls. On committal by the Juvenile Courts, they must be under 17 years of age. Each of the three boys' Approved Schools has a maximum accommodation for 120 boys, and for the girls school 50. The boys' schools are classified according to age groups computed at the time of admission. All these approved schools are Federal Institutions.[85]

---

[85] *Juvenile Courts Ordinance* (*op. cit.*) is a federal law; and courts dealing with criminal and civil matter are Federal Courts established under the *Courts Ordinance, 1948.*

The system of training, retraining, and re-education is based very much on the British system. The juvenile committed has to serve a period of three years, but the Board of Visitors, may, by virtue of the power conferred upon it, authorize his/ her release or licence after 12 months of detention. After this the discharged juvenile remains under the supervision of a Probation Officer until the expiry of the original Court Order of detention or until he reaches the age of 18 years. Those ordered to reside in an Approved School for being in need of care and protection are to remain there for a period of three years or until they attain the age of 18 years, whichever is longer. The Principal of the Approved School may, however, before the expiry of the statutory period, apply to the Juvenile Court for the revocation of the Order. The court may then grant a substitute order placing the juvenile, after release from the institution, under the supervision of a probation for a period not exceeding three years.

The total number in the four Approved Schools in West Malaysia is 580 (530 in the boys schools and 50 in the girls schools) at the end of 1966.

The training program can be divided into four phases: (*i*) reception and information; (*ii*) training facilities; (*iii*) observation of progress; and (*iv*) aftercare.

Henry Gurney Schools. As has been said earlier, these are Borstal Institutions managed by the Prisons Department. In West Malaysia there are two establishments, one for boys and the other for girls.

Committal is on a Juvenile Court Orderly, a Sessions Court,[86] or a High Court. The Juvenile Courts Ordinance lays down two clear priniciples to ensure that the committal orders are not indiscriminately made. First, the nature of the offense must be grave enough to merit the detention of such a character that removal from his surrounding is necessary. Secondly, the length of a Henry Gurney School Order is not to exceed three years. Full responsibility is, however, placed on the Commissioner of Prisons, who, on the advice of the Institution

[86]A Sessions Court is also a Subordinate Court, higher than Magistrate Court. The President of a Sessions Court sits as Chairman of the Juvenile Court. A High Court has unlimited power in both original jurisdiction and appellate jurisdiction.

Discharge Board, may terminate the detention at any stage
after the offender has served his/her first year. Although the
order specifies three years as the maximum, the average time
spent by the inmate is around two years. To be released before
serving his full term is considered a privilege and not a right.
Release from the institution is followed by aftercare supervision by a Probation Officer until the statutory period of detention has lapsed.

This open social treatment is primarily aimed at assisting
the individual to integrate with the wider community, but the
service leaves much to be desired. Its importance cannot be
overstressed considering the appreciable number of discharged
inmates who have no proper homes or jobs to go to. On the
other hand, if during the period of supervision the licencee
fails to adhere to the conditions laid down, his licence may be
revoked and the licencee recalled for further training to complete the unexpired residual period of the original detention
order. The number of such recalls is however negligible—only
three in 1966. The number of offenders undergoing Borstal
training at the end of 1966 was 450 boys and 35 girls.

The Henry Gurney School for girls is an open institution
converted from a private home. The small unit offers splendid
opportunity to the staff to carry out more individualized
treatment. The atmosphere is less restrictive and training provided is understood to be geared to the inmates' needs, interest, and employability, such as housekeeping. Links with
the outside community are continuously encouraged. Attention
is paid to their exchange of letters and visits by relatives and
friends, since girls are generally believed to be more prone to
emotional outbursts. The number of inmates fluctuates between
25-35, and ages of girls range between 14-20 years.

Methods of Capital Punishment

The law forbids passing or recording sentence of death on any
juvenile below the age of 17 years.[87] Death sentence on adults
is carried out by means of hanging.

Legal Provisions. With regard to the procedure of carrying

---

[87]*Juvenile Courts Ordinance, op. cit.,* Section 16.

out death sentence, it is laid down in the Criminal Procedure Code as follows: "A warrant of death sentence under the Seal of the Court is made out and directed to the Officer-in-charge of the prison. The prisoner is detained until a further warrant for execution. If there is no appeal, the Judge who passed the sentence of death shall inform the Mentri Besar[88] of the State giving his reason why the sentence of death should or should not be carried out."

If there is an appeal, the judge shall forward to the Court of Appeal a report in writing together with notes of evidence taken at the trial where the appeal is dismissed by the Court of Appeal. The Mentri Besar, on receipt of the proceedings, shall transmit the same to the Ruler of the State in Council for approval. Death sentence may be commuted into any other punishment by the Ruler in Council.

At the execution of the death sentence the Medical Officer in charge of the prison, the Superintendent of prison concerned, shall be present together with a Minister of Religion, and the relatives of the condemned prisoner if they so desire. All death sentences in West Malaysia are carried out in the Federal Capital, i.e. Kuala Lumpur.

The Court may order a youthful offender to be whipped with not more than ten strokes of a light cane or rattan within the court premises and in the presence, is he desires, of the parent or guardian of such offender. This provision of law, however, is very little used, probably because some courts consider it to run counter to public opinion. But in offenses like rape or involving injury to the complainant, High Courts do not hesitate to order whipping.

Methods of Punishment in Prisons. Prison staffs are encouraged to rely on firmness and humanity in the maintenance of discipline rather than on repressive force of authority. Prison superintendents in dealing with breaches of discipline make use of force wherever this appear to be unavoidable.

Punishment may only be ordered by the Officer-in-charge. Apart from cautions, forfeiture of remission and forfeiture or postponement of privileges, other permitted punishments are restricted diet, exclusion from associated work, stoppage of earn-

---

[88]Chief Minister of the State in Malaysia.

ings, and confinement to a cell for prescribed periods of time.

In the case of grave offense such as mutiny or gross personal violence to an officer, special provision is made for the
Commissioner of Prisons or the Visiting Justices[89] to decide on
the punishment. Handcuffs and other mechanical restraints
may not be used as a punishment but only as a restraint when
it is necessary to prevent the prisoner from injuring himself
or others. As punishment for aggravated prison offense, the
Officer-in-charge of the prison may order the guilty prisoner
to be subjected to (i) corporal punishment and (ii) confinement
in a punishment cell on prescribed punishment diet.

The prison rules provide that no prisoner shall be punished
until he has had an opportunity of hearing the charge or complaint against him. To secure sound discipline and control, the
rule provides that every opportunity should be given to the
prisoner to be acquainted with the rules and regulations concerning his obligations and welfare on reception.

Punishment Methods in Henry Gurney Schools. Within the
institution the inmate is subjected to various methods of discipline and control, and in this connection any report of
breach of conduct by the inmate requires to be dealt with by
the Superintendent. But the inmate, when reported upon, shall
be given an opportunity to explain himself. The list of offenses
against institutional discipline is enumerated in the rules and
they cover disobedience towards the staff, idleness or negligence at work, using indecent language, escape or attempt to
escape from legal custody, and inciting inmates to committing
personal violence against staff, or other inmates.

Punishments include (i) removal of the inmate to the Penal
Grade; (ii) Deprivation of privileges for a period not exceeding
one month; (iii) loss of stage or grade for a period of three
months; (iv) confinement to a room for three days; and (v)
placing the offender on a restricted diet.

Where the offense is of a graver nature power for punishment can be exercised by the Visiting Committee[90] when the

---

[89]The members are appointed by the Mentri Besar or Chief Minister
of the State. All Magistrates in the district where the prison is situated
shall be ex-officio members.

[90]Board of Visitors are appointed by the Minister concerned.

power of the Superintendent is considered insufficient. In this category, escape from legal custody is one of the specific types of offenses. The above types of punishment may be used—but on a higher degree—and whipping with a light cane may also be ordered by the Visiting Committee.

Power to award corporal punishment is vested in the Visiting Committee, but the execution is carried out by the staff. The Commissioner of Prisons has power to reduce any disciplinary award by the Visiting Committee or by the Superintendent.

Where confinement to a room, corporal punishment, or restriction of diet is ordered as a method or punishment, the rules require that the certificate of the Medical Officer be first obtained to ensure that the inmate is in a fit condition of health to sustain the punishment. Moreover, the rule forbids the use of any mechanical restraint as a punishment on any inmate. Violent inmates may be confined temporarily in a special room by the Superintendent.

Punishment in Approved Schools. Like Henry Gurney School[91] Rules, the rules for Approved Schools made under the Juvenile Courts Ordinance, which came into force in 1949, have undergone little changes since then, and some of the provisions are obviously out of date.

As far as discipline and punishment in an Approved School are concerned the general principles laid down emphasize the need for discipline to be maintained by the personal influence of the Superintendent and staff. This shall be provided by a system of rewards and privileges. Whenever punishment is necessary, the following methods may be applied: (*i*) forfeiture of rewards or privileges (including pocket money) or temporary loss of recreation; (*ii*) alteration of meals for a period not exceeding 3 days; (*iii*) separation from other boys/girls (but no boy or girl under 12 years of age shall be kept in separation; and (*iv*) corporal punishment is to be used as a last resort and, if used, to be kept to the minimum.

Only the Superintendent or his authorized staff may carry out corporal punishment and when this is carried out, it shall not be inflicted in the presence of other boys/girls. The cane used must be approved and the strokes limited according to

[91]Formerly known as Advanced Approved Schools.

age of the boys/girls, and in the case of boys caning to be applied to the lower portion if not on the palm. In all cases involving girl inmates caning shall be applied on the hands.

It is emphasized that other than authorized persons no member of the staff shall inflict any kind of corporal punishment; this term refers to striking, cuffing, shaking, or any physical form of violence. Any staff who commits a breach of this rule renders himself liable to be dismissed. (The practice, however, deviates in varying degrees from what is prescribed.) In this connection, wise selection of staff with due regard to their personality and professional training is very important.

PROBATION AND PAROLE SYSTEM

Probation as a form of treatment/punishment is relatively new in this country,[92] notwithstanding the fact that the provision for this is contained in the Criminal Procedure Code[93] which has been in use since 1902. Probation, as a judicial discretionary order, may be made either under the Criminal Procedure Code or the Juvenile Courts Ordinance.[94]

As a result of the introduction of the Juvenile Courts Ordinance, the court, as a general practice, has made a distinction between the adults and juveniles in so far as granting of probation is concerned. In respect of adults to be discharged conditionally or unconditionally, the court derives its power from the Criminal Procedure Code. Here again the legislation contains two separate provisions making a distinction between conviction and non-conviction.[95] For juvenile offenders, the probation order is made by a Juvenile Court which has jurisdiction to hear all cases concerning persons under 17 years of age.

[92]The first batch of probation officers, numbering 12, were appointed by the Government in 1950 after the coming into force of the *Juvenile Courts Ordinance*.

[93]*Criminal Procedure (Amendment) Ordinance* of 1947 applies to all the Malay States. Its origin is the Indian Criminal Procedure Code.

[94]This Ordinance 38/47, though passed by the Federal Legislative Council in 1947, did not become law until December, 1949.

[95](a) Sec. 294 of the CPC carries conviction and (b) Sec. 173A does not carry conviction. A conviction, generally speaking, is a disqualification and results in dismissal from Government Service.

The probation officers appointed for the purposes under the law are employed by the Ministry of Welfare Services but they are also answerable to the court by whom they are entrusted with the duties of supervision. The case load of adult probation is relatively small since the court makes little use of probation for adults, or discharges the offender without a condition of supervision; while the Juveniles Courts make greater use of this type of treatment.

TABLE XII

CASE LOAD OF PROBATIONERS

Year	Adults	Juveniles	Total	Rate
1960	54	254	308	
1961	35	257	292	—5.2%
1962	72	315	387	+2 2%
1963	41	368	409	+33%
1964	11	407	417	+35%
1965	22	338	360	+17%

SOURCE: Annual Reports of Department of Social Welfare, Federation of Malaya.

The average case load of a probation officer is 20 although the figure fluctuates from town to town, and a heavier case load is generally concentrated in the larger urban area. Together with cases under supervision whilst on licence from the Borstals and the Approved Schools, the case load per officer is about 35.

No parole law[96] has been passed in this country for adult prisoners. Instead of this, a remission system is in use.[97] With regard to young persons committed to Henry Gurney Schools[98] and Approved Schools, the law allows them to be released on licence, regarded as parole. The eligibility is a minimum year of stay in the institution. In the case of Henry Gurney Schools, the power rests with the Commissioner of

[96]The question of whether or not parole for adult prisoners should be introduced was considered by the government in 1964, but apparently this idea has been shelved.

[97]A prisoner sentenced to imprisonment which exceeds one month is entitled to remission amounting to one-third of his/her sentence.

[98]Also referred to as Borstals in this article.

Prisons who normally acts on the advice of the Institutional Discharge Board. The Commissioner also has power of recall, which he can exercise when any licencee has failed to observe the conditions laid down.

Similarly, the duration of Court Order for an Approved School is three years but as soon as the youngster has served for a year or more,[99] he is eligible to be considered for release on licence. The power to grant this release on licence is vested with the Board of Visitors. With this object in view, the Board is required to review not only the progress made by each boy or girl but also all the circumstances of the case (including home surroundings) as often as may be necessary, in any case at least once annually.

The table below shows the number of adults and young persons on parole from these two types of juvenile institutions.

TABLE XIII

ADULTS AND YOUNG PERSONS UNDER SUPERVISION WHILST ON LICENCE FROM APPROVED SCHOOLS AND HENRY GURNEY SCHOOLS

	Adults		Young persons		Total	Rate
	Females	Males	Females	Adults		
1960	2	52	15	385	454	
1961	—	35	11	447	493	+8.6%
1962	—	27	5	407	439	—3.3%
1963	—	22	6	334	362	—20%
1964	—	41	7	355	403	—11%
1965	—	22	7	308	337	—26%

SOURCE: Annual Reports of Department of Social Welfare, Federation of Malaya.

Probation Eligibility

As mentioned earlier, there are two pieces of legislation under which an offender may be released on probation: (a) the Criminal Procedure Code and (b) the Juvenile Courts Ordinance.

With regard to adults, the court derives its judicial sanction from the Criminal Procedure Code and this provision of the Code appears to be applied rather negatively in that the

[99] The average length of stay is two and a half years.

person so discharged, though with conditions, is seldom asked to be supervised physically by a probation officer. This defect, if it can be so regarded, is now being corrected. Before this method of disposal is considered, the court often makes it a point to call for a pre-sentence report. This generally applies to the young adult offenders between the age of 17-21 years, whom the court considers it to be unwise to send to prison if they are first offenders and their crime is not considered very serious. The infrequent use of probation for adults can be partly due to misconception of some courts, to regard this method as only being suitable to children and young persons.

In the context of Juvenile Courts Ordinance, probation implies a method of treating offenders who are released to be of good behavior upon conditions prescribed by the court. One of the most important basic elements is supervision by a probation officer. The Juvenile Court is limited by law to order probation because the court has no power to try any offense punishable with death.[100]

The definition and principles of probation generally applicable to other countries like Great Britain are implied in the Ordinance. Probation order can only be made after conviction, and the probationers may be returned to the court upon violation of the conditions. Probation as a method of disposal by the court is not a legal right but is determined by judicial discretion. It is often misconceived by the public as a form of judicial leniency or clemency.

The court in assessing offenders for probation treatment is greatly assisted by the probation officer who gives a comprehensive picture of the offender to the court in a pre-sentence report. There is no strict policy laid down as to who are eligible. Nevertheless the court seems to regard it as suitable for the first offender, and one whose offense is not so grave as to merit harsher punishment. The practice varies from one court to another, but in general it is still a prevailing practice for the court to be sceptical about probation being an effec-

---

[100]See *Juvenile Courts Ordinance, op. cit.*, Section 16: Sentence of death shall not be pronounced or recorded against a person convicted of an offense, when the person is a child or young person, but in lieu thereof the court, shall sentence him to be detained during the pleasure of the Ruler of the State.

tive measure of social treatment, or to cling on to the outdated view that punishment must fit the crime rather than the
offender.

Nevertheless the court is guided by the principles of the
individual's potentials to adjust under the supervision of the
probation officer. In addition to the considerations of the
triviality of the offense, and the age of the offender, the court
pays regard to the antecedents, character, mental condition,
the associations of the offender, and the motives behind the
offense. Of importance also are the resources available and
the adequacy of supervision. The court is likely to grant probation where the chances of a job for the offender are good
and where parents are willing to co-operate towards re-education and rehabilitation of the individual. Selection of offenders
poses many problems. Facts presented to courts contain hidden
meanings, e.g. the first offender may exist in name only, but
may actually be a recidivist of long standing who has so far
evaded identification. Generally psychopaths, alcoholics, drug
addicts, sex delinquents, professional or hardened extortioners,
thugs, and members of secret societies are considered bad
risks.

Parole

As had been mentioned earlier, the law to grant parole for
adult prisoners does not exist in this country.[101] The features
of parole, however, apply to juveniles released on licence from
Borstal and Approved Schools after serving an indeterminate
form of sentence. Release on licence is therefore a conditional
release like parole.

Eligibility for Release on Licence. The minimum period to
be served is one year before the inmate is eligible for release
on licence. Other factors like the inmate's conduct and progress in the school, and the prospects of his adaptation to the
outside environment, are also taken into account. Towards
this assessment, the inmate is given opportunity of an annual

---

[101]The system of remission is in use—it is automatic unless the prisoner has committed a grave offense for which his remission may be for-
feited.

home leave during which time the attitude of his parents/guardians and the prospects of employment, if need be, are studied and carefully assessed. For the older inmates, employment as a pre-requisite is logical since a large number of youngsters often relapse into crime because of the difficulty to secure jobs.

With the younger children, immediate employment may be less important, so long as the parents/guardians are willing to take them back and to assist the supervising officer in the aftercare of the youngsters. The responsibility of aftercare for persons to be released on licence has been partly placed on the School Board.[102] They are required to "endeavor to place the youngster in a hostel or other suitable lodging, and to find employment if necessary." In this respect, a useful function is served by the Probation Hostel which often can serve as a half-way home or temporary lodging home for youngsters who have jobs but who have no satisfactory accomodation.

In connection with preparation for release on licence, the good superintendent is one who makes it a point to discuss with the pre-released youngster the various issues like work opportunity, the community attitude, the community resources, and the problems of living independently. The assurance of the superintendent has often proved to be a source of strength and a means of overcoming initial difficulties faced by the youngster, who normally views the outside world with fear and uncertainty after he has been stigmatized and confined.

Problems Relating to Probation and Parole

There has been no evaluative study of probation as it is used in West Malaysia. Probation as a form of treatment is not much used by the court, e.g. of the 2,613 juveniles charged in courts in West Malaysia in 1960, only 226 (8.6 per cent) were placed on probation, and in 1965 of the 2,620, only 178 (7 per cent) were placed on probation. In the same years the committals to institutions were 11 per cent and 15 per cent. This does

[102]The Board of Visitor in an Approved School, or the Institutional Board in a Borstal:

not, however, suggest that probation is less successful than institutional treatment though the court seem to prefer committals to probation. One possible reason for the preference by courts is that probation is regarded as being more suited for first offenders and less vicious offenders, determined by the nature of the act.

Generally speaking, the department responsible for carrying out probation service claims high degree of success in its work.[103] "Of the 784 closed cases 51 were registered as failures. Expressed in percentage, there were therefore 93.5% successes as against 6.5% failures. Of the number of adults whose orders expired during the year, 23 were recorded as successes and 4 as failures. This gives nearly 85%."

The definition of "success" adopted in this report was that if the probationer had not committed any offenses during the period of probation, his case would then be termed as success.

In this sense, the definition is rather loose since it is not necessary that there must be a police record before a person can be termed a failure. Secondly, it is not sufficient to confine to behavior manifested during the period of probation only. The behavior subsequent to expiration of probation is equally important if not more.

With regard to release on licence, this has not been measured reliably in terms of success or otherwise. However, according to a survey[104] conducted in 1961—involving 608 boys and 45 girls who were assessed for their conduct—12 months after their release from Approved Schools, the finding shows that 467 boys (76.8 per cent) and 40 girls (88.9 per cent) were classified as "success." Undoubtedly the results were very encouraging both to the government and to the tax-payers. The definition used for "success" was based upon ability and performance "to re-establish oneself in society, keep out of the law, earn an honest living, or lead a sobre, wholesome settled life," and those who could not were termed as "failures." This is a loose definition and application to the survey found many loopholes with the result that anyone who at the time of the survey had

[103]*Annual Report of Department of Social Welfare, 1960*

[104]Unpublished Report on "the Statistical Survey on Boys and Girls, Discharged from Approved Schools," Department of Social Welfare, 1961.

not committed any further offense (or convicted) was loosely labeled as success.

Problems of failure in probation and release on licence may be attributed to the following factors.

Wrongful Selection of Offender. It is emphasized that there can be no simple categorical guide to the determination of the suitability of a particular offender for probation, though it is generally accepted that the bulk of failures come from those who possess lengthy previous careers of criminal association, like members of secret societies. First offenders are generally preferable, but it is also realized that a previous failure on probation does not necessarily render an offender unsuitable.

Like probation, the selection of a licencee is important, but it is impossible to formulate a reliable interim to the suitability of a person to be considered for licence. Normally, factors taken into account are the persons, length of stay, conduct and progress in the school, prospects of employment, and if possible, assurance of parents or guardians to assist in aftercare supervision.

Case Load. To perform his functions competently, the case load of the officer should be reasonable. The present average case load can be put around 35 though this varies from town to town and from state to state. The majority of officers are entrusted with multiple duties which means that besides his court work he is required to attend to other duties arising from public assistance, work with handicapped people, adoption, children's work, etc. Furthermore, case load is often influenced by the distance which the officer has to travel.

Misconception of Probation. The initial problem of making probation successful can also be seen to lie in the misconception of probation. As has been indicated earlier, this misconception that probation is a form of leniency, or as a "let-off," exists even among judicial officers and this explains why as a method of treatment the tendency is to apply it more readily to the young. But in actual fact the essence of probation is that each case should be considered on its own merit.

In general, this misconception which persists among officials charged with the enforcement of the law arises from the persistent primitive view towards the treatment of offenders.

Problem of Employment. Employment for probationers and

licencees from Approved Schools and Borstals remains one of the most acute problems. The highest rate of failure appears to come from those who want jobs but cannot find them. This problem is also aggravated by failures on the part of probationers and licencees to hold on to jobs which they have secured. Public prejudice also militates against rehabilitative prospects of people who have been convicted. It is not uncommon to find employers fighting shy of probationers and licencees because they hold the persistent view "once a thief, always a thief."

Non-cooperation of Parents. Generally, families of probationers and licencees also contribute to failures. Inadequate parents, illiterate and ignorant parents, are not expected to be able to play their role satisfactorily or offer adequate facilities for bringing up their own children. One other handicap lies in language difficulty, which makes case work relationship almost impossible when the supervising officer is of a different cultural group.

STUDY OF CRIMINOLOGY IN MALAYSIA

In the University of Malaya,[105] no courses on criminology and penology are being offered. This University is relatively new compared to the University of Singapore and perhaps the main reason why such courses are not yet made available is because the need for it has not been felt. A few years ago, there was a report in the local newspaper that some members of the legal profession had urged the University of Malaya to consider providing a course on criminology. Nothing has been heard of since then.

To some extent, a few selective subjects are offered to the undergraduates in the University of Singapore through its Law faculty and the Department of Social Work and Social Administration. Law students in the third academic year are given the option of a series of lectures and seminars described as criminal science covering the basic concepts of law, crime, and punishment/treatment. For the undergraduates in the Department of Social Work and Social Administration, sub-

---

[105]Established in 1961 as the national university of the country.

jects like principles and methods of social work, psychology, law relating to social work, and social service and problems are relevant to criminology. The subjects are basic in scope and are primarily intended for practising social workers. A distinction is made between the Diploma of Social Studies, Part I, and Diploma in Social Studies, Part II. Those completing the two year course are conferred with a Diploma Part I, while Diploma Part II is conferred on anyone who has successfully completed the third year advanced-level course. The latter covers an in-depth study of subjects like sociology of law, criminal etiology, penology, probation and parole, and institutional services.

The reasons why few law students choose optional papers like criminal science is that it has little material incentive and practical utility.

Although full-time courses are not provided in the University of Malaya or Singapore, it is not to be misconstrued that no interest is paid to the problem of crime and delinquency. Each concerned government department like the Police, Prisons, and Social Welfare Department run training courses for their officers. These training schemes are designed for the differential needs, level of education, and degree of responsibility of the officers. The Police Department has the most systematic scheme and basically their courses are provided at various centers for law enforcement officers.[106]

First, the Basic Training Depot in the Federal Capital is for probationary inspectors, general duty recruits and general duty women recruits. Secondly, the Higher Training Center at Police College in Selangor holds courses for prosecuting officers and Criminal Investigation Department officers. Thirdly, the Department of Chemistry—an independent Government Department—assists in training police officers in forensic science. And fourthly, there are the Overseas Training courses for selected officers. At the Department of Social Welfare, basic and advanced training is given to officers who are assigned to work in the field of probation, parole of juveniles discharged from approved schools and Henry Gurney School, and institutional work with juvenile delinquents.

[106]See *Official Year Book*, *op. cit.*, 1964.

For the year 1965, no less than 32 per cent of the 104 technical staff of the Department attended a training course of some
kind or other.[107] The training service of this Department
operates under the belief that learning is a continuous process
and in the context of social work, therefore, it should continue
throughout the entire span of the social worker's career.

Current Problems

Reference has already been made to the fact that few students
in the Law Faculty at the University of Singapore choose
criminal science as an optional subject. This has been attributed to the absence of material incentive and practical utility.

First and foremost, criminology is relatively new and has not
been accepted as a science. The argument over the approach to
the subject persists.[108] The crimonologist believes that fear of
punishment does not restrain crime. The psychoanalyst tries to
show that crime is a disease, but the law persistently deals with
the criminal as a normal person. The aim of criminal justice is
not clear whether it exists for punishment or treatment. This
explains a great deal of inconsistency in our sentencing policy
and correctional systems. If it exists for punishment, then why
should there be any need for study? Too many judges still insist
upon the retributive theory in one form or another. They go
so far as to argue that satisfaction of public desire for vengeance
is legitimate. This kind of philosophy does not create any justification for it to be made an important subject. To crown it
all, an easy way out is to attribute it to lack of funds; hence any
project in this direction is on a very low-scale of priority.

Another reason perhaps is that crime is generally not regarded as a major problem. In West Malaysia out of nearly
8,000,000, people the daily average prison population is 3,000
and the daily average inmate population in juvenile corrective
institutions is 800. The police and social workers hold the view
that juvenile delinquency is not yet a serious problem. Despite
this the government is actively interested in reviewing the measures being used to deal with the problem in any shape or size.

[107] *Annual Report of Department of Social Welfare, 1965.*
[108] Roscoe Pound, "Inherent and Acquired Difficulties in the Administra-
tration of Punitive Justice," *Crime and Delinquency*, Vol. 10, No. 4, 1964.

For social workers, specialization is limited in scope, because of a policy of the Department which has turned all social-welfare personnel to multiple social workers. This means that the social worker has to deal with problems in all areas of needs, child care, adoption, public assistance, matrimonial disputes, and probation. Interchange of personnel from one field of interest and operation to another has also weakened scope and opportunity for individual specialization in any field.

As a social science, criminology is extremely new, even in the most developed countries. The word is seldom used and where it is mentioned, it gives rise to ambiguity. Psychological studies, like psychiatry, are viewed by many with suspicion and are labelled as Western concepts. It has not made all the impact that it should because their studies and findings are thought to be irrelevant to an agricultural type of economy. Another barrier to study may stem from the fatalistic philosophy inherent among the more conservative and less-literate Malaysians.

Consequently, personnel engaged in prisons, probation, and institutional work are often paid less than those in the general public service. The argument is based upon the fact that personnel in correctional services have lesser academic qualifications compared with other civil servants. So long as this remains, it is doubtful if intelligent young men will find sufficient incentive in choosing correctional work as their career.

Research Courses

In the University of Singapore, one of the requirements for students doing the course of social work and social administration is the production of a thesis based on original research in their second academic year. Over the years, ample material has been collected and their findings must contain important sociological, psychological, and criminological information. It would produce enormous results of beneficial value if further research on these materials could be carried out to establish correlation. The studies so far have tended to be too individualized and coordination of these fragmented studies may prove very useful.

Other selective areas of study have from time to time been carried out by the concerned government department. As an example the Department of Social Welfare has produced an interesting study to evaluate Approved School methods in rehabilitating juvenile offenders. Studies and reports compiled by the University of Singapore and the Department of Social Welfare, are for restricted use only. Free access to the public and those interested would be welcome, mainly to stimulate interest in the subject.

Joint efforts and close liaison between the University and the relevant government departments are desirable and necessary if criminological research is to be more meaningful and to provide effective measures for crime control and treatment. What seems of immediate importance under a joint project is (*i*) to assess if crime is a problem for the community; (*ii*) to identify the causative factors in crime; and (*iii*) to seek improvement and evaluation on the measures now being used for rehabilitating offenders.

These tasks can only be accomplished with the co-operation of all concerned—the police, the courts, the prisons, probation and institutional services, and the University.

GENERAL SOCIAL POLICIES

Broadly speaking, two methods may be discussed. The first method aims at preventing commission of crimes and the second aims at preventing repetition of crimes by means of legislation.

Preventive Measures

These aim at preventing commission of first crimes through the following measures.

Police School Liaison Program. Recently the police have launched a program known as Police School Liaison Program whereby school children can be taught to respect law and become law-abiding citizens of tomorrow. It is now realized that it is easier to inculcate good and healthy values in younger children than in adults. The background of the present day criminals who form the prison population indicates that disrespect for law and social order has its origin in childhood and adolescence itself. To correct the wrong image of the police, the program seeks to remove the impression, perhaps rightly formed, that the policeman is not a friend of the public. Hence, the primary objective of the School Liaison Program is to influence the young child to identify the police as a law enforcement agency guided by principles of honesty, fairness, firmness.[109] The program requires the police to participate in the various school and youth movements, to assist parents, teachers, and children in sorting out society or delinquency influence. With this end in view, police officers in the district are encouraged to give talks not only on their own functions but on the duty and obligations of the citizens. Policemen on beat duty or in their relation with the public, especially school children, are urged to demonstrate their friendly attitude to gain the confidence of those they are supposed to serve.

New System of Policing. With a view to preventing crime a new system, known as the Salleh system,[110] has been recently introduced after a successful experiment which was carried out in 1968 in a densely populated new satellite town called Petaling Jaya in the State of Selangor. By this system, decentralization of policemen at station or district level is necessary. Policemen would have to live amongst the inhabitants in the neighborhood and not in centralized barracks. This enables the policemen to identify themselves with the local inhabitants so that they can be more readily accepted as friends. They need to convince the public that they would use their authority wisely, and their response to public call for service must be swift and prompt. The plan envisages greater effectiveness in their role because of the new interest and enthusiasm infused into their work.

Social and Economic Planning. Rapid population growth is a factor that has to be checked if the country is to avoid the ill effects of over-population. With the present annual increase of 3 per cent efforts are being made by the government to bring it down to 2 per cent. Although the Family Planning Board is in theory, not a government department

[109]Unpublished Report from the Inspector General of Police, Malaysia, 1968.

[110]It was introduced by the first Malaysian Inspector General of Police in 1968, and thus bears his name.

it receives almost full subsidy from the government for its operating expenses.

In the field of economic growth, the government is resolved to redouble its efforts in several directions, "the Government," the Deputy Prime Minister is reported to have said, "will pursue with vigor the development of agricultural land in both West and East Malaysia and will continue to utilise fully the substantial land resources for economic and social advancement."[111]

Malaysia's productivity in the economic field has brought about one of the highest per capita incomes in Asia. Despite this, the unemployment situation has caused grave concern to the government and for the year 1969 the economic review shows that fewer new jobs had been created than originally anticipated. The unemployment figure was nearer 6 per cent of the total labor force of 3,342,000 at the end of 1968 which means the total unemployed is nearly 200,000. The mid-term review of the First Malaysia Plan 1966 to 1970 further reveals significant degrees of under-employment in agriculture, commerce, and service industries.

The government realizes that a more dynamic economy is extremely vital, for if this does not happen increasing number of people will be driven to employment when withdrawal of Britain's military forces begin in two or three years time. Nearly 17,000 workers are employed by the British Forces in Malaysia. To promote trade and industry for the economic development of the country and to ensure that the returns from government efforts in such promotions contribute to the national economic prosperity, the Ministry of Commerce and Industry has actively stepped up its activities.[112] One of these is to promote industrialization throughout the country—either from local capital or foreign investments—with the provision of adequate incentives as a measure to diversify national economy. To meet this increased responsibility, Parliament has voted a sum of $7,215,860 for

[111]*Straits Times*, February 3, 1969, when the Deputy Prime Minister of Malaysia introduced the 1969 development estimates in the House of Parliament.

[112]*Budget Summary of Federal Government Expenditure*, 1969, p. 77.

the year 1969 as against $5,861,582 for 1968.[113]

Youth Services. Such services as provided by the government through its Ministry of Youth, Sports and Culture, can contribute towards prevention or reduction in delinquency. Stress, of late, has been laid upon provision of suitable recreational facilities for teenagers so as to offer effective counter attractions to the lure of anti-social influence to the youth. In a seminar on "Children in Need of Treatment" held in Kuala Lumpur,[114] one of the resolutions passed was to urge the government to provide recreational facilities wherever needed—particularly in the housing estates where, in the absence of outlets to their energies, there is the danger of children forming into sub-cultural gangs. The Government Youth Club program aims mainly at uplifting the social, economic, and educational conditions for its youth. The provision of facilities for wholesome leisure-time activities, participation in rural development and in other community service projects could also check tendencies of youth to migrate to urban areas with possible consequent ill-effects.

In the past, education tended to be too strongly biased towards academic education but the new system has tried to strike a happy balance between the two. In several secondary schools, and their number is increasing, vocational training is also provided. Another example of trying to adjust training to practical needs is seen in the Pioneer Corps for unemployed youth recruited mainly from rural areas.[115] The Ministry is expanding in terms of its activities to provide basic leadership, technical and vocational training for Malaysian youths who are to be equipped for active and effective participation in the economic, agricultural, industrial, and social development of the country.

Youth Employment Service. The Ministry of Labor has a section to give vocational guidance to school leaders by suggesting types of employment which will provide the best

[113] *Ibid.*, p. 78.

[114] Organized by the Department of Social Welfare in 1963 with both professional social workers and voluntary workers participating.

[115] The National Youth Pioneer Corps was formed in 1966. A large proportion of the trainees have found employment after graduation. See *Report of the Ministry of Youth, Sports and Culture, 1968.*

opportunities for the development of their capabilities and interest. The object of this service is to help them to find employment suited to their educational qualifications, aptitude, interest, and personality and it also provides advice to boys and girls who have just started work.

In addition to this, the Ministry of Labor through its central apprenticeship board, which was established in 1956, maintains a register of apprentices, exercises a general supervision over their apprenticeship contracts, and issues final certificates of proficiency at the end of training. This service is designed to prepare young apprentices for effective employment after they have completed a training course.

Care of Children. The various laws governing the care of children recognise that the family is the best guarantee for the happiness and well-being of the child. Provision is made for the child to be taken care of in the event that the family system breaks down, temporarily, or permanently. The Children and Young Persons Ordinance of 1947 places statutory responsibility on the Department of Social Welfare to provide children in every area of need, be it the child who is neglected, cruelly treated, abandoned, or exploited in one way or another. For the year 1968, there were 600 children in the Government Children's Homes, and 552 children were enjoying the Foster Allowance Schemes operated by the Federal Department of Social Welfare, not counting the large number of recipients under the individual State Schemes.[116]

The Adoption Ordinance is designed to guarantee that the adopted child will have the full opportunities to enjoy himself as other children. The Juvenile Courts Ordinance regards the child with a problem as one in need of help rather than one to be punished. Apart from these statutory duties, the officials of the department advice regarding problem children and help in other multifarious duties connected with welfare of families and children. Contribution towards childcare also comes from the many well-established voluntary organizations, like the Convent Orphanages. Salvation Army Children's Homes, and a host of others. They were supported

[116]*Budget Summary of Federal Government Expenditure, op. cit.*, p. 203.

by grants from the Ministry of Welfare Services to a tune of 5ラ 2,000 for the year 1968.

General Welfare and Public Assistance Schemes. The scheme operated individually by each state has the aim of preserving the family unit. The idea is to keep the family unit intact even under adverse conditions so that the recipient could work towards re-establishing and restoring his normal functioning capacity. As a new development, emphasis is now laid on giving subsidy to children from poor families to buy books, to help pay their school fees, transport and examination fees, so that children who can benefit from education are not forced to leave school and thus become easy prey to the criminal world.

Legislation

Prevention of repetition of crime exists in several Acts and Enactments. In order of importance, "Prevention of Crime Ordinance 13/59" should be mentioned first. The object and scope of this Ordinance "is to provide for the more effectual prevention of crime in the Federation and for the control of criminals, members of secret societies and other undesirable persons."

Powers of arrest and remand are vested with the police who may without warrant arrest any person if he has reason to believe that ground exists for the holding of an inquiry. On production before a Magistrate, the arrested person may be remanded in police custody if the Magistrate is satisfied that there is ground for the arrested person to be subjected to an inquiry.

The Inquiry Officer[117] shall inquire and report in writing to the Minister whether there are reasonable grounds for believing that such person is a member of any of the registrable categories.[118] A person who is registered under any of

[117]An Inquiry Officer is appointed by the Minister charged with responsibility for internal affairs and he is normally a qualified Advocate and Solicitor employed by the court and never a Police Officer.

[118](a) These cover all members of unlawful societies; (b) all persons below 21 years of age who have been convicted on at least three occasions of offenses involving dishonesty or violence; (c) all persons who

the categories may by order of the Minister be subjected to police supervision for a period not exceeding five years. A registered person who contravenes the order made by the Minister shall be liable upon conviction to imprisonment for a term between two and five years.

The Restricted Residence Enactment[119] also gives considerable power to the government in dealing with criminals for the prevention of further crimes. The object and scope of this Enactment is to provide enforcement of orders regarding residence of those so restricted by exclusion from certain parts of the country. Power under this Enactment is given to the Mentri Besar or the State to make an order for habitual criminal to reside in a particular place within the State if the Mentri Besar or Chief Minister has reasonable ground to believe that such an order is necessary.

The recommendation for such an order is normally made by the police after it has satisfied itself that restricting a person as to his residence would prevent further crime. The effect of this order is similar to that made under Prevention of Crime Ordinance. This Enactment is more restrictive in scope because it covers only a state and not the whole country. Police is also given power under the Criminal Procedure Code to take steps to disperse unlawful assembly of five or more persons likely to cause a disturbance in the public peace. The police officer may use force if necessary where civil force is not sufficient to disperse the unlawful assembly. Military force may also be used.

Under the Criminal Procedure Code a Supreme Court or Sessions Court may, in addition to sentencing a person to imprisonment, order him to undergo police supervision after the expiration of the term for a period of not more than three years. A Magistrate may in addition to passing sentence of imprisonment, order a person to be supervised by police for a period not exceeding one year. A person subjected to the

---

have been dealt under the Restricted Residence Enactment of the Federated Malay States; (*d*) certain offenses under the Penal Code; and (*e*) offenses under the Corrosive and Explosive Substance and Offensive Weapons Ordinance, 1958.

[119]*Restricted Residence Enactment*, Chapter 39, passed in June, 1933.

supervision of the police is required to report to the Officer-in-charge of the district once a month and to obtain permission before he changes his place of residence. The penalty for breach of the supervision order is imprisonment for one year.

Sentencing Policy of the Court. The effectiveness of the judicial policy with regard to young adult offenders between the age of 17-21 has yet to be assessed. The Subordinate Courts have been asked to examine alternative methods in dealing with this group of offenders, as it has been acknowledged that short-term imprisonment has been found to be fairly negative.

Little or nothing could be done by the prison authority to rehabilitate the prisoners. In Malaya, almost 50 per cent of the total prison population are serving sentences of six months or under. Such short term imprisonment, it has been argued, may acclimatize the first offender to prison conditions and tends to make him hardened or indifferent to the rehabilitative aspects of imprisonment so that he slowly gravitates into recidivism.[120] Being aware of this danger, there was a suggestion from the former Chief Justice in 1954 that consultation with the Probation Officer may be desirable as the background report of the convicted young offender may contain possibility of his being dealt with in a more satisfactory manner, such as probation with supervision and other conditions attached to the order.

SUMMARY AND CONCLUSION

As a background to this paper, the brief history of Malaysia, together with its people and its social system, is intended to promote a greater understanding and appreciation of the problem of crime and delinquency, and of the various measures adopted to deal with the inevitable imperfection universally found in all societies. However, with a population of nearly 10,000,000 people, Malaysia has reason to be proud of the fact that despite the multi-racial composition of its people, and their divergent background, there is unity in diversity, and respect for law is a distinct feature in the life of its people.

[120]United Nations, *The Open Correctional Institutions in Asia and the Far East*, Japan, 1965.

This may thus explain the absence of crime as a major problem.

In attempting to establish definitions of the terms "crime" and "criminal" reference has to be made to the existing criminal law. It could, however, be seen that the Penal Code, Juvenile Courts Ordinance, and other Acts of Parliament do not necessarily supply us with a very satisfactory answer. Nevertheless, a crime has now come to be regarded as an offense against the State. The definition of a juvenile delinquent is necessarily more flexible for not only is a child over seven years of age liable to penal prosecution for any public wrong he commits, but his anti-social behavior particularly towards parents, can also lead him to be subjected to judicial process, though primarily, this measure is intended for his own good.

An attempt to present crime statistics raises basic difficulties. It must be remembered that the general statistics of crime and criminals are probably the most unreliable and most difficult of all. Therefore, it is impossible to determine with accuracy the amount of crime in any given area and at any particular time. One is well aware of the fact that a large proportion of crimes committed go undetected, or unreported, and where reported may not be officially recorded. With this in mind, it is stressed that any record of crimes kept by the police or any other law enforcement agencies can at best be regarded as an index of the crimes committed; but even this is unsatisfactory for various reasons. For this paper, further difficulty was added by the non-availability of information from other law enforcement agencies except the police. In so far as the police is concerned, only record of true seizable offenses reported to them is available. As shown earlier there is a gradual rise in the number of seizable offenses from 31,399 in 1960 to 46,861 in 1967. The pattern of crime over the years seems constant with offenses against property being prevalent.

The section on "Theories of Crime Causation" vividly shows the basic difficulty in defining the causal problem, considered by many to be unique in the entire realm of criminology. Crime Causation is a subject about which there is a great deal of confusion. Each point of view seems, to a considerable extent, to be based upon a deep-rooted conviction which makes objectivity difficult to achieve. Whatever view one takes, psychological, psycho-analytical, biological or sociological, there is ample evidence to show that each point of view is correct to a point. In fact, there is no facet of social life which does not have a bearing on criminality or delinquency. The multi-causal theory in attempting to explain the matter more scientifically has of course nullified the outdated theory of the "inborn criminal."

With the transformation of penological concept and practice over the last three decades, the barbaric and brutal form of punishment has come to be replaced by a system in accord with modern needs colored by humanitarian and reformative philosophy. Punishment as the primary sanction of the criminal law has been modified and more constructive forms of punishment like releasing offenders on probation are in use. Experience has shown that harsh punishment sanctioned by theories of retaliation, retribution and deterrence, does not necessarily create respect for law. Social attitude towards criminals has changed considerably and due to the impact of modern psychology, criminal law today is even prepared to accept that criminals in some instances are psychological patients. The penal development in the Malaysian prisons has been a logical process characterized by the abolition of corporal punishment of penal servitude, of rigorous and simple imprisonment, and creation of Borstal training for youngs offenders.

The section on the functions of the courts highlights the relationship between the courts and the executive organ, and emphasizes the need to guarantee fundamental rights of its citizens if democracy as enshrined in the Constitution is to work well. The administration of criminal justice can be said to be in safe hands because not only is independence of the judiciary guaranteed, but also the judges, prosecutors, and magistrates who man the machinery are people qualified for the task they perform. The hierarchy of courts and judges with scale of jurisdiction does not alter the fact that each court in the exercise of its jurisdiction is a separate entity, and each judge or magistrate acts independently, without consultation, except when there is an appeal to a higher court. The trial method, as one can see, is based upon the sporting theory of justice and in practice is regarded as a game in which the two parties fight a battle of words against each other with the court acting as a referee to decide which has a better cause. Where counsel is required, the law permits the defendant to employ his own counsel, and under certain circumstances—like offense carrying death penalty—even the State may provide one for him. All persons dissatisfied with the decision of any court again enjoy the unlimited right of appeal. Not only justice must be done, but it must be seen to be done. One of the rights which the citizens enjoy is the right to a public trial. With the Juvenile Court, however, the position is different not because of denial of this right but because of the belief that any public trial will expose children to further criminality and harm their future as a result of stigma attached to crime.

The functions of the Royal Malaysia Police, as already explained in outline, include the maintenance of law and order, the prevention of detection of crime, and the apprehension and prosecution of offenders. Of particular interest is the work of the Criminal Investigation Department which is concerned with the last two functions. Much is to be said in favor of the preventive role of police, but if its relationship with the public is to be improved and maintained, as I am sure every policeman would like to see, then they must make it a point to demonstrate their goodwill and exemplary conduct and behavior in order to win the confidence of the public. Public are often blamed and one of the reasons for increase in crime has been partly attributed to the public for not offering resistance to criminals and failing to report crimes to police authorities.

What role do the Malayan prisons play today to be in accord with modern penological thinking? In tracing development of the prison up to the present the section on prisons reveals the progress that has been made in this field. It is gratifying to note that with the unification of the different prisons into a central system of control and administration in 1949, followed by the more enlightened Prisons Ordinance and Rules passed in 1953, the present approach to prisoners has embodied the principles laid down by the United Nations known as the UN "Standard Minimum Rules." Although its declared policy that prisoners are not sent to prison solely for punishment but for the more punitive aim of rehabilitation may have given rise to mixed feelings, but should not the community be pleased if the purpose of imprisonment is "to establish in the prisoners to lead a good and useful life on discharge?" Any plan by the prisons authorities to experiment on opening more correctional constitutions—now universally regarded as one of the most constructive, humane and economical developments in penology—should receive support.

Coming to probation as a suitable alternative method to imprisonment, we find that the number of probationers for the years 1961-1966 remains below 400, when the prison population for the same period is nearly 3,000 per year. This is nearly eight times more. Compared with England, according to figures collected by the Howard League for Penal Reform, the daily average prison population is less than 25,000 whereas there are now approximately 50,000 persons on probation at any given time. Could the lack of use reflect the continuous desire for vengeance by the public when a wrong has been done? Because of the conflicting aim of criminal justice, it is not surprising to find some judges who would use probation freely, while others condemn the system. It would seem necessary at this stage for more probation officers to be appointed from people with not only sound academic training but with the right personality, for this should lead to higher success rates and command confidence not only of the public but of the judges.

While it may be regretted that there are limited facilities for training in criminology, penology, and juvenile delinquency work, one has to be realistic about the matters. The various government departmental facilities, together with those available at the University of Singapore, would appear adequate for the moment. With development in penological thinking, and gradual recognition that criminology can be studied scientifically, there will come a time when greater facilities will be provided for those who would like to choose a carrier in the field of prevention of crime and treatment of offenders.

With regard to the prevention of crime and delinquency, two principal methods exist to prevent commission of first crimes as well as to prevent their repetition. The two methods are necessarily inter-related. In examining the measures, co-ordination and co-operation between the government depart-ments concerned is vital but if they are to be effective, the public must not be left out altogether. The varions social and economic policies seek to strengthen family life and in this respect the valuable contribution of the voluntary agencies cannot be overstressed.

Suggestions and Recommendations

A number of issues emerging from this study have been raised here. While it would be useful to try and suggest possible solutions to the many-sided problems, the following comments and observations are meant to help stimulate further dis-cussion.

A Unified Approach. First and foremost, any program or policy of prevention of crime and treatment of offenders needs to have the participation of all concerned—the courts, the police, the prison administrator, the tax-payers, and per-haps the offender himself. In England, and in many other countries, there is an annual meeting held under the auspices of the Lord Chief Justice, and attended by judges, magistrates, justices of the peace, criminologists, prison psy-chologists, sociologists, and lawyers, at which problems of common interest are discussed. A conference of this nature is necessary in Malaysia if a combined unified approach is desired. A lesson can perhaps be learned from the Selangor Discharged Prisoners Aid Society which has made it a practice to invite the Chief Justice to address its members as well as invited representatives from other government departments at its annual conference. Seminars organized by the various Ministries on topics relevant to crime prevention and treatment now usually have representation by all bodies concerned; this is to be encouraged.

Training of Lawyers and Judges. The need for lawyers, judges, magistrates, to be better informed about the treatment of offenders has been increasingly felt. Dr R.M. Jackson, a very learned critic of the English Legal System, has said: "An English criminal trial properly conducted is one of the best products of our land provided you walk out of the court before a sentence is given. If you stay to the end you may find that it takes far less time and inquiry to settle a man's prospects in life than it has taken to find out whether he took a suitcase out of a parked motorcar."

This suggests that some aspects of criminology would be valuable for inclusion in the curriculum of law schools, a practice adopted by many countries. In Japan it is now understood to be the policy of Ministry of Justice to send public prosecutors, judges of district courts, and law enforcement-officers, in addition to correctional workers, for a refresher course at the United Nations Asia Far East Institute which runs regular short term courses on prevention of crime and treatment of offenders.

One appreciates that judges are not wholly unresponsive to other means of penal measure though there may be a misconception that retribution ought to be the dominant philosophy. The objects of criminal justice now lay stress that punishment, whether with pain or without, inflicted on a person because of a crime is only the means and not the end of criminal justice.

Arising from this, the question is sometimes asked, "Is there a need for appointment of special juvenile court judges?" This question stems from recognition of the fact that if juvenile delinquents are not handled correctly, the adult criminal population will remain high. There is a view that perhaps the question should now be examined with the view to appointing Juvenile Court judges with specialized training in child psychology and sociology. The persons who fill such vacancies should not only be qualified in academic learning but should have a warm personality and sympathetic understanding of the child and his needs.

Changes in the Law. Touching on police supervision contained in the Criminal Procedure Code which the court can add to imprisonment under certain circumstances, it can be suggested that, this particular provision should be replaced by probation supervision. Police supervision is usually negative. While it may prevent a person from committing further crime, it is not likely to affect rehabilitation in the supervisee. This has also been confirmed by the Prisons Inquiry Commission (Singapore).[121]

> The commission has received ample evidence that police
> supervision is extremely disliked by prisoners who have
> even stated to the commission that they would prefer to
> serve the period of supervision within the prisons rather
> than be subjected to the surveilance of the police. There
> is a widespread view that police supervision has no value
> to the police and certainly it has no value at all even to the
> prisoner trying to adjust himself into society.

Parole. As mentioned earlier, there is no parole law for adult
prisoners. Parole would appear to have distinctive advantages
over the remission system. The former provides compulsory
supervision of prisoners discharged on parole, whereas the latter
offers no facility of supervision for the discharged prisoner.
The Malaysian Government looked into the possibility of
introducing parole in 1964 but nothing has been heard since.
Perhaps financial considerations caused the idea to be shelved.

One of the resolutions adopted by the second United
Nations Congress on the Prevention of Crime and the Treatment of Offenders held in London in 1960 resolves that "it is
desirable to apply the principle of release before the expiration
of the sentence subject to conditions to the widest possible
extent as a practical solution of both the social and the
administrative problem created by imprisonment."

The theory of punishment stresses the value of indeterminate sentence as is now applicable to juvenile delinquents
committed to juvenile corrective institutions. The period of
corrective training imposed should be determined not so much
by the seriousness of the instant crime or even of the prisoners' past criminal record, but rather in relation to the time
considered necessary to reform the prisoner.[122]

Social Work in Prisons. It is being increasingly felt that social
work should form an integral part of the modern prison administration. A proper approach will be to appoint trained social

[121] See *Report of the Prisons Inquiry Commission*, State of Singapore,
1960.
[122] J. Li Edwards, "A New Doctrine in Criminal Punishment," *Law
Quarterly Review*, Vol. 72, 1956.

workers to deal with such problems as may arise. Merely calling prison officers as social workers is avoiding the real problem. The need for expert social work in prison cannot be overstressed for it is only trained people who can deal with the intricate emotional problems presented by those incarcerated. Theoretically speaking, prison welfare service and aftercare service extended to paroles should be viewed as a continuous rehabilitative process. The former primarily operates in the institution while the latter operates in the open. It must be stressed that the duty of society does not end with the prisoner's release. There should be governmental or private agencies capable of helping the discharged prisoner towards his social rehabilitation.

The present concept of aftercare as practised by the Discharged Prisoners Aid Society is too narrow and is often thought of in terms of largely meeting the material needs of the prisoner. More important than this is to provide case-work service to give moral help for overcoming the prisoner's emotional problems. Mere material help leaves the real problem unsolved. Even the shift of emphasis in their role has been advocated by the Selangor Discharged Prisoners Aid Society in its recent annual report.

In this connection, too much dependence must not be placed on volunteers although certain Discharged Prisoners Aid Societies are taking a keen interest in some aspects of aftercare work. There should be an active lead and support from the government. No voluntary body with its limited humane and economic resources can ever be in a position to render service of such a magnitude. The treatment of offenders is a matter of public interest and even if semi-governmental or voluntary organizations are entrusted with important functions in the field, policy-making is likely to remain a purely governmental responsibility almost everywhere.[123] Finally, in so far as training of officers for this sort of work is concerned a constant liaison and co-ordination between the Ministry of Social Welfare and the Prisons Department is vital.

Medical and Psychiatric Work in Prisons. The important role

---

[123]United Nations, *International Review of Criminal Policy*, No. 23, 1965, p. 35.

which medical officers can play in prisons cannot be overstressed. It would appear that every large prison needs a full-time
medical officer who can contribute much to the rehabilitative
measures of the prisons. The present practice of having prisons
served by visiting medical officers cannot be regarded as satisfactory. His responsibilities are not merely limited to treating
sick prisoners but by his daily contact with them he can assert
a considerable amount of influence in determining the atmosphere of the prison. With regard to psychiatric service, the
position is much worse—the whole prison service being without a psychiatrist. In the whole country, it is said, there are
only four trained psychiatrists serving two large mental hospitals with a patient population of nearly 7,000.

With the total prison population being 3,000 for West
Malaysia, there is a definite need for either a psychiatrist or a
psychiatric social worker, to begin with. The fact that prisoners
are not on the whole easy patients justifies the employment
of qualified personnel,—without undermining the role of the
non-specialist custodial staff. Frequently the courts, while
passing the verdict, hope that the sentenced accused could
receive psychiatric treatment. Since this facility is not available,
there is no wonder if the psychiatric prisoner does not respond
to the training programme. In the absence of reliable statistics
to classify abnormal prisoners for psychiatric treatment, it is
not possible to guage the extent of the present problem. In
any case the number appears serious enough to be of concern
to prison officers who seem to have resigned to an attitude
of hopelessness or indifference. The need for psychiatric service
could also apply to Approved Schools and the Borstals.

Trained Personnel for Institution Work. The quality of an
institution depends entirely upon the people who operate it.
It is important to obtain for the prisons and juvenile institutions a staff of wise, humane, and dedicated men who are
prepared to understand the prisoners' character and special
needs and capable of exercising a wholesome moral influence
over them.[124] This body of men and women must appreciate
that their working material is human lives. Modern penology

[124]*Report of the First United Nations Congress on the Prevention of
Crime and the Treatment of Offenders,* Geneva, 1955.

places emphasis upon the reform and rehabilitation of offenders, and "the purpose of a prison is to protect society against crime and this purpose is not served if the offender returns to society unfitted to lead a normal life and earn an honest living."[125]

The staff must not regard prisoners as a group of men to be controlled, counted, locked and unlocked. "If this is so, the conflict between the criminal and society will be continually re-enacted."[126]

Finally it has to be strongly stressed that there should be a unified approach in the prisons, that is to say, the body of officers carrying out different functions will have one common aim solely oriented towards the reform of the offender.

Importance of Police Work. How much confidence does the police command in the general public? So often the general public is blamed for failing to co-operate with the police in its work in crime prevention, detection, and arrest. On the other hand, the police have been severely criticized for their wrong approach, though such criticisms are not always constructive. There is need for closer understanding with the public, and the police is well advised to strive harder to build a good image for itself. The public need to be convinced that police work does not merely consist in arresting the criminal but also in preventing commission of offenses. In this connection, the police involvement in community projects, youth and boys' clubs is certainly to be encouraged.

Social Work and Delinquency. There is a strong view that social work has a big role to play in preventing delinquency and crime. Unfortunately the number of social workers engaged in preventive work in this field is rather inadequate. It is too much to expect a handful of (around 20) officers to attend to (nearly 800) probationers and juvenile licencees. The majority of probation officers feel frustrated as they have to concentrate mainly on the making of pre-sentence reports. As multiple social workers they have other equally pressing duties to perform. Much of the work in supervision may be described as meeting statutory requirement with little application of genuine

---

[125]*Prisons and Borstals* (London: HMSO, 1957), p. 10.
[126]Winifred A. Alkin, *op. cit.*, p. 133.

case-work principles and practice because of pressure of work. It is obvious that if the standard of probation and aftercare work is to be raised and maintained, there needs to be a more realistic policy of increasing the officers quantitatively, and improving their work qualitatively. Malaysia is indeed fortunate to have nearly 90 per cent of the 20 odd or so probation personnel trained at university level, with qualification in social studies. Unless there is a high standard, should the court be blamed if it does not have much faith in the probation staff as it ought to?

Arising from the call for more probation officers and social workers an argument is put forward for a less expensive form of treatment for offenders. Probation is not only less expensive, but it also avoids the shattering impact of imprisonment on human personality. Another advantage is the fact that it offers a more individualized approach and treatment program than the penal institution can provide. Unfortunately, we still see some judicial officers holding the view that punishment should fit the offense rather than the offender. While we cannot be certain that a more humanitarian form of treatment like probation would be more effective than (the punitive form of treatment like) imprisonment in reducing recidivism, there is no reason to believe that less severe punishment will be less effective. The argument for more severe punishment is not always based on logic but emotionally colored by the retributive and deterrent theory of punishment.

Use of probation is also compatible with making treatment more realistic and not only less expensive. The disposition in court cases seems too much guided by convention and traditional belief and not always related to the modern needs of the community. There is a wrong belief that it is easier to control delinquents and at the same time offer protection to society if the offender is committed to institutions. But the problems of both society and the delinquent lie clearly in free society.

For treatment of juvenile offenders, a more realistic scheme could perhaps be linked up with some community, rural or work programs. The pioneer youth corp of West Malaysia initiated by the Ministry of Youth, Sports and Culture, could perhaps be modified to include suitable probationers for vocational and agricultural training rather than just being open to unemployed youth. In this connection, it is relevant to mention that juvenile institutions like Approved Schools and Borstals could with some changes in policy and legislation prepare their inmates for participation in community programmes like FLDA[127] schemes for landless youth. Sense of responsibility and faith in training programs also needs to be strengthened among parents.

Research. There is a great need for research into the causes of crime and the effectiveness of the various methods used in treating offenders. This could perhaps be done on a joint basis by the different departments concerned like the police, prison, the courts, Social Welfare Department, Education Department, and the local University. As an alternative, the task could be performed by a separate and independent agency.[128] Each department, as indicated earlier, tends to pursue its interest in a water-tight compartment without regard to co-ordination. The University of Singapore—through its Departments of Social Work and Social Administration—has ample data of criminological value collected from field-work carried out by graduating students. What is important is to have them co-ordinated.

The various ad hoc studies carried out by the Department of Social Welfare in West Malaysia—dealing with the intelligence of delinquents in Approved Schools and the effectiveness of Approved School training—show encouraging possibilities, and subsequent follow-up on a wider scale is recommended. There is general lack of experts duly trained for research in the field of treatment of offenders, with the result that even where some investigations are completed, they fail to contribute substantially to the knowledge needed by the practitioners. It is obviously necessary to devise a plan for the training of people competent to carry out research. It is also useful to build up

[127]Federal Land Development Authority which provides land for landless people.

[128]D. N. Ray, Director, Central Bureau of Correctional Services, Government of India, discusses "The Need for a National Agency to Promote Sound Policies, for the Prevention of Crime and Treatment of Offenders, with Particular Reference to India," in *International Review of Criminal Policy*, No. 23, 1965, United Nations publication.

a system of interchange of personnel between the various departments on the one hand and universities on the other, if a central national agency is created.

Criminological research, in order to be of value to the government, must not be detached from actual practice in prevention, control, and treatment of crime and delinquency. We should avoid a situation whereby the practitioner has ground to accuse the researcher of pursuing his investigation only within an academic framework unrelated to the practical requirements and needs of the community. It would be wrong for the government to refuse funds if the projects could lead to saving of thousands of dollars which are bound to be spent unnecessarily on ineffective methods. Human behavior is unpredictable, and the government must be prepared to consider the initial expenditure fair, and if necessary to be spread over a longer period, so that a worthwhile assessment can be made.

Future Implications and Conclusion

There is indication that Malaysia is trying to deal with this problem in the light of its own social, economic, and cultural background and traditions. The question is often asked, "Is there likely to be an increase in crime and delinquency in the future?" We have seen urban conditions being more prone to produce young offenders than rural conditions. As there appears to be a shift in population from rural areas to the towns and suburbs, it will be reasonable to expect an increase unless, of course, conditions of employment in towns improve. The government is aware of this and with its stepped up industrialization program, it hopes to meet the challenge. At the same time rural programs are intensified to check the uhealthy migration of people to the town.

The breaking of family ties also exposes young people to various forms of stresses and strains. We have reason to believe that family ties in Asian homes are not going to break up so easily. A fear frequently expressed is that children who do not go to schools could become potential recruits for juvenile crimes and on this basis the government is right in establishing more and more schools to ensure that every child who needs to go to school is given a place. Where children after primary education are not considered suitable for the academic stream, vocational schools with a technical bias are strongly recommended to absorb them.

While it is apparent that Malaysia is steadily moving towards more humane social concepts of treatment for those who have succumbed to crime, it is considered important to introduce measures which can help prevent crime. The political, social, and economic stability which the country now enjoys does seem to offer prospects that respect for law and order will continue to prevail.

BIBLIOGRAPHY

Malaysian Constitutional Documents.
Official Year Books Malaysia, 1960-1967.
Juvenile Courts Ordinance and Rules, No. 38/47.
Malayan Penal Code.
Malayan Criminal Procedure Code.
Courts Ordinance, No. 43 of 1948.
Courts of Judicature Act, 1963.
Police Act, 1967.
The Prison Ordinance and Rules, 1953.
Advocates and Solicitors Ordinance, No. 4 of 1947.
Prevention of Crime Ordinance, No. 13/59.
Restricted Residence Enactment, Chap. 39 of 1933.
Children and Young Persons Ordinance, No. 33 of 1947.
Annual Reports of Department of Social Welfare, 1960-1965.
Annual Reports of Royal Malaysia Police, 1962, 1965, 1966 (for restricted use)
Annual Reports of Discharge Prisoners' Aid Society, Selangor, 1964, 1965.
Extract of Annual Report of Prisons Department, 1963.
Malaysia Year Book, 1967
United Nations. *The Open Correctional Institution in Asia and the Far East* prepared by The United Nations Asia and Far East Institute for the Prevention of Crime and Treatment of Offenders, Japan, 1965.
Report of the Treatment of Children in Need, issued by Department of Social Welfare, 1963.
HUANG SU MIEN (Miss). "Judicial Review of Administrative Action by the Prerogative Orders." Published by *University of Malaya Law Review.* Vol. 2, No. 1, July, 1960.
T. T. B. KOH. "The Sentencing Policy and Practice of Singapore Courts" in *University of Malaya Law Review,* Vol. 7, No. 5, December, 1965.
A. A. G. PETFRS. *Comparative Survey of Juvenile Delinquency in Asia and The Far East.* U.U.A.F.E.I. Series, Tokyo 1968.
Report of the Prisons Inquiry Commission, State of Singapore, 1960.
LI EDWARDS, "A New Doctrine in Criminal Punishment" in the *Law Quarterly Review,* Vol. 72, 1956.
United Nations. *International Review of Crime Policy,* No. 23 of 1965, *Prisons and Borstals,* HMSO, London, 1957.
WINIFRED A. ALKIN, *English Penal System.*

D. N. RAY. "The Need for a National Agency to promote sound policies for the prevention of crime and treatment of offenders in India", *International Review of Criminal Policy*, No. 23 of 1965.

Unpublished Report on *the Statistical Survey on boys and girls discharged from approved schools*. Department of Social Welfare, 1961

Unpublished *Survey on Population of Sungei Besi Approved School*, Selangore, 1962.

SUTHERLAND, CRESSY. *Principles of Criminology.*

Report of the First United Nations Congress on the Prevention of Crime and the Treatment of Offenders Geneva, 1955.

Report of the Second United Nations Congress on the Prevention of Crime and the Treatment of Offenders, London, 1960.

Unpublished Report *Juvenile Delinquency in Malaya* by Hanif Omar of the Royal Malaysia Police Force, 1964.

WALTER RECKLESS. *Criminal Behavior*, 1940.

HEALY and BRONNER. *New Light on Delinquency and its Treatment.*

CYRIL BURT. *The Young Delinquent.*

JOHN SLAWSON. *The Delinquent Boy.*

DICKSON, M. G. *Young Offenders in Sarawak and Sabah.* Borneo Literature Bureau.

SHELDON and ELEANOR GLUECK. *Delinquents in the Making.*

PAUL W. TAFAN. *Juvenile Deliquency.*

CHARLES GORING. *The English Convicted.*

W. I. THOMAS. *The Unadjusted Girl*, 1923.

SHAH CLIFFORD, and MCKAY, H.D. *Juvenile Delinquency and Urban Areas*, 1942.

W. H. NAGE. *Juvenile Delinquency in Thailand*, Bangkok, 1967.

Report on *The Present State of Juvenile Delinquency and Counter Measures in Japan*, Ministry of Justice, 1965.

Chambers Encyclopedia, "The Meaning of Punishment."

RICHARD WINSTEDT. *Malaya and Its History.*

Sir RICHARD WINSTEDT and Dr P. E. JOSSELIN DE JONG, "A Digest of Customary Law from Sungei Ujong, Negri Sembilan," published in the *Journal of the Malaya Branch of the Royal Asiatic Society.*

ROSCOE POUND. "Inherent and Acquired Difficulties in the Administration of Punitive Justice," published in *Crime and Delinquency Journal*, U.S.A., Vol. 10, No. 4 of 1964.

Dewan Ra'ayat Debates [House of Representatives], No. 12, 19th August, 1963.

Budget Summary of Federal Government Expenditure, 1969, Government of Malaysia.

Straits Times [local newspaper] 26th February, 1969.

Straits Times [local newspaper] 3rd February, 1969.

Sunday Times [local newspaper] 6th December, 1964.

CHAPTER 10

THE PHILIPPINES

ALEJANDRO F. DE SANTOS

Alejandro F. De Santos, a lawyer-professor-writer, is widely known in the Philippines. De Santos received his Bachelor of Laws from the University of the Philippines in 1940, and his Master of Laws in 1949 from the University of Manila. In 1959, he received another Master of Laws degree from the University of California. He was admitted to the Philippine Bar in 1940 and since then has been practising law. From 1946 to 1962 he held a professorial post at the University of Manila. In addition, he is Professorial Lecturer and Bar Reviewer at Ateneo de Manila University, San Beda College, and University of the East. In 1968, he became Chief Legal Counsel of Metropol (Association of Police Chiefs in Manila and Metropolitan areas). His distinguished work in the field of law was recognized and he became the first Filipino Awardee of Walter Perry Johnson Research Fellowship in Law. De Santos' published books include Handbook on Statutory Construction *(1948),* Handbook on Agency *(1948),* Quizzers in Remedial Law *(2 volumes) (1954),* Special Remedies *(1956), and* Handbook in Special Proceedings *(1957). He published many articles, some of which include: "Philippine Doctrine of Precedents" (1956), "The Hearsay Rule in the Philippines" (1956), "Evolution of the House Rental Laws" (1948), and "The Doctrine of Forum non Convenience" (1957).*

THE PHILIPPINE ELECTIONS[1] following the termination of World War II have focused attention to the sad state of peace and order in the country.

The party out of power had always pointed to the failure of the incumbent administration to improve law and order conditions in the country. Before the war the Philippines was prosperous as the people were happy and secure in their homes and places of work; however, during the war and immediately thereafter conditions deteriorated. Segments of society which had achieved recognition for fighting, robbing, killing, and sabotaging the Japanese and their administration found it difficult to adjust to the conditions ushered in by the termination of hostilities. Gangs had formed, criminal syndicates had come into existence, and the moral fiber of the Filipino's character had all but reached the breaking point.

THE PHILIPPINE SOCIETY AND THE MAKE-UP OF THE FILIPINO

The character of present day Philippine society was brought about by a series of domestic and foreign influences which are still discernible. When Magellan landed on the Philippine soil on the feast day of St Lazarus, March 17, 1521; the archipelago was peopled by the *aetas*,[2] the Indonesians, the Malays, and a few hundred Chinese, and Japanese.

The *aetas*—Philippine aborigines, believed to have come to the country by crossing the land bridges from mainland Asia some 25,000 to 30,000 years ago—were already in the mountains and hinterlands when the Spaniards came.

The Indonesians who came in two waves, one between 5,000 and 6,000 years ago, and the second between 1,000 and 2,500 years ago had also been driven to the hinterlands by the Malays who first came to the Philippines around the 3rd century B.C. The Indonesians, or their descendants, were found in scattered groups in different parts of the archipelago. The Indonesian strain is visible among the Apayaos, Ibanags,

---

[1] Elections are held every two years. Those for national officials alternate with the elections for provincial and municipal officials.

[2] Negritos, or small negroes. They resemble the pygmies of New Guinea and the East Indies and, undoubtedly, are related in race to the Ethiopians of Africa.

Gaddangs, Ilongots, Kalingas and Tingians of Luzon,[3] and also among the Tagbanuas, Mandayas, Bukidnons, Atays, Kalamianes, Bagobos, Manobos, Tirurays, Ismals and Bila-ans of the Visayas and Mindanao.

Spanish Culture

The Malays continued migrating to the Philippines from Java and Sumatra up to the 14th century. They had established settlements over all the principal islands of the Philippine archipelago and were already engaged in trade with the Chinese and Japanese by the time the Spaniards came. They were the first Philippine settlers to build houses on wooden posts above the water, they knew pottery-making, and had highly developed weapons, tools, utensils and ornaments.

At the time of the coming of the Spaniards, the different settlements were already known as "barangays" and were made up of around 30 to 100 families. Each barangay was an independent unit with its own ruler, called the "rajah." Society was made up of the nobility, the freemen, and the slaves. Barangays sometimes allied with each other for common protection and welfare.

The pre-Spanish Filipinos had their own alphabet and wrote on leaves, tree bark, polished bamboo and metals with pointed sticks. They had written laws and observed, in addition, customs and traditions. Their religion recognized many gods but the principal deity was known as "Bathala."

Two of the ancient Filipino-written legal codes have survived, the Maragtas Code of 1250 A.D. and the Kalantiao Code of 1433 A.D. The codes covered subjects which could be found in modern jurisprudence and included subjects such as family relations, inheritance, property and property rights, marriage and divorce, adoption, contracts, partnerships, loans, usury, and crimes and their punishments. Felonies and misdemeanors were distinguished. Serious offenses included murder, robbery, sorcery, insult, rape, and arson; and were punishable

---

[3]The Philippine archipelago is made up of over 7,000 islands. The biggest are Luzon which lie in the north, and Mindanao in the south. Between Luzon and Mindanao are several comparatively smaller islands referred to as the Visayas.

with death, slavery, burning at the stake, and confiscation of property. Minor offenses included petty theft, adultery, dishonesty or cheating in business dealings and perjury; these were punished with whipping, exposure to ants, swimming for hours in a river, and other small fines. Recidivism was recognized and the recidivist or criminal repeater was given a heavier punishment.

Spanish Rule: Spanish Law

Serious settlement of the Philippines started in 1556 when Philip II ascended to the throne of Spain. Thirteen years earlier Villalobos, who headed one of the expeditions to the archipelago, named it Islas Filipinas after Philip, who was then the crown prince of Spain. By 1576 the Spanish conquest of the Philippines was completed and the Spanish administration, with its seat in Manila, was already well established. Government of the Philippines under Spain was highly centralized. Sovereignty rested in the king although immediate concern was lodged with the Ministry of Overseas Territories. Actual government was, however, carried on by the Governor General or "Adelantado." He exercised executive, administrative, legislative, and judicial powers. He executed the laws coming from Spain, he issued decrees and executive orders, and he also presided over the Royal Audiencia or the Supreme Court. He was also the highest military officer in the islands and the exercise of his almost unlimited powers caused upheavals and revolts during the almost four centuries of Spanish rule.

The Royal Audiencia was not only a court of last resort but also a superior council which advised the Governor General on matters of State. And in the absence of the Governor General, the Royal Audiencia administered civil matters while a Lieutenant General took charge of military affairs. Other instrumentalities of government were the Board of Authorities, the Council for Administration, the Council of Primary Instruction, the Board of Health, the Board of Agriculture, the Board of Privileges, the Board of Commerce and Industry, and the Office of the Secretary of the Central Government.

There were no political subdivisions as provinces and municipalities in the Philippines until the last decades of the 19th century. The country was divided into parcels of land called "encomiendas" and given to deserving Spaniards, called "encomenderos," who were charged with the task of looking after the spiritual and temporal welfare of the natives. Some of the encomenderos proved worthy of the trust reposed in them and helped greatly in converting the natives to Christianity, improving their conditions of living and providing them tools for self-education. The majority, however, heaped abuses so that complaints finally reached the Crown. The Provincial Reform Decree of 1886 created provinces and provincial governments. These were headed by "alcaldes mayores" who were not only executive but also judicial officers whose decisions were appealed to the Royal Audiencia.

During the last two decades of the 19th century, Spain introduced all kinds of reforms in the Philippines in an attempt to stem the rising spirit of revolt. Notable among these were extension of the Spanish Penal Code in 1887, the Civil Code and the Code of Commerce in 1889, the Becerra Law extending local autonomy to some Philippine towns in 1889, and the Maura Law creating municipal tribunals or councils in 1893. These reforms, however, came too late, and on August 25, 1896, the Philippine Revolution against Spain broke out. The hostilities were temporarily ended when the Pact of Baik-na-Bato was signed on December 14 and 15, 1897, by Governor Primo de Rivera representing the Spanish Government, and Pedro A. Paterno representing the Revolutionary Government.

The reforms, which the revolutionists believed would follow the signing of the Pact of Baik-na-Bato, did not materialize. The uprising was renewed early in 1898. As this resumption of hostilities spread, the United States of America on April 25, 1898, formally declared war on Spain and the American fleet under Admiral Dewey entered Manila Bay on April 30, and by May 1, had engaged the Spanish fleet in battle. The Spanish fleet was routed by eleven o'clock in the evening of that day and Patricio Montojo, the Spanish Admiral, raised the flag of truce. For lack of land troops, Admiral Dewey was able to occupy and hold only Manila Bay and the fort at Cavite. The Filipinos, who had been promised assistance by the American Consul in Hongkong, prosecuted the fight against the Spaniards with unrestrained vigor and controlled almost all of the country except the City of Manila and the nearby surrounding towns. On June 12, 1898, an independent Philippines was proclaimed at Malolos, Bulacan, under the leadership of General Emilio Aguinaldo.

While the Americans and the Filipinos were allies for a while, President McKinley decided to colonize the Philippines. On December 10, 1898, Spain and the United States of America concluded the Treaty of Paris whereby Spain formally ceded the Philippines to America despite the fact that almost the entire archipelago was no longer under her rule. The Revolutionary Government having been ignored, it did not take long for hostilities to break out between the Filipinos and the Americans. American sovereignty over the islands was not firmly implanted until 1901, when the leaders of the Revolutionary Government were defeated and captured in battle. On July 4, 1901, civil government replaced the military regime.

American Rule

American rule was benevolent and prepared the Filipinos for self-government. The general framework was patterned along democratic lines which separated the executive, legislative, and judicial departments into co-equal and co-sovereign bodies. While the executive powers were lodged in the American Governor-General, the bicameral legislature was composed entirely of Filipinos elected by popular suffrage, and the Supreme Court was presided over by a Filipino Chief Justice, although the Americans in the court always outnumbered the Filipinos by one. The aspiration of the Filipinos for independence was achieved with the passage of the Tydings-McDuffie Law on March 24, 1934. The law ushered in the Philippine Commonwealth[4] which was to precede the grant of full independence ten year later. With the termination of World War II and the Japanese Occupation,[5] independence was formally

[4]The Philippine Commonwealth was inaugurated on November 15, 1935.

[5]The Japanese Occupation commenced on January 2, 1942 and lasted up to July, 1945, when General MacArthur declared the Philippines fully liberated.

granted when the Republic of the Philippines was proclaimed on July 4, 1946.

The Philippine Republic

The government of the Republic of the Philippines is basically that of the Commonwealth as created by the Constitution which was approved by popular suffrage on May 14, 1934. The three departments of government remained separate and independent of each other, but with a system of checks and balances similar to that of the American Constitution. By the amendment of 1948, the legislature was converted from unicameral to bicameral with a Senate of 24 senators elected at large, and lower house of representatives from the 102 electoral districts allocated to the different provinces.

American rule brought about the peculiar legal system that exists in the Philippines today. The tenets of the civil law, implanted by almost four centuries of Spanish domination, met and clashed with the traditions of the common law. During the first two decades of American rule clashes between the two systems, in the process of merger, were reflected in decisions of the Supreme Court. The conflict finally culminated in the emergence of a hybrid legal system.[6]

The codes[7] containing dispositions of the substantive law remain basically of the Spanish Law. The laws governing procedure[8] are patterned after those of the United States, although there is no jury and questions of facts and law are tried by a single judge.

[6]Eugene A. Gilmore, *Philippine Jurisprudence* (American Bar Association Journal, 1930), pp. 92-93; George A. Malcolm, *Philippine Law* (11 Illinois Law Review 1916-17), pp. 331, 387; Charles S. Lobingier, *Blending Legal Systems in the Philippines* (21 Law Quarterly Review, 1905), p. 401.

[7]The Civil Code, the Revised Penal Code, the Revised Administrative Code as regards political subdivisions of the country.

[8]The Revised Rules of Court of 1964 are based on the Federal Rules Service of 1938, the California Code of Civil Procedure, and the Fields Code of 1848. The rules of evidence are 90 per cent Anglo-American.

The Filipino Today

The population of the Philippines has increased steadily from 1948 to the present at the rate of 3.4 per cent a year. The census of 1948 showed a population of a little over 19 million while present estimates place the population at 35 million. Over 90 per cent of the people are Christians and the rest are Muslims and pagans.[9] The Filipino family is patriarchal and family ties are strong.

There are over 80 dialects spoken in the islands although the four principal dialects are Tagalog, Cebuano, Ilocano, and Pampango. About 36 per cent of the population speak English which was the medium of instruction used since the start of American occupation. Tagalog has been made the national dialect and is now called the Filipino language. It is a required subject in all schools from the primary grades up to collegiate level. It is estimated that 48 per cent of the population can understand, if not actually speak, Filipino. The difficulty of communication and regionalism have also contributed to the problems of the country.

The cities are the main centers of population. Manila, which is the principal city, has a day population of almost three million. Quezon City, the capital of the Philippines, has an estimated population of over a million. In the Visayas, Cebu City is the most thickly populated, while in Mindanao are the cities of Davao and Zamboanga. With the exception of Quezon City, all of these are port cities.

The Filipinos as a people are courteous, hospitable and gregarious. They are patriotic. The men are trained to be brave from childhood, while modesty and chastity are traditional traits of Filipino women. The Filipinos are, however, a fun loving people. They are indolent with a propensity to gambling. They enjoy fiestas and indulge in extravagant merry-making. Like most Orientals they are fatalistic.

Philippine society has always been characterized by the existence of strong family ties. Family relationship is a factor

[9]According to the 1948 census 82.9 per cent are Roman Catholics, 7.6 per cent are Aglipayans or members of the Filipino Independent Church, 2.3 per cent are Protestants, 4.1 per cent are Muslims, 1.8 per cent are pagans, and 1.3 per cent are unclassified.

which influences to a marked degree the social, political and economic life of the Filipino. The individual will sacrifice his personal interests and aspirations for the family, while the members of the family will go to great lengths to enhance the future of the individual. There is no marked distinction as to the husband's side or the wife's side of the family. Marriage is invariably considered an alliance of two groups. The "compadre" system or ritual of co-parenthood, created by the selection of sponsors at weddings and baptisms, expands kinship and has proved a bane and a blessing to the Philippines.

Although the growth of a middle class has been noted, Philippine society is essentially a two-class society. The upper class forms approximately 5 per cent of the population. This is made up of the land owners and members of prestigious families. Their members have had better education and the capital to undertake business ventures. It was inevitable that they came to dominate the economic and business fields. They could influence elections and appointments to public office, and their proteges, in turn, look after their interests in dealings with the government political dynasties, where the husband is a congressman or senator while the wife or son is the governor of their home province, have become an accepted fact in certain areas. Where election or appointment to public office is influenced to a marked degree by family ties and capitalized regionalism, where business opportunities and economic advancement depend on kinship, it is not difficult to see the failure in government administration and the birth of causes for ferment in Philippine society, which account for the rising tide of criminality and the continued deterioration of peace and order.

PHILIPPINE CRIMINAL LAW

At the time of the Philippine Revolution, Philippine criminal law was to be found chiefly in the Spanish Penal Code of 1870 which was extended to the Philippines by the Royal Decrees of September 4, 1884 and December 17, 1886. It took effect on July 14, 1887.[10] In 1927 a committee undertook the

---

[10]U.S. *vs.* Tamparong, 31 Phil. 321 (1915).

revision of the Spanish Penal Code, together with the special penal laws then in existence. The draft prepared by the committee was later on enacted into the Revised Penal Code and became effective on January 1, 1932.

Concept of Crime

Article 3 of the Revised Penal Code defines felonies as follows: "Acts and omissions punishable by law are felonies (*delitos*). Felonies are committed not only by means of deceit (*dolo*) but also by means of fault (*culpa*). There is deceit when the act is performed with deliberate intent; and there is fault when the wrongful act results from imprudence, negligence, lack of foresight, or lack of skill."

The above article contemplates a felony as having three elements: (*a*) there must be an act or omission; (*b*) that this act or omission be performed by means of deceit, that is, with deliberate intent, or by means of fault, i.e., through negligence or imprudence; and (*c*) that the act or omission be punishable by law.

The maxim of the criminal law, "Actus non facit reum nisi mens sit rea," is recognized in Philippine criminal law. Harboring an evil intent unaccompanied by an act is not punishable. Every crime, therefore, must show the union of the act or omission and the mental element called criminal intent. For a felony to exist it is not enough that the accused has done what the law prohibits or has failed to do what the law commands. It is necessary that the act or omission be committed by means of deceit (*dolus*) or by means of fault (*culpa*).[11]

There is *dolus* when the act or omission is free, intelligent, and intentional. *Doluce* involves three elements: freedom, intelligence, and intent.[12]

To act with freedom means to act with deliberation, with the power to choose between two or more things—to act not by reason of necessity. Thus a person who acts coerced by physical force is not a criminal; should the law declare him to be such, the people's conscience would revolt against it.

---

[11] U.S. *vs.* Ah Chong, 15 Phil. 488 (1910).
[12] Pacheco, *Codigo Penal*, Vol. 1, p. 74.

The law exempts from criminal liability one who acts under compulsion of an irresistible force,[13] or under the impulse of an uncontrollable fear of an equal or greater injury.[14]

To act with intelligence means awareness of what is right and what is wrong. The imbecile, the lunatic, and the infant may act voluntarily, but they are not possessed of sufficient ken to judge the morality of their acts, or see the dividing line between the licit and the illicit, or foresee the consequences of their acts, or perceive whether they are prohibited by law or not. Thus, the law exempts from criminal liability those who are mentally unbalanced,[15] children under nine years of age,[16] children over nine but under fifteen—unless they acted with discernment[17]—and those who acted under a mistake of fact.[18]

Intent, as an element of *dolus*, has been held by the Philippine Supreme Court as synonymous with malice or criminal intention. It has been considered as the moral element of the crime. The absence of malice, negligence, or imprudence, in the commission of acts defined as punishable under the penal laws, exempts the action from criminal liability.[19] Criminal intent, however, does not always require proof. The commission of an unlawful act gives rise to the presumption that it was done with criminal intent, and it is incumbent on the actor to disprove such presumption.[20]

The State alone has the right to declare what acts are criminal within certain well-defined limitations. The State has a right to specify what act or acts shall constitute a crime, as well as what proof shall constitute *prima facie* evidence of guilt, and then to put upon the defendant the burden of showing that such acts are innocent and are not committed with any criminal intent.[21]

---

[13]Art. 12, No. 5, Revised Penal Code.
[14]Art. 12, No. 6, Revised Penal Code.
[15]Art. 12, Par. 1, Revised Penal Code.
[16]Art. 12, Par. 2, Revised Penal Code.
[17]Art. 12, Par. 3, Revised Penal Code.
[18]U.S. *vs.* Ah Chong, 15 Phil. 488 (1910).
[19]*Ibid.*
[20]U.S. *vs.* Tria, 17 Phil. 303 (1910).
[21]U.S. *vs.* Luling, 34 Phil. 725 (1916).

Juvenile Delinquents

As earlier noted, Philippine Penal law considers infancy as affecting the intelligence of the actor. According to the Revised Penal Code, the following are exempt from criminal liability: First, a person under nine years of age. Secondly, "a person over nine years of age and under fifteen, unless he has acted with discernment, in which case, such minor shall be proceeded against in accordance with the provisions of article 80 of this Code." And, thirdly, "when such minor is adjudged to be criminally irresponsible, the court, in conformity with the provisions of this and the preceding paragraph, shall commit him to the care and custody of his family who shall be charged with his surveillance and education; otherwise, he shall be committed to the care of some institution or person mentioned in said article 80."[22]

Although there is no indication whatsoever that the above quoted provision of the Revised Penal Code has influenced juvenile delinquency in the Philippines, it is undeniable that crimes committed by minors have increased in volume and intensity in the past 10 to 15 years. Physical injuries, theft and robbery were the most prevalent of juvenile crimes reported to the police. Police ascribe the increasing number of these crimes to economic factors, and the lack of school and recreational facilities. Certain sectors of the police consider as a source of delinquent behavior the children of "important persons" who engage in illegal activities for excitement and who are able to escape punishment because of their family's influence. Aware of the tremendous proportions which juvenile delinquency can reach and proliferate into, the government,

[22]Article 80 of the Revised Penal Code was preceded by Public Act No. 1438, enacted on January 11, 1904, and was known as the Juvenile Delinquent Act. Under this article the trial court proceeds to hear the evidence but instead of pronouncing a judgment of conviction suspends all further proceedings and commits the child to the custody of a public or private benevolent institution under the supervision of the Secretary of Social Welfare, until he reaches the age of majority or sooner ordered by the court to be released. If the child has behaved properly, he is ordered released, but if he has proved to be incorrigible the court imposes the judgment corresponding to the crime he has committed.

in addition to creating social welfare offices and organizations, has started to create juvenile courts in major cities and centers of population.

Executive Order Number 67, issued by Philippine President Ferdinand E. Marcos on May 28, 1967, took cognizance of the need for an integrated system of crime reporting and accordingly established it. Almost an year after this, the Committee on the Integration and Co-ordination of Official Statistics on Crimes finally adopted the Nation-Wide Uniform Crime Case Report, together with a manual of instruction. The President approved the crime case report and issued Executive Order Number 127, dated May 6, 1968, officially establishing the Nation-Wide Uniform Crime Case Report System. The first such official report, released in April, 1969, covered the period from July 1, 1968, to December 31, 1968. The case report has eight major parts, namely (i) heading; (ii) suspect's or offender's data; (iii) victim's data (iv) property destroyed/stolen/ recovered; (v) offense data; (vi) police investigation; (vii) prosecution; and (viii) authentication.

Uniform Crime Reporting

One phase of the crime report covering the volume of crimes reported for the last six months of 1968 divided the Philippines into ten regions and tabulated the crimes as shown in Table I.

Other Bases for Classification

The crime tables also classified the data received in relation to suspect or offender on the basis of (a) age; (b) connection with alcohol; (c) where suspect resisted arrest; (d) attendance in school, below 21; (e) civil status; (f) number of dependents; (g) educational attainment; (h) membership with gangs; (i) income level; (j) nationality; (k) occupation; (l) criminal record; (m) religion; (n) sex; (o) size of family; and (p) type of work. In relation to the victim, the classification of data received was based on (a) age; (b) connection with alcohol;

TABLE I

VOLUME OF CRIMES REPORTED BY REGION BY PROVINCE
SEMI-ANNUAL REPORT (JULY-DECEMBER, 1968)

Region	Crimes vs person	Crimes vs property	Crimes vs chastity	Others	Total
REGION I	253	292	6	192	743
Manila	253	292	6	192	743
REGION II	382	215	23	174	794
Abra	15	8	3	9	35
Benguet	54	52	5	27	138
Ifugao	11	6	—	5	22
Ilocos Norte	73	40	5	48	166
Ilocos Sur	90	14	1	10	115
Kalinga Apayao	9	6	—	—	15
La Union	126	73	8	68	275
Mt Province	4	16	1	7	28
REGION III	281	225	27	120	653
Batanes	—	1	—	—	1
Cagayan	79	42	7	32	160
Isabela	166	149	17	74	406
Nva Vizcaya	36	33	3	14	86
REGION IV	957	868	137	497	2,459
Bataan	54	52	3	18	127
Bulacan	152	116	36	69	373
Nva Ecija	106	176	28	96	406
Pampanga	99	121	18	43	281
Pangasinan	262	175	25	112	575
Tarlac	213	190	21	135	559
Zambales	70	38	6	24	138
REGION V	852	596	132	476	2,056
Batangas	54	33	11	28	126
Cavite	42	52	4	12	110
Laguna	193	139	32	107	471
Marinduque	57	28	11	47	143
Mindoro Occ	24	25	4	17	70
Mindoro Or	46	16	3	9	74
Palawan	61	41	8	53	163
Quezon	270	196	38	156	660
Rizal	105	66	21	47	239
REGION VI	526	431	67	394	1418
Albay	101	72	11	49	233
Camarines Norte	64	42	6	50	162
Camarines Sur	138	138	24	91	391
Catanduanes	7	10	1	25	43

Masbate	95	79	11	109	294
Sorsogon	121	90	14	70	295
REGION VII	575	345	24	363	1,307
Aklan	68	19	2	35	124
Antique	46	22	2	25	95
Capiz	36	12	1	6	55
Iloilo	109	76	4	54	243
Negros Occ	273	198	13	219	703
Romblon	43	18	2	24	87
REGION VIII	916	566	72	483	2,037
Bohol	115	77	7	50	249
Leyte Norte	232	147	9	128	516
Leyte Sur	188	83	9	71	351
Negros Or	5	2	1	2	10
Samar Eastern	134	91	16	64	305
Samar Norte	63	47	3	32	145
Samar Western	145	78	19	110	352
REGION IX	611	321	44	350	1,326
Agusan	61	18	3	17	99
Bukidnon	87	49	9	55	200
Camiguin	11	6	3	10	30
Lanao Norte	98	70	9	43	220
Lanao Sur	5	2	2	5	14
Mis Occ	64	51	5	50	170
Mis Or	62	40	3	39	144
Surigao Nte	70	19	2	13	104
Surigao Sur	153	66	8	118	345
REGION X	747	383	87	297	1,513
Cotabato Nte	180	76	24	76	356
Cotabato Sur	120	33	7	16	176
Davao Nte	116	83	11	52	262
Davao Or	56	24	4	33	117
Davao Sur	82	74	13	44	213
Sulu	14	3	1	2	20
Zambo Nte	42	31	8	28	109
Zambo Sur	137	58	19	46	260
TOTAL	6,100	4,241	619	3.346	1,4306

(c) civil status; (d) educational attainment; (e) occupation; (f) criminal record; (g) sex; and (h) type of work.

A further classification of offense data used the following bases: (a) type of crime by days of the week; (b) motive/cause; (c) special events; (d) time of commission; (e) type of place of commission; (f) weapons or means used; and (g) firearms used. Considering that the period covered by the report is only six months no specific conclusions can be essayed.

No centralized compilation being available prior to July 1, 1968, reports from different police agencies gave information from which certain conclusions may be drawn as regards the volume of crime and their incidence.

Criminal Investigation Section

From the Criminal Investigation Section of the Philippine Constabulary, the following table shows the crime volume from 1964 to the third quarter of 1968:

TABLE II
COMPARATIVE CRIME VOLUME, 1964-68

Type of crimes	1964	1965	1966	1967	1968 (January-September)
I. INDEX CRIME	11,851	9,495	9,234	7,859	6,964
Murder	2,065	1,943	1,789	2,102	1,354
Homicide	2,677	2,035	2,519	2,629	1,800
Robbery	1,623	876	887	860	868
Rape	234	155	203	103	153
Theft	2,276	1,201	1,785	882	708
Parricide	94	49	66	175	80
Physical injuries	2,882	3,236	1,985	1,108	2,001
II. OTHERS	5,237	3,628	4,373	3,505	2,370
TOTAL	17,088	13,123	13,607	11,364	9,334

The figures given in the above table do not include those of the City of Manila.

The statistics from the Manila Police Department covering five fiscal years, are reported in Table III.

From the foregoing reports of the Philippine Constabulary and the Manila Police Department one cannot help but notice the increasing volume of crime. It is also noted that while crimes against persons account for almost fifty per cent of the crimes reported in the rural areas, in the city of Manila, crimes against property come to over eighty per cent of the total crime volume and crimes against persons account for only a little over sixteen per cent.

According to the Philippine Constabulary, crime frequency in the Philippines, including all chartered cities and the Manila

TABLE III

Crimes	1963-64	1964-65	1965-66	1966-67	1967-68
I. GENERAL LAWS	30,994	32,401	33,623	42,759	36,409
(A) *Major offenses*	9,423	9,423	8,098	9,275	10,305
Robbery	2,303	2,325	1,625	2,402	2,833
Theft	4,513	4,636	4,421	4,220	4,897
Estafa and falsification	1,197	1,144	823	984	1,020
Murder	218	184	182	258	264
Homicide	635	620	698	925	901
Parricide and infanticide	12	8	5	13	13
Serious physical injuries	403	350	179	302	183
Rape	71	99	104	104	116
Abduction	36	43	49	32	60
Seduction	35	14	12	27	18
(B) *All other general laws*	21,571	22,978	25,729	33,484	26,104
II. CITY ORDINANCES	44,400	52,949	62,069	103,049	49,311
TOTAL	75,394	85,350	95,892	145,808	85,720

metropolitan area, covering a five-year period (1962-66), is as follows: (*a*) 17 homicide murder cases in one (1) day; (*b*) 32 physical injury cases in one (1) day; (*c*) 39 robbery/theft cases in one (1) day; (*d*) 1 rape case in one (1) day; (*e*) 1 kidnapping case every ten (10) days; and (*f*) 188 minor offenses in one (1) day.

Excluding the Manila metropolitan area, the crime frequency for the rest of the Philippines, covering the same five-year period, is as follows: (*a*) 13 murder cases in one (1) day; (*b*) 6 physical injury cases in one (1) day; (*c*) 5 robbery/theft cases in one (1) day; (*d*) 2 rape cases every five (5) days; and (*e*) 1 kidnapping case every fifteen (15) days.

Manila Police Department Reports

The report of the Manila Police Department on crime frequency in the city is given in Table IV.

PC-MPD Reports Compared

The reports of the Philippine Constabulary covering almost

TABLE IV
CRIME RATE PER 100,000 INHABITANTS

Offenses	1963-64	1964-65	1965-66	1966-67	1967-68
I. GENERAL LAWS	2,440.4	2,469.5	2,494.3	3,049.8	2,596.7
(A) Major offenses	741.9	718.2	597.1	661.5	734.8
Crimes vs. person	99.8	88.5	78.4	106.8	96.9
Murder	17.1	14.0	13.4	18.4	18.8
Homicide	50.0	47.2	51.4	65.9	64.1
Parricide and infanticide	0.9	0.6	0.3	0.9	0.9
Serious physical injuries	30.9	26.6	13.2	21.5	13.02
Crimes vs. property	630.9	616.9	506.5	543.1	624.1
Robbery	181.3	177.2	119.8	171.5	202.2
Theft	355.2	353.3	326.0	301.5	344.4
Estafa and falsification	94.2	87.1	60.6	70.1	72.6
Crimes vs. chastity	11.1	11.8	12.1	11.6	13.8
Rape	5.5	7.5	7.6	7.4	8.2
Abduction	2.8	5.2	3.6	2.2	4.1
Seduction	2.7	1.0	0.8	1.9	1.3
(B) All other general laws	1,698.5	1,758.9	1,897.1	2,388.3	1,861.9
II. CITY ORDINANCES	3,496.1	4,035.7	4,577.3	7,350.2	3,517.1
TOTAL	5,936.5	6,505.3	7,071.7	10,400.0	6,113.8

a five-year period show a constant crime volume in the rural areas, while the records of the Manila Police Department show that the crime volume for the five-year period (1963-64 to 1967-68) has gone up. In so far as the major offenses are concerned, it appears that the crime volume in Manila is almost the same as that of the entire rural areas of the country.

Philippine Constabulary reports show that in 1966, 95.6 per cent of the crimes reported in the rural areas were committed by males, while only 4.3 per cent were committed by females. For the fiscal year 1966-67, Manila Police Department records show that 85.5 per cent of the crimes were committed by males and 14.2 per cent were committed by females. The offenses commonly committed by females in the urban and rural areas are vagrancy, prostitution, and physical injuries.

Juvenile Delinquency Reports

The search for statistics pertaining to crimes committed by juveniles failed to yield any complete compilation by any government agency. There were, however, two reports which carried useful data. The first is the Survey of Youthful Offenses in Cities and Provincial Capitals from January to December, 1961, prepared and released by the Philippine Youth Welfare Coordinating Council. The second is the semi-annual Nationwide Uniform Crime Report of the Philippine Constabulary covering the period of July 1 to December 31, 1968.

From the Survey, the following tables give the breakdown of total apprehensions of youthful offenders from the ages of 9 to 21, and the breakdown of total apprehensions of youthful offenders from the ages of 9 to 16.

TABLE V

APPREHENSIONS AS TO OFFENSES COMMITTED
(EXCLUDING MANILA)

Offenses	9—21 Years		Total
	Male	Female	
Murder	42	0	42
Parricide	4	0	—
Physical injuries	969	30	999
Robbery	331	5	336
Theft	1,547	115	1,660
Estafa	135	14	149
Homicide	124	2	126
Disobedience to parents	93	43	136
Malicious mischief	216	2	218
Unjust vexation	105	4	109
TOTAL	3,566	215	3,781

The number of offenders in the 16-21 years old bracket was given at 2,627 without classification according to sex. The total apprehensions in Manila for 1961, for the major offenses listed above, therefore, reached 3,577—which almost equalled the total apprehensions for the same offenses for the rest of the country.

TABLE VI

POSSIBLE JUVENILE DELINQUENTS
(EXCLUDING MANILA)

Offenses	9—16 years		Total
	Male	Female	
Murder	4	0	4
Parricide	0	0	0
Physical injuries	173	9	182
Robbery	82	5	87
Theft	597	59	656
Estafa	17	5	22
Homicide	12	0	12
Disobedience to parents	79	27	106
Malicious mischief	70	0	70
Unjust vexation	14	1	15
TOTAL	1,048	106	1,154

NOTE. If broken down, the offenses would be disturbed as follows: (1) Of the age 9-12 years, 152 are males, 17 are females, or a total of 169. (2) In the 13-16 bracket, 896 are males and 89 are females, making a total of 985. (3) The 16-21 year olds have 2,518 males and 109 females, or a total of 2,627.

TABLE VII

APPREHENSIONS IN MANILA, 1961

Offenses	9—12 years		13—16 years		Total
	Male	Female	Male	Female	
Murder	0	0	0	0	0
Parricide	0	0	0	0	0
Physical injuries	42	3	45	1	91
Robbery	26	0	55	0	81
Theft	216	24	413	28	681
Estafa	16	0	29	4	49
Homicide	0	0	3	0	3
Disobedience to parents	0	1	3	1	5
Malicious mischief	7	0	20	0	27
Unjust vexation	3	0	10	0	13
TOTAL	310	28	578	34	950

The Survey found the total number of apprehensions of

youthful offenders for 1961 to have reached a total of 18,902, but hesitated to declare the incidence to be low in the absence of accurate population data. Violators increase as age advances. Youthful offenses are more pronounced in cities than in the provincial capitals. The greater number of apprehensions (over 75 per cent), were for violation of municipal ordinances. Crime frequency was more marked during summer and holiday seasons when the youth have more time as schools are closed.

The frequency of crimes, in which first offenders were apprehended, was shown by the Survey to be:

Parricide—3; murder—43; homicide—88; unjust vexation—101; estafa—117; disobedience to parents—124; malicious mischief—158; robbery—265; physical injuries 715; theft—1,359; and other laws, special laws and ordinances—2,529.

Those apprehended with previous conviction were as follows:

Parricide—0; murder—1; homicide—0; unjust vexation—3; estafa—6; malicious mischief—7; robbery—26; physical injuries—49; theft—147; and other laws, special laws and ordinances—107.

The Nationwide Uniform Crime Report, as earlier stated, covered only the period of July 1 to December 31, 1968. Unlike the Survey of 1961 which bracketed the youthful offenders at 9-12, 13-16 and 16-21 years, this report bracketed them at below 15, 15-19, and 20-24 years. For the whole Philippines, the data gathered by the NUCR is shown in Table VIII.

The fact that in the cities and suburbs crimes against property outnumber crimes against persons—while in the rural areas crimes against persons prevail over crimes against property —holds true even as to the youthful offenders. It is also noted that as the age bracket goes up, so does the volume of crimes. Of the nationwide total of 9,904 crimes against persons, almost 33 per cent were committed by offenders within the age group of 15 to 24. With respect to crimes against property, of the estimated total of 8,752, almost 40.5 per cent were committed by the same age group. And in crimes against chastity, out of 932 nationwide cases 207 (22.5 per cent) were committed by this same age group. The high ratio of offenses committed

Table VIII

Type of crimes	Below 15 years	15-19 years	20-24 years	Below 15 years	15-19 years	20-24 years	Below 15 years	15-19 years	20-24 years	below 15 years up and RP-wide
CRIMES VS PERSONS	69	1,064	2,113	36	723	1,491	12	135	262	9,904
Murder	8	100	188	2	77	137		12	29	966
Homicide	4	99	215	4	81	167		1	16	994
Homicide TRI	1	9	61	1	7	45		1	4	353
Parricide	3	3	5	2	3	4				47
Murder A F	3	53	107		42	83		3	7	589
Homicide A F	8	144	287	6	107	211		15	39	1,379
Parricide A F		1	3		1	2				30
Serious physical injury	3	86	185	1	46	134		7	20	786
Less serious physical injury	5	165	356	2	130	261		8	20	1,547
Slight physical injury	39	404	706	18	229	447	12	88	127	3,213
CRIMES VS. PROPERTY	236	1,494	1,714	98	930	1,036	39	225	367	8,752
Robbery	30	294	342	13	184	210	5	46	69	1,466
Robbery A F	1	8	8	1	3	6		4	2	48
Robbery in band	2	8	41	1	8	30	1		6	196
Theft	166	788	651	62	502	453	24	100	81	3,207
Theft qualified	25	200	205	15	131	136	5	26	32	1,323
Swindling/Estafa	3	41	98	1	14	50	2	15	37	709
Malicious mischief	7	116	163	4	79	114	1	22	30	829
Damage to property	2	39	206	1	9	37	1	12	110	974
CRIMES VS. CHASTITY	6	131	207	5	85	153		20	23	932
Rape	3	47	72	3	27	52		6	6	181
Abduction/seduction		35	45		16	33		11	7	
Lasciviousness	3	49	90	2	42	68		3	10	380
OTHERS	33	636	1,352	20	385	765	10	154	391	1,460
TOTAL	344	3,325	5,386	159	2,123	3,445	61	534	1,043	26,336

by youthful offenders as compared to the overall crime volume —undoubtedly reflects the turmoil and unrest which characterizes the younger generation of the country.

THEORIES OF CRIME CAUSATION

There is a dearth of material on crime causations in the Philippines. There is not a single paper written on criminology by any student or scholar of worth prior to World War II. Criminality in the Philippines, then, was not the problem that it is today. Macaraig,[23] writing in 1938, after examining statistics covering the years 1906 to 1935, concluded that it was difficult to maintain the position that there had been an increase or decrease in crimes. He wrote that the most he could do was to point out tendencies which show that some crimes have increased in number while others have decreased.

Philippine Papers

Writing in 1918, Justice Ignacio Villamor of the Supreme Court expressed his views on the causes of crimes in the following manner[24]:

The commission of crime has been a subject of serious investigation, and several causes have been attributed to it. There is no doubt that many social factors and conditions play their part in the making of a criminal. Thus, the fluctuating economic and political conditions, religion and morals, have a share in developing a criminal type. These causes are external, bearing their influence upon a criminal subject, but there are equally forceful causes which are found in the person himself.

Biological research has come to an acceptable conclusion that life traits and tendencies are transmitable from person to person of the same lineage, and this theory is borne out by the fact that certain abnormalities in the structure of an organism determine, to some extent, criminal conduct.

[23]Serafin Macaraig, *Introduction to Sociology*, 1938.
[24]Ignacio Villamor, *Criminality in the Philippine Islands 1903-1908* (Manila : Bureau of Printing, 1909).

Thus, organic processes in the viscera at times throw out of order certain regular functions, and the deranged condition causes abnormal conduct.

They are physical and internal conditions which find expression in muscular actions, but the study of psychology shows that certain mental traits and processes contribute to the commission of crime. In short, crime has many causes which may be accepted as more or less uniform in different countries. It is not finally concluded whether the internal or external class of causes are more fundamental, but it is safe to assume that each contributes to the other.

There are all indications in present day Philippine society that the conclusions of the former justice are still valid.

Economic Factors

Economic straits undoubtedly contribute to the commission of crimes in the Philippines. Unemployment has been, for the past decade, an extremely serious problem in the country. The number of job openings have not kept pace with the number of job applicants. A survey made in 1965 (when the total population was estimated at Rs 30,000,000) showed that more than 700,000 persons were out of work. This figure included 216,000 men with families and 484,000 single individuals.[25] College graduates do not find jobs immediately available after leaving the institutions of learning. And quite a number, due to economic necessity, take up jobs which may have no direct relation to the subject of their schooling. Where there is economic dislocation, the streets swell with the ranks of the unemployed whose idle hands and worried minds, tortured by the pangs of hunger, make them "ripe for almost anything."

While serious attempts have been made by one administration after another to achieve industrial peace, recent years have shown unrest in factories and business establishments which have given way to strikes and acts of violence.

[25]P. A. Zapanta, "Unemployment Agony," *Sunday Times Magazine,* Manila, July 17, 1966.

Politics

Politics and political sentiments undoubtedly contribute to the overall crime situation in the country today. For one thing, the high cost of being elected to a public office breeds corruption before and after election. For another, seeds of hate are sown in the electoral process and the harvests invariably carry crimes of violence. Renato Constantino, a writer known for the acuteness of his insight and depth of his analytical powers, had this observation to make on corruption in Philippine politics:

Our matter-of-fact acceptance of corruption is nowhere more evident than in the conduct of our elections. We affirm as an elementary truth the proposition that only a man with money should run for office because no one will work for him unless he can give out the pesos (and sometimes the dollars). There is corruption, too, in the idea that a vote for a candidate is a favor granted him and not an exercise of the right of choice. The validity of party platforms, the examination of a candidate's views, and the consideration of basic issues, seldom play an important part in the voter's choice. He is cowed down by a show of strength and wealth.

One of the most pathetic pictures of corruption is that of a poor voter boasting of the money his candidate is using to buy up the people's votes. The poor man is corrupt but has nothing to show for his corruption except the vicarious thrill of being associated with wealth for a brief period. Indeed, our whole attitude towards elections is corrupt. As rabid followers of this or that candidate, we distort truth, fabricate lies, justify and sometimes participate in all kinds of shady schemes to gain victory. We are more moral about basketball games (expecting fair refereeing and clean playing) than about elections.

The wonder of it is that after the fever of the campaign, we complain about the quality of our leadership. That is unfair. We have no right to expect honor from dishonor, impartial statesmanship from rabid partisanship, intellectual integrity from dishonesty. Thus, in practically every election in the past, we got exactly what we wanted. . . .

Another bad consequence of the lack of opportunity for employment in the economic field is that the government becomes the biggest dispenser of business contracts as well as employment. This makes of government such a rich plum that to secure it, many men are willing to indulge in the most corrupt election practices. Its position as the biggest employer results in another form of corruption. The pressure on politicians to provide jobs for their men is so great that merit and seniority in the civil service are set aside. This corrupts both the deserving and undeserving employees or job-seekers because they must rely on "padrinos" instead of doing a good job or improving their qualifications. With the destruction of the merit system, we develop the worst type of bureaucrat, interested only in personal advancement, doing the minimum amount of work, obsequious and servile to his superiors, and eager to use the resources of government for his private benefit.[26]

Environmental Factors

These factors also contribute to crime causation. Strong family ties, while a tempering factor in certain situations, provide the catalyzer in some instances. Newspapers have editorialized cases of "compartmentalized justice" pointing to the children of the rich and influential who had been treated with "velvet gloves" by the police and prosecution authorities.

Mariano O. Patalinjug of the Philippines Free Press criticizes the present state of things in these words:

In the major cities, the sons of those who belong to the powerful establishment are reported to be making a career of robbery, raping and killing, and getting away with it. There is no law. There is no peace. There is no order. Nobody feels safe and secure anymore. Life has become precarious and cheap in our country. The wheels of justice grind slowly, much too slowly. And when they do, they move for the rich and the powerful.[27]

[26] Renato Constantino, *The Filipinos in the Philippines*, Quezon City, Philippines, 1966, pp. 84, 92-93.
[27] October 28, 1966.

Other Factors

Lack of sufficient schools has also been pointed out by the police as a contributing factor to juvenile delinquency in the country. As of 1960, it was estimated that as much as 50 per cent of the children who should be in school were out of school. Police reports show that most juvenile crimes were committed by out-of-school children. Vibar, a police scholar, holds the view that alcohol is a major contributing factor to criminality in the City of Manila in particular and the country in general. He also calls attention to the growing incidence of criminal cases where prohibited drugs have played a significant role.[28]

From the Philippine Constabulary Data Processing Unit the factors considered as causative of crimes may be noted in Table IX.

Constantino, tracing the breakdown of peace and order to the overall corruption which he found to have reached all levels of Philippine society within the government and without, concludes that corruption is merely the effect and not the cause of the other problems besetting the country today. He concludes by pointing out the basic cause as follows:

Moralists, civic leaders, and politicians bewail these various forms of corruption but they have not looked at it as an integrated whole. They appeal for a regeneration, for a phoenix rising out of the ashes. In their obsession to impose a new system of morals or to introduce a new political dispensation, they overlook the fact that corruption is not the cause of our present plight. Corruption is merely the consequence of a more basic problem—the problem of our colonial economy and thinking.

The Philippine situation today is a classic example of the effects of colonial rule on the habits, predispositions, and morals of a people. To eliminate the effect, you must eliminate the cause. Only a resolute nationalism can break the chains we ourselves have helped to forge. Only a deter-

---

[28] Eliseo Vibar, "Crime and Delinquency" (Unpublished Lecture before the National Committee for the Prevention of Alcoholism in the Philippines, May 14, 1964).

TABLE IX

TYPE OF CRIMES BY MOTIVE/CAUSE
RP—WIDE
SEMI-ANNUAL REPORT (JULY-DECEMBER, 1968)

Type of crimes	Agrarian trouble	Alcohol	Family trouble	Insanity	Land trouble	Labor dispute	Material gain	Misunderstanding	Narcotics	Passion/jealousy	Politics	Revenge/grudge	Trial	Unknown	Total
CRIMES VS. PERSONS	28	1,466	214	22	92	28	180	1,861	9	240	11	1,018	977	2,506	8,662
Murder	7	81	14	5	15		28	78	1	30	3	180		317	775
Homicide	2	233	25	3	11	3	43	273		28	1	120		356	1,111
Homicide TRI		2						2		2			383	13	402
Parricide		5	23	2			2	4		5				8	51
Murder AF		76	8	2	15	3	9	63	2	13	2	121		162	489
Homicide AF	3	242	19	3	14	7	27	331	1	21	2	183		326	1,179
Parricide AF		5	12	1				3		6		1		4	32
Serious physical injury		112	10	1	8	3	9	99		17		54	193	189	695
Less serious physical injury	3	241	51	2	10	1	18	270	2	41		104	197	308	1,228
Slight physical injury/malt	13	469	72	3	19	11	44	738	3	78	3	220	204	823	2,700

															Total
CRIMES VS. PROPERTY	15	297	13	13	84	14	6,096	103	7		2	123	587		7,355
Robbery	4	38	1		5	2	1,396	8				12			1,466
Robbery A F		2					32								34
Robbery in band		8	1	1	1		114	1	1						127
Theft	4	30	12		25	1	2,643	11	8	3		11			2,726
Theft qualified	3	6	1	5	3		883	8	3			7			938
Swindling/estafa		32	2			1	564	7	7						612
Malicious mischief	4	170	8	2	33	5	235	<7	1			92	1		617
Damage to property		11			5		210	1				1	587		835
CRIMES VS. CHASTITY	3	67	2	3			5	755				8		587	843
Rape	2	20	2	2				290				1	8		315
Abduction/seduction	1	4	2	1				149				3	1		160
Lasciviousness		43					5	316	5			4	4		368
OTHERS	30	936	111	10	121	25	582	630	101	225	15	343	62	1,727	4,918
TOTAL	76	2,766	340	48	297	67	6,858	2,599	117	220	28	1,502	1,626	4,233	21,778

mined effort to set a nationalistic course for our national life will finally free us of the corruption born of our political, economic, and cultural bondage.

Our corruption is essentially a consequence of our semicolonial status. Those who try to solve this evil in our society have been dealing with an effect. They have been treating the manifestations of a disease without striking at the disease itself. This is, at best, a palliative measure comparable to relying on an anti-pyretic to cure a fever when what the patient needs is a drug to combat the infection that manifests its presence by the fever. You may succeed in reducing the fever and making the patient temporarily less uncomfortable. But until you eliminate the infection itself, the fever will not disappear permanently.

However, if you do not attend to the infection, it may yet get out of hand, with disastrous consequences. Thus mere palliatives in the form of government reorganizations, anti-graft campaigns, and pious exhortations from grandstand or pulpit may temporarily contain the spread of corruption. But as long as the evil that breeds it remains untouched, new forms of corruption will inevitably arise and re-enforce the old. The longer we postpone a realistic appraisal of our present status, the more difficult it will be to make the first step toward a real cure for our corrupt society.[29]

PENAL PHILOSOPHY

The Revised Penal Code of the Philippines was enacted in December, 1930 and came into effect on January 1, 1932. It was based mainly on the Spanish Penal Code of 1870 which in turn was based on the early Spanish Penal Code of 1848. Therefore, in so far as the philosophic foundation is concerned, the Revised Penal Code of the Philippines is at least a hundred years old.

Classical vs. Positivist School

The main criterion of this Code is that the basis of criminal

[29] Renato Constantino, *op. cit.*

liability is human free will and the reason for the imposition of a penalty is retribution. The Spanish Penal Code of 1870 belonged to the Classical or Juristic School of Europe. Its framers saw man as an essentially moral creature with an absolute free will to choose between good and evil. They held to the view that man should only be adjudged and held accountable for wrongful acts, so long as that free will appears unimpaired. Thus, the Spanish Penal Code of 1870 placed more stress upon the effect or result of the felonious act than upon the man himself, and attempted to establish a mechanical and direct proportion between crime and penalty. The result was a beautiful symmetrical pattern where the particular act was attached to a multitude of penalties with different gradations. The offender was unimportant—to all intents he was a mere abstract being. This view met a lot of criticism from the forerunners of the positivist school such as Lombroso, Garofalo, and Ferri.

The Positivist School considered free will as a myth, a figment of the imagination, a debatable matter. Its advocates held the view that man is subdued occasionally by a strange and morbid phenomenon which constrains him to do wrong in spite of, or contrary to, his volition. Consequently, the central idea of all positivist thinking is the defense of the community from anti-social activities whether actual or potential, against the morbid type of man whom they called a "socially dangerous person." Thus, positivist philosophy chose a different approach to forestall the social danger and to achieve social defense for the community. Man, to them, was the primary consideration, while the deed was secondary. With these premises, the positivists viewed crime as essentially a social and natural phenomenon which cannot be treated and checked by the application of abstract principles of law and jurisprudence, nor by the imposition of a punishment fixed and determined *a priori*; but rather through the enforcement of individual measures after a through personal investigation conducted by a competent body of psychiatrists and social scientists.

Judge Guillermo Guevara, a member of the Committee which drafted the Revised Penal Code of 1931 and of the Code Commission which drafted the proposed Code of Crimes of

1958,[30] pointed to the "deadly conflict" between the Classical or Juristic School, and the Positivist or Realistic School as the first and most exacting task in undertaking the preparation of the Code of Crimes.

Laureta[31] asserts that the answers of the two schools to the question, "Whom should we punish?" reveal that the conflict between them is more apparent than real. He develops this thesis by explaining that the contradiction is the result of their failure to realize that while they are addressing themselves to the same question, they are concerned with it in different ways, and hence the divergent answers.[32] Quoting Rawls,[33] Laureta simplifies his thesis with this illustration of the conversation between a father and his son about J's imprisonment went: "The son asks, 'Why was J put in jail yesterday?' The father answers, 'Because he robbed the bank at B. He was duly tried and found guilty. That is why he was put in jail yesterday."[34] But suppose that "the son had asked a different question, namely, 'why do people send other people to jail'? Then the father might answer, 'To protect good people from bad people,' or 'To stop others from doing things which would make it uneasy for all of us; for otherwise, we wouldn't be able to go to bed at night and sleep in peace."[35]

Thus, Laureta concludes that the first answer sounds remarkably "like the retributive view," and is the characteristic—and indeed, the only—reply which a judge can and does make when applying the law to a particular case before him. While the second sounds "like the utilitarian view," and is the kind of answer which a legislator may be expected to make when proposing the establishment of a practice or an institution, such as criminal law.[36]

---

[30] *Code of Crimes* (Manila: Bureau of Printing, 1958), p. 1.

[31] Jose C. Laureta, *On Punishment, or on Opposing Theories of Criminal Law: Classical vs. Positivist* (Working Paper for the Conference on Criminal Law Reform, 1965), Diliman, Quezon City.

[32] *Ibid.*

[33] Rawls, "Two Concepts of Rules," *64 Philosophical Reviews*, 1955, pp. 3-4.

[34] *Ibid.*, pp. 5-6.

[35] *Ibid.*

[36] Laureta, *op. cit.*

The judge looks to the past solely to determine whether "guilt" is present, for unless this condition is there, the rule he is seeking to enforce would be inapplicable and any attempt to punish the accused would be illogical. The legislator, on the other hand, looks to the future and looks mainly for the advantages and disadvantages resulting from the laws and institutions which were established for the attainment of social ends.

Punishment, if it is the end, has no meaning for the positivists, for the mere infliction of suffering has only a negative value. It is whether punishmeat can yield consequences as deterrence of wrong doing, compensation of victims, reformation of offenders, or satisfaction of vindictive impulses, that has significance and bearing to them. Consequently, when the classicists consider the punishment as the ultimate of retributive justice, the other school criticizes the position taken as hollow and unsatisfactory. On the other hand, as the positivists take the position that dangerousness to society, rather than the notion of guilt, has any relevance to the problem of punishment, the classicists criticize them as utterly mistaken for this would allow the imposition of punishment on one who may be legally innocent of crime.

Convinced that both schools of thought cannot claim perfection and monopoly of the true and rightful approach toward the administration of criminal justice, the Code Commission stated the guiding principle they followed in preparing a Code of Crimes for the Philippines.

After a deliberate and careful study of the vast field of criminal science, the Commission came to the conclusion that no particular school of thought or theory could claim perfection and monopoly of the true and rightful approach toward the administration of criminal justice. To adhere entirely to the idea of moral blame and retribution; to assess retribution by means of a mechanical balance, attempting to measure beforehand the punishment or repression in terms of years, months and days; and to lay stress upon the act rather than upon the actor, as is done by the classical Penal Code of 1870, and the existing Revised Penal Code, would make one play the role of a physician who claims to be able to cure all ills with a stereotyped prescription, without regard to the peculiar and personal conditions of the patient.

On the other hand, to look upon each anti-social act as the pure and simple manifestation of an influence or force which is entirely independent from human free will, and to make the penal sanction rest upon no other consideration than the frightful character or dangerousness of the subject would create the absurdity of discarding every vestige of ethics in determining the innocence or guilt of an accused and of entrusting the administration of criminal justice to social scientists rather than to trained and professional jurists.

Whatever validity or force there may be in the theory of morbid influence upon a human being, it is undisputable that there is such a thing as justice at the base of man's conscience which demands that evil be condemned and good rewarded.

The foregoing reasons, among others, kept the Commission from committing itself entirely to either of the two opposing schools of thought. The Commission prefers to follow the path of Criminal Politic which may be considered as the *giusto mezzo* or the happy medium between the two extreme theories.

The Code of Crimes proposed by the Code Commission has, however, been sleeping in one of the Congressional committees for the past 11 years, the feeling being that the proposed Code is too revolutionary and would give judges too much discretion in the imposition of a sentence.

Proposals of Philippine Lawyers

In 1965, the College of Law of the University of the Philippines,[37] convened a conference on Criminal Law Reform.[38] A set of working papers was prepared and finally a draft of a penal code was presented for public consideration. The draft did not espouse changes as sweeping as those of the Code

[37]Held on July 14, 15, and 16, 1965.
[38]*Proposed Penal Code of the Philippines*, U.P. Law Center, U.P. Diliman, December 29, 1966.

Commission. It presereved the basic philosophy of the existing
Code under which criminal conduct and its responsibility rest
on the concept of moral guilt or conscious wrongdoing which
must be dealt with primarily for retributive and punitive, and
incidentally for reformatory, purposes. The changes were limited to dispensing with outmoded portions of the existing Code
and streamlining and strengthening the same against the tides of
modern-day conditions and developments. The draft, it can be
said, crystallized the thinking of the legal profession as to
needed changes. It may not, therefore, be out of place to quote
here at length the limits and objectives of the proposed
changes:

(*i*) *What act or behavior ought to be made criminal and how
should it be defined?* Amendment and change along this line
have been made in two ways: first, by the introduction of
new articles; second, by expanding the scope of existing provisions. In either case, prime consideration has been directed
to the frequency of the behavior; its injuriousness; the need
to protect individual or constitutional rights, the public
interest, and peace and order; its novelty or that of the
means or method of committing it. The first way is illustrated by Article 213, penalizing public officers who shall be
financially interested in transactions or engage in any profession or occupation which constitutional or statutory
provisions prohibit them from being financially interested or
engaging in; Article 270, which penalizes the selling of
minors; and Article (312) 311[39] which penalizes what is
commonly known as "squatting." Notable examples of
changes effected in the second way are (*a*) the addition of
a new paragraph to Article (125) 121 which, to stress that
the right to counsel is fundamental and essential to a fair
trial, would penalize any public officer or employee who
shall fail to inform any person detained by him of the cause
of his detention, or shall in any manner prevent him from

---

[39]The number within brackets refers to the number of the article
under the present code; the one outside the brackets is the new number
substituted in this draft. This observation holds throughout this preface
and this draft.

communicating with his attorney, next of kin or friend privately at any time of the day or night, after such communication has been requested by the person detained or by another acting on his behalf; (*b*) the inclusion of air piracy and air mutiny in Articles (122) 118 and (123) 119; (*c*) issuance, in addition to procurement, of a search warrant without just cause under Article (129) 125; (*d*) the inclusion of officers exercising quasi-judicial functions among those who may be punished under Articles (204)202 and (205) 203 for rendering, knowingly or through ignorance or negligence, an unjust judgment, order, decree, or resolution; (*e*) the expansion of the concept of delay in the administration of justice to that of delay in the performance by any public officer of his official functions;[40] (*f*) the inclusion of deceitful employment of sex stimulants as a means of committing rape;[41] and (*g*) the addition of television as a means of committing libel.[42]

(*ii*) *What provisions have generated confusion and controversy in their application and interpretation by the courts, and hence call for a satisfactory clarification?* Accordingly, the concept of qualified rebellion is introduced to abate dissatisfaction with the Supreme Court's ruling that the crime of rebellion cannot be combined with murder, robbery, kidnapping or other crimes committed in the course of a rebellion, these crimes being absorbed by and forming part and parcel of, rebellion (People *v.* Hernandez, 52 O.G. 5506, 1956; People *v.* Geronimo, 53 O.G. 68, 1956. This ruling is criticized on two major counts: first, it posits the absurd situation of a lesser crime, rebellion, absorbing a capital offense like murder; second, the penalty imposed is disproportionately too light considering the gravity of the acts committed. Under the concept of qualified rebellion introduced in this draft, the penalty to be imposed would be either the penalty corresponding to the gravest offense or that of reclusion temporal to death, depending on the nature of the acts committed.

In the same manner, this draft also seeks to correct the

[40]See Art. (207) 204.
[41]See Art. 335.
[42]*Ibid.*

unsatisfactory and hairsplitting ruling that the crime committed was only theft, not robbery, in a case where a showcase was broken and the offender put in his hand to take out the watches, on the theory that entry was neither effected nor intended (People v. Adorno [CA], 40 O.G. 567, 1941). Similar acts are here made robbery, regardless of intention to enter or success of entry.

(*iii*) *What provisions have proven to be unjust in their operation and hence must be corrected?* A notable instance is Article 29. Under the present Code, this article credits, in the service of their sentences consisting of deprivation of liberty, offenders who have undergone preventive imprisonment with only one-half of the period of such preventive imprisonment. This is so even if, as it has often happened, the offender has served preventive imprisonment equal to or even longer in duration than that of his sentence. And yet in the great majority of cases, it is not the detainee's fault that his case is not disposed of with dispatch and so he has to be confined indefinitely; it is rather due to the hopelessly slow working of our machinery of justice. To avoid this unjust situation and in recognition of the fact that, although not a penalty, detention also constitutes a deprivation of liberty, the article is amended so as to credit the offender with the entire period of his preventive imprisonment.

(*iv*) *What provisions should be deleted for having become obsolete or for being superfluous?* For instance, *destierro* (banishment) is abolished as a penalty throughout the Code, it having become manifestly ineffective because of the advances in means of transportation. So is bond to keep the peace, which is superfluous since there is no felony in the Code for which bond to keep the peace is prescribed as a penalty.

(*v*) *What measures should be adopted to give more efficiency to certain provisions of the Code which are frequently violated?* This is done by attaching more severe penalties or by instituting methods which would make prosecution of offenders less difficult. This is specifically illustrated by the proposals relative to arson for which severer penalties are imposed in all its forms and presumption of its commission is established under certain conditions.[43] Another illustration is the abolition of the rule that the maximum duration of a convict's sentence "shall not be more than threefold the length of time corresponding to the most severe of the penalties imposed upon him,"[44] for the reason that it has actually encouraged habituality and professionalism in crimes like swindling, theft, gambling, and malversation.

(vi) *What provisions must be simplified by eliminating unnecessary distinctions which have often made their application difficult and cumbersome?* Under the present provision on complex crimes,[45] for instance, light felonies may not be combined with grave or less grave felonies with which they concur. As a consequence, each one of such light felonies has to be prosecuted separately from each other and from the concurrent grave or less grave offenses, giving rise to a multiplicity of actions. This rule is changed in this draft so that light felonies may be combined, and be prosecuted in a single action, with grave or less grave offenses resulting from the same act. Care, however, has been taken to add a proviso that the penalty to be imposed shall not be more severe than the aggregate of the penalties that would be imposed if the concurrent crimes were prosecuted and punished separately. This is for the purpose of preventing the imposition of a disproportionately much higher penalty where one of the concurrent crimes is a light felony. Another instance is the provision on arbitrary detention,[46] which is simplified by providing only two, instead of four, different penalities.

(vii) *What differences in the nature, circumstances or results of the criminal act, or in the character or situation of the offender should determine the variance in penalty?* For example, one who is guilty of administering opium to another is proposed to be dealt with differently from the victim who, but for the need to treat him, should not be considered guilty of using the drug.[47]

[43]See Arts. (320) 319—(326) 325, and Art. 326.
[44]See Art. (70) 68.
[45]See Art. (48) 47.
[46]See Art. (124) 120.
[47]See Arts. (190) 187, 188, (191) 189, and (192) 190.

(viii) What acts should be given a different qualification or character from that which they are presently given so that the commensurate penalty may be imposed? Under the present Code, certain acts, such as taking of property by snatching or cutting through the clothing of the victim or taking anything from a person who has been killed or hurt in an accident, or on the occasion of war, riot, fire, typhoon, or any other calamity, may only constitute theft. As proposed in this draft, such acts would now constitute robbery.[48] Likewise, the kidnapping or detaining of a human being for the purpose of enslaving him is presently characterized as slavery to which the penalty attached is only *prision mayor* and a fine not exceeding 10,000 pesos. To qualify and punish the act as kidnapping or serious illegal detention, for which a much severer penalty is imposed, it is deleted from the present provision on slavery.[49]

(ix) What penalties should be standardized? To correct the disparity between the penalties for arbitrary detention, on the one hand, and serious illegal detention and forcible abduction, on the other, the penalty for the former crime is raised to at least approximate that of the latter.[50] This is justified on the ground that both acts constitute deprivation of liberty. In fact, a public officer who commits arbitrary detention owes a greater duty to respect individual rights than a private individual committing serious illegal detention.

(x) What provisions of the Code need to be harmonized with each other or with other laws? Accordingly, Article 180 of the present Code, covering false testimony, is amended so that it may be applied to prosecutions for violations of special laws.[51] The provision penalizing the removal, sale or pledge of mortgaged property is expanded to include immovable or real property, in addition to personal property, in view of the fact that the Civil Code classifies as immovables by incorporation or destination certain property which

[48]See Art. 297.
[49]See Arts. (272) 271 and (267) 265.
[50]See Arts. (124) 120 and (267) 265.
[51]See Art. (180)177.

can be removed to the prejudice of the mortgagee.[52]

Penalties and Indeterminate Sentence Law

With particular reference to penalties and the Indeterminate
Sentence Law as they are presently understood and applied in
the Philippines, the exposition of Justice Arsenio Solidum of the
Court of Appeals during a recent judicial conference[53] cannot
be improved upon.

Penalty is the punishment inflicted by law for its violation.
In its general sense, penalty signifies pain; juridically speaking, penalty means the suffering undergone, because of the
action of human society, by one who commits a crime. The
different theories justifying penalty are: (*i*) prevention, that
is the principal purpose of the State in punishing the criminal is to restrain the danger to society and the public caused
by the criminal acts of the offender; (*ii*) self-defense, by
which the State has the right to punish a criminal so as to
protect society from the threat and wrong inflicted by the
criminal; (*iii*) reformation, according to which, it is the duty
of the State to correct and reform the criminal; (*iv*) exem-
plarity, that is the criminal has to be punished as an
example to deter others from committing crime; and (*v*)
justice, which is based on the theory that crime must be
punished by the State, as an act of retributive justice and
vindication of the absolute right and moral law violated by
the criminal.

The characteristics of a just penalty are: (*i*) It must be
productive of suffering with the limitation that the integrity
of the human personality be not affected, because penalty
should be a restriction to freedom since the offender in violating the law, merely abuses such freedom; hence, the code
rejects those penalties which violate the physical integrity of
man and those other penalties which injure his moral in-

---

[52]See Art.(320) 319.

[52]*Proceedings of the Judicial Conference on the Application and Graduation of Penalties under the Revised Penal Code and the Indeterminate
Sentence Law*, U.P. Law Centre, Diliman, Quezon City, 1965.

tegrity; (*ii*) it must be commensurate with the offense, according to which, different crimes must be punished with different penalties and that each crime must be punished by a more or less severe penalty in harmony with its greater or lesser criminality; (*iii*) it must be personal, that is it should be imposed only upon the offender so that no one may be punished for the crime of another; (*iv*) it must be legal, that is it must be the consequence of a judgment rendered according to law; (*v*) it must be certain so that no one may escape its effects; (*vi*) it must be equal to all, which means that the same penalty must be applied to the rich and to the poor as well as to the powerful and to the humble.

According to the Constitution of the Philippines, "Excessive fines shall not be imposed or cruel or unusual punishment inflicted." The prohibition of cruel and unusual punishments is generally directed not so much against the amount or duration as against the character of the punishment. A penalty is not cruel and unusual simply because it prescribes a term of imprisonment that may strike us as out of proportion to the injury done and the degree of malice shown by the defendant. To be such, the punishment must not only be unusual but must also be cruel. Unusual punishments which are not cruel are not prohibited. And in order to be cruel and unusual the punishment must inflict moral or physical torture. Mere severity in a punishment is no test for unconstitutionality. As examples of cruel and unusual punishments, we have those inflicted at the whipping post or in the pillory, burning at the stake, breaking on the wheel, crucifixion and the like.

According to Article 21 of the Revised Penal Code, the penalty that may be imposed for any felony should be that prescribed by law prior to its commission. In other words, no matter how immoral or reprehensible an act may be, if at the time of its commission there is no law punishing the said act, the offender cannot be punished and the only thing that the court can do is to dismiss the case and acquit the accused. But the court, as provided by Article 5 of the same Code, is required to report to the Chief Executive, through the Department of Justice, the reasons which induced it to believe that the act should be made the subject of penal legislation. However, the accused may be punished under a law passed after the commission of the crime if such law is more favorable to him and he is not a habitual delinquent in accordance with Article 22 of the same Code. On the other hand, even if the court is of the opinion that a strict enforcement of the provisions of the Revised Penal Code would result in the imposition of a clearly excessive penalty, considering the degree of malice and the injury caused by the offense, it is the duty of the court to impose the penalty provided by law for such offense and submit to the Chief Executive, through the Department of Justice, such statement imposed upon the defendant. The reason is that it is a well-established rule that courts are not concerned with the wisdom, efficacy or morality of laws. That question falls exclusively within the province of Congress which enacts them and the Chief Executive who approves or vetoes them. The only function of the judiciary is to interpret the laws and, if not in disharmony with the Constitution, to apply them. Consequently, as the Supreme Court has stated in one case, while members of the judiciary as citizens or judges, may regard certain laws harsh, unwise or morally wrong and may recommend to the proper authority or the department concerned their amendment, modification or repeal, still, as long as said laws are in force, they must apply and give them effect as ordained by the law-making body.

The penalty provided by law for the commission of a crime can be imposed only when the accused is found guilty of the offense, because once the accused is acquitted, the court has absolutely no authority or jurisdiction to impose any penalty upon him; not even a reprimand for such reprimand, however slight it may be, constitutes a penalty. But should the court find that the acts proven to have been committed by the accused—although unethical, immoral, or otherwise reprehensible—do not constitute a crime within the purview of our penal law, and hence the court is constrained to acquit him, the court may with unquestionable propriety express its disapproval or reprehension of those acts to avoid the impression that by acquitting the accused it approves or admires his conduct.

In the imposition of the penalty, the court, in its decision, must specify the kind of penalty imposed, although it is not necessary to mention the particular provision of law applicable to the offense. Hence, it is not correct for the court, in a case involving the commission of a crime punished by the Revised Penal Code, to merely sentence the accused to suffer a certain number of years of imprisonment as is usually done when the offense is penalized by a special law. For in addition to the number of years of imprisonment to which the accused may be sentenced, the court must specify the kind of penalty imposed; for example, five years of *prision correccional* or ten years of *prision mayor*. The reason is that without mentioning the specific penalty imposed, it cannot be determined what accessory penalties will have to be undergone by the accused, for such accessory penalties need not be expressly imposed by the court in its decision as the same are impliedly included in the imposition of the principal penalty. The penalty must not be imposed in the alternative but absolutely and unconditionally. An example of an alternative penalty is in a case of swindling where the court, after finding the accused guilty, sentenced him either to pay the offended party the amount swindled or to undergo the corresponding penalty. An example of an indefinite penalty is in a case of murder where the Supreme Court was scandalized with the trial court's imposition of the penalty "from *reclusion perpetua* to death." Consequently, in order that the penalty will be in strict accord with the provisions of the Revised Penal Code, it must not only be imposed absolutely and unconditionally but must also specify the number of years of imprisonment and the kind of penalty imposed.

We will now discuss the main feature of this article which is the computation of the penalty under the Indeterminate Sentence Law. It must be remembered that this Law is for the benefit of the accused and its application, with certain exceptions, is mandatory when the penalty imposed upon the accused exceeds one year of imprisonment. Its purpose according to the Supreme Court is "to uplift and redeem valuable human material, and prevent unnecessary and excessive deprivation of personal liberty and economic usefulness." The criminal should be considered, first, "as an individual" and, second, as "a member of society." But this law is applicable only when the penalty imposed consists of deprivation of liberty, like imprisonment. It does not apply to penalties consisting of restriction of liberty like *destierro*[54] (exile), or deprivation of rights like suspension or disqualification. On the other hand, in as much as this law, as already stated, is principally for the benefit of the accused, should its application result in prolonging the penalty unnecessarily, its provision shall not be applied.

The Indeterminate Sentence Law applies to crimes punishable either by special laws or by the Revised Penal Code. Two penalties have to be imposed—the minimum and the maximum. Where the offense is punishable by special law, Section 1 of the Act provides that the court shall sentence the accused to an indeterminate sentence, the maximum term of which shall not exceed the maximum fixed by said law and the minimum shall not be less than the minimum term prescribed by the same. Thus, in a case where the accused is convicted of the crime of illegal possession of firearms of small caliber, the penalty for which is from one to five years, the court may sentence the offender to an indeterminate sentence, the minimum of which shall not be less than one year and the maximum not to exceed five years. The meaning of this is that you may select any number of years as the minimum so long as it is not less than the minimum, and the maximum does not exceed the maximum penalty provided by law. For obvious reasons, the maximum must always be higher than the minimum. Specifically, the court may sentence the accused to suffer an indeterminate penalty to say, from two to four years. On the other hand, when the offense is punishable by the Revised Penal Code, the same section provides that the court shall sentence the accused to an indeterminate sentence, the maximum term of which shall be that which, in view of the attending circumstances, is to be properly imposed under the rules of said Code and the minimum shall be within the range of the penalty next lower in degree to that prescribed by the

[54]People *vs*. Almeda, CA G.R. No. L-1563, June 18, 1938.

Code for the offense. In this connection, one basic principle that should be remembered is that in finding the range of the minimum penalty to be imposed where the offense is punishable by the Revised Penal Code, the basis must always be the penalty provided by law for the offense. To determine the range of such minimum requires familiarity with the different rules of the Revised Penal Code regarding the graduation of penalties. The Indeterminate Sentence Law applies only to divisible penalties which have fixed duration and which can be divided into periods. It does not apply to indivisible penalties, like *reclusion perpetua*, which do not have any fixed duration and which cannot be divided into periods.

Now, in graduating the divisible penalties it can be stated generally that when the penalty provided by law for the offense is composed of one or more divisible penalties to be imposed to their full extent, the penalty next lower in degree shall be that immediately following the lesser of the penalties prescribed in the respective graduated scales mentioned in Article 71 of the Revised Penal Code; that where the penalty prescribed is composed of three periods of different divisible penalties, the penalty one degree lower shall be composed also of three periods, starting after the minimum; that where the penalty is composed of two periods, the penalty one degree lower shall also be composed of two periods counted after the lesser of the penalties; and that if the penalty is composed of one period, the penalty one degree lower shall consist also of one period which is the one immediately following the prescribed penalty.

FUNCTIONS OF THE COURT

The Philippines is a republican state.[55] Its form of government, therefore, adheres to the principle of separation of powers. Accordingly, the functions of government are divided into three distinct classes, the executive, the legislative, and the judicial. Within the limits of its own sphere, each department is supreme. Absolute separation, however, is not possi-

[55]Constitution, Art. II, Sec. 1.

ble. While the Constitution sets the limits of independence of each department, it also confers upon each of them certain powers by which to restrain the others from exceeding their authority. The result is a system of checks and balances.[56]

Philippine Courts

The Constitution vests judicial power in "one Supreme Court and in such inferior courts as may be established by law."[57] Courts inferior to the Supreme Court created by law are: the Court of Appeals; the Courts of First Instance; the Juvenile and Domestic Relations Court; the City and Municipal Courts; the Criminal Circuit Courts; the Court of Tax Appeals; the Court of Industrial Relations; and the Court of Agrarian Relations.

Philippine courts exist to decide actual controversies, to enforce rights and duties between individuals or between individuals and the State, as defined and regulated by substantive law. Unlike the administrative agencies or officers, which are also called upon to administer the law after deciding on the expediency of their actions, the courts confine themselves to ascertaining the respective rights and duties of the litigants by determining what law is applicable to their dispute.[58] With regards to criminal cases, however, whenever a court has knowledge of any act which it may deem proper to repress and which is not punishable by law, it shall render the proper decision and shall report to the President of the Philippines, through the Secretary of Justice, the reasons which induce the court to believe that the said act should be made the subject of penal legislation. Similarly, when a too strict enforcement of the provisions of the Revised Penal Code would result in the imposition of a clearly excessive penalty, taking into consideration the degree of malice and the injury caused by the offense, the Court shall submit such statement as may be deemed proper, to the President, through the Secretary of Justice,

---

[56]Alejandrino vs. Quezon, 46 Phil. 83 (1924).

[57]Art. VIII, Sec. 1.

[58]Lorenzo M. Tanada and Francisco Carreon, *Political Law of the Philippines* (Manila: Central Book Supply, 1962), Vol. 2, p. 477.

without suspending the execution of the sentence.[59]

The Supreme Court. Following the establishment of American rule, the Philippine Commission enacted the Judiciary Act of 1901. This law created a Supreme Court composed of a Chief Justice and six associate justices which supplanted the *Audiencia Territorial de Manila.* In the Administrative Codes of 1916 and 1917, the composition of the court was increased to nine and it also provided for the qualifications of the justices, the regular terms of the court, vacation period, and exclusive administrative control of all matters affecting the court's internal operation. The legislature also made provisions for sessions of the court *in banc* and in divisions, one to dispose of civil cases, and the other criminal cases. The Constitution abolished the division of the Supreme Court and increased its membership to one Chief Justice and ten Associate Justices. The Constitution also conferred the Supreme Court with jurisdiction over certain cases which Congress is precluded from diminishing. Six justices constitute a quorum for the consideration of ordinary cases and the concurrence of six results in judgment. However, in two special cases—namely, to pass upon and declare a treaty or statute unconstitutional, and in the review of criminal cases where death or life imprisonment has been imposed by the lower courts—the required quorum is eight. Failure of eight justices to concur in these cases results in sustaining the constitutionality of the treaty or statute and in the commutation of a death sentence into life imprisonment.[60]

Court of Appeals. This Court which was created by Commonwealth Act Number 3,[61] primarily to lessen the Supreme Court's load in disposing of appealed cases involving questions of fact, was originally composed of one Presiding Judge and ten appellate judges. It sat in two divisions but could sit *in banc* to resolve motions for consideration of the rulings of a division. Executive Order Number 37, dated March 10, 1945 abolished this court. It was recreated by Republic Act Number 52 as a body composed of one Presiding

[59]Revised Penal Code, Art. 5.
[60]Judiciary Act of 1948, as amended. R.A. No. 2613, Sec. 17.
[61]Took effect on February 1, 1936.

Justice and fourteen Associate Justices.[62] It sat in divisions of threes for the purpose of judgment but sat *in banc* for adopting resolutions for internal administration.

Republic Act Number 1605[63] increased the total composition of the Court to 18, and still later, Republic Act Number 5204 brought the Court of Appeals to its present composition of one Presiding Justice and 23 Associate Justices.[64] It sits in eight divisions of threes. To arrive at a judgment there must be unanimity among the members of the division. In the event of a dissent, the Presiding Justice designates two other members of the court to sit with the division concerned, thereby creating a special division of five. The case is reheard and three out of five votes carry the verdict.[65]

The increase in the number of divisions of this court was deemed expedient by Congress to ease the burden of the Supreme Court which, with the emergence of quasi-judicial bodies whose decisions were by statute appealable to the highest court, was accumulating a backlog in its docket. A number of these appeals have been transferred to the enlarged Court of Appeals.[66]

Court of First Instance. While the Supreme Court and the Court of Appeals, primarily appellate courts, also enjoy original jurisdiction over certain cases, the workhorses of the Philippine judiciary are the Courts of First Instance. They are courts of original as well as appellate jurisdiction.[67] They exercise general jurisdiction and can take cognizance of civil, criminal, and admiralty cases. Probate and other special proceedings also come within their original jurisdiction. They hear land registration and naturalization cases,

[62]Took effect on October 4, 1946.

[63]Took effect on August 23, 1956.

[64]Took effect on June 15, 1968.

[65]RA. No. 296, as amended, Sec. 33.

[66]R.A. No. 5434, transferred appeals from the CAR, violations of the Minimum Wage Law, Department of Labor, Section 23, Land Registration Commission, Securities and Exchange Commission, Social Security Commission, Civil Aeronautics Board, Patent Office, Agricultural Inventions Board.

[67]Decisions of the inferior courts within the province are appealable to the Court of First Instance of the province where a *trial de novo* is held.

and dispense relief at law and equity. They are trial courts
of record.

For the purposes of Courts of First Instance, the Phlilip-
pines has been divided by the Judiciary Act of 1948[68] into
16 judicial districts. The division has not been made on any
definite basis. Some districts are made up of several provinces
while the city of Manila is a judicial district in itself. The
number of branches or *salas* in each district is not the same.
Under the present law there are a total of 243 Courts of
First Instance all over the archipelago.

Juvenile and Domestic Relations Courts. Quezon City, the
capital of the Republic, and Manila have each a Juvenile
and Domestic Relations Court. These courts have exclusive
original jurisdiction over all criminal cases arising within
their territorial limits where the accused at the time of trial
is below 16 years of age.[69] They also exercise jurisdiction
over matters pertaining to persons and family relations such
as actions for acknowledgment of children, guardianship,
legal separation, support, change of name, administration,
and dissolution of the conjugal partnership.

The Inferior Courts. Every municipality and municipal
district has a Municipal Court and every chartered city has
a City Court. In chartered cities the City Court may have
several branches. In Manila and Quezon City some branches
of the City Court hear only traffic cases. These inferior
courts are generally courts not of record. Their jurisdiction
over civil cases is limited to a maximum claim of pesos 10,000.00
exclusive of interests and costs. Their criminal jurisdiction
extends over petty or minor offenses and infractions of municipal and city ordinances.[70]

---

[68]Republic Act No. 296, amended. Took effect on June 17, 1948.
[69]Republic Act No. 1401.
[70]In criminal cases, justices of the peace and judges of municipal
courts of chartered cities have original jurisdiction over (*a*) all violations of municipal or city ordinances committed within their respective
territorial jurisdiction; (*b*) all criminal cases (arising under the laws
relating to gambling and management or operation of lotteries; assaults where the intent to kill is not charged or evident upon the trial;
larceny, embezzlement and estafa where the amount of money or property stolen, embezzled, or otherwise involved, does not exceed the

Circuit Criminal Courts. Due to persistent clamor regarding the slow disposition of criminal cases, Congress in 1968 enacted Republic Act Number 5179 creating Criminal Circuit Courts. Sixteen branches were created distributed all over the archipelago's 16 judicial districts. Their jurisdiction extended over the following criminal cases:

(*i*) Crimes committed by public officers, crimes against persons and crimes against property as defined and penalized under the Revised Penal Code, whether simple or complexed with other crimes.

(*ii*) Violations of Republic Act Number 3019 (Anti-Graft and Corrupt Practices Law) and Republic Act Number 1379 (Unexplained Wealth of Government Officers and Employees).

(*iii*) Violations of Sections 3601, 3602, and 3604 of the Tariff and Customs Code (unlawful importation, fraudulent practices against customs revenue; making false return on importations) and Sections 174, 175, and 345 of the National Internal Revenue Code (possession and removal of smuggled goods; venalities of Bureau of Internal Revenue officers, agents, and employees).

Current reports indicate success in the speedy disposition of cases by the Circuit Criminal Courts. Postponements are discouraged, trials are continuous, and the judges are enjoined to decide the cases within 30 days from the time they are submitted for decision. Some cases involving capital offenses have been tried in less than two weeks and decisions have been handed down forthwith. Whether the judgments speedily handed down can stand review by the appellate courts still remains to be seen as up to this date no reports of disposition by the appellate courts have been compiled.

---

sum or value of two hundred pesos; sale of intoxicating liquors; falsely impersonating an officer; malicious mischief; trespass on government or private property; threatening to take human life; and illegal possession of firearms); and (*c*) all other offenses except violation of election laws in which the penalty provided by law is imprisonment for not more than six months, or a fine of not more than 200 pesos, or both.

Appointments to the Judiciary

The justices of the Supreme Court and all judges of inferior courts are appointed by the President of the Philippines with the consent of the Commission on Appointments.[71] Justices of the Supreme Court and of the Court of Appeals must be at least 40 years of age, must have been for ten years or more a judge of a court of record, or engaged in the practice of law for the same period in the Philippines. While he need not be a natural born citizen, he must at least be, at the time of appointment, a Filipino citizen for the last five years.[72] No person can be appointed judge of the Courts of First Instance, Criminal Circuit Courts, Juvenile and Domestic Relations Court, Court of Industrial Relation, and Court of Agrarian Relations unless he has been a citizen of the Philippines for ten years and has practiced law in the country for a period of not less than ten years, or has held during a like period, within the Philippines, an office requiring admission to the practice of law as an indispensable requisite.[73]

City Court and Municipal Court judges must at least be 25 years old, citizens of the Philippines, of good moral character and must have not been convicted of any felony. In addition, they must have practiced law in the Philippines for at least five years or have held during a like period, within the Philippines, an office requiring admission to the Philippine Bar as an indispensable requisite.[74]

All justices and judges hold office during good behavior, until they reach the age of 70 years, or become incapacitated to discharge the duties of their office. They receive compensation as fixed by law which may not be diminished during their continuance in office.[75]

[71]The Commission on Appointments is a constitutional body composed of 12 Senators and 12 Congressmen, elected by each House of Congress on the basis of proportional representation of the political parties therein.

[72]Sec. 11, Republic Act No. 296, as amended by Republic Act No. 1186.

[73]Sec. 4, Republic Act No. 296.

[74]Sec. 71, Republic Act No. 296, as amended by Republic Act No. 2613.

[75]Sec. 9, Art. VIII, Constitution of the Philippines.

Criminal Prosecutions

Criminal prosecutions are initiated with the filing of complaints or informations.[76] Cases falling within the jurisdiction of the Court of First Instance require the holding of a preliminary investigation before the accused is held for trial.[77] In the provinces, preliminary investigations are conducted by the municipal judges or the provincial fiscals.[78] In chartered cities, the preliminary investigations are conducted by the city fiscals or city attorneys.[79] They have the authority to dismiss cases where the evidence does not establish a *prima facie* case.[80] The accused is invariably entitled to the assistance of counsel during the preliminary investigation,[81] a right that at times contributes to the delay of the process as the investigation loses its summary character and is converted into a full dress trial.

Fiscals or Public Prosecutors are all appointed by the President of the Philippines with the consent of the Commission on Appointments. They must be Filipino citizens, members of the Philippine Bar, and must have practiced law in the Philippines, or held the position of clerk of court, law clerk in a Bureau of the National Government or an office requiring the services of a lawyer, for a period of at least five years.[82] In the case of provincial fiscals or chief City Attorneys, the period of practice requirement is six years instead of five.[83]

All criminal prosecutions are conducted in the name of the People of the Philippines and while the offended parties may engage the services of private practitioner to look after their interests, the Public Prosecutor retains direction and control

[76]Rule 110, Sec. 1, Rules of Court in the Philippines.

[77]Rule 112, Sec. 1, Rules of Court in the Philippines.

[78]Rule 112, Sec. 2, Rules of Court in the Philippines.

[79]Rule 112, Sec. 14, Rules of Court in the Philippines.

[80]Rule 112, Sec. 6, Rules of Court in the Philippines.

[81]Rule 112, Secs. 11, 14, 15, Rules of Court in the Philippines.

[82]Sec. 1675, Revised Administrative Code, as amended by Republic Act No. 2673.

[83]Sec. 1673, Revised Administrative Code, as amended by Republic Act No. 2673.

over the case.[84] The trial may be actively conducted by the lawyer of the offended party upon motion of the Public Prosecutor and with the approval of the trial judge—the Public Prosecutor, however, retaining direction and control at all times.[85]

The Trial

The ordinary trial of a criminal case is attended not only by the trial judge, the parties and their lawyers, but also by the clerk of court, the court stenographers, and the bailiff. There may also be an interpreter. The clerk of court keeps the calendar of the court, attends to the marking of the exhibits, keeps minutes of the proceedings, and safeguards the court records. The stenographers take down the proceedings either in shorthand or by steno-type machine. They are officially required to transcribe their notes only in the event of an appeal, although it is customary for them to furnish transcript to parties asking for the same upon the payment of agreed fees.[86] Most trials call for an interpreter as the stenographers usually take notes only in English or Spanish. Very few, as yet, can take shorthand or steno-type notes in Philipino. Moreover, the Philippines is a multi-lingual country and it is not uncommon to have witnesses in a case speaking in two or three different tongues. The bailiff keeps order in the court and enforces orders coming from the bench. Court processes and written orders are, however, served on the parties by the Sheriff of the Province or City and his deputies.

Admission to the Bar

Law is a very popular profession in the Philippines. Admission to the legal profession is directly under the jurisdiction of the Supreme Court.[87] An average of 1,500 candidates have been

[84]Rule 110, Secs. 1, 4 and 15, Revised Rules of Court in the Philippines.

[85]People vs. Liggayu, 97 Phil. 865, Oct. 31, 1955.

[86]The regular rate is U.S. $0.25 a page containing an average of 200 words. If the transcription is made in rush, the rate is doubled or tripled.

[87]Art. VIII, Sec. 13, Constitution of the Philippines.

taking the bar examinations every year since liberation. Of this number 20 to 25 per cent make the passing grade. A candidate who fails in three attempts cannot apply for the examinations without attending a one-year refresher course and pre-bar review classes in a recognized law school.[88] To be admitted to the bar examinations, the candidate must be a Filipino citizen, had regularly studied law for four years and successfully completed all prescribed subjects in a law school or university recognized by the Secretary of Education. Before entering law school, he must have earned a bachelor's degree in arts or sciences with any of the following subjects as major or field of concentration: political science, logic, English, Spanish, history and economics.[89]

The bar examinations which are given by a Committee headed by a Justice of the Supreme Court cover the following subjects: Civil Law (15 per cent); Labor and Social Legislation (10 per cent); Mercantile Law (15 per cent); Criminal Law (10 per cent); Political Law and International Law (15 per cent); Taxation (10 per cent); Remedial Law (20 per cent) and Legal Ethics and Practical Exercises (5 per cent).[90] The passing average is 75 per cent provided the candidate does not obtain a grade below 50 per cent in any subject.[91] The Supreme Court can always refuse admission to a candidate on grounds of bad moral character.[92]

There is no integrated bar in the Philippines. The new lawyer, following his oath taking in the attorney's roll in the office of the Clerk of the Supreme Court, may start practice on his own, singly or with friends or relatives. He may also join an established law firm as an assistant attorney with a view to gaining experience. Others present themselves to the trial courts as available to appear for indigent persons facing criminal charges. Still others enter the government service as clerks and researchers, passing the bar examination being the equivalent of a first grade civil service eligibility.

[88]Rule 138, Sec. 16, Revised Rules of Court in the Philippines.
[89]Rule 138, Secs. 5 and 6, Revised Rules of Court in the Philippines.
[90]Rule 138, Secs. 9 and 14, Revised Rules of Court in the Philippines.
[91]Rule 138, Sec. 14, Revised Rules of Court in the Philippines.
[92]Rule 138, Sec. 2, Revised Rules of Court in the Philippines.

The procedure in Philippine courts is basically the adversary system. Although there is no jury, witnesses are called by the contending parties and subjected to direct and cross-examination under oath. Evidence is admitted or rejected in accordance with a set of rules copied mainly from the California Code of Civil Procedure.

Rights of the Accused

The Bill of Rights in the Philippine Constitution guarantees to every person the right to due process and the equal protection of the laws.[93] He cannot be held to answer for a criminal offense without due process of law.[94] Before conviction, he is entitled to bail, except in capital offenses when the evidence of guilt is strong.[95] Neither can excessive bail be required for his provisional liberty.[96] In all criminal prosecutions the accused shall be presumed innocent until the contrary is proved, and shall enjoy the right to be heard by himself and counsel, to be informed of the nature and cause of the accusation against him, to have a speedy and public trial, to meet the witnesses face to face, and to have compulsory process to secure the attendance of witnesses on his behalf.[97] No person shall be compelled to be witness against himself.[98] Excessive fines shall not be imposed, nor cruel and unusual punishment inflicted.[99] Nor shall a person be twice put in jeopardy of punishment for the same offense.[100] And free access to the courts shall not be denied to any person by reason of poverty.[101]

Appeal

Every accused who is found guilty by the trial court can always

[93]Art. III, Sec. 1 (1), Constitution of the Philippines.
[94]Art. III, Sec. 1 (15), Constitution of the Philippines.
[95]Art. III, Sec. 1 (16), Constitution of the Philippines.
[96]*Ibid.*
[97]Art. III, Sec. 1 (17), Constitution of the Philippines.
[98]Art. III, Sec. 1 (18), Constitution of the Philippines.
[99]Art. III, Sec. 1 (19), Constitution of the Philippines.
[100]Art. III, Sec. 1 (20), Constitution of the Philippines.
[101]Art. III, Sec. 1 (21), Constitution of the Philippines.

appeal to a higher court. The prosecution cannot appeal if the defendant would be placed thereby in double jeopardy.[102] From a judgment of conviction handed down by the City or Municipal Court an appeal may be taken to the Court of First Instance of the province or district. A trial *de novo* is held by the Court of First Instance. Should the Court of First Instance affirm the decision, the judgment is no longer appealable except by petition for review filed with the Court of Appeals. Such petition will be given due course only if it shows *prima facie* that the court below has committed errors of fact or of fact and law that would warrant reversal or modification of the judgment or decision sought to be reviewed.[103]

A case originally tried by the Court of First Instance must be decided within 90 days from submission.[104] If the accused is not satisfied with the judgment he can appeal to the Court of Appeals by simply filing a notice of appeal within 15 days from promulgation or notice of the judgment.[105] The trial court elevates the records to the Court of Appeals. As soon as the transcript of the evidence is received by the appellate court a notice is sent to the appellant's counsel for the filing of his brief. He is given 30 days within which to file his printed brief.[106] Indigent appellants are allowed to file typewritten or mimeographed briefs.[107] The appellants brief must point out the errors committed by the trial court and must include a copy of the appealed decision as appendix.[108]

The prosecution is represented in the Court of Appeals by the Office of the Solicitor General. This office prepares the reply brief.[109] Unless any of the parties ask for oral argument, or the appellate court on its own motion requires it, the appeal is deemed submitted for decision upon the filing of the reply-brief.[110] The appellate court may reverse, affirm, or modify the

[102]Rule 122, Sec. 2, Revised Rules of Court in the Philippines.
[103]Republic Act No. 5433.
[104]Sec. 5, R.A. 296.
[105]Sec. 1, Rule 122.
[106]Sec. 3, Rule 124.
[107]Sec. 7, Rule 124.
[108]*Ibid,*
[109]Sec. 1661, Revised Administrative Code. The OSG is the law office of the Government; it is under the Department of Justice.
[110]Sec. 1, Rule 48.

judgment and increase or reduce the penalty imposed by the trial court, or remand the case to the Court of First Instance for new trial or retrial, or dismiss the case.[111]

Automatic Appeals. Where the Court of First Instance has sentenced the accused to death or life imprisonment, the records are elevated to the Supreme Court on automatic review. In other cases, the appellant may also elevate the case to the Supreme Court on pure questions of law.[112] The procedure for appeals from the Court of First Instance to the Supreme Court is the same as that from the Court of First Instance to the Court of Appeals.[113]

A decision of the Court of Appeals, whether rendered in an original case or an appealed one, can only be elevated to the Supreme Court on petition for certiorari, the questions to be raised being limited to questions law.[114]

Output of Trial Courts

The delay in the judicial process has been one of the constant criticisms levelled at Philippine courts. There is some truth in this as criminal cases have been known to drag on and on for years.[115] Postponements are at times easy to obtain. The clogged dockets of the court allow cases to be heard only an hour or two each month and "amicable" settlements though prohibited in criminal cases have been tolerated by some judges with the tacit assent of the government prosecutors.

Statistics, in Table X, XI and XII from the Office of the Judicial Supervisor, Department of Justice, show the never ending race between the disposal of cases and the filing of new ones.

[111]Sec. 11, Rule 124.

[112]Sec. 17 (1), Republic Act No. 296, as amended by Republic Ac No. 5440.

[113]Rule 125, Sec. 1, Revised Rules of Court in the Philippines.

[114]Rule 45, Revised Rules of Court in the Philippines.

[115]One of the cases most often referred to was that of the Politbur defendants, charged and tried for treason in 1951, sentenced to death b the trial court in 1953, imprisoned up to 1969 when the Supreme Cour finally found them guilty of simple rebellion which carried a prison ter of 10 years.

TABLE X

CASES FILED AND DISPOSED OF AND PENDING IN
THE COURTS OF FIRST INSTANCE

FY 1963 TO FY 1968

	Total all cases	Criminal cases	Ordinary civil cases	Sp. proc. and all others
Pending July 1, 1962	84,708	47,779	21,622	25,377
Filed in FY 1962-63	46,523	23,870	11,560	11,093
Disposed of FY 1962-63				
(172 Judges)	47,311	26,462	8,950	11,899
Pending July 1, 1963	83,920	35,187	24,232	24,920
Filed in FY 1963-64	43,588	21,677	9,605	12,306
Disposed of FY 1963-64				
(170 Judges)	46,936	23,463	10,402	13,071
Pending July 1, 1964	80,572	33,267	22,931	24,374
Filed in FY 1964-65	44,856	22,913	11,627	10,116
Disposed of FY 1964-65				
(167 Judges)	43,856	22,240	10,571	10,844
Pending July 1, 1965	81,774	33,940	24,187	23,646
Filed in FY 1965-66	47,318	23,198	12,510	11,610
Disposed of FY 1965-66				
(179 Judges)	47,166	22,900	11,280	12,986
Pending July 1, 1966	81,925	24,238	25,417	22,270
Filed in FY 1966-67	47,794	24,506	13,168	10,120
Disposed of FY 1966-67				
(191 Judges)	46,589	24,055	11,057	10,577
Pending July 1, 1967	83,130	34,689	26,628	21,813
Filed in FY 1967-68	51,629	25,789	13,120	12,720
Disposed of FY 1967-68	49,418	24,130	12,694	12,594
Pending July 1, 1968	85,341	36,348	27,054	21,939
Filed July to December 1968	27,139	13,860	7,518	5,961
Disposed of July to December 1968 (224 Judges)	26,694	14,072	6,272	6,350
Pending as on December 31, 1968	84,417	35,111	24,138	25,168

TABLE XI

STATISTICS OF CASES FILED AND DISPOSED OF AND PENDING IN THE CITY COURTS

FY 1965 to FY 1968

	Total	Criminal	Civil
Pending July 1, 1962	62,600	55,120	7,480
Filed in FY 1962-63	87,000	74,500	12,500
Disposed during FY	88,500	75,000	13,500
Pending July 1, 1963	61,100	54,620	6,480
Filed in FY 1963-64	88,500	75,000	13,500
Disposed during FY	89,500	76,000	13,500
Pending July 1, 1964	60,100	53,620	6,480
Filed in FY 1964-65	90,800	77,500	13,300
Disposed during FY	91,500	79,000	12,500
Pending July 1, 1965	59,400	52,120	7,280
Filed in FY 1965-66	94,500	82,000	12,500
Disposed during FY	93,000	81,500	11,500
Pending July 1, 1966	60,900	52,620	8,280
Filed in FY 1966-67	96,000	78,000	18,000
Disposed during FY	92,000	75,500	16,500
Pending July 1, 1967	64,900	55,120	9,780
Filed in FY 1967-68	98,000	79,150	18,850
Disposed during FY	89,800	74,400	15,400
Pending July 1, 1968	73,100	59,870	13,230

Critique of Philippine Judicial System

No less than the Chief Justice of the Philippines, the Honorable Roberto Concepcion, has commented on the defects of the Philippine judicial system and expounded on the significance of the needed ethical and technical application of law enforcement to achieve suitable conditions of peace and order. He specifically pointed out the need for (*i*) minimizing partisan political considerations in the appointments to the judiciary; (*ii*) rendering prompt decisions on the part of the Judges; (*iii*) improvement of public prosecution; (*iv*) adequate compensation for public defenders; (*v*) re-orientation of practitioners to assist rather than obstruct the courts in the administration of justice; and (*vi*) orientation of Philippine society toward the government and its commands.

TABLE XII

STATISTICS OF CASES FILED AND DISPOSED OF AND PENDING IN THE MUNICIPAL COURTS

FY 1963 to FY 1968

	Total	Criminal	Civil
Pending July 1, 1962	44,000	33,700	10,300
Filed in FY 1962-63	74,000	63,000	11,000
Disposed during FY	73,500	62,500	11,000
Pending July 1, 1963	44,500	34,200	10,300
Filed in FY 1963-64	74,000	64,000	10,000
Disposed durind FY	75,000	64,500	10,500
Pending July 1, 1964	43,500	33,700	9,800
Filed in FY 1964-65	76,500	65,000	11,500
Disposed during FY	75,500	64,500	11,000
Pending July 1, 1965	44,500	34,200	10,300
Filed in FY 1965-66	76,000	65,000	11,000
Disposed during FY	77,500	65,500	12,000
Pending July 1, 1966	43,000	33,700	9,300
Filed in FY 1966-67	75,280	65,500	9,780
Disposed during FY	77,400	66,500	10,900
Pending July 1, 1967	40,880	32,700	8,180
Filed in FY 1967-68	75,200	65,000	10,200
Disposed during FY	75,900	65,800	10,100
Pending July 1, 1968	40,180	31,900	8,280

The Chief Justice pointed out the following as the leading factor which lent to the breakdown of peace and order: the glamorization of racketeers, unscrupulous and violent movie idols, spectacular public performers, and others as opposed to the more modest achievements of teachers, artisans, obedient public servants and law-abiding citizens. He pictured present Philippine society as an acquisitive society and one where the desire for rapid success too frequently breeds a disregard for the normal process, thereby developing its anticipated concomitant—violence, social disruption, and disregard for law.[116]

[116]Speech delivered before the Women Lawyers' Association of the Philippines, October 26, 1966.

Law Enforcement Agencies

The President of the Philippines as chief executive is the highest officer of the land charged with the enforcement of law. As Commander-in-Chief of the Armed Forces he can call on the armed forces to suppress lawless violence, invasion, or rebellion.[117] All law enforcement agencies are in effect under his control and supervision. He is the person ultimately responsible for the state of peace and order throughout the archipelago. If the security of the country requires it, he can suspend the writ of *habeas corpus*,[118] place any or all parts of the nation under martial law,[119] and order the expulsion of undesirable aliens.[120]

National Security Council and the NICA

Directly under him, and a part of his cabinet, are the Executive Department and the Departments of National Defense and Justice. There is also the National Security Council which advises him on the security of the State. Another unit of his office is the National Intelligence Co-ordinating Agency. The NICA coordinates all intelligence respecting government activities. It submits intelligence estimates on peace or order situation at home and abroad. While its activities have recently extended to smuggling control, it was primarily intended as a staff agency to be the focal point of all intelligence and security information and not as an operational agency.

Philippine Constabulary

The largest police agency is the Philippine Constabulary. It is a segment of the Armed Forces of the Philippines composed of 16,000 officers and men. It was created in 1901, long before the Philippines had an army, and was intended primarily as a national police force for the preservation of peace, law, and order in the Philippines. The Philippine Constabulary is directly under the Department of National Defense.

---

[117]Article VII, Sec. 10 (2), Constitution of the Philippines.
[118]*Ibid.*
[119]*Ibid.*
[120]Forbes *vs.* Chuoco Tiaco, 16 Phil, 534 (1910).

When the Philippines became a Commonwealth, Commonwealth Act Number 343 (approved on June 23, 1938), constituted the Philippine Constabulary as a national police force. Since its inception it has alternated among a variety of functions including military, police, and civil. Its dispersion throughout the archipelago made it the logical government agency to enforce national laws and maintain peace and order particularly in remote areas where local police forces are weak or non-existent. Today, the Constabulary represents the basic internal security force of the country.

Its chain of command starts with a Chief and a deputy Chief, thence to the regional commanders of the twelve Constabulary zones into which the archipelago has been divided. Each zone is composed of several provinces, each province having its provincial commander. As stated earlier, the provincial commander co-ordinates and co-operates with the provincial governor in the enforcement of laws intended for the maintenance of peace and order.

The Constabulary Headquarters at Camp Crame, Quezon City, offers facilities for the inspection and licensing of all firearms issued to non-military persons, a ballistics laboratory, a laboratory for the study of questioned documents, a medico-legal staff, and a Criminal Investigation Section.

Philippine Navy

Segments of the Philippine Navy have also been charged to assist in the enforcement of laws and regulations pertaining to navigation, immigration, customs revenue, opium and other prohibited drugs, quarantine, fishing, and neutrality in neutral waters. They do patrol work in territorial waters and can inspect fishing boats and other watercraft.

National Bureau of Investigation

As an office under the Department of Justice, the Division of Investigation was created on November 13, 1936, and conceived as a police agency similar to the Federal Bureau of Investigation. It was made up of college graduates, mostly lawyers, and certified public accountants. It made such an auspicious start in the solution of crimes and apprehension of criminals, gaining a reputation of being incorruptible, that legislation expanded it into a Bureau by virtue of Republic Act Number 157 (approved on June 19, 1947). It was still enlarged in 1960 by Republic Act Number 2678. The NBI "investigates and detects violation of law on its own initiative or upon proper request." Its goals are: to train municipal police officers in modern methods of crime detection and investigation, to expand and improve its capabilities so that it can assist local law enforcement entities, to provide a modern crime laboratory for the mutual benefit of all law enforcement agencies, and to maintain an effective system of keeping track of crime and criminal by keeping accurate data on criminal information and records.

The Bureau is headed by a Director and an Assistant Director who are both appointed by the President with the confirmation of the Commission on Appointments. It has at present personnel strength of over 1,000 persons, including agents, crime laboratory technicians, finger-print specialists, communications technicians, and clerks. No person can be appointed to the Investigation Division of the Bureau unless he is a *bona fide* member of the Philippine Bar or a Certified Public Accountant. The services extended by the National Bureau of Investigation include (*a*) General Investigation; (*b*) Technical Services; (*c*) Records Services; and (*d*) Specimen for Examination and/or Analysis.

In comparison to other police investigative agencies in the world, as of 1966, the NBI covers the largest unit area in square miles and the largest number of people, per agent:

TABLE XIII

Agency	Number of people per agent	Number of square miles per agent
Surete	840	4.2
Scotland Yard	8,600	0.7
FBI	28,500	382.0
NBI	185,000	939.0

It has an annual budget of around pesos 5,000,000. The Bureau has a well-earned reputation among local as well as foreign law enforcement agencies.

Provincial and Municipal Executives

The executive officer in the different provinces are the provincial governors elected once every four years by the voters of the province. They are charged with the execution of the laws by the provincial officers. A Philippine Constabulary provincial commander is assigned to every province to co-operate with the governor for the maintenance of peace and order in the province. The provincial governor, in the public interest, can ask the President to place any local police force under PC control.

The cities and municipalities have their own local police departments. As of 1966, the total police force of 47 cities and 1,378 municipalities reached over 31,000 officers and men. Manila, with a total force of 3,000 officers and men, has the biggest police department, while Uyugan and Ivana, in Batanes province, have only one police officer each.

Peace and order in the cities and municipalities is the responsibility of the municipal or city mayors. They have full control over the municipal police, including the selection and employment of police chiefs and their men, subject to civil service qualifications.[121]

All the police agencies in the Philippines bewail the lack of sufficient funds to improve their services. Salaries of personnel are low and, therefore, fail to attract capable persons who would want to make a police job as a career. Low salaries have also made police officers more susceptible to corruption, thereby giving them a poor image. Paucity of funds also accounts for lack of modern equipment, means of transportation, and communication. In many cities and municipalities, reliance on civic organizations for donations of equipment has become the rule rather than the exception. Investigative methods tend to be crude and third degree is not uncommon. As many of the police officers are not civil service eligibles,

---

[121]Police Act of 1966, Republic Act No. 4864, took effect on September 8, 1966.

every incoming mayor is able to put his own men in the police force, thereby making them subject to his political influence most of the time. And in majority of municipalities where there is no appropriation for municipal lawyers, the police officers who may know very little about the law are the ones charged with undertaking the prosecution of criminal cases.

FUNCTIONS OF THE PRISON

While the natives of the Philippines had written codes of crimes long before the Spaniards came, no system of prisons existed even after their coming. There were no prisons to house the offenders because the nature of the punishment for infraction of the laws was on the whole retributive and did not contemplate imprisonment for purposes known today. The Code of Kalantiao punished felonies and misdemeanors with death, incineration, mutilation of the fingers, slavery, flagellation, being bitten by ants, submerging in a river for a fixed time, and other arbitrary punishment. And those who did not fulfil their sentences were burned.

The Spanish Era

As government control and Christianity spread over the archipelago, royal orders and decrees directed the establishment of penitentiaries. Four principal ones were founded, one at Manila, another at Cavite, a third in Zamboanga, and a fourth at Marianas Islands. Penal colonies were also opened at San Ramon in Zamboanga, Balabac, and Cotabato.

In 1847, the construction of Bilibid Prison in Manila was started. This prison structure was planned with a central building and brigs spreading out like radial spokes of a wheel. This Bilibid Prison became the central confinement place for the prisoners up to 1941. Five years earlier the construction of the New Bilibid Prison had started at Muntinglupa in Rizal. It had a total acreage of 551 hectares and had a complex of buildings. Barely a year before the outbreak of World War II, the prisoners were transferred to the new Bilibid Prison and the old Bilibid was given to the city of Manila which now uses it as a City Jail.

Present Prison System

No significant legislation regarding prisons and prisoners were enacted during the American regime, and to date the prison system in the Philippines is governed by the Revised Administrative Code of 1917. The prison organization, as it exists today, is seen in the following chart:

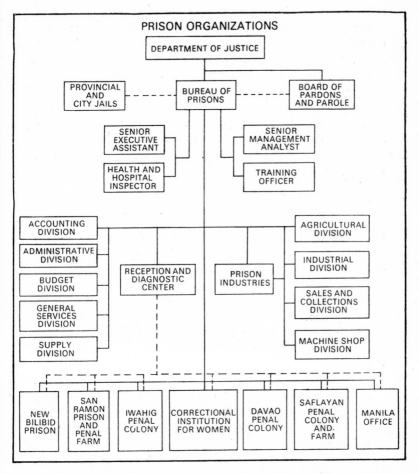

The Bureau of Prisons exercises general supervision and control of national, city, and provincial jails and of all penal settlements. It is charged with the safe keeping of all prisoners confined therein or committed to its custody. The primary objectives of the Bureau are: the physical rehabilitation of the prisoners, their moral and social development, and their training in some gainful occupation for which they may be vocationally inclined—all with the view of effecting their reformation and conversion into useful citizens.

The Reception and Diagnostic Center undertakes to analyze the personality and the factors contributing to the criminality of each offender, and to determine the type of institutionalization and treatment program best suited to each prisoner. It conducts researches geared to contribute to a better understanding of the cause of crime, the prevention of delinquency, and the rehabilitation of prisoners.

The Agricultural Division and the Industrial Division undertake to train the prisoners in gainful occupations. Agricultural products are used to supplement the needs of the prison while industrial products are sold to government offices and to the general public.

Classification of Prisoners

Under date of January 7, 1959, the Secretary of Justice approved a set of rules for the treatment of prisoners. These rules contained the following classification of prisoners:

Section 1. Prisoners shall be classified into any of the following classes:

(a) *A detention prisoner*—any prisoner either (i) awaiting trial, (ii) undergoing trial, or (iii) whose sentence is on appeals.

(b) *A third class prisoner*—any prisoner (i) previously committed for three or more times as a sentenced prisoner, provided that imprisonment for non-payment of a fine shall not be considered, or (ii) one who has been reduced from a higher class.

(c) *A second class prisoner*—any prisoner (i) newly arrived, or (ii) demoted from first class, or (iii) promoted from the third class.

(d) *A first class prisoner* is one (i) whose known character and credit for work while in detention earned assignment to this class upon commencement of sentence, or (*ii*) who has been promoted from the second class.

The rules also required separate dormitories whenever facilities permit, for the following: "(*a*) sentenced prisoners, (*b*) detention prisoners, (*c*) juvenile prisoners, (*d*) third class prisoners, (*e*) habitual delinquents and recidivists, (*f*) sexual deviates, (*g*) infirmed, aged and invalids, (*h*) patients, (*i*) mentally abnormal or insane, and (*j*) those sentenced to capital punishment."

Irrespective of class or rank, each prisoner is assigned to a security group, as follows:

(*a*) *Maximum security*—(*i*) Any prisoner who is on detention or who is sentenced to death and whose sentence is under review by the Supreme Court; (*ii*) while the prisoner is in the Reception and Diagnostic Center; (*iii*) when the prisoner is under disciplinary punishment; and (*iv*) irrespective of length of service of sentence when the institution Classification Board deems the prisoner in need of maximum measures.

(*b*) *Medium security*—Any prisoner whose conduct and character requires only ordinary surveillance and who does not fall under maximum security.

(*c*) *Minimum security*—(*i*) Any prisoner classified as colonist or trusty as provided for by law; (*ii*)Minimum A—when in the judgment of the Classification Board a prisoner, though as yet not eligible for classification as a colonist or trusty, has maintained a conduct and character warranting trust and whose work assignment requires such classification; and (*iii*) Minimum B—if the prisoner has been classified under Minimum A and whose work assignment requires his sleeping outside the prison compound but within the prison reservation.

Congestion in Penal Colonies. A problem of recent years was the clashes between gangs within the penitentiaries. According

---

[122]Atty. L.E. Fernandez, Chief, Documents Division, Bureau of Prisons.

to a ranking official [122] at the New Bilibid Prison there are at present twelve gangs[123] in the prison, and the prisoners belonging to the same gang—first offenders or otherwise—are lodged together in the same brigade or dormitory. This policy was adopted because inmates belonging to different gangs always quarrel when confined in the same cell. Fortunately, these gang clashes do not exist in the penal colonies. Thus, the prison officials attribute these disorders to congestion in the prison.

Of the penal colonies, San Ramon Penal Prison and Penal Farm is the oldest, having been founded in 1869 by Captain Ramon Blanco of the Spanish Royal Army. While intended originally to house only political prisoners who were not shot or exiled to Guam during the Spanish Regime, it is not both a confinement center for prisoners from Mindanao and a receiving station for the Bureau in Mindanao.

Sablayan Penal Colony, created in 1955, is the most recent of such colonies. The prisons at Muntinglupa could accommodate only 3,000 inmates, but an unusual increase in the prison population in 1955 persuaded the President to create by proclamation the Sablayan Penal Colony. It has its own superintendent and is reported to be the fastest growing penal colony.

Rehabilitation

For the male convicts, the penal colony system has proved the most effective measure for rehabilitation. From the table given earlier it will be noted that there are four penal colonies presently in operation: San Ramon in Zamboanga, Iwahing in Palawan, Tagum in Davao, and Sablayan in Occidental Mindoro.

A prisoner transferred to a penal colony is no longer called a prisoner but a colonist. To qualify as such, he must be a first class prisoner for at least a year preceding the completion of a period equivalent to one-fifth of maximum time imposed in the sentence of the court, or seven years in the case of life sentence. However, even without the foregoing qualifications,

[123]Of the total prison population of 3,199, as of January 10, 1969.

the Director of Prisons may approve the transfer to a colony of a prisoner recommended by the Reception and Diagnostic Center as (a) a fair security risk; (b) physically and psychologically fit to absorb the rehabilitative program in the colony; and (c) such assignment is therapeutically indicated.

The colonist is free of physical security measures. His discipline is relaxed and easy but firm, intended to develop his self-discipline and self-restraint. He has a number of privileges, among which are: good-conduct time allowance; to have his wife and children with him in the colony, or if he is not married, his fiancee, with transportation at government expense; to handle his own money; to receive part of the proceeds of his produce; and to receive upon discharge a six hectare parcel of land titled in his name.

Correctional Institution for Women. Female prisoners are kept at the Correctional Institution for Women. The establishment consists of a complex of buildings situated on an 18 hectare lot just outside of Manila. It has a program for the rehabilitation and reform of the prisoners which covers pre-release treatment, aftercare and assistance to prisoners' dependents. All types of vocational training are extended as a part of pre-release treatment. Numerous activities are scheduled to promote the maintenance of family and social relatives. Guidance counselling is extended to erring inmates and solutions to personal and family problems are patiently sought and applied. Relatives of the prisoners are invariably invited to the discussions and their views are taken into consideration. Government agencies—like the Presidential Committee for the Rehabilitation of Prisoners, and the Field Services of the Department of Social Welfare—and private civic groups—like Friendship, Inc., and the Catholic Women's League—participate in the overall effort to rehabilitate these female prisoners.

Youth Correctional and Detention Centers. Under Article 80 of the Revised Penal Code, persons under 16 years of age at the time of the commission of the offense, after the reception of evidence in the proper proceedings, are not pronounced guilty but ordered committed to the custody or care of a public or private benevolent or charitable institution. There they remain until reaching the age of maturity. Periodic reports are submitted to the court. If the minor behaves and complies with

the conditions imposed by the court, he is ordered finally discharged by the committing court upon reaching 21 years of
age. Otherwise, the court may sentence him in accordance
with the penalty prescribed by law for the crime committed
by him.

Youth correctional and detention centers, as these public
institutions under the Social Welfare Administration are called,
operate with little funds, which is the major obstacle they
have to face. At a hearing before a Congressional Committee,
a witness, Sister Elizabeth Moriarte of the Religious of the
Sacred Heart, disclosed that Youth Reception Center in
Manila "is really a prison" instead of a correctional institution.
"There does not seem to be any supervision of the children."
She reported that accommodations were sub-standard, citing
that eight boys shared a single bed. However, she added, that
even this was better because then the "children no longer
have to sleep on the concrete floors" or "stand for their
meals." This witness also pointed out the absence of medical
aid and gave this report:

> One day, I went there and I found a little boy in one of the
> detention rooms where he was locked. He was crying and
> obviously very sick. His eyes were swollen and he had a
> high temperature. He had measles. We wanted to help him
> but there was no doctor, no anything. They did not even
> have aspirins, that was worst. We wanted to give him a
> sponge bath but there was no soap, no towels, no basin.
> The only thing we could get was an old shirt which they
> wet. That was the only help they could give that boy.
> Fortunately, a woman doctor turned up unexpectedly and
> gave a prescription. We went to buy it for the boy. That
> boy would have died within two or three days.

This same witness gave a first-hand account of conditions
in Welfareville, another police institution for the juvenile
offenders, as follows: "Then I went to Welfareville and again
there were about 100 in prison there with nothing to do. There
were small boys and there was one man 23 years old. There
is supposed to be a school but there is no real training going
on. These boys need special help but there were no psychia-

trists and guidance counsellors." She concluded by saying that the Youth Reception and Detention Centers are "simply training criminals."

An official of the Youth Reception Center tried to make some clarifications regarding the prison-like atmosphere of the center.

> In working with these minors, the Center is assisted by police officers from the Manila Police Department charged with the sole function of providing security. It is understandable, therefore, when outsiders visiting the institution are prone to believe that situations obtaining in the Center are similar to those in ordinary prisons. The number of security officers assigned to the task is limited, thereby making it difficult for us to set them free from their dormitories, except on certain time of the day (during recreation time and gardening) and in certain areas within the compound.
>
> Much as we desire to keep up with the modern trend of handling juvenile delinquents, we regret to inform the Committee that the personnel, especially the security officers, have liabilities in cases of escape.

One thing is certain, that unless concrete steps are taken by the government to modernize and update these youth reception and detention centers, what may now be a mere charge, that it is a training place for criminals, could become a reality.

Provincial and Municipal Jails

Most provincial capitals have a provincial jail annexed to the provincial capitol or situated in its immediate vicinity. They are called provincial jails and are used to house provincial prisoners and detained persons awaiting trial in the Courts of First Instance of the province. A provincial prisoner is one, other than those awaiting trial, who is serving a final sentence of not less than 31 days but not exceeding one year. Subsidiary imprisonment is not reckoned in determining the prisoner's classification and if he has been imposed two sentences, the aggregate of which is more than one year, he is not considered a provincial prisoner.

Municipal buildings in several towns, including provincial capitols, have their own municipal jails, directly under the supervision of the local police chiefs. They house the municipal or city prisoners. This class of prisoners includes any person detained or sentenced for violation of a municipal or city ordinance; a person detained pending trial before the municipal or city court; a person detained by order of the municipal judge pending preliminary investigation for a crime cognizable by the Court of First Instance; and a person sentenced to imprisonment of not more than 30 days.

Those prisoners who do not fall into the category of provincial or municipal prisoners, and those convicted for violations of the Customs Laws are classified as national prisoners and committed to the national penitentiaries.

Capital Punishment

Capital punishment is provided for by the Revised Penal Code and some special statutes as punishment for several serious offenses. As in other jurisdictions, debates periodically come up in public forums urging the abolition of the death sentence. Prior to 1924, death sentences imposed by the courts were carried out by hanging; however, by virtue of Public Act Number 3104 (approved on March 17, 1925), the method of execution was changed to that of electrocution. Since then it has been used on and off depending on the decision of the Chief Executive and the exercise of his power of extending executive clemency. From January 16, 1904 to February 4, 1968, nearly 168 prisoners have been executed—both through hanging and electrocution.

PROBATION AND PAROLE SYSTEM

In 1933, the Philippine Legislature enacted Public Act Number 4221, known as the Probation Act, and Public Act Number 4225, known as an amendatory act, to the Indeterminate Sentence Law. The First provided for a system of probation and the second provided for a system of parole. In 1937, however, the constitutionality of the Probation Act was raised, and the Supreme Court (in the case of People of the Philippines vs.

Hon. Jose O. Vera, *et al.*),[124] declared the said law unconstitutional for constituting undue delegation of legislative power and for denying equal protection of the laws.

Probation System

It is, however, inaccurate to state that there is no system of probation in the Philippines. Article 80 of the Revised Penal Code, which refers to juvenile delinquents, actually established a probation system for juvenile offenders. When a minor is found to be delinquent, he becomes a ward of the court and continues as such until he attains majority or is sooner discharged by the court. Where the period of probation ends favorably, because the conditions imposed upon the minor have been complied with, he is returned to the court in order that the same may order his final release. If the minor fails to behave properly during the probation period, he is returned to the court in order that the same may render the judgment corresponding to the crime committed by him.

The following table shows the number of youthful offenders sent by the Juvenile and Domestic Relations Court of Manila to Welfareville on probation and the number of probationers who were returned to the court upon reaching the age of majority and sentenced to serve in the penitentiary:

TABLE XIV

	Sent to Welfareville	Returned to the court
1964-65	580	9
1965-66	565	0
1966-67	749	2
1967-68	676	0

Parole System

As discussed earlier, under the Indeterminate Sentence Law the court shall sentence an accused to an indeterminate sentence, the maximum term of which shall be that which, in view of the attending circumstances, could be properly imposed under the

[124] 65 Phil. 59, 1937.

rules of the Revised Penal Code, and to a minimum which shall be within the range of the penalty next lower to that prescribed by the Code; and if the offense is punished by any other law, the court shall sentence the accused to an indeterminate sentence, the maximum term of which shall not exceed the maximum fixed by law and the minimum shall not be less than the minimum prescribed by the same.

After serving the minimum term imposed by the court, the prisoner becomes entitled to apply for parole. In the Philippines, parole is considered a reward for the good conduct and manifestations of reform on the part of the prisoner. It is also believed that a system of parole improves institutional discipline and serves as an incentive to continued good behavior after release of the prisoner—since the privilege is revocable and the prisoner can be reincarcerated.

Board of Pardons and Parole

Applications for parole are considered by the Board of Indeterminate Sentence, renamed Board of Pardons and Parole, composed of the Secretary of Justice and four members—a sociologist, a clergyman or educator, a psychiatrist and one more qualified person. At least one member must be a woman.[125]

Once every six months, the officers of the Bureau of Prisons forward to the Board of Pardons and Parole the records of all prisoners who have served the minimum term of their sentences. The cases are then apportioned by the Board to parole officers for investigation before deliberation by the whole body of each individual case. On scheduled dates, the prisoners appear before the Board for questioning and further investigation. The matters looked into by the Board are: (*i*) the facts and circumstances surrounding the commission of the crime, and the prisoner's version of the case; (*ii*) his history, family life, environment, education, former habits, associates, occupation, and such other factor influences as are available to the Board; (*iii*) his apparent mentality and heredity; (*iv*) his general health and condition; (*v*) his attitude towards discipline and towards society as evidenced by his institutional record; (*vi*) previous convictions

---

[125]Republic Act No. 4203, Sec. 3.

and the probability of committing the crime again; and (*vii*) reports of the prison officials regarding the prisoner and his work.

The Board also considers pre-parole reports coming from interested agencies, religious and church affiliates of the prisoner, and other organizations to which the prisoner might pertain.

The Board authorizes the release of the prisoner on parole if it is convinced that the prisoner is fitted by his training for release, that there is a reasonable probability that he will live and remain at liberty without violating the law, and that such release will not be incompatible with the welfare of society.[126] The release may be subject to conditions prescribed by the Board.

The parolee may be placed under surveillance during the remaining term of his sentence or until final discharge by the Board. The officials designated by the Board to keep the parolee under surveillance shall report to it regarding the latter's conduct.[127] Due to lack of funds, municipal judges in the towns and rural areas are designated as parole officers to whom the parolees report periodically. In the event the parolee violates the conditions of his parole, he is re-arrested and required to serve the unexpired portion of his sentence.[128]

TABLE XV

Fiscal year	Prison population	Parolees
1958-59	13,152	4,673
1959-60	13,578	2,764
1960-61	14,099	2,549
1961-62	14,508	2,717
1962-63	15,032	3,156
1963-64	16,168	2,514
1964-65	17,214	2,953
1965-66	17,703	3,150
1966-67	19,201	2,877
1967-68	19,221	3,936

[126]*Ibid.*
[127]Sec. 6.
[128]Sec. 8.

Table XV shows the proportion of parolees to the existing prison population over a period of 10 years.

Due to lack of statistics, it is difficult to say whether the probation and parole systems in the Philippines have been successful or not. With regards to juvenile delinquents only those previously convicted of theft show a significant reversion to crime. In 1961, out of 1,337 juveniles arrested for theft, 147 showed previous convictions for the same offense.

A paper[129] submitted to a Senate Committee studying penal reforms found the following problems in relation to the parole system and the Indeterminate Sentence Law.

There are still many among our trial judges who do not know how to apply the Indeterminate Sentence Law properly (many judges in fact rely solely on the recommendation of the prosecutor on the penalty to be imposed upon the convict). This regrettable situation has led to indeterminate sentences which are either too short or too long or where the gap between the minimum and the maximum sentence is very small or very wide.

In order that parole may be effective, the confinement and treatment in the penal institution must prepare for it. Unless the offender has been so dealt with that his attitude toward society has changed and he is thoroughly equipped to rejoin the community, parole in many cases will fail. Presently, our penal institutions are doing little or nothing to prepare prisoners for parole.

While the members of the Board of Pardons and Parole are striving to make wise selections of prisoners to be released on parole through a thorough study of the prisoner's institutional record and interview of the prospective parolee, still it must be admitted that their decisions are based on imperfect knowledge. This is so because the members of the prison staff, whose psychiatrical, psychological, sociological, educational and other reports form the basis of the parole board members' decisions are far from competent,

[129]Report submitted to the Senate Committee on Justice entitled "Penal Institutions, how They Affect the Individual in Particular and Society in General (1968-69)."

vitiating the reliability of their reports. It has even been said that these reports are prepared not by the prison staff but by other prisoners. Moreover, the records of the prisoners are usually incomplete.

The success of a parole system is dependent on the degree to which the state is willing to finance truly effective parole supervision. As stated elsewhere in this report, we have only a few parole officers all of whom hold office in Manila. Supervision over parolees in the provinces and other cities is delegated to municipal and city judges whose effort in this regard is limited to requiring the parolee to report to him once a month or every two months and noting such report on the back of the parolee's discharge on parole.

Many parolees revert to crime because of the community attitudes toward any one who has been in a penal or correctional institution. Too often the public acts as though it believes that "once a crook, always a crook" is invariably true. The government itself is unwilling to employ parolees.

STUDY OF CRIMINOLOGY IN THE PHILIPPINES

Criminology as a course of study is quite new in the Philippines. The first school to offer a course in Criminology was the Philippine College of Criminology. It started as a unit of the Manila Law School, and was granted a licence as an independent college by the Department of Education in 1954. The enrollment of this college swelled from about a hundred in 1954 to over four thousand male and female students at the end of the school year 1968-69. It graduated 180 students with the degree of Bachelor of Science in Criminology and two with the degree of Master in Criminology last April, 1969.

The four-year bachelor's course carries a curriculum requirement of 141 units. In the freshman year, outside of the cultural subjects, those related to criminology are: Introduction to Criminology, Police Photography and Laboratory, Introduction to Law and Legal History, and Constabulary Science and Tactics. In the second year there are: Logic, Forensic Chemistry, Modern Criminal Investigation, Criminal Law, General Psychology, Legal Medicine, and Principles of Economics. In the junior year the students take up Criminal Psychology, Police Organization and Administration, Polygraph Laboratory, Criminal Procedure, Juvenile Delinquency and Crime Prevention, Vice and Rackets Investigation, and Criminal Psychiatry. In the senior year, among the required subjects are: Prison Management and Administration, Police Ethics and Human Relations, Correction, Probation and Parole, Criminal Evidence, Police Personnel Management, and Police Reports, Forms and Records Management.

A graduate of the four-year course is eligible for admission to any recognized law school in the Philippines. He is able to find employment in the police departments of the different cities and municipalities after taking a civil service examination. Graduates can also apply for positions in the National Bureau of Investigation. Some have been employed by banks for their training in examining questioned documents, others in ballistics and finger printing sections of the different government police organizations. Still others join security service organizations and private investigation agencies.

The Faculty of the Philippine College of Criminology includes a former justice of the Supreme Court, and well-known police officers from the Manila Police Department, the National Bureau of Investigation, the Police Commission and the Judge Advocate General's Office of the Armed Forces of the Philippines. There are also medico-legal officers from the Department of Justice, psychiatrists from established hospitals, former prison officials, chemists and photographers.

Records of the Department of Education showed that there are at present five other institutions of learning in Manila offering the four year course leading to the degree of Bachelor of Science in Criminology. There are 19 other schools located in the different cities of the archipelago while 18 schools have filed applications with the Department of Education to offer the said course. It is estimated that the total enrollment in the existing schools is slightly over 20,000 students.

The main problem of these schools is the lack of books for the use of students. While the libraries of these schools meet the requirements of the Department of Education as to the number of volumes, 99 per cent of their books are from foreign sources. There are no printed books by local authors

THE PHILIPPINES 841

on the subjects of study. Except for mimeographed manu-
scripts by some Faculty members, most of the books are not
easily available even from the book stores. And books from
abroad are priced way above the means of the ordinary student.

Candidates for the Master's Degree in Criminology are
required to submit these as a pre-requisite for graduation. But
there are very few of them and most seem to deal on criminal
law rather than criminology. No systematized nor serious
research on criminology has really been undertaken to date.

The Philippine Constabulary Data Processing Unit has
been placed under the National Economic Council and has
an office force of less than ten persons. It is engaged primarily
in compiling reports from different police agencies and interpretation of data is still in its initial stage.

SOCIAL POLICIES TOWARDS CRIME: PAST AND PRESENT

The average Filipino citizen reads the front page of the
morning papers reporting another killing or a well-planned
robbery. Momentarily, he feels aghast or stunned by the
brutality of the killing or the boldness with which the robbery
was executed, and then, unconcernedly turns to the comic
page to see whether Popeye has taken his daily dose of
spinach, or to the sports page to see which golfer has broken
par in some tournament course. He lives in a state of unconcern—this crime can happen to others, not to him, so why
bother. Moreover, this is a matter for the police and not for
him. Multiply this reader a thousandfold and you can have
a picture of Philippine society's attitude towards the rising
tide of criminality in the country today.

A shooting takes place in broad daylight on a downtown
street, witnessed by several persons. They narrate the event
with vivid details to their cronies and friends over a cup of
coffee or in a cocktail lounge. Yet, when the police start looking for clues and inquiring after witnesses, no one comes
forward to help it. Why? Again, the average citizen feels that
this is not his concern. Perhaps he is also afraid of being involved. He does not enjoy the thought of going to the police
station to identify suspects. He disdains the very thought of
going to court to testify and be interrogated by pugnacious

lawyers. He does not want to be identified; for, after all, the accused are notorious criminals, and there is always a possibility that he and his family may be the object of revenge.

Society's Unconcern and Government's Lack of Definite Policy

If the greater mass of society is unconcerned about the rising tide of criminality, would it not be natural to expect that the social policies regarding criminality and juvenile delinquency would also be one of unconcern? In a way, the peaceful nature of the people and the prosperity that characterized the country's agricultural economy must have contributed to this sense of lethargy in the past. Writing in 1938, Macaraeg said: "All foreigners who have come to our shores and American government officials who have had a chance to come in close contact with our people unanimously agree that we are a peaceful people. Our crime record in the Philippines is lower as compared with Japan and with either the United States, Germany or other European countries."

But conditions then were very different from today. A great war intervened when the Filipinos were forced to kill and rob and steal to survive, to clothe, and feed their families. Economic dislocation came about. Entrepreneurs saw hope in industrialization and the old agricultural economy had to be revised. But industrialization brought its own peculiar problems. The rapid increase of population, the convergence in cities and industrial centers, the propagation of a new ideology, all these came to a Philippines whose social policies were still geared to pre-war conditions. Thus, in 1966, President Marcos making the State of the Nation Address, when he assumed office, said:

There is a very disturbing upsurge in the incidence of criminality in our country. The crime clock indicates murder and homicide every hour, theft every 30 minutes, robbery every hour, sexual offenses, estafa and falsification every two hours. Speed in the investigation of complaints, prosecution of criminals and adjudication of cases is far from satisfactory and there is a backlog of more than 80,000 cases pending in our courts.

There are other crimes whose pernicious influence rests not so much on their rate of incidence, but more importantly, on their adverse effects on the national economy. I refer particularly to the problem of smuggling—that cancerous evil that has wrecked havoc on our economy and weakened the moral fiber of our people.

These threats to our security are further aggravated by the state of preparedness of our military and police establishments which is far from adequate.[130]

From 1938 to 1966 there seems to have been no definite policy adopted by the government with respect to crime and delinquency prevention outside of those related to the broad and general objectives of improving the economy, raising the level of education of the masses, and maintaining peace and order. In the past, it was believed that the threat of punishment, cruel and severe without doubt, was enough to discourage or deter crime. Vengeance and retribution, and the protection of the existing social order, was considered the philosophical basis behind the penalty which society through the governmental agencies imposed upon the wrongdoer. But human experience over the years has shown that the threat of punishment alone did not and could not prevent or eradicate crime. There are many factors which affect human behavior and lead to the commission of crimes. Not the act alone, but the wrongdoer, is of primary concern. It took the Philippines some fifty years to realize the necessity for a well-geared social welfare program to lessen, if not eliminate, factors that egg an individual into the commission of crimes.

The Socio-economic Program

In 1968 the Social Welfare Administration[131] was elevated to cabinet level. It is charged with the duty to extend assistance to the needy which will include increased allotment of basic needs, family counselling, community welfare services to pro-

---

[130]State of the Nation Address of President Marcos on January 24, 1966 (Manila: Bureau of Printing, 1968), pp. 6-7.
[131]Republic Act No. 5416, took effect on May 25, 1968.

mote the rehabilitation, and social adjustment of the individual and his relocated family—and to inculcate in them a sense of self-discipline, community consciousness, co-operation, and civil responsibility. It is also bound to rehabilitate the homeless, wayward women, beggars and negative lepers.

For children, the social welfare program contemplates help to needy children on a national scale which includes placement under foster homes, adoption and guardianship services, institutional care and rehabilitation of abandoned and/or orphaned children; probation and parole services for the treatment and rehabilitation of juvenile offenders, supervision and licensing of child-caring institutions, codification of child welfare laws, and updating of such legislation in accordance with modern trends in child and youth welfare.

Since its elevation to cabinet level, the Social Welfare Administration has undertaken a crash program for the benefit of over three million out-of-school youths to control juvenile delinquency, the establishment of regional youth and community centers, and a home for unwed mothers.

The efforts of the Social Welfare Administration have, however, met with obstacles in the form of insufficient budgetary support, dumping of political protegees among its personnel, politically influenced allocation of assistance, and the lack of skilled and sufficiently-trained social workers.

Land Reform. Land reform has also been undertaken as a part of the socio-economic program to improve the lot of the common man. However, efforts to bring about a more equitable distribution of lands during the past thirty years have not resulted in appreciable success. The Homestead Law[132] tried to encourage the development of virgin areas and afford every farmer a chance to own his own farm. The Philippine Rice Share Tenancy Act,[133] and its amendments, tried to give the tenants a bigger share in the harvest and to break the institution of absentee-landlordism. The Land Reform Code,[134] patterned after those of Japan and Taiwan, sought the break up of large estate, outlaw the *kasama* or harvest sharing system,

[132]Public Act No. 926, October 7, 1903.
[133]Public Act No. 4054, February 27, 1933.
[134]Republic Act No. 3844, August 8, 1963.

and pave the way to eventual ownership of family-sized farms
by the tenant-farmers. Agrarian Courts—oriented by law to
resolve all doubts in favor of the tenant and against the landlords, created to expedite achievements of the Code's objectives—have not really accomplished much more than to sow
confusion into an already confused situation, favoring thereby
the intrusion in the farm areas of elements said to be commu-
nist oriented.

Strong family ties militate against farmers moving to other
areas to open virgin lands and own homesteads of their own.
Regionalism seems to be another contributing factor to this
problem. And so religious beliefs. Christians fear to move into
areas in Mindanao, where there are vast uncultivated lands,
because of big Muslim or non-Christian groups. Areas where
most of the early settlers are Ilocanos do not welcome
Cebuanos and Tagalogs, and vice versa.

Prices of landed estates increased by all kinds of administrative charges, and in some cases connivance between the land-
owner and the government negotiators render eventual acquisition of family-sized farms by the farm workers well nigh
impossible.

Propensity to gambling and the prospect of hard work under
an unfriendly climate also dampen pioneering spirits to venture
into virgin forest areas to hew out farms and homesteads.

From Agricultural to Industrial Economy. The shift of the
nation from agriculture to industrialization has also brought
about social problems which have influenced the frequency of
crime. As in the case of the farm workers, the government
has enacted laws to enhance and promote the well-being of the
factory workers. There is the Court of Industrial Relations[135]
to hear, mediate, and arbitrate labor disputes, and there is an
Industrial Peace Act[136] to emphasize and declare what are the
rights of the working masses. In addition, there is the Social
Security System,[137] patterned after that of the United States
(except unemployment benefits), for all employees in the
private sector and there is the Government Service Insurance

[135]Commonwealth Act No. 103, October 29, 1936.
[136]Republic Act No. 875, June 17, 1953.
[137]Republic Act No. 1161, June 18, 1954.

System for the employees of the government offices. These institutions are charged with the duty to assist the ordinary wage earner in obtaining financial assistance from the education of their children up to the construction of their family homes. But the accomplishment of the objectives of these institutions, to be considered satisfactory by the masses, will take years of long and sincere dedication.

The Police Act of 1966

To achieve and attain a higher degree of efficiency in the organization, administration and operation of local police agencies—with the end in view that peace and order may be maintained more effectively and the laws enforced with more impartiality—the Police Act of 1966[138] created a Police Commission composed of a chairman and two members, all appointed by the President with the consent of the Commission on Appointments. The original appointees were extended terms of seven, five, and three years. Subsequent appointees shall hold office for seven years without re-appointment. Thus, continuity in policies is assured though a new member joins the Commission every two years following the expiration of the first three years of the Commission's existence. The POLCOM, as the body has come to be called, advises the President on all matters involving local police administration, examines and audits on a continuing basis the performance, activities and facilities of all local police agencies throughout the country, organizes and develops police training programs, and operates police academies. Among its other prerogatives is to review the findings of local POLCOM units[139] in administrative cases, filed against erring police officers and agents.

Policy regarding Peace and Order

Assessing the peace and order situation at the beginning of 1969, President Ferdinand Marcos, in his State of the Nation Address, said:

[138]Republic Act No. 4864, approved on September 6, 1966.
[139]Composed of an officer of the Philippine Army, the City or Municipal Treasurer, and a City or Municipal Councilor.

The problem of maintaining peace and order is not a monopoly of the Philippines. It is a worldwide phenomenon that increases in intensity and extent as a society becomes a complex organism; as population increases; as peoples of varied cultures mingle and live together; as technology encroaches on traditional ways of life. These changes create not only the conditions for a better material of life; they create, too, social problems, the most grievous of which are criminality and juvenile delinquency.

Accordingly, he stated the policies that the Administration will follow in resolving the crime problem of the country. These include "(*i*) Improving our capability for crime prevention; (*ii*) improving law enforcement, and (*iii*) improving the administration of justice."

The objectives of these policies, he likewise enumerated, are to

(1) arouse, promote and maintain an active public concern for the prevention of crime and juvenile delinquency; (2) to integrate and coordinate the activities and projects of community organization into the national crime prevention program; (3) to improve the caliber of the manpower resources of police agencies; (4) to develop inter-police agency teamwork and cooperation; (5) to win the support of the citizen in the peace and order campaign; (6) to make the judicial system more effective by introducing changes that will facilitate the processing of criminal cases; (7) to enhance the dignity of the courts by protecting the judiciary and the prosecuting agencies from pressure groups; (8) to eliminate the backlog of pending cases; and (9) to emphasize correctional treatment of prisoners and to reduce recidivism by strengthening rehabilitation, counselling, educational and vocational training activities.

SUMMARY AND CONCLUSION

The young Republic of the Philippines with its legacy of Spanish and American legal systems is beset by numerous problems, one of which is the rising tide of criminality. Its pre-

Spanish culture of Indonesian and Malay origins have almost been obliterated by four hundred years of Spanish subjugation and fifty years of American rule, though its ancient written laws recognized principles in criminal law and penology which are still valid today. American rule has been benevolent and ushered in among the inhabitants, now numbering 35 millions, a democratic form of government and way of life.

World War II brought economic dislocation and a change in the moral fiber of the Filipino's character. Respect for law and order which was noted by all pre-war visitors seemed to have deteriorated after the war. Lawlessness and corruption in sectors of the government have occupied the newspaper headlines and the authorities seemed at a loss to find the proper solutions.

The police agencies lack co-operation and harmony. There are areas where overlapping of functions can be noted, which act as irritants to the strained relation among police agencies. No centralized system of crime reporting was in existence till the middle of 1968. No accurate data as regards the crime and juvenile delinquency on a national scale was available. No serious study of crime causation had been undertaken during the last 50 years and even its prison system operates under a law which is over 50 years old.

The penal laws of the country lean towards the Classical rather than the Positivist School. However, studies have been initiated and amendments are quite probable within the near future. Realization that the individual wrongdoer is just as important as the wrongful act has started to affect the attitude towards crime, its causes, and its punishment. There is a probation law of sorts for the juvenile offenders and a system of parole for the adult convicts. No punishment which is cruel or unusual may be inflicted.

The judicial structure operates on the adversary system of procedure. Lower courts are allocated their jurisdictions over offenses ranging from minor offenses such as infractions of ordinances to the more serious ones as homicide and murder. Appeals are provided for up to the highest court of the land. Cases, however, drag and the backlog in the courts' dockets appears to be ever present. The increase in the number of trial judges does not appear to be a solution, although the recently created criminal circuit courts bring promise of alleviating the unsatisfactory situation.

Criminology as a course of study has gained popularity in recent years but the facilities of the schools appear inadequate. Unless better-trained teachers and adequate study materials are made available, these would amount to nothing more than preparatory institutions for students intending to go to law school.

The government has finally realized that social and economic factors affect criminality to a marked degree. Of late, policies have been announced which emphasize improving the social condition of the working masses which have converged on industrial centers that came into existence with the shift from an agricultural to an industrial economy.

The need for serious study of crime, its causes and prevention, is a pressing one—a study which will co-ordinate all sectors of the government and the community as a whole. The people must be made aware of the problems which beset the country, and their suggestions for solutions must come voluntarily. The problem of peace and order is not of the government alone. It is about time that the Filipinos realize the need for an organized effort to solve this problem, if their country is to survive the threat of anarchy.

BIBLIOGRAPHY

Address on the State of the Nation, January 24, 1966 (Manila: Bureau of Printing, 1968).

A Nation of Achievers, State of the Nation Address, January 22, 1968 (Manila: Bureau of Printing, 1968).

The Challenge Accepted, Excerpts from Major Speeches of President Ferdinand E. Marcos in 1966.

Commentaries on the Revised Rules of Court, Ruperto Martin.

IGNACIO VILLAMOR. *Criminality in the Philipine Islands 1903-1908*, (Manila: Bureau of Printing, 1909).

————. *Crime and Moral Education* (Manila: Bureau of Printing, 1918).

H. B. JACOBINI & ASSOCIATES. *Governmental Services in the Philippines*, Institute of Public Administration, U. P. 1956.

The Filipino in the Philippines, Renato Constantino, Quezon City, 1966.

The Fookien Times Yearbook 1964, Fookien Times Co., Inc. (Manila: October, 1964).

The Fookien Times Yearbook 1968, Fookien Times Co., (Manila: October, 1968).

Nation-wide Uniform Crime Case Report Manual, G. Rangel & Sons, Manila, 1968. PC Data Processing Unit, Hqr. P. C. Camp Crame, Q. C., Philippines.

Nation-wide Uniform Crime Report (July-Dec. 1968). PC Data Processing Unit, Q. C., 1969 (Unpublished).

Proceedings of the Judicial Conference on the Application and Graduation of Penalties.

Proposed Code of Crimes, Code Commission (Manila: Bureau of Printing, 1958).

Proposed Penal Code of the Philippines, U. P. Law Center, College of Law, U. P. Diliman, Quezon City, Dec. 29, 1966.

Report submitted by the Senate Committee on Justice entitled Penal Institutions, how they affect the Individual in Particular and Society in General, 1968-59.

Rules for the Treatment of Prisoners (Manila: Bureau of Printing, 1960).

Survey of Philippine Law Enforcement, Office of Public Safety, AID, Dept. of State, Washington, D.C. 20523, December, 15 1966.

Under the Revised Penal Code and the Indeterminate Sentence Law, U. P. Law Center, College of Law, U. P. Diliman, Quezon City, 1965.

Working Paper for the Conference on Criminal Law Reform, U. P. Law Centre, College of Law, U. P. Diliman, Quezon City, July, 1965 (Unpublished).

CHAPTER 11

UNITED STATES OF AMERICA

The following excerpts are a mere sampling from the two governmental publications: The Challenge of Crime in a Free Society, *by the President's Commission on Law Enforcement and Administration of Justice, U. S. Government Printing Office, Washington, D.C., 1967; and* Crime in the United States: Uniform Crime Reports, *1968, by Federal Bureau of Investigation, U.S. Department of Justice, Washington D.C. The former project, especially, is so lengthy and exhaustive, in its treatment of criminality—from the overall viewpoint as well as in particular crime problems of minute detail—that the limited space allowed in this text permits only a sketchy selection of passages. The editor hopes that the brief passages taken from* CCFS *will serve out to point out the richness of this work, indicating what many of the best minds in the United States consider to be "the challenge of crime in a free society."*

THERE IS MUCH CRIME in America, more than ever is reported, far more than ever is solved, far too much for the health of the nation. Every American knows that. Every American is, in a sense, a victim of crime. Violence and theft have not only injured, often irreparably, hundreds of thousands of citizens, but have directly affected everyone. Some people have been impelled to uproot themselves and find new homes. Some have been made afraid to use public streets and parks. Some have come to doubt the worth of a society in which so many people behave so badly. Some have become distrustful of the government's ability, or even desire, to protect them. Some have lapsed into the attitude that criminal behavior is normal human behavior and consequently have become indifferent to it, or have adopted it as a good way to get ahead in life. Some have become suspicious of those they conceive to be responsible for crime: adolescents, Negroes, drug addicts, college students, or demonstrators; policemen who fail to solve crimes; judges who pass lenient sentences or write decisions restricting the activities of the police; and parole boards that release prisoners who resume their criminal activities.

The most understandable mood, into which many Americans have been plunged by crime, is one of frustration and bewilderment; for "crime" is not a single simple phenomenon that can be examined, analyzed, and described in one piece. It occurs in every part of the country and in every stratum of society. Its practitioners and its victims are people of all ages, incomes, and backgrounds. Its trends are difficult to ascertain. Its causes are legion. Its cures are speculative and controversial. An examination of any single kind of crime, let alone of "crime in America," raises a myriad of issues of the utmost complexity.

Consider the crime of robbery, which, since it involves both stealing and violence or the threat of it, is an especially hurtful and frightening one. In 1965 in America there were 118,916 robberies known to the police, 326 robberies a day; a robbery for every 1,630 Americans.[1] Robbery takes dozens of forms, but suppose it took only four: forcible or violent purse-snatching by boys, muggings by drug addicts, store stickups by people with a sudden desperate need for money, and bank robberies by skillful professional criminals. The technical, organizational, legal, behavioral, economic, and social problems that must be addressed, if America is to deal with any degree of success with just those four kinds of events and those four kinds of persons, are innumerable and refractory.

[1]*Editor's Note.* In 1968 there were 261,730 robberies known to the police; one robbery committed every two minutes, at a rate of 131 per 100,000 inhabitants; in cities over 250,000 the robbery rate was 433 per 100,000. *Uniform Crime Report,* 1968 (Washington: Government Printing Office, 1969), pp. 13, 29.

The underlying problems are ones that the criminal justice system can do little about. The unruliness of young people, widespread drug addiction, the existence of much poverty in a wealthy society, and the pursuit of the dollar by any available means are phenomena which the police, the courts, and the correctional apparatus cannot confront directly. They are strands that can be disentangled from the fabric of American life only by the concerted action of the whole society; for unless society makes a concerted effort to change the general conditions and attitudes that are associated with crime, no improvement in law enforcement and administration of justice, subjects which the President's Commission was specifically asked to study, will be of much avail.

Of the everyday problems of the criminal justice system itself, the most delicate and perhaps the most difficult concern the proper ways of dealing individually with individuals. Arrest and prosecution are likely to have quite different effects on delinquent boys and on hardened professional criminals. Judging occasional robbers and habitual robbers by the same standards is clearly inappropriate. Rehabilitating a drug addict is a procedure that has little in common with rehabilitating a holdup man. In short, there are no general prescriptions for dealing with "robbery" either. Keeping streets and parks safe is not the same problem as keeping banks secure. Investigating a mugging, and tracking down a band of prudent and well-organized bank robbers are two entirely distinct police procedures. The kind of police patrol that will deter boys from street robberies is not likely to deter men with guns from holding up storekeepers.

Robbery is only one of 29 crimes on which the Federal Bureau of Investigation reports in its annual Uniform Crime Reports.[2] Each of the 29 categories of crime confronts the community and the criminal justice system, in a greater or a lesser degree, with unique social, legal, correctional, and law enforcement problems. Taken together they raise a multitude of questions about how the police, the courts, and corrections should be organized; how their personnel should be selected,

[2]*Editor's Note*. The correct figure used in the *Uniform Crime Report* currently is 29 rather than 28 which was formerly used.

trained, and paid; what modern technology can do to help their work; what kinds of knowledge they need; what procedures they should use; what resources they should be given; and what should be the relation between the community and the various parts of the criminal justice system.

CRIME: ITS UNDERSTANDING AND PREVENTION

A skid-row lying drunk in a gutter is crime. So is the killing of an unfaithful wife. A Cosa Nostra conspiracy to bribe public officials is crime. So is a strong-arm robbery by a 15-year-old boy. The embezzlement of a corporation's funds by an executive is crime. So is the possession of marijuana cigarettes by a student. These crimes can no more be lumped together for purposes of analysis than can measles and schizophrenia, or lung cancer and a broken ankle. As with disease, so with crime: if causes are to be understood, if risks are to be evaluated, and if preventive or remedial actions are to be taken, each kind must be looked at separately. Thinking of "crime" as a whole is futile.

In any case it is impossible to answer with precision questions about the volume or trends of crime as a whole, or even of any particular kind of crime. Techniques for measuring crime are, and probably always will be, imperfect. Successful crime, after all, is secret crime. The best, in fact almost the only, source of statistical information about crime volumes is the Uniform Crime Reports of the Federal Bureau of Investigation. The UCR is the product of a nationwide system of crime reporting that the FBI has painstakingly developed over the years. Under this system local police agencies report the offenses they know of to the FBI; the UCR is a compilation of these reports. The compilation can be no better than the underlying information that local agencies supply to the FBI. And because the FBI has induced local agencies to improve their reporting methods year by year, it is important to distinguish better reporting from more crime.

What the UCR shows is a rise in the number of individual crimes over the years at a rate faster than the rise in America's population. It shows an especially rapid rise in crimes against property. Moreover, Commission surveys of the experience of the public as victims of crime show that there is several times as much crime against both property and persons as is reported to the police. Even in areas having the highest rates of crime in our large cities, the surveys suggested that citizens are victimized several times as often as official records indicate. As might be expected, crimes the public regards most serious, particularly those involving violence, are generally better reported than less serious crimes.

While it is impossible to offer absolute statistical proof that every year there are more crimes per American than there were the year before, both available statistics and the facts of social change in America suggest that this is so.

Kinds of Crime

Obviously, the most serious crimes are the ones that consist of or employ physical aggression: wilful homicide, rape, robbery, and serious assault. The injuries such crimes inflict are grievous and irreparable. There is no way to undo the damage done to a child whose father is murdered or to a woman who has been forcibly violated. And though medicine may heal the wounds of a victim of mugging, and law enforcement may recover his stolen property, they cannot restore the feeling of personal security violently wrested from him. The most damaging effect of a violent crime is fear, and that must not be belittled. Suddenly becoming the object of a stranger's violent hostility is as frightening as any other class of experience.

The UCR estimates that in two-thirds of the cases of wilful homicide and aggravated assault, the criminals and the victims are known to each other; very often they are members of the same family. Studies of rape indicate that in perhaps half the cases the criminal and victim are acquainted. Robbery is the principal source of violence from strangers.

Controlling violent crime presents a number of distinct problems. Since these crimes occur on private premises, as most murders and rapes and assaults do, they are not susceptible to deterrence by police patrol. Most often they are passionate culminations of quarrels between acquaintances or relatives, hence there is little that can be done to increase the deterrent effect of the threat of punishment. More than nine-tenths of all murders are cleared by arrest, and a high proportion of those arrested are convicted. Yet people continue to commit murders at about the same rate year after year. Almost a third of all robberies are committed by juveniles and are, therefore, one aspect of the enormously complicated phenomenon of juvenile delinquency. Some robberies are committed by drug addicts, and a certain number of rapes are committed by sexually pathological men (or boys). Effective treatment for these diseases, in the community or in the criminal justice system, has not yet been found. Finally, more than one-half of all wilful homicides and armed robberies, and almost one-fifth of all aggravated assaults, involve the use of firearms. As long as there is no effective gun-control legislation, violent crimes and the injuries they inflict will be harder to reduce.

Only 13 per cent of the total number of Index Crimes in the UCR for 1965 were crimes of violence.[3] The remaining 87 per cent were thefts: thefts of $50 or over in money or goods, automobile thefts, and burglaries (thefts that involve breaking into or unlawfully entering private premises). Of these three kinds of stealing, burglary was the most frequent; 1,173,201 burglaries were reported to the FBI in 1965,[4] approximately one-half of them involving homes, and one-half commercial establishments. Burglary is expensive; the FBI calculates that the worth of the property stolen by burglars in 1965 was some $284 million.[5] Burglary is frightening; having one's home broken into and ran sacked is an experience that can unnerve almost anyone. Finally, burglars are seldom caught; only 25 per cent[6] of the burglaries known to the police in 1965 were solved, and many more remained unreported.

Since burglary is so frequent, so costly, so upsetting, and so difficult to control, it makes great demands on the criminal justice system. Preventing burglary demands imaginative methods of police patrol, and solving them calls for great

[3]*Editor's Note.* These figures were unchanged in 1968.

[4]*Editor's Note.* In 1968 the figures were 1,828,900 burglaries. *Uniform Crime Report, 1969*, p. 17.

[5]*Editor's Note.* "$545 million in 1968." *Uniform Crime Report, 1969*, p. 17.

[6]*Editor's Note.* "19% in 1968." *Uniform Crime Report, 1969*, p. 31.

investigative patience and resourcefulness. Dealing with individual burglars appropriately is a difficult problem for prosecutors and judges; for while burglary is a serious crime that
carries heavy penalties and many of its practitioners are habitual or professional criminals, many more are youthful or
marginal offenders to whom criminal sanctions in their most
drastic form might do more harm than good. Burglars are
probably the most numerous class of serious offenders in the
correctional system. It is a plausible assumption that the pre-
valence of the two crimes of burglary and robbery is a significant, if not a major, reason for America's alarm about crime.
Bringing them within manageable bounds, and finding effective ways of protecting the community from these two crimes,
would do much to make "crime" less frightening as a whole.

Larceny—stealing that does not involve either force or
illegal entry—is by far the most frequent kind of stealing in
America. It is less frightening than burglary because to a
large, perhaps even to a preponderant extent, it is a crime of
opportunity, a matter of making off with whatever happens to
be lying around loose: Christmas presents in an unlocked
car, merchandise on a store counter, a bicycle in a front yard,
and so forth. In so far as this is so, it is a crime that might
be sharply reduced by the adoption of precautionary measures
by citizens themselves. The reverse side of this is that it is an
extremely difficult crime for the police to deal with. Unlike
the cases of breaking and entering by force, there are seldom
physical clues to go by, and the likelihood of the victim
identifying the criminal is far less than in the case of a face-to-
face crime like robbery. Only 20 per cent[7] of reported major
larcenies are solved, and the solution rate for minor ones is
considerably lower.

A unique feature of the crime of automobile theft is that,
although only a quarter of all automobile thefts—and there
were 486,568 reported to the FBI in 1965—are solved, some
87 per cent of all stolen automobiles are recovered and returned to their owners.[8] The overwhelming majority of auto-

[7]*Editor's Note.* "18% in 1968." *Uniform Crime Report, 1969,* p. 31.

[8]*Editor's Note.* "In 1968, 777,800 auto thefts, 86% recovered. 19% of
auto thefts were solved in 1968, concerning identity of the offender." *Uniform Crime Report, 1969,* pp. 31-36.

mobile thefts are for the purpose of securing temporary transportation, often for "joyriding."

More than 60 per cent of those arrested for this crime in 1965 were under 18 years of age, and 88 per cent were under the age of twenty-five.[9] However, a Commission study of professional criminals indicates that, automobile theft for the purpose of stripping automobiles of their parts or for reselling automobiles in remote parts of the country is a lucrative and growing part of professional crime. What is especially suggestive about these facts is that, while much automobile theft is committed by young joyriders, some of it is calculating, professional crime that poses a major law enforcement problem. The estimated value of the unrecovered stolen automobiles in 1965 is in excess of 100 million dollars.[10] In other words, coping with automobile theft, like coping with every kind of serious crime, is a matter of dealing with different people who have different motives. No single response, by either the community or the criminal justice system, can be effective.

These three major crimes against property do not tell the whole story about stealing. In fact, the whole story cannot be told. It is not known how much embezzlement, fraud, loan sharking, and other forms of thievery from individuals or commercial institutions is prevalent, or how much price-rigging, tax evasion, bribery, graft, and other forms of thievery from the public at large is existent. The Commission's studies indicate that the economic losses caused by crimes are far greater than those caused by the three Index Crimes against property. Many crimes in this category are never discovered, they just get lost in the complications and convolutions of business procedures. Many others are never reported to law-enforcement agencies. Most people pay little heed to crimes of this sort when they worry about "crime in America," because those crimes do not, as a rule, offer an immediate, recognizable threat to personal safety.

However, it is possible to argue that, in one sense, such crimes are the most threatening of all—not just because they

[9]*Editor's Note.* "In 1968, 61% were under 18, 79% were under 21."

[10]*Editor's Note.* "In 1968, the estimated value is in excess of 100 million dollars." *Uniform Crime Report, 1969,* p. 28.

are so expensive, but because of their corrosive effect on the moral standards of American business. Businessmen who defraud consumers promote cynicism towards society and disrespect for law. The Mafia or Cosa Nostra or the Syndicate, as it has variously been called, is deeply involved in business crime, and protects its position by bribery and graft and, all too often, assault and murder. White-collar crime and organized crime are subjects about which the criminal justice system, and the community as a whole, have little knowledge. Acquiring such knowledge in a systematic way is an extremely high-priority obligation of those entrusted with protecting society from crime.

"Crimes without victims," crimes whose essence is providing people with goods or services that, though illegal, are in demand, are peculiarly vexatious to the criminal justice system. Offenses, like gambling, narcotics, and prostitution are not only numerous, but they also present policemen, prosecutors, judges, and correctional officials with problems they are ill-equipped to solve. Since such crimes have no direct victims, or at any rate no victims with complaints, investigating them obliges policemen to employ practices like relying on informants who may turn out to be accomplices, or walking the streets hoping to be solicited by prostitutes. These practices may be legal, but they are surely distasteful and they can lead, in addition, to discriminatory enforcement or out-and-out corruption.

When offenders of this sort are arrested, correction or punishment seldom has much effect on them; they resume their activities as soon as they return to the street. Yet offenses of this sort cannot be ignored. Gambling is an activity that is controlled by organized criminals and is a major source of their wealth and power. The growing use of drugs, especially by young people, is a matter of profound concern to almost every parent in America and, of course, the distribution of narcotics is also an important part of the activities of organized crime. Often the statutes that deal with these offenses are obsolete or ambiguous and the treatment programs are still in an experimental stage. The connection between these offenses and social conditions is little understood. Finding ways of dealing with crimes without victims is not only a task for the criminal justice system but for legislators, doctors, sociologists, and social workers as well.

Finally, there are "petty offenses" and "breaches of peace" like public drunkenness and public quarreling, which are the most frequent of all crimes. Most Americans have never actually seen a serious crime committed, but every American has seen a petty offense. Such offenses are undoubted public nuisances against which the public has every right to protect itself. Yet a curious thing about them is that usually the only person who suffers real damage from one of these crimes is the offender himself. Breaches of peace are the most exasperating everyday problem of the criminal justice system. Petty offenders—many of whom, like chronic alcoholics, are repeated and incurable lawbreakers—occupy much of the time of policemen, clog the lower courts, and crowd city and county jails.

Crime and Social Conditions

Two facts stand out from a study of the UCR and every other examination of American crime: one, that most crimes, wherever they are committed, are committed by boys and young men, and, two, that most crimes, by whomever they are committed, are committed in cities. Over three-quarters of the 1965 arrests for Index Crimes in the UCR, plus petty larceny and negligent manslaughter, were of people less than 25 years old, more 15 year-olds were arrested for those crimes than people of any other age, and 16 year-olds were a close second. Of 2,780,015 "offenses known to the police" in 1965— these were Index Crimes—some two million occurred in cities, more than half a million occurred in the suburbs, and about 170,000 occurred in rural areas. The number of city crimes per hundred thousand residents was over 1,800 in cities, almost 1,200 in suburbs and 616.9 in rural areas.[11] In short, crime is evidently associated with two powerful social trends; the increasing urbanization of America and the increasing numerous-

[11]*Editor's Note.* "In 1968, 76.1% of the arrests for Index Crimes were of people less than 25 years of age. The largest group of arrestees were in the 13-14 year-old age group followed by the group age 16, and then the group age 15. 13-14 year-old groups are taken together in the UCR figures, but the 15 and 16-year olds are considered separately. In 1968 there were

ness, restlessness, and restiveness of American youth. The two trends are not separate or distinct. They are interrelated with each other in many ways, and are also intimately associated with the trend of increasing affluence. An abundance of material goods provides an abundance of motives and opportunities for stealing, which is the fastest growing crime.

For as long as crime statistics of any kind have been compiled, they have shown that males between the ages of 15 and 24 are the most crime-prone group in the population. For the last five years, as a result of the "baby boom" that took place after the Second World War, the 15-24 age group has been the fastest growing group in the population.

The fact that young people make up a larger part of the population than they did ten years ago accounts for some of the recent increase in crime. This group will continue to grow disproportionately for at least 15 more years. Therefore, it is probable that crime will continue to increase during this period, unless there are drastic changes in general social and economic conditions, and in the effectiveness of the criminal justice system. However, population changes cannot account for the sharp increase that is reported in juvenile and youth crime, nor can the probability that police reporting is more complete every year. There have been marked improvements in police efficiency and correctional resourcefulness in many localities in recent years, which, other things being equal, might have reduced crime. It may be that young people are not only more numerous than ever, but more crime-prone.

What appears to be happening throughout the country, in the cities and in the suburbs, among the poor and among the well-to-do, is that parental, and especially paternal, authority over young people is becoming weaker. The community is accustomed to rely upon this force as a guarantee that children will learn to fit themselves into society in an orderly and peaceable manner, that the natural and valuable rebelliousness of young people will not express itself in the form of warring violently on society or any of its members. The programs and activities

---

4,466,600 Index Crimes known to the police—3,823,000 occurred in cities, 350,000 in suburbs, and 294,000 in rural areas. The number of city crimes per hundred thousand inhabitants was 2,803, the suburban rate was 1,358, and the rural rate was 780." *Uniform Crime Report*, pp. 31, 58.

of almost every kind of social institution with which children come in contact—schools, churches, social-service agencies, youth organizations—are predicated on the assumption that children acquire their moral standards, and fundamental attitudes toward life in their homes. The social institutions provide children with many opportunities: to learn, to worship, to play, to socialize, and to secure expert help in solving a variety of problems.

However, offering opportunities is not the same thing as providing moral standards. The community's social institutions have so far not found ways to give young people the motivation to live moral lives; some of them have not even recognized their duty to seek for such ways. Young people who have not received strong and loving parental guidance, or whose experience leads them to believe that the society is callous at its best or a racket at its worst, tend to be unmotivated and unscrupulous. They are ill-prepared to cope with the many ambiguities and inadequacies of life in the community. Boredom corrodes ambition, and cynicism corrupts those with ethical sensitivity.

There is no dearth of such irritants in the day-to-day life. Poverty and racial discrimination, bad housing and commercial exploitation, the enormous gap between ideals and achievements, and the many distressing consequences and implications of these conditions are national failings that are widely recognized. Their effects on young people have been greatly aggravated by the technological revolution of the last two decades, which has greatly reduced the market for unskilled labor. A job, earning one's own living, is probably the most important factor in making a person independent and responsible.

Today, education is a prerequisite for all but the most menial jobs; and a great deal of education is essential for really promising ones. Thus, there are two continually growing groups of discontented young people: those whose capacity or desire for becoming educated has not been developed by their homes or schools (or both), and who, therefore, are unemployed or even unemployable; and those whose entry into the adult working world has been delayed by the necessity of continuing their studies long past the point at which they have become physically and psychologically adult. Young people today are sorely discontented in the suburbs and on the campuses as well as in the slums.

There is, however, no doubt that young, as also older people, more often seek to express this discontent criminally in the slums. The reason is not hard to find. The conditions of life there, economic and social, conspire to make crime not only easy to engage in, but easy to justify too. A man who lives in the country or in a small town is likely to be conspicuous, under surveillance by his community, and therefore under its control. A city man is often almost invisible, socially isolated from his neighborhood, and therefore incapable of being controlled by it. He has more opportunities for crime, much more than in a small community, for he rubs constantly, abrasively, and impersonally against other people. He is likely to live his life unnoticed and unrespected, and his hopes unfulfilled. He can fall easily into resentment against his neighbors and against society, and may get a feeling that he is in a jungle where force and cunning are the only means of survival.

There have always been slums in the cities, and they have always been the hotbeds of crime. What has made this condition even more menacing in recent years is the fact that the slums, with all their squalor and turbulence, have more and more become ghettos, neighborhoods in which racial minorities are sequestered with little chance of escape. People who, though declared by the law to be equal, are prevented by society from improving their social conditions—even when they have the ability and the desire to do so—are left with little respect for law and society.

It is with the young people and the slum dwellers, who have been embittered by these painful social and economic pressures, that the criminal justice system preponderantly deals. Society insists that individuals are responsible for their actions, and the criminal process operates on that assumption. However, society has not devised ways for ensuring that all its members have the ability to assume responsibility. It has let too many of them grow up untaught, unmotivated, and unwanted.

The criminal justice system has a great potential for dealing with individual instances of crime, but it was not designed to eliminate the conditions in which crime usually breeds. It needs to be amended. Warring on poverty, inadequate housing, and unemployment, is warring on crime. A civil rights law is a law against crime, just as medical, psychiatric, and family-connselling services are services against crime. Broadly speaking, every effort, schooling for instance, to improve life in America's "inner cities" is an effort against crime. A community's most enduring protection against crime is to right the wrongs and cure the illnesses that tempt men to harm their neighbors.

No system, however well staffed or organized, no level of material well-being for all, will rid a society of crime if it is not accompanied by a widespread ethical motivation, and a widespread belief that the government and the social order deserve credence, respect, and loyalty.

SYSTEM OF CRIMINAL JUSTICE

The system of criminal justice used in America is not a monolithic, or even a consistent, system. It was not designed or built in one piece at one time. It is based on the philosophic core that a person may be punished by the government if, and only if, it has been proved by an impartial and deliberate process that he has violated a specific law. Around that core layer upon layer of institutions and procedures, some carefully constructed and some improvised, some inspired by principles and some by expediency, have accumulated. Parts of the system—magistrate's courts, trial by jury, bail—are of great antiquity. Other parts—juvenile courts, probation and parole, professional policemen—are relatively new. The entire system represents an adaptation of the English common law to America's peculiar structure of government, which allows each local community to construct institutions that fill its special needs. Every village, town, county, city, and State has its own criminal justice system, in addition to the Federal system. None of these are precisely alike in their operation.

Any criminal justice system is an apparatus society uses to enfore the standards of conduct necessary to protect individuals and the community. It operates by apprehending, prosecuting, convicting, and sentencing those members who violate the basic rules of group existence. The action taken against lawbreakers works in three ways beyond the immediately punitive purpose: it removes dangerous people from the community, it deters others from criminal behavior, and it gives society an opportunity to transform lawbreakers into law-abiding citizens. What distinguishes the system of one country from that of another is the extent and the form of protections it offers to individuals in determining guilt and imposing punishment. Our system of justice deliberately sacrifices much in efficiency and even in effectiveness in order to preserve local autonomy and to protect the individual. Sometimes it may seem to sacrifice too much. For example, the American system was not designed with Cosa Nostra-type criminal organizations in mind, and it has been notably unsuccessful to date in preventing such organizations from preying on society.

The criminal justice system has three separately organized parts—the police, the courts, and corrections—and each has distinct tasks. However, these parts are by no means independent of each other. What each one does and how it does has a direct effect on the work of the others. The courts must deal, and can only deal, with those whom the police arrest; the business of corrections is with those delivered to it by the courts. How successfully correction reforms convicts determines whether they will once again become police business and influences the sentences the judges pass; police activities are subject to court scrutiny and are often determined by the court decisions. Thus, reforming or reorganizing any part or procedure of the system changes other parts or procedures. Moreover, the criminal process, the method by which the system deals with individual cases, is not a hodgepodge of random actions. It is rather a continuum—an orderly progression of events— some of which, like arrest and trial, are highly visible and some of which, though of great importance, occur out of public view.

The popular, or even the lawbook, theory of everyday criminal process usually over simplifies or overcomplicates the happening. Thus, when an infraction of the law occurs, a policeman finds, if he can, the probable offender, arrests him and brings him promptly before a magistrate. If the offense is minor, the magistrate disposes it off; if it is serious, he holds the defendant for further action and admits him to bail. The case then is turned over to a prosecuting attorney who charges the defendant with a specific statutory crime. This charge is subject to review by a judge at a preliminary hearing of the evidence; and if the offense charged is a felony, by a grand jury that can dismiss the charge, or affirm it by delivering it to a judge in the form of an indictment. If the defendant pleads "not guilty" to the charge he comes to trial; the facts of his case are marshalled by prosecuting and defense attorneys and presented, under the supervision of a judge, through witnesses, to a jury. If the jury finds the defendant guilty, he is sentenced by the judge to a term in prison, where a systematic attempt is made to convert him into a law-abiding citizen; or to a term of probation, under which he is permitted to live in the community as long as he behaves himself.

Some cases, especially those involving "major" offenses like a serious act of violence or theft involving a large amount of property, generally proceed this way. However, not all major cases follow this course, and, in any event, the bulk of the daily business of the criminal justice system consists of offenses that are not major—of breaches of peace, crimes of vice, petty thefts, and assaults arising from domestic or street-corner or bar-room disputes. These and most other cases are disposed of in much less formal and much less deliberate ways.

The theory of the juvenile court is that it is a "helping" social agency, designed to prescribe carefully individualized treatment to young people in trouble, and that its procedures are therefore nonadversary. Here again there is, in most places, a considerable difference between theory and practice. Many juvenile proceedings are no more individualized and no more therapeutic than adult ones.

What has evidently happened is that the transformation of America from a relatively relaxed rural society into a tumultuous urban one has presented the criminal justice system in the cities with a volume of cases too large to be handled by traditional methods. One result of heavy caseloads is highly visible in city courts, which process many cases with excessive haste and many others with excessive slowness. In the interest of effectiveness as well as fairness to individuals, justice should be swift and certain; instead, too often in city courts today it is hasty or faltering. Invisibly, the pressure of numbers has effected a series of adventitious changes in the criminal process. Informal shortcuts have been used. The decision making process has often become routinized. Throughout the system the importance of individual judgment and discretion, as distinguished from stated rules and procedures, has increased. In effect, much decision making is being done on an administrative rather than on a judicial basis. Thus an examination of how the criminal justice system works, and a consideration of the changes needed to make it more effective and fair, must highlight the desirability and the extent to which invisible, administrative processes depart from visible, traditional procedures.

The Police

It is worth noting that law-enforcement policy is made by the policeman, for they cannot and do not arrest all the offenders they encounter; it is doubtful whether they arrest most of them or not. A criminal code, in practice, is not a set of specific instructions to policemen but a more or less rough map of the territory in which they work. How an individual policeman moves around that territory depends largely on his personal discretion.

That a policeman's duties compel him to exercise personal discretion several times every day is evident. Crime does not look the same on the street as it does in a legislative chamber. How much noise or profanity makes conduct "disorderly" within the meaning of the law? When must a quarrel be treated as a criminal assault: at the first threat, or at the first shove, or at the first blow, or after blood is drawn, or when a serious injury is inflicted? How suspicious must conduct be before there is "probable cause," the constitutional basis for an arrest? Every policeman, however complete or sketchy his education, is an interpreter of the law.

Every policeman, too, is an arbiter of social values, for he meets situation after situation in which invoking criminal sanctions is a questionable line of action. It is obvious that a boy throwing rocks at a school's windows is committing the statutory offense of vandalism, but it is often not clear whether a policeman will better serve the interests of the community and of the boy by taking him home to his parents or by arresting him. It raises questions like : Who are the boy's parents? Can they control him? Is he a frequent offender who has responded badly to leniency? Is vandalism so epidemic in the neighborhood that he should be made a cautionary example? With juveniles especially, the police have to exercise a great deal of discretion.

The manner in which a policeman works is influenced by practical matters: the legal strength of the available evidence, the willingness of victims to press charges and witnesses to testify, the temper of the community, and the time and information at the policeman's disposal. Much is at stake in how the policeman exercises this discretion. If he judges conduct not suspicious enough to justify intervention, the chance to prevent a robbery, rape, or murder may be lost. If he overestimates the seriousness of a situation or his actions are controlled by panic or prejudice, he may hurt or kill someone unnecessarily. His action may even touch off a riot.

The Magistrate

In direct contrast to the policeman, the magistrate before whom a suspect is first brought usually exercises less discretion than the law allows him. He is entitled to inquire into the facts of the case, into whether there are grounds for holding the accused. He seldom does. He seldom can. The more promptly an arrested suspect is brought into magistrate's court, the less likelihood there is that much information about the arrest other than the arresting officer's statement will be available to the magistrate. Moreover many magistrates, especially in big cities, have such congested calendars that it is almost impossible for them to subject any case, barring exceptions, to prolonged scrutiny.

In practice the most important things, by far, that a magistrate does are to set the amount of a defendant's bail and in some jurisdiction to appoint counsel. Too seldom does either action get the careful attention it deserves. In many cases the magistrate accepts a waiver of counsel without insuring that the suspect knows the significance of legal representation.

Bail is a device to free an untried defendant and at the same time make sure he appears for trial. That is the sole stated legal purpose in America. The Eighth Amendment to the Constitution declares that it must not be "excessive." Appellate Courts have declared that not just the seriousness of the charge against the defendant, but the suspect's personal family, and employment situation, as they bear on the likelihood of his appearance, must be weighed before the amount of his bail is fixed. Yet more magistrates than not set bail according to standard rates: so and so many dollars for such and such an offense.

The persistence of money bail can best be explained not by its stated purpose but by the belief of police, prosecutors, and courts that the best way to keep a defendant from committing more crimes before trial is to set bail so high that he cannot obtain his release.

The Prosecutor

The key administrative officer in the processing of cases is the prosecutor. Theoretically, the examination of the evidence against a defendant by a judge at a preliminary hearing, and its re-examination by a grand jury, are important parts of the process. Practically speaking, they are rarely so because a prosecutor seldom has any difficulty in making a *prima facie* case against a defendant. In fact most defendants waive their rights to preliminary hearings, and more often than not grand juries indict precisely as prosecutors ask them to. The prosecutor wields almost undisputed sway over the pretrial progress of most cases. He decides whether to press a case or drop it. He determines the specific charge against a defendant. When the charge is reduced, as it is in as many as two-thirds of all cases in some cities, the prosecutor is usually the official who reduces it.

In the informal, non-criminal, non-adversary juvenile justice system there are no "charges," or, in most instances, defense counsel. An arrested youth is brought before an intake officer who is likely to be a social worker or, in smaller communities, before a judge. On the basis of an informal inquiry

into the facts and circumstances that led to the arrest, and of
an interview with the youth himself, the intake officer or the
judge decides whether or not a case should be the subject of
formal court proceedings. If he decides it should be, he draws
up a petition, describing the case.

In very few places is bail a part of the juvenile system; a
youth whose case is referred to court is either sent home
with orders to reappear on a certain date, or remanded to
custody. This decision, too, is made by the screening official.
Thus, though these officials work in a quite different environment and according to quite different procedures from magistrates and prosecutors, they in fact exercise the same kind of
discretionary control over what happens before the facts of a
case are adjudicated.

The Plea and the Sentence

When a prosecutor reduces a charge it is ordinarily because
there has been "plea bargaining" between him and a defense
attorney. The issue at stake is how much the prosecutor will
reduce his original charge, or how lenient a sentence he will
recommend, in return for a plea of guilty. There is no way
of judging how many bargains reflect the prosecutor's belief
that a lesser charge or sentence is justified, and how many
result from the fact there may be in the system at any given
moment ten times as many cases as there are prosecutor's, or
judges, or courtrooms to handle them, should every one come
to trial. In form, a plea bargain can be anything from a series
of careful conference to a hurried consultation in a court-house
corridor. In content it can be anything from a conscientious
exploration of the facts and dispositional alternatives available
and appropriate to a defendant, to a perfunctory deal. If the
interests of a defendant are to be properly protected while
his fate is being thus invisibly determined, he obviously needs
just as good legal representation as the kind he needs at a
public trial. Whether or not plea bargaining is a fair and
effective method of disposing of criminal cases depends heavily
on whether or not defendants are provided early with competent and conscientious counsel.

Plea bargaining is not only an invisible procedure but, in some jurisdictions, a theoretically unsanctioned one. In order to satisfy the court record, a defendant, his attorney, and the prosecutor will at the time of sentencing often ritually state to a judge that no bargain has been made. Plea bargaining may be a useful procedure, especially in congested urban jurisdictions, but neither the dignity of the law, nor the quality of justice, nor the protection of society from dangerous criminals is enhanced by its being conducted covertly.

In the juvenile system there is, of course, no plea bargaining in the sense described above. However, the entire juvenile process can involve extra-judicial negotiations about disposition. Furthermore, the entire juvenile process is by design invisible. Though intended to be helpful, the authority exercised is often coercive; juveniles, no less than adults, may need representation by counsel.

An enormously consequential kind of decision is the sentencing decision of a judge. The law recognizes the importance of fitting sentences to individual defendants by giving judges, in most instances, considerable latitude. For example the recently adopted New York Penal Code, which went into effect in the autumn of 1967, empowers a judge to impose upon a man convicted of armed robbery any sentence between a five-year term of probation and a 25-year term in prison. Even when a judge has presided over a trial during which the facts of a case have been carefully set forth and has been given a probation report that carefully discusses a defendant's character, backgrond, and problems, he cannot find it easy to choose a sentence. In perhaps nine-tenths of all cases there is no trial; the defendants are self-confessedly guilty.

In the lower or misdemeanor courts, the courts that process most criminal cases, probation reports are a rarity. Under such circumstances judges have little to go on and many sentences are bound to be based on conjecture or intuition. When a sentence is part of a plea bargain, which an overworked judge ratifies perfunctorily, it may not even be his conjecture or intuition on which the sentence is based, but a prosecutor's or a defense counsel's. Perhaps the greatest lack judges suffer from when they pass sentence is not time or information, but correctional alternatives. Some lower courts do not have any probation officers, and in almost every court the caseloads of probation are so heavy that a sentence of probation means, in fact, releasing an offender into the community with almost no supervision. Few States have a sufficient variety of correctional institutions or treatment programs to inspire judges with the confidence that sentences will lead to rehabilitation.

Corrections

The correctional apparatus to which guilty defendants are delivered is in every respect the most isolated part of the criminal justice system. Much of it is physically isolated; its institutions usually have thick walls and locked doors, and often they are situated in rural areas, remote from the courts where the institutions' inmates were tried and from the communities where they lived. The correctional apparatus is isolated in the sense that its officials do not have everyday working relationships with officials from the system's other branches, like those that commonly exist between policemen and prosecutors, or prosecutors and judges. It is isolated also in the sense that what it does with, to, or for the people under its supervision is seldom governed by any but the most broadly written statutes, and is almost never scrutinized by appellate courts. Finally, it is isolated from the public partly by its invisibility and physical remoteness; partly by the inherent lack of drama in most of its activities, but perhaps most significantly by the fact that the correctional apparatus is often used—or misused—by both the criminal justice system and the public as a rug under which disturbing problems and people can be swept.

The most striking fact about the correctional apparatus today is that, although the rehabilitation of criminals is presumably its major purpose, the custody of criminals is actually its major task. On any given day there are well over a million people being "corrected" in America, two-thirds of them on probation or parole and one-third of them in prisons or jails. However, prisons and jails are where four-fifths of correctional money is spent and where nine-tenths of correctional employees work. Furthermore, fewer than one-fifth of the people who work in State prisons and local jails have jobs that are not essentially either custodial or administrative in character.

Several jails have nothing but custodial and administrative personnel. Of course many jails are crowded with defendants who have not been able to furnish bail and who are not considered by the law to be appropriate objects of rehabilitation because it has not yet been determined that they are criminals who need it.

What this emphasis on custody means in practice is that the enormous potential of the correctional apparatus of making creative decisions about its treatment of convicts is largely unfulfilled. This is true not only of offenders in custody but also of offenders on probation and parole. Most authorities agree that while probationers and parolees need varying degrees and kinds of supervision, an average of no more than 35 cases per officer is necessary for effective attention; 97 per cent of all officers handling adults have larger caseloads than that. In the juvenile correctional system the situation is somewhat better. Juvenile institutions, which typically are training schools, have a higher proportion of treatment personnel, and juvenile probation and parole officers generally have lighter caseloads. However, these comparatively rich resources are very far from being sufficiently rich.

Except for sentencing, no decision in the criminal process has more impact on the convicted offender than the parole decision, which determines how much of his maximum sentence a prisoner must serve. This again is an invisible administrative decision that is seldom open to attack or subject to review. It is made by parole board members who are often political appointees. Many are skilled and conscientious, but they generally are able to spend no more than a few minutes on a case. Parole decisions that are made in haste and on the basis of insufficient information, in the absence of parole machinery that can provide good supervision, are necessarily imperfect decisions. And since there is virtually no appeal from them, they can be made arbitrarily or discriminatorily. Just as carefully formulated and clearly stated law-enforcement policies would help policemen, charge policies would help prosecutors and sentencing policies would help judges, so parole boards perform their delicate and important duties.

In sum, America's system of criminal justice is overcrowded and overworked, undermanned, underfinanced, and very often misunderstood. It needs more information and more knowledge. It needs more technical resources. It needs more co-ordination among its many parts. It needs more public support. It needs the help of community programs and institutions in dealing with offenders and potential offenders. It needs, above all, the willingness to re-examine old ways of doing things, to reform itself, to experiment, to run risks, and to dare. It needs vision.

FOUNDATIONS OF A CRIME CONTROL PROGRAM

The many specific needs of the criminal justice system—for manpower, for equipment, for facilities, for programs, for research, for money—are interrelated.

Resources

Each one of the needs must be filled with the others in mind. Equipment cannot be operated, facilities manned, programs initiated, or research conducted without personnel of many different kinds. It would be useless to seek to recruit more and better personnel if there were not more and better jobs for them to do. Programs cannot be conducted without equipment and facilities, and cannot be conducted effectively without research. Above all, money is needed for everything.

The problem of personnel is at the root of most of the criminal justice system's problems. The system cannot operate fairly unless its personnel are fair. It cannot operate swiftly and certainly unless its personnel are efficient and well-informed. The system cannot make wise decisions unless its personnel are thoughtful. In many places—many police departments, congested urban lower courts, the understaffed county jails, the entire prison, probation and parole appartus—more manpower is needed. Probably the greatest need, in view of the increasing and overdue involvement of defense counsel in all kinds of cases, is for lawyers who can handle criminal cases. Everywhere skilled, trained, and imaginative manpower is needed. Some positions are hard to fiil. Often the salary is low and the working conditions are difficult.

In addition, an odd and injurious notion is widepread that there is something disreputable about being a policeman, or a criminal lawyer, or a prison guard. The fact is that there are few fields in which people have more opportunities to do important and responsible work than the criminal justice system. Recruiting such people in large numbers, training them fully and giving them the pay, the opportunities for advancement, and the responsibility they deserve is a matter of great urgency.

Too much of the system is physically inadequate, antiquated, or dilapidated. This condition goes beyond the obvious obsolescence of many correctional institutions, and the squalor and congestion of many urban lower courts—which make it difficult to treat defendants or convicts humanely. The system's personnel often must work with poor facilities: recordkeeping systems that are clumsy and inefficient, communications equipment that makes speedy action difficult, and an absence of all kinds of scientific and technological aids. Furthermore, in few States is there the variety of correctional facilities that could make a variety of correctional programs possible. Most institutions are almost entirely custodial in a physical sense—with high walls, locked gates, and barred windows. New kinds of institutions, less forbidding in character and situated within reach of the community, are an immediate and pressing need.

Probably the single greatest technical limitation on the system's ability to make its decisions wisely and fairly is that the people in the system often are required to decide issues without enough information. A policeman who has just set out in pursuit of a speeding and suspicious looking car should be able to get immediate information as to whether or not the car is wanted; a judge about to sentence a criminal should know everything about him that the police know; and the correctional authorities to whom that criminal is delivered should know everything about him that the judge knows. When they make dispositional decisons, judges and correction officials should be able to draw on the experience of the system. Existing procedures must be made more efficient; and new procedures must be devised, so that information can flow more fully and swiftly among the system's many parts.

Finally, the nature of crime and the means of controlling it are subjects about which a suprisingly small amount of research has been done. What "deterrence" really means and involves, how different kinds of criminals are likely to respond to different kinds of treatment, what the objective effects of making various kinds of marginal behavior criminal have been, how much of the juvenile justice system's informality can be preserved without sacrificing fairness—and a multitude of other abstruse questions of this kind—are almost totally unanswerable today. There is almost as great a lack of operational knowledge. It is impossible to state accurately, for example, what proportions of police time are spent on the different sorts of police work, or how large a proportion of the drunks that come before lower courts are chronic offenders, or what personal characteristics best qualify a man to be an effective correctional official.

This lack of firm data of almost every kind has been the greatest obstacle to the Commission's work, in many instances requiring it to base its recommendations on fragmentary information, combined with the experienced judgment of those who have worked in this field. The process of change cannot await all the answers the Commission would like to have had. The criminal justice system is faced with too urgent a need for action to stand back for a generation and engage in research. At the same time self-education is one of the system's crucial responsibilities. Only by combining research with action can future programs be founded on knowledge rather than on informed or perceptive guesswork.

Moreover, once knowledge is acquired, it is wasted if it is not shared. An east coast city must be able to draw on a west coast city's experience, a judge on a policeman's. Scattered about the country today are many individuals and groups with special knowledge about one aspect or another of law-enforcement and the administration of justice. Often no one else in the system knows that these individuals and groups could have important information. Sometimes these individuals and groups are themselves not aware, through lack of contact with the rest of the system, that they know something no one else knows. The system must devote itself to acquiring and diffusing knowledge, with special emphasis on exploring ways in which the criminal justice system and the universities can work together.

Public Involvement and Support

Each time a citizen fails to report an offense, declines to take the commonsense precautions against crime his police department tells him to, is disrespectful to an officer of the law, shirks his duty as a juror or performs it with a biased mind or a hate-filled heart, or refuses to hire a qualified man because he is an exconvict, he contributes his mite to crime. That much is obvious. A further duty of every citizen is to familiarize himself with the problems of crime and the criminal justice system so that when legislatures are considering criminal laws or appropriations for the system he can express informed views, and when politicians make crime an election issue he will not be panicked or deceived. The money that is needed to control crime will come, ultimately, from the public. That too, is obvious.

Beyond this, controlling crime depends to a great degree on interaction between the community and the criminal justice system. The need for the system and the universities to work together on research into crime and the ways to prevent or control it has been mentioned. Similarly, effective policing of slums and ghettos requires programs designed to improve relations between the police and the residents of such neighborhoods and enable them to work together. Community-based correctional programs require that organizations of many kinds, and individuals as well, involve themselves actively in the job of reintegrating offenders into the life of the community. Programs designed to reduce juvenile delinquency require the same kind of public involvement.

Above all, the Commission inquiries have convinced it that it is undesirable that offenders travel any further along the full course from arrest to charge, to sentence, to detention, than is absolutely necessary for society's protection and the offenders' own welfare. Much of the congestion throughout the system from police stations to prisons, is the result of the presence in the system of offenders who are there only because there is no other way of dealing with them. One of the system's greatest needs is to establish institutions and agencies to which policemen, prosecutors, and judges can refer various kinds of offenders, without being compelled to bring the full force of criminals sanctions to bear on them. Doubtless, devising and instituting alternative ways of treating offenders is a long and complicated process. It must begin with an understanding by the community of the limited capacity of the criminal justice system for handling the whole problem of "crime." Until the public becomes fully aware of what the system can do and what it cannot do, it can scarcely give the system the help it needs.

Willingness to Change

The inertia of the criminal justice system is great. More than 30 years ago the Wickersham Commission described the scandalous way in which justice was being administered in many of the country's "lower" courts, and urged that they be abolished; few of them have been abolished and many of the remaining ones are still a scandal. For centuries the imposition of money bail has discriminated against poor defendants, but only in the last few years has the movement to eliminate money bail for most defendants gained any momentum, and even so money bail is still used for almost everyone in the overwhelming majority of courts. State prisons that were built before 1850, and became obsolete before 1900, are still in operation.

Police departments continue to insist that all policemen start their careers at the bottom and rise through the ranks slowly, despite the clearly damaging effect this has on the recruitment and effective use of able personnel. A third of the arrests and convictions in America every year are for drunkenness, though for many years almost everyone in the criminal justice system and out of it has recognized that the criminal process is an irrational means of dealing with drunks. The list of examples could extend for pages.

Many of the criminal justice system's difficulties stem from its reluctance to change old ways or, to put the same proposition in reverse, its reluctance to try new ones. The increasing volume of crime in America establishes conclusively that many of the old ways are not good enough. Innovation and experimentation in all parts of the criminal justice system are clearly imperative with respect to entire agencies and specific procedures. Court systems need reorganization and case-docketing

methods need improvement; police-community relations programs are needed and so are ways of relieving detectives
from the duty of typing their own reports; community-based
correctional programs must be organized and the pay of prisons guard must be raised. Recruitment and training organization and management, research and development all require
re-examination and reform.

The Commission believes that the first step toward improvement is for officials in all parts of the system to face their
problems. The lower courts never will be reformed if their
officials do not grapple with the hard fact that the quality of
justice that is dispensed in them is disgracefully low. Any
program to rehabilitate prisoners must begin with the acknowledgement of the fact that most prisons today do not even
try do this job. Until the police recognize that they exercise
great discretion about whom they arrest and how they investigate, no effort to ensure that that discretion is exercised wisely can be made. It is futile to consider ways of making plea
negotiation an open, regular procedure as long as prosecutors
and defense attorneys state ritually to judges that pleas are
not negotiated.

The Commission finds, first, that America must translate
its well-founded alarm about crime into social action that will
prevent crime. It has no doubt whatever that the most significant action that can be taken against crime is action designed
to eliminate slums and ghettos, to improve education, to
provide jobs, and to make sure that every American is given
the opportunities and the freedoms that will enable him to
assume his responsibilities. We will not have dealt effectively
with crime until we have alleviated the conditions that stimulate it. To speak of controlling crime only in terms of the
work of the police, the courts and the correctional apparatus,
is to refuse to face that widespread crime implies a widespread
failure by society as a whole.

Secondly, the Commission finds that America must translate
its alarm about crime into action that will give the criminal
justice system the wherewithal to do the job it is charged with
doing. Every part of the system is undernourished. There is
too little manpower and what there is, is not well enough
trained or well enough paid. Facilities and equipment are in-

adequate. Research programs that could lead to greater knowledge about crime and justice, and therefore to more effective
operations, are almost nonexistent. To lament the increase in
crime and at the same time to starve the agencies of law enforcement and justice is to whistle in the wind.

Thirdly, the Commission finds that the officials of the criminal justice system itself must stop operating, as all too many
do, by tradition. They must re-examine what they do. They
must be honest about the system's shortcomings with the
public and with themselves. They must be bold and willing to
take risks in order to make advances.

CRIME FACTORS AND CRIME STATISTICS

Uniform Crime Reports give a nationwide view of crime based
on police statistics made possible by the voluntary cooperation of local law-enforcement agencies. Since the factors
which cause crime are many and vary from place to place,
readers are cautioned against drawing conclusions from   direct
comparisons of crime figures between individual communities
without first considering the factors involved. The national
material summarized in this publication should be used, however, as a starting point to determine deviations of individual
cities from the national averages.

Crime is a social problem and the concern of the entire
community. The law enforcement effort is limited to factors
within its control. Some of the conditions which will affect
the amount and type of crime that occurs from place to place
can be briefly summarized as: density and size of the community population and the metropolitan area of which it is a
part; composition of the population with reference particularly to age sex and race; economic status and mores of the
population; relative stability of population, including com-
muters, seasonal, and other transient types; climate, including
seasonal weather conditions; educational, recreational, and
religious characteristics; effective strength of the police force;
standards governing appointments to the police force; policies
of the prosecuting officials and the court's; attitude of the
public toward law-enforcement problems; and the administrative and investigative efficiency of the local law enforcement

agency, including the degree of adherence to crime reporting standards.

Crime Capsule

Almost 4.5 million serious crimes recorded during 1968, a 17 per cent rise over 1967.

Risk of becoming a victim of serious crime increased 16 per cent in 1968 with over two victims per each 100 inhabitants.

Firearms used to commit over 8,900 murders, 65,000 assaults, and 99,000 robberies in 1968.

Since 1964 use of a firarm in murder up 71 per cent; in aggravated assault up 117 per cent. Armed robbery 1964-68 up 113 per cent.

Daytime burglaries of residence rose 247 per cent from 1960 to 1968.

Property valued at more than 1.7 billion dollars stolen as a result of 261,730 robberies, 1,828,900 burglaries, 3,442,800 larcenies, and 777,800 auto thefts. Police recoveries, however, reduced this loss by 50 per cent.

Arrests of juveniles for serious crimes increased 78 per cent from 1960 to 1968, while number of persons in the young age group, 10-17, increased 25 per cent.

Arrests for Narcotic Drug Law violations in 1968 over four times as great as 1960. Narcotic arrests 1968 over 1967 up 64 per cent, influenced again primarily by marijuana arrests.

Percentage of police solutions of serious crimes declined 7 per cent in 1968, and since 1960, has had an overall decline of 32 per cent.

Sixty-four law-enforcement officers murdered by felons in 1968. Since 1960, 96 per cent of the 475 police officers were killed by use of firearms.

In 1968, rate of 2.1 police employees per 1,000 inhabitants compared to rate of 2.0 in 1967.

Careers in Crime. Study disclosed 63 per cent of offenders realeased to the street in 1963 rearrested within five years, with 43 per cent being rearrested within one year following release.

Seventy per cent of persons under 25 years of age released in 1963 were rearrested within five years.

Thirty-nine per cent of offenders having an arrest in either 1967 or 1968 for an Index Crime offense had been previously charged with one or more serious offenses.

Forty-six per cent of 94,467 offenders arrested in 1967 or 1968 had been imprisoned on a prior charge.

Five-year follow-up indicates 69 per cent of the narcotic offenders released in 1963 were rearrested.

With regards to "crime and population," 1960-1968, per cent change over 1960—crime up 122 per cent, crime rate up 99 per cent, and population up 11 per cent.

In terms of "crimes of violence," 1960-1968, per cent change over 1960—violent crime up 106 per cent, rate up 85 per cent; "crime against property," 1960-1968, per cent change over 1960—property crime up 124 per cent, rate up 101 per cent.

Index Crimes. The Uniform Crime Reporting Program employs seven crime classifications to establish an index to measure the trend and distribution of crime in the United States. These crimes—murder, forcible rape, robbery, aggravated assault, burglary, larceny $50 and over in value, and auto theft—are counted by law-enforcement agencies as the crimes become known to them. These crimes were selected for use in the Crime Index because, as a group, they represent the most common local crime problem.

It is believed desirable to point out that there is no way of determining the total number of crimes which are committed. Many criminal acts occur which are not reported to official sources. In view of this fact, the best source for obtaining a count of crime is the next logical universe, namely, crimes which come to police attention. The crimes used in the Crime Index are those considered to be most consistently reported to police and computations of crime trends and crime rates are prepared using this universe—offenses known to police.

In calendar year 1968 almost 4.5 million serious crimes were reported to law-enforcement agencies, a 17 per cent national increase over 1967. The violent crimes as a group made up 13 per cent of the Crime Index total and rose 19 per cent, with murder up 13 per cent, forcible rape 15 per cent, robbery 30 per cent, and aggravated assault 11 per cent. Each of the voluminous property crimes recorded an increase, which contributed to the 17 per cent rise in this group of offenses representing 87 per cent of the Crime Index total. Individually, burglary was up 14 per cent, larceny $50 and over in value increased 21 per cent, and auto theft continued its upward trend by recording a 19 per cent increase. Since 1960, the violent crimes as a group have increased 106 per cent, property crimes 124 per cent, and the combined total 122 per cent in volume.

As in prior years the suburban areas continued to show a sharp rise in the volume of crime with a 17 per cent increase over 1967. The large core cities having populations in excess of 250,000 were up 18 per cent in volume and the rural areas registered an 11 per cent upswing. The largest American cities over one million population registered an average increase of 16 per cent. As noted in prior issues, while the suburban areas continued to record sharp upswings in the volume of crime, a much higher volume of crime occurs in the large cities.

Crime rates relate the incidence of crime to population. From a more realistic point of view, a crime rate should be considered as a count of victims. The discussion that follows will demonstrate that the risk of becoming a victim of crime in this country is increasing and that population growth cannot alone account for the crime increases.

The national Crime Index rate rose from 1,922 offenses per 100,000 population in 1967 to 2,235 in 1968, a 16 per cent increase in the victim rate. The rise in the national crime rate since 1960, or the risk of being a victim of one of these crimes has nearly doubled. As already discussed, many factors influence the nature and extent of crime in a particular community. A crime rate only takes into consideration the numerical factor of population and does not incorporate any of the other elements which contribute to the amount of crime in a given area. The statistical tables in this article disclose that the varying crime experiences, especially among large cities and suburban communities, are affected by a complex set of involved factors and are not solely limited to numerical population differences. The text tables reveal the variation in crime experience by geographic region and particularly large core cities as contrasted with the suburban and rural areas.

The overall crime rate increase in 1968 was attributable to the upward climb of violent crimes, as well as crimes against property. Each crime category recorded a rate increase ranging from 10 per cent in aggravated assault to 28 per cent in robbery. The number of crimes per unit of population is, as expected, highest in the large metropolitan centers and in those areas where populations are growing the fastest. Since 1960, the rate for crimes of violence as a group increased 85 per cent and property crime rate rose 101 per cent.

Clearance. In this program police clear a crime when they have identified the offender, have sufficient evidence to charge him and actually take him into custody. Crime solutions are also recorded in exceptional instances when some element beyond police control precludes the placing of formal charges against the offender—such as the victim's refusal to prosecute—or local prosecution is declined because the subject is being prosecuted elsewhere for a crime committed in another jurisdiction. The arrest of one person can clear several crimes or several persons may be arrested in the process of clearing one crime.

The percentage of Index Crimes cleared by law-enforcement agencies in 1968 was a substantial 7 per cent below the clearance percentage in 1967. Whereas police nationally cleared 22.4 per cent of these offenses in 1967, this dropped to 20.9 per cent in 1968. The decrease was noted in every Crime Index offense. "Crimes cleared by arrest," 1968, against the person—cleared, murder 86 per cent, negligent manslaughter 80 per cent, forcible rape 55 per cent, aggravated assault 66 per cent; and against property—cleared, robbery 27 per cent, burglary 19 per cent, larceny 18 per cent, auto theft 19 per cent. "Crime and crimes cleared," 1960-1968, per cent change over 1960—crime index up 122 per cent, index type arrests up 60 per cent, crimes cleared up 51 per cent, and clearance rate down 32 per cent.

Age. Nationally, persons under 15 years of age made up 10 per cent of the total police arrests; under 18, 26 per cent; under 21, 39 per cent; and under 25, 50 per cent. In the

TABLE I
NATIONAL CRIME, RATE, AND PER CENT CHANGES

Crime index offenses	Estimated crime, 1968		Per cent change over 1967		Per cent change over 1960	
	Number	Rate per 100,000 inhabitants	Number	Rate	Number	Rate
TOTAL	4,466,600	2234.8	+17.5	+16.3	+121.7	+ 98.9
Violent	588,800	294.6	+19.1	+17.8	+106.5	+ 85.3
Property	3,877,700	1,940.0	+17.2	+16.1	+124.2	+101.2
Murder	13,650	6.8	+12.9	+11.5	+ 51.7	+ 36.0
Forcible rape	31,060	15.5	+14.6	+13.1	+ 84.3	+ 64.9
Robbery	261,730	131.0	+29.5	+28.3	+143.7	+118.7
Aggravated assault	282,400	141.3	+11.5	+10.4	+ 85.8	+ 66.8
Burglary	1,828,900	915.1	+13.9	+12.8	+103.8	+ 82.8
Larceny $50 and over	1,271,100	636.0	+21.4	+20.2	+151.1	+125.3
Auto theft	777,800	389.1	+18.8	+17.6	+138.8	+114.3

suburban areas, the involvement of the young age groups in police arrests is again markedly higher than the national figures with the under 15 age group represented in 13 per cent; under 18, 35 per cent; under 21, 50 per cent; and under 25, 62 per cent. In the rural areas the distributions were lower for the younger age groups, with the under 15 age group being involved in 5 per cent; under 18 in 22 per cent; under 21 in 40 per cent; and those under 25, 53 per cent of total police arrests. When only the serious crimes are considered, nearly one-fourth of all arrests in 1968 were for persons under the age of 15 and almost one-half were under 18 years of age.

The younger the age group, the higher the repeating rate has been documented many times, as it is here. Lastly, "per cent repeaters," by age group—under 20, 72 per cent; 20-24, 69 per cent; 25-29, 67 per cent; 30-39, 63 per cent; 40-49, 54 per cent; 50 and over, 40 per cent; total all ages, 63 per cent.

CRIME IN AMERICA

The most natural and frequent question people ask about crime is "why?" They ask it about individual crimes and about crime as a whole. In either case it is an almost impossible question to answer. Each single crime is a response to a specific situation by a person with an infinitely complicated psychological and emotional make-up who is subject to infinitely complicated external pressures. Crime as a whole is millions of such responses. To seek the "causes" of crime in human motivations alone is to risk losing one's way in the impenetrable thickets of the human psyche. Compulsive gambling was the cause of an embezzlement, one may say, or drug addiction the cause of a burglary, or madness the cause of a homicide; but what caused the compulsion, the addiction, the madness? Why did they manifest themselves in those ways at those times?

There are some crimes so irrational, so unpredictable, so explosive, so resistant to analysis of explanation that they can no more be prevented or guarded against than earthquakes or tidal waves.

At the opposite end of the spectrum of crime are the carefully planned acts of professional criminals. The elaborately organized robbery of an armored car, the skillfully executed jewel theft, or the murder of an informant by a Cosa Nostra "enforcer" are so deliberate, so calculated, and so rational, that understanding the motivations of those who commit such crimes does not show us how to prevent them. How to keep competent and intelligent men from taking up crime as a life work is as baffling a problem as how to predict and discourage sudden criminal outbursts.

To say this is not, of course, to belittle the efforts of psychiatrists and other behaviorial scientists to identify and to treat the personality traits that are associated with crime. Such efforts are an indispensable part of understanding and controlling crime. Many criminals can be rehabilitated. The point is that looking at the personal characteristics of offenders is only one of the many ways, and not always the most helpful way, of looking at crime.

It is possible to say, for example, that many crimes are "caused" by their victims. Often the victim of an assault is the person who started the fight, or the victim of an automobile theft is a person who left his keys in his car, or the victim of a loan shark is a person who lost his rent money at the race track, or the victim of a confidence man is a person who thought he could get rich quick. The relationship of victims to crimes is a subject that so far has received little attention. Many crimes, no matter what kind of people their perpetrators were, would not have been committed if their victims had understood the risks they were running.

From another viewpoint, crime is "caused" by public tolerance of it, or reluctance, or inability to take action against it. Corporate and business—"white-collar"—crime is closely associated with a widespread notion that, when making money is involved, anything goes. Shoplifting and employee theft may be made more safe by their victims' reluctance to report the police—often due to a recognition that the likelihood of detection and successful prosecution are negligible. Very often slum residents feel they live in territory which it is useless for them even to try to defend. Many slum residents feel overwhelmed and helpless in the face of the flourishing vice and crime around them; many have received indifferent treatment from the criminal justice system when they have attempted to do their duty as complainants and witnesses; many fear reprisals, especially victims of rackets. When citizens do not get involved, criminals can act with relative impunity.

In a sense, social and economic conditions "cause" crime. Crime flourishes, and always has flourished, in city slums, those neighborhoods where overcrowding, economic deprivation, social disruption and racial discrimination are endemic. Crime flourishes in conditions of affluence, when there is much desire for material goods and many opportunities to acquire them illegally. Crime flourishes when there are many restless, relatively footloose young people in the population. Crime flourishes when standards of morality are changing rapidly.

Finally, to the extent that the agencies of law-enforcement and justice, and such community institutions as schools, churches, and social service agencies, do not do their jobs effectively, they fail to prevent crime. If the police are inefficient or starved for manpower, otherwise preventable crimes will occur; if they are overzealous, people better left alone will be drawn into criminal careers. If the courts fail to separate the innocent from the guilty, the guilty may be turned loose to continue their depredations and the innocent may be criminalized. If the system fails to convict the guilty with reasonable certainty and promptness, deterrence of crime may be blunted. If correctional programs do not correct, a core of hardened and habitual criminals will continue to plague the community. If the community institutions that can shape the characters of young people do not take advantage of their opportunities, youth rebelliousness will turn into crime.

The causes of crime, then, are numerous and mysterious and intertwined. Even to begin to understand them, one must gather statistics about the amounts and trends of crime, estimate the costs of crime, study the conditions of life where crime thrives, identify criminals and the victims of crime, and survey the public's attitudes toward crime. No single way of describing crime describes it well enough.

On the average, the likelihood of a serious personal attack on any American in a given year is about one in 550; together with the studies available they also suggest that the risk of serious attack from spouses, family members, friends, or acquaintances is almost twice as great as it is from strangers on the street. Commission and other studies, moreover, indicate that the risks of personal harm are spread very unevenly. The actual risk for slum dwellers is considerably more; for most Americans it is considerably less.

Except in case of wilful homicide where, the figures describe the extent of injury as well as the number of incidents, there is no national data on the likelihood of injury from attack. More limited studies indicate that while some injury may occur in two-thirds of all attacks, the risk in a given year of injury serious enough to require any degree of hospitalization of any individual is about one in 3,000 on the average, and much less for most Americans. These studies also suggest that the injury inflicted by family members or acquaintances is likely to be more severe than that from strangers. The risk of death from wilful homicide is about one in 20,000.

Criminal behavior accounts for a high percentage of motor vehicle deaths and injuries. In 1965 there were an estimated 49,000 motor vehicle deaths. Negligent manslaughter, which is largely a motor vehicle offense, accounted for more than 7,000 of these. Studies in several States indicate that an even higher percentage involve criminal behavior. They show that driving under the influence of liquor is probably involved in more than one-half of all motor vehicle deaths, and more than

13 per cent of the 1,800,000 non-fatal motor vehicle injuries each year.

Factors Affecting the Reporting of Crime

From the time that police statistics first began to be maintained in France in the 1820's, it has been recognized that the validity of calculations of changes in crime rates was dependent upon a constant relationship between reported and unreported crime. Until the Commission surveys, no systematic effort of wide scale had ever been made to determine what the relationship really was. As shown earlier, these surveys have now indicated that the actual amount of crime is several times that reported to the police, even in some of the precincts with the highest reported crime rates. This margin of unreported crime raises the possibility that even small changes in the way that crime is reported by the public to the police, or classified and recorded by the police, could have significant effects on the trend of reported crime. There is strong reason to believe that a number of such changes have taken place within recent years.

Changing Expectations. One change of importance in the amount of crime that is reported in our society is the change in the expectations of the poor and members of minority groups about civil rights and social protection. Not long ago there was a tendency to dismiss reports of all but the most serious offenses in slum areas and segregated minority group districts. The poor and the segregated minority groups were left to take care of their own problems. Commission studies indicate that whatever the past pattern was, these areas now have a strong feeling of need for adequate police protection. Crimes that were once unknown to the police, or ignored when complaints were received, are now much more likely to be reported and recorded as part of the regular statistical procedure.

The situation seems similar to that found in England. The University of Cambridge's Institute of Criminology, which in 1963 conducted an exhaustive study of the sharp rise in crimes of violence, concluded in its report that: One of the main causes for an increase in the recording of violent crime appears to be a decrease in the toleration of aggressive and violent behavior, even in those slum and poor tenement areas where violence has always been regarded as a normal and accepted way of settling quarrels, jealousies, or even quite trivial arguments.

Police Practice. Perhaps the most important change for reporting purposes that has taken place in the last 25 years is the change in the police. Notable progress has been made during this period in the professionalization of police forces. With this change, Commission studies indicate, there is a strong trend toward more formal actions, more formal records and less informal disposition of individual cases. This trend is particularly apparent in the way the police handle juveniles, where the greatest increases are reported, but seems to apply to other cases as well. It seems likely that professionalization also results in greater police efficiency in looking for crime. Increases in the number of clerks and statistical personnel, better methods for recording information, and the use of more intensive patrolling practices also tend to increase the amount of recorded crime. Because this process of professionalization has taken place over a period of time and because it is most often a gradual rather than an abrupt change, it is difficult to estimate what its cumulative effect has been.

Insurance. Another factor that probably increases the amount of reporting for some crimes is the sizable increase in insurance coverage against theft. It is difficult to evaluate this factor. However, because many persons believe that they must report a criminal event to the police in order to collect insurance, more reporting seems likely. Insurance is usually involved in auto theft cases.

Factors Indicating an Increase in Crime

Many factors affect crime trends but they are not always easy to isolate. Murder is a seasonal offense. Rates are generally higher in summer, except for December, which is often the highest month and almost always 5 to 20 per cent above the yearly average. In December 1963, following the assassination of President Kennedy, murders were below the yearly average by 4 per cent, one of the few years in the history of the UCR that this occurred. Since 1950 the pace of auto thefts has increased faster than car registrations. During World War II, however, when there was rationing and a shortage of cars, rates for auto theft rose sharply. And in 1946 when cars came back in production and most other crimes were increasing, auto thefts fell off rapidly.

Changing Age Composition. One of the most significant factors affecting crime rates is the age composition of the population. In 1965 more than 44 per cent of all persons arrested for forcible rape, more than 39 per cent for robbery, and more than 26 per cent for wilful homicide and aggravated assault were in the 18 to 24 year age group. For property crimes the highest percentages are found in the under 18 group—nearly 50 per cent of all those arrested for burglary and larceny and more than 60 per cent for auto theft.[12]

For most of these offenses the crime rate per individual in these age groups is many times that in older groups. Of course the differences are based on arrest figures, and the national figures on offenses cleared by arrest show that 75 to 80 per cent of burglaries, larcenies, and auto thefts are unsolved. It is possible that older persons committing offenses against property are more successful at evading arrest, so that the age figures for arrests give a somewhat biased picture.

Because of the unusual birth rate in the post-war years, the youthful high-risk group—those in their teens and early twenties—has been increasing much faster than other groups in the population. Beginning in 1961, nearly one million more youths have reached the ages of maximum risk each year than did so in the prior year. Thus the volume of crime and the overall crime rate could be expected to grow whether the rate for any given age increased or not.

Commission studies based on 1960 arrest rates indicate that between 1960 and 1965 about 40 to 50 per cent of the total increase in the arrests reported by UCR could have been expected as the result of increases in population and changes in the age composition of the population.

[12]*Editor's Note.* "1968 figures indicate that this trend, toward a preponderance of youthful criminals, is steadily increasing." *Uniform Crime Report*, 1968, p. 33.

Urbanization. Rates for most crimes are highest in the big cities. Twenty-six core cities of more than 500,000 people, with less than 18 per cent of the total population, account for more than half of all reported Index Crimes against the person and more than 30 per cent of all reported Index Property Crimes. One of every three robberies and nearly one of every five rapes occurs in cities of more than one million. The average rate for every Index Crime except burglary is at least twice as great--and often more—in these cities as in the suburbs or rural areas. With a few exceptions, average rates increase progressively as the size of the city becomes larger.

Suburban rates are closest to those of the smaller cities except for forcible rape where the former are higher. Suburban rates appear to be going up as business and industry increase —shopping centers are most frequently blamed by local police officials for rises in suburban crime.

Although rural rates are lower generally than those for cities, the differences have always been much greater for property crimes than for crimes against the person. Until the last few years rural rates for murder were close to those of the big cities; rural rates for murder and rape still exceed those for small towns.

The country has for many years seen a steady increase in its urban population and a decline in the proportion of the population living in rural areas and smaller towns. Since 1930 the rural population has increased by less than 2 per cent while the city population has increased by more than 50 per cent. The increase in the cities and their suburbs since 1960 alone has been about 10 per cent. Because of the higher crime rates in and around the larger cities, this trend toward urbanization has a considerable effect on the national rate for most Index Crimes. Commission studies show that if metropolitan, small city, and rural crime rates for 1960 had remained constant through 1965, the increase that could have been expected due to urbanization would have been about 7 to 8 per cent of the increase reported by the UCR.

It would obviously tell us a great deal about the trend of crime if we could analyze all together the changes that have been taking place in urbanization, age composition of the population, number of slum dwellers, and other factors such as sex, race, and level of income. The Commission has spent a considerable amount of time trying to make this kind of analysis. However, it was unable to analyze satisfactorily more than one or two factors in conjunction with each other on the basis of present information. As more factors were brought into the analysis, the results differed in some instances substantially from those obtained when only one factor was analyzed. It also seemed clear that as the number of factors was increased, a more accurate picture of the effect of changing conditions on the rate of crime emerged.

On the basis of its study, the Commission estimates that the total expected increase in crime from 1960 to 1965 from these kinds of changes would be at least half, and possibly a great deal more, of the total increase in crime rates actually observed. The Commission's study clearly indicates the need for fuller reporting of arrest information and for the development of more compatibility between police statistics and information collected by other statistical agencies. The FBI has already made substantial progress in this direction in recent years but further steps are still needed.

Increased Affluence. Another change that may result in more crime is increasing affluence. There are more goods around to be stolen. National wealth and all categories of merchandise have increased in terms of constant dollars more than fourfold since 1940—significantly more than the population or the rate of reported theft.

Increased affluence may also have meant that property is now protected less well than formerly. More than 40 per cent of all auto thefts involve cars with the keys inside or the switch left open. A substantial percentage of residential burglaries occur in unlocked houses. Bicycles, whose theft constitutes 15 per cent of all reported larcenies, are frequently left lying around. Larceny of goods and accessories from cars accounts for another 40 per cent of all reported larceny.

Increase in some business thefts can be directly attributed to less protection. The recent rise in bank robbery seems due in large part to the development of small, poorly protected branch banks in the suburbs.

In retail establishments, managers choose to tolerate a high percentage of shoplifting rather than pay for additional clerks.

Discount stores, for example, experience an inventory loss rate almost double that of the conventional department store. Studies indicate that there is in general more public tolerance for theft of property and goods from large organizations than from small ones, from big corporations or utilities than from small neighborhood establishments. Restraints on conduct that were effective in a more personal rural society do not seem as effective in an impersonal society of large organizations.

Inflation has also had an impact on some property crimes. Larceny, for example, is any stealing that does not involve force or fraud. The test of the seriousness of larceny is the value of the property stolen. The dividing line between "grand" and "petty" larceny for national reporting purposes is $50. Larceny of $50 and over is the Index Offense that has increased the most over the history of the UCR, more than 550 per cent since 1933. Because the purchasing power of the dollar today is only 40 per cent of what it was in 1933, many thefts that would have been under $50 then are over $50 now. UCR figures on the value of property stolen, for example, indicate that the average value of a larceny has risen from $26 in 1940 to $84 in 1965.

Other Countries. Crime is a worldwide problem. For most offenses it is difficult to compare directly the rates between countries because of great differences in the definitions of crime and in reporting practices. It is clear, however, that there are great differences in the rates of crime among the various countries, and in the crime problems that they face. These differences are illustrated to some extent by the homicide rates for a number of countries. The comparisons show only the general range of difference, as definitions and reporting even of homicide vary to some extent. In the years covered by the table, Colombia had the highest rate for all countries and Ireland the lowest.

A comparison between crime rates in 1964 in West Germany and the north central United States, prepared by the FBI, indicates that the Federal Republic, including West Berlin, had a crime rate of 0.8 murders per 100,000 inhabitants, 10.6 rapes, 12.4 robberies, 1,628.2 larcenies, and 78.2 auto thefts, as opposed to 3.5 murders per 100,000 inhabitants for north central United States, 10.5 rapes, 76.2 robberies, 1,337.3

larcenies, and 234.7 auto thefts.

Assessing the Amount and Trend of Crime

Because of the grave public concern about the crime problem in America today, the Commission has made a special effort to understand the amount and trend of crime and has reached the following conclusions:

First, the number of offenses—crimes of violence, crimes against property, and most others as well—has been increasing. Naturally, population growth is one of the significant contributing factors in the total amount of crime.

Secondly, most forms of crime—especially crimes against property—are increasing faster than population growth. This means that the risk of victimization to the individual citizen for these crimes is growing, although it is not possible to ascertain precisely the extent of the increase. All the economic and social factors discussed above support, and indeed lead to, this conclusion.

The Commission found it very difficult to make accurate measurements of crime trends by relying solely on official figures, since it is likely that each year police agencies are to some degree dipping deeper into the vast reservoir of unreported crime. People are probably reporting more to the police as a reflection of higher expectations and greater confidence, and the police in turn are reflecting this in their statistics. In this sense more efficient policing may be leading to higher rates of reported crime. The diligence of the FBI in promoting more complete and accurate reporting through the development of various procedures of the professional police has clearly had an important effect, but while this task of upgrading local reporting is under way, the FBI is faced with the problem—in computing national trends—of omitting for a time the places undergoing changes in reporting methods and estimating the amounts of crime that occurred in those places in prior years.

Thirdly, although the Commission concluded that there has been an increase in the volume and rate of crime in America, it has been unable to decide whether individual Americans today are more criminal than their counterparts 5, 10, or 25 years ago. To answer this question it would be necessary to make comparisons between persons of the same age, sex, race, place of residence, economic status, and other factors at the different times; in other words, to decide whether the 15-year-old slum dweller or the 50-year-old businessman is inherently more criminal now than the 15-year-old slum dweller or the 50-year-old businessman in the past. Because of the many rapid and turbulent changes over these years in society as a whole and in the myriad conditions of life which affect crime, it was not possible for the Commission to make such a comparison. Nor do the data exist to make even simple comparisons of the incidence of crime among persons of the same age, sex, race, and place of residence at these different stages.

Fourthly, there is a great deal of crime in America, some of it very serious, that is not reported to the police, or in some instances by the police. The national survey revealed that people are generally more likely to report serious crimes to the police, but the per cent who indicated they did do so ranged from 10 per cent for consumer fraud to 89 per cent for auto theft. Estimates of the rate of victimization for Index Offenses ranged from two per 100 persons in the national survey to 10 to 20 per 100 persons in the individual districts surveyed in three cities. The surveys produced rates of victimization that were from 2 to 10 times greater than the official rates for certain crimes.

Fifthly, what is needed to answer questions about the volume and trend of crime satisfactorily are a number of different crime indicators showing trends over a period of time to supplement the improved reporting by police agencies. The Commission experimented with the development of public surveys of victims of crime and feels this can become a useful supplementary yardstick. Further development of the procedure in needed to improve the reliability and accuracy of the findings. However, the Commission found that these initial experiments produced useful results which justify more intensive efforts to gather such information on a regular basis. They should also be supplemented by new types of surveys and censuses which could provide better information about crime in areas where such information is lacking, such as crimes by or against business and other organizations. The

Commission also believes that an improved and greatly expanded procedure for the collection of arrest statistics would
be of immense benefit in the assessment of the problem of
juvenile delinquency.

Sixthly, throughout its work the Commission has noted
repeatedly the sharp differences in the amount and trends of
reported crimes against property as compared with crimes
against persons. It has noted that while property crimes are
far more numerous than crimes against the person, and so
dominate any reported trends, there is much public concern
about crimes against persons. The more recent reports of the
UCR have moved far toward separating the reporting of these
two classes of crime altogether.

In order to get over this problem, the Commission has recommended the following: (*i*) The present Index of reported
crime should be broken into two wholly separate parts, one
for crimes of violence and the other for crimes against property. (*ii*) In principle, the development of additional indices to
indicate the volume and trend of such other important crime
problems as embezzlement, fraud, crimes against trust, crimes
of vice that are associated with organized crime, is recommended. The Commission urges that consideration be given to practical methods for developing such indices. (*iii*) The Commission
also urges that the public media and others concerned with
crime be careful to keep separate the various crime problems
and not to deal with them as a unitary phenomenon. Whenever possible, crime should be reported relative to population
as well as by the number of offenses, so as to provide a more
accurate picture of risks of victimization in any particular
locality.

Seventhly, the Commission believes that age, urbanization,
and other shifts in the population already under way will
operate over the next 5 to 10 years to increase the volume of
offenses faster than population growth. Further dipping into
the reservoirs of unreported crime is likely to combine with
this real increase and will show even greater growth in reported crime rates. Many of the basic social forces that tend to
increase the amount of real crime are already taking effect and
are for the most part irreversible. If society is to be successful
in its desire to reduce the amount of real crime, it must find

new ways to create the kinds of conditions and inducements—social, environmental, and psychological—that will bring about a greater commitment to law-abiding conduct, respect for law on the part of all Americans, and a better understanding of the great stake that all men trust in the honesty and integrity of their fellow citizens.

Economic Impact of Crime

One way in which crime affects the lives of all Americans is that it costs all of them money. Of course, economic costs alone cannot determine attitudes or policies toward crime. The costs of lost or damaged lives, of fear and of suffering, and of the failure to control critical events cannot be measured in dollars and cents. Nor can the requirements of justice and law-enforcement be established solely by use of economic measures. A high percentage of a police department's manpower may have to be committed to catch a single murderer or bombthrower. The poor, unemployed defendant in a minor criminal case is entitled to all the protections the American constitutional system provides—without regard to monetary costs.

However, economic factors relating to crime are important in the formation of attitudes and policies. Crime in the United States today imposes a very heavy economic burden upon individual members and the community as a whole. Risks and responses cannot be judged with maximum effectiveness until the full extent of economic loss has been ascertained. Researchers, policymakers, and operating agencies should know which crimes cause the greatest economic loss, which the least; on whom the costs of crime fall, and what the costs are to prevent or protect against it; whether a particular or general crime situation warrants further expenditures for control or prevention and, if so, what expenditures are likely to have the greatest impact.

The number of policemen, the size of a plant security staff, or the amount of insurance any individual or business carries are controlled to some degree by economics—the balance of the value to be gained against the burden of additional expenditures. If the protection of property is the objective, the economic loss from crime must be weighed directly against the cost of better prevention or control. In view of the importance and the frequency of such decisions, it is surprising that the cost information on which they are based is as fragmentary as it is. The lack of knowledge about which the Wickersham Commission complained 30 years ago is almost as valid today.

Some cost data are now reported through the UCR and additional data are available from individual police forces, insurance companies, industrial security firms, trade associations, and others. However, the total amount of information is not enough in quantity, quality, or detail to give an accurate picture.

The information available about the economic cost of crime is most usefully presented not as an overall figure, but as a series of separate private and public costs. Knowing the economic impact of each separate crime aids in identifying important areas for public concern and guides officials in making judgments about priorities for expenditure. Breakdowns of money now being spent on different parts of the criminal justice system, and within each separate part, may afford insights into past errors. For example, even excluding value judgments about rehabilitative methods, the fact that an adult probationer costs 38 cents a day and an adult offender in prison costs $5.24 a day suggests the need for re-examining current budget allocations in correctional practice.

Economic Impact of Individual Crimes. The picture of crime as seen through cost information is considerably different from that shown by statistics portraying the number of offenses known to the police or the number of arrest. According to these figures (*i*) organized crime takes about twice as much income from gambling and other illegal goods and services as criminals derive from all other kinds of criminal activity combined; (*ii*) unreported commercial theft losses, including shoplifting and employee theft, are more than double those of all reported private and commercial thefts; (*iii*) of the reported crimes, wilful homicide, though comparatively low in volume, yields the most costly estimates among those listed on the UCR Crime Index; (*iv*) a list of the seven crimes with the greatest economic impact includes only two, wilful homicide and larceny of $50 and over (reported and unreported), of the offenses included in the Crime Index; and (v) only a small proportion of the money expended for criminal justice agencies is allocated to rehabilitative programs for criminals or for research.

Employee theft, embezzlement, and other forms of crime involving business, which appear in relatively small numbers in the police statistics, loom very large in dollar volume. Direct stealing of cash and merchandise, manipulation of accounts, and stock records, and other forms of these crimes, along with shoplifting, appear to constitute a tax of 1 to 2 per cent on the total sales of retail enterprises, and significant amounts in other parts of business and industry. In the grocery trade, for example, the theft estimates for shoplifting and employee theft almost equal the total amount of profit. Yet Commission and other studies indicate that these crimes are largely dealt with by business itself. Merchants report to the police fewer than one-quarter of the known offenses. Estimates for these crimes are particularly incomplete for non-retail industries.

Fraud is another offense whose impact is not well conveyed by police statistics. Just one conspiracy involving the collapse of a fraudulent salad oil empire in 1964 created losses of $195-$175 million. Fraud is especially vicious when it attacks, as it so often does, the poor or those who live on the margin of poverty. Expensive nostrums for incurable diseases, home-improvement frauds, frauds involving the sale or repair of cars, and other criminal schemes create losses which are not only sizable in gross but are also significant and possibly devastating for individual victims. Although a very frequent offense, fraud is seldom reported to the police. In consumer and business fraud, as in tax evasion, the line between criminal conduct and civil fraud is often unclear. And just as the amount of civil tax evasion is much greater than the amount of criminal tax fraud, the amount of civil fraud probably far exceeds that of criminal fraud.

Cost analysis also places the crimes that appear so frequently in police statistics—robbery, burglary, larceny, and auto theft—in somewhat different perspective. The number of reported offenses for these crimes account for less than one-sixth the estimated total dollar loss for all property crimes and would constitute an even lower percentage if there were any accurate way of estimating the very large sums involved in extortion, blackmail, and other property crimes.

This is not to say, however, that the large amounts of police time and effort spent in dealing with these crimes are not important. Robbery and burglary, particularly residential burglary, have importance beyond the number of dollars involved. The effectiveness of the police in securing the return of better than 85 per cent of the $500 million worth of cars stolen annually appears to be high, and without the efforts of the police the costs of these crimes would doubtless be higher. As with all categories of crime, the total cost of property crimes cannot be measured because a large volume of them go unreported; however, Commission surveys suggest that the ones that are unreported involve less money per offense than those that are reported.

The economic impact of crimes causing death is surprisingly high. For 1965 there were an estimated 9,850 homicide victims.[13] Of the estimated 49,000 people who lost their lives in highway accidents, more than half were killed in accidents involving either negligent manslaughter or driving under the influence of alcohol. An estimated 290 women died due to complications resulting from illegal abortions (nearly one-fourth of all maternal deaths). Measured by the loss of future earnings at the time of death, these losses totalled more than $1½ billion.

The economic impact of other crimes is particularly difficult to assess. Anti-trust violations reduce competition and unduly raise prices; building code violations, pure food and drug law violations, and other crimes affecting the consumer have important economic consequences, but they cannot be easily described without further information. Losses due to fear of crime, such as reduced sales in high crime locations are real but beyond measure.

Economic impact must also be measured in terms of ultimate costs to society. Criminal acts causing property destruction or injury to persons not only result in serious losses to

[13]Editor's Note. "In 1968, 13,650." Uniform Crime Report, 1968, p. 6.

the victims or their families but also the withdrawal of wealth or productive capacity from the economy as a whole. Theft on the other hand does not destroy wealth but merely transfers it involuntarily from the victim, or perhaps his insurance company, to the thief. The bettor purchasing illegal betting services from organized crime may easily absorb the loss of a 10-cent, or even 10-dollar, bet. But from the point of view of society, gambling leaves much less wealth available for legitimate business. Perhaps more important, it is the proceeds of this crime tariff which organized crime collects from those who purchase its illegal wares that form the major source of income required by organized crime to achieve and exercise economic and political power.

Crime and the Inner City

One notable fact in this regard is that the common serious crimes that worry people most—murder, forcible rape, robbery, aggravated assault, and burglary—usually happen in the slums of large cities. Innumerable studies of cities in all regions of the country have traced the variations in the rates for these crimes. The results, with monotonous regularity, show that the offenses, the victims, and the offenders are found mostly in the poorest, most deteriorated, and socially disorganized areas.

Studies of the distribution of crime rates in cities and of the conditions of life most commonly associated with high crime rates have been conducted for well over a century in Europe and for many years in the United States. The findings have been remarkably consistent. Burglary, robbery, and serious assaults occur in areas characterized by low income physical deterioration, dependency, racial and ethnic concentrations, broken homes, working mothers, low levels of education and vocational skill, high unemployment, high proportions of single males, overcrowded and substandard housing, high rates of tuberculosis and infant mortality, low rates of home ownership or single family dwellings, mixed land use, and high population density. Studies that have mapped the relationship of these factors and crime have found them following the same pattern from one area of the city to another.

Crime rates in American cities tend to be highest in the city center and decrease in relationship to distance from the center.

The big city slum has always exacted its toll on its inhabitants, except where those inhabitants are bound together by an intense social and cultural solidarity that provides a collective defense against the pressures of slum living. Several slum settlements inhabited by people of oriental ancestry have shown a unique capacity to do this. However, the common experience of the great successive waves of immigrants of different racial and ethnic backgrounds that have poured into the poorest areas of our large cities has been quite different.

An historic series of studies by Clifford R. Shaw and Henry D. McKay of the Institute of Juvenile Reasearch in Chicago documented the disorganizing impact of slum life on different groups of immigrants as they moved through the slums and struggled to gain a foothold in the economic and social life of the city. Throughout the period of immigration, areas with high delinquency and crime rates continued to be so, even though members of new nationality groups successively moved in to displace the older residents. Each nationality group showed high rates of delinquency among its members who were living near the center of the city and lower rates for those living in the better outlying residential areas. Also for each nationality group, those living in the poorer areas had more of all the other social problems commonly associated with life in the slums.

This same pattern of high rates in the slum neighborhoods and low rates in the better districts is true among the Negroes and members of other minority groups who have made up the most recent waves of migration to the big cities. As other groups before them, they have had to crowd into the areas where they can afford to live while they search for ways to live better. The disorganizing personal and social experiences with life in the slums are producing the same problems for the new minority group residents, including high rates of crime and delinquency. As they acquire a stake in urban society and move to better areas of the city, the crime rates and the incidence of other social problems drop to lower levels.

However, there are a number of reasons to expect more crime and related problems among the new migrants to the city than among the older immigrants. There have been major changes in the job market, greatly reducing the demand for unskilled labor, which is almost new migrants have to offer. At the same time the educational requirements for jobs have been rising. Discrimination in employment, education, and housing, based on such a visible criterion as color, is harder to break than discrimination based on language or ethnic background.

What these changes add up to is that slums are becoming ghettos from which escape is increasingly difficult. It could be predicted that this frustration of the aspirations that originally led Negroes and other minority groups to seek out the city would ultimately lead to more crime. Such evidence as exists suggests that this is true.

Employee Theft. According to security experts for retail and other commercial establishments, theft by employees accounts for a considerably larger volume of theft than shoplifting. Theft of merchandise or equipment by employees is particularly hard to control because detection is so difficult. Employees have opportunities for theft every working day, whereas the shoplifting customer cannot steal merchandise regularly from the same establishment without arousing suspicion.

Employee theft is also a problem in many industrial concerns. A recent survey by the National Industrial Conference Board of 473 companies indicated that 20 per cent of all companies and nearly 30 per cent of those with more than 1,000 employees had a serious problem with employee theft of tools, equipment, materials, or company products. More than half of the companies with a problem of employee thefts indicated trouble with both white and blue-collar workers.

In neighborhood establishments surveyed by the Commission only 14 per cent reported the discovery of any employee dishonesty. Among those, 40 per cent estimated losses at no more than $50 a year. Most managers or owners surveyed were making attempts to establish the honesty of employees before hiring them. Nearly one-third made an effort to check references or to clear the employee with the local police department but 74 per cent did not report to the police the discovery of theft by their own employees, preferring to discharge the employee or handle the matter in some other way by themselves.

The Professional Criminal

Professional criminals think of themselves as very different from the habitual, amateur offenders whose persistent criminality resembles their own, but who do not have the skills or contacts to make a good living at crime in comparative safety from the law. Professional criminals engage in a wide variety of common law property offenses, including those involving the use of force or its threat, and those in which the stealing is accomplished by stealth or by manipulating the victim. They spend their full energies on crimes. Often they may be hired to do special jobs by the established figures in the world of organized crime, but they are not regarded as permanently part of that world.

A pilot study of professional crime in four cities sponsored by the Commission found that the way the professional criminal spends his time varies with his standing in the profession. The small-time professional spends virtually all of his time directly engaged in crime. He develops criminal opportunities, sells goods he has stolen, or procures tools or equipment needed for his next "job." It is an active but relatively planless life of crime on a day-by-day basis.

The more successful professional criminals spend a greater proportion of their time on planning and other preparation. A single promising "caper" can take weeks or months to plan and execute. But this calculation pays off in higher "scores" and lower risks of arrest. The most successful professional gangs even employ specialists to develop criminal prospects for them.

Although all professionals probably are more technically competent than most, if not all, habitual or amateur criminals, they differ widely in their professional abilities. At one end of the spectrum are the big-time jewel thieves and the "big con" men who manipulate wealthy victims into parting with hundreds of thousands of dollars. At the other are the petty thieves, "short con" operators, pickpockets, and shoplifters.

The Commission's study found that professional criminals, particularly the less successful, generally do not operate in the same groups or gangs over sustained periods. Different technical skills are needed for different crimes and circumstances. To meet this fluctuating need for skills there is an "employment" system operating out of the bars and restaurants that professional criminals habituate. These places serve as job placement centers.

Even professional crime is a risky business. The Commission's study found that the professional criminal's need for ready capital often opens him to severe exploitation by loan sharks. Most often this problem arises as a consequence of an arrest. To meet the cost of the premium for his bond and initial legal fees he must engage in more frequent criminal activity, often more risky than his ordinary line of work. If rearrested he will have additional costs, and this pattern may be repeated many times over before the professional is brought to trial.

Professional crime could not exist except for two essential relationships with legitimate society: the "fence" and the "fix." These are the mutually profitable arrangements between professional criminals and members of legitimate society. The fence arranges the redistribution of stolen goods; the fix gives the professional criminal sufficient immunity from law-enforcement agencies to enable him to practice his profession with reasonable safety.

The professional thief aims to sell stolen goods. Although he often retails his own stolen wares, he many also sell to receivers who resell the stolen goods. Sale to a fence may cost the thief 75 per cent of the value of the goods, but it reduces the risk of their being stolen from him or of his being arrested with them in his possession. He also avoids the risks involved in the retail process. In addition, large quantities of goods—goods that are perishable or otherwise—quickly lose their value, and goods for which there is a specialized demand, require a division of labor and level of organization beyond the capacity of an individual thief.

Fencing takes care of one problem of the professional criminal but the fix is even more important to him. The professional's connections and the problems to be solved determine whether he deals directly with the official himself, uses an attorney as an intermediary, or deals with the local fixer who has political connections and may be tied in with organized crime. Provided he can pay the price, the professional is often able to purchase excellent protection.

Professional crime ordinarily uses cash as the bribe, but sometimes a case may be fixed on credit or as a favor. Often professional criminals offer enforcement authorities testimony or information in return for a dismissed or reduced charge. This may be a "fix" in the criminal view, but to law enforcement it is an indispensable and legitimate means of combating crime.

Unquestionably professional criminals, because they work regularly at crime, account for a large share of thefts, particularly the costly thefts, that occur. The control of this type of criminality requires new forms of police intelligence operations, which some police departments are beginning to develop. Furthermore, this type of work needs to be supplemented by much more intensive research on professional criminality as a way of life.

"White-Collar" Offender and Business Crime

Inevitably, crimes reflect the opportunities people have to commit them. Whether a person has access to a criminal opportunity or not depends very much on who he is, what work he does and where he lives. Most of the crimes discussed in this report, those that have most aroused the public, are the common crimes of violence or theft that threaten people in the streets and in their homes. These are the crimes that are the easiest for the poor and the disadvantaged to commit; these are the crimes they do commit as the arrest statistics and the information about offenders on probation, parole, or in prison clearly disclose. They also are the crimes that make up the greatest part of the cases processed by the higher criminal courts.

However, there is another set of crimes that are connected with the occupational positions people have. They are committed in the course of performing the activities of particular jobs and exist as opportunities only for people in those occupations. Within this great reservoir of actual and potential crimes, the rather vague term "white-collar crime" is now commonly used to designate 'those occupational crimes committed in the course of their work by persons of high status and social repute. It thus differentiates these offenders and their crimes from those committed by low-status or disreputable persons.

The white-collar criminal is the broker who distributes fraudulent securities, the builder who deliberately uses defective material, the corporation executive who conspires to fix prices, the legislator who peddles his influence and vote for private gain, or the banker who misappropriates funds in his keeping. Arrest, court, or prison statistics furnish little information about the frequency and distribution of these offenses or about the characteristics of these offenders. The reason is that they are only rarely dealt with through the full force of criminal sanctions. This is an area of criminal activity where the standards of what is right and what is wrong are still evolving, and where society is still testing the effectiveness of less drastic sanctions for controlling undesirable conduct on the part of individuals or corporations. The newness, complexity, and difficulties of controlling many aspects of the white-collar crime problem can be seen most clearly when the offender is not an individual but a corporation.

During the last few centuries economic life has become vastly more complex. Individual families or groups of families are not self-sufficient; they rely for the basic necessities of life on thousands or even millions of different people, each with a specialized function, many of whom live hundreds or thousands of miles away. The manufacture and distribution of goods and the provision of services at low cost and high quality has resulted in giant business enterprises with billions of dollars in assets and in unions with hundreds of thousands of members.

Until the late 19th century, the economic life of this country was largely unregulated. At that time, the depredations of the "robber barons" made clear that business enterprise had to be regulated in order to protect not only the public but business itself. Regulations also became necessary for other purposes: to raise standards of health and safety, to stabilize prices in war time, to assist the poor and ignorant to obtain decent housing and other necessities, and to maintain the economy at a high level of production.

And so today virtually every aspect of business life is regulated in some way. There are anti-trust laws, food-and-drug laws, safety and health laws, licensing provisions for numerous kinds of businesses, housing codes, and a multitude of other regulatory statutes. Some of them, like the anti-trust laws, are sometimes enforced through criminal sanctions. The defendant is tried in a criminal court under criminal rules of procedure and, if an individual, can be sentenced to imprisonment or a fine, or, if a corporation, to a fine. Less serious violations, of housing codes for example, are minor offenses handled in the lower courts and punished usually by small fines. On the other hand, many regulatory laws, such as some labor laws, are enforced by administrative agencies outside the criminal system. Typically, the agency holds a hearing and, if a violation is found, either itself imposes or asks the court to impose an administrative remedy. This remedy might be an order to abandon an improper practice or suspension of a license. Frequently, such remedies are enforced by court injunction. Non-compliance with administrative or court orders may be a violation of the criminal law. While there is considerable debate as to what regulatory laws should be deemed criminal in nature, the crucial fact is that these laws are violated on a vast scale, sometimes in deliberate disregard of the law, sometimes because businessmen, in their effort to come as close to the line between legality and illegality as possible, overstep it.

It is impossible to ascertain even approximately the amount of business crime because it is almost certain that only a small proportion of it is detected. However, its pervasiveness is suggested by two studies. Edwin H. Sutherland examined decisions of the courts and regulatory commissions under the anti-trust, false advertising, patent, copyright, and labor laws as they applied to 70 of the country's largest corporations over their history averaging approximately 45 years. He found that 980 adverse decisions had been rendered against these corporations. Every one of the 70 corporations had at least one decision against it; 98 per cent of the 70 corporations had two or more decisions against them; 90 per cent had four or more decisions against them. About 60 per cent of the 70 corporations had been convicted by criminal courts; the average number of convictions per corporation was four.

Another study examined blackmarket violations during World War II. It indicated that appoximately one in every 15 of the three million business concerns in the country had serious sanctions imposed on them for violations of price regulations. The evidence suggested further that the total volume of violations was much larger than was indicated by officially imposed sanctions.

Business crime imposes three kinds of costs on society. First, physical injury or even death can come from tainted foods and harmful drugs sold in violation of the Pure Food and Drug Act, local health laws, and various safety laws and housing codes.

Secondly, financial losses are produced, for example, by the marketing of worthless, defective, or injurious products in violation of Post Office Department regulations, by frauds that violate the rules of the Securities and Exchange Commission, and by the sale of goods based on misrepresentation in advertising. The price-fixing by 29 electrical equipment companies alone probably cost utilities, and therefore, the public, more money than is reported as stolen by burglars in a year.

Thirdly, as serious as the physical and financial costs of corporate crime may be, it is probable that they are less serious than the damage it does to the country's social, economic, and political institutions. Restraint of trade tends to undermine the principles of free enterprise that the anti-trust laws are intended to protect. For example, the damage from the price-fixing conspiracy in the electrical equipment industry was not limited to the direct extra costs imposed. As Judge T. Cullen Ganey declared in sentencing the defendants: "This is a shocking indictment of a vast section of our economy, for what is really at stake here is the survival of the kind of economy under which this country has grown great, the free enterprise system."

Serious erosion of morals accompanies violations of this nature. It is reasonable to assume that prestigious companies that flout the law set an example for other businesses and influence individuals, particularly young people, to commit other kinds of crime on the ground that everyone is taking what he can get. If businessmen who are respected as leaders of the community can do such things as break the anti-trust laws or rent dilapidated houses to the poor at high rents, it is hard to convince the young that they should be honest.

Reducing the scope of business crime is peculiarly difficult. The offenses are often extremely hard to detect, especially since there is often no victim but the general public, or at least victims do not know that they have been victimized. Merely determining whether or not an offense has been committed frequently involves extremely complicated factual investigation and legal judgment.

Perhaps most important, the public tends to be indifferent to business crime or even to sympathize with the offenders when they have been caught. As one executive convicted and sentenced to jail in the electrical equipment conspiracy said: "On the bright side for me personally have been the letters and calls from people all over the country, the community, the shops and offices here, expressing confidence in me and support. This demonstration has been a warm and humbling experience for me." It is unlikely that a convicted burglar would receive such letters and calls.

The Commission has not been able to investigate in detail the many different kinds of business crime and anti-social conduct and so it cannot recommend specific measures for coping with them. This would require separate analysis of virtually every aspect of the American economy and its regulatory laws. However, it is clear that such studies are needed to improve enforcement of statutes governing many kinds of business practice. The studies should conduct research into the scope of illegal and immoral conduct; consider non-criminal sanctions to deal with it; propose methods for strengthening administrative agencies; explore the need for higher penalties, including both fines and jail sentences, for serious violations;

and discover whether new substantive law is needed to deal with harmful activity that is not, or may not, now be illegal.

Most important, however, it is essential that the public becomes aware of the seriousness of business crime. Without such awareness and the resulting demand for action, legislatures, courts, and administrative agencies will continue, as is now usually the case, to treat business offenses as relatively minor mistakes. The laws relating to business activities should be enforced as vigorously as those relating to the more traditional forms of crime.

CONCLUSION

The Commission cannot say that the public's fear of crime is exaggerated. It is not prepared to tell people how fearful they should be; that is something each person must decide for himself. People's fears must be respected; certainly they cannot be legislated. Some people are willing to run risks that terrify others. However, it is possible to draw some general conclusions from the findings of the surveys.

First, the public fears most the crimes that occur least often, crimes of violence. People are much more tolerant of crimes against property, which constitute most of the crimes that are committed against persons, or households, or businesses. Actually, the average citizen probably suffers the greatest economic loss from crimes against business establishments and public institutions, which pass their losses on to him in the form of increased prices and taxes. Nevertheless, most shoplifters never get to court; they are released by the store managers with warnings. Most employees caught stealing are either warned or discharged, according to the reports of businesses and organizations in the Commission's survey in three cities.

Secondly, the fear of crimes of violence is not a simple fear of injury or death or even of all crimes of violence, but, at bottom, a fear of strangers. The personal injury that Americans risk daily from sources other than crime are enormously greater. The annual rate of all Index Offenses involving either violence or the threat of violence is 1.8 per 1,000 Americans. This is relative to the total accidental injuries calling for medical attention or restricted activity of one day or more, as reported by the Public Health Service. A recent study of emergency medical care found the quality, numbers, and distribution of ambulances and other emergency services severely deficient, and estimated that as many as 20,000 Americans die unneccessarily each year as a result of improper emergency care. The means necessary for correcting this situation are very clear and would probably yield greater immediate return in reducing death than would expenditures for reducing the incidence of crimes of violence. But a different personal significance is attached to deaths due to the wilful acts of felons as compared to the incompetence or poor equipment of emergency medical personnel.

Furthermore, most murders and assaults are committed by persons known to the victim, by relatives, friends, or acquaintances. Indeed on a straight statistical basis, the closer the relationship the greater the hazard. In one sense the greatest threat to anyone is himself, since suicides are more than twice as common as homicides.

Thirdly, this fear of strangers has greatly impoverished the lives of many Americans, especially those who live in high-crime neighborhoods in large cities. People stay behind the locked doors of their homes rather than risk walking in the streets at night. Poor people spend money on taxis because they are afraid to walk or use public transportation. Sociable people are afraid to talk to those they do not know. In short, society is to an increasing extent suffering from what economists call "opportunity costs" as the result of fear of crime. For example, administrators and officials interviewed for the Commission by the University of Michigan survey team, report that library use is decreasing because borrowers are afraid to come out at night. School officials talked of parents not daring to attend PTA meetings in the evening, and park administrators pointed to unused recreation facilities. When many persons stay home, they are not availing themselves of the opportunities for pleasure and cultural enrichment offered in their communities, and they are not visiting their friends as frequently as they might. The general level of social interaction in the society is reduced.

When fear of crime becomes fear of the stranger, the social order is further damaged. As the level of sociability and mutual trust is reduced, streets and public places can indeed become more dangerous. Not only will there be fewer people abroad but those who are abroad will manifest a fear of and a lack of concern for each other. The reported incidents of bystanders indifferent to cries for help are the logical consequence of a reduced sociability, mutual distrust, and withdrawal.

However, the most dangerous aspect of a fear of strangers is its implication that the moral and social order of society are of doubtful trustworthiness and stability. Everyone is dependent on this order to instil in all members of society a respect for the persons and possessions of others. When it appears that there are more and more people who do not have this respect, the security that comes from living in an orderly and trustworthy society is undermined. The tendency of many people to think of crime in terms of increasing moral deterioration is an indication that they are losing their faith in society. And so the costs of the fear of crime to the social order may ultimately be even greater than its psychological cost to individuals.

Fourthly, the fear of crime may not be as strongly influenced by the actual incidence of crime as by other experiences generally. For example, the mass media and overly zealous or opportunistic crime fighters may play a role in raising fears by associating the idea of "crime" with a few sensational and terrifying criminal acts. Past research on the mass media's connection with crime has concentrated primarily on depictions and accounts of violence in the mass media as possible causes of delinquency and crime. Little attention has thus far been given to what may be a far more direct and costly effect —the creation of distorted perceptions of the risk of crime and exaggerated fears of victimization.

The greatest danger of an exaggerated fear may well reside in the tendency to use the violent crime as a stereotype for crimes in general. For example, there may be a significant interplay between violence and the mass media and the reporting of general crime figures. Publicity about the total of these figures without distinguishing between the trends for property crime and those for crimes against persons may create mistaken ideas about what is actually happening.

If burglaries and larcenies increase sharply while violent crimes decrease or remain stable, the total figures will follow the property crime figures, since crimes against property are more than four-fifths of the total. Yet under these conditions people may interpret the increases in terms of the dominant stereotype of crimes of violence, thus needlessly increasing their fears. They may not only restrict their activities out of an exaggerated fear of violence but may fail to protect themselves against the more probable crimes. The fact is that most people experience crime vicariously through the daily press, periodicals, novels, radio and television, and often the reported experiences of other persons. Their fear of crime may be more directly related to the quality and the amount of this vicarious experience than it is to the actual risks of victimization.

The Commission believes that there is a clear public responsibility to keep citizens fully informed of the facts about crime so that they will have facts to go on when they decide what the risks are and what type of precautionary measures they should take. Furthermore, without an accurate understanding of the facts, they cannot judge whether the interference with individual liberties which strong crime control measure may involve is a price worth paying. The public obligation to citizens is to provide this information regularly and accurately. And if practices for disseminating information give wrong impressions, resources should be committed to developing more accurate methods.

Finally, public concern about crime need not have only the adverse effects that have been described so far. It can be a powerful force for action. However, making it one will not be easy. The Commission's Washington survey asked people whether they had ever "gotten together with other people around here, or has any group or organization you belong to met and discussed the problem of crime or taken some sort of action to combat crime." Only about 12 per cent answered affirmatively, although the question was quite broad and included any kind of group meeting or discussion. Neither did most persons believe that they as individuals could do anything about crime in their own neighborhoods. Only slightly over 17 per cent thought that they could do either a lot or just something.

Most people feel that the effort to reduce crime is a responsibility of the police, the courts, and perhaps other public agencies. This was even true to some extent of administrators and officials of public agencies and utilities who were interviewed in the three city precinct surveys. However, when these officials were pressed they were able to think of many ways in which their organizations might help reduce crime, such as co-operating to make law-enforcement easier, donating and helping in neighborhood programs, providing more and better street lighting, creating more parks with recreational programs, furnishing more youth programs and adult education, and promoting integration of work crews and better community relations programs.

A NATIONAL STRATEGY

America can control crime. This report has tried to say how. It has shown that crime flourishes where the conditions of life are the worst, and that therefore the foundation of a national strategy against crime is an unremitting national effort for social justice. Reducing poverty, discrimination, ignorance, disease and urban blight, and the anger, cynicism, or despair those conditions can inspire, is one great step toward reducing crime. It is not the task, indeed it is not within the competence, of a Commission on Law-Enforcement and Administration of Justice to make detailed proposals about, housing education, civil rights, unemployment, welfare, or health. However, it is the Commission's clear and urgent duty to stress that forceful action in these fields is essential to crime prevention, and to adjure the officials of every agency of criminal justice—policemen, prosecutors, judges, correctional authorities—to associate themselves with, and labor for, the success of programs that will improve the quality of American life.

This report has shown that most criminal careers begin in youth, and that therefore programs that will reduce juvenile delinquency and keep delinquents and youthful offenders from settling into lives of crime are indispensable parts of a national strategy. It has shown that the formal criminal process, arrest to trial to punishment, seldom protects the community from offenders of certain kinds and that therefore, the crimi-

nal justice system and the community must jointly seek alternative ways of treating them. It has shown that treatment in
the community might also return to constructive life many
offenders who quite appropriately have been subjected to formal process.

It has also been pointed out in the report that legislatures
and, by extension, the public, despite their well-founded alarm
about crime, have not provided the wherewithal for the criminal justice system to do what it could and should do. It has
identified the system's major needs as better qualified, better
trained manpower; more modern equipment and management;
closer co-operation among its functional parts and among its
many and varied jurisdictions; and, of course, the money
without which far-reaching and enduring improvements are
impossible.

It has been emphasized again and again in the report that
improved law-enforcement and criminal administration is
more than a matter of giving additional resources to police
departments, courts, and correctional systems. Resources are
not ends. They are means, the means through which the agencies of criminal justice can seek solutions to the problems of
preventing and controlling crime. Many of those solutions
have not yet been found. We need to know much more about
crime. A national strategy against crime must be in large part
a strategy of search.

On the whole the report concentrates on cities, for that is
where crime is most prevalent, most feared, and most difficult
to control. On the whole the report dwells on the criminal
justice system's deficiencies and failures, since prescribing remedies was what the Commission was organized to do. Some
States and cities are doing much to improve criminal administration; their work is the basis for many of the report's recommendations. Finally, because it is a national report, it is
not and cannot be a detailed manual of instructions that police
departments, courts and correctional systems need only to
follow step by step in order to solve their problems. It is of
necessity a general guide that suggests lines along which local
agencies can act.

Planning—The First Step

A State or local government that undertakes to improve its criminal administration should begin by constructing, if it has not already done so, formal machinery for planning. Significant reform is not to be achieved overnight by a stroke of a pen; it is the product of thought and preparation. No experienced and responsible State or city official needs to be told that. The Commission's point is not that each individual action against crime should be planned, but that all of a State's or a city's actions against crime should be planned together, by a single body. The police, the courts, the correctional system, and the non-criminal agencies of the community must plan their actions against crime jointly if they are to make real headway.

The relationships among the various parts of the criminal justice system—and between the system and the community's other institutions, governmental and non-governmental—are so intimate and intricate that a change anywhere may be felt everywhere. Putting into effect the Commission's recommendation for three entry "tracks" in police departments could involve the rewriting of civil service regulations, the revision of standard police field procedures, the adjustment of city budgets, and possibly the passage of enabling legislation. A reform like organizing a Youth Services Bureau to which the police, the juvenile courts, parents and school officials, could refer young people will require an enormous amount of planning. Such a bureau will have to work closely with the community's other youth-serving agencies. It will affect the caseloads of juvenile courts, probation services, and detention facilities. It will raise legal issues of protecting the rights of the young people referred to it. It could be attached to a local or State government in a variety of ways. It could offer different kinds of service. It could be staffed by different kinds of people. It could be financed in many different ways.

Furthermore, concerted and systematic planning is not only a necessary prelude to action, it is a spur to action. The best way to interest the community in the problems of crime is to engage its members in planning. The best way to mobilize the community against crime is to lay before it a set of practical and coherent plans. This report often has had occasion to use the word "isolation" to describe certain aspects of relationship between the criminal justice system and the community. State and city planning agencies could do much to end that isolation. In every State and every city, an agency, or one or more officials, should be specifically responsible for planning improvements in crime prevention and control and encouraging their implementation.

It is impossible, of course, to prescribe in a national report the precise forms that State or city planning agencies should take. No two states have identical constitutions, or penal codes, or crime problems. State-city relationships vary from State to State, and often within States according to the size of cities. County governments have more or less power, depending on the State. Municipal government takes many forms. However, there are certain principles that are universally applicable. The Commission has made the following recommendations:

First, much of the planning for action against crime will have to be done at the State level. Every State operates a courtsystem and a corrections system, and has responsibility for certain aspects of law-enforcement. State legislatures, as a rule, control local finances. The states are in the best position to encourage or require the co-ordination or pooling of activities that is so vitally necessary in metropolitan areas and among rural counties.

Secondly, the planning will also have to be done at the municipal level. The problems of the police and, to a certain extent, of the jails and the lower courts are typically city problems. Welfare, education, housing, fire prevention, recreation, sanitation, urban renewal, and a multitude of other functions that are closely connected with crime and criminal justice are also the responsibility of cities. In some cities members of the mayor's or the city manager's staff, or advisory or interdepartmental committees, co-ordinate the anti-crime activities; but in most of the cities there is as yet little planning or work being done in this field.

Thirdly, close collaboration between State and city planning units is obviously essential. Representatives of a State's major cities should serve on its body, and staff members of the State body should be available to the city bodies for information and advice. Money, manpower, and expertise are in too short supply to be squandered in activities that duplicate or overlap each other and, conversely, when there is no collaboration there is always a risk that some important field of action will be overlooked.

Fourthly, however much the structure and composition of planning units vary from place to place, all units should include both officials of the criminal justice system and citizens from other professions. Plans to improve criminal administration will be impossible to put into effect if those responsible for criminal administration do not participate in their making. On the other hand, as this report has repeatedly stressed, crime prevention is the task of the community as a whole and, all parts of the criminal justice system can benefit from the special knowledge and points of view of those outside it. Business and civic leaders, lawyers, school and welfare officials, persons familiar with the problems of slum dwellers, and members of the academic community are among those who might be members of planning boards, or who might work with such boards as advisers or consultants.

Fifthly, planning boards must have sufficient authority and prestige, and staffs large enough and able enough, to permit them to furnish strong and imaginative leadership in making plans and seeing them through.

The first thing any planning unit will have to do is to gather and analyze the following facts: statistics about crime and the costs and caseloads of the criminal justice system; knowledge about the programs and procedures being used in its own jurisdiction, and about those that have proved successful elsewhere; data about the social conditions that appear to be linked with crime; and information about potentially helpful individuals and organizations in the community.

In few States or cities has information of this kind been compiled systematically. Gathering facts will be an invaluable process for any planning body, not only because of the importance of the facts themselves, but also because they will have to be collected from people and organizations experienced in crime prevention and criminal administration, like judges, correctional officials, police officials, prosecutors, defense counsel, youth workers, universities, foundations, civic organizations, service clubs, neighborhood groups.

Those people and organizations can be combined into a network of support for the changes the planning body will propose. Such a network will be able to do much to overcome resistance to change, or fear of it, inside and outside the criminal justic system, by showing how changes can be made carefully and practically.

On the basis of the facts it gathers, the planning body will be able to appraise objectively and frankly the needs of its State or city and the resources that are available for meeting those needs. It would ask, for example, whether in its jurisdiction police training is adequate; whether the lower and juvenile courts are failing in any of the ways cited by the Commission; whether the correctional system is beginning to make fundamental improvements of the sort the Commission has recommended.

It will discover needs that can be met rapidly by putting into effect programs that have succeeded in other places; for example, bail reform projects, systems for the assignment of defense counsel to indigents, police standards commissions, rehabilitation programs in jails, and sentencing institutes for judges. An excellent model of how much a planning body can do is the work of the President's Commission on Crime in the District of Columbia, which undertook a comprehensive study of the criminal justice system and other agencies concerned with crime and delinquency in the District, and made detailed recommendations for change.

One caution about planning bodies, the Commission feels must be exercised, is that they should not postpone changes that can be made immediately. For example, most police departments could immediately add legal advisers to their staffs, or launch police-community relations programs. In many cities there is no question about whether more prosecutors and probation officers are needed in the lower courts; they clearly are and they should be provided without delay. Sentencing councils could be organized with no more effect than it would take for a number of judges to arrange to meet regularly. There are other recommendations that one jurisdiction or another could put into effect at once without elaborate planning. Simple changes that have been recommended should be immediately introduced, not only because justice demands it, but because these will contribute to creating a climate in which complicated, long-range reform will be feasible.

Major Lines for State and Local Action

The following pattern has been outlined for better and quicker action against crime.

Money. The most urgent need of the agencies of criminal justice in the States and cities is money with which to finance the multitude of improvements they must make. As is set forth in the following part of this article, the Commission believes that federal financial support of improved criminal administration in the States and cities is necessary and appropriate. But even more essential is an increase in State support. Plans for change must include realistic estimates of financial requirements and persuasive showings of the gains that can be achieved by spending more on criminal administration.

A central task of planning bodies and the network of agencies and individuals working with them will be to mobilize support, within legislatures and by the public, for spending money on innovation and reform. The collaboration of police, prosecutors, correctional officials, and others involved in the agencies of justice is crucial in this, for they know best how vital the need for greater resources is, and how little is accomplished by identifying scapegoats or resorting to simplistic answers as solutions to the complicated problems of crime and criminal justice.

Personnel. The Commission has found that many of the agencies of justice are understaffed. Giving them the added manpower they need is a matter of high priority for protection of public safety and of the rights of individuals accused of crime. But even more essential is a dramatic improvement in the quality of personnel throughout the system. Establishment of standard-setting bodies, such as police standards commissions that exist in several States, is one way to approach this problem. Better and more numerous training programs are another. State and city planning groups must consider to what extent each operating agency can and should provide its own training and to what extent metropolitan, statewide, or regional programs should be developed instead.

If the agencies of justice are to recruit and retain the able, well-educated people they badly need, they will have to offer them higher pay and challenging and satisfying work. For example, it is clear to the Commission that until the single recruitment and promotion "track" that now prevails in all police forces is abandoned, upgrading of the police will be extremely difficult. Thus, one of the first and most difficult tasks of planning bodies will be to consider major changes in the personnel structures of the agencies of justice.

Meeting the Challenge. This report has described how modern urban life has burdended the criminal justice system with a range of almost entirely new problems. It has attempted to suggest promising ways of dealing with them. For example, it outlines a model for future development in corrections that predicates treatment on a new kind of facility: a small institution, located in the community it serves, that can be used flexibly for short-term incarceration and as a base for intensive community treatment. It has proposed police communication centers that take advantage of modern technology. It has described how necessary it is, in the interest of preventing delinquency, for the community to reassess the current practices of schools, welfare departments, and housing officials, particularly in poor neighborhoods. It has recommended as a new alternative to criminal disposition for less serious juvenile offenders, Youth Services Bureaus that would provide them with a variety of treatment services and keep them from being grouped with serious criminals. It has proposed greatly strengthened community relations programs to improve respect for law and increase police effectiveness in the highest crime neighborhoods of America's cities.

In addition, broader methods of meeting problems presented by the increasing complexity and anonymity of life in large urban areas are obviously important. Thus, some cities may wish to consider developing procedures or agencies—of which the ombudsman, which has proved useful in a number of other countries, is only one possible model—to assist citizens in understanding and dealing with the many official bodies that affect their lives. These are only a few important examples of the many new services the Commission recommends that State and local planning bodies develop.

In many instances establishing new programs will be costly. The Commission has therefore recommended that the emphasis of proposed Federal financial aid be placed on innovation. The Commission further recommends that State and local governments carefully consider the feasibility and desirability of devotion to new programs increasing proportions of the funds allocated to crime control.

Organization and Procedures of Agencies of Justice. An important matter for planning units and operating agencies to consider is how the police, the courts, and corrections can improve their organization and their operations. Since there are throughout the country many examples to draw on, and since legislative action often will not be required, early and substantial improvements can be made. Such of the Commission's proposals—as those for regularizing the procedures in pre-trial disposition of cases and in sentencing; for providing clearer guidance by police chiefs to field officers on such matters as the making of arrests in domestic disputes, drunkenness, and civil disturbance situations; and for developing a "collaborative" regime within prisons—can be considered almost at once, and acted upon without legislative action and, in many instances, without significant increases in spending.

The success of such changes where they have been introduced should greatly help the agencies in States and cities where they have not been made to act promptly. Planning bodies and other State and local groups may find themselves chiefly providing support, encouragement, and continuing pressure for change. In some cases it may be desirable for State or local agencies to obtain suggestions from recognized professional or governmental groups such as the International Association of Chiefs of Police or the Bureau of Prisons as one means of identifying specific needs and possible ways of meeting them.

Law Reform. While many improvements in the system of criminal justice do not require legislative action other than the appropriation of funds, others do require new laws or changes in existing laws. Proposals for court reoganization may even require constitutional change. Therefore, at an early stage in their work, planning bodies should appraise the needs for legislative change. The letter could include such diverse actions as enacting new gun control laws, amending existing laws to aid in organized crime prosecutions, changing legal disabilities of former prisoners, and enacting controls over dangerous drugs that are uniform with Federal law.

More general and fundamental re-evaluation is also called for. A number of State legislatures, including those in Illinois, California, and New York, have recently completed or are now engaged in major revisions of their criminal codes. For States that have not yet addressed themselves to this problem, the carefully formulated provisions of the American Law Institute's Model Penal Code serve as a valuable starting point. In many places there are bar associations and other groups with continuing interest in law revision; clearly such groups should be involved in the planning process. Governors and State legislatures should also give strong consideration to appointing law revision commissions comparable to that established by the Congress for review of all Federal criminal statutes.

Role of the Federal Government

Although criminal administration is primarily a State and local responsibility, the Federal Government's contribution to the national efforts against crime is crucial. The Federal Government carries much of the load of financing and administrating the great social programs that are America's best hope of preventing crime and delinquency, and various of its branches concern themselves actively with such specific criminal problems as preventing juvenile delinquency, and treating drug addiction and alcoholism.

The Federal Government has the direct responsibility for enforcing major criminal statutes against, among other things, kidnapping, bank robbery, racketeering, smuggling, counterfeiting, drug abuse, and tax evasion. It has a number of law-enforcement agencies, a system of criminal courts, and a large correctional establishment. Some of the Commission's recommendations, notably those concerning organized crime, drug abuse, firearms control, the pooling of correctional facilities, and of police radio frequencies, are addressed in part to the Federal Government.

The Federal Government has for many years provided information, advice, and training to State and local law enforcement agencies. These services have been extremely important. In many towns and countries, for example, the Federal Bureau of Investigation's on-site training programs for police officers and sheriffs are the only systematic training programs available. The Department of Justice, under the Law Enforcement Assistance Act of 1965, has begun to give State and city agencies financial grants for research, for planning, and for demonstration projects.

The Commission wants not only to endorse warmly Federal participation in the effort to reduce delinquency and crime, but to urge that it be intensified and accelerated. It believes further that the Federal Government can make a dramatic new contribution to the national effort against crime by greatly expanding its support of the agencies of justice in the States and in the cities.

Federal Prevention Programs. The Federal Government is already doing much in the field of delinquency prevention. An Office of Juvenile Delinquency and Youth Development, which funds research and demonstration projects by both governmental and non-governmental State and local agencies, is an important part of the Department of Health, Education, and Welfare. The office is supporting projects, to give only a few examples, aimed at providing job training and opportunities to delinquents; enabling school drop-outs to continue their education; controlling the behavior of youthful gangs; involving young people in community action; devising alternatives to juvenile court referral, and finding ways to give delinquents the support and counselling they do not get from their families. The same Department's Children's Bureau has for years given technical aid to police and juvenile court personnel. The Vocational Rehabilitation Administration in the Department has recently developed job-training programs specifically designed for delinquent young people. The Commission is convinced that efforts like these are of great immediate, and even greater potential, value, and urges that they be strengthened.

Other Federal programs of greater scope work against delinquency and crime by improving education and employment prospects for the poor and attacking slum conditions, associated with crime. Such work and job-training programs as the Neighborhood Youth Corps, the Job Corps, the Youth Opportunity Centers, and Manpower Development and Training Act programs provide training, counselling, and work opportunities essential to break the pattern of unemployability that underlies so much of crime today. The Elementary and Secondary Education Act programs and the Head Start work with preschool children are aimed at readying disadvantaged children for school, improving the quality of slum education, and preventing dropping out. Community action programs and the new Model Cities Program are concerned with strengthening the social and physical structure of inner cities, and thus ultimately with delinquency and crime prevention. As already pointed out, a community's most enduring protection against crime is to right the wrongs and cure the illnesses that tempt men to harm their neighbors.

An Expanded Federal Effort. In the field of law-enforcement and administration of justice the Federal contribution is still quite small, particularly in respect to the support it gives the States and cities, which bear most of the load of criminal administration. The present level of Federal support provides only a tiny portion of the resources the States and cities need to put into effect the changes this report recommends. The Commission has considered carefully whether or not the Federal Government should provide more support for such programs, and has concluded that it should do so. In reaching this conclusion it has been persuaded, first, by the fact that crime is a national, as well as a State and local, phenomenon; it often does not respect geographical boundaries. The FBI has demonstrated the high mobility of many criminals. Failure of the criminal justice institutions in one State may endanger the citizens of others. The Federal Government has already taken much responsibility in such fields as education and welfare, employment and job training, housing and mental health, which bear directly on crime and its prevention.

Moreover, simply in terms of economy of effort, and of feasibility, their are important needs that individual jurisdictions cannot or should not meet alone. Research is a most important instance. Careful experimentation with and evaluation of police patrol methods, for example, or delinquency prevention programs, means assembling and organizing teams of specialists. They can best be marshalled with the help of the Federal Government. It is also important to make available the sort of information that every jurisdiction in the country needs access to every day, like wanted person and stolen property lists, and fingerprint files. Furthermore, the Federal Government can do much to stimulate pooling of resources and services among local jurisdictions.

Next, most local communities today are hard-pressed just to improve their agencies of justice and other facilities at rate that will meet increases in population and in crime. They cannot spare funds for experimental or innovative programs or plan beyond the emergencies of the day. Federal collaboration can give State and local agencies an opportunity to gain on crime rather than barely stay abreast of it, by making funds, research, and technical assistance available and thereby encouraging changes that in time may make criminal administration more effective and more fair.

The Federal program the Commission visualizes is a large one. During the past fiscal year the Federal Government spent a total of about $20 million on research into crime and delinquency, and another $7 million, under the Law-Enforcement Assistance Act, on research and demonstration projects by local agencies of justice. The Commission is not in a position to weigh against each other all the demands for funds that are made upon the Federal Government. And so it cannot recommend the expenditure of a specific number of dollars a year on the program it proposes. However, it does see the program as one on which several hundred million dollars annually could be profitably spent over the next decade. If this report has not conveyed the message that sweeping and costly changes in criminal administration must be made throughout the country in order to effect a significant reduction in crime, then it has not expressed what the Commission strongly believes.

The Commission's final conclusion about a Federal anti-crime program is that the major responsibility for administering it should lie with the Department of Justice, and that the official who administers it for the Attorney General should be a Presidential appointee, with all the status and prestige that inheres in such an office. In the Department of Justice alone among Federal agencies there is a large existing pool of practical knowledge about the police, the courts, and the correctional system. The Federal Bureau of Prisons and the Federal Bureau of Investigation, each of which is already expanding its own support of State and local agencies, are parts of the Department of Justice. The Department of Justice has a Criminal Division, one of whose most important sections is concerned with organized crime and racketeering. It has the recently established Office of Criminal Justice, which has concentrated on criminal reform. Many of the research and demonstration portions of the Commission's program are already authorized under the Law-Enforcement Assistance Act, which is administered by the Department of Justice. If it is given the money and the men it will need, the Department of Justice can take the lead in efforts against crime.

In proposing a major Federal program against crime, the Commission is mindful of the special importance of avoiding any invasion of State and local responsibility for law-enforcement and criminal justice, and its recommendation is based on the judgment that Federal support and collaboration of the sort outlined below are consistent with scrupulous respect for—and indeed strengthening of—that responsibility.

The Commission's Program

The program of Federal support that the Commission recommends would meet the following eight major needs: State and local planning; education and training of criminal justice personnel; surveys and advisory services concerning organization and operation of criminal justice agencies; development of co-ordinated national information systems; development of a limited number of demonstration programs in agencies of justice; scientific and technological research and development; institutes for research and training personnel; and grants-in-aid for operational innovations.

(i) *State and Local Planning.* The Commission believes that the process of State and local planning outlined in the preceding section of this chapter should be a prerequisite for the receipt of Federal support for action programs. It believes further that such planning should itself receive Federal support, and it recommends that planning grants be made available for this purpose. The Department of Justice has already made grants of up to $25,000 to a number of State planning committees formed during the past year. It is clear that planning support in considerably larger amounts will be necessary if States and cities are to conduct a careful assessment of their needs and of ways to meet them.

(*ii*) *Education and Training.* This report has emphasized many times the critical importance of improved education and training in making the agencies of criminal justice fairer and more effective. The Federal Government is already involved to a limited degree in providing or supporting education and training for some criminal justice personnel. The FBI provides direct training of police officers at its academy in Washington and in the field. The Department of Justice's new Law-Enforcement Assistance program has supported police curriculum development and training demonstration projects; the Department of Health, Education, and Welfare has done some research on education and training in the fields of juvenile corrections, mental health, and delinquency prevention; and the Department of Labor has recently intiated in a few large cities programs under the Manpower Development and Training Act to help prepare young men from slum areas for police work.

The Commission believes that Federal financial support to provide training and education for State and local criminal justice personnel should be substantially increased. Such support might take several forms. In the field of medicine forgivable loans have been used to help defray the costs of college education and to provide an incentive for further work in the field. Another plan would be to subsidize salary payments to personnel on leave for training or longer study programs, or to their interim replacements. Curriculum development programs like those conducted by the National Science Foundation are also much needed if those from different parts of the criminal justice system are to be jointly instructed in such subjects as, for example, the treatment of juveniles or the problems of parolees.

A seminar for police chiefs, sponsored by the Office of Law-Enforcement Assistance and held at the Harvard Business School in the summer of 1966, exposed the chiefs to the methods and insights of modern business administration in a way that they felt was invaluable, and created new interest in the managerial problems of the police among professors at the school. Such advanced programs hold great promise for breaking down the isolation in which many criminal justice agencies now operate.

The Departments of Police, Administration of Justice, and Corrections badly need some promising programs for education and training on the following lines:

Police. State police standards commission programs to establish minimum recruitment and training standards, and to provide training, particularly through the establishment of regional academies or programs for medium and small size communities; graduate training in law and business administration for police executives through degree courses or special institutes; curriculum development and training for instructors in police academies and police training programs; special training programs in such critical problems as organized crime, riot control, police-community relations, correctional supervision of offenders being treated in the community, the use by police and juvenile court intake personnel of social agencies in the community; and programs to encourage college education for police in liberal arts and sciences, including scholarship and loan support, and curriculum development to guide college police-science programs away from narrow vocational concentration.

Administration of Justice: Special programs to educate and train judges, prosecutors, and defense counsel for indigents; orientation in correctional and non-criminal dispositions for prosecutors and judges; and training for court administrators.

Corrections. Education and training of rehabilitative personnel, including teachers, counsellors, and mental health personnel; training custodial personnel for rehabilitative roles; and education and orientation of personnel for research and evaluation in experimental treatment methods.

As these examples indicate, it is proposed that Federal aid

in this area would be directed toward meeting special needs of training new types of personnel, developing programs if none now exist, and encouraging the acquisition of advanced skills.

(*iii*) *Surveys of Organization and Operations.* Many criminal-justice agencies willing to consider making changes are not sure what their needs are or how their practices compare to the best practice of the field. They need experienced advice about how to put changes into effect. State and local officials whom the Commission has consulted have pointed out that ineffectual administration can negate otherwise promising attempts to increase effectiveness against crime, and have urged that the Federal program help with this problem.

Management studies already have a long history in law-enforcement. Organizations like the IACP and the Public Administration Service have conducted them since the 1920's. The Children's Bureau has provided specialized assistance to many of the juvenile courts. In corrections, the Bureau of Prisons provides increasingly extensive consulting services to local authorities, having recently set up a special office to do so. The Justice Department's new Office of Criminal Justice has been able, with a relatively small amount of explanation and advice, to help stimulate local bail reform efforts. These valuable services have touched but a few of the thousands of agencies that could benefit by surveys and expert advice.

The Commission does not believe that the Federal Government itself should provide the staff to conduct studies or advise the very large number of local agencies that might wish such services. Federal assistance should be aimed instead at developing State or regional bodies with the skills to perform these services. In addition, the Federal Government could contract with private groups to conduct surveys and studies. Advice and studies by expert groups could become a valuable adjunct to the continuing work of State and local planning bodies. For example, they could assist police agencies that desire to reorganize their community relations programs, or correctional agencies seeking to establish halfway houses. In such cases, the studies might be a forerunner to more substantial grant-in-aid support.

(*iv*) *Information Systems.* Another way in which the Federal Government can collaborate with State and local criminal justice systems is by helping to improve the collection and transmission of information needed by the police, courts, and correction agencies in their day-to-day work. The FBI already makes much important data available to local police agencies from its fingerprint files. The National Crime Information Center, now being developed by the FBI, will provide instantaneous response to computer inquiry by local agencies for information on stolen automobiles, wanted persons, certain identifiable types of stolen property, and the like.

In addition to this "hot" information, data on offenders needed by prosecutors, courts, and correctional authorities should be collected and made centrally available. The goal should be to develop an index drawn from the records of the criminal justice agencies across the country. With such an index a sentencing judge, for example, could learn where information might be found bearing on an offender's response to treatment in other jurisdictions. Disclosure of the information itself would remain, as at present, entirely within the discretion and control of the individual agency that held it. This would help avoid the dangers of developing national "dossiers," but would greatly speed collection of data for making decisions on disposition of cases—a major source of present delays and injustice.

At the State and local levels, enforcement activities against organized crime groups are for the most part non-existent or primitive. A principal need in this field is an effective system for receiving, analyzing, storing, and disseminating intelligence information. Many of organized crime's activities are national in scope, and even its small operations usually spill across city, county, and State lines. If investigators and prosecutors in separate jurisdictions are to make any headway at all against crime, they must work together; especially they must share information. There should be within the Department of Justice a computerized, central organized crime intelligence system that handles information from all over the country. This system should be the center of a federally supported network of State and regional intelligence systems, such as those now being developed in New York and in the New England States.

In addition to information needed for operations, there

should be available on a centralized basis statistical information on the criminal justice system itself. This is needed for assessing requirements and effectiveness. The FBI's Uniform Crime Reports service should be closely co-ordinated with this program, which also would include court, probation, prison, and parole statistics on such information as numbers and dispositions of cases, time intervals, and costs. Complementing such data would be special intensive surveys—of crime victims or insurance claims, for example—designed to ascertain more accurately the patterns of crime.

There are at present no centralized crime statistics apart from the UCR, although for many years it has been generally agreed in the field that the absence of information on all aspects of the criminal system has seriously impeded important research. Correlation of comprehensive statistics with surveys and other new methods for analyzing facts about crime is important not only to develop a national picture of crime's seriousness, but to provide a gauge by which police and other agencies can accurately determine the effect of their efforts on the amount of crime. The victimization survey undertaken by the Commission has shown the feasibility and usefulness of such surveys, in combination with UCR data, as the basis for statistical indices as comprehensive as those prepared by the Federal Government in the labor and agricultural fields.

(v) *Special Demonstration Projects.* The Federal administering agency should be authorized to finance in a few places major demonstration projects designed to show all cities and States how much major changes can improve the system of criminal justice. For example, support could be provided to a police force that was prepared, on the basis of an organization study, to make fundamental personnel, management, and operational changes ; or to a State or city wishing to plan for entirely new combinations of service between community-based correctional institutions and non-criminal agencies. The demonstration project authorization should also be broad enough to support co-operative programs under which various jurisdictions share needed services, such as police dispatching or short-term detention facilities, or even totally pooled police services.

In the earlier stages of the Federal program, these few major projects could serve at the primary laboratories for research and training, and the experience gained through them would provide a reference point for much of the work done by States and local communities under operational grants-in-aid. Thus, there should be special authorization for the systematic dissemination of the results of demonstration projects and for bringing State and local officials from other areas together to see model programs in operation.

(*vi*) *Science and Technology.* This report has shown that the skills and techniques of science and technology, which have so radically altered much of modern life, have been largely untapped by the criminal justice system. One extremely useful approach to innovation is the questioning, analytical, experimental approach of science. Systems' analysis, which has contributed significantly to such large-scale government programs as national defense and mass transportation, can be used to study criminal justice operations and to help agency officials choose promising courses of action.

Modern technology can make many specific contributions to criminal administration. The most significant will come from the use of computers to collect and analyze the masses of data the system needs to understand the crime control process. Other important contributions may come, for example, from flexible radio networks and portable two-way radios for patrol officers; computer assisted command-and-control systems for rapid and efficient dispatching of patrol forces; advanced fingerprint recognition systems; innovations for the police patrol car such as mobile teletypewriters, tape recorders for recording questioning, and automatic car position locators; alarms and surveillance systems for homes, businesses and prisons; and criminalistics techniques such as voice prints, neutron activation analysis and other modern laboratory instrumentation.

The Federal Government must take the lead in the effort to focus the capabilities of science and technology on the criminal justice system. In the first place, it can sponsor and support a continuing research and development program on a scale greater than any individual agency could undertake alone. Such a program will benefit all agencies. Secondly, it should stimulate the industrial development, at reasonable prices, of the kinds of equipment all agencies need. A useful technique might be to guarantee the sale of first production runs. Thirdly, it should provide funds that will enable criminal justice agencies to hire technically trained people and to establish internal operations research units. And, fourthly, it should support scientific research into criminal administration that uses the agencies as real-life laboratories.

(vii) *Research.* There is need for research of all kinds. There should be Federal support for specific research projects by individual scholars, and by universities or research organizations. In many instances such projects should be carried out in conjunction with large police departments, correctional institutions, or other operating agencies. In addition to such project grants, the Commission believes the Federal Government should provide support for a number of institutes specifically dedicated to research into crime and criminal justice. Such institutes would bring together top scholars from the social and natural sciences, law, social work, business administration, and psychiatry and would be able to deal with the criminal justice system, from prevention to corrections, as a whole. Presumably most of these research institutes would be located at universities, although one or more might be independent.

These institutes would serve as the foundation for the other parts of the Federal program described here, both in the substance of the research they undertook and in the availability of their staff members as top-level consultants. They could provide training, through special seminars or degree courses, for senior administrators and specialist personnel. They could undertake studies of the effectiveness of various education and training programs. They could provide much of the data needed to conduct organization and operations studies, and seek and test new techniques for implementation. They could take major responsibility for analyzing data developed by the national information systems and they would propose and evaluate important new demonstration programs and provide consulting services.

(viii) *Grants-in-aid Support for New Programs.* In addition to the forms of support described above, a major part of the Federal program should be grants-in-aid for a broad range of innovative State and local programs. The standards of this part of the program should preclude continuing support for such normal operational expenses as those for basic personnel compensation, routine equipment like police cars, or replacement of physical facilities like jails and courthouses. Support would instead be given to major innovations in operations, including especially the co-ordination of services among parts of the system of criminal administration and among agencies in different jurisdictions.

The possibilities for such programs are as wide as the range of innovations State and local authorities propose to undertake. They might include: new police operations such as the storefront Community Service Officer program, sophisticated communications equipment; and regional laboratory facilities; construction and operation of new corrections facilities to serve as a nucleus for community-based programs; and temporary salary support for new specialized personnel, such as computer experts, court management specialists, and classification or treatment experts for correctional facilities.

The Commision is confident that this eight-point programme, if fully implemented, will do much to bring crime under control.

Role of Citizens and their Organizations

Given enough time and money, specialists can do dramatic things. They can prolong human life. They can make deserts bloom. They can split the atom. They can put men on the moon. However, specialists alone cannot control crime. Crime is a social problem that is interwoven with almost every aspect of American life; controlling it involves changing the way schools are run and classes are taught, the way cities are planned and houses are built, the way businesses are managed and workers are hired. Crime is a kind of human behavior; controlling it means changing the minds and hearts of men. Controlling crime is the business of every American institution. Controlling crime is the business of every American.

That every American should co-operate fully with officers of justice is obvious. The police cannot solve crimes that are not reported to them; the courts cannot administer justice fairly and surely if citizens will not serve as witnesses and jurors. In an earlier society the peace was kept, for the most part, not by officials but by the whole community. Constables were citizens who served their community in turn and magistrates were local squires. That society no longer exists except, perhaps, in a few remote rural areas. But the complexity and anonymity of modern urban life, the existence of professional police forces and other institutions whose official duty it is to deal with crime, must not disguise the need—far greater today than in the village societies of the past—for citizens to report all crimes or suspicious incidents immediately; to co-operate with police investigations of crime; in short, to "get involved."

The Chicago Police Department has had much success with "Operation Crime-Stop," a formal campaign to involve citizens. A special police emergency number that connects callers directly to a dispatcher has been established and widely publicized. Citizens are urged to report suspicious occurrences and are given official commendation when they do report or help the police in other ways. Washington, D.C., and several other cities have similar programs. In some cities taxi drivers and other citizens with radios in their vehicles are organized to assist the police by transmitting information useful in apprehending offenders. Under some State statutes active concealment of a felony is itself an offense as it was at common law. Even if there are no special programs or penalties; every citizen should recognize that he is duty bound to assist the police.

People can do much to insure their own safety and that of their families and belongings by reducing the opportunities for crime. Many crimes would not occur if individuals had proper locks on their doors and windows and enough lighting to discourage prowlers, and if they took such simple preventive action as not letting newspapers or milk bottles accumulate as a sign that a house is unoccupied. Keys left in the ignition or an unlocked ignition account for more than 42 per cent of the cars that are stolen.

The citizen's responsibility runs far deeper than co-operating with officials and guarding against crime. Much more important is a proper respect for the law and for its official representatives. People who sneer at policemen, people who "cut corners" in their tax returns, landlords who violate housing codes, parents who set bad examples by their own disrespect for the law, or who wink at their children's minor offenses, contribute to crime. Delinquents—and adult criminals as well—often try to justify their actions by saying that the only difference between them and "respectable citizens" is that they were unlucky enough to be caught.

Participation by industry, Religious Institutions, and Other Private Groups. As members of groups and organizations outside the official agencies of justice, citizens can play even a greater part than they can as individuals in helping to reduce crime. Private businesses, welfare agencies and foundations, civic organizations, and universities can contribute much toward impelling official agencies to reform themselves. There are some impressive examples of what such groups can do when they turn their attention to crime.

In Chicago and New York the YMCA and other agencies supported by contributions pioneered the concept of "detached workers" for juvenile gangs. Research projects conducted by the Vera Institute of Justice in New York sparked the bail reform movement, and the Institute is now exploring new ways of handling drunks. Law schools and bar associations have led the development of legal aid and defender programs. Church groups in St. Louis and Chicago opened the first halfway houses for released prisoners. The student service organization at Harvard University was one of the first groups to run regular programs to teach prison inmates. Such projects indicate that private groups have a growing interest and involvement in crime problems, but they still do far less about crime than about such matters as health, education, or recreation.

Business, Industry, and Labor Unions. Business and industry are in a particularly favorable position to help the criminal justice system. They have the financial and technical resources that are essential both for developing new equipment to modernize law-enforcement and justice, and for devising means to protect against crime. The jobs they can provide can do much to prevent delinquency and reintegrate offenders into society.

The Commission's task force on science and technology explored a number of ways in which industry might apply technological innovations to protecting lives and property from crime. It discussed with the automobile industry, for example, such new ways to combat auto theft as ignitions that buzz when a key is left in a turned-off lock, or expel the key; special shielding around ignition cables to prevent "jumping"; and steering column or transmission locks. Automobile manufacturers have already assured the Commission that they will incorporate such devices in future models.

The same sort of effort is needed on such problems as making alarm systems less expensive and less susceptible to false alarms. Alteration of telephone equipment to permit free dialing to the police from public telephones, adoption of a uniform police number, and development of equipment that would automatically record the location from which the call is made are other examples of how private business could contribute to reducing crime.

There are several noteworthy recent examples of successful programs in which business, industry, and organised labor have collaborated with correctional authorities. For example, at the Federal penitentiary at Danbury, Conn. , the Dictograph Corp. trains in the penitentiary and then employs, on work release or parole, micro-soldering technicians for hearing aid manufacture; IBM trains key punch operators, programers and systems analysts, hiring some itself while others are employed elsewhere; and the International Ladies' Garment Workers' Union has established a program to train sewing machine repairmen on machines furnished by several local companies, and provides a card to graduates enabling them to find employment upon release.

The experience of the Bureau of Prisons with these programs indicates that there is a vast, largely untapped willingness on the part of business and labor to co-operate in employment programs in corrections. This bodes well for the success of the growing number of work-release programs in various States, and represents an encouraging change from industry's and labor's traditional hostility toward prison industries, expressed in restrictive State and Federal laws on prison industry activities. If employers overcome their reluctance to hire—and unions to admit persons with arrest or conviction records —and if irrational prohibitions on licensing such persons for occupations and trades are removed, correctional agencies will have much more chance to succeed in their task.

The co-operation of business and labor is also essential to make jobs available to young people from slum areas and to help give them the skills and attitudes necessary for success-ful integration into working life. Several companies have run programs for the Job Corps; many more have provided jobs through the Neighborhood Youth Corps and the Youth Opportunity Centres, both programs of the Department of Labor. But here, as with employment of offenders, much more can be done through less formal, entirely private, initiative. Chambers of commerce, labor union locals, and service clubs are logical bases for community programs to advise young people about employment and place them in jobs.

Individual employers, too, can contribute substantially to crime prevention through special programs to train and hire young people who have had some trouble with the law. There are obvious risks, though many can be offset through bonding— arranged perhaps with government guarantees. However much recruitment, training, and employment programs for delin-quents and ex-convicts may cost, the price cannot possibly be as great as that paid for the almost total failure, up to now, to bring criminals and potential criminals back into the working world.

Private Agencies and Foundations. Private social service agen-cies and foundations, concerned with counselling, health, and welfare aid, have long carried major responsibility for delin-quency prevention. Professional associations such as the International Association of Chiefs of Police, the National Council on Crime and Delinquency, the ABA and local bar associations, the American Law Institute, and others have led for many years the attempt to raise standards and rationalize the criminal justice system. In recent years a number of pri-vate organizations like the Ford Foundation have supported research and demonstration projects in various parts of the criminal area, bridging the gap between agencies active in the field and those that concentrate on planning and standard setting. Work of all these sorts is vitally necessary for compre-hensive progress in reducing crime. Private groups can identify needs and problems that have not been officially recognized and undertake programs that would be too experimental or controversial for public agencies.

There are, of course, distinct discouragements to work by private social agencies in the criminal area. Usually progress is very difficult to achieve. Those who need to be helped are often hostile, sometimes dangerous, and seldom promise to be truly outstanding citizens even if rehabilitated.

It is not surprising, then, that most private agencies, with very limited resources, have concentrated on serving persons whose problems are less intractable than those of the delinquent or the criminal. But the extent to which official agencies, even some anti-poverty programs, continue to shun people with criminal records emphasizes the importance of attention to the criminal area by private agencies that can better afford than official ones to risk the failures that are a necessary consequence of experimental work.

Religious Institutions. The important contribution churches, synagogues, and other religious institutions can make to crime prevention is evident. They are leading exponents and guardians of the community's moral and ethical standards. They have the ability to understand and teach in their largest context the great principles of honesty and honor, of compassion and charity, of respect and reverence, that underlie not only the country's laws but its entire being. They have the power to move men's spirits and sway their minds.

They have the power, too, to do many practical things. Many religious institutions and inner-city churches have done valuable work with youth gangs and released offenders. A particularly noteworthy contribution has been made by the Faith Opportunities Project of the Chicago Conference on Religion and Race. This project, partially financed by the Office of Economic Opportunity, makes a point of finding deserting fathers, particularly those who have deserted because they are unemployed, finding them jobs, and returning them to their families. During one six-month period 2,500 families were reunited, and 89 per cent of them remained that way for at least 90 days.

Community and Professional Organizations. The most dramatic example in the country of a citizens' group that has addressed itself forcefully and successfully to the problems of crime and criminal justice is the Anti-Crime Crusade in Indianapolis. In 1962, the day after a 90-year-old woman had been hit on the head and robbed on the street, 30 Indianapolis women, representing a cross section of the community, met to devise ways of making the streets safer. The organization, which has no dues, no membership cards, no minutes and no bylaws, now involves some 50,000 women, in 14 divisions. It has stimulated the city to improve street lighting. It has secured jobs for young people, helped school dropouts return to school, involved thousands of adolescents in volunteer work for social service agencies and clinics. It has organized campaigns for cleaning up the slums. It has sponsored police recruits. It has observed the operation of the courts and publicized their shortcomings. It has helped parole officers with their work. It has campaigned for pay raises for policemen and formed block clubs to improve slum neighborhoods. This list is only a random selection of the crusade's activities, and only an indication of what concerned citizens can do.

Every group in a community can do something about crime or criminal justice. PTA's and other school groups, for example, could concentrate on the school's role in delinquency prevention and reintegration of offenders; volunteer parents could promote closer contact with slum parents, lead field trips and other activities to compensate for culturally deprived backgrounds, tutor in remedial work, and serve as teacher aides. Suburban groups might pair with those in the inner city for such projects. Hospitals could join together to institute treatment centers for narcotics and drunkenness offenders. Businessmen's groups would be well suited to conducting employment programs. Neighborhood clubs and settlement houses have set up recreation centre and a wide range of other services. All of these efforts must be greatly strengthened, an endeavor that will require increased financial support by government and private foundations.

Bar associations and other professional groups have an important role in encouraging legislatures and official agencies to implement changes such as those recommended by this report. A special bar association group in Illinois, for example, drew up that State's pioneering new criminal code. This IACP has been active in promoting police standards and training councils. The National Council of Juvenile Court Judges has promoted reforms in juvenile justice. The American Bar Foundation is now publishing a series of volumes reflecting an intensive 10-year study of law-enforcement and criminal justice in three States, most of it completely new and of great importance.

Colleges and universities. Higher education has played an uneven part in criminal justice. A few law schools have engaged for years in research, and in representation of indigent defenders; their professors have been responsible for a major share of modern criminal legislation and much of the informed criticism of the criminal process. On the other hand, until recently, little emphasis was given to preparing students to practice criminal law. Universities like the University of California at Berkeley and Michigan State University have had police science departments for several decades, but they have existed too much in isolation from the rest of the academic community. To a large extent, the same thing is true of teaching and research in the corrections' field.

All operating agencies of justice urgently need the close contact with academic thought that could be achieved through use of faculty consultants; seminars and institutes to analyze current problems and innovations; advanced training programs for judges, police administrators, and correctional officers; and more operational research projects and surveys conducted in conjunction with agencies of justice.

CONCLUSION

At its end, as at its beginning, this report on crime and criminal justice in America must insist that there are no easy answers. The complexity and the magnitude of the task of controlling crime and improving criminal justice is indicated by the more than 200 specific recommendations for action, and the many hundreds of suggestions for action, that this report contains. These recommendations and suggestions are addressed to cities, to States, to the Federal Government; to individual citizens and their organizations; to policemen, to prosecutors, to judges, to correctional authorities, and to the agencies for which these officials work. Taken together these recommendations and suggestions express the Commission's deep conviction that if America is to meet the challenge of crime it must do more, far more, than it is doing now. It must welcome new ideas and risk new actions. It must spend time and money. It must resist those who point to scapegoats, who use facile slogans about crime by habit or for selfish ends. It must recognize that the government of a free society is obliged to act not only effectively but fairly. It must seek knowledge and admit mistakes.

Controlling crime in America is an endeavor that will be slow and hard and costly. But America can control crime if it will.

TABLE OF RECOMMENDATIONS

The Commission's study of the nature, volume, and trends of crime in America reveals at many points the need to develop additional and improved information and understanding about it. To assist each city administration and agency of justice in insuring that its citizens are being informed of the full rate of crime in their community, the Commission recommends that cities and police departments that have not already done so adopt centralized procedures for handling reports of crime from citizens and establish the staff controls necessary to make such procedures effective. To promote a clearer public understanding of the differences between crimes of violence and property crimes, the Commission recomends that the trend in the FBI's Uniform Crime Reports toward separate treatment of these crime categories be carried further and that the present Index of reported crime be broken into wholly two separate parts.

(1) Adopt centralized procedures in each city for handling crime reports from citizens, with controls to make those procedures effective.

(2) Separate the present Index of reported crime into two wholly separate parts, one for crimes of violence and one for crimes against property.

Juvenile Delinquency and Youth Crime

The most effective way to prevent crime is to assure all citizens full opportunity to participate in the benefits and responsibilities of society. Especially in inner cities, achievement of this goal will require extensive overhauling and strengthening of the social institutions influential in making young people strong members of the community—schools, employment, the family, religious institutions, housing, welfare, and others. Careful planning and evaluation, and enormous increases in money and personel are needed to expand existing programs of promise and to develop additional approaches.

Such efforts are especially crucial for those youths, now too often overlooked, who have already demonstrated delinquent tendencies. The community must not wait until such tendencies manifest themselves in serious criminal acts. Measures short of formal adjudication can help such youths find their way to appropriate assistance programs, and minimize the reinforcing and stigmatizing effects of full criminal treatment. For this purpose Youth Services Bureaus should be established to co-ordinate and provide needed programs. The bureaus should accept both delinquents and non-delinquents but devote special resources to intensive treatment of delinquents.

The formal juvenile justice system should concentrate on those cases in which a need for coercive court authority has been demonstrated. Proceedings in these more serious cases must be characterized by safeguards commonly accepted as necessary to protect persons subject to coercive State authority, including counsel, confrontation of complainants, and exclusion of improper evidence. At all stages in the juvenile justice system, there is need for greater clarification and regularization in the exercise of discretion. Detention pending court determination, for example, must be based on clearly articulated standards and reduced to a minimum. The police in their dealings with juveniles should attempt to divert cases from the criminal process wherever appropriate and without coercive stationhouse adjustment procedures. In exercising discretion the police should also observe the most scrupulous standards of procedural fairness and personal impartiality.

Housing and Recreation
(3) Expand efforts to improve housing and recreation.

Families
(4) Develop methods to provide minimum income.

(5) Revise welfare regulations so that they contribute to keeping family together.

(6) Insure availability of family-planning assistance.

(7) Expand counselling and therapy.

(8) Provide assistance in problems of domestic management and child care.

(9) Develop activities that involve the whole family together.

Involving Youths in Community Life
(10) Involve youths in community activities.

(11) Employ young people as subprofessional aids.

(12) Establish Youth Services Bureaus to provide and co-ordinate programs for delinquents and non-delinquents.

(13) Increase involvement of religious institutions, private social agencies, other groups in youth programs.

(14) Provide residential centers.

Schools
(15) Provide financial support for needed personnel and facilities.

(16) Improve the quality of teachers and facilities.

(17) Reduce racial and economic segregation.

(18) Compensate for inadequate preschool preparation.

(19) Develop better means for dealing with behavior problems.

(20) Use instructional material more revelant to inner city life.

(21) Encourage students capable of higher eduction to pursue their education.

(22) Revise programs for students not going to college.

(23) Expand job placement by schools.

(24) Increase contacts between the school and the community.

Employment

(25) Prepare youth more adequately for employment.

(26) Provide easily accessible employment information.

(27) Eliminate irrational barriers to employment.

(28) Create new job opportunities.

Juvenile Justice System

(29) Formulate police department guidelines for handling of juveniles.

(30) Train police officers in handling of adolescents.

(31) Limit police custody of juveniles to instances where there is objective specific suspicion.

(32) Maintain confidential records of all frisks and extended interrogations of juveniles.

(33) Limit stationhouse adjustment of cases by police.

(34) Provide alternatives to adjudication through Youth Services Bureau.

(35) Increase referrals to community agencies.

(36) Employ voluntary preliminary conference at intake.

(37) Adopt consent decree as alternative to adjudication.

(38) Narrow juvenile court jurisdiction over non-criminal matters.

(39) Restrict prehearing detention and provide separate detention facilities for juveniles.

(40) Provide particularised notice in advance of hearings.

(41) Provide counsel wherever coercive action is possible.

(42) Divide court hearing into adjudicatory and dispositional proceedings.

Police

Widespread improvement in the strength and caliber of police manpower, supported by a radical revision of personnel practices, are the basic essentials for achieving more effective and fairer law-enforcement. Educational requirements should be raised to college levels and training programs improved. Recruitment and promotion should be modernized to reflect education, personality, and assessment of performance. The traditional, monolithic personnel structure must be broken up into three entry levels of varying responsibility and with different personnel requirements, and lateral entry into advanced positions encouraged.

The need is urgent for the police to improve relations with the poor, minority groups, and juveniles. The establishment of strong community relations programs, review of all procedures in light of their effect on community relations, recruitment of more minority group members, and strengthening of community confidence in supervision and discipline, all aim at making the police more effective in high-crime areas. Increased effectiveness also requires that law-enforcement improve its facilities and techniques of management—particularly that it utilize manpower more efficiently, modernize communications and records, and formulate more explicit policy guidelines governing areas of police discretion. The pooling of services and functions by police forces in each metropolitan area can improve efficiency and effectiveness.

Community Relations

(43) Establish community relations, units in departments serving substantial minority population.

(44) Establish citizen advisory committees in minority-group neighborhoods.

(45) Recruit more minority-group officers.

(46) Emphasize community relations in training and operations.

(47) Provide adequate procedures for processing citizen grievances against all public officials.

Personnel

(48) Divide functions and personnel entry and promotion lines among three kinds of officers.

(49) Assess manpower needs and provide more personnel if required.

(50) Recruit more actively, especially on college campuses and in inner cities.

(51) Increase police salaries, especially maximums, to competitive levels.

(52) Consider police salaries apart from those of other municipal departments.

(53) Set as goal requirement of baccalaureate degree for general enforcement officers.

(54) Require immediately baccalaureate degrees for supervisory positions.

(55) Improve screening of candidates to determine character and fitness.

(56) Modify inflexible physical, age, and residence recruitment requirements.

(57) Stress ability in promotion.

(58) Encourage lateral entry to specialist and supervisory positions.

(59) Require minimum of 400 hours of training.

(60) Improve training methods and broaden coverage of non-technical background subjects.

(61) Require one-week yearly minimum of intensive inservice training and encourage continued education.

(62) Require 12-18 months' probation and evaluation of recruits.

(63) Establish police standards commissions.

Organization and Operations

(64) Develop and enunciate policy guidelines for exercise of law-enforcement discretion.

(65) Clarify by statute authority of police to stop persons for questioning.

(66) Include police formally in community planning.

(67) Provide State assistance for management surveys.

(68) Employ legal advisers.

(69) Strengthen central staff control.

(70) Create administrative boards of key ranking personnel in larger departments.

(71) Establish strong internal investigation units in all departments to maintain police integrity.

(72) Experiment with team policing combining patrol and investigative duties.

(73) Adopt policy limiting use of firearms by officers.

Pooling of Resources and Services

(74) Provide areawide communications and records co-ordination.

(75) Pool and co-ordinate crime laboratories.

(76) Assist smaller departments in major investigations.

(77) Explore pooling or consolidation of law-enforcement in all counties or metropolitan areas.

Courts

A number of important reforms are necessary to enable courts to operate with the dignity and effectiveness which many of them now lack. Substantial changes in the processing of criminal cases and increases in the number and caliber of judges, lawyers, and administrators are essential to fairer and more effective justice. To rationalize procedures in the crucial and often neglected pretrial stage, bail practices must be re-formed; guilty plea negotiation regularized; and discovery expanded. Early diversion of appropriate cases to non-criminal treatment should be encouraged. Sentencing reforms—such as revision of criminal codes, improved fact-gathering, sentencing councils and institutes for judges—are needed to promote consistent and informed decisions.

The right of defendants to counsel must be extended and defense counsel's role broadened. Improvements must be made in the methods used to select, compensate, and educate counsel. Better procedures are needed to remove judges from political influence and supervise their performance. Several Commission recommendations are aimed at strengthening prosecutors' offices, and encouraging better formation of policy guidelines and procedures for the exercise of discretion. State governments should take a more vigorous role in co-ordinating local prosecution through stronger State attorney generals and the creation of State councils of prosecutors.

Court structures should be reformed to unify felony and misdemeanor courts, overhaul or abolish the justice of the peace system, and provide firm, central administrative responsibility within the courts. The procedures used by the courts to monitor and schedule their work should be modernized and professional talent brought to the administration of courts.

The Lower Courts

(78) Unify felony and misdemeanor courts.

(79) Increase judicial manpower and modernize physical facilities.

(80) Provide prosecutors, defense counsel, and probation officers in courts now lacking them.

(81) Abolish or overhaul State justice of the peace and U.S. commissioner systems.

Initial Stages of a Criminal Case

(82) Establish bail projects.

(83) Enact comprehensive State bail reform legislation.

(84) Establish stationhouse release and summons procedures.

(85) Improve decisions on which defendants should and should not be charged.

(86) Insure fair and visible negotiated guilty pleas.

(87) Develop and share dispositional information early in case.

Court Proceedings

(88) Establish standards for publicity in criminal cases.

(89) Expand pretrial discovery by defense and prosecution.

(90) Provide single, simple State postconviction procedure.

(91) Extend prosecution's right to appeal from pretrial rulings suppressing evidence or confessions.

(92) Enact general witness immunity statutes and co-ordinate immunity grants under them.

(93) Eliminate special standards of proof in perjury cases.

Sentencing Policies and Procedures

(94) Revise sentencing provisions of penal codes.

(95) Consider whether to retain capital punishment.

(96) Establish probation services in all courts for presentence investigation of every offender.

(97) Permit defense counsel broader access to presentence reports.

(98) Expand sentencing institutes and conferences.

(99) Abolish jury sentencing in non-capital cases.

(100) Institute procedures for promoting just and uniform sentencing.

Officers of Justice

(101) Improve selection of judges through better screening.

(102) Provide judicial tenure of at least 10 years.

(103) Establish commissions on judicial conduct with power to discipline or require retirement.

(104) Institute salary and selection reforms for prosecutors.

(105) Co-ordinate local prosecutors through State attorneys general and prosecutor's councils.

(106) Establish programs for training prosecutors.

(107) Extend early provision of counsel for indigents.

(108) Institute State-financed, co-ordinated assigned counsel or defender systems.

(109) Expand training programs for defense counsel.

Court Scheduling, Management and Organization

(110) Create single, unified State court systems.

(111) Centralize administrative responsibility.

(112) Institute timetable for completion of criminal cases.

(113) Utilize experts in business management and business machine systems.

(114) Improve facilities and compensation for witnesses and jurors.

Corrections

The wholesale strengthening of community treatment of offenders and much greater commitment of resources to their rehabilitation are the main lines where action is needed to make correctional treatment more effective in reducing recidivism. Correctional programs of the future should be built around small centers, located in the communities they serve. These would be better suited than present facilities for flexible treatment, combining the short-term commitment sufficient for most offenders with a variety of partial release or community corrections programs in which job training, educational and counselling services would be provided or co-ordinated by the center's staff. Careful screeing and classificatión of offenders is essential so that handling can be individualized to suit the needs in each case. So, too, is greater emphasis on evaluation of the effect of various programs on different offenders.

Much can be done to advance corrections toward such goals with existing facilities, but large increases in skilled diagnostic, rehabilitation, and research personnel are needed immediately. A new regime should be inaugurated in institutions to involve all staff, and encourage inmates to collaborate as much as possible, in rehabilitation. Prison industries give more meaningful work experience. Counselling, education and vocational training programs for inmates must be strengthened. Greater use should be made of release for work and education, of halfway houses, and of similar programs to ease the offender's reintegration in society.

Community-based Corrections

(115) Make parole and probation supervision available for all offenders.

(116) Provide for mandatory supervision of released offenders not paroled.

(117) Increase number of probation and parole officers.

(118) Use volunteers and sub-professional aides.

(119) Develop new methods to reintegrate offenders by mobilizing community institutions.

(120) Make funds available to purchase services otherwise unobtainable for offenders.

(121) Vary caseload size and treatment according to offender needs.

(122) Develop more intensive community treatment programs as alternative to institutionalization.

Correctional Institutions

(123) Establish with State and Federal funds small-unit institutions in cities for community-oriented treatment.

(124) Operate institutions with joint responsibility of staff and inmates for rehabilitation.

(125) Upgrade education and vocational training for inmates.

((126) Establish State programs to recruit and train instructors.

(127) Improve prison industries through joint State programs and Federal assistance.

(128) Expand graduated release and furlough programs.

(129) Integrate local jails and misdemeanant institution with State corrections.

(130) Provide separate detention facilities for juveniles.

(131) House and handle persons awaiting trial separately from convicts.

(132) Provide separate treatment to special offenders groups, through pooling or sharing among jurisdictions.

Correctional Decision-making

(133) Strengthen diagnostic and screening resources.

(134) Appoint parole boards solely on basis of merit, providing training and requiring full-time service.

(135) Develop standards and procedures to insure fairness to offenders in decisions affecting them.

Research and Training

(136) Improve university research and training in corrections.

Organized Crime

Success in combating organized crime will require a greater commitment of resources and imagination at all levels of government, directed toward investigation and prosecution and also toward attacking criminal syndicates through regulatory laws. A co-ordinated network of investigative and prosecutive units is needed, provided with legal tools necessary for gathering evidence—including investigating grand juries and the power to grant witnesses immunity. Investigation must be carried out with a broader focus than merely the prosecution of individual cases; research for building longer range plans should draw on sociologists, economists, and experts from other disciplines.

Proof of Criminal Violations

(137) Impanel annual investigative grand juries.

(138) Provide right of appeal for grand juries to obtain special investigators and prosecutors.

(139) Enact general witness immunity statutes and co-ordinate immunity grants.

(140) Eliminate special standards of proof in perjury cases.

(141) Clarify law regarding wiretapping and eavesdropping.

(142) Provide power to impose extended sentences on organized crime leaders.

(143) Extend prosecution's right to appeal from pretrial rulings suppressing evidence or confessions.

(144) Establish Federal residential facilities to protect witnesses.

Investigation and Prosecution Units

(145) Form organized crime intelligence units in offices of State attorney generals and local police departments.

(146) Assign special prosecutorial manpower to organized crime cases.

(147) Create computerized central Federal intelligence office.

(148) Expand staff of Organized Crime and Racketeering (OCR) Section in U.S. Justice Department.

(149) Give OCR Section authority over U.S. attorneys on organized crime cases.

(150) Furnish Federal technical assistance and training to local jurisdictions.

(151) Provide Federal assistance for development of State and regional intelligence systems.

(152) Encourage research.

(153) Create permanent joint congressional committee on organized crime.

(154) Establish permanent State and citizens crime commissions.

Non-criminal Controls

(155) Use existing regulatory authority against businesses

controlled by organized crime.

(156) Encourage private business groups to prevent and uncover criminal business tactics.

(157) Increase new coverage on organized crime.

(158) Brief local government officials regularly on organized crime.

Narcotics and Drug Abuse

The growing problem of narcotics and drug abuse in this country must be attacked by strengthening all approaches: law-enforcement, rehabilitation and treatment of drug users, and public education on the dangers involved. This is partly a matter of increased resources, such as for customs control; for the Bureaus of Narcotics (especially to strengthen its long-range intelligence); and for expansion of treatment. There is also need for intensified research, and for careful implementation, evaluation, and co-ordination of the many new and promising programs for contol.

Enforcement

(159) Increase staffs of Bureaus of Customs and Narcotics.

(160) Adopt State drug abuse control legislation.

(161) Amend Federal drug abuse control law to strengthen record-keeping provisions.

(162) Revise sentencing laws to give adequate flexibility.

Research and Education

(163) Undertake research with respect to regulation of drugs.

(164) Conduct research at National Institute of Mental Health (NIMH) on marijhuana use.

Drunkenness

Present efforts to find alternatives to treatment of drunkenness within the criminal system should be pursued vigorously. One of the most promising possibilities is the construction of detoxification centers with medical services and therapy for short-term detention. A network of aftercare facilities and services should also be established to which referrals could be made after diagnosis at a detoxification center.

(165) Eliminate criminal treatment of drunkenness when not accompanied by disorderly or otherwise unlawful conduct.

(166) Establish civil detoxification centers.

(167) Co-ordinate and extend aftercare programs.

(168) Expand research.

Control of Firearms

The increasing violence in the country demands that governments, at all levels, strengthen control of possession and sale of the firearms that contribute to that violence. Additional laws requiring registration of firearms and permits for those who possess or carry them, prohibiting their sale to and possession by certain potentially dangerous persons, and preventing transportation and sale of military-type weapons are needed. Such restrictions would not need to interfere with legitimate sporting or antique-collecting interests.

(169) Enact laws prohibiting transportation and possession of military-type weapons.

(170) Prohibit potentially dangerous persons from acquiring firearms.

(171) Require registration of handguns, rifles, and shotguns.

(172) Require permit for possessing or carrying a handgun.

(173) Prohibit interstate sale of handguns and regulate such sales of other firearms.

Science and Technology

The potential contributions of science and technology in the field of law-enforcement and criminal justice have scarcely been tapped; a strong research program to develop them is necessary. This program should be initiated through Federal support. It should cover both basic research studies and systems' analysis, and development of specific technological innovations. The Commission's task force on science and technology explored a number of specific areas where science might make a contribution, particularly in increasing law-enforcement effectiveness. It found a number of lines for improving police response-time for apprehension of crminals. Co-ordinated information systems covering immediate-response inquiries, law-enforcement criminal records information, and statistics on criminal justice agency operations should be established.

Police Operations

(174) Undertake studies in large police departments of crimes, arrests, and operations.

(175) Permit public access to police callboxes.

(176) Establish single, uniform police telephone number.

(177) Develop computer-assisted command-and-control systems.

(178) Develop police radio networks.

(179) Require metropolitan areas to co-ordinate requests to FCC for additional frequencies.

(180) Make greater use of multichannel radio trunks.

(181) Consider allocation portions of TV spectrum to police use.

(182) Establish Federal project to underwrite initial costs of new radio equipment.

(183) Initiate research on new fingerprint recognition system.

(184) Undertake experiments to improve statistical procedures for manpower allocation.

Court Operations

(185) Expand pilot use of simulation studies of court systems.

Correctional Operations

(186) Develop statistical aids for sentencing and treatment.

Information Systems

(187) Establish criminal information systems.

(188) Establish National Criminal Justice Statistics Center.

General Federal Research and Assistance

(189) Sponsor science and technology research and development program.

(190) Co-ordinate establishment of equipment standards.

(191) Provide technical assistance to criminal justice agencies.

(192) Support operation research staff in large criminal justice agencies.

(193) Support scientific and technological research in research institute.

Research

Expanded research is essential for preventing crime and improving the effectiveness of criminal justice. It must be conducted by operating agencies; universities, foundations, and research corporations; private industry; and government institutes. It must attempt a more complete assessment of the volume, nature, and causes of crime. It must look more carefully at the way the criminal justice system operates. Change need not await upon the gaining of such knowledge; only through innovation and evaluation of operations can most of it be obtained.

(194) Organize research units in criminal justice agencies.

(195) Give public and private support to criminal research institutes in various parts of the country.

(196) Expand research efforts of universities, foundations, and other private groups.

(197) Provide funds to individuals and organizations with promising research programs.

(198) Establish a National Foundation for Criminal Research.

SUMMARY

This report is about crime in America—about those who commit it, about those who are its victims, and about what can be done to reduce it.

The report is the work of 19 commissioners, 63 staff members, 175 consultants, and hundreds of advisers. The commissioners, staff, consultants, and advisers come from every part of the country and represent a broad range of opinion and profession.

In the process of developing the findings and recommendations of the report the Commission called three national conferences, conducted five national surveys, held hundreds of meetings, and interviewed tens of thousands of persons.

The report makes more than 200 specific recommendations—concrete steps, which the Commission believes can lead to a safer and better society. These recommendations call for a greatly increased effort on the part of the Federal Government, the States, the countries, the cities, civic organizations, religious institutions, business groups, and individual citizens. They call for basic changes in the operations of police, schools, prosecutors, employment agencies, defenders, social workers, prisons, housing authorities, and probation and parole officers.

But the recommendations are more than just a list of new procedures, new tactics, and new techniques; they call for a revolution in the way America looks at crime.

Many Americans take comfort in the view that crime is the vice of a handful of people. This view is inaccurate. In the United States today, one in six boys is referred to the juvenile court. A Commission survey shows that in 1965 more than two million Americans were received in prisons or juvenile training schools, or placed on probation. Another Commission study suggests that about 40 per cent of all male children now living in the United States will be arrested for a non-traffic offense during their lives. An independent survey of 1,700 persons found that 91 per cent of the sample admitted they had committed acts for which they might have received jail or prison sentences.

Many Americans also think of crime as a very narrow range of behavior. It is not. An enormous variety of acts make up the "crime problem." Crime is not just a tough teenager snatching a lady's purse. It is a professional thief stealing cars "on order." It is a well-heeled loan shark taking over a previously legitimate business for organized crime. It is a polite young man who suddenly and inexplicably murders his family. It is a corporation executive conspiring with competitors to keep prices high. No single formula, no single theory, no single generalization can explain the vast range of behavior called crime.

Many Americans think controlling crime is solely the task of the police, the courts, and correction agencies. In fact, as the Commission's report makes clear, crime cannot be controlled without the interest and participation of schools, businesses, social agencies, private groups, and individual citizens.

What, then, is America's experience with crime and how has this experience shaped the country's way of living? A new insight into these two questions is furnished by the Commission's National Survey of Criminal Victims. In this survey—the first of its kind conducted on such a scale—10,000 representative American households were asked about their experiences with crime, whether they reported those experiences to the police, and how those experiences affected their lives.

An important finding of the survey is that there is far more crime than ever is reported. Burglaries occur about three times more often than they are reported to police. Aggravated assaults and larcenies over $50 occur twice as often as they are reported. There are 50 per cent more robberies than are reported. In some areas, only one-tenth of the total number of certain kinds of crimes are reported to the police. Seventy-four per cent of the neighborhood commercial establishments surveyed do not report to police the thefts committed by their employees.

The existence of crime, the talk about crime, the reports of crime, and the fear of crime have eroded the basic quality of life of many Americans. A Commission study conducted in high crime areas of two large cities found that 43 per cent of the respondents stay off the streets at night because of their fear of crime; 35 per cent do not speak to strangers any more because of their fear of crime; 21 per cent use cars and cabs at night because of their fear of crime; and 20 per cent would like to move to another neighborhood because of their fear of crime.

The findings of the Commission's national survey generally support those of the local surveys. One-third of a representative sample of all Americans say it is unsafe to walk alone at night in their neighborhoods. Slightly more than one-third say they keep firearms in the house for protection against criminals. Twenty-eight per cent say they keep watch-dogs for the same reason.

Under any circumstance, developing an effective response to the problem of crime in America is exceedingly difficult. And because of the changes expected in the population in the next decade, it will become more difficult in the years to come. Young people commit a disproportionate share of crime and the number of young people in our society is growing at a much faster rate than the total population. Although the 15- to 17-year-old age group represents only 5.4 per cent of the population, it accounts for 12.8 per cent of all arrests. Fifteen and sixteen year olds have the highest arrest rate in the United States. The problem in the years ahead is dramatically fore-told by the fact that 23 per cent of the population is 10 or under.

Despite the seriousness of the problem today and the increasing challenge in the years ahead, the central conclusion of the Commission is that a significant reduction in crime is possible if the following objectives are vigorously pursued:

First, society must seek to prevent crime before it happens by assuring all Americans a stake in the benefits and responsi-bilities of American life, by strengthening law enforcement, and by reducing criminal opportunities.

Secondly, society's aim of reducing crime would be better served if the system of criminal justice developed a far broa-der range of techniques with which to deal with individual offenders.

Thirdly, the system of criminal justice must eliminate exist-ing injustices if it is to achieve its ideals and win the respect and co-operation of all citizens.

Fourthly, the system of criminal justice must attract more people and better people—police, prosecutors, judges, defense attorneys, probation and parole officers, and corrections offi-cials with more knowledge, expertise, initiative, and integrity.

Fifthly, there must be much more operational and basic research into the problems of crime and criminal administra-tion, by those who are within and without the system of cri-minal justice.

Sixthly, the police, courts, and correctional agencies must be given substantially greater amounts of money if they are to improve their ability to control crime.

Seventhly, individual citizens, civic and business organizations, religious institutions, and all levels of government must take responsibility for planning and implementing the changes that must be made in the criminal justice system if crime is to be reduced.

In terms of specific recommendations, what do these seven objectives mean?

Preventing Crime

The prevention of crime covers a wide range of activities: eliminating social conditions closely associated with crime; improving the ability of the criminal justice system to detect, apprehend, judge, and reintegrate into their communities those who commit crimes; and reducing the situations in which crimes are most likely to be committed.

Every effort must be made to strengthen the family, now often shattered by the grinding pressures of urban slums.

Slum schools must be given enough resources to make them as good as schools elsewhere and to enable them to compensate for the various handicaps suffered by the slum child, so that he can be rescued him from his environment.

Present efforts to combat school segregation, and the housing segregation that underlies it, must be continued and expanded.

Employment opportunities must be enlarged and young people provided with more effective vocational training and individual job counselling. Programs to create new kinds of jobs—such as probation aides, medical assistants, and teacher helpers—seem particularly promising and should be expanded.

The problem of increasing the ability of the police to detect and apprehend criminals is complicated. In one effort to find out how this objective could be achieved, the Commission conducted an analysis of 1,905 crimes reported to the Los Angeles Police Department during a recent month. The study showed the importance of identifying the perpetrator at the scene of the crime. Eighty-six per cent of the crimes with named suspects were solved, but only 12 per cent of the unnamed suspect crimes were solved. Another finding of the study was that there is a relationship between the speed of response and certainty of apprehension. On the average, response to emergency calls resulting in arrests was 50 per cent faster than response to emergency calls not resulting in arrest. On the basis of this finding, and a cost effectiveness study to discover the best means to reduce response time, the Commission recommends an experimental program to develop computer-aided command-and-control systems for large police departments.

To insure the maximum use of such a system, headquarters must have a direct link with every onduty police officer. Because large scale production would result in a substantial reduction of the cost of miniature two-way radios, the Commission recommends that the Federal Government initiate a development program for such equipment and that it consider guaranteeing the sale of the first production lot of perhaps 20,000 units.

Two other steps to reduce police response time are recommended: (i) police callboxes, which are locked and inconspicuous in most cities, should be left open, brightly marked, and designated "public emergency callboxes"; and (ii) the telephone company should develop a single police number for each metropolitan area, and eventually for the entire United States.

Improving the effectiveness of law enforcement, however, is much more than just improving police response time. For example a study in Washington, D.C., found that courtroom time for a felony defendant who pleads guilty probably totals less than one hour, while the time from his initial appearance to his disposition is four months.

In an effort to discover how courts can best speed the process of criminal justice, the known facts about felony cases in Washington were placed in a computer and the operation of the system was simulated. After a number of possible solutions to the problem of delay were tested, it appeared that the addition of a second grand jury—which, with supporting personnel, would cost less than $50,000 a year—would result in a 25 per cent reduction in the time required for the typical felony case to move from initial appearance to trial.

The application of such analysis—when combined with the Commission's recommended timetable laying out timespans for each step in the criminal process—should help court systems to ascertain their procedural bottlenecks and develop ways to eliminate them.

Another way to prevent crime is to reduce the opportunity to commit it. Many crimes would not be committed, indeed many criminal careers would not begin, if there were fewer opportunities for crime.

Auto theft is a good example. According to FBI statistics, the key had been left in the ignition or the ignition had been left unlocked in 42 per cent of all stolen cars. Even in those cars taken when the ignition was locked, at least 20 per cent were stolen simply by shorting the ignition with such simple devices as paper clips or tinfoil. In one city, the elimination of the unlocked "off" position on the 1965 Chevrolet resulted in 50 per cent fewer of those models being stolen in 1965 than were stolen in 1964.

On the basis of these findings, it appears that an important reduction in auto theft could be achieved simply by installing an ignition system that automatically ejects the key when the engine is turned off.

A major reason that it is important to reduce auto theft is that stealing a car is very often the criminal act that starts a boy on a course of lawbreaking.

Stricter gun controls also would reduce some kinds of crime. Here, the Commission recommends a strengthening of the Federal law governing the interstate shipment of firearms and enactment of State laws requiring the registration of all hand-guns, rifles, and shotguns, and prohibiting the sale or ownership of firearms by certain categories of persons—dangerous criminals, habitual drunkards, and drug addicts. After five years, the Commission recommends that Congress pass a Federal registration law applying to those States that have not passed their own registration laws.

New Ways of Dealing with Offenders

The Commission's second objective—the development of a far broader range of alternatives for dealing with offenders—

is based on the belief that, while there are some who must be completely segregated from society, there are many instances in which segregation does more harm than good. Furthermore, by concentrating the resources of the police, the courts, and correctional agencies on the smaller number of offenders who really need them, it should be possible to give all offenders more effective treatment.

A specific and important example of this principle is the Commission's recommendation that every community consider establishing a Youth Services Bureau, a community-based center to which juveniles could be referred by the police, the courts, parents, schools, and social agencies for counselling, education, work, or recreation programs and job placement.

The Youth Services Bureau—an agency to handle many troubled and troublesome young people outside the criminal system—is needed in part because society has failed to give the juvenile court the resources that would allow it to function as its founders hoped it would. In a recent survey of juvenile court judges, for example, 83 per cent said no psychologist or psychiatrist was available to their courts on a regular basis and one-third said they did not have probation officers or social workers. Even where there are probation officers, the Commission found, the average officer supervises 76 probationers, more than double the recommended caseload.

The California Youth Authority, for the last five years, has been conducting a controlled experiment to determine the effectiveness of another kind of alternative treatment program for juveniles. There, after initial screening, convicted juvenile delinquents are assigned on a random basis to either an experimental group or a control group. Those in the experimental group are returned to the community and receive intensive individual counselling, group counselling, group therapy, and family counselling. Those in the control group are assigned to California's regular institutional treatment program. The findings so far: 28 per cent of the experimental group have had their paroles revoked, compared with 52 per cent in the control group. Furthermore, the community treatment program is less expensive than institutional treatment.

To make community-based treatment possible for both adults and juveniles, the Commission recommends the development of an entirely new kind of correctional institution: located close to population centers; maintaining close relations with schools, employers, and universities; housing as few as 50 inmates; serving as a classification center, as the center for various kinds of community programs and as a port of re-entry to the community for those difficult and dangerous offenders who have required treatment in facilities with tighter custody.

Such institutions would be useful in the operation of programs—strongly recommended by the Commission—that permit selected inmates to work or study in the community during the day and return to control at night, and programs that permit long-term inmates to become adjusted to society gradually rather than being discharged directly from maximum security institutions to the streets.

Another aspect of the Commission's conviction, that different offenders with different problems should be treated in different ways, is its recommendation about the handling of public drunkenness, which, in 1965, accounted for one out of every three arrests in America. The great number of these arrests—some two million—burdens the police, clogs the lower courts, and crowds the penal institutions. The Commission therefore recommends that communities develop civil detoxification units and comprehensive aftercare programs, and that with the development of such programs, drunkenness, not accompanied by other unlawful conduct, should not be a criminal offense.

Similarly, the Commission recommends the expanded use of civil commitment for drug addicts.

Eliminating Unfairness

The third objective is to eliminate injustices so that the system of criminal justice can win the respect and co-operation of all citizens. Our society must give the police and the correctional agencies the resources and the mandate to provide fair and dignified treatment for all.

The Commission found overwhelming evidence of institutional shortcomings in almost every part of the United States.

A survey of the lower court operations in a number of

large American cities found cramped and noisy courtrooms, undignified and perfunctory procedures, and badly trained personnel overwhelmed by enormous caseloads. In short, the Commission found assembly line justice.

The Commission found that in at least three States, justices of the peace are paid only if they convict and collect a fee from the defendant, a practice held unconstitutional by the Supreme Court 40 years ago.

The Commission found that approximately one-fourth of the 400,000 children detained in 1965—for a variety of causes including truancy, smoking, and running away from home— were held in adult jails and lockups, often with hardened criminals.

In addition to the creation of new kinds of institutions— such as the Youth Services Bureau and the small, community-based correctional centers—the Commission recommends several important procedural changes. It recommends counsel at various points in the criminal process.

For juveniles, the Commission recommends providing counsel whenever coercive action is a possibility.

For adults, the Commission recommends providing counsel to any criminal defendant who faces a significant penalty— excluding traffic and similar petty charges—if he cannot afford to provide counsel for himself.

In connection with this recommendation, the Commission asks each State to finance regular, statewide assigned counsel and defender systems for the indigent.

Counsel also should be provided in parole and probation revocation hearings.

Another kind of broad procedural change that the Commission recommends is that every State, county, and local jurisdiction provide judicial officers with sufficient information about individual defendants to permit the release without money bail of those who can be safely released.

In addition to eliminating the injustice of holding persons charged with a crime merely because they cannot afford bail, this recommendation also would save a good deal of money. New York City alone, for example, spends approximately $10 million a year holding persons who have not yet been found guilty of any crime.

Besides institutional injustices, the Commission found that while the great majority of criminal justice and law-enforcement personnel perform their duties with fairness and understanding even under the most trying circumstances, some take advantage of their official positions and act in a callous, corrupt, or brutal manner.

Injustice will not yield to simple solutions. Overcoming it requires a wide variety of remedies including improved methods of selecting personnel, the massive infusion of additional funds, the revamping of existing procedures and the adoption of more effective internal and external controls.

The relations between the police and urban poor deserve special mention. Here the Commission recommends that every large department—especially in communities with substantial minority population—should have community-relations machinery consisting of a headquarters planning and supervising unit and precinct units to carry out recommended programs. Effective citizen advisory committees should be established in minority group neighborhoods. All departments with substantial minority populations should make special efforts to recruit minority group officers and to deploy and promote them fairly. They should have rigorous internal investigation units to examine complaints of misconduct. The Commission believes it is of the utmost importance to insure that complaints of unfair treatment are fairly dealt with.

Fair treatment of every individual—fair in fact and also perceived to be fair by those affected—is an essential element of justice and a principal objective of the American criminal justice system.

Personnel

The fourth objective is that higher levels of knowledge, expertise, initiative, and integrity be achieved by police, judges prosecutors, defense attorneys, and correctional authorities so that the system of criminal justice can improve its ability to control crime.

The Commission found that one obstacle to recruiting better police officers was the standard requirement that all candidates—regardless of qualifications—begin their careers at the lowest level and normally remain at this level from two to five years before being eligible for promotion. Thus, a college graduate must enter a department at the same rank and pay and perform the same tasks as a person who enters with only a high school diploma or less.

The Commission recommends that police departments give up single entry and establish three levels at which candidates may begin their police careers. The Commission calls these three levels—the "community service officer," the "police officer," and the "police agent."

This division, in addition to providing an entry place for the better educated, would also permit police departments to tap the special knowledge, skills, and understanding of those brought up in the slums.

The community service officer would be a uniformed but unarmed member of the police department. Two of his major responsibilities would be to maintain close relations with juveniles in the area where he works and to be especially alert to crime-breeding conditions that other city agencies had not dealt with. Typically, the CSO might be under 21, might not be required to meet conventional education requirements, and might work out of a store-front office. Serving as an apprentice policeman—a substitute for the police cadet—the CSO would work as a member of a team with the police officer and police agent.

The police officer would respond to calls for service, perform routine patrol, render emergency services, make preliminary investigations, and enforce traffic regulations. In order to qualify as a police officer at the present time, a candidate should possess a high school diploma and should demonstrate a capacity for college work.

The police agent would do whatever police jobs were most complicated, most sensitive, and most demanding. He might be a specialist in police community-relations or juvenile delinquency. He might be in uniform patrolling a high-crime neighborhood. He might have staff duties. To become a police agent would require at least two years of college work and preferably a baccalaureate degree in the liberal arts or social sciences.

As an ultimate goal, the Commission recommends that all

police personnel with general enforcement powers have baccalaureate degrees.

While candidates could enter the police service at any one of the three levels, they could also work their way up through the different categories as they meet the basic education and other requirements.

In many jurisdictions there is a critical need for additional police personnel. Studies by the Commission indicate a recruiting need of 50,000 policemen in 1967 just to fill positions already authorized. In order to increase police effectiveness, additional staff specialists will be required, and when the community service officers are added manpower needs will be even greater.

The Commission also recommends that every State establish a commission on police standards and to provide financial and technical assistance for local police departments.

In order to improve the quality of judges, prosecutors, and defense attorneys, the Commission recommends a variety of steps: taking the selection of judges out of partisan politics; the more regular use of seminars, conferences, and institutes to train sitting judges; the establishment of judicial commissions to excuse physically or mentally incapacitated judges from their duties without public humiliation; the general abolition of part-time district attorneys and assistant district attorneys; and a broad range of measures to develop a greatly enlarged and better trained pool of defense attorneys.

In the correctional system there is a critical shortage of probation and parole officers, teachers, caseworkers, vocational instructors, and group workers. The need for major manpower increases in this area was made clear by the findings from the Commissions national corrections survey. It revealed that less than 3 per cent of all personnel working in local jails and institutions devote their time to treatment and training; eleven States do not offer any kind of probation services for adult misdemeanants, six offer only the barest fragments of such services, and most States offer them on a spotty basis; and two-thirds of all State adult felony probationers are in caseloads of over 100 persons.

To meet the requirements of both the correctional agencies and the courts, the Commission has found an immediate

need to double the country's pool of juvenile probation officers, triple the number of probation officers working with
adult felons, and increase sevenfold the number of officers
working with misdemeanants.

Another area with a critical need for large numbers of expert criminal justice officers is a complex one, viz. of controlling organized crime. Here, the Commission recommends that
prosecutors and police in every State and city where organized crime is known to, or may, exist develop special organized
crime units.

Research

The fifth objective is that every segment of the system of
criminal justice devote a significant part of its resources for
research to insure the development of new and effective
methods of controlling crime.

The Commission found that little research is being conducted into such matters as the economic impact of crime; the
effects on crime of increasing or decreasing criminal sanctions;
possible methods for improving the effectiveness of various
procedures of the police, courts, and correctional agencies.

Organized crime is another area in which almost no research has been conducted. The Commission found that the
only group with any significant knowledge about this problem
was that of law-enforcement officials. Those in other disciplines—social scientists, economists, and lawyers, for example—
have not until recently considered the possibility of research
projects on organized crime.

A small fraction of 1 per cent of the criminal justice
system's total budget is spent on research. This figure could
be multiplied many times without approaching the 3 per cent
industry spends on research, much less the 15 per cent the
Defense Department spends. The Commission believes it
should be multiplied many times.

That research is a powerful force for change in the field of
criminal justice perhaps can best be documented by the history
of the Vera Institute in New York City. Here the research of
a small, non-government agency has in a very short
time led to major changes in the bail procedures of approxi-

mately 100 cities, several States, and the Federal Government.

Because of the importance of research, the Commission recommends that major criminal justice agencies—such as State court and correctional systems and big-city police departments—organize operational research units as integral parts of their structures.

In addition, the criminal justice agencies should welcome the efforts of scholars and other independent experts to understand their problems and operations. These agencies cannot undertake needed research on their own; they urgently need the help of outsiders.

The Commission also recommends the establishment of several regional research institutes designed to concentrate a number of different disciplines on the problem of crime. It further recommends the establishment of an independent National Criminal Research Foundation to stimulate and coordinate research and disseminate its results.

One essential requirement for research is more complete information about the operation of the criminal process. To meet this requirement, the Commission recommends the creation of a National Criminal Justice Statistics Center. The Center's first responsibility would be to work with the FBI, the Children's Bureau, the Federal Bureau of Prisons, and other agencies—in order to develop an integrated picture of the number of crimes reported to police, and the number of persons arrested, the number of accused persons prosecuted, the number of offenders placed on probation, in prison, and subsequently on parole.

Another major responsibility of the Center would be to continue the Commission's initial effort to develop a new yardstick to measure the extent of crime in our society as a supplement to the FBI's Uniform Crime Reports. The Commission believes that the Government should be able to plot the levels of different kinds of crime in a city or a State as precisely as the Labor Department and the Census Bureau now plot the rate of unemployment. Just as unemployment information is essential to sound economic planning, so some day may criminal information help official planning in the system of criminal justice.

Money

Next, the police, the courts, and correctional agencies will require substantially more money if they are to control crime better.

Almost all of the specific recommendations made by the Commission will involve increased budgets. Substantially higher salaries must be offered to attract topflight candidates to the system of criminal justice. For example, the median annual salary for a patrolman in a large city today is $5,300. Typically, the maximum salary is something less than $1,000 above the starting salary. The Commission believes that the most important change that can be made in police salary scales is to increase maximums sharply. An FBI agent, for example, starts as $8,421 a year and if he serves long and well enough can reach $16,905 a year without being promoted to a supervisory position. The Commission is aware that reaching such figures immediately is not possible in many cities, but it believes that there should be a large range from minimum to maximum everywhere.

The Commission also recommends new kinds of programs that will require additional funds, like Youth Services Bureaus, greatly enlarged misdemeanant probation services, and increased levels of research.

The Commission believes some of the additional resources —especially those devoted to innovative programs and to training, education, and research—should be contributed by the Federal Government.

The Federal Government already is conducting a broad range of programs—aid to elementary and secondary schools, the Neighborhood Youth Corps, Project Head Start, and others—designed to attack directly the social problems often associated with crime.

Through such agencies as the Federal Bureau of Investigation, the Office of Law Enforcement Assistance, the Bureau of Prisons, and the Office of Manpower Development and Training, the Federal Government also offers comparatively limited financial and technical assistance to the police, the courts, and corrections authorities.

While the Commission is convinced that State and local

governments must continue to carry the major burden of criminal administration, it recommends a vastly enlarged program of Federal assistance to strengthen law-enforcement, crime prevention, and the administration of justice.

The program of Federal support recommended by the Commission would be directed to eight major needs: (*i*) state and local planning; (*ii*) education and training of criminal justice personnel; (*iii*) surveys and advisory services concerning the organization and operation of police departments, courts, prosecuting offices, and corrections agencies; (*iv*) development of a co-ordinated national information system for operational and research purposes; (*v*) funding of limited numbers of demonstration programs in agencies of justice; (*vi*) scientific and technological research and development; (*vii*) development of national and regional research centers; and (*viii*) grants-in-aid for operational innovations.

The Commission is not in a position to recommend the exact amount of money that will be needed to carry out its proposed program. It believes, however, that a Federal program totaling hundreds of millions of dollars a year during the next decade could be effectively utilized. The Commission also believes the major responsibility for administering this program should lie with the Department of Justice.

The States, the cities, and the counties also will have to make substantial increases in their contributions to the system of criminal justice.

Responsibility for Change

Lastly, individual citizens, social-service agencies, universities, religious institutions, civic and business groups, and all kinds of governmental agencies at all levels must become involved in planning and executing changes in the criminal justice system.

The Commission is convinced that the financial and technical assistance program it proposes can and should be only a small part of the national effort to develop a more effective and fair response to crime.

In March of 1966, President Johnson asked the Attorney General to invite each Governor to form a State committee on criminal administration. The response to this request has been encouraging; more than two-thirds of the States already have such committees or have indicated their intention to form them.

The Commission recommends that in every State and city there should be an agency, or one or more officials, with specific responsibility for planning improvements in criminal administration and encouraging their implementation.

Planning agencies, among other functions, play a key role in helping State legislatures and city councils decide where additional funds and manpower are most needed, what new programs should be adopted, and where and how existing agencies might pool their resources on either a metropolitan or regional basis.

The planning agencies should include both officials from the system of criminal justice and citizens from other professions. Plans to improve criminal administration will be impossible to put into effect unless those responsible for criminal administration help make them. On the other hand, crime prevention must be the task of the community as a whole.

While this report has concentrated on recommendations for action by governments, the Commission is convinced that governmental actions will not be enough. Crime is a social problem that is interwoven with almost every aspect of American life. Controlling it involves improving the quality of family life, the way schools are run, the way cities are planned, and the way workers are hired. Controlling crime is the business of every American institution. Controlling crime is the business of every American.

Universities should increase their research on the problems of crime, private social welfare organizations and religious institutions should continue to experiment with advanced techniques of helping slum children overcome their environment, labor unions and businesses can enlarge their programs to provide prisoners with vocational training, and professional and community organizations can help probation and parole workers with their work.

The responsibility of the individual citizen runs far deeper than co-operating with the police, or accepting jury duty, or insuring the safety of his family by installing adequate locks—

important as they are. He must respect the law, refuse to cut corners and reject the cynical argument that "anything goes as long as you don't get caught."

Most important of all, he must, on his own and through the organizations he belongs to, interest himself in the problems of crime and criminal justice, seek information, express his views, use his vote wisely, and have a sense of involvement.

In sum, the Commission is sure that America can control crime if it will.

CHAPTER 12

VENEZUELA

JUAN MANUEL MAYORCA, H.

Dr Juan Manuel Mayorca h. is a well-known scholar who specializes in law, criminology, and legal sociology in Venezuela. He received his Master's degree in Criminology and Doctor in Law degree from the University of Lovaina, Belgium, in 1960-1961 respectively. In addition to his law practice, he has taught in various universities in Venezuela, namely Aadres Bello Catholic University (UCAB), the School of the Formation of Technical Judicial Police, Teresiano College, Central University of Venezuela, and San Jose de Tarbes College. He has published a number of books which include Criminology: Static Part *(1963),* Introduction to the Study of Prostitution*(1967),* Thus I Believe *(1967), and* This World is Ours *(1968). At present Dr Mayorca is serving in the Ministry of Justice, Republic of Venezuela.*

AN OFFENSE PRESENTS TWO kinds of characteristics: "generic" (which correspond to social anomalies), and "specific". As we shall be talking about the latter throughout this chapter, we will discuss here only the former.

GENERIC CHARACTERISTICS OF OFFENSES

Following are the characteristics that fall in this group:
An Offense is Constant. Some authorities[1] prefer to speak of

---

[1]As discussed by Van Der Bruggen, *Course de Sociologie Criminelle* (Course of Criminal Sociology) (Louvaina: Three Circles Publications, 1958).

it as being "perpetual," or endurable indicating the offense's extension in time. The term constant is more acceptable, as only some types of offenses have been truly perpetual. The acceptance of this characteristic does not assume even the most remote entailment with the sociological and cartographic schools of criminal sociology.[2] These doctrines support the idea of cycle, period, or rhythm of crime as the more or less natural product of each society. We believe, together with other authorities, that throughout all eras the punishable deed is constant and that it obeys variable elements, but that this does not mean a cyclical repetition or the negation of the free will to change these forms of behavior.

It is important not to incur certain contradictions. If it is man who makes social life, who brings it into existence (because it is essential to his own nature or because he arrives at it by artificial means), it is man who with his behavior makes it change in one way or another. The fact that man is subject to social pressures—which sometimes are overwhelming and which often place him like an insignificant particle in the midst of a hurricane—is no argument from which to deduce, on a general plane, that freedom does not exist for man. This freedom is not conceived as the quality to decide without interference or to choose without pressures, but is understood as a potential quality of the subject. The corollary of freedom is social change, and therefore "social cycles" are only valid in the proportion in which they reflect the change of trends of those who originate, move, and act during the so-called "periods." There is social and anti-social change in the proportion that man changes and bends his behavior and the institutions in his own benefit; but until this moment no important laws, with the possibility of demonstration, can be pointed out in relation to this matter.[3]

[2]L. Lacassagne, *Precis de Medecin Legal* (Summary of the Legal Doctor) (Paris : University Presses of France, 1906)

[3]Alois Dempf has already warned; "Today social laws and predictions are poetry. Novelists warn us with frightening tales against the ant-like state of total bureaucratization. They offer us a few optimistic

An Offense is Complex. In all social phenomena, simple explanations are generally simplistic; or, as Lepp says referring to similar matters: "Simplicity is almost always falsity."[4] The possibility of establishing for any social phenomenon perfectly determined causes, whose effects can be perfectly determined, seems Utopian. Many times in the field of crime apparently clear causes are, in a certain manner, the results or effects of other phenomena. Divorce, which certainly is an element in juvenile delinquency, is the product of a series of social elements such as loss of values, impiety, and legal case in obtaining it. To put it in another way, that which seems to be a direct cause is in reality derived, or an effect of collateral situations.

This complexity should not alarm us because it derives (*a*) from the intricacy of human behavior, from which society springs; and (*b*) from social dynamics, which is interconnected in itself and which is becoming more and more complex throughout history and civilization.

This difficulty of understanding the anti-social act or of measuring it, obstructs the analysis but does not make it impossible. From the point of view of the subject who is acting, there generally occurs a concealment, a "smoke-screen" (when the sanction mechanisms function more or less automatically), in the period following the anti-social behavior in order to elude the responsibility and the sanction which derive from the same. The social investigator, who in matters of anti-social behavior generally acts a posteriori, finds acts and phenomena which are perfectly tangible but which almost always lack an author.

It is thus easy to attribute to clearly "subjective" conduct (in the sense that it obeys individual motives) acts which are repeated and without a known author. On the other hand, the complexity of anti-social behavior has its most tangible proof in the grouping and specialization which can be observed as a trend in modern times in the field of sociology. The

---

Utopias, as all Utopias used to be." [*Sociologia de la Crisis* (Sociology of Crisis) (Madrid: Castilla S.A., 2nd edition, 1951)].

[4]Ignace Lepp, *La Nueva Moral* (The New Morality) (Buenos Aires: Carlos Lohle Publications, 1964).

idea which is contributed by criminology in its specialized studies seems to be capable of being extended to the whole field of offenses. In the same way, one should not speak of "criminals" in a strict and scientific sense but the criminal categories, one should not accept pure criminality in general, but classes or spheres of the same.[5]

The fact that the juvenile and the adult move in different spheres of criminality is no accident. Nor is it by chance that juvenile gangs and feminine or feminine-like organizations are formed for specific types of anti-social actions, which do not necessarily constitute unlawful behavior. The fact that in our time, in a great part of the world, the moral crisis is more obvious in the classes placed higher economically; the loss of an economic conscience or justice in the value of material things in the proletariat or lower classes of the developing countries; and, finally, the absence of conscience which links the so-called middle classes; are if not perfectly proven facts, interesting symptoms for the study of anti-social behavior by groups.

Offenses are Exceptional. Within the innumerable totality of acts which are realized daily within a specific society, the act which tends to disarrange it, no matter how often we see it repeated, is an exception.

Only a very limited kind of human behavior attacks order and succeeds in overcoming the pressures which are exerted by religion, morals, law, and sometimes even social conventions. Only the pessimistic sociologists, most of them unfashionable in our era, insist on the thesis of the generalization of anti-social behavior. One can say that as a general rule, social correctives fulfil their standardizing task mentioned by Emile Durkheim.[6] The anti-social act is precisely the exception.

[5]The acceptance of this thesis does not imply a contradiction with the terminology which we have been using and which we will use throughout. To develop such a theme would involve the study of situations which correspond to specialized disciplines outside the confines of this article.

[6]Emile Durkheim, *Regles de la Methode Sociologique* (Rules of the Sociological Method), 13th edition (Paris: University Presses of France, 1956).

This is so evident that the opposite position implies a total absence of security, and of the possibility of devoting oneself to activities which make human life possible (work, feeding, education, and procreation), as well as an encouragement of the anguish of this century. The existence of this exception is no less true, nor is the alarm which it must produce in all persons worried about the advance of society. But this alarm must be placed within just boundaries under penalty of falling into unfounded hysteria.

From the historical point of view the exceptionality of the criminal act is interesting because it explains in part the evolution of humanity. We have already indicated that the dynamic character of life and of the social institutions makes all studies difficult. This same dynamic element causes the exceptional anti-social behavior to show a marked trend.

Offenses Tend to Grow. Inexhaustible laws and new sciences, institutions recently formed, the search for ideals of justice which are really demandable within social life, all these are only roads which the man of this century is opening in order to submit social life to the order which seems to have been lost. Those who deny the trend toward growth of the social anomaly, because they are optimists, deny not only the increasing growth of the population in a large part of the earth, but also the advance of poverty and a high index of delinquency during the past fifty years.

For North-American Sociology (and specifically, in the opinion of Ward, in his *Contemporary Sociology*), social life, in its most essential mechanism, is formed by forces of association and dissociation, forces which have always existed. When we speak of a trend toward growth we simply mean an increment in these negative or disconnecting forces; we do not imply that the other forces have disappeared.

Offenses are Universal Phenomena. It would suffice to indicate that offenses are products of human behavior, a specific result of the conduct of man, and that therefore they will exist and have existed in all societies. This does not imply identity of the different forms of anti-sociality. It has a common base which is its subject, but it is influenced by the diverse historical, social, political, economic, and religious circumstances of each period and place. The phenomenon as such is universal, but the way in which it presents itself in each moment of history, can be quite different, similar or antagonistic to the form adopted in a moment in the past or in the future. The help of history is basic in this matter and therefore the acceptance of this attribute, or the lack of it, depends upon the innumerable historical proofs which may be submitted.

The mechanisms of segregation or sanction will have operated in each society in face of the diverse aspects presented by the anti-social act and its author or authors, when it was possible to determine the same. Certainly one has to warn that to focus the different situations outside the historical conditions in which they are forged, leads to false conclusions. All these characteristics, applicable in principle to the unlawful act occuring in any society or period, present variations (in quality and in quantity) in accordance with the historical, cultural, geographic, political, religious, and other circumstances of each country, We will now study briefly some of these circumstances in relation to Venezuela.

Historical Evolution of Venezuela

The discovery and conquest of Venezuela were accomplished by Spain towards the end of the 15th and the beginning of the 16th century. There was an unorganized native population, with a more or less primitive culture, to which the African Negro was incorporated. The object of the conquest was the hope that the later will mix without distinctions with the white Spaniard and the native.

Colonization was accomplished by Spain through the system of encomienda and free labor, to which were added instruction in the Catholic religion and rudimentary knowledge. The process of cultural inter-relation, thus started, culminated with the beginnings of Emancipation.

Around 1810 an emancipation movement was born, based upon the ideas of the French Revolution and later on the North-American Constitution. This came at a time when the Spanish monarchy was decaying. After a long fight and under the direction of Simon Bolivar, the Liberator, this movement culminated in the independence of the country in 1824. The

Liberator, creator of Pan-Americanism, extended his activities to Colombia, Ecuador, Panama, and Peru which he also separates from the Spanish Metropolis after changing high Peru into Bolivia.

After a great deal of internal conflict, the Republic, born as a system from independence, achieved stability in this century.

Today, Venezuela is a country of one million square kilometers, with a fast-growing population which, according to recent statistics, has already reached 9,686,486 inhabitants. The population is distributed in 20 States, two Territories, and one Federal District. The country and its people have several peculiar characteristics of which the following need to be highlighted.

First, it has a well-established egalitarian society without any kind of racial segregation.

Secondly, its low cultural level is explained by the traditional neglect of education, which was started systematically only about 20 years ago. The present index of illiteracy is 23.7 per cent for the population of over 15 years of age.

Thirdly, there has been a fast growth and expansion of the large cities, especially of the capital, accompanied by the disorders which are involved in the phenomenon of urbanization, when plans have not been prepared in accordance with the speed of said ecological phenomenon (lack of housing, rural exodus, sub-employment and unemployment).

Fourthly, the population is 96 per cent Catholic. The popular faith is more the result of tradition than of a clear concept of the truths and vitality of the said religion. Remnants of African and of native belief can be observed occasionally.

Fifthly, politically speaking, the Venezuelan loves liberty, at least in its formal aspects (exercise of the vote, certain amount of freedom of the press, etc.). In the past ten years the average citizen of the country has begun to understand that freedom includes something more than the capacity to dissent and to govern. He has understood that it is necessary to be organized in order to exercise this right.

Sixthly, from the point of view of organization of power, the country is a democratic Republic based upon the representative system, with the executive and the legislative powers renewed every five years by universal, direct, and secret ballot. The judicial power will be stuided in the following pages. According to the law, the functions of repressive police, of judicature, of prevention of crime, and of a penitentiary system belong to the National Authority.

And, seventhly, from the economic point of view, a large part of its history has evolved with a basis in agriculture and cattle raising. Mining became a source of riches only as an exception. As a nation, Venezuela started to base its economy upon its oil deposits during the second decade of this century. At present, the process of industrialization tends to develop with the accompanying diversification of production, complexities, and changes which this implies.

CRIMINAL LAW

In the penal legislation in force in Venezuela, the term "crime" does not exist. What is more, in none of the legal texts of the last 65 years has this expression been used in order to describe the forms of human behavior under legal sanction.

Definition of Crime

This word is used for certain acts especially condemned by society and speculated upon by newspapers. One speaks about "crime" in the case of some very aggravating homicides, in the case of violation or corruption of minors and, in general, in all those cases in which the victim presents a special weakness for the author of the act. Technically our legislation only accepts the terms "offenses" and "faults" as elements of the classification of the penal infraction. The classification called bipartite is accepted in our terminology. For this reason, according to Article 1 of the Penal Code, *"punishable acts are divided into offenses and faults"*.[7] Then, the idea of crime, expressed in other legislations in order to indicate the punishable acts of greatest seriousness and therefore of longest and harshest penalty (even capital punishment

[7] *Penal Code of Venezuela* (Reformation of 1964), Ministry of Justice.

in many cases), would correspond in Venezuelan legislation
to certain forms considered as offenses.

To give definitions of offense is also a technique not used
in our legislation. These concepts have been fashioned by
doctrines (interpretations by scholars about penal subjects),
which often have taken into account the jurisprudence of the
courts of the Republic. But, at the universities, as well as
in judicial documents, the definitions of offense which have
been most successful, correspond to those given by religious
authors of treatises. In choosing the definition of offense a
great role is played by the similarity of focus, or of philosophical school or attitude, which may exist between the person
who quotes and the person quoted. The penal definition of
offense is as follows: "One calls offense any unlawful act
which is imputable, and of proven culpability in ordinary
procedure and upon which falls a penal sanction through
a firm and confirmed sentence."[8]

It is worth noting here that the above definition does not
include a series of acts which are subject to penal sanctions
in many countries and which in Venezuela are subject to
special laws and measures which are outside the penal sphere.
This refers to all behavior which results in a correctional
regimen (among which stand our habitual vagrancy, homo-
sexuality, and others), a name which involves what is technically called "security measures."

In accordance with the law of Vagrants and Perverts,[9] the
Executive and its police agencies are empowered to apply
sanctions in work colonies via non-judicial procedure, to the
persons who engage in the said acts. This system is excessi-
vely irregular in spite of conforming to a rather anachronistic
law and it attacks individual liberty in a great number of cases,
and gives the Executive a weapon which is not always managed with technique and skill.

[8]The personal works in which this definition has been reproduced
with some variations are: Juan Manuel Mayorca, "Criminología, Parte
Estática" (Criminology, Static Part), Gráfica Americana, Caracas, 1963;
"Introductión al Estudio de la Prostitutión" (Introducción to the Study
of Prostitution), Gráfica Americana, second edition, Caracas, 1967.

[9]Ley de Vagos y Maleantes (Law of Vagrants and the Corrupt), Ministry of Justice, Caracas, Venezuela, 1961.

On the other hand, experience demonstrates that lack of success which the application of this Law has had in Venezuela, as shown by the high index of recurrence. Possibly this is due to the lack of adequate treatment in the short period during which many persons who pose a certain danger to society are committed.

The preceding definition does not cover either the punishable acts committed my minors, even if the same are subject to a special penal procedure. The Penal Code establishes a scale, which goes from total exemption from penalty (unlawful acts performed by minors under 12 years of age) to a diminution of half or one-third of the punishment if it concerns minors between the ages of 12 and 18 years—18 years being the age when they can be fully punished. The Law also establishes an exception of the minor who commits the act between 12 and 15 years of age, as it declares him irresponsible unless it appears that he acted with discernment.[10]

Therefore, minors who commit punishable acts between the ages of 12 and 18 years, are subject to a special regimen. The fundamental descriptive characteristics of this regimen are the following: (*i*) special procedures entrusted to the Juvenile Courts; (*ii*) fulfillment of the sanction in establishments of re-education and of special treatment; (*iii*) minimum publicity of the act, the Law indicating that neither photos nor elements of identification of the minor will be published; (*iv*) as they are not considered delinquents, this term is kept for the adult and therefore one does not speak of "juvenile delinquency" but of "minors in irregular situation."

In fact—and this in any case is an artifice of the law-maker—this idea has resulted in being rather romantic and old-fashioned in practice. Reality has shown the formation of genuine unlawful organizations by juveniles and the action, in many cases fraudulent, of young and very dangerous delinquents. On the other hand, as we will see in the following pages, nowadays the average age of the delinquent has gone down. It is useful to indicate here that 72 per cent of the minors, held in one of the special establishments of the metropolitan area between the years 1964 and 1967, performed their acts between the ages of 12 and 15 years.

[10]*Penal Code of Venezuela,* Articles 69, 70, and 71.

CRIME STATISTICS

Following are the statistics of crime in Venezuela in various categories :

TABLE I

GENERAL SUMMARY

Year	Prisoners*	Sentenced†	Men		Women		Total††
1958	5,924	2,955	5,741	96.91%	183	3.09%	6,412,000
1959	7,067	2,477	6,852	96.96%	215	3.04%	6,607,000
1960	7,331	2,501	7,097	96.60%	234	3.40%	6,808,000
1961	7,804	2,564	7,547	96.71%	257	3.29%	7,612,000
1962	8,217	2,659	7,989	97.23%	228	2.77%	7,872,000
1963	8,391	2,438	8,169	97.35%	222	2.65%	8,144,000
1964	9,219	2,429	8,966	97.26%	253	2.74%	8,427,000
1965	11,454	2,650	10,723	97.62%	330	2.88%	8,722,000
1966	12,340	2,989	11,987	97.14%	353	2.86%	9,030,000
1967	13,044	2,977	12,723	97.54%	321	2.46%	9,352,000
1968	13,089	3,167	12,745	97.37%	343	2.63%	9,500,000

*The word "Prisoners" used in this table and in the following, refers to judicial detention and not simply to police detention. The idea of arrest is not used in the Venezuelan statistics. We have given all the totals in *absolute numbers* and in percentages (%) as it is done in our system.

†A sentenced person is one who has received a firm sentence and who has been delivered to the administrative authorities in order to fulfil his penalty. From a penal point of view there is no appeal he can exercise.

††This estimated information of our cumulative growth has been included, with source in the Demographic Analysis of the Ministry of Development.

TABLE III

Offenses	1964		1965		1966		1967		1968	
	Number	Per cent	Number	Per cent	Number	Per cent	Number	Per cent	Number	Per cent
AGAINST PERSONS										
Homicides	3,187	34.53	3,073	26.82	3,112	25.32	3,146	24.12	3,102	23.70
Injuries	1,711	18.54	1,723	15.04	1,672	13.57	1,688	12.94	1,414	10.80
Other	18	0.20	42	0.37	3	0.02	70	0.54	22	0.18
AGAINST PROPERTY										
Theft	1,881	20.38	2,912	25.42	2,381	19.29	2,782	21.33	2,676	20.44
Robbery	986	10.68	892	7.79	1,069	8.66	1,180	9.04	1,021	7.80
Other	294	3.19	767	6.70	754	0.11	597	4.58	949	7.25
AGAINST CONVEN-TIONAL MANNERS										
Violations	348	3.77	419	3.66	488	3.63	530	4.06	507	3.87
Other	182	1.97	269	2.35	298	2.41	535	4.10	319	2.44
OTHER OFFENSES*	622	6.74	955	8.34	952	7.71	832	6.38	808	6.17

*In the category "Other Offenses" the following are included: Offenses against liberty, against public property, against the security of the nation, against public order and faith, against the administration of justice. The statistics on this matter have just begun to be collected and it is impossible to give exact data for each type of offense.

TABLE II

OCCURRENCE OF UNLAWFULNESS

Offenses	1958		1959		1960		1961		1962		1963	
	Number	per cent	Number	Per cent	Number	Per cent	Number	Per cent	Number	Per cent	Number	Per cent
AGAINST PERSONS												
Homicides	2,599	43.87	2,871	40.63	2,961	40.39	3,071	39.35	3,132	38.12	3,069	36.57
Injuries	1,583	26.72	2,165	30.64	1,927	24.29	1,942	24.88	1,750	21.30	1,517	18.08
Other	62	1.05	17	0.24	10	0.14	10	0.13	17	0.21	18	0.21
AGAINST PROPERTY												
Theft	759	12.81	1,052	14.89	1,325	18.07	1,565	20.05	1,907	23.21	2,001	23.85
Robbery	120	2.03	269	3.81	284	3.87	382	4.89	501	6.10	631	7.52
Other	196	3.31	125	1.77	233	3.18	236	3.03	209	2.54	281	3.35
AGAINST CONVEN-TIONAL MANNERS												
Violations	247	4.17	308	4.35	242	3.30	285	3.65	292	3.55	350	4.17
Other	70	1.18	97	1.37	105	1.43	98	1.26	131	1.59	182	2.17
OTHER OFFENSES	288	4.86	163	2.30	244	3.35	215	2.75	278	3.38	342	4.08

TABLE IV

AGES

Year	18-24	25-29	30-34	35-39	40 and over*	Penal population
1958	731	1,474	1,281	930	1,230	5.646
1959	1,522	1,528	1,280	960	1,220	6,510
1960	1,190	1,600	1,405	1,000	1,570	6,775
1961	1,368	1,660	1,487	940	1,670	7,125
1962	893	1,801	1,600	1,460	1,495	7,249
1963	2,531	1,721	1,559	1,020	1,560	7,554
1964	2,935	2,113	1,612	1,025	1,534	8,768

Year	18-23	24-27	28-32	33-37	38-42	43-47	48-52	53 and over	Penal population
1965	2,307	2,879	2,166	1,478	870	533	310	911	10,342
1966	2,890	1,702	2,545	1,620	593	636	358	577	11,069
1967	3,188	1,918	3,073	2,018	675	827	427	919	11,711
1968	2,717	1,646	2,498	943	1,339	779	423	486	13,089

*Includes the ages that were not declared and those not confirmed. As a mere reference, in the last four years of statistics (1963-67) for 1,800 youths subject to re-education this is the distribution by age of minor's less than 18 years old: 12 years—4.2 per cent; 13 years—9.9 per cent; 14 years—17.8 per cent; 15 years—21.9 per cent; 16 years—20.3 per cent; 17 years—20.8 per cent; and 18 years—4.5 per cent.

TABLE V*

ECONOMIC FACTOR OF THE PRISONER

Weekly family income	Number of prisoners	Per cent
From 1 to 50 Bolivares	307	27.89
From 51 to 100 Bolivares	242	21.98
From 101 to 200 Bolivares	265	24.07
From 201 to 300 Bolivares	123	11.17
From 301 to 400 Bolivares	60	5.45
From 401 to more	63	5.72
Did not declare	41	3.72
TOTAL	1,101	100.00

LODGINGS		
Have	565	51.69
Do not have	530	48.14
Did not declare	9	0.27
TOTAL	1,104	100.00

LAST SALARY RECEIVED (WEEKLY AVERAGE)		
1 to 20	58	5.51
21 to 40	239	22.72
41 to 60	157	14.93
61 to 80	135	12.83
81 to 100	114	10.84
101 to 120	64	6.08
121 to 140	73	6.94
141 to 160	42	3.99
161 to 180	40	3.80
181 to 500	130	13.36

*Unofficial data from our book *Criminologia* (criminology) (Gráfica Americana: 1963, Caracas, p. 277). All the cases studied are sentenced delinquents.

TABLE VI
PROSTITUTION*

PROSTITUTION AND OFFENSE	Per cent
Infanticide	49.00
Homicide	42.00
Abortion	6.00
Other	3.00
PROSTITUTION AND AGE OF INITIATION	
Before 15 years	3.00
From 16 to 20 years	40.40
From 21 to 25 years	31.70
From 26 years on	24.90
PROSTITUTION AND CIVIL CONDITION	
Single	92.70
Married	6.10
Divorced	0.60
Widowed	0.60
PROSTITUTION AND ASOCIALITY	
Imprisonment due to the same trade	34.45
For lack of documentation or vagrancy	34.51
For drunkenness and scandal	31.04
REPETITION OF OFFENSE	
A single imprisonment or arrest	30.50
From two to four arrests	38.40
From 5 up	31.10

*The above data are not official. They correspond to our study *Introduccion al Estudio de la Prostitucion* (Introduction to the Study of Prostitution). (Mayorca Jr., Juan Manuel, *Gráfica Americana* Caracas, 2nd edition, 1967) which discusses 1,527 cases.

TABLE VII

Year	Denuntiations	Imprisonments	Per cent
1958*	6,558	Unknown data	
1959	26,647	16,291	61.13
1960	40,169	19,341	48.14
1961	42,565	17,383	40.83
1962	38,005	17,851	46.97
1963	34,292	12,454	36.34
1964	29,730	13,820	46.49
1965	29,696	14,729	49.60
1966	33,540	21,023	62.28
1967	44,687	23,982	53.67
1968	48,329	26,268	54.40

Year	Vehicles Stolen	Recovered	Per cent
1958	Official data unknown		
1959	4,209	3,137	74.53
1960	6,369	3,734	58.62
1961	6,931	4,479	64.62
1962	6,876	4,933	71.74
1963	6,436	5,110	79.34
1964	5,058	4,622	91.40
1965	5,422	4,152	76.60
1966	5,140	3,529	68.66
1967	3,679	2,740	74.48
1968	4,767	2,467	51.80

*The information corresponding to 1958 is partial as on that date the Technical Body of Judicial Police was created. The denuntiations and imprisonments correspond to the whole country and include the theft of vehicles.

TABLE VIII

DRUNKENNESS AND OFFENSE

Year	Total Offenses	Drunkenness	Per cent Annual	Occurrence Monthly	Daily
1958	177,664	27,005	4.9	900	74
1959	197,612	33,592	6.1	1,120	92
1960	198,851	30,436	5.5	1,015	83
1961	216,798	31,840	5.8	1 061	87
1962	225,296	34,101	6.2	1,137	93
1963	239,278	39,625	7.2	1,321	109
1964	241,005	44,032	8.0	1,468	121
1965	249,324	51,350	9.3	1,712	141
1966	256,118	54,738	9.9	1,825	150

TABLE IX
MORTALITY DUE TO ALCOHOLISM
ACCORDING TO AGE GROUPS

Year	Total	Up to 29	30-39	40-49	50-59	60-69	70 and over
1958	567	51	94	130	118	114	60
1959	574	52	69	118	132	117	86
1960	560	54	53	91	136	130	96
1961	550	69	45	116	121	120	79
1962	567	75	62	101	131	111	87
1963	536	40	54	110	129	118	85
1964	595	74	78	95	124	128	96
1965	611	63	93	122	145	112	76
1966	633	58	85	107	157	134	92

THEORIES OF CRIMINAL CAUSALITY

The term "causality" implies the study of the causes of any phenomenon. In accordance with the acceptance of the term in Spanish, "cause" is that which is considered the source or origin of something. In the Third International Congress of Criminology, Von Henting said that cause of an offense was "the agent which determines, due to its incidence, the appearance of a new force or a new object." By putting it across in this manner and by applying the term cause to social matter, he represents a certain formulation derived from determinism. For example, the cause of the fall of an object is the attraction which earth exerts on its mass. This attraction *determines* the fall of the object. For this reason it seems preferable to speak of "factors" in criminology, understanding as such the total of facts of different kinds which are present at the formation of the criminal phenomenon.

Criminological Schools

Setting out from the Positivist school (1871), criminology has acquired autonomy and received a special impetus.[11] Whithin this new science, the study of unlawful factors forms

[11]Date of publication of *The Delinquent Man* by Lombroso.

the central object of the same.   If we give a short outline of the orientations of the best-known criminologists, we can summarize the hypotheses of contemporary criminological thought in the following three bases :

Hypothesis of a Constitutional Base. It is represented basically by the Harvard school, which, in questions of criminal anthropology, has followed the investigations of Lombroso. (Professor Hooton dedicated twelve years of his life to studying 13,873 delinquents and 3,203 non-delinquents; the Criminal Biological Compilation Center of Bavaria has also made its contributlon in this field.)

Recent discoveries in modern genetics have opened new vistas in the study of this subject. The chromosomatic hypothesis seems to be the most forceful of these ideas.

The psychological hypotheses merits a special place within the constitutional explanation. Born from the studies of Itar, Sequin, and Felix Voisin, it arrives at firm statements with the works of Binet, and Simon, until it reaches its definitive formulation in Freud, Adler, Jung, and their modern followers. We can sum up the Constitutional Course in the following outline manner:

First, life of the human being, and therefore of the delinquent, is nothing else but a complex series of stimuli and reactions; on the other hand, an intricate nervous process is evident, which allows man to choose in his life of intercourse.

Secondly, study of the personality of each concrete delinquent is very important. The individual antecedents are of great interest as data, for they help to arrive at determined illnesses. For their part, the psychological investigation has to cover the so called "changes of character" in which the origin of the offense is found by many. Freudian inspiration is reborn, as many times "the acts are nothing else than simple rationalizations of unconscious motivations."

Thirdly, social life is not forgotten. It does not have the category of cause of delinquency. It is simply a condition or a "supplementary stimulus." One attempts to prove this with a rather feeble statement that in any community whatsoever it is precisely the minority which is considered as agent of offense and that, if the social environment were the cause, it would be the majority.

Fourthly, the behaviour of the delinquent is nothing else but a more or less direct reflex of his personality, which has been formed in the first seven years of his life. Therefore, the true criminogenic factors exist since the foetal period. These factors are of psychic, nutritional, and hereditary character.

Fifthly, given the factors, the concept which one has of the delinquent and the importance of the biological and psychological fact, criminology cannot obtain clear statements without a method which manages to find out the personality of the delinquent and his psycho-biologic antecedent. Therefore, basically, sciences which could contribute towards this direction are anthropology, embryology, experimental and clinical psychology, and psychiatry.

Sixthly, crime is an individual phenomenon and not a social one. Therefore, any criminal study has to be eminently subjective.

Hypothesis of a Sociological Base. Starting with the work of Quetelet (1796-1874), the development of modern statistics and the influence of Comte's thoughts, the social environment begins to gain importance in the explanation of the criminological problem. This fact, and the more modern development of well-defined ideas in the field of criminal sociology, has made many people establish distinctions with regard to the social environment.

The reality is that "social environment" is a term of many meanings and covers the most diverse influences. Thus, according to the distinction drawn by Etiene De Greef,[12] there is (*i*) the environment in general "which includes all the circumstances of the world which surround us and which produce common influences for all the citizens of a given country." (*ii*) The personal environment "which, on the contrary, comprises the group of persons which surround the individual, and which produces particular and generally decisive influences." In this point of the classification, De Greef further distinguishes between Family Environment of Origin ("where the world takes place in the conscience of

---

[12]Etiene De Greef, *Introduccion a la Criminología* (Introduction to Criminology), Brussels, 1946.

the child and history is born at the same moment that he appears"; therefore the family implies a geographical idea like street where one is born, the frontiers of the house or apartment); Occasional Environment (constituted by the school, the university, or even the military service, and the first manufacture or shop); and the environment of choice or acceptance (which is the definitive environment chosen by the subject).

All these "environments" are of an objective character, but for the subject each one is represented by fictitious influences. Though not quite precise sociologically when we speak of this course, social environment in general covers all the concepts of the classification. We make this distinction because each author refers to one in particular. Here then, one should understand as social that which the foetus finds upon being born and leaves when dying, and which substantially exists outside himself.

Perhaps the words of Louis Lacassagne, "the criminal is a microbe and society is his culture,"[13] represent the global focus of the idea which can be summed up in the following words:

First, the majority of the North-American authors as well as the criminologists of a marked socialist tendency "cheat" —to use a phrase from Sellin—the problem of the personality of the delinquent as an organic and thinking subject. It is not that this situation is not important, but that it is only of secondary order.

Secondly, life of man, and therefore of the delinquent, is moved by reflexes to stimuli of social life. More exactly, it is a reflex to the social fact, which for the Soviets is confined to the economic factor. For some North-American schools this life of the subject is only a mass of "reflexes and customs."

Thirdly, the behavior of the delinquent is, basically, a product of the apprenticeship of a cultural model. This postulate, created as to apprenticeship by E. Durkheim and as to imitation by Gabriel Tarde, is developed with its own characteristics by each author.

[13]Louis Lacassagne, *op. cit.*

Fourthly, crime is a social phenomenon in reality and as such can be studied without reference to a determined individual conduct. It is patrimony of social life in general. Its study is limited to searching in society prior anti-social acts.

Fifthly, the expressions of national criminality (unlawful incidence, considered qualitatively and quantitatively for each country) arise from demographic, geographic, economic, and political influences.

Sixthly, using the appropriate methods of criminology and with the special help of criminal sociology and statistics, the central theme for both courses is to establish the relationship which exists between the political geography, the demography, and the economy of a certain country and the criminal behavior of a concrete individual.

Hypothesis of a Mixed Base. The two preceding courses do not exclude one fact, viz. that the criminal phenomenon is complex; and therefore they do not assert a simple solution. There is causal preference (be it constitutional or social) but there is always a plurality. There does not exist a unique fact which explains by its sole influence the unlawful beginning. This is the basis of a new idea that to crime as such (and to offense in general) factors of both type provide assistance.

Thus, in the first place, crime is a complex phenomenon. Any partial (or "specialized") explanation is truly impotent in explaining the totality of the phenomenon.

Secondly, only general criminology, with its specific methods and helped by its auxiliary sciences, can explain how offenses are born and produced. From this same criminology, the science which will give directions for the prevention of crime, that is, criminal policy, will take its foundation.

Thirdly, within this idea there is no opposition to the acknowledgement that there are cases in which the biological fact in itself or the psychological causality alone are sufficient in order to explain certain isolated acts of criminality. It is admitted that the sociological explanation is incomplete in anti-social signs such as the violation of minors or offenses with an eminently psychic base. Taken singly, certain cases which happened during the post-war era are the consequence of the destruction, misery, and anguish produced by factors almost exclusively exogenous, but under normal conditions they would have a valid constitutional explanation. But in none of these hypothetical cases one can generalize conclusions and demonstrate them as true theses. According to Jean Pinatel,[14] this is a mistake which many scholars have made.

Fourthly, it is true that one should not speak of "delinquency in general" and give worldwide directions which should be applied like a mathematical catalog of prevention and causal explanation of the offense. It is thus established that what one is concerned with in practical terms is the study of concrete delinquents. These human beings, complex in their psyche, heredity, and temperament, are even more difficult to understand when they enter into contact with the social environment. This environment changes not only within the space of the frontiers of a country but also in time. From this it follows that the variable social conditions also make a dynamic study of the genesis of unlawfulness necessary—as suggested by the great German penologist Edmund Mezger who, in 1939, outlined a study plan in his work *Criminal Policy*. It should be clear that the fact that we speak of the "concrete" delinquent, should not make one suppose that in this idea the casuistical study tends to predominate. The case corroborates the general hypothesis, issuing from an analytical and synthetical study, produced by the comparison of experiences in the light of different doctrinal focuses, but is not in itself the object of criminological study.

Fifthly, it is important to indicate that this course, known also as the "unitarian idea," admits of gradation and shades. Criminality results with a typical exogenous content in countries which have not reached their development but which are carrying out diverse socio-economic processes in order to attain it. The economic factor plays an important and primary role. This fact obscures some offenses of endogenous content which appear accidentally. Causality is more varied in industrialized countries. But in any case, this is only an emphasis of the investigation, an adaptation of its general focus.

[14]Jean Pinatel, *La Criminologie* (Criminology) (Paris : Spes Publications, 1960).

PENAL PHILOSOPHY

The philosophical principles which inspired the Constitution and the penal laws in Venezuela have gone through a long evolution.

Philosophical Foundation and its Historical Development

This evolution can be divided into five periods, which are all antecedents of the principles that have inspired the judicial edicts of the country.

First Period. Among primitive populations[15]—some of which can be studied in present communities in spite of the more or less direct modifications which the different cultures have undergone—crime presents itself as an outrage against the manes of the family or the divine principles of the clan or group. Thus there is a violation of the law which is of a religious character. This does not imply impunity if it is committed by a member of the nascent human society; that which changes in this case is the punishment, which will be greater if the author is a stranger. Therefore, this group performs, under the pretense of private justice, a vengeance which does not arise from the previously considered laws. The conditions form an extreme casuistry. Normally, this "vendetta" represents a much greater sanction than the act in itself and sometimes extends to the relatives and the goods of the offender. The idea of imputableness or intentionality does not play any role at all. After studying very old documents, Olof Kimberg[16] affirms that, on the contrary, "in the face of certain facts it (the absence of internationality) can be aggravating instead of attenuating." Responsibility, therefore, is measured by the act and by its consequence, the damage. It seems certain that the acts which had the greatest incidence in

---

[15]See Radbruch, *Historia de la Criminalidad* (History of Criminality) (Barcelona: Bosch Publications, 1955, pp. 5, 20, and 100; and Malinowoski, *Crimen y Costumbre en la Sociedad Salvaje* (Crime and Custom in the Society of Savages) (Barcelona : Bosch Publications, 1956).

[16]Olof Kimberg, *Problemas Fundamentales de la Criminología* (Basic Problems of Criminology), (Toulousse: Cuyas Publications, 1959), p. 2.

these primary communities were injury, homicide, and theft, in their different forms of qualification.

Second Period. In this period, worship becomes more formal and the offense is considered as an outrage against the social gods. The punishment becomes a collective attribute, as the whole group to which the victim belongs considers itself offended. But a qualification is added to the crime, as a nascent idea: it is a voluntary act and if the damage is produced independently from the volitional act, it is considered as produced by chance. The motives of the criminal act are synthetized in "violation of peace." Therefore, the collective sanction will have a double purpose; on the one hand, corporal punishment of the author, and on the other, that which Roman law will call "compositio" that is, the reparation of the damage caused to the group. The first purpose is represented by different corporal punishments (exile and obligation of pardon), the second is a payment in kind, money, or in temporary or perpetual rendering of service. Kimberg admits that in these groups exist "real social authorities organized against crime."

We put classical Greece in this period, even if she, together with the Roman culture, attained a higher grade of evolution. There the idea of mental illness appears with the work of Hippocrates, to be completed and developed in Rome by the physician, Aretaius. It is conceived as "an illness of the soul" of extraterrestial origin, qualified as "demoniacal possession." Therefore, the names which will be given to the different mental insanities will be furia, larvatia, linfatis, etc. But Greece dates this evolution a little due to the fact that even if she is the first country to admit the existence of mental illness, she is not going to exempt the "possessed by the demon" from punishment, thus negating the advance created by the old Germanic law. But on the other hand, the Hellenic culture shows another advance, by forming, as Momsen says, "the first group in which a tribunal exists," that of the Heleasts. It will occupy itself with the judging of criminal acts, that is, "those which constitute an outrage against morality and the gods."[17] In the performance of this instrument of justice

[17]Theodore Momsen, *Le Droit Penal Romain* (Roman Penal Law), Vol. I, Paris, 1907, p. 88.

occurs what can be considered the first infamy. In the year 399 B.C. Socrates is condemned to drink hemlock or to retract in public the affront caused to the morality of the gods.

The Jews will use again the idea of crime as a voluntary act. For the Hebrew culture, the act of the minor is compared with those of the lunatic and the deaf-mute, who "being unable to want but able to think" are not responsible. The theory of motive as an eminently subjective act begins to gain a place. The motive has been wanted and thought by the criminal, and therefore one deduces—it being accepted by Hebrew legislation—that the lunatic could be punished if it could be proven that the act was committed during a lucid interval. On the other hand, the punishment has become an almost mathematical reparation of the damage caused. Retaliation,as created by Hamurabi, already shows signs of positive vigor, though the Jews accept and give birth to the very modern idea of variety in the punishment over the "eye for an eye" in a literal sense. Different kinds of punishment, like exile or stoning, are used for the same act, according to its gravity, realization or intention.

One hears frequently, and this seems to come from Poitiers, that the Romans "were giants in civil law and dwarfs in penal law." But if a comparison is made with the other ancient cultures, this idea does not appear to be a historical truth, at least insofar as it refers to crime and criminology in general. Thus Marquiset,[18] says with reason: "Only a nation with such a positive spirit (that of the Romans) could have built such an admirable edifice of the criminal sciences."

The Roman jurists started by making the following distinctions: In the first place, there were crimes which were an outrage against the religious law (faz), and which regulated the relationship of man with the gods, and which in principle were irrelevant to society, as they were only subject to the sanction of conscience.

Secondly, Roman medicine creates for penal law (which will be collected in the times of Marcus Aurelius) the idea of non-responsibility as applied to the mentally ill. The mental

[18]Jean Marquiset, *Le Crime* (Crime) (Paris: University Presses of France, 1957), p. 10 and following.

illnesses will be defined in the work of Aretaius and they
will be typified as insanity, dementia, menlancholy, and fatui-
tas, the latter represented by the rather vague behavior of
the "mente-captus."

Thirdly, only Rome and her thinkers will classify, with a
basis in Aristotle, the extensive idea of "character" in order
to try to observe what relationship there is between character
and the behavior of the criminal. One speaks then of three
types of men: lymphatic, sanguineous, and nervous.

Fourthly, it is also Roman law which establishes definitively
and in a clear and precise way a catalog of crimes, attribu-
ting to each a different consequence—perhaps arbitrary and
barbarous—but which represents a great advance over other
nations.

Fifthly, as can be found in the *Pandectas Justininea* and in
Ulpiano's work, it is also Rome which defines the most important crimes. For the moment, the gravest crime is injury
in a strict sense, which is an attempt against the life or the
physical integrity of the individual (homicides and wounds),
or against his honor (defamation and injury of today). Therefore, even if it is true that in the ancient nations prior to
Rome there was a sanction for the offense to honor, only in
Roman law was this placed as an attempt against the integrity
of the person.

Sixthly, in Roman society it was demonstrated and accepted that crime, besides material motives, may have motives of
an immaterial type, for example, to defame the moral personality of a person.

Third Period. Upon the fall of the Roman Empire, law is
spread through the Germanic and Gallic cultures. The Roman
idea of crime will undergo a deep transformation due to the
appearance of Christianity. This is a changing period full of
high and low points which will continue to develop until the
end of the Middle Ages. One could say that Christian philosophy and its application to life goes through two periods; first,
an initial one during which penalties are softened and the
ideas relating to prisons and penitentiaries in general evolve
more around the concept of social reparation than of punishment—even though this idea does not disappear completely.
But the other period is somewhat pernicious. Penal law conti-

nues to be customary and therefore remains, in the hands of a judge (human being with errors), the application of a justice moved more than once by personal interest and passion. The commandment of the Master, to measure with the same yardstick with which one is measured, is forgotten.

One arrives at the Middle Ages, when a system of judgments is implanted through which prior tortures and chastisements of the accused try to bring the convincement of the truth to the judge. All the ferocities appear, against which rise the voices of two great champions of modern penology and penal doctrine, viz. Marquis Cesar de Beccaria (in his small but wise work *De los Delitos y de las Penas* [Of Offenses and of Punishments]), and John Howard (in his "State of Prisons"). This period is full of incredible paradoxes. It is even thought that animals can be active subjects of real criminal acts and therefore brought to justice. We see then how mice which came to an Italian city are placed on the dock of some tribunal, and an elephant which escaped from a circus is accused and constrained to repair damages due to his acts in a French town.

On the other hand, the evolution of the idea of offense is influenced by the political change, change by which the temporal and spiritual powers are often united in one person. One speaks thus of crimes of divine lese-majesty, forgetting the Roman differentiation between rights and morals, and giving birth to so many vitiated processes of the Middle Ages. The term was so extensive that the interpretation of a judge was enough to include in the same category the revolutionary activities of a Joan of Arc and those of any soothsayer. Witchcraft, an old practice of humanity not even erradicated in civilized nations and not even persecuted in some, is punished with the penalty called "of the skin and the hair."

In his work Rousselet has enumerated the qualifications of criminal acts as made in France.[19] In the first place are the crimes of divine lese-majesty which included blasphemy, atheism, heresy, injury, abuses of sacraments, simony, profanation of sacred vessels, and violation of sepulchers. In the second

[19]Rousselet, *Histoire de la Justice* (History of Justice) (Paris: University Presses of France,1963), p. 25 and following.

place are the crimes of human lese-majesty which include attempt against the person of the King and his family, against the honor of the royal family, the lack of respect for official orders, attack on the sovereignty of the Crown (not the nation) peculation, extortion, prevarication of functions, falsification of money, and all enterprise "against the State." As can be seen by some of the titles, the denominations are so extensive that any kind of action is covered by each concept.

In the third place, there are the crimes "against private persons" which include, without distinction by act, crime in a strict sense (homicides), poisoning of waters and poisoning as the way to carry out a concrete homicide, abduction, rape, incest, sodomy, fraud, arson and certain types of theft.

We are not going to refer to the penalties. It is enough to say that they have the character of exemplary punishment and that the work of Beccaría abounds in this theme. Due to this character, a person, for a single act, could be subjected to such crude sanctions following one upon the other, that the penalties which were to be applied in second or third place almost always implied an act of sadism in the judgment; or, as Carnelutti says, a "violation of civility"[20] as they fell upon the cadaver of the culprit, who died with the application of a single part of the sentence, lacking the strength to tolerate the tortures of the inquisitorial process.

Fourth Period. This is a period of political influences. The Rights of Man, remembered by the thinkers of the French Revolution, will have a notable influence upon the evolutionary development of the concepts of crime, criminal, motive, and sanction. The category of "crime of less-majesty" is abolished, and in its place "the crimes against public affairs" (internal security of the State and against public peace) are incorporated as the first important chapter of the French Code of 1810. The crimes against private persons (offenses against goods and against persons) are put in the second place. The principle "Nullum Crimen Nulla Poena sine lege" enters in force, and the obligation to be judged by natural judges is made official.

[20]Carnelutti Francesco, *Las Miserias del Proceso Penal* (The Miseries of the Penal Process), Breviarios de Derecho, No. 24, EJEA, Buenos Aires, 1952, p. 14.

Fifth Period. In this period, following the French Revolution to the present day, an offense is transformed into a judicial entity. The different schools, mainly the Italian and the German, will discourse upon the characteristics of the penal infraction. Doctrine will influence legislation and jurisprudence being the source of greater importance in the Anglo-Saxon system which, based upon cases, will determine the concept of offense.

Present Penal Philosophy

In schematic form, the principles which inspire the present system, as foreseen in the National Constitution[21] and the Penal Code in force, are the following (*i*) In Venezuela the death penalty is forbidden, and is considered as a perpetual and opprobious punishment (Articles 58 and 60; Paragraph 7 of the National Constitution). This takes for granted that under no circumstance can human life be violated and the State guarantees this individual right. (*ii*) Personal liberty and security are inviolable and therefore nobody can be imprisoned or detained, unless taken infraganti if he is not presented with a written order of the court officials authorized by the law (Article 60, Paragraph 1 of the National Constitution). (*iii*) No civil act can lead to the deprivation of liberty if it is not legally an offense which merits such a penalty (Article 60 of the National Constitution). (*iv*) Nobody can be held in solitary confinement or subject to proceedings which cause physical or moral suffering. The Constitution considers this behavior punishable in Paragraph 3 of its Article 60. (*v*) The Right of defense is inviolable in every State and grade of the process (Article 68 of the National Constitution). (*vi*) In Venezuela it is obligatory to be judged by official judges, who are established in accordance with territorial jurisdiction and competence in the matter (Article 69 of the National Constitution). (*vii*) Nobody can be condemned to suffer a type of sanction which has not been established prior to the act in the penal law (Article 69 of the National Constitution).

[21]*Constitucion Nacional de la Republica de Venezuela* (National Constitution of the Republic of Venezuela) Gaceta Official, January 23, 1961.

Besides the above-mentioned constitutional provisions, it has to be indicated that, in penal matters, the principle of non-retroactivity of the law has also been established (Article 2 of the Venezuelan Penal Code).

In the same manner, the Constitution legalized the general principle of law known as "judged thing," which implies that "nobody can be judged for the same acts due to which he has been judged previously" (Article 60, Paragraph 8).

Our Basic Bill also legalizes the obligation of the right to defense, the guarantees of a process, and of some lapses in time, in order to allow the citizen to submit himself to justice without substantial loss in the rest of his activities.

On the other hand, in penal matters, the Code establishes as an indispensable requirement for the application of sanctions all that refers to responsibility. Offense is a plainly conscious act and whoever is deprived of conscience, be it partially or totally, will carry out a behavior, which although damaging in many cases (possibly subject to civil reparation) may not always be unlawful according to the appraisal of the judge. In this matter there is the influence of natural maturity, measured by the coming of age—which is variable in all legislation—and this determines the punishment, ranging from a total exemption to other attenuated forms.

FUNCTIONS OF THE COURT

In Venezuela, the judicial power is independent from all the other branches of the public power, as it refers to the exercise of its functions. It is thus legalized in Article 203 of the National Constitution in force. The law which governs it was enforced from June 30, 1956 and is called, "Organic Law of the Judicial Power." Between 1956 and the present, the general Law has been modified and specified respectively by Decree-Laws (in periods of de-facto government) and some Regulations. The National Constitution of 1961 dedicates Title VII to this function.

In spite of the fact that judges and judicial functionaries enjoy certain stability, up to this date there exists no law of the Judicial Career.

The independence of the judicial power does not suppose

an absence of relationship with the other branches of power. The link with the executive power is essentially of an economic character as the judicial functionaries receive their remuneration through entries included in the National Budget in the section corresponding to the Ministry of Justice. Also, this Ministry inspects the working of the courts of the country. There are close links with the legislative power insofar as (*a*) it is the Congress which names the Attorney General of the nation; and (*b*) it is the Supreme Court of Justice who decides about the submission to a judicial decision of legislators who have committed acts capable of depriving them of parliamentary immunity.

Objectives, Organization, and Classification of the Courts

Be it in unipersonal or in collegiate Courts (the latter less frequent within the Venezuelan system), in accordance with Article 4 of the Organic Law which governs this matter, to the Judicial Power corresponds the cognizance of "all cases and matters, be they civil, mercantile, penal, of labor, of minors, military, political, administrative, or fiscal, whoever be the persons who intervene."

This is the first objective indicated by the competent law, viz. the knowledge of all these cases, classified by matter, about which there exists a controversy, solved in a friendly way or out of court. We could say that this is the general purpose of the courts which function in the Republic.

A second objective is, evidently, to decide about these controversies through sentences or judgments arising from the cognizance of the cases stated in the lawsuits and based upon the proofs which are furnished.

As a third objective, the courts become the executors of their own decisions or the sentences of other courts, national as well as foreign, when all the requirements which the Law imposes—in order that the decisions of foreign courts may be valid in Venezuela (Exequatur)—have been fulfilled.

In the last place and as an important objective, the Judicial Power has competence to "intervene in all the non-contentious acts indicated by the Law; and perform all the correctional and disciplinary attributes indicated by it."[22]

Article 2 of the Organic Law establishes that Judicial Power is performed through the following agencies: (*i*) the Federal Court and the Court of Repeal; (*ii*) the Courts of Ordinary Jurisdiction; and (*iii*) the Courts of Special Jurisdiction.

Supreme Court. Starting with the Constitution of 1961, the first of the agencies mentioned has come to be called Supreme Court of Justice, and performs the functions of highest judicial agency of the country. At present it has three tribunals: Civil Tribunal, Penal Tribunal, and Political-Administrative Tribunal. In each case, it is a collegiate Tribunal, formed by five judges, and has a Secretariat. As to its specific activities, it is governed by internal rules.

In order to be a magistrate of the Court, one is required, in accordance with Article 213 of the National Constitution, to be (*i*) Venezuelan by birth; (*ii*) a lawyer; and (*iii*) be at least 30 years of age. There it is also established that the law which will govern all judicial careers can determine other conditions, such as to have experience due to exercise of the profession, of the judicature or a University professorship, in judicial matters. The magistrates of the Court are elected by the National Congress for a period of nine years, being renewed by thirds every three years. The substitutes, who have to fill temporary or accidental vacancies, are also named by the Congress.

The attributes of this highest agency of Justice in Venezuela are thus enumerated in Article 215 of the Constitution:

(*i*) To declare if there is merit or not for the institution of legal proceedings against the President of the Republic or whoever is in his place, and, in an affirmative case, to continue cognizance of the case with prior authorization of the Senate until definitive sentence.

(*ii*) To declare if there is merit or not for the institution of legal proceedings against the members of Congress or the Court itself, of the Ministers, the Attorney General, the Solicitor General or the Controller General of the Republic, the Governors, and the chiefs of diplomatic missions of the Republic, and, in affirmative case, to pass the proceedings to

[22]*Organic Law of the Judicial Power*, Article 4.

the competent ordinary Tribunal, if the offense is ordinary; or to continue cognizance of the case until definitive sentence if it is concerned with political offenses, excluding that established in Article 144 with regard to members of Congress.

(*iii*) To declare the total or partial invalidity of the national laws and other acts of the legislative bodies which clash with this Constitution.

(*iv*) To declare the total or partial invalidity of the State laws, the municipal ordinances and other acts of the deliberating bodies of the states or townships, which clash with this Constitution.

(*v*) To resolve the differences which may exist among different legal requirements and declare which of them has to prevail.

(*vi*) To declare the invalidity of the regulations and other acts of the National Executive when they are in violation of this Constitution.

(*vii*) To declare the invalidity of the administrative acts of the Executive, when such is the case.

(*viii*) To reconcile the controversies in which one of the parties is the Republic or a state or township, when the other party is one of these same entities, unless they are controversies between township of the same state, in which case the law may attribute its cognizance to another Tribunal.

(*ix*) To decide the conflicts of competence between courts, be they ordinary or special, if there is no other court which is superior and common to both of them in order of hierarchy.

(*x*) Take cognizance of the recourse of "Repeal."
This enumeration is not restrictive as the Article concludes with an additional clause numbered (xi) which reads: "The others that the Law may attribute to it."

Ordinary Courts. The Venezuelan Courts[23] can be classified as follows, according to their hierarchy: (*a*) Superior Courts, (*b*) Courts of First Instance, (*c*) District or Departmental Courts, (*d*) Municipal or Parish Courts, and (*e*) Courts of Instruction.

---

[23]The term tribunal or court does not change the category, although the tendency at present is to call the agencies of justice by the name of "Tribunals."

The above classification only follows the order in which one takes recourse to them. In accordance with the importance, a lawsuit can be started, in civil as well as in mercantile matters, in a Municipal or Parish Tribunal, District or Departmental one, or in one of First Instance; the Superior Court or Tribunal is reserved for cognizance in appeal of the questions tried in the agencies that are immediately below.

In penal matters, the ordinary organization is as follows: (a) Supreme Court of Justice (Penal Tribunal), (b) Superior Court—Penal, (c) Courts or Tribunals of First Instance—Penal, and (d) Courts of Instruction.

From the point of view of judicial mechanics and in penal matters, the Tribunals of Instruction obtain the necessary evidence, compile the file with the help of the competent police agencies, and send them to the ordinary tribunal (Judge of the case which is the First Instance) in order that the same may pronounce verdict as to the culpability or innocence of the one subjected to judgment. All this operates in accordance with a form of process which will be discussed later.

Special Courts. Outside ordinary jurisdiction, as judicial activity for a more limited category of persons, there are courts which have special functions at the same time that they are subject to the requirements of the Constitution and the laws which have created them. The matters of which they take cognizance and the proceedings of some of them present certain modalities and therefore they are placed outside the general picture. The Military Tribunals, the Fiscal Tribunals, the Leasehold Tribunals, and the Juvenile Courts are some of the bodies that fall in this category. It cannot be considered a real tribunal, but there also exists with similar functions the Commission against the illicit enrichment of public functionaries and employees, whose activity is governed by the same denomination, although it cannot be considered a real Tribunal. The following chart will be helpful in understanding the Venezuelan judicial organization.

Qualifications of Judges and the Attorney General

In order to be a judge of an ordinary court of the Republic, it is necessary to fulfil the following requirements: (a) to be a

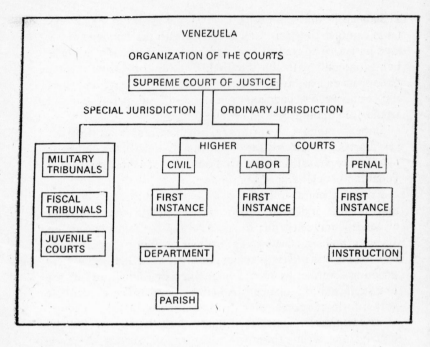

lawyer in the case of the titulars, as this condition is not demanded from the substitutes; (*b*) to be Venezuelan; (*c*) to be
at least 21 years of age; (*d*) to have full enjoyment of civil and
political rights (which can only be lost through civil incapacita-
tion or through a sentence which makes impossible the performance of political rights); and (*e*) to have a conduct above
reproach. Furthermore, the law establishes (Article 33) that
the following are impediments to performing this charge, besides
the fact of not fulfilling some of the above conditions: (*a*) to be a
member of the military (they can be judges of military courts);
(*b*) to be a minister of any cult; (*c*) to be the leader or activist
of a political party; and (*d*) to have any physical impediment
which makes impossible the complete performance of the function. This last impediment is only important in grave and
notorious cases.

In many cases, the courts (especially those situated in very
remote places) are discharged by persons who do not have the
title of lawyer. This fact, becoming less frequent, is for several
reasons mentioned in the same article of the organic Law of

the Judicial Power. Besides the poor remuneration of these charges (a fact which is being improved), there was a lack of titled persons who wanted to discharge them. The situation has changed notably with the graduating classes of the seven law schools which exist at present in the country.

In principle, the same requirements which are demanded for a judge, are applicable to the Department of Justice, until the time there appears a special law to regulate these aspects. Nevertheless, the general functions of the Department of Justice (presided by the Attorney General of the Republic) are established in Article 220 of the National Constitution, which enumerates them as follows: (*i*) to watch that the constitutional rights and guarantees are respected; (*ii*) to watch for the celerity and good progress of the administration of justice and that the laws are applied honestly in the courts of the Republic, in the penal processes and in those in which public order and convential manners are involved; (*iii*) to perform penal action in the cases in which petition from a party is not necessary in order to commence the lawsuit or to prosecute it, this without impairing the capability of the court to proceed officially when the law determines it; (*iv*) to watch that there is a correct fulfilment of the laws and of the guarantee of human rights in the jails and other types of prison; (*v*) to commence the lawsuits which may be necessary in order to make effective the civil, penal, administrative or disciplinary responsibility which the public functionaries may have incurred in the performance of their functions; and (*vi*) other functions which the laws may attribute to it.

It is important to indicate that the Attorney General of the Republic, in representation of his Department, annually gives account to the National Congress.

Obligations and Rights

Title II of the organic Law of the Judicial Power, in 17 articles, establishes the obligations of the judges, which can be summarized as follows: (*a*) to keep conventional manners and, therefore, to avoid any kind of acts which might lessen his dignity as magistrate; (*b*) to reside in the place where he performs his functions and in a radius of at least 15 kilometers of the seat of the court; (c) to give audience five days a week for at least during four hours on each of those days; (d) to sign the documents and to authorize the official communications; (e) to abstain from giving an opinion in matters which due to their function are subject to sentences; (f) with the authorization of the court, they can perform the functions of notaries or registrars, especially in places where no such offices exist; and (g) the judges cannot, under any pretext and not even in the character of consultants, practise the profession of lawyer, not even through third persons. All these obligations are subject, in case of non-fulfillment, to sanctions which go from a simple warning, passing through the fine, to the compiling of a file with penal sanctions for the perpetration of offenses which give rise to the same.

From the point of view of rights, the judges can (a) charge the amounts which the Law of Judicial Fees fixes for finished acts; (b) request the assistance of public forces, if this is necessary, in order to fulfil his decisions; (c) enjoy vacations of one month every year; (d) be re-elected to their office and enjoy the immovability established by the Constitution, as long as they do not commit faults which make them unsuitable for the post; and (e) enjoy retirement after 25 years of activity in the judicature. The amount of the same is variable, being the usual practice to grant it for an amount of no less than half the last salary after 20 years of service.

Internal System of the Lawyers. As we have seen, in Venezuela in order to be a Judge it is necessary in principle to have the title of lawyer. The same thing tends to be required for the functions of attorney general of the Justice Department, public defender of prisoners, notary, and registrar. From a single career, five years in length, there appear possibilities for different professions which in other countries have already reached a justified specialization. There is a certain tendency to leave the career of the law as a basis for these activities and to give post-graduate courses for each of the specialized professions that can be discharged. Once the title is obtained and registered in an Office of Public Registry, the lawyer has to be registered in the Bar Association of his locality in order to be able to work in his profession and in accordance with a condition laid down by the Constitution. The Bar Association is a trade union which through a new law created a special institute for the social protection of the profession. This social protection and the registration in the Institutó de Previsión del Abogado (Impre-Abogado) are indispensable requirements for the signature or approval of any kind of documents in which the laws order the reviewing of the act by a lawyer. Besides the registration and approval of the bar association and the Instituto de Previsión, all Venezuelans or foreigners who have a title and reside in the country can perform their profession freely.

Elements of the Venezuelan Penal Process[24]

Within the known lawsuit systems, the one accepted by our country is of a mixed character because it combines elements of the system called accusatory and of the inquisitive one. The first is characterized by being (a) oral; (b) public; (c) via popular juries; and (d) with contradiction by the parties. The second (inquisitive system) presents the opposite characteristics of being (a) written; (b) it is not public; (c) properly said, there is no contradiction by the parties; and (d) there are no popular juries, as all the aspects inherent to the decision, correspond to permanent agencies of the State.

The mixed system represents a combination of the two mentioned above. On the one hand, it is *essentially* written, to such a degree that many of the oral acts which may occur during the same, in order to be valid, will have to be incorporated into the file in written form. But there are acts which have to be oral through express mandate of the law, for example, the act of pleading. In the second place the penal process has two parts: first, the indictment which is secret and where only the accused and his counsel can be informed of what is being considered; and, secondly, the Plenary which is totally public except in those cases in which the facts to be discussed may cause disturbances.

Finally, the function of deciding always remains in hands

---

[24]The law which governs the matter is the *Code of Institution of Criminal Proceedings*, the reformed version of December 15, 1961, of the same being in force.

of a pre-existing agency, the judge. As has already been said, sometimes this function falls upon several persons (Collegiate Tribunals), but juries do not exist. Referring to the contradiction by the parties, it should be mentioned that in the summary part of the process it is almost imperceptible. It becomes more evident starting with the investigatory declaration delivered by the accused. In the Plenary the accused can accept the facts, deny them completely, or accept them in part. As a guarantee of the rights of the citizen during the summary, the Constitution allows him to omit any declaration which may be used to his detriment until he is assisted by his counsel.

Penal action ("judicial power to stimulate and to promote the decision of the jurisdictional agency about a determined relationship of Penal law," according to the writer Florian) is characterized in the Venezuelan system by being *public* (given the interest which is pursued and the organism to which one recurs); *singular*, as from each penal act only a single action of this kind arises; *indivisible*, when it is a case of offenses which are of action not reserved to private persons; *irrevocable*, because once the lawsuit is initiated by a private person (if such is the case), even if he should renounce its continuation, the State has an interest in it and will carry it to the consummation of the judgment (except in offenses of action which through legal exception are reserved to private persons, called "offenses of private action"); and finally, penal action is *autonomous*, it is born from our own capacity as citizens.

In principle, this action is in hands of the State, which performs it officially in the greater part of the offenses. In other instances, the State proceeds based upon a denunciation from a private person who knows of the realization of an act which he presumes punishable. Exceptionally, as already mentioned, the private person performs the action as the injured party (accusation) and indicates the subject or subjects whom he points out as authors of the presumably punishable act. As a practical rule for distinguishing the way of proceeding, the law stipulates that as long as the Penal Code does not indicate that an accusation is required in order to proceed, the offense is of public action. Therefore, the offenses of private action are

an exception. Thus, the process is opened and it will be started
with the indictment, which begins with the act of prosecuting.
This is an instruction to the investigating agencies to the effect
that they exhaust their techniques in the clarification of.the act
stated. This act supposes that the judge has determined his
competence and the capacity of the accuser, that the action is
not prescribed, and that the act to be investigated is invested
with a penal character. During the summary one will try to
(a) assure that an offense has been committed; (b) determine
the person on which falls justified evidence of culpability; (c)
assure that the persons presumed guilty do not escape the
action of justice; and (d) preserve the elements of judgment
(tracks, etc.) which would get lost in time or by fraudulent
action.

The indictment, then, concludes in the following ways: by
decree of detention or of subjection to judgment, with the
conditions which the law fixes for one or the other; by decree
which will order to leave open the investigation, when the end
which the summary pursues has not been fulfilled and within
the time limits established by law; and by the decree which
declares "that there are no merits to continue the investigation." In these cases the Plenary is opened.

During this second period, the following will begin to act: the
prosecutor of the Department of Justice as a *bona fide* party
which he is within the process, be it in order to formulate
charges or in order to abstain from doing the same; the experts,
who are helpers of justice in specific matters, with special
value in all referring to the probatory questions; and the
counsel, who, even if he has already acted, now has a definitive and fundamental character. In this lapse of time, counsel
and prosecutor prepare the elements of judgment which will
form the convincement of the judge in order to decide. The
clarity of argumentation is essential because in case of doubt,
the benefit will be for the accused. Once the sentence has been
pronounced, if the accused is not satisfied because he considers
himself innocent or because the penalty imposed on him is
unjust, he can make an appeal to the higher competent court.
In certain offenses of some degree of seriousness, the decision
has to be sent to the higher court in the character of consultation, in order that it may confirm or revoke the decision of

the trial judge, even if the interested party does not appeal.

FUNCTIONS OF THE POLICE

In Venezuela there exist a large number of Corps and Organizations which, in a strict sense, perform police actions. On the other hand, there is no basic co-ordination of the functions of many of these groups.

Organization of the Police in Relation to the Government Offices

Taking as an example any of the cities (over 200,000 inhabitants) we find the following Police Corps:

Local Organizations. They are represented by the Municipal Police Forces, authorized by the State Governors (Local Executive Power), and basically have these functions: (*i*) task of surveillance in the jurisdiction, in order to *avoid* the commission of offenses as well as the routine disturbances of public order; (*ii*) control of the offenses included in the Penal Code and in the local ordinances (norms valid within the confines of the districts); and (*iii*) overseeing of the places where delinquents or dangerous subjects gather frequently (gambling places, bars, zones of tolerance), though generally, this activity is performed by functionaries out of uniform.

National Police Forces. Under this title are included all those organizations which, according to the law which creates them and by the character of their functions, practice the latter in all of the National Territory. These comprise:

(*i*) *The General Police Administration* (Dirección General de Politiciá. It is authorized by the Ministry of Internal Relations (called State Secretariat elsewhere), whose basic function is the keeping of public order and tranquility. This objective of general policy covers, first, summary court proceedings and routine investigations in the offenses which are attempted against the security of the State, of the public functionaries, and in general the offenses with political motives. Secondly, surveillance and control of foreigners. Thirdly, everything concerning the carrying of arms, in accordance with the law about arms and explosives. Fourthly, all the other police functions not entrusted to any other official corps or agency.

(*ii*) *Co-operative Armed Forces* (Fuerzas Armadas de Cooperacíon). In other countries they fulfil their functions under the names of National Gendarmerie, Civil Guard, and Carabineer Corps. In Venezuela they are a branch of the army, with the basic functions of protection of the national frontiers and highways, as well as prosecution of contraband offenses and all matters relating to summary court proceedings due to this offense.

(*iii*) *Technical Corps of Judicial Police*. (El Cuerpo Técnico de Policía Judicial). The Statute which creates it (Decree Number 48 of February 20, 1958) indicates that this organization is an auxiliary body of the judicial power, with the obligation of fulfilling the functions which the Code of Institution of Criminal Proceedings establishes (Article 74-A).

This Corps is more prevalent and has a wider sphere of action, as it does not issue from the executive and lacks political functions. Insofar as its budget is concerned, it is part of the Department of Justice. According to internal regulations of the Technical Corps of Judicial Police[25] it has as "special mission, to collaborate in the investigation of offenses, to impede their continuation and their being carried to ulterior consequences, to identify and to apprehend those presumed guilty, and to insure and keep the proofs necessary for the application of the law. In the fulfilling of these functions, it is subordinated to the judges of instruction." One could say that this is the national frame of action. The whole of penal justice is based upon the investigations of the Judicial Police, and specifically in the greater part of the offenses, in those of this Corps.

But the Technical Corps of Judicial Police also has functions in the international sphere, co-operating in the repression of crime with international authorities and organizations, "in the terms and conditions established in the treaties signed by Venezuela, or in their defect, by the norms of International Law."

Conditions and Duties of the Members of the Corps. In order to join the Technical Judicial Police Corps, one is required

---

[25]Internal Regulation of the Technical Corps of Judicial Police, Articles 2 and 3.

(*a*) to be Venezuelan; (*b*) to be in the age group of 21-60 years; (*c*) to have good antecedents; (*d*) to have capacity proven in examinations for the position to which one aspires; (*e*) to be physically able; (*f*) not to be leader or activist of a political party; (*g*) to have a ticket of military registration; and (*h*) to post bonds in certain cases.

In order to be Director, Assistant Director, and Judicial Counsellor it is also necessary to be a lawyer, as these offices, as well as that of Secretary General, are filled by the National Executive through the agency of the Department of Justice.

All members of the Technical Corps of Judicial Police are subject to fulfilling the following duties: (*a*) to try for the improvement of their professional education; (*b*) to observe absolute reserve and discretion in matters of the service; (*c*) to maintain relations of harmony and co-operation with similar organizations; (*d*) to use towards the public proceedings in accordance with the culture and the objectives of the Corps; and (*e*) to care and keep with great pains the goods which belong to the Institution, especially the arms.

Powers of the Judicial Police. It has already been pointed out that the penal process is secret (Summary) in its first period. During the same, all the situations pertinent to the enlightenment of the facts are investigated, with the Judicial Police acting as the investigating agency. When for any reason this organism acquires knowledge of an unlawful act, it will go immediately to the place where the offense was committed, inform the judicial authority and, without delay, will try to maintain the probatory elements.

Immediately afterwards it will take informative declarations from the informants, summon the witnesses, and practice investigations. In case a preventive detention has been made, the Code of Institution of Criminal Proceedings (Art. 75-H) indicates that the citizen has to be placed at the orders of the Court of Instruction "in a lapse of time no longer than 8 days, to be counted from the date of detention."

On the other hand, it is established in the Decree which constitutes the Technical Corps of Judicial Police that, in the headquarters of the same there will be no premises for detainees, who, placed under the orders of the competent judge, have to go without delay to the nearest penal establishment.

Later on, during the trial the judge will call the functionaries of the Judicial Police in order that they make their declaration. In any case, the confession made by the accused in front of the Judicial Police, if it is not ratified by the accused during the process, will only have the value of simple circumstantial evidence and therefore is not complete proof.

Internal Structure of the Judicial Police. The main offices of the Corps, issuing from the management and the assistant management, are Division of Offenses against property; Division of Offenses against Minors; Division of Offenses against Persons; Division of Vehicles; Division of Narcotics; Section of Denunciations; and Body of Counsellors.

As internal services, in order to fulfil the above activities, there are the following departments: control of transmissions; patrols; legal medicine; police laboratory; photography; fingerprinting; handwriting experts, cryptographers and planimetry; ballistics, arms and explosives; and statistics.

Evidently, all the divisions count in their turn with a section of police interrogation, and the advice of national as well as foreign technicians hired for this purpose.

Due to the nature of the functions and the diversification of the police organizations, it is impossible to give statistical data about the total number of police forces in the country; therefore, the proportion which exists in relation to the citizens in general is not known.

PENITENTIARY SYSTEM

According to the Venezuelan Penal Code (Article 8) "penalties are divided mainly into corporal and non-corporal." When the legislator defines the first kind, he identifies them with those penalties which restrict freedom, such as penitentiary, prison, arrest, banishment to a penal colony, confinement, and expulsion from the territory (Article 9 of the Penal (Code).

The non-corporal penalties are not defined in the law, but one can deduce that they are those which do not imply a restriction of freedom. This idea is corroborated by Article 10 of the Penal Code, which enumerates them under 11 categories.

The law which regulates all penitentiary activity is called Law of the Penitentiary System (1961). In this law the competent administrative agency is determined, before which the condemned is placed for the fulfillment of the penalty imposed by a firm sentence. In Venezuela this agency is the Department of Justice, which is concerned with the organization and functioning of the penitentiary services.

We could summarize the purposes which the penalty is supposed to fulfil according to the law, besides the fact that in the sentence it is considered a sanction for the offense committed. These objectives, as indicated in the first articles of the Law of the Penitentiary System, are (a) to try for the rehabilitation of the punished; and (b) to obtain the re-adaptation of the same through the treatments established by the law. These purposes, and the treatment in general, are fulfilled taking into account the minimal regulations on the subject approved by the United Nations.[26] These can be summarized as follows: (a) classification of the punished before the internment; (b) criminological diagnosis; (c) penitentiary grouping, in accordance with the nature of the penalties, an affinity between the diagnosis and the treatment; (d) remunerated work, according to the vocation and the capability of the prisoner; (e) integral education; (f) medical assistance; and (g) norms of discipline.

A characteristic note of the Venezuelan system, besides the classification and grouping, is its progessiveness. According to the Constitution (Article 60, Ordinal 7th), no Venezuelan can be condemned to perpetual or opprobrious penalties. On the other hand, for a long time now and through various reforms, the principle which prohibits capital punishment has been maintained. The maximum penalty the Constitution admits is 30 years.

Internal Organization

We can classify the prison establishments in the following categories:

---

[26]"Minimal Regulations for the Treatment of Prisoners and Related Recommendations," Geneva, 1955.

Juridical Detainment Places. These are not meant for fulfilling a sentence, but are centers of seclusion for persons which are in the process. Sometimes they are a part or an annex of a place for fulfilling sentences, and are also known as "Public Jails."

National Penitentiaries and Jails. These are centers for the fulfillment of penalties which come under the degree of security of the establishment, and are subject to the rehabilitation system.

Establishments for Women. These are managed with female personnel only and generally with a connecting orphan asylum. The Law of the Penitentiary System establishes special norms for the women, type of custodians, the protection they merit during the internment, and the general services of the law which are applicable to them. At present there is an establishment called National Institute of Feminine Orientation, which receives 80 per cent of the female delinquents of the country. The remainder are placed in the female annexes of the two national jails.

Establishment for Young People. There are two kinds of establishments for young delinquents: First, detainment places for minors of less than 18 years, controlled and guided by the Venezuelan Children's Council. (This category lies outside the scope of the present article, as minors of less than 18 years are not considered delinquents). Secondly, special establishments for subjects between 18 to 21 years of age, and 21 to 25 years of age—if the criminological diagnosis of the latter category recommends grouping them with those of less age, in case they are not repeaters.

Establishments for the Mentally Ill. All those who show symptoms of mental illness during their imprisonment have to fulfill their sentence in special establishments, generally incorporated with penitentiaries of medium security and called Psychiatric Penitentiary Annexes. If the mental illness is considered to be longterm and difficult to cure, then the patient has to be transported to a psychiatric institute, which is not a penitentiary. The law also foresees the creation of *opeu* establishments and of *agricultural colonies.*

In reality, one can indicate that the 25 penitentiary establishments of the country correspond to places of maximum and medium security.

Rehabilitation System

Besides the general characteristics already indicated, if can be mentioned here that the entire rehabilitation process is based upon the following elements:

Work. (*i*) As a general rule, penitentiary work is obligatory. Preferably, its purpose is educational and it tends to be established as work-therapy. The law indicates (Art. 16) that under no circumstances "it will have a distressing character." (*ii*) The working day in the penitentiary, as well as everything referring to the health and the security of the punished, is ruled by the requirements of the Labor Law. (*iii*) Work has to be remunerated fairly, taking into account the educational function, productivity, and capability of the prisoner. (*iv*) According to what is specified in Article 19 of the Law of the Penitentiary System, this remuneration has to be utilized for the acquisition of objects for personal use; consideration of the needs of the family of the prisoner; formation of his own capital, which he will be able to enjoy upon his release; and, finally, "to compensate partially for the cost of his internment, in the measure that the amount of the assigned renumeration allows for the same." (*v*) The work has to be directed according to the demands of the development of the country.

Education. (*i*) One starts with the assumption that education has to be integral and obligatory at the level of primary instruction, putting emphasis on alphabetization and on the understanding of patriotic subjects (history, geography, and civics). (*ii*) Education has to be adapted to the official programs in force and to be adequate to the levels of the students. Those older than 50 and those mentally deficient can be exempted from this obligation. (*iii*) Included as elements of cultural extension we find choirs, bands, orchestras, and other artistic and literary competitions. (*iv*) Sports are obligatory, for they encourage the spirit of solidarity, inculcate respect for norms, and provide stimulus to success.

Medical Assistance and Living Conditions. (*i*) The living environment of the prisoner has to be harmonious with the human level to which one wants to promote him. Urbanity, personal cleanliness, hygiene and the development of good customs "are an integral part of the treatment," says the law. (*ii*) The diet and the uniforms are subject to inspection by the medical group, in order that they may be adequate for the general treatment. (*iii*) The punished is compelled to receive complete medical assistance—when he enters, or at any moment when he wishes it, as well as when he is subjected to special disciplinary measures due to misbehavior—during his imprisonment.

LIBERTY WITH BAIL AND LIBERTY UNDER VIGILANCE

The Venezuelan Code also provides for provisional and/or conditional liberty.

Liberty with Bail

Liberty with bail is defined as that "which is given to the indicted during the trial, under the condition that he does not absent himself from the place of trial or the place in which the penal establishment where he was detained is located, the conditions to be at the disposition of the Tribunal; in guarantee of which he has to give a guarantor of notoriously good behavior and responsibility."[27]

This presupposes that freedom with bail or provisional liberty, as it is also called, is, in a certain way, a right of the indicted which can be exercised during any period of the proceedings, once the decree of detention has been firmly established. Nevertheless, the following conditions have to be fulfilled in order to make this right effective:

(*i*) *The seriousness of the punishable act.* It is a principle accepted by the legislation that liberty with bail only follows when "in the charges, an offense, which may merit penalty of imprisonment or an offense with a penalty of prison or arrest for over two years as a maximum limit, is imputed to the suspect."[28] However, the above limitation as to maximum

[27]Arminio Borjas, *Exposición del Código de Enjuiciamiento Criminál Venezuelano* (Interpretation of the Venezuelan Code of Institution of Criminal Proceedings), Vol. III, p. 11.

[28]*Venezuelan Code of Institution of Criminal Proceedings*, Art. 320.

penalty is not applied in the offenses of omission (those
committed through want of experience, imprudence, negligence,
and non-observance of regulations), as the same rule cited
indicates that this liberty can be given for this type of offense
even if "they may merit a penalty depriving of liberty, which
may exceed three years as its maximum limit." This type of
liberty can also be given in offenses, whose penalty of prison
or arrest is greater than two years but less than three, "only
if no circumstances of treachery, premeditation or aggravation
occur."

(*ii*) *The dangerousness of the indicted.* Therefore the article
mentioned above says that provisional liberty will not be given
when the subject is a repeater and if he had committed bad
behavior prior to the offense. The matter has to be adduced
and proven by the Prosecutor of the Department of Justice.

(*iii*) *The competence of the Tribunal.* Article 321 of the Code
of Institution of Criminal Proceedings says that "the tribunal
which has competence to give provisional liberty is the one
that has the jurisdiction of the process at the moment in which
the request for liberty is made, or the one which knows in
appeal of the decree which denies this liberty."

(*iv*) *Objects of liberty with bail.* In accordance with a recent
interpretation,[29] we can summaries its objects in the following
terms: (*a*) *purpose in relation to the lawsuit,* through which one
insures that the accused will present himself to the tribunal
whenever the same requires it, at the same time that his liberty is guaranteed, presuming his innocence; (*b*) *softening the
severity* of preventive detention; and (*c*) *to lighten the weight
of preventive detention* upon the judicial prisons and internment places.

In Table X is given some statistical data about liberty with
bail according to the Memoirs of the Department of Justice.

Problems of Liberty with Bail. Given the criterion of the
seriousness of the punishable act, which seems to depend
upon the dangerousness of the indicted, it is frequently observed that, in the first place, many occasional delinquents,
of rural extraction and those who commit homicides under

[29]Héctor Nieves, "La Libertad Provisional" (Provisional Liberty)
Relación Criminológica, Year 1, No. 1, Valencia, Venezuela, 1968.

TABLE X

Year	Provisional liberties
1964	2,931
1965	3,218
1966	1,889
1967	2,181
Yearly Average	2,555
TOTAL	10,219

the influence of alcohol, cannot enjoy this right due to the graveness of the applicable penalty (Penal Code, Article 407, from 12 to 18 years). Secondly, the crowding in the prisons could be reduced through the application of more elastic norms in the matter, with prior reform of the corresponding trial dispositions. (One has to remember that in Venezuela, of each 10 persons who are in prison, only two are there fulfilling a sentence. To many of the eight remaining, who are in process, the benefit of conditional liberty could be applied if the legislation would allow it). Thirdly, the present system of liberty with bail makes the process more expensive and creates maintenance expenses of the suspect as long as the trial lasts. And, fourthly, the congestion of the prisons, due to the reasons already given, is an inadequate treatment of the condemned, as there is lack of sufficient space for the application of the regimen.

Liberty under Vigilance or Conditional Liberty

There is no legal definition of this judicial institution. In 1961 it appeared for the first time in Venezuela, legalized in the Law of the Penitentiary System in force. One can get an idea of the same through interpretation of several articles which speak about it. As already mentioned, one of the characteristics of the Venezuelan penitentiary system is the *progressiveness* of the treatment. Thus, the penalty has to be fulfilled in a stepping-stone fashion, whenever possible. In contrast with pardon or "administrative grace," liberty under vigilance or conditional liberty is not a formula for extinguishing the penalty, but a form of fulfilling it. It is supposed to be a last period of fulfillment and implies an early release of the person who meets the conditions for choosing it.

Conditions. The Law establishes two categories of punished who can choose conditional liberty (Article 77), with different requirements for each.

(*i*) In the subjects sentenced to penalties of *up to 5 years,* the following conditions have to be fulfilled: that he has served three-fourths of his penalty; that he has fulfilled at least two years of the penalty in the penitentiary establishment of his destination; that he merits this benefit due to his behavior, a negative diagnosis of dangerousness, and psycho-criminological prognosis favorable to liberation; and that he offers guarantees to make an honest living in liberty.

(*ii*) In the subjects sentenced to penalties *over 5 years in length,* the following requirements are demanded: that he has served two-thirds of the penalty; that he has fulfilled at least half of his penalty in the penitentiary establishment to which he has been destined; and the others established by the cases treated before.

There is a special case under the law which is outside the general question stated in the above two categories. It is that of persons 70 years of age, who can obtain conditional liberty, no matter what the duration of the penalty, if they have fulfilled half of the same. In those cases of old persons who cannot demonstrate their chronological age, liberty can be given if there is a negative diagnosis of dangerousness, and a medical report which accredits a physiological age higher than 70 years.

One can loose conditional liberty, with or without deduction of the time enjoyed in liberty, in any of the following cases: (*a*) bad conduct of the freed; (*b*) non-fulfillment of the obligations inherent in the benefit; and (*c*) relapse, be it of the offense that produced the application of the penalty (specific), or of any other offense (generic). These cases will be heard and decided by the Board which had agreed to the conditional liberty.

In all cases of conditional liberty the fulfillment of the formality established in Article 81 of the Law of the Penitentiary Regimen is required, that is, the publication of the decision in the Official Gazette.

STUDY OF CRIMINOLOGY IN VENEZUELA

We can say without risk of error, that the systematic study of criminology, considered as an autonomous science, started in Venezuela less than 10 years ago. Prior to that, only general notions of the discipline were discussed during conferences and lectures from the positivist point of view, and as issuing from penal law.

Twenty years ago one seldom found texts or even articles about the subject. In a very scattered fashion, some scholars of the early period of the Republic (Fermín Toro, for example, in the first half of the 19th century) talked about Norms of Social Prophylaxis. More recently, José Gil Fortoul could be considered as a forerunner of this science in the country.

The first systematic explanation of Criminology was given by the lawyer, José Rafael Mendoza who gave a course for the body of officers of the Armed Forces of Cooperation.[30] Later on, a certain degree of consciousness of the value of criminology was awakened in young graduates.

Criminology in the Universities

After this period, criminology began to be incorporated into the different faculties of several Venezuelan Universities. Towards 1962, the Central University of Venezuela and the Catholic University, "Andrés Bello," incorporated the subject in the curriculum of the career in law. In the first it is in the form of a monographic course. In the second it is an obligatory course for the post-graduates in penal law.

More recently, the School of Law of the University of Carabobo opened its Center of Penal and Criminological Investigations where the subject is acquiring increasing value. Today, in this Center as well as in the Central University, there are monographic courses in areas like General Criminology; Introduction to Criminology; Criminal Sociology; Criminogesis of Juvenile Delinquency; the Dangerous State; Criminal Psychology and Psychiatry; and Course about As-

---

[30]José Rafael Mendoza, *Curso de Criminologia*, Gráficas Mariegas, Madrid 1951.

pect; of Criminogesis. All these expositions are in courses of one year in length for students who have passed or are studying in the third year of their program.

At present, the University of Santa María (Caracas) has incorporated the subject as an obligatory course, substituting for the course of Legal Medicine, which was studied traditionally. There is a project to incorporate criminology in the School of Law of the Central University of Venezuela, with the same purpose and rank as in the University of Santa María. The Schools of Psychology (of the Central University as well as of the Catholic University) give courses about different aspects of criminology, as a complementary subject in the formation of psychology. The same has been done in the Schools of Sociology of the two universities mentioned above.

Investigations. Since criminology is a new subject on the campuses, its research and systematic publications are more recent still. There are already some monographs or Manuals of General Criminology. The one which the author of this article published in 1963 has already been mentioned. Elio Gómez Grillo's monograph, entitled *Introduction to Criminology* (1964), is very valuable.

As systematic and periodic investigations we have to mention here those which have appeared in *Revista de Policía Científica* (Magazine of Scientific Police, which has already published 20 numbers, covering different aspects of criminology, criminal law and penal law); *El Anuario* (The Yearbook of the Institute of Penal and Criminological Sciences, published by the Central University of Venezuela); and the *Relacion Criminológica* (Criminological Report, which promises to be one of the best publications about criminological investigations on the Continent, in view of its quality and specialization).

On the other hand, there are monographs of learned Venezuelans about criminological aspects, published as specialized works or within collections or magazines of a general type. Among these are the *Magazine of the Faculty of Law of the Central University of Venezuela* (38 issues); the *Magazine of the Department of Justice* (58 issues), and the *Magazine of the office of the Attorney General of the Department of Justice* (9 issues).

Problems in the Study of Criminology

In general one notices an extra ordinary difficulty in obtaining truthful sources, which guarantee the results, in any type of criminological study or investigation. To date the biographies of delinquents are unknown and the *curricula vitae* are rather incomplete. One has begun to make the first prognosis and the follow-ups. The official statistics, which have been a source for this article, are not constant in the type of information which they furnish and sometimes they present serious doubts.

Another important problem in the study of criminology in the country is posed by the excessive ties which many criminological studies have with the activity of the State. This is explainable to some extent, because everywhere in the world the State has "criminological laboratories" at its disposals (jails, police, tribunals). On other occasions the State carries out studies in order to justify its activities. This, however, is improper. The studies should be made previously in order to guide the State action.

A third problem is born out of the type of formation present in Venezuela. There are a group of criminologists who have a fund of knowledge, but frequently there is a lack of auxilliary personnel. It is difficult to find statisticians of criminality, psycho-criminologists, and specialized social workers. Very often these professions are looked upon by the public, in a rather disrespectful manner.

Fourthly, from the point of view of the public, criminology and its studies lack an "image". It is therefore difficult to motivate the citizens, the enterprises, and the foundations, national as well as international, as to the value of general criminology, and even of concrete investigations. This is due to many reasons: (*a*) the empiricism which has dominated our science for many years; (*b*) the broadcasting of erroneous ideas about the discipline; and above all because of (*c*) a strong hedonistic feeling of the Venezuelan donor, who looks for practical and immediate rather than deep and long-term results.

Fifthly, for a long time, the study of criminology was neglected in university circles, because it was not independent and also was poorly remunerated. In many cases this is still true.

Sixthly, the big enemy of Venezuelan scientific criminology is its methodology. In self-criticism, it has to be acknowledged that the greater part of the studies made have been failures as far as the investigating techniques go. This is the result of the reigning darkness as to the specific methodology of criminology.

PREVENTION OF OFFENSE

As a concept, prevention is all activity which tends to avoid the realization of punishable acts (activity *a priori*) or the repetition of offenses (activity *a posteriori*).

Till about 15 years ago, Venezuela did not have a preventive policy against offenses. The State activity placed emphasis upon the repression of the offense, certainly not infrequent in a traditional society, attached to conventional ways of life. Earlier than 1950, there were no concrete plans about prevention *a priori*, with a date earlier than 1950.

In reference to *a posteriori* prevention, the firts investigations were done between 1940 and 1958. This period can be summarized as follows:

(*i*) Creation of the Commission for the Prevention of Delinquency, in order to make the preliminary studies; (*ii*) process of humanization of the jails—which were used until 1936 as centers of internment for politicians who did not agree with the dictatorial system, after which a transitional period toward the new republican way of life opens culminating in 1941; and (*iii*) beginnings of the specialized prison treatment and of the first establishments for fulfilling it.

This period, during which the Department of Justice is created (until 1955 it is only a branch of the Ministry of Internal Relations), is more a time of organization, of first steps in investigation as well as in action, than one of true realizations.

Prevention a Priori (*1958-1968*)

Venezuelan criminality has a strong exogenous base. Therefore, the elements of the environment, in general, acquire a special value. It has been observed that rural criminality is related basically to the degree of illiteracy of the peasant, his idea of honor and of manliness (machismo), alcoholism, and emotional motives. On the other hand, delinquency in the urban zones is explained by elements of disorganization of the family, prostitution, gambling, and alcoholism—the influence of the latter being especially notorious in traffic offenses.

During this period, the first centers of protection of children were created and used (Venezuelan Council of the Child). The first private organizations, which in certain fields, perform their beneficial action in favor of the marginal groups of society, also made their appearance. The first campaigns against offenses were carried out, with the help of the advertising media, especially to diminish offenses in the urban regions. New police bodies were formed in accordance with new techniques and knowledge for the prevention of offenses. Judges were initiated in the auxiliary disciplines of penal law, in order to have a better understanding of the problems of crime.

Plans for the Future

At the time of writing this article Venezuela is in the process of starting a new constitutional period. The team of men who, together with the President-elect, assumed power in March 1969, had to submit to the Program of Government presented to public opinion in the pre-election period, while the advisory team devoted itself to the task of implementing the said program.

In accordance with what is explained in the same, the following significant features can be outlined:

(*i*) Unification of the police bodies, as public security is considered the primary need of the country.

(*ii*) Realization of an ambitious housing plan (510,000 units in 5 years) because, among other things, the lack of housing is a constant element in the creation of tensions for the Venezuelan population, which very often are elements of crime that should not be ignored.

(*iii*) Programming of an anti-alcholic policy, derived from statistical observation, which reflects the fact that Venezuela has one of the highest indices of per capita alcohol consumption in the world.

(*iv*) Implementation of a policy which will not only control legal gambling—guaranteeing the citizen the absence of frauds and deceitful management of the money which he invests in this manner—but at the same time see to it that the earnings obtained by the State institutes which control this activity, are re-invested in works of social welfare and collective benefit.

(*v*) Policy of social and sanitary prophylaxis in relation to prostitution.

(*vi*) Increase at the popular level of sport activities and support to the private organizations dedicated to the same. It helps in avoiding juvenile leisure produced by the splits and dissolutions of the family, the crisis of authority, and double shifts at school.

(*vii*) Preparation of the project concerning health, because it is considered that many of our social ills (and delinquency among them) having their more remote origin in the frequent lack of orientation and therapy for lighter disorders of conduct.

(*viii*) Advancement of the moral level of population while engaging it in the task of general improvement through its voluntary action, chanelled through the Secretariat of the National Volunteers. Other measures of a preventive type have not so far been announced due to the nature of the same and the state of political transition in the country.

SUMMARY AND CONCLUSION

Crime in Venezuela is an essentially growing problem, while the investigations being made out have been most inadequate uptil the year 1961. From 1961 until the time of writing this article, many lawyers, sociologists, psychologists, and psychiatrists, and criminologists have shown a promising interest in results, which will be visible in the years to come.

It would be useful if national funds as well as contributions from foundations were to be made available for this activity and also for the constitution of the Center of Criminological Investigations, which would co-ordinate this activity and would plan on the national level the policy against crime.

It is necessary to start by establishing an office which would gather sources for any future investigation, improving the existing ones, and implementing methods from cybernetics. It is also necessary to interest the public in the problem of delinquency and in its solution. It would be worthwhile utilizing the mass media for this purpose, at the same time using them as re-educators of anti-social behavior. This is especially valid for television.

Moreover, the different religious authorities corresponding to the different faiths, especially the Catholic faith—which are intermediate bodies of society—have a preventive duty against offense, which has not been fully realized.

In conclusion it may be said that the search for an explanation of criminality in Venezuela, as in most of the developing countries, is geared towards the socio-economic causes of the offense.

BIBLIOGRAPHY

BORJAS, ARMINIO. *Exposición de Código de Enjuiciamiento Criminal Venezolano.* (Exposition of the Code of the Venezuelan Criminal Adjudication). Biblioamerican Editorial. Caracas, Venezuela.

CARNELUTTI, FRANCESCO. *Las Miserias del Proceso Penal.* (The Miseries of the Penal Process). Briefs of the Law, No. 24, E.J.E.A. Buenos Aires, Argentina, 1952.

Cuerpo Tec'nico De Policía Judicial. (Technical Body of Judicial Police). Scientific Police Magazine. Caracas, Venezuela, 1963-68 (20 numbers).

DE GREEFF, ETIENE. *Introduction a la Criminologia* (Introduction to Criminology). Van der Plast Editors. Brussels, Belgium, 1946.

DEMPF, ALOIS. *Sociología de la Crisis.* (Sociology of Crisis) 2nd Edition, Castilla, S. A., Madrid, Spain, 1951.

DURKHEIM, EMILE. *Régles de la Methode Sociologique.* (The Rules of the Sociological Method). University Presses of France. Paris, France, 1956. Edition XIII.

GOMEZ GRILLO, ELIO. *Introducción a la Criminología.* (Introduction to Criminology). Publications of the Central University of Venezuela. Caracas, Venezuela, 1964.

Instituto De to Ciencias Penales Y Criminológicas. (Institute of Penal and Criminoiogical Sciences). 1968 Annual. Publication of the Central University of Venezuela. Caracas, Venezuela.

KIMBERG, OLOF. *Problem Fundamentaux de la Criminologie.* (Fundamental Problems of Criminology). Cuyás Publications. Toulousse, France, 1959,

LACASSAGNE, LOUIS. *Précis de Médecin Legal.* (Summary of the Legal Doctor). University Presses of France. Paris, France, 1906.

LEPP, IGNACE. *La Nueva Moral.* (The New Morals). Carlos Lohlé Publications. Buenos Aires, Argentina, 1964.

MALINOWSKI, B. *Crimen y Costumbre en la Sociedad Salvaje.* (Crime and Custom in Primitive Society). Bosch Publications. Barcelona, Spain, 1956.

MARQUISET, JEAN. *Le Crime.* (Crime). University Presses of France. Paris, France, 1957.

MAYORCA, JUAN MANUEL. "Criminología, Parte Estática" (Criminology, Static Part), *Gráphica Americana* (or Scale). Caracas, Argentina, 1963.

———. *Introducción la Estudio de la Prostitución.* (Introduction to the Study of Prostitution), 2nd Edition, *Gráphica Americana,* 1967.

MENDOZA, JOSE RAFAEL. *Curso de Criminología* (Criminology Course). Mariegas Graphs. Madrid, Spain, 1961.

MOMSENM, THEODORE. *Le Droit Penal Romaine.* (The Roman Penal Law). A. Frontenmoing, Editors. Paris, France, 1907. Tomo 1.

NIEVES, HECTOR. *La Libertad Provisional.* (Provisional or Temporary Liberty). Article appearing in the magazine, "Criminal Relationship." Year 1, No. 1. Valencia, Venezuela, 1968.

PINATEL, JEAN. *Criminologie.* (Criminology). Spes Publications. Paris, France, 1960.

RADBRUCH Y GWIGNER. *Historia de la Criminalidad.* (The History of Criminality). Bosch Publications. Barcelona, Spain, 1955.

ROUSSELET, X: *Histoirire de la Justice.* (History of Justice). University Presses of France. Paris, France, 1963.

VAN DER BUGGEN. *Course de Sociologie Criminell.* (Course of Criminal Sociology). Louvain, Belgium, 1958. Three Circles Publications.

Código De Enjuiciamiento Criminal (Reforma) [Code of Criminal Adjudication (Reformation)]. Official Publication of the Ministry of Justice. Caracas, Venejuela, 1961.

Codigo Penal de Venezuela, Reforma de 1964. (The Penal Code of Venezuela, Reformation of 1964). Official Publication. Publication of the Ministry of Justice.

Constitución Nacional de la Republica de Venezuela. (The National Constitution of the Republic of Venezuela). Official Newspaper of January 23, 1961.

Lay de Régimen Penitenciario. (Law of the Penitentiary Regime). Official Publication of the Ministry of Justice. Caracas. Venezuela, 1961.

Lay de Vagos y Maleantes. (Law of Vagrants and the Corrupt). Official Publication. Publication of the Ministry of Justice. Caracas, Venezuela, 1956.

Memorias del Ministerio de Justicie. (Memoirs of the Ministry of Justice). Caracas, Venezuela, 1955-1968.

Ley Organica del Poder Judicial. (Organic Law of Judicial Power). Official Publication of the Ministry of Justice. Caracas, Venezuela, 1956.

Reglamento Interno del Cuerpo Técnico de Policia Judicial (Internal Bylaws of the Technical Body of Judicial Police). Official Publication of the Ministry of Justice. Caracas, Venezuela.

"Reglas Minimas para el tratamiento de los reclusos y recomendaciones relacionadas " (Minimum Rules for the Treatment of the Recluse and Related Recommendations). Publications of the Organization of the United Nations. Geneva, Switzerland, 1955.

INDEX

Abrahmson, David, family tension, cause of criminal behavior, 680, 680n
Adeer, 997
Aguinaldo, General Emilio, 767
Alkin, Winifred, 685
American Negroes, bias against, 904; *see also* United States of America
Anglo-American Law, 594
Annual conference of the Japanese Association of Sociology (1968), Waseda University, 643n
Aretaius, Work of, 1003, 1005
Aristotle, 545, 553
Atavism, theory of, 550
Atonement, principle of, 552-554,
Auto theft, in USA, 967

Beat system, feature of, 713-714; implementation of, 714; *see also* Malaysia, police organization
Beccaria, 554
Belgium, criminology in, 603
Binet, works of, 997
Black marketing, study of, 911
Bolivar, Simon, liberator of emancipation movement in Venezuela, 985-986
Bonifacio de vitalinis (Excess, transgressio) in Germany, 540
"Breaches of peace," cause of crime, 861
Bronner, on the relationship between personal traits and delinquency, 678, 683
Burt, cyril, 679
Business crimes, 910-913; scope of, 912, 914; three kinds of costs on society, 911-912

California Youth Authority, role of, 968
Capital punishment, in Germany, 508-509; in Italy, 577; in Japan, 588, 631-632; in the Philippines, 834; in Malaysia, 692-693, 722-726
Carmignani, 555
Cicero doctrine, 553
"Circondario," 558n
Citizens, role of, 938-945
Colleges and Universities (USA), role of, 945
Colombia, highest crime rate in, 895
Commercial smuggling, in Italy, decrease of, 538; in West Malaysia, 676
Community and the police, relationship between, 878, 880, 971; and professional organizations. (USA), role of, 943-945
Confucianism, 643-644
Constabulary Data, Processing Unit (the Philippines), 841
Constantino, on cause of crimes in the Philippines, 788
"Contravenzion," usage of, 538, 540
Correction practices, in the Philippines, 831-832; in USA, 854, 873-875, 973-974, 954-956
Corruption, cause of crime, 786-787
Crime/crimes, and educational system, 687-688; and poverty, relationship between, 685-686; classical and positive schools views, 555-557; classification of, 662; Colposo (without intention of the consequences),

496; studies of criminology in, 514-519; Third Reich period, 485

"Giudizio Direttissimo," types of penal processual in Italy, 566-567

Glueck Sheldon, positive school of, 680

Goddard, H. H., on human efficiency and levels of intelligence, 682, 682n

Goring, Charles, on criminal tendency cause, 681

"Grand Countumier" of Charles VI, 540

Grillo, Goomez, 1032

Grozio, works of, 554

Guevara, Guillermo, 792

Halt, Thomas, study of delinquents by, 689-690

Healy, on the relationship between personal traits and delinquencies, 683

Hebrew Culture, 1004

Hegal, on penalty, 484

Hellenic culture, 1003

Henry Gurney Schools (Borstal Training Institution), 666, 697, 746, 720-721; punishment methods of, 724-725; training programmes of, 722; see also Malaysia

Heredity, and criminality, 680; and environment, controversy over, 680-681

Hiroyuki Iwai, Dr, research on criminological studies by, 607

Hoche, on criminology, 478

Home and family, role in determining the behavior of the child, 678-680

Hoshino, 642

Hooton, Prof., 997

Howard, John, on penal doctrine, 1006

Howard League for Penal Reforms, figures collected by, 749

"Illuminismo," ideology of, 554-555

Increase affluence, favor of increase of crime rate, 894-895

Indeterminate sentence law, in the Philippines, features of, 804-806, 835, 838; see also the Philipines

Indian Evidence Act, 663

Inflation, impacts on property crimes, 895

Ireland, low crime rate in, 895

Iswasaburo Takano, 605

Italian Crimino-anthropological School and French Crimino-sociological School, contradiction between, 478

Italy, Assize Court, functions and powers of, 559; Attorney General, powers of, 561, 567; capital punishment, 577; code of, 1890, 166; constitution of, 573; correctional system Act, 571; court of appeal, power and functions of, 559, 560; court of causation, power and functions of, 560; crime, legal definition of, 538-548; crime causation theories of, 545, 551-552; crime index of, 546-548; crime reporting, decrease of, 537-538; crimes of rape, 538; criminal etiology, socio-economic factors of, 550; criminal law in, 538-539, types of, 538; Defence Group, 581; employment, 535-536; gross income, 536-537; institutions for security measures for, 572-573; judicial system in, 558-561, 561-564; judicial system Act, 561; Justice Ministry, functions of, 563-564; judiciary independence of, 564; juvenile categories of, 544; juvenile delinquency, legal definition of, 544-545; juvenile detention homes of, 576-577; lawyer system in, 564-566; methods of rehabilitation in, 573-576; national net income,